MANAGEMENT RIGHTS

MANAGEMENT RIGHTS

A LEGAL AND ARBITRAL ANALYSIS

MARVIN HILL, JR.
Associate Professor of Industrial Relations
Northern Illinois University

ANTHONY V. SINICROPI
John F. Murray Professor of Industrial Relations
University of Iowa

The Bureau of National Affairs, Inc. Washington, D.C. 20037

Authorization to photocopy items for internal or personal use, or the internal or personal use of
specific clients, is granted by BNA Books for libraries and other users registered with the Copyright
Clearance Center (CCC) Transactional Reporting Service, provided that $0.50 per page is paid
directly to CCC, 21 Congress St., Salem, MA 01970. 0-87179-504-3/86/$0 + .50

Library of Congress Cataloging in Publication Data

Hill, Marvin.
    Management rights.

    Includes index.
    1. Collective labor agreements—United States.
2. Arbitration, Industrial—United States.
3. Management rights—United States.   4. Labor laws
and legislation—United States.   I. Sinicropi, Anthony V.
II. Title.
KF3408.H55   1986   344.73′0189   86-8229
ISBN 0-87179-504-3   347.304189

Printed in the United States of America
International Standard Book Number: 0-87179-504-3

Preface

This text, in substantial part, relies on arbitration awards published by The Bureau of National Affairs, Inc. (BNA) and/ or by Commerce Clearing House (CCH). To the extent that these awards are not representative of the thinking of the arbitral community,[1] the conclusions drawn by the authors may be suspect. An analysis by Stieber, Block, and Corbitt[2] of 759 discharge cases[3] published in *Labor Arbitration Reports* (BNA) and/or in *Labor Arbitration Awards* (CCH) in 1979, 1980, and 1981 revealed that in both publications the final outcomes and awards were not representative of final outcomes and awards in unpublished cases, at least when judged by the results in a collection of unpublished cases decided by Michigan arbitrators. (To the extent that the constituencies, practices, and local statutory restrictions for Michigan arbitrators differ from those of arbitrators nationwide, the findings are, of course, not reliable.) The study also indicated that in terms of actual proportion of types of cases to the whole, published decisions tend to underrepresent public sector cases, cases involving female grievants, and cases involving employees in the service occupations.

Cases published by BNA showed a significantly higher grievance denial rate than the rate for the Michigan "control" group, while cases published by CCH showed an even more significant lower denial rate than that for the unpublished

---

[1]The authors invite the arbitral and academic community to submit data in support of the contention that published awards are not representative of the thinking of the industrial relations community.

[2]Unfortunately, the study was limited to arbitration decisions regarding discharges. The findings therefore may not be indicative of the relationship between published and unpublished decisions for other issues presented in grievance arbitration.

[3]Stieber, Block & Corbitt, "How Representative Are Published Decisions?" Proceedings of the 37th Annual Meeting of NAA, 172–92 (BNA Books, 1984).

decisions. However, the combined grievance denial rate in cases published by BNA and CCH was found to be quite representative of the overall denial rate for the unpublished cases. As pointed out by Stieber and his colleagues, this suggests that if one wishes to draw conclusions from published cases, both cases published by BNA and cases published by CCH should be examined. The authors have done this.[4]

Further, the authors have reviewed a number of unpublished decisions, many involving the airline and coal industries, and, when relevant, cite them in the text. In addition, the authors consulted many scholarly articles—particularly those appearing in the proceedings of the National Academy of Arbitrators, in law reviews, and in other journals in the industrial relations area—in an attempt to ascertain the thinking of arbitrators on issues discussed in this text. These also are cited where appropriate.

Finally, the authors researched decisions of the NLRB and of state and federal courts involving management rights and arbitration and discuss them in the text where relevant. In the authors' view, any text on management rights would be deficient without some knowledge of the views of the judiciary, especially where the NLRB continues to defer a decision in unfair labor practice cases pending the rendering of an award by an arbitrator who, in turn, frequently looks to the law in resolving a grievance. Indeed, the authors found an ever-increasing number of arbitrators "applying law," especially law derived from fair employment decisions by the courts, even when disposition of a case was not deferred by the NLRB.

At the same time, the authors have found a disturbing trend by the judiciary in the area of management rights. When the parties' contract is silent on a particular matter, some courts have not hesitated to overturn arbitrators' decisions implying limitations on managerial discretion, rather than applying traditional standards of review as outlined by the Supreme Court in the *Steelworkers Trilogy* decisions.[5] These

---

[4]Some arbitration cases have been published by both BNA and CCH. In such instances, only the LA (BNA) cite is provided for cases discussed in this text.
[5]Steelworkers v. American Mfg. Co., 363 U.S. 564, 46 LRRM 2414 (1960); Steelworkers v. Warrior & Gulf Nav. Co., 363 U.S. 574, 46 LRRM 2416 (1960); Steelworkers v. Enterprise Wheel & Car. Corp., 363 U.S. 593, 46 LRRM 2423 (1960). The *Trilogy* is discussed at length in Hill & Sinicropi, Remedies in Arbitration, 13–20 (BNA Books, 1981).

courts have thus taken a strict "reserved rights" approach in determining the rights of management vis-a-vis unions, even where arbitration awards theoretically are entitled to some deference. For the above reasons, in addition to an understanding of arbitral thinking, an understanding of the law as it relates to managerial discretion is imperative.

It is the authors' hope that this integrative approach to a study of issues relating to management rights will prove to be sufficiently comprehensive that readers searching for answers to specific questions will a) obtain if not the answers at least some guidance as to where to find them, and b) discover whether there are other questions they should be seeking the answers to as well.

For the convenience of readers, the United States Arbitration Act is reprinted as Appendix A, followed by the Uniform Arbitration Act as Appendix B. A list of titles of proceedings of the annual meetings of the National Academy of Arbitrators is provided as Appendix C, to supplement the abbreviated titles used in footnotes.

Acknowledgments

Our debts are many and we again wish to thank our families who continue to be patient with us while time demanded our efforts for this text. Thanks must be extended to our research assistants: Richard Quist and Chuck Nave of the College of Law, Northern Illinois University; Diana Beck and Pat Walz, graduate students at the Industrial Relations Institute, University of Minnesota; and Joseph Humsey, College of Law, University of Iowa. A special thanks to BNA's Tim Darby, a fine editor who actually reads footnotes.[1] Like Marvin's German shepherd, he is always watching and he cannot be fooled. Finally, we wish to thank our colleagues at work, many of whom write and publish science fiction and believe that we only moonlight as professors. All of you we still love.

---

[1]"No passion in the world is equal to the passion to alter someone else's draft." H.G. Wells.

Summary Table of Contents

Detailed Table of Contents

Part II
Employee Privacy Concerns

Part I

Management Rights
in Perspective

Chapter 1

The Concept of Management Rights: An Overview

Introduction

No area of labor-management relations evokes so much emotion and controversy as does "management rights," for it is the concept of management rights and its counterpart—the union's quest for job security and other substantive protections for its members—that are at the core of the conflict between labor and management. Cullen and Greenbaum have observed:

> [T]he management rights issue is one of those exceptions on which the cleavage of opinion is so deep that the contending parties cannot even agree in principle. Not only is the economic power of the parties on the line, but their self-esteem, their standing in the eyes of others, and some of the values each deems important in a free society may all be called into question whenever the rights issue is open for debate. Small wonder, then, that agreement on management rights is hard to come by on any level, whether in lofty principle or . . . in the real world of legislatures, courts, and collective bargaining.[1]

Unquestionably the control of the workplace, the rules that govern the working (and, at times, the non-working) environment of employees, and the rights, duties, responsibilities and privileges of the parties are all at stake when the

---

[1]Cullen & Greenbaum, Management Rights and Collective Bargaining: Can Both Survive?, at 17 (N.Y. State Sch. Indus. & Lab. Rel. Cornell U., ILR Bull. No. 58, 1966).

3

rights of management and the rights of employees are at issue. To understand the root causes of this conflict, the goals and purposes of management and labor must be considered.

In the tradition of Adam Smith, management has been described as being dedicated to the goal of profit maximization. Indeed, many prominent economists view profit maximization as the only legitimate goal of managers who, if not owners themselves, are the guardians of the financial interests of stockholders.[2] If this is an accepted predicate, it follows (in the eyes of many observers) that management must have control over all decision-making factors of the enterprise if it is to operate efficiently. Economic efficiency, in turn, requires maximum flexibility to make unencumbered decisions involving the commitment of resources and the direction of the work force. Professor Neil Chamberlain puts it this way:

> Management requires initiative, and initiative requires discretion and the exercise of judgment, and, if that judgment is exercised fairly, it should be upheld even though the union— equally fairly—would have it otherwise. In this case its views are not given equal treatment with management's and I don't see how they can be if organized sanity is to be preserved.[3]

Perhaps the dilemma facing labor and management in this area is best summarized by Chamberlain. After stating that "[t]he issue of managerial prerogatives has arisen precisely because the 'inherent' right of unions to organize and bargain has run counter to the 'inherent' right of management to manage,"[4] Chamberlain goes on to stress the nature of authority or managerial decision making under collective bargaining and its effect on efficiency:

> This aim of management [control] is based on efficiency concepts, in which the functioning parts of the business organism—including of course the personnel—have their assigned roles. In the business organism there can be only one mind and one nerve center if the various parts are to be coordinated into a harmonious whole. The union, however, constitutes a second

---

[2]See, e.g., Friedman, "The Social Responsibility of Business Is to Increase Its Profits," N.Y. Times Magazine, Sept. 13, 1970, at 33, 122–26.

[3]Chamberlain, "Discussion—Management's Reserved Rights," Proceedings of the 9th Annual Meeting of NAA, 138, 140 (BNA Books, 1956).

[4]Chamberlain, The Union Challenge to Management Control, 4 (Harper, 1948).

center of authority, which speaks in terms of welfare rather than efficiency.[5]

Often management assesses its ability to be efficient and in control by determining how much flexibility it has with regard to decision making, particularly when directing the work force is at issue. Employers maintain that any union penetration into this area is an intrusion of management's inherent right to manage. Union advocates argue that the right to direct the work force, where it involves wages, hours, or working conditions is only a procedural right that does not imply some right over and above labor's right. On this point, former Supreme Court justice Arthur Goldberg argues as follows:

> [The right to direct] is a recognition of the fact that somebody must be boss; somebody has to run the plant. People can't be wandering around at loose ends, each deciding what to do next. Management decides what the employee is to do. However, this right to direct or to initiate action does not imply a second-class role for the union. The union has the right to pursue its role of representing the interest of the employee with the same stature accorded it as is accorded management. To assure order, there is a clear procedural line drawn: the company directs and the union grieves when it objects. To make this desirable division of function workable, it is essential that arbitrators not give greater weight to the directing force than the objecting force.[6]

At the same time employees, acting through their unions, often view management behavior as unpredictable and unfair. Cullen and Greenbaum, for example, point out that if efficiency and low costs are the only goals of our society, then perhaps society should outlaw unions and let management make all the decisions on wages, hours, and working conditions. This argument is posed by union leaders to those who accuse them of invading management's right to manage.[7]

Thus the conflict is born. The dual union objective of pre-

---

[5]Id. at 134. Chamberlain lists six other management beliefs that motivate it to resist union penetration into its unilateral decision-making preserve: 1) union penetration threatens the business organization itself by destroying the unified final authority of management; 2) unions prevent management's ability to discharge its responsibilities; 3) union penetration endangers the efficiency of the industrial organization; 4) the union may act irresponsibly if and when it gains shared rights to manage; 5) the union lacks adequate leadership; and 6) there could be negative long-run consequences of union penetration. Id. at 131–37.

[6]Goldberg, "Management's Reserved Rights: A Labor View," Proceedings of the 9th Annual Meeting of NAA, 118, 120–21 (BNA Books, 1956).

[7]Cullen & Greenbaum, supra note 1, at 4.

dictability of managerial behavior and job-security protections
for employees challenges management's dual goals of organizational flexibility and efficiency. Within this relationship
management invariably attempts to negotiate an agreement
in which its exclusive and explicit rights are incorporated in
the labor contract.

In addition to explicit management rights that have their
genesis in the language of the labor agreement, there are those
"implied," "residual," or "reserved" rights that exist within
the relationship between the parties but are not found within
the four corners of the agreement. These inherent management rights arise and, under certain conditions, are sometimes
lost, by the operation of custom or past practice of the parties,
or what is frequently referred to as the "common law of the
shop."

The "reserved rights theory"—the doctrine that holds that
management's authority is supreme in all matters except those
it has expressly agreed to share with or relinquished to the
union—has been the topic of much debate. Such rights are
often challenged on the basis of 1) the reasonableness of the
specific management right, or 2) the equitable administration
and application of that inherent right. Arbitrator Sidney Wolff
poses the question and answers it this way:

> [W]hile management has the right to manage subject to the
> contractual limitations, is there not implied—if not ex-
> pressed—the requirement that management will exercise that
> right in good faith. . . .
> Management may subcontract, for example, but is it not
> to do so in good faith depending on the needs of its business
> rather than from an intent merely to take work away from its
> unionized employees, to cause them to lose their jobs, to de-
> moralize them—all to the end of destroying the union?
>
> . . .
> All will agree that it is an obligation of a party to a contract
> not to enter upon a course of conduct the effect of which is to
> avoid performance under that contract and to render it null
> and void. This is well settled in ordinary contract law. How
> much more applicable is it to a labor contract intended to main-
> tain a proper stable working relationship between a company,
> its employees, and the union![8]

Adopting Arbitrator Wolff's reasoning, it is argued that

---

[8]Wolff, "Discussion—Management's Reserved Rights," Proceedings of the 9th
Annual Meeting of NAA, 129, 131–32 (BNA Books, 1956).

management has an implied obligation in exercising its inherent rights, when challenged by the union, to demonstrate that these rights are reasonably related to the safe and efficient operation of the business, and that the application of such rights has been consistent and equitable. Prasow and Peters, who inquired into this area at some length, discuss the reserved management rights controversy as follows:

> The very heart of the conflict between the parties is the application of what has become best known as the "theory of management reserved rights." The reserved-rights doctrine is the basic frame of reference for interpreting the collective agreement, accepted even by those who are quick to challenge it whenever it is enunciated as a full-blown theory.
> Stated in an unqualified simplistic form, the reserved-rights theory holds that management's authority is supreme in all matters except those it has expressly conceded in the collective agreement and in all areas except those where its authority is restricted by law. Put another way, management does not look to the collective agreement to ascertain its rights; it looks to the agreement to find out which and how many of its rights and powers it has conceded outright or agreed to share with the union. The reserved-rights theory is somewhat analogous to the Tenth Amendment of the United States Constitution.[9]

Professor Dennis Nolan has argued that arbitrators, faced with questions of interpretation arising from issues that are not addressed in the contract, sometimes hold that management retains all rights not limited by the agreement.

> Usually termed the "reserved rights doctrine," this principle is based on the argument that because the employer possessed all rights to run the business before the union came on the scene it must still possess those the union did not succeed in limiting. If this were not so, it would mean either that all such rights passed *sub silentio* to the union or that they simply disappeared, and neither of these possibilities is very reasonable.[10]

Prasow and Peters also submit that an important corol-

---

[9]Prasow & Peters, Arbitration and Collective Bargaining: Conflict Resolution in Labor Relations, 2d Ed., 33–34 (McGraw-Hill, 1983).

[10]Nolan, Labor Arbitration Law and Practice, 164–65 (West, 1981). Nolan goes on to assert that a large majority of arbitrators follow this doctrine with a few qualifications, one of which is that an employer may not use a reserved right to destroy others that are specified in the contract. Other qualifications include 1) the reserved rights principle applies only to situations where no contract provision is applicable, and 2) reserved rights can be limited by a past practice, unless the contract provides otherwise. Id. at 165.

lary to the reserved-rights theory is that of "implied obligations."

> The "doctrine of implied obligations" is an important corollary to the reserved-rights theory of management. The implied-obligations doctrine acknowledges the employer's right to alter or abolish employee benefits when the contract is open for negotiations, but once a new contract has been signed, he is no longer free to withdraw existing benefits. He has an implied obligation to maintain them, including those benefits which were not revoked by him during negotiations and to which the contract makes no reference.[11]

Underpinnings of Management Rights Theory

Various historical and theoretical bases are cited as a justification for recognizing the reserved-rights doctrine. The idea that rights not specifically given away are retained is not just a twentieth century concept. The reserved-rights theory of management's powers has a parallel in the sixteenth century theory of the "divine right of kings." Under that concept, subjects owed the king a duty of passive obedience. Just as "divine right came to mean that the subject's duty of submission was absolute,"[12] so did the term "management rights" come to mean (to many) that management has absolute control of the enterprise, unless provided otherwise in the written contract. (However, the practice today of making irresponsible management action generally answerable to the grievance procedure also has its historical antecedents, even within the ambit of the "divine rights" theory. Stated another way, just as the duty of passive obedience did not mean that the king could do whatever he chose,[13] the better view is that management cannot exercise its prerogatives in an unreasonable manner.)

The political concept of sovereignty is closely allied to the divine right concept, actually representing an extension of the theory to the state as a corporate entity. A sovereign has been defined as "a person, body, or state in which independent and supreme authority is vested."[14] While sovereignty-rooted ar-

---

[11]Prasow & Peters, supra note 9, at 43.
[12]Sabine, A History of Political Theory, 394–95 (Holt, Rinehart & Winston, 1950).
[13]Id.
[14]Black's Law Dictionary, 5th Ed., Rev., 1252 (1979).

guments at one time were a powerful force against private-sector collective bargaining, they have long since been abandoned in favor of a national labor policy supporting bargaining.[15] However, the sovereignty doctrine has clearly been responsible in part for the delay in the development of collective bargaining in the public sector.[16] In effect, the doctrine reinforced the notion (especially in public-sector management) that managerial discretion was equivalent to the discretion of a sovereign, and that what the sovereign does not voluntarily relinquish it retains.

In addition to political theory, analyses of the historical development of laws surrounding the employment relationship also have provided a basis for the development of a theory of management rights. In early Roman law master and servant relationships were taken literally. The rights of the servant were not his own but those of his "paterfamilias"—the head or master of the family. The paterfamilias was absolute ruler of the household with authority over life and death. The ancient doctrine gradually faded away as the world became more civilized and, by the fourteenth century, the erosion of the paterfamilias doctrine was virtually complete.[17] While few would argue that modern-day organizations should be accorded similar power, the idea of an absolute ruler in a master-servant (employment) relationship has its parallel in the reserved-rights theory.

Toward the end of the nineteenth century the idea of contract, which was a dominant force in American common law, spilled over to employment relations.[18] Justice required, according to this legal theory, that each individual be free to use his or her natural powers in bargains and exchanges and promises. This concept of freedom of contract in large part had evolved from the laissez-faire economic philosophy of the times—what was good for private enterprise was good for the general welfare. Any interference with the right to contract was looked upon with suspicion, except in those select cases where the bargain struck interfered with like action on the part of others

---

[15]Weitzman, The Scope of Bargaining in Public Employment, 9 (Praeger, 1975).
[16]Id. See also Smith, Edwards, & Clark, Jr., Labor Relations Law in the Public Sector: Cases and Materials, 7–24 (Bobbs-Merrill, 1974).
[17]See Hill, "Arbitration as a Means of Protecting Employees From Unjust Dismissal: A Statutory Proposal," 3 N. Ill. U.L. Rev. 111, 113 (1982), citing R. Pound, Legal Immunities of Labor Unions, 17 (American Enterprise Ass'n, 1957).
[18]Pound, An Introduction to the Philosophy of Law, 133–68 (Yale U. Press, 1943).

or with some court-designated "natural" right. Since the emphasis was on the self-sufficiency of the individual in securing his or her economic gains, it is not surprising that management was accorded great discretion in directing the working force.

Modern Considerations

Apart from these arguments based on historical considerations, others simply take the pragmatic view that management's right to operate its business as it sees fit is not a right that needs to be rooted in some historic genesis. Rather, it is a right inherent in management's responsibility to preserve the stockholders' investment.[19] In this regard, an analysis of the modern-day conflict between management and labor may be made in terms of the institution of private property. Historically, the ownership and control of property has implied economic and political power over others. This property-right concept has been given more extensive treatment by Cullen and Greenbaum:

> Management . . . primarily bases its claims for unfettered authority on the rights and responsibilities of property ownership. In this view an essential feature of any free society, and particularly one with a free-enterprise economy, is the guarantee that the owner of property has the right to use it as he sees fit, provided only that he is not violating any law. If you want to paint your car with zebra stripes or drive it only on Thursdays or give it away tomorrow, "that's your business." . . .
> When ownership is separated from control, as in the corporation, the professional manager is regarded as an agent of the stockholder-owner and therefore is entitled to exercise the owner's property rights. In fact, the manager is seen as having a legal responsibility to the owners that prevents him from sharing their property rights with anyone else, even if he wanted to.
> Moreover, property rights have important values beyond their claim to legality. As a simple matter of equity, it only seems fair to many people that, since the owner puts up the money for a business and runs the risk of losing it all if the business fails, he should have a free hand in making the decisions that will spell his success or failure.[20]

---

[19]Prasow & Peters, supra note 9, at 46.
[20]Cullen & Greenbaum, supra note 1, at 8.

Chamberlain disputes the validity of the property-rights theory as a basis for removing certain subjects from the realm of collective bargaining by arguing that wages and hours are hardly the only subjects affecting employees and that mere property ownership cannot control terms of employment:

> "Property rights confer only a control over things, not over people. The owner or manager of a plant can, it is true, decide for himself how he would like to employ his physical capital .... But he cannot, on the strength of his ownership of physical assets, force workers to conform to his decisions. He can only seek to induce them."[21]

An interesting, more contemporary variation of the property-rights notion concerns the argument that to today's workers, jobs are their most valuable possession and consequently should be subject to minimum protections.[22] The employee's property "is his ability to be productive and his right to sell his skills," and if employees cannot sell their work freely, they lose control of their "property" and their destiny.[23] This point is frequently made in relation to proposals to institute a "just cause" for dismissal standard to replace the long-standing notion that non-union employees may be discharged "at will" and for any reason, or for no reason at all simply because they have no common-law property right to continued employment.[24] As Cullen and Greenbaum note, if employees acquire rights in their job by virtue of long service, "many labor-management disputes over principles and rights dissolve into routine commercial hassles between two sets of property owners!"[25]

With few exceptions courts, cognizant of an economic and social climate that glorified the value of laissez-faire economics, have traditionally tailored the common law in line with the interests of management. Courts were reluctant to recognize that the institution of private property could encompass intangible interests of a worker with respect to his or her job security. Proponents of the reserved-rights theory have contended that arbitrators should follow the common-law model

---

[21]Chamberlain, The Labor Sector, 344 (McGraw-Hill, 1965), as quoted in Cullen & Greenbaum, supra note 1, at 14.
[22]See Drucker, "The Job as a Property Right," Wall St. J., Mar. 4, 1980, at 24, col. 4.
[23]Wellington, Labor and the Legal Process, 12 (Yale U. Press, 1968).
[24]The common law "at-will" rule is discussed at length in Chapter 4.
[25]Cullen & Greenbaum, supra note 1, at 10.

in determining the respective rights of labor and management when the agreement is silent.

The controversy over the precise nature and origin of management rights has extended to many forums. In an often-quoted piece from the proceedings of the National Academy of Arbitrators, vice-president of Bethlehem Steel and management advocate James Phelps, and Arthur Goldberg, then general counsel to the United Steelworkers of America and later Supreme Court justice, outlined their views.[26] In that exchange, Phelps argued that the term "management rights" refers to the "residue of management's pre-existing functions which remains after the negotiation of a collective bargaining agreement." According to Phelps, absent such an agreement, management has absolute discretion in the hiring, firing, and organization and direction of the working forces, subject only to such limitations as may be imposed by law.[27]

Phelps submitted that management rights provisions serve the useful function of enabling the arbitrator to "cite or quote explicit language which . . . would otherwise be implied"; he added that such language also "helps to avoid shop frictions and to prevent charges that the management indulges in legalistic hocus-pocus."[28] Phelps summarized his position on management's reserved rights as follows:

> The job of management is to manage. The operation of the enterprise at its maximum efficiency is management's responsibility and obligation. If a management believes that, in order to discharge its obligations, it must retain in full measure the so-called prerogative of management, it has the right to refuse to agree in collective bargaining to restrict those rights. If the management should agree to limit its exclusive functions or even to delegate certain of its duties to a union, it can enter into an agreement that will clearly define how far it has agreed to go.
>
> However, this is an area that is peculiarly unsuitable for the development of any theoretical conception of a common law of contract interpretation. To read into the mere act of signing a contract implications that may never have been considered by either party is repugnant to the basic concept of the collective bargaining agreement that is a voluntary act of the parties. That can be avoided only by interpreting the contract as the

[26]Phelps, "Management's Reserved Rights: An Industry View," and Goldberg, "Management's Reserved Rights: A Labor View," Proceedings of the 9th Annual Meeting of NAA, 102, 118 (BNA Books, 1956).
[27]Phelps, id. at 105.
[28]Id. at 113–14.

parties write it—an instrument containing specific and limited restrictions on the functions that management would otherwise be free to exercise. To the extent that the parties have not seen fit to limit management's sphere of action, management's rights are unimpaired by the contract.[29]

Arthur Goldberg, of course, takes a much narrower view of management rights. For his part, he noted the following:

> Too many spokesmen for management assume that labor's rights are not steeped in past practice or tradition but are limited strictly to those specified in a contract; while management's rights are all-inclusive except as specifically taken away by a specific clause in a labor agreement.
>
> This view of the history of rights is not accurate; nor is it reasonable. Labor always had many inherent rights, such as the right to strike . . . . Failure of management to recognize such rights does not indicate that they did not exist. . . .
>
> Collective bargaining does not establish some hitherto non-existing rights; it provides the power to enforce rights of labor which the labor movement was dedicated to long before the institution of arbitration had become so widely practiced in labor relations.
>
> I cannot agree, therefore, that management's reserved rights were all-embracing to the exclusion of any labor right. The bit of historical fiction that some of my management colleagues attempt to write is neither accurate nor well-founded. As I understand it, it goes something like this: First, there was management. Its power was supreme. Then came unions and challenged this absolute power. Management's rights are diminished only to the extent that labor's challenge . . . is measured, the story goes, only by specific contract clauses wherein a right is specifically established for labor. No other right for labor exists.
>
> I cannot agree to this appraisal of the reserved rights of management.[30]

Regarding management rights clauses, Goldberg said:

> The rights reserved to management, usually in management clauses, should be viewed in proper context. These clauses do not confirm some notion of labor's inferior position in the bargaining process or in the administration of a contract. They merely establish affirmatively certain areas in which it is the company that acts, not the union, without implying any greater weight to the direction than to the grievance.[31]

Goldberg also noted the need for reciprocity of recognition:

---

[29]Id. at 117. Phelps did recognize that where the parties' agreement contained no management reserved rights clause, it would have to be implied. Id. at 113–14.
[30]Goldberg, supra note 26, at 118–19.
[31]Id. at 121.

Management determines the product, the machine to be used, the manufacturing method, the price, the plant layout, the plant organization, and innumerable other questions. These are reserved rights, inherent rights, exclusive rights which are not diminished or modified by collective bargaining . . . .

Our ability to have this accepted without question depends on equally clear acceptance by management of the view that the exercise of these rights cannot diminish the rights of the worker and the union.[32]

In an address before the National Academy of Arbitrators, management advocate Andrew Kramer correctly pointed out that the position that one should not imply an obligation out of a collective bargaining agreement was disapproved years ago.[33] In 1962, in *Teamsters Local 174 v. Lucas Flour Co.*,[34] a collective bargaining agreement provided for arbitration over "any difference as to the true interpretation of this agreement," and also stated that "during such arbitration, there shall be no suspension of work." Further, that same article provided that "should any difference [not covered in the first section] arise between the employer and the employee, same shall be submitted to arbitration." The union called a strike to protest the dismissal of an employee, and the employer successfully sued the union for damages in state court. Addressing the issue whether a strike over an arbitral issue is in breach of a collective bargaining agreement even if the agreement does not contain an explicit promise not to strike, the Supreme Court implied the existence of a no-strike clause from an agreement to submit disputes through a negotiated grievance procedure. The Court, citing *Steelworkers v. Warrior & Gulf Navigation Co.*,[35] noted that a contrary holding "would be completely at odds with the basic policy of national labor legislation to promote the arbitral process as a substitute for economic warfare" and would "do violence to accepted principles of traditional contract law."[36]

Numerous other commentators, many cited and discussed elsewhere in this text, have pointed out that both courts and arbitrators have long implied obligations under a "silent" col-

---

[32]Id. at 123.
[33]Kramer, "External Law and the Interpretive Process," Proceedings of the 38th Annual Meeting of NAA, 149 (BNA Books, 1986).
[34]369 U.S. 95, 96, 49 LRRM 2717, 2718 (1962).
[35]363 U.S. 574, 46 LRRM 2416 (1960).
[36]369 U.S. at 105, 49 LRRM at 2721–22.

lective bargaining agreement. David Feller, addressing the arbitrator's function under silent labor agreements, writes:

> These limitations [embodied in the collective bargaining agreement] need not be express. The very nature of the agreement and the complex organization which it governs often require substantial implication, if only because of the impossibility of setting out in words all of the understandings and practices which the parties necessarily assume in executing it. An agreement, for example, may have no provision limiting the employer's right to discharge employees. If, however, it contains seniority provisions which appear to grant security of employment and the right to preference in both the filling of vacancies and in the choice of employees for layoffs, an arbitrator may find that it implicitly contains an undertaking not to discharge an employee without proper cause. Similarly, the agreement may contain no provision with respect to the contracting out of work. An arbitrator may nevertheless find that in some circumstances by contracting out certain types of work the employer has violated the implicit understanding not to undercut the wage or other provisions of the contract. Note that in the latter case there often is no contention that contracting out is per se a violation of the agreement. Absent restriction, the employer clearly has the right to contract out as part of his right to manage the plant. The question is whether he has exercised that right "in such a way as to frustrate the basic purposes of the Agreement or make the Agreement impossible to perform."[37]

In his dissent in *Lucas Flour*, Justice Hugo Black arguably rejected the implied obligation view of management rights:

> . . . I have been unable to find any accepted principle of contract law—traditional or otherwise—that permits courts to change completely the nature of a contract by adding new promises that the parties themselves refused to make in order that the court-made contract might better fit into whatever social, economic, or legal policies the courts believe to be so important that they should have been taken out of the realm of voluntary contract by the legislative body and furthered by compulsory legislation.[38]

Black said it was "fiction" to imply a no-strike obligation where none is set forth in the contract:

> Both parties to collective bargaining discussions have much at stake as to whether there will be a no-strike clause in any

---

[37]Feller, "A General Theory of the Collective Bargaining Agreement," 61 Calif. L. Rev. 663, 748–49 (1973) (footnotes omitted).
[38]369 U.S. at 108, 49 LRRM at 2723.

resulting agreement. It is difficult to believe that any desire of employers to get such a promise and the desire of the union to avoid giving it are matters which are not constantly in the minds of those who negotiate these contracts. In such a setting, to hold—on the basis of no evidence whatever—that a union, without knowing it, impliedly surrendered the right to strike by virtue of "traditional contract law" or anything else is to me just fiction.[39]

Consistent with Black, and as pointed out by Kramer, in cases involving fundamental management rights it may be unrealistic to assume implied restrictions against management action absent evidence of an agreement or understanding to do otherwise. Kramer states:

> Part of the concept of implied obligation seems to be based on the notion that parties give the arbitrator authority to fill in the "gaps" of their agreement. I must seriously question whether it is still appropriate, twenty-five years after the Trilogy, to assume that in all cases parties still intend to leave such "gaps" in their agreement for an arbitrator to fill. In cases where you have sophisticated parties who have negotiated for many years, I think it is unrealistic to assume that they have not given conscious and serious thought to both what is, and is not, contained in their agreement.
> Parties who have executed numerous agreements governing myriad issues should not be presumed to have ignored industrial realities when a particular item is absent and there is a subsequent dispute over alleged implied obligations. Normally parties do not negotiate in a vacuum and the failure to include certain restrictions in an agreement can be proof in and of itself of an *intent* not to limit management's freedom of action.[40]

Kramer concludes by urging that an arbitrator today should be careful not to imply restrictions without analyzing whether the silence represents a recognition that management's action was not intended to be proscribed.

Other management advocates go further and submit that silence is to be equated with the retention of power for management, period. Owen Fairweather, in the 1983 edition of his often-cited text *Practice and Procedure in Labor Arbitration*, carries the banner for the reserved rights theory and asserts that the construction rule is as follows:

> When an arbitrator construes a labor agreement provision

---

[39]Id.
[40]Kramer, supra note 33, at 161.

under the residual rights doctrine or the parol evidence rule, he or she will hold that, if there is no negotiated written provision restricting management's right to take specific action, then there is no restriction on management's action.

. . .

Arbitrators have pointed out that the residual rights construction principle operates even where there is no clause in the agreement specifically reserving to management the right to manage. . . .

The parol evidence rule and the residual rights doctrine are further articulations of the arbitrator's jurisdiction and authority. The arbitrator must find a restriction imposed on management contained within the four corners of the agreement, simply because the arbitrator has been hired to interpret the terms of the written labor agreement and prescribe how they are to be applied to resolve a particular grievance.[41]

And so the debate continues, especially in the public sector where, as pointed out by Charles Killingsworth, "the intensity and the heat engendered by a management rights clause are directly related to the stage of development of a collective bargaining relationship."[42]

Focus of Study

George Torrence, in a text on management rights, argues that the expression "management rights" is loaded with controversy and, to the uninformed, it is all too easy to conclude that the major reason management makes such a fuss over these rights is pride, principle, or prejudice.[43] Specifically, Torrence contends that management rights concerns "the very practical matter of having and preserving the right of management to run the business efficiently and profitably."[44]

In operating a business and directing the work force, however, this much is clear: few management rights are absolute. As noted by Killingsworth, the pristine view of management rights—the view that management goes to the bargaining

---

[41]Fairweather, Practice and Procedure in Labor Arbitration, 2d Ed., at 211–13 (BNA Books, 1983) (footnotes omitted). Zack and Block, in Labor Agreement in Negotiation and Arbitration (BNA Books, 1983), contend that "[t]he more prevalent view is that those rights not specifically negotiated away from management by the union remain unfettered and within the control of the employer." Id. at 56.

[42]Killingsworth, "Management Rights and Union-Concerted Action," in Arbitration in Practice, ed. Zack, 81, 82 (ILR Press, N.Y. State Sch. Indus. & Lab. Rel. 1984).

[43]Torrence, Management's Right to Manage, 3 (BNA Books, 1968).

[44]Id.

table with all rights in the labor-management relationship—
"is based on a mistaken assumption as to the status of management and labor in the absence of a collective bargaining
agreement."[45] Besides being accountable to stockholders, customers, and the community at large, management has to be
guided by some sense of fairness and equity to its employees.
An insensitivity to common-sense notions of fairness will not
only result in a diminished labor supply, but will give renewed
meaning to the often-invoked saying that "it is management
that gives birth to unions."

Moreover, to the dismay of many companies and governmental bodies, through collective bargaining agreements unions
have imposed substantial barriers to unilateral decision making in areas that were once sacred prerogatives of management. Even in the absence of a union or a collective bargaining
agreement, federal and state statutes exert an ever-increasing
effect on the exercise of managerial discretion in all phases
of the employment relationship. This effect is so evident that
no text on management rights would be complete without
integrating the effect of legal constraints on managerial decision making. For example, it would be of little utility to
discuss management's power to require employee polygraph
examinations without noting that many states have now statutorily precluded any use of a lie detector test as a condition
of employment.[46]

The authors have accordingly approached the subject of
management rights by examining the major forces—collective
bargaining agreements as interpreted by arbitrators and the
law—that constrains managerial decision making. To this end
we have focused on the traditional areas of management rights,
such as hiring, evaluating, discipline and discharge, subcontracting, and even plant and work relocation.

We have also elected to direct attention to an area that
has been ignored within a management rights context but
which nevertheless presents an ever-increasing problem for
both management and labor—accommodating the rights of
management with the privacy concerns of employees. For example, management's right to regulate the off-duty conduct
of employees; or to require employees to submit to a polygraph,

---

[45]Killingsworth, supra note 42, at 82.
[46]See Chapter 9.

medical, or even a psychiatric examination; or to conduct searches or surveillance is an important area of inquiry.

In this effort we have attempted to present an integrative approach to the problem of what rights of both management and labor remain after the negotiation of a collective bargaining agreement. As expected, much of our focus is directed to the rights of the parties when the agreement is silent. The problem in most cases involving management rights issues is determining when the omission of a provision can be considered a conscious and deliberate choice of the parties.[47] Although there are not many absolutes, a number of discernible trends in the area of management rights are worthy of investigation and analysis.

---

[47]Wellington, supra note 23, writes: "As Lon Fuller has observed, when courts, in finding implied terms in contracts, talk of intention, they frequently are not talking about 'conscious and deliberate choice' but rather are discussing 'the manner in which current mores and conceptions of fairness can be said to influence the shape and conduct of parties without their being aware of the existence of alternatives.' " Id. at 115, citing Lon L. Fuller, Basic Contract Law, at 764 (West, 1947).

Chapter 2

The Role of Past Practice

Few questions in contemporary American labor arbitration are more difficult than determining when a past practice exists and when, if ever, it should be given the same status as if it were included in the written contract. In 1960 the United States Supreme Court approved the inclusion of past practices as part of the total bargaining of parties. The late Justice William O. Douglas, in *Steelworkers v. Warrior & Gulf Navigation Co.*,[1] stated:

> The labor arbitrator's source of law is not confined to the express provisions of the contract, as the industrial common law—the practice of the industry and the shop—is equally a part of the collective bargaining agreement although not expressed in it.[2]

Arbitrator Arthur Jacobs stated both the principle and the rationale for according deference to the parties' past practices in *Coca-Cola Bottling Co.*:[3]

> A union-management contract is far more than words on paper. It is also all the oral understandings, interpretations and mutually acceptable habits of action which have grown up around it over the course of time. Stable and peaceful relations between the parties depend upon the development of a mutually satisfactory superstructure of understanding which gives operating significance and practicality to the purely legal wording of the written contract. Peaceful relations depend, further, upon both parties faithfully living up to their mutual commitments as

---

[1]363 U.S. 574, 46 LRRM 2416 (1960).
[2]46 LRRM at 2419.
[3]9 LA 197 (1947).

20

embodied not only in the actual contract itself but also in the modes of action which have become an integral part of it.[4]

Likewise, Arbitrator Whitley McCoy, in *Esso Standard Oil Co.*,[5] declared that under certain circumstances custom can form an implied term of contract, stating:

> Where the Company has always done a certain thing, and the matter is so well understood and taken for granted that it may be said that the Contract was entered into upon the assumption that that customary action would continue to be taken, such customary action may be an implied term.[6]

Arbitrator Marlin Volz likewise recognized that the contractual relationship between the parties normally consists of more than the written word. Volz noted that day-to-day practices mutually accepted by the parties' collective bargaining agreement, particularly where these practices are not at variance with any written provision, are long-standing, and were not changed during contract negotiations.[7]

Describing past practice "as an umbrella for a great variety of problems," Arbitrator Alex Elson has asserted that past practice is actually a merger of a variety of concepts, all of which have their analogy in the law. These include: (1) reliance on custom or usage, (2) the application of at least one facet of the parol evidence rule (that parol evidence is not admissible to vary a clear and unambiguous contract but may be taken into consideration when ambiguity exists), and (3) the doctrines of contemporaneous construction, laches, and estoppel.[8]

Although there is little dispute that an arbitrator may consider the parties' past practice in rendering an award,[9] the

---

[4]Id. at 198.

[5]16 LA 73 (1951).

[6]Id. at 74.

[7]Metal Specialty Co., 39 LA 1265, 1269 (1962).

[8]Elson, "Discussion—Past Practice and the Administration of Collective Bargaining Agreements," Proceedings of the 14th Annual Meeting of NAA, 58, 58–59 (BNA Books, 1961).

[9]See, e.g., Office & Professional Employees Local 212 v. Curtiss-Wright Corp., 52 LRRM 2252 (N.Y. Sup. Ct., 1962)(in applying contract language to specific grievance, arbitrator must necessarily go beyond the literal wording of the contract); Furniture Workers v. Virco Corp., 257 F.Supp. 138, 50 LRRM 2681, 2685 (E.D. Ark., 1962)("Before he could interpret the contract, the arbitrator had to determine what the contract was, and he had a right to consider not only the formal agreement but collateral materials as well, including the actual practices prevailing in the Virco plant. . . . In finding that 'the contract' consisted of the formal agreement, the pamphlet, the bulletin, and the actual practices of the Company and in construing the entire contract and applying it to Rigdon's grievance, the arbitrator did nothing that

relationship between past practice and the rights of the parties under the agreement remains uncertain. Dean Harry Shulman may have expressed this most clearly when he declared that "commonly, inquiry into past practice . . . produces immersion in a bog of contradictions, fragments, doubts, and one-sided views."[10]

This chapter examines those issues most likely to be encountered in a typical arbitration case where custom or practice, Justice Douglas's "industrial common law," is alleged to have some effect. The importance of such an inquiry is clear: management requires the freedom and flexibility to respond to changing economic, technological, and operational conditions and, at the same time, the union needs the stability and security created by recognizing established past practices. The desires of management for flexibility and of the bargaining unit for stability often clash, and this conflict is invariably illustrated in the reported cases dealing with past practices.

Establishing a Past Practice

In *George Wiedemann Brewing Co.*,[11] Arbitrator Volz stated that "an analysis of the facts in each case is a more dependable guide in deciding the question than the application of some general formula." Still, various tests have been used by arbitrators as an aid in determining whether a custom or practice should be binding on the parties.

Arbitrators' Standards

Some decisions enforce only those practices concerning "major" conditions of employment. Elkouri and Elkouri have

---

he was not supposed to do."); Procter & Gamble Indep. Union v. Procter & Gamble, 195 F.Supp. 64, 48 LRRM 2443, 2445 (E.D. N.Y., 1961) ("There is no question that arbitrators may, in reaching their conclusion, consider past practices at the plant as well as in the industry generally and also 'bring to bear considerations which are not expressed in the contract as criteria for judgment,'" citing United Steelworkers v. Warrior & Gulf Navigation Co., 363 U.S. 574, 46 LRRM 2416 (1960)); NLRB v. Rockaway News Supply Co., 345 U.S. 71, 31 LRRM 2432, 2434 (1953)("Substantive rights and duties in the field of labor-management do not depend on verbal ritual reminiscent of medieval real property law."); Printing Indus. of Washington, D.C., Inc., Union Employers Div. v. Typographical Union No. 101 (Columbia), 353 F.Supp. 1348, 82 LRRM 2537, 2538 (D.D.C., 1973) ("The incorporation of past industry practice was within the arbitrator's authority and based on his wide knowledge and expertise in these matters.").
   [10]Ford Motor Co., 19 LA 237, 242 (1952).
   [11]54 LA 52, 55 (1969).

suggested a comparable test. They would enforce only those practices that involve employee benefits.[12] Both of these tests arguably encourage the arbitrator to "bootstrap" by characterizing the practice in a way that is itself dispositive, rather than providing a reason for a decision.

A review of published awards indicates that arbitrators have cited guidelines or standards that a course of conduct must meet before it can be regarded as a binding past practice. These standards have been best expressed by Arbitrator Richard Mittenthal in an address before the National Academy of Arbitrators. In relevant part the standards are as follows:

> First, there should be *clarity* and *consistency*. A course of conduct which is vague and ambiguous or which has been contradicted as often as it has been followed can hardly qualify as a practice. . . .
> Second, there should be *longevity* and *repetition*. A period of time has to elapse during which a consistent pattern of behavior emerges. Hence, one or two isolated instances of a certain conduct do not establish a practice. Just how frequently and over how long a period something must be done before it can be characterized as a practice is a matter of good judgement for which no formula can be devised.
> Third, there should be *acceptability*. The employees and the supervisors alike must have knowledge of the particular conduct and must regard it as the correct and customary means of handling a situation. Such acceptability may frequently be implied from long acquiesence in a known course of conduct. . . .
> One must consider, too, the *underlying circumstances* which give a practice its true dimensions. A practice is no broader than the circumstances out of which it has arisen, although its scope can always be enlarged in the day-to-day administration of the agreement. . . .
> And, finally, the significance to be attributed to a practice may possibly be affected by whether or not it is supported by *mutuality*. Some practices are the product, either in their inception or in their application, of a joint understanding; others develop from choices made by the employer in the exercise of its managerial discretion without any intention of a future commitment.[13]

Another representative and often-quoted set of criteria was promulgated by Arbitrator Jules Justin who declared that a past practice, in order to be binding on both parties, must

---

[12]Elkouri & Elkouri, How Arbitration Works, 4th Ed., 444 (BNA Books, 1985).

[13]Mittenthal, "Past Practice and the Administration of Collective Bargaining Agreements," Proceedings of the 14th Annual Meeting of NAA, 32–33 (BNA Books, 1961) (emphasis in original).

be (1) unequivocal, (2) clearly enunciated and acted upon, and (3) readily ascertainable over a reasonable period of time as a fixed and established practice accepted by both parties.[14] Similarly, after reviewing a "welter of decisions," Lester Block concluded that three requirements are essential: (1) the practice must be unequivocal, (2) it must have existed over a reasonably long period of time, and (3) it must have been mutually accepted by the parties.[15]

While all sorts of variables may lead an arbitrator to accept or reject the existence of a past practice, those most often discussed, and deserving of special note, are (1) knowledge, (2) longevity and repetition, (3) mutuality, and (4) the underlying circumstances giving rise to the practice (or changes in these circumstances).

Knowledge

A genuine past practice requires that both parties had some intention of dealing with a recurring problem in a particular way, although, as noted by arbitrator Berthold Levy, "at least one of them may not have manifested it affirmatively and might even be surprised to discover that such an intention existed on its part."[16] The rationale for the requirement of knowledge has been expressed by Arbitrator Levy as follows:

> The theoretical basis of the past practice doctrine is that the contract has been interpreted by the parties in a particular way and that their interpretation is found by its reflection in their conduct. But one party cannot by its conduct bind the other party unless that other is aware of the nature of the conduct; hence the requirement of knowledge.[17]

Rarely, if ever, will a party that is contesting the existence of a past practice concede knowledge of it. The arbitrator must instead draw an inference from the evidence. In this respect

---

[14]Celanese Corp. of Am., 24 LA 168, 172 (1954). See also Arkansas Power & Light Co., 81-1 ARB ¶8039 (Sisk, 1980), 3181; Pacific Sw. Airlines, 83-2 ARB ¶8474 (Richman, 1983), at 5113.

[15]Block, "Customs and Usages as Factors in *Arbitration Decisions*," N.Y.U. 15th Annual Conference on Labor, 313 (1962).

[16]United States Indus. Chems. Co., 76 LA 620, 622 (Levy, 1981); Pacific Sw. Airlines, 83-2 ARB ¶8474 (Richman, 1983)("Not only has the practice been open and notorious, but it has included officers of the prior bargaining agent as persons who have been called on their days off for first standby scheduling. It is impossible for the Union to claim that it did not have knowledge of the practice." Id. at 5115.).

[17]United States Indus. Chems. Co., supra note 16, at 622.

credibility considerations often enter the determination of whether a party had knowledge of a custom or practice. An employee, for example, may be hard pressed to argue before an arbitrator that he had no knowledge of the company's layoff policies when he had been a shop steward for 17 years and was privy to all layoff notices.[18]

Longevity and Repetition

This criterion is perhaps the most difficult to apply. An arbitrator is not expected to rule that a course of conduct constitutes a binding past practice when that conduct occurred only one or two times over a short period of time. Nonetheless, there are reported decisions where only one incident was found sufficient to establish a binding past practice.[19] Similarly, the mere fact that a pattern has been repeated time after time over many years is no assurance that an arbitrator will conclude that the conduct manifested such a degree of longevity and repetition to constitute a past practice. For example, Arbitrator Tim Bornstein, in *Moore Co.*,[20] ruled that an employer could unilaterally discontinue a 25-year "handshake" agreement under which the profits derived from an in-house vending machine were disbursed among several in-plant unions. The arbitrator reasoned that there are a number of ways for the parties to preserve past practices without identifying and describing them expressly in the contract, including use of a "maintenance of benefits" provision in the written agreement. Since the parties had not negotiated such a provision, despite the fact that the contract was silent concerning such practices,[21] the arbitrator stated that, regardless of his personal sense of fairness, he had no authority to write into the collective bargaining agreement an important practice where the parties for 25 years had elected to leave it outside their written contract.

The best that can be said is that longevity and repetition

---

[18]See, e.g., United States Indus. Chems. Co., 76 LA 620 (Levy, 1981); Union-Tribune Publishing Co., 85-1 ARB ¶8292, at 4211–12 (Weckstein, 1985) ("[T]he Grievant's testimony was credible and her understanding justified that she was unaware of any past practice or policy requiring her to call in by 6:00 p.m. on a sick day . . . ."

[19]See, e.g., Kennecott Copper Corp., Utah Div., 34 LA 763 (Kadish, 1960).

[20]72 LA 1079 (1979).

[21]See text accompanying notes 135–41 infra for a discussion of maintenance-of-standards clauses.

are but two variables considered by arbitrators in deciding whether a past practice exists and that the better view is that only one or two isolated instances of conduct are insufficient to establish a past practice. Each case will turn on its own facts and circumstances. One practitioner summarized this area as follows:

> The practical question, of course, is how to measure this "longevity and repetition"; just how long must a particular custom or practice be followed by the parties before it has "ripened" into a binding condition of employment? From the nature of things, it would seem that once again this is a factor for the good judgment of the arbitrator. No precise formula or "time limitation" can reasonably be specified. While it does not shed a great deal of light on a possible solution to say that it must be a "significant" period of time, that the practice should be long established, that it should be readily ascertainable over a "reasonable period of time" or that the practice must have existed for a sufficient length of time to establish a "pattern," it is not at all feasible to devise a more concrete measuring stick.[22]

In this same respect, Prasow and Peters have argued:

> [A] long and enduring past practice is not likely to be invalidated by a few exceptions. Not many practices could stand the test of undeviating uniformity. Most arbitrators will usually hold that a practice is binding if it shows a clear, predominant pattern. Infrequent exceptions will not normally upset the practice unless they are discriminatory. In the latter event, the arbitrator may either hold the company responsible for adverse effects of the discriminatory treatment or invalidate the practice.[23]

Mutuality

There is little dispute that in order for a past practice to be binding on the parties, there must be "mutuality" between them concerning that practice. Indeed, some authority suggests that mutuality, or a "meeting of the minds," is even more critical where the alleged past practice is one which purports to infringe upon a basic or fundamental management

---

[22]McLaughlin, "Custom and Past Practice in Labor Arbitration," 18 Arb. J. 205, 209–10 (1963). See also Latrobe Steel Co., 85-1 ARB ¶8308, at 4278 (Creo, 1985)("There can be no binding past practice in something new since there is not even a past history.")

[23]Prasow & Peters, Arbitration and Collective Bargaining: Conflict Resolution in Labor Relations, 2d Ed., 167 (McGraw-Hill, 1983).

right, such as the right to control the nature of the business or to effect a plant closing.[24]

Perhaps the most often-quoted discussion of mutuality and past practice is that by Dean Harry Shulman in *Ford Motor Co.*,[25]

> A practice, whether or not fully stated in writing, may be the result of an agreement or mutual understanding. And in some industries there are contractual provisions requiring the continuance of unnamed practices in existence at the execution of the collective bargaining agreement. . . . A practice thus based on mutual agreement may be subject to change only by mutual agreement. Its binding quality is due, however, not to the fact that it is past practice but rather to the agreement in which it is based.[26]

Dean Shulman further noted:

> [T]here are other practices which are not the result of joint determination at all. They may be mere happenstance, that is, methods that developed without design or deliberation. Or they may be choices by Management in the exercise of managerial discretion as to the convenient methods at the time. In such cases there is no thought of obligation or commitment for the future. Such practices are merely present ways, not prescribed ways, of doing things. The relevant item of significance is not the nature of the particular method but the managerial freedom with respect to it. Being the product of managerial determination in its permitted discretion such practices are, in the absence of contractual provision to the contrary, subject to change in the same discretion. The law and the policy of collective bargaining may well require that the employer inform the Union and that he be ready to discuss the matter with it on request. But there is no requirement of mutual agreement as a condition precedent to a change of practice of this character.[27]

Dean Shulman went on to argue that a contrary holding would place a past practice on a par with the written agreement and create the anomaly that, while the parties expend a great effort in negotiating the details of an agreement, they unknowingly and unintentionally commit themselves to unstated and perhaps more important past practices.

---

[24]Willamette Indus., Inc., 78 LA 1137 (Milentz, 1982), citing Shell Oil Co., 44 LA 1219, 1222 (1965); see Saginaw Mining Co., 76 LA 911, 914 (Ruben, 1981); Browning-Ferris Indus., Inc., 68 LA 1347, 1353 (Teple, 1977).

[25]19 LA 237 (1952).

[26]Id. at 241.

[27]Id. at 241–42. In this regard, see Arbitrator L.S. Mewhinney's application of Dean Shulman's analysis in American Petrofina Oil & Ref., 71 LA 852 (1978) at 855–56.

Similarly, Arbitrator David Kaplan, in *Immigration & Naturalization Service*,[28] declared:

> Many arbitrators are of the opinion that once it has been conclusively demonstrated that a "past practice" does in fact exist, then such a past practice rises to the level of an express contractual provision. Such demonstration of proof however must also show that *both* parties have by their conduct *mutually* agreed, in effect, to modify or amend the written agreement.[29]

Arbitrators have discussed the concept of mutuality and the manner in which a neutral determines whether it exists in a particular bargaining relationship. For example, in *Burdick Corp.*,[30] Arbitrator William Petrie stated:

> In weighing evidence relating to the past practice, arbitrators will look closely to the degree of *mutuality* present in each case. A unilaterally adopted practice or change of practice, will not be regarded as persuasive evidence of a mutually agreed-upon interpretation of the contract, unless there is evidence of acceptance or acquiescence by the other party. ... Had the Union been informed of the change of practice, any failure to promptly protest the non-payment would have been strong evidence of mutuality.[31]

Some arbitrators have inferred mutuality from the length of time that the practice has been operative. Thus, in *Weston Paper & Manufacturing Co.*,[32] Arbitrator George Bowles declared:

> In brief, the Union established a consistent past practice for time off for Executive Board members for a meeting to prepare for a later membership meeting. This practice is of sufficient duration and specificity that one can infer mutuality, that is, agreement between the parties of its existence. Hence, it is entitled to protection.[33]

The important point to stress is that not every practice which develops over an extended period of time can be considered a consensual and binding past practice. This point was best expressed by Arbitrator Mittenthal in *Wyandotte Chem-*

[28]78 LA 842 (1982).
[29]Id. at 847 (emphasis in original).
[30]76 LA 611 (1981).
[31]Id. at 618–19 (emphasis in original).
[32]76 LA 1273 (1981).
[33]Id. at 1277.

ical Corp.[34] In that case the union claimed that the company was required to assign certain tasks to a specific class of employees on the basis of a past practice. Arbitrator Mittenthal, addressing the mutuality requirement, had this to say:

> For a practice, to be enforceable, must be supported by the *mutual agreement* of the parties. Its binding quality is due not to the fact that it is a past practice but rather to the agreement on which it is based. Yet, there are many practices which are not the result of joint determination at all. . . .
>
> . . . Only those [practices] which are supported by mutual agreement may, apart from any basis in the contract, be considered binding conditions of employment. They must be continued until changed by mutual consent. To treat all practices as binding conditions of employment, without regard to the matter of mutuality, would be to place past practice on an equal footing with the written Agreement, a result which the parties could hardly have contemplated. There is, after all, no provision in this Agreement which specifically requires this continuance of existing practices. The arbitrator certainly has no authority to write a "past practice" clause into the Agreement under the guise of contract interpretation.
>
> . . .
>
> . . . The mere exercise of this discretion in a given way over a period of time cannot by itself produce later restrictions on such discretion. Or, to express the point in the context of this case, merely because the Company had seen fit twice to assign the disputed work to Yard Department personnel does not mean that it may not assign the work to anyone else. In the absence of clear and convincing evidence that the work assignment practice is supported by mutual agreement, I have no choice but to deny the grievance.[35]

This mutuality can be either express or implied. For example, one party may announce the practice at bargaining sessions with explicit concurrence from the other side. Alternatively, there may be some memorandum of understanding in existence. Frequently, however, the arbitrator will have the task of determining mutuality from the conduct of the parties over an extended period of time.

In any event, most arbitrators have held that the burden rests upon the party asserting a binding prior practice to establish the existence as well as the specific details of the prac-

---

[34]39 LA 65 (1962).
[35]Id. at 67–68 (emphasis in original).

tice at issue.[36] Richard McLaughlin, reporting his research on the subject, stated that "there is no question that the burden of proving the existence and mutual acceptance of a past practice is upon the party alleging it." He went on to contend:

> In many cases, the alleged practice will be cherished by the employees as an "important condition of work." On the other hand, the employer may feel it is simply an "inherent right of management" which he is free to terminate at will. It may involve thousands of dollars or thousands of man-hours. It is for this reason that the burden of proving the existence and application of a past practice will ordinarily be no small task.[37]

And when the evidence is of equal weight on both sides, the case will be resolved against the party having the burden.[38]

Underlying Circumstances

No past practice, even one having considerable longevity and frequently repeated, is given effect after the underlying circumstances that gave rise to the practice have changed. A past practice always depends upon the continuation of the factual circumstances that gave rise to the practice in the first instance.

Thus, in *Dravo Corp.*,[39] Arbitrator Clair Duff ruled that a reduction in crew size did not violate an established past practice when an employer discontinued assignment of a handyman-painter to assist spray painters following the introduction of new painting equipment. The arbitrator reasoned that signficant changes occurred in both the equipment and working procedures (the underlying circumstances) which destroyed the existence of the former practice, if one ever existed.

---

[36]Shell Oil Co., 44 LA 1219, 1224 (Turkus, 1965); Kelsey-Hayes Co., 74 LA 50, 53 (Heinsz, 1980); Saginaw Mining Co., 76 LA 911, 914 (Ruben, 1981) quoting Chief Umpire Selby in Arbitration Review Board Decision, 78–2 (1979) (" 'party claiming a past practice has the obligation to assume the burden of persuasion that there was a past practice and what its nature and scope of coverage and application may be. That proof should show that the practice is unequivocal, clearly enunciated and acted upon, and readily ascertainable over a reasonable period of time as a fixed and established practice accepted by both parties.' "); City of Minneapolis, 82 LA 956, 960 (Ver Ploeg, 1984) ("party carries a heavy burden when it tries to prove the existence of a past practice"); Pepsi-Cola Bottlers of Akron, Inc., 82 LA 1026, 1029 (Feldman, 1984).

[37]McLaughlin, supra note 22, at 217–18.

[38]Rockwell Int'l Corp., 82 LA 42 (Feldman, 1984).

[39]76 LA 903 (1981).

And in *W.E. Plechaty Co.*,[40] Arbitrator Roger Abrams held that the past practice of not subcontracting work when employees were on layoff was not binding where the circumstances giving rise to the practice—availability of equipment—were not present.

Arbitrator Miles Ruben, in *Saginaw Mining Co.*,[41] pointed out that "when a change in the set of conditions that gives rise to the practice takes place, a change in the practice may be made to the extent that the changed conditions affect the practice."[42] Arbitrator Ruben held that an employer's annual Christmas distribution of hams to employees, which had taken place without interruption for at least 10 years, constituted a past practice that grew out of and was dependent upon the continued financial success of the corporation. Despite a maintenance-of-standards clause in the agreement, the arbitrator ruled that, due to the company's financial loss that year, the employer was not obligated to distribute hams. Arbitrator Ruben also directed the company to resume the practice the following year unless it experienced another loss.

Determining when the circumstances that gave rise to a practice no longer exist can be difficult. A gradual erosion of the conditions may leave some former conditions still operative. The arbitrator must reconstruct the events that gave rise to the practice and then determine if there remains any utility in maintaining the former practice.

Silence in Later Bargaining

Professors Cox and Dunlop once wrote that "a collective bargaining agreement should be deemed, unless a contrary intention is manifest, to carry forward for its term the major terms and conditions of employment, not covered by the agreement, which prevailed when the agreement was executed."[43]

---

[40]78 LA 404 (1982).

[41]76 LA 911 (1981).

[42]Id. at 915, citing Sioux Tools, Inc., 64 LA 571 (Fitzsimmons, 1975); Three Rivers Mgmt. Corp., 68 LA 547 (McDermott, 1977); Proform, Inc., 67 LA 493, (Render, 1976); Western Auto Supply Co., 63 LA 569 (Petrie, 1974); Lord Baltimore Press, 72-1 ARB ¶8096 (Cahn, 1972). See also City of Harper Woods, 81-2 ARB ¶8494 (Roumell, 1981) ("[I]t is widely recognized that should the underlying basis or understanding for the past practice disintegrate, the practice, no longer being applicable, loses its binding nature." Id. at 5171). St. Regis Paper Co., 85-1 ARB ¶8141 (Byars, 1985) ("In the instant case the particular circumstances of the dispute have not arisen before and, therefore, have not become a part of the parties' practice." Id. at 3586.)

[43]Cox & Dunlop, "The Duty to Bargain Collectively During the Term of an Existing Agreement," 63 Harv. L. Rev. 1097, 1116–17 (1950).

This principle has been expressed by numerous arbitrators. For example, in *Jafco, Inc.*,[44] the employer discontinued paying time and one-half for Sunday work without discussing the matter at negotiations. Even though the agreement was silent on the issue of premium pay for Sunday work, the arbitrator found that there was a past practice and ordered the practice reinstated and awarded back pay for the grievants. In sustaining the grievance the arbitrator found that the employer was obligated to discuss the issue with the union during negotiations rather than change a term and condition of employment after negotiations had concluded. The arbitrator declared that "by remaining silent the Employer knew, or should have known, that the Union in reliance on the past practice would not seek to renegotiate [the agreement]."[45]

Likewise, Arbitrator David Borland, in *Edward C. Levy Co.*,[46] ruled that it was improper for an employer to prorate the Christmas bonus of those employees who did not work a full year. The arbitrator pointed out that during the negotiations for the new agreement no discussion of the issue occurred and, as such, no notice of a discontinuance could have been provided to the union. More important, the arbitrator noted that "any obligation the Company believes the Union might have had to raise the issue was dissipated by a failure to notify the Union of any anticipated change."[47]

Perhaps the best summary on this issue is provided by Arbitrator Samuel Chalfie, who declared:

> A collective bargaining agreement is not negotiated in a vacuum. Rather it is negotiated in a setting of past practices and prior agreements. It may be reasonably assumed that the parties, in shaping bargaining demands as to wages and employee benefits, do so with silent recognition of existing unwritten benefits and working conditions.[48]

[44]82 LA 283 (Armstrong, 1984).
[45]Id. at 286.
[46]81 LA 529 (1983).
[47]Id. at 536.
[48]Diamond Nat'l Corp., 52 LA 33, 35 (1969). See also Eau Claire County, 76 LA 333, 335 (McCrary, 1981)("the parties will be presumed to have been aware of the instant practice as bargaining for the current agreement took place in the context of the practice. In addition, due to the parties' awareness of the instant practice and the Company's failure to repudiate the practice during the negotiations, it is reasonable to conclude that the parties intended for the practice to continue in force."); A.O. Smith Corp., 23 LA 27, 32 (Prasow, 1954) ("It is a well-settled principle of industrial arbitration that where past practice has established a meaning for language that is subsequently used by the parties in a new agreement, the language will be presumed to have the meaning given it by past practice."); Duquesne Brewing

Prior Awards

Although arbitration awards involving different parties but similar issues do not have the precedential force of judicial decisions, many principles for applying and interpreting language commonly found in collective bargaining agreements have evolved from published awards. The resulting "industrial common law" frequently provides solutions to union-management problems. These published awards form the basis for many of the industrial rules adopted by both arbitrators and practitioners, although many unpublished awards also find their way into hearings and briefs as a foundation for arguments based on "precedent."

The relatively relaxed arbitral version of *stare decisis*, or giving authoritative force to prior awards when a similar issue arises between different parties, is to be distinguished from the stronger application of *res judicata*, or refusing to permit the merits of the same event or incident to be relitigated. When an arbitrator has rendered an award in a dispute between the *same* parties on a similar issue, the treatment of the prior award tends to move from that of *stare decisis* to that of *res judicata*. Issuance of the initial arbitration award generally bars any subsequent *court* action on the merits of the same event. In a like manner, arbitrators recognize and apply *res judicata* concepts where the same parties are involved and the same issue was presented in an earlier arbitration. In such cases, it is often held that adherence to prior awards is desirable because of the need for finality, stability in labor-management relations, and consistency in contractual interpretation.[49] Perhaps the principle was best expressed by Arbitrator Jack Johannes, who stated that "whether Ar-

---

Co., 54 LA 1146, 1149 (Krimsly, 1970)("[I]n utilizing the same language in the present contract that it had in the past contract, the Union carries with it the same interpretation as provided in that past language, and the Company had the right to rely on accepting this same language, that the procedure used under that language in the prior contract would be acceptable in the present contract."); Trans-Buckeye Sheet & Strip Steel Co., 85-1 ARB ¶8214 (Spilker, 1985)("The practice derives its binding effect from the fact that it represents a substantial economic benefit to the employees and the recognized and consistent response to situations involving insurance coverage for disabled employees. Here, the practice at issue was unilaterally instituted by the Company, and since it has continued for some 27 years and there was no evidence that it was discussed during negotiations, the logical assumption is that the Parties intended to maintain the *status quo*." Id. at 3897 (emphasis in original).).

[49]See, e.g., Board of Educ. of Cook County, 73 LA 310, 314 (Hill, 1979); General Tel. Co. of Ohio, 70 LA 240, 244 (Ellmann, 1978); Vestal & Hill, "Preclusion in Labor Controversies," 35 Okla. L. Rev. 281 (1982).

bitrators speak of *res judicata, authoritative force, heavy precedential value,* or *stare decisis,* the weight of arbitral opinion is strongly in favor of holding a prior arbitration award which involves the same issues, parties and contract provisions, controlling of the subsequent case."[50]

Issues of preclusion arise in past practice cases where a party is urging that a prior award between the same parties is dispositive of a past practice issue in a second arbitration. The argument may take one of two different forms. A party may assert that a prior arbitration on the same issue renders the second grievance procedurally not arbitrable. Alternatively, an argument may be made that the prior award goes to the merits of the second grievance rather than to its arbitrability, and resolves the issue. Either way, the existence of the award may preclude a party from relitigating an issue or a claim in a subsequent grievance proceeding.

Failure to File a Grievance

There is some authority for the proposition that a union's failure to file a grievance may be construed as acceptance of a past practice. For example, under a past practice of considering an employee a "voluntary quit" when he walks off the job, one arbitrator sustained the discharge of an employee who punched out and left the plant early after arguing with his foreman. The arbitator reasoned that although under common standards the penalty was too severe, in similar cases the union either did not pursue the matter or dropped any complaints short of arbitration, thus implying agreement with management.[51]

Another arbitrator expressed this principle as follows:

> "It is generally accepted that actual practice, if continued without protest over a substantial period of time, is compelling evidence of intent. . . . Having expressed no objections to the

---

[50]Atlantic Richfield Co., 79 LA 764, 768 (Johannes, 1982).
[51]Eltra Corp., 76 LA 62, 68 (Raymond, 1981). See also White Mfg. Co., 74 LA 1191 (LeBaron, 1980); Arco Pipe Line Co., 85-1 ARB ¶8237 (Marcus, 1985); Associated Wholesale Grocers, Inc., 82-1 ARB ¶8240 (Mikrut, 1982).

practice, the Union has in effect accepted the interpretation [of the employer]."[52]

Likewise, Arbitrator Marvin Feldman, in *Teledyne Monarch Rubber*,[53] ruled that management had the right to assign non-unit personnel to reset microprocessor equipment with new software where in the past the union failed to grieve management's programming of microprocessor equipment. The reasoning of the arbitrator is particularly instructive:

> It might be further noted that the bargaining unit had never grieved for such work during their entire course of bargaining history at the facility, which dates back some eight years at the time of hearing and which had been accomplished, according to Company testimony, over a thousand times by management personnel. Thus it appears that the bargaining unit, while it may choose to police the contract of collective bargaining as it sees fit from time to time, cannot waive a right forever and then attempt to grieve one workload when the workload has been accomplished a thousand times at least prior without protest. . . . [F]ailure of the bargaining unit to protest such activity as it was occasioned throughout the course of years at the facility leads this arbitrator to believe that as a matter of fact the bargaining unit realized over that period of years that they as a matter of fact had no right to the workload which is grieved in this particular matter at this particular time.[54]

It should be noted, however, that a union may elect not to grieve a practice for numerous reasons that have nothing to do with the merits of a case. Thus, the better rule is that acquiescence should not be presumed only from the failure to file a grievance. The problem for the arbitrator then becomes one of determining when failure to act can fairly be equated with active acceptance of the other party's course of conduct.

In this regard, a union is not forever precluded from insisting upon compliance with the contract where a past practice is in apparent conflict with the written agreement. A study of arbitral authority indicates that a union desiring to

---

[52]Port Drum Co., 82 LA 942, 944–45 (Holman, 1984), quoting Willys Motors, Inc., 22 LA 289 (Allen, 1954). See also Merchants Fast Motor Lines, Inc., 85-1 ARB ¶8215 (Sartain, 1985)("[I]t is clear that a long-continued practice that is reasonably (or wholly) consistent and has never been protested may and often does throw light on what was in fact meant by the provision." Id. at 3900.). Amax Chem. Corp., 85-1 ARB ¶8286 (Sartain, 1985)(citing the Union's failure to file a grievance over an 18-year period); Red Wing Shoe Co., 85-1 ARB ¶8095 (Bognanno, 1985)("[The company's] interpretation has gone unchallenged in the grievance process and evidences the parties' intent." Id. at 3387.).
[53]75 LA 963 (1980).
[54]Id. at 965.

secure contractual compliance would be advised to notify the employer that continued violations will give rise to a grievance. Any impact that failure to file a grievance might have on arbitration will then be less than if no notice had ever been given.

Failure to Exercise a Contractual Right

The issue of waiver frequently arises in past practice cases through the failure to exercise a contractual right. The better view is that the non-use of a right does not entail its loss and that management or a labor organization can assert or reassert a right under the agreement, or even recapture a right which has not yet ripened into a past practice. As stated by Arbitrator Burton Turkus:

> Viewed in its best light for the Union, the evidence is that the Employer was able to fill its overtime needs on a voluntary basis and thus found it unnecessary to vindicate its right to require such work. Indeed, insistence upon this right did not become necessary until changing Union and employee attitudes, increased production, a tight labor market and the need to meet competition created a situation in which it was problematic whether production schedules could be met without requiring overtime.
>
> In these circumstances, I shall not find that the Employer waived its contractual right simply because it did previously choose not to enforce that right and test it in arbitration. The failure over a long period of time to exercise a legitimate function of management is not a surrender of the right to start exercising such right nor does it operate as a past practice or mode of action which becomes an implied term or integral part of the labor agreement of the parties. Mere non-use of a contractual right does not entail a loss of it.[55]

A major exception to this principle exists where there has been laxity in enforcing grievance-procedure time limits. The better weight of arbitral authority suggests that, absent notice, a party cannot insist on strict compliance with the time limits to the detriment of the other side.[56] However, not all

---

[55]Colt Firearms Div., 52 LA 493, 496 (1963). See also Immigration & Naturalization Serv., 78 LA 842, 847 (Kaplan, 1982); Transamerica Delaval, Inc., 84 LA 190, 194 (Brisco, 1985).

[56]See, e.g., Printing Indus. of Metro Washington, D.C., 77 LA 911 (Epstein, 1981)("[T]he short delay in the filing of the ... grievance was certainly in accord with the parties' practices." Id. at 916.); District of Columbia Dept. of Corrections, 77 LA 793 (Lipton, 1981); Associated School Bus Serv., 72 LA 859 (Krebs, 1979).

courts agree that a party can be estopped from insisting on compliance with time limitations despite past non-enforcement. For example, in *Detroit Coil Co. v. Machinists Lodge 82*,[57] the Sixth Circuit considered the validity of an award that held a grievance arbitrable despite noncompliance with the time limits outlined in the collective bargaining agreement. The arbitrator reasoned that the parties in the past had not enforced the time limits. The appellate court acknowledged that "an arbitrator can look for guidance beyond the express terms of the contract to the past application of that contract."[58] It stated, however, that there was no evidence in the record which would allow the arbitrator to conclude that the parties to any extent waived compliance with the time limits and, accordingly, the court of appeals reversed the lower court's decision sustaining the award. Even though the arbitrator outlined specific instances where the parties had waived the time limits, the court nevertheless concluded that the arbitrator's award failed to draw its essence from the agreement.

Parol Evidence Rule

The parol evidence rule is not a rule of evidence but a substantive rule of contract interpretation. Simply stated, the rule excludes any evidence of agreements or understandings made prior to or contemporaneous with the parties' written agreement where the evidence is used to add to, vary, or alter the terms of a written agreement that is intended to be the final and complete integration of the parties' bargain.

It must be emphasized that the parties' intent is critical. If the parties did not intend the written agreement to be the final integration of the bargain, the rule is not applicable.[59]

The rule has applicability in past practice cases where one party is introducing evidence which, if credited, would alter the terms of the written contract. A question arises as to its use where the practice at issue is not covered in the written contract. One view is that prior or contemporaneous

---

[57] 594 F.2d 575, 100 LRRM 3138 (CA 6, 1979).

[58] 100 LRRM at 3141.

[59] In our text, Evidence in Arbitration, 52 (BNA Books, 1980), we write: "One way to ascertain whether a written agreement was intended to be the complete integration of the bargain would be by direct reference to the agreement itself. For example, the agreement may contain a 'completeness of agreement' clause, otherwise known as a 'zipper' clause."

agreements upon which the contract is silent are not foreclosed because they do not vary the terms of the written contract. According to this line of thinking, a party may appropriately introduce any evidence relating to the establishment of a past practice when the agreement is silent on the issue. Adopting this view, one arbitrator notes:

> Such agreements may have been added inducements or consideration to enter into the contract. It also means that agreements that arise subsequent to the adoption of the contract language are admissible to vary the terms of the written contract in order to evidence that the parties subsequently modified the contract or entered into a novation.[60]

An opposing view argues that even where the contract is silent, agreements that were made prior to or contemporaneous with the written contract should be excluded if used to alter the written agreement in any way. According to this view the contract is altered when something is added that is not mentioned in the written agreement itself.

Because an established past practice represents an agreement of the parties, evidence of custom or practice should be admissible to show that a modification of the contract took place. Thus, even where the issue is addressed in the written agreement, a party may appropriately introduce evidence of a practice and not run afoul of the parol evidence rule where the agreements, statements, and understandings took place after the adoption of the written contract. While the practice may not be held to take precedence over the written agreement, the parol evidence rule should not preclude an arbitrator from considering the evidence in this regard.

Applying a Past Practice

Once a party has demonstrated the existence of a past practice, the issue then arises as to the effect to be given that practice. A review of arbitration awards and court decisions reveals four primary uses or applications of past practices: (1) to clarify ambiguous language in the parties' agreement; (2) to implement general contractual language; (3) to establish an enforceable condition of employment where the con-

---

[60]Total Petroleum, Inc., 78 LA 729, 736–37 (Roberts, 1982).

tract is silent on the issue; or (4) to modify or amend apparently unambiguous language in the agreement.

Clarifying Ambiguous Language

There is little dispute that a past practice may be used to clarify ambiguous contractual language. Arbitrator Mittenthal expressed the reasoning for resorting to past practice when the contract is ambiguous as follows:

> How the parties act under an agreement may be just as important as what they say in it. To borrow a well-known adage, "actions speak louder than words." From the conflict and accommodation which are daily occurrences in plant life, there arises "a context of practices, usages, and rule-of-thumb interpretations" which gradually give substance to the ambiguous language of the agreement. A practice, once developed, is the best evidence of what the language meant to those who wrote it. . . . The real significance of practice as an interpretative aid lies in the fact that the arbitrator is responsive to the values and standards of the parties. A decision based on past practice emphasizes not the personal viewpoint of the arbitrator but rather the parties' own history, what they have found to be proper and agreeable over the years.[61]

The more difficult question is determining when language is ambiguous. As noted by one authority, language does not become ambiguous merely because the parties disagree over the meaning of a phrase, for that would encourage them to contest the clearest provision in the hope of a favorable arbitration award.

> "The test most often cited is that there is no ambiguity if the contract is so clear on the issue that the intentions of the parties can be determined using no other guise than the contract itself. The test borders on a tautology, however, for it comes perilously close to a statement that language is clear and unambiguous if it is clear on its face. Perhaps a better way of putting it would be to ask if a single, obvious and reasonable meaning appears from a reading of the language in the context of the rest of the contract. If so, that meaning is to be applied."[62]

Arbitrator Robert Mueller, in *Community Mental Health Center of Linn County*,[63] has offered the following test:

---

[61]Mittenthal, supra note 13, at 37 (citations omitted).
[62]Hill & Sinicropi, supra note 59, at 52–53, quoting Nolan, Labor Arbitration Law and Practice, 163 (West, 1979).
[63]76 LA 1236 (1981).

To test whether or not a particular provision or provisions
of a contract are clear and unambiguous or are in fact ambiguous, one must take a particular provision and examine the
manner of its application throughout the contract to determine
whether or not it has been afforded a consistent application.[64]

Another arbitrator, holding that the employer was bound
by a past practice, had this to say:

Inasmuch as there has been no previous history or any discussion or negotiations by the parties concerning this portion of
the agreement, it is my conclusion that there can be no mis-
understanding as to the interpretation of the contract provisions as they have been previously applied.[65]

The courts have likewise sanctioned the use of past practice to clarify ambiguous language. For example, the Fifth
Circuit, in *Boise Cascade Corp. v. Steelworkers Local 7001*,[66]
held that a lower court exceeded the proper scope of judicial
review when it vacated an award because it did not draw its
essence from the collective bargaining agreement. The arbitrator had ruled that the contract was ambiguous and that
the past practice favored the union. The lower court determined that the language at issue was clear and unambiguous
and thus the arbitrator exceeded his authority when he resorted to extrinsic evidence. Reversing the lower court, the
Fifth Circuit declared that the arbitrator's determination that
the contract was ambiguous and that extrinsic evidence favored the union's position "cannot be said to have no foundation in reason or fact." The appellate court also stated that
the "no additions or alterations" clause cannot be read as
precluding the arbitrator from considering extrinsic evidence
to explain an agreement that may rationally be considered
ambiguous. In the words of the court:

An arbitrator faced with the task of interpreting an arguably
ambiguous contract provision may look to extrinsic evidence
for assistance. The Supreme Court in *Warrior & Gulf* stated:
The labor arbitrator's source of law is not confined to the
express provisions of the contract, as the industrial common
law—the practices of the industry and the shop—is equally

---
[64]Id. at 1238.
[65]DeBourgh Mfg. Co., 75 LA 814, 815 (Kapsch, 1980).
[66]588 F.2d 127, 100 LRRM 2481 (CA 5, 1979).

a part of the collective bargaining agreement although not expressed in it.[67]

The limited scope of judicial review of arbitrators' decisions does not mean that an arbitrator's finding that an agreement is ambiguous is immune to challenge in the courts. In this respect the Sixth Circuit, in *Morgan Services, Inc. v. Clothing & Textile Workers Local 323*,[68] stated:

> Insofar as the Union argues that the construction of ambiguities in collective bargaining agreements is a task for arbitrators and not for courts, it is correct. But insofar as it argues that the threshold determination that a given provision is ambiguous is *exclusively* a question for the arbitrator, it errs. If the Union's position were accepted, then the rule that arbitrators cannot ignore or modify unambiguous contract provisions would be wholly nugatory; an arbitrator could easily circumvent this rule by making a finding that a provision is ambiguous when in fact it is not. The initial question of whether an ambiguity exists is amenable to judicial review to the same extent and in the same manner as other decisions or arbitrators. That is, the determination that an ambiguity exists will be reviewed to determine whether the decision draws its essence from the agreement. . . . This is to be contrasted to the situation in which an arbitrator adopts one of several possible conflicting constructions of an unclear provision in a collective bargaining agreement. In the latter situation, courts will rarely, if ever, substitute their own judgment for that of the arbitrator.[69]

In contrast to the arbitrator, the appellate court found that an employer had exclusive authority to determine sanctions for insubordination under an agreement that provided that "[a]ny employee may be discharged without redress if proven guilty of . . . insubordination."

The Seventh Circuit likewise has ruled, in *Textron, Inc., Burkart Randall Division v. Machinists Lodge 1076*,[70] that

---

[67]100 LRRM at 2483, citing Warrior & Gulf Navigation Co., 363 U.S. 574, 46 LRRM 2416, 2419. See also Television & Radio Artists v. Storer Broadcasting Co., 660 F.2d 151, 108 LRRM 2727 (CA 6, 1981); Rainbow Glass Co. v. Teamsters Local 610, 663 F.2d 814, 108 LRRM 3038 (CA 8, 1981)("Because a collective bargaining agreement is a generalized code covering the entire employment relationship and governing a myriad of cases, its draftsman cannot anticipate all the contingencies and problems that may require resolution under the terms of the agreement. . . . The gaps that naturally arise in the labor agreement may be filled by examining sources outside the four corners of the contract. . . . Such an examination is often essential to ascertain the intent of the parties under the current contract and determine their rights and obligations." 108 LRRM at 3041 (citations omitted).).
[68]724 F.2d 1217, 115 LRRM 2368 (CA 6, 1984).
[69]115 LRRM at 2372 n.8 (emphasis in original; citations omitted).
[70]648 F.2d 462, 107 LRRM 2836 (CA 7, 1981).

when an explicit contractual provision restricts the arbitrator's use of past practice to elucidate the meaning of contractual provisions, an arbitrator exceeded his authority if, in rendering an award, he relied solely on the company's practice. The court of appeals remanded the case to the arbitrator for clarification in accordance with its opinion.

Implementing General Language

In negotiating an agreement there are invariably some items that cannot be made specific. For example, rather than outline all the situations that can give rise to discipline and discharge, the parties usually include a provision in the contract that limits managerial discretion to imposing discipline or discharge only for just or proper cause. Likewise, past practices would appear especially appropriate in interpreting a provision that provides that a leave of absence may be granted "for any valid reason."[71] Another example is a provision to the effect that an employer will distribute overtime on an equal basis "to the extent practicable under the circumstances of each assignment."

The examples present situations where all the possibilities that may take place during the term of the agreement cannot be anticipated by the parties. The "gaps" are accordingly left to the arbitrator to fill in based, in whole or part, on what the practice has been between the parties.

Establishing Conditions of Employment

Whether a past practice can be used to establish an enforceable condition of employment separate from any basis in the agreement depends upon one's view of management rights and the collective bargaining agreement. Under the "reserved rights" theory, management retains all powers except those expressly conceded in the collective bargaining agreement or restricted by law. Under this theory management does not look to the agreement to ascertain its rights but, rather, the agreement is consulted to find out what rights it has ceded to

---

[71]Northern Ind. Pub. Serv. Co., 80 LA 41 (Winton, 1982).

the union.[72] Illustrative of this view is *Moore Co.*,[73] a decision in which Arbitrator Tim Bornstein stated:

> Certainly in the early days of labor arbitration there was a tendency for arbitrators to bend the terms of a collective bargaining contract to achieve what arbitrators viewed as a "just result." It was in this context that some arbitrators held that a past practice was binding on the parties, even though it had no basis whatever in the contract. That view, which was based primarily on a sense of natural justice rather than contract interpretation, is frankly of doubtful legality. While the literature of labor arbitration, especially the proceedings of the National Academy of Arbitrators, is full of thoughtful discussions on this subject, the prevailing view today is—I believe—that a past practice that has *no basis whatever* in the contract is not enforceable.[74]

Likewise, Arbitrator B. J. Speroff, adopting the reserved rights theory, declared:

> To state "To deny this grievance signals the Company that they can say anything, do anything, or sign anything, without being held accountable" is absolutely correct so long as there is nothing in the corpus of the contract that denies them those actions. In short, all rights and prerogatives not expressly forbade the Company—such as the right to contract out work—redound to the benefit of the Company.[75]

Another arbitrator commented that:

> [T]he disputed portions of the collective bargaining agreement under which this controversy has arisen do not address the specific question of how seniority is to affect the scheduling of work when the plant shuts down for the purpose of conducting annual inventory. Absent such specification, it would appear that the "residual rights theory" of management would be applicable in that ". . . where the union fails to attempt or fails to obtain such limitation on management's rights, the employer continues to possess all such rights undiminished."[76]

And Arbitrator John Boyer, in *Minnesota Mining & Manufacturing Co.*,[77] stated:

---

[72]See, e.g., the discussion by Arbitrator Howlett in Diecast Corp., 75 LA 66, 72–73 (1980).
[73]72 LA 1079 (1979).
[74]Id. at 1088 (emphasis in original).
[75]Air Prods. & Chems., Inc., 81 LA 465, 467 (Speroff, 1983).
[76]Olin Corp., 81 LA 585, 587 (Mikrut, 1983), citing Baer, Practice and Precedent in Labor Relations (Lexington, 1972).
[77]81 LA 338 (1983).

It is axiomatic in dispute resolution that managerial autonomy or rights may only be restricted or limited through direct negotiation and/or concession in the bargaining process. Such philosophy and principle were enunciated by the often quoted Neutral Lewis E. Solomon nearly two (2) decades past as follows:

> Collective bargaining agreements, generally, are devised to establish and grant certain rights to employees, which rights they would not otherwise have under common law. It is also a normal and well recognized principle in the interpretation of such Agreements that the rights of management are limited and curtailed only to the degree to which it has yielded specified rights. The right of Management to operate its business and control the working force may be specifically reserved in a labor agreement. However, even in the absence of such a specific reservations clause, as the case is here, those rights are inherent and are nevertheless reserved and maintained by it and its decisions with respect to the operations of the business and the direction of the working forces may not be denied, rejected or curtailed unless the same are in clear violation of the terms of the contract, or may be clearly implied, or are so clearly arbitrary or capricious as to reflect an intent to derogate the relationship.[78]

The other view is that the collective bargaining agreement subsumes existing conditions of employment. Under the "implied obligations" theory of managerial rights, an employer may alter or abolish any employee benefit only after the contract has expired. During the term of the agreement, however, the employer is no longer free to withdraw existing benefits. The employer has the implied obligation to maintain the benefits that were not revoked during negotiations even though the contract makes no reference to them.

Both the reserved rights theory and the implied obligations doctrine find support in the reported decisions.[79] If one is of the view that management retains all rights not ceded to the union, then management will be free to change or eliminate any past practice during the term of the collective bargaining agreement. A person subscribing to the implied

---

[78]Id. at 341, citing Fairway Foods, Inc., 44 LA 161, 164 (1965) (emphasis omitted).

[79]" 'Management reserved right' is but another term for a practice outside the bargain between the parties. When such a reserved right becomes part of their bargain, it is said to have ripened into a binding practice. In short, a binding practice is a reserved right plus mutuality. Mutuality, when the contract is silent on a practice, is the essential ingredient which transforms the practice into an implied obligation." Prasow & Peters, supra note 23, at 167.

obligations theory will reason that the written agreement is not the source of all rights and obligations and, accordingly, some types of past practices may not be unilaterally eliminated during the term of the parties' contract.

There is authority for the proposition that in situations where the parties' agreement is silent, the line between those practices that will be enforced and those which are not binding is drawn on the basis of whether the matter under consideration involves a basic management right or whether it involves a benefit of peculiar personal value to the employees.

For example, in *Le Blond Machine Tool, Inc.*,[80] Arbitrator Frank Keenan ruled that the matter of an attendance policy was a basic management function, clearly involving the direction of the work force. The employer accordingly had the right unilaterally to institute a new system for dealing with absences and tardiness.

And in *Zimmer Manufacturing Co.*,[81] the arbitrator held that an employer had the unilateral right to split the lunch time for its production employees from one to two periods. The arbitrator reasoned that where a past practice involves a management right, as opposed to a "working condition," it may be unilaterally eliminated. Framing the issue as whether the time at which the employees have their lunch is a working condition or an operations method, the neutral concluded that the right to schedule work is a management prerogative which could unilaterally be changed by the employer. The arbitrator pointed out that the employer could not unilaterally alter the length of the lunch hour, since that would be considered a working condition over which the company must bargain.[82]

Some decisions have held that an employer cannot unilaterally change a past practice that constitutes some "benefit" to the employees. Thus, in *Virginia Stage Lines, Inc.*,[83] the company, in recognition of a driver's good safety record, awarded a gold pin containing a small diamond. The number

---

[80]76 LA 827, 834 (1981).
[81]75 LA 16 (Kiok, 1980).
[82]See, e.g., Tecumseh Prods. Co., 81 LA 483, 486 (Seidman, 1983)("The matter involved here [rotation of oven tenders] is one peculiarly connected with the methods of operations and direction of the working force. It does not directly confer any pecuniary benefit of personal value to the employees."); Koppers Co., 73 LA 837 (Morgan, 1979)(upholding unilateral elimination of fire barrels as source of outside heat as an "operational method" rather than a "working condition.").
[83]80 LA 16 (Wahl, 1982). In this regard, see the analysis of Arbitrator John Boyer, Jr., in CF Indus., Inc., 80-2 ARB ¶8423 (1980).

of diamonds would increase in accordance with a schedule based on the number of years of driving with no chargeable accidents. When the company changed the composition of the pin by substituting a simulated stone for the diamonds, the union filed a grievance. Arbitrator Wahl ruled that the issuance of a safety award pin with a diamond constituted a benefit to the employees which the company could not eliminate.

Similarly, in *Tecumseh Products Co.*,[84] Arbitrator L.D. May ruled that the employer could not unilaterally transfer food and other vending machines in light of a 10-year practice of positioning the machines on the shop floor. As a remedy, the employer was directed to return the vending machines to their original location.

Prasow and Peters[85] argue that it is important to differentiate between benefits initiated unilaterally by management which become binding conditions of employment and other benefits which, regardless of how much employees rely upon these, may be withdrawn at management's discretion. Benefits of the latter type, according to Prasow and Peters, may be subdivided into (1) gratuities (for example, a Christmas bonus) and (2) unintended benefits, which are incidental by-products of the organization of production and services (the use of a parking lot by employees).

The issue, of course, is what type of practices may be withdrawn by management and which type of customs are binding on the parties during the term of the agreement. To say that "gratuities" and "incidental benefits" may be withdrawn is a conclusion. It only moves the necessary analysis back one more step. When is something a "gratuity," or what is an "incidental by-product" of the organization? For example, in 1984 the NLRB declared that a Christmas bonus consistently paid over a number of years is a term of employment, even though it was not expressly provided for in the bargaining agreement. Accordingly, it could not be discontinued by the employer before the union was given an opportunity to bargain.[86] Application of this principle by arbitrators may

---

[84]80 LA 568 (1983).

[85]Prasow & Peters, supra note 23, at 142–67.

[86]Stroehmann Bros. Co., 268 NLRB 1360, 115 LRRM 1150, 1151 (1984)(an employer that previously gave a cash Christmas bonus to its employees violated the statute by instead giving them food). See also Harvstone Mfg. Co., 272 NLRB 939 117 LRRM 1447 (1984)(a three-member Board held that an employer did not

lead to a result different than that suggested by Prasow and Peters, at least where a practice is longstanding and the bonus is tied to the seniority of the employee.

The reported decisions indicate that once an arbitrator concludes a past practice involves a "gift," rarely will it be held to be an enforceable custom, at least in those cases where the agreement does not include a maintenance-of-standards provision. Thus, in *Vulcan Iron Works, Inc.*,[87] Arbitrator Ralph Roger Williams held that an employer did not violate the parties' agreement when it unilaterally discontinued a 20-year practice of giving employees a Thanksgiving turkey. The arbitrator found that the agreement did not require the employer to give turkeys to the unit employees (the company continued to make the "gift" to the salaried employees). He pointed out that the turkeys' value was not listed on the employees' W-2 tax forms, and that the employees did not report their value as income. In short, the turkey was a gift subject to unilateral discontinuance by the employer.[88]

When the so-called "benefit" is considered a part of the employee's overall compensation package, and not merely a gratuity, arbitrators have ruled that the past practice has become an implied term of the wage agreement and not subject to modification without consent of both parties, at least during the term of the agreement. For example, when a bonus is treated as income, with social security and income taxes withheld, an arbitrator may infer that the practice has ripened into an enforceable condition of employment that cannot be unilaterally changed by management.

A benefit may also be considered as part of the employees' total compensation package where the employer, at bargaining sessions, cites the benefit as a fringe enjoyed by the unit. In *Board of Public Utilities*,[89] Arbitrator Henry Grether ruled that a municipal utility could not unilaterally discontinue its

violate its bargaining obligation when it unilaterally discontinued Christmas bonuses, prizes, and parties, since these items are in the nature of gifts rather than terms and conditions of employment), and Aeronca, Inc., 650 F.2d 501, 107 LRRM 2687 (CA 4, 1981)(upholding discontinuance of past practice of giving employees Christmas turkey without bargaining with union, where court found that union waived right in bargaining by inclusion of zipper clause in agreement and rejection of maintenance-of-standards provision).

[87]79 LA 334 (1982).
[88]See also D.E. Thomas, Inc., 81-2 ARB ¶8405 (Towers, 1981)(upholding discontinuance of Christmas turkey following parties' entrance into their first bargaining agreement).
[89]76 LA 446 (1981).

10-year practice of providing unit employees with free coffee where the employer, during negotiations, cited the free coffee custom as a fringe to its employees.

Arbitrator Ruben, in a well-researched opinion, noted that some arbitrators, applying these tests, have considered it important whether the benefit was treated as wages subject to federal income and Social Security tax withholding, or whether a deduction was claimed by the employer on its income tax returns. According to Ruben, still other decisions have been influenced by whether the NLRB deemed the so-called "benefit" a "condition of employment" which, under Taft-Hartley, could not be unilaterally discontinued by the company without notification to the union and an opportunity to bargain. One arbitrator even found it material to the decision whether the employer reported the annual employee distribution as a "benefit plan" to the Department of Labor.[90]

While guidelines in this area are difficult to enunciate, some common trends can be identified as to when an arbitrator will give effect to a past practice under a contract that is silent. Without more, a gratuity that is not treated as income by the employer will generally not form a basis as an independent enforceable condition of employment, although exceptions may be found. When a benefit is considered part of the employees' overall compensation package and is treated as such by the company's accountants, an arbitrator will likely conclude that it cannot be unilaterally withdrawn during the term of the agreement. A minority of arbitrators have even concluded that the employer must obtain agreement from the union before the benefit can be withdrawn even after the contract has expired.

Where a practice does not concern the employer-employee relationship, e.g., a decision concerning the elimination of part of a business or a choice of the particular product to manufacture, few arbitrators would bind the company to the prior custom of operating a portion of the business or continuing to produce a specific product. They would reason that a practice was never formed or alternatively, if formed, the practice could not operate to deprive management of its inherent right to determine its operations. In the last analysis this may simply be another way of restating the "major-minor" test, i.e., that

---

[90]Saginaw Mining Co., 76 LA 911 (Ruben, 1981).

when the employee benefit is major (a fringe benefit such as insurance), it may not be withdrawn during the term of the agreement.

One problem with the "management rights" versus "employee benefits" test is that the distinction does not easily lend itself to application. Frequently the exercise of a basic management right, such as directing the working force, also impinges upon some type of benefit enjoyed by the bargaining unit. For example, in *Foremost-Gentry*,[91] Arbitrator Adolph Koven considered the effect of a past practice of allowing senior employees to refuse holiday work. The agreement contained no provision regulating the manner in which holiday work must be offered. Arbitrator Koven ruled that the company could not assign senior employees to work on a holiday against their wishes. An argument can be made that there was both a basic management right and a benefit at issue and that it is of little utility merely to conclude that the arbitrator will not enforce a past practice when basic management rights are being exercised.

Accordingly, arbitrators may in certain cases use the major-minor test as a bootstrap to justify a conclusion already reached. If an arbitrator decides that a practice should be enforced, he or she will conclude that it is a major benefit to the employees; otherwise, it will be called minor.[92]

Resolving Conflicts With Contract Language

Perhaps the most difficult case facing an arbitrator is where a long-standing practice directly conflicts with the express terms of the parties' agreement. There are, of course, agreements that explicitly address the issue. The following provisions illustrate some of the possibilities in this respect:

> A local condition or practice which is inconsistent with or which goes beyond the provisions of this Agreement established after the date of this Agreement shall not be recognized or enforced unless and until it is reduced to writing and approved by the Staff Representative of the Union and the Vice President of the Company.[93]

* * *

---

[91]75 LA 1067 (1980).
[92]See, e.g., Mittenthal, supra note 13, at 53.
[93]Inland Steel Mining Co., 75 LA 1208, 1210 (Beilstein, 1980).

A past practice which is in violation of a specific provision of the Agreement shall have no further force and effect.[94]

* * *

When a current practice or policy of the Employer conflicts with the provisions of this contract, the contract shall prevail. However, mutually agreed to or acceptable policies and practices different from the provisions described in this Agreement shall be controlling where they remain mutually acceptable following the effective date of this Agreement. When a policy or practice is no longer acceptable to one party, it shall serve notice on the other party at the Agency or Local Union level of its intent to declare the contract provisions controlling. If the other party desires to maintain the policy or practice, the parties shall meet to resolve this difference. . . . Failing resolution, the contract provisions shall apply.[95]

Arbitrators are of differing views when confronted with a conflict between a past practice and the agreement. One view is that a past practice can never be used to alter, change, or otherwise modify clear, unambiguous language. Arbitrator Fred Witney has expressed this view as follows:

In the case at hand, however, to base a decision on practice would ignore an accepted and fundamental principle of the arbitration process. When contractual language written in clear and unambiguous terms conflicts with practice, the contractual language prevails rather than the practice.[96]

Likewise, Arbitrator Jules Justin, in the often-quoted *Phelps Dodge Copper Products Corp.* decision,[97] stated:

Plain and unambiguous words are undisputed facts. The conduct of Parties may be used to fix a meaning to words and phrases of uncertain meaning. Prior acts cannot be used to change the explicit terms of a contract. An arbitrator's function is not to rewrite the Parties' contract. His function is limited to finding out what the Parties intended under a particular clause. The intent of the Parties is to be found in the words which they, themselves, employed to express their intent. When the language used is clear and explicit, the arbitrator is constrained to give effect to the thought expressed by the words used.[98]

Similarly, Arbitrator Ralph Roger Williams, in *Cherokee Electric Cooperative*,[99] declared:

---

[94]TRW, Inc., 74 LA 5 (Mewhinney, 1980).
[95]Illinois Dep't of Pub. Aid, 74 LA 132, 134 (Gruenberg, 1980).
[96]Illinois Dep't of Transp., 76 LA 875, 882 (1981).
[97]16 LA 229 (1951).
[98]Id. at 233.
[99]75 LA 519 (1980).

The Company correctly stated in its brief that a past practice may be used in the interpretation or construction of contract language, and may establish an implied contract provision. But a past practice cannot change clear and unequivocal provisions of a written contract with which the practice conflicts.[100]

A contrary view holds that a past practice may take precedence over clear contractual language. Those arbitrators who subscribe to this view usually reason that the parties, by their conduct, can amend the written agreement. As stated by one arbitrator:

> It is clear that the Arbitrator cannot modify the labor agreement. The contract is between the Employer and the Union. They wrote it and they can modify it. Modification usually takes place in a written form. It is also generally accepted in arbitration that the parties may modify an existing agreement by their actions whether or not such modification is in writing. I thus find that the parties by their actions effectively modified the written agreement by their actions in a binding past practice.[101]

In this case the arbitrator ruled that the behavior of the parties was sufficient to amend the contract even though the agreement provided that any modification must be in writing and ratified by the membership.

Similarly, in *White Manufacturing Co.*,[102] the arbitrator considered a conflict between a past practice of not paying the full cost of employees' safety shoes and language that provided that the employer was to pay the full cost of shoes for each 12-month period. In holding that the past practice was operative, Arbitrator Howard LeBaron reasoned that the practice of setting a limit for safety shoe purchases had been in effect a full two years before the grievance was filed. Moreover, the

---

[100]Id. at 521. See also Mead Paper, 74 LA 699, 704 (Kruger, 1980)("Although the Employer relied on past practice, in part, in making its decision to offer the senior qualified employee in the department the Sunday work, past practice must give way to the Agreement and the intent of the parties."); Veterans Admin., 81 LA 946, 948 (Dunn, 1983)("While custom and past practice, as well as bargaining history, may be used to determine the intent of contract language which is *ambiguous*, they will not be used to give meaning to a provision which is *clear* and *unambiguous*.")(emphasis in original); Minnesota Mining & Mfg. Co., 81 LA 338, 343 (Boyer, 1983); Transamerica Delaval, Inc., 84 LA 190, 192 (Brisco, 1985)("If the contract language is clear, the intent of the parties is manifest and past practice generally cannot be used to alter or amend clear contract language. It is the intent of the parties which governs resolution of contract interpretation disputes, not the predilection of the arbitrator . . . .").

[101]Hercules Prods., Inc., 81 LA 191, 193 (Goodman, 1983).

[102]74 LA 1191 (LeBaron, 1980).

union, at a prior bargaining session, had described a range of allowable costs for safety shoes. Citing an article by Arbitrator Benjamin Aaron,[103] the arbitrator concluded that a modification of the parties' agreement may take effect by the unilateral action of the employer which is tacitly approved by the union.

Arbitrator Marlin Volz, in *United States Envelope*,[104] found that the parties had entered into a "special agreement" that was in conflict with the written contract. In holding that the past practice took precedence over the written agreement, Volz reasoned that the best evidence of the existence of a special agreement was that a practice was followed for eight years without a grievance being filed to challenge it. In addition, the arbitrator pointed out that the practice was continued without change through several contract negotiations. Arbitrator Volz also noted that the union had sought unsuccessfully to secure a change in prior negotiations.

The Court of Appeals for the Ninth Circuit, in *Certified Corp. v. Teamsters Local 996*,[105] held that an oral modification of a written collective bargaining agreement is allowable even in the face of a provision requiring that any modification must be in writing. The court stated that in dealing with collective bargaining agreements, "courts should not be preoccupied with principles which might apply to an ordinary contract." The appellate court found that this "contract rule" is not contrary to federal labor policies and, in fact, effectuates the federal policy of maintaining industrial peace.[106]

In those select cases where there is a conflict between a past practice and clear contractual language, the better weight of authority is that the practice will prevail only if the record is clear that the parties mutually agreed to amend the written agreement. In the words of Arbitrator Richard Mittenthal, "the modification is justified not by the practice but rather by the parties' agreement, the existence of which may possibly be inferred from a clear and consistent practice."[107] The presumption should always favor the written contract since, other

---

[103]Aaron, "The Uses of the Past in Arbitration," Proceedings of the 8th Annual Meeting of NAA, 1–23 (BNA Books, 1955); also found in Los Angeles Inst. of Indus. Rel., USLA, Reprint No. 50, 1955.
[104]63 LA 645 (1974).
[105]597 F.2d 1269, 101 LRRM 2584 (CA 9, 1979).
[106]101 LRRM at 2585.
[107]Mittenthal, supra note 13, at 43.

considerations being equal, there is no better indication of the parties' intention than their written agreement. As stated by one arbitrator, "the highest quantum of proof will ordinarily be required in order to show that the parties intended by their conduct to amend or modify clear and unambiguous contractual language. . . .[108]

Resolving Conflicts with Management Rights

The subject matter of the practice at issue and how it relates to the management rights clause is important in any discussion of past practice. Other considerations being equal, a practice that involves some phase of employer-employee relations is more likely to be enforced by an arbitrator than a custom that has little or nothing to do with the basic employment relationship. Practices that affect the method of payment to employees, the application of seniority to layoffs, or how overtime is distributed, for example, are more likely to be enforced than a practice involving the number of employees who are assigned to a particular shift or the question of whether the company must continue to operate at its present location.

The key to this determination is often found in the management rights clause. As an example, if the management rights provision declares that "the company retains the sole and exclusive right to make all working assignments, including, but not limited to, the number of employees on a shift," it will be more difficult for a union to argue successfully that the employer improperly reduced crew size pursuant to a past practice than would be the case absent this clause.

In such situations, the final outcome will depend on the arbitrator's view concerning the nature of the labor agreement, the reserved rights theory, and the relevance of bargaining history on the subject. The reported decisions indicate that arbitrators do examine the management rights clause in determining whether the subject matter at issue has been reserved to management. Even if the past practice involves an employee benefit as opposed to a basic management right, a management rights clause that explicitly reserves to management discretion over the subject matter will often be accorded great weight by an arbitrator.

---

[108]Total Petroleum, Inc., 78 LA 729, 737 (Roberts, 1982).

When there is some dispute as to whether a practice has been reserved to management, arbitrators tend to resolve the ambiguity in favor of management to the extent that the practice involves the exercise of a fundamental management right. To this end, there are some management rights considered by many arbitrators to be so clearly fundamental rights that they are retained by the company even in the absence of an express contractual reservation. These rights are considered to be part of the company's residuum of managerial authority and cannot be limited without express contractual authority. The decision to close part of a business, for example, has been held to be a right that can be exercised by management without prior bargaining with a union.[109]

Eliminating a Past Practice

There are any number of ways that a past practice can be eliminated. A practice may be eliminated when the circumstances that gave rise to it no longer exist,[110] or where the parties, dissatisfied with the past practice, negotiate language that makes the former custom a nullity. Alternatively, the parties may negotiate language that allows management the right to unilaterally eliminate or change practices at any time. Finally, the parties can engage in conduct that results in an arbitrator concluding that a practice is no longer operative. The more common methods of eliminating practices are discussed in this section.

Contractual Authority

Frequently, the parties will negotiate explicit language that permits the employer to unilaterally change or alter any past practice. For example, in *City of Tampa*,[111] the agreement contained the following management rights provision:

> "Except as expressly limited by any provision of this Agreement, the City reserves and retains exclusively all of its normal and inherent rights with respect to the management of its op-

---

[109]First Nat'l Maintenance Corp. v. NLRB, 452 U.S. 666, 107 LRRM 2705 (1981). See Chapter 15, infra, for a discussion of business closings and relocations.
[110]See the discussion in "Underlying Circumstances," supra notes 39–42 and accompanying text.
[111]74 LA 1169 (Wahl, 1980).

erations, whether exercised or not, including, but not limited to, its rights . . . to alter or vary past practices and otherwise to take such measure as the City may determine to be necessary to the orderly and efficient operation of its various operations, functions and services."[112]

The effect of this and similar provisions is to create a presumption in favor of the employer when a past practice is changed. Given sufficient evidence that the change was for a legitimate business reason, it would be difficult for a neutral to sustain a grievance charging that the employer was, under the agreement, bound by a past practice.[113]

Bargaining Conduct

There are a number of situations where a party, during contract negotiations, engages in conduct that subsequently results in an inference being drawn with respect to a past practice. Some of the more frequent occurrences are discussed below.

Objections to Continuation

There is authority that if during contract negotiations either party should object to the continuation of a practice, it could not reasonably be inferred from the execution of a new contract that the parties intended the practice to remain in force.[114] As stated by Arbitrator Mittenthal:

> Without [the parties'] acquiesence, the practice would no longer be a binding condition of employment. In face of a timely repudiation of a practice by one party, the other must have the practice written into the agreement if it is to continue to be binding.[115]

---

[112]Id. at 1171.
[113]See, e.g., Olin Corp., 80 LA 1279 (Tharp, 1983), where the arbitrator held that the union could not rely on a past practice when it had recently agreed to a new and expanded management rights provision allowing the employer to establish or continue policies and to change or abolish policies, practices, or procedures; Ethyl Corp., 83 LA 602 (White, 1984)(holding that the parties by adopting a booklet of 150 pages of written working agreements intended to eliminate the necessity of relying upon oral agreements or unwritten past practices).
[114]Mittenthal, supra note 13, at 56; Eau Claire County, 76 LA 333 (McCrary, 1981); School Dist. of Beloit, 82 LA 177 (Greco, 1984).
[115]Mittenthal, supra note 13, at 56.

Arbitrator Mittenthal goes on to cite an exception to this principle:

> Consider next a well-established practice which serves to clarify some ambiguity in the agreement. Because the practice is essential to an understanding of the ambiguous provision, it becomes in effect a part of that provision. As such, it will be binding for the life of the agreement. And the mere repudiation on the practice by one side during the negotiation of a new agreement, unless accompanied by a revision of the ambiguous language, would not be significant. For the repudiation alone would not change the meaning of the ambiguous provision and hence would not detract from the effectiveness of the practice.[116]

This position represents the better weight of authority among arbitrators.

Rejection of Inclusion in Contract

Arbitrators have uniformly held that a party should not be allowed to secure through arbitration that which it was unable to obtain in bargaining. Some neutrals have therefore cited the unsuccessful attempt by a party to include a custom or practice in the written contract as evidence that the practice lacks mutuality and should not be enforced. This view was expressed by one arbitrator when he said that "it has long been recognized that actions speak louder than words, and one does not ask for something which he believes he already has."[117]

The bellwether case on this issue is *Torrington Co. v. Automobile Workers, Metal Products Workers Local 1645*,[118] a decision by the U.S. Court of Appeals for the Second Circuit. During renegotiation of a collective bargaining agreement, the union sought an express provision reinstating the company's past practice of permitting employees time off with pay to vote in elections. The successor agreement contained no mention of paid time off for voting, the union having apparently dropped its demand for an election-day pay provision. The new agreement did, however, contain a much less restrictive arbitration clause than the old agreement and the union elected to take the issue of paid time off for voting to arbitration. The arbitrator held that the benefit was a firmly estab-

---

[116]Id. at 56.
[117]Hospital Serv. Plan of N.J., 66-3 ARB ¶9096 at 6882 (Scheiber, 1966).
[118]362 F.2d 677, 62 LRRM 2495 (CA 2, 1966).

lished past practice, that the company had the burden of changing this policy by negotiating with the union, and that in the recent negotiations the parties had not agreed to terminate this practice. Finding further that the past practice was not within management's prerogative under the management functions clause of the agreement, the arbitrator ruled the practice valid.

The Second Circuit upheld the district court's decision vacating the arbitration award, stating that "while it may be appropriate to resolve a question never raised during negotiations on the basis of prior practice in the plant or industry, it is quite another thing to assume that the contract confers a specific benefit when that benefit was discussed during negotiations but omitted from the contract."[119] The appellate court concluded that the arbitrator had added a provision to the parties' contract since the issue he decided had been the subject of negotiation but had not been included in the written agreement.

Grievance Settlements

The settlement of a prior grievance on the same issue that is the subject of a later arbitration is usually indicative of the parties' interpretation of the agreement and, as such, an arbitrator may hold them bound by the prior settlement.[120] When one side specifies that the settlement is "without prejudice," however, the better rule is not to hold the settlement indicative of the parties' interpretation.[121] Thus, when a party settles a grievance short of arbitration and, at the same time, makes it clear to the other side that a practice will not be controlling in the future, that party may be able to defend effectively against the enforcement of that practice in a subsequent arbitration.[122]

Failure to Specify Practice at Bargaining

A bargaining strategy frequently used by employers is to request during contract negotiations that the union cite any

---

[119]62 LRRM at 2499.
[120]See, e.g., Sparta Area Schools, 81 LA 957, 960 (Roumell, 1983).
[121]Ohio Steel Foundry Co., 36 LA 445, 446 (Dworkin, 1961).
[122]Tarkett, Inc., 81 LA 943 (Seltzer, 1983).

past practice that it believes is controlling between the parties.
The union's subsequent failure to point out a practice at bargaining may lead to an inference by an arbitrator that the
practice has no effect.

Zipper Clauses

"Zipper" clauses, otherwise known as integration or com-
pleteness-of-agreement clauses, are frequently included in an
agreement. Common examples include the following:

> This contract may be amended only by written agreement be-
> tween the Company and the Union. No practice which has de-
> veloped, either with or without the consent of the Company,
> shall be considered part of this contract unless same is in writ-
> ing and is included in this contract.[123]

> * * *

> [I]t is agreed that no such right, function or prerogative shall
> be limited by any past or present practice or course of conduct
> or otherwise than by the express provisions of this Agree-
> ment. . . .[124]

Both the NLRB and courts have held that zipper clauses
are neither against public policy nor repugnant to Taft-
Hartley.[125] In *NLRB v. Tomco Communications, Inc.,*[126] the
Ninth Circuit, ruling that an employer could rightly insist on
a zipper clause in the contract, declared:

> An integration, or "zipper," clause seeks to close out bargaining
> during the contract term and to make the written contract the
> exclusive statement of the parties' rights and obligations. It is
> nothing but a diluted form of waiver, and so is governed by the
> same principles that apply to a management functions clause.[127]

When the agreement is silent regarding a past practice
but contains a zipper clause, both arbitrators and courts have
held that the practice has no effect, although there is a split
of authority on this issue. One court expressed the principle
as follows:

> Although the non-inclusion of the practices in the bargaining
> agreement does not necessarily compel the conclusion that past

---

[123]Hayssen Mfg. Co., 82 LA 500, 503 (Flaten, 1984).
[124]Hesco Indus., Inc., 81 LA 649, 651 (Chapman, 1983).
[125]Radioear Corp., 214 NLRB 362, 87 LRRM 1330, 1332 (1974).
[126]567 F.2d 871, 97 LRRM 2660 (CA 9, 1978).
[127]97 LRRM at 2664.

practices are not impliedly so incorporated, the existence in a contract of a broad integration clause, if it means anything, does clearly negate the notion that the parties meant to include any terms or conditions, including those based *only* on past practices, not specifically incorporated in the written contract or reasonably inferable from its provisions. We think that this provision is dispositive of this case.

The court went on to state:

[W]here a collective bargaining agreement not only makes no mention whatever of past practices but does include a broad integration clause, an award which incorporates into the agreement, as separately enforceable conditions of the employment relationship, past practices which antedate the effective date of that agreement cannot be said to "draw its essence from the collective bargaining" agreement.[128]

More recently, a three-member Board, in *Columbus & Southern Ohio Electric Co.,*[129] held that an employer did not violate the duty to bargain with the union when it unilaterally eliminated a Christmas bonus that employees had received for nearly 40 years. The Board found that the union had waived its right to bargain over the matter by agreeing to the following zipper clause:

It is the intent of the parties that the provision of this Agreement will supersede all prior agreements and under-standings, oral or written, expressed or implied, between such parties and shall govern their entire relationship and shall be the sole source of any and all rights or claims which may be asserted in arbitration hereunder or otherwise.
The Union for the life of this Agreement hereby waives any rights to request to negotiate or to bargain with respect to any matters contained in this Agreement.[130]

It is of note that Member Zimmerman pointed out that when the union, during bargaining, requested a list of all matters that were subject to this clause, the employer refused to make such a list, stating that its intention was to wipe the slate clean before the new contract went into effect.[131]

A difficult question arises where the past practice contin-

---

[128]County of Allegheny v. Allegheny County Prison Employees Indep. Union, 476 Pa. 27, 381 A.2d 849, 96 LRRM 3396, 3399–4000 (1977)(reinstatement of lunch privileges ordered by arbitrator barred by integration clause of collective bargaining agreement)(emphasis in original; citations omitted).
[129]270 NLRB 686, 116 LRRM 1148 (1984).
[130]116 LRRM at 1148.
[131]Id. at 1149 n.4.

ues after adoption of the zipper clause. One view holds that the practice is not cancelled. The reasoning is that even though the parties may have attempted to cancel the past practice with specific language or by the use of a zipper provision, by continuing the past practice the parties obviously intend for the past practice to continue and be part of the new agreement.[132]

The other view holds that no past practice can survive the negotiation of a "completeness of agreement" clause and negotiation of such a provision cancels and supersedes any other agreement and past practice. The reasoning is that there is no better indication of the parties' intent than the words they use and that these words take precedence over the actual conduct of the parties.[133]

In discussing the effect of a zipper clause, former NLRB General Counsel John S. Irving has argued that there is a clear distinction between a situation where a party to a contract wishes to preserve the status quo and one where a party wishes to change it. As noted by Irving:

> In those cases involving a unilateral change, the employer relies on the existence of a zipper clause in the collective bargaining agreement not to establish that the contract precludes bargaining over the new subjects during the term of the contract, but rather to establish that the contract gives the employer unfettered power to change any term or condition not contained in the contract. The board has clearly stated that a zipper clause will not ordinarily be construed to grant the employer such unfettered power.[134]

The better rule is that the existence of a zipper clause alone will not preclude a finding that a past practice is effective between the parties. Moreover, similar to the position taken by the Board's former general counsel, the authors believe the mere existence of a zipper clause should not be sufficient to support a ruling that a past practice, not mentioned

---

[132]Jenison Pub. School Dist., 81 LA 105, 110 (Roumell, 1983).

[133]See Hogan, "Past Practice and Administration of Collective Bargaining Agreements," Proceedings of the 14th Annual Meeting of NAA, 63–65 (BNA Books, 1961).

[134]"Reports on Case-Handling Developments at NLRB," Labor Relations Yearbook–1979, 263 (BNA Books, 1980); Commonwealth v. Commonwealth Labor Rel. Bd., 82 Pa. Cmmwlth 330, 474 A.2d 1213 (1984) (union waiver of the right to bargain on mandatory subjects during term of agreement will not be found in a boiler-plate waiver clause alone); NLRB v. Southern Materials Co., 447 F.2d 15, 77 LRRM 2814 (CA 4, 1971).

in the contract, can be unilaterally eliminated during the term of the agreement.

Maintenance-of-Standards Clauses

Many collective bargaining agreements contain contractual provisions requiring the continuance of unnamed past practices in existence at the execution of the agreement. The following is a representative sample of such maintenance-of-standards provisions:

"Except where abolished by mutual agreement of the parties, all prior practices and custom not in conflict with this Agreement shall be continued. . . ."[135]

* * *

"The Company agrees that all conditions of employment in his individual operation relating to wages, hours of work, overtime differentials and general working conditions shall be maintained at not less than the highest minimum standards in effect at the time of the signing of this Agreement, and the conditions of employment shall be improved whenever specific provisions for improvement are made elsewhere in this Agreement."[136]

* * *

"Except as this Agreement shall otherwise provide, all terms and conditions of employment applicable on the signing date of this Agreement as established by the rules, regulations and/ or written policies of the Board in force on said date, shall continue to be so applicable during the term of this Agreement. Unless otherwise provided in this Agreement, nothing contained herein, shall be interpreted and/or applied so as to eliminate, reduce, or otherwise detract from any teacher benefit existing prior to its effective date. . . .[137]

A limited type of maintenance-of-standards provision may declare that the employer agrees not to arbitrarily or capriciously change any rights or working conditions not specifically referred to in the written agreement.[138]

---

[135]Saginaw Mining Co., 76 LA 911, 914 (Ruben, 1981) (citing Article XXVI, Section (b) of the National Bituminous Coal Wage Agreement of 1978). See also Burnside-Graham Ready Mix Co., 85-1 ARB ¶8230 (Mulhall, 1985) ("[T]he company and Union agree *to continue and to keep in force*, for the duration of that agreement, *the established past practices* that now exist. . . ." Id. at 3960–61, quoting from Joint Exhibit No. 2, an agreement extending provisions of an existing collective bargaining agreement to employees in another facility (emphasis added by arbitrator in quoting original).).
[136]Stokely-Van Camp, Inc., 74 LA 691, 694 (Stern, 1980).
[137]Ringgold School Dist. v. Ringgold Educ. Assn., 489 Pa. 380, 414 A.2d 118, 106 LRRM 3066, 3066–67 (1980).
[138]City of Tampa, 74 LA 1169 (Wahl, 1980).

Sunshine Mining Co.,[139] a case reported by Arbitrator Cornelius Peck, illustrates the effect of a maintenance-of-standards provision. In that case the parties' agreement provided:

> "All present local practices, understandings or supplements or working conditions which grant to the employees benefits and protections not otherwise provided by the Agreement, shall remain in effect unless changed by mutual agreement. . . ."[140]

Arbitrator Peck ruled that an employer had no right to unilaterally discontinue a 16-year practice of giving employees a turkey at Christmas. The arbitrator reasoned that the gift of turkeys was a "local practice" and a "benefit" within the meaning of the above language.

There is authority to the effect that an unsuccessful attempt by the union to secure a maintenance-of-standards clause in the agreement will be considered by an arbitrator as evidence that no past practice ever existed or, alternatively, if it did exist, that it was repudiated by the employer's rejection of the union's claim during bargaining. A number of arbitrators, however, hold that a proposed maintenance-of-standards provision which was not incorporated into the agreement would not, in and of itself, preclude the union from raising the past practice issue in a subsequent arbitration.[141]

Expiration of the Agreement

Arbitrator Pearce Davis, commenting on the duration of a past practice, argued what is believed to be the better rule in this area:

> If there has been an award supporting past practice as established under a contract, it seems to me that such an award cannot generally be held to be effective beyond the termination date of the existing contract if one party or the other gives notice of desire to alter the practice. It appears reasonable to conclude that established past practice, like any contract provision, is potentially terminable when the period of the general agreement runs its course.[142]

---

[139]79-2 ARB ¶8476 (1979).
[140]Id. at 5084.
[141]Associated Wholesale Grocers, Inc., 81 LA 1126, 1128 (O'Reilly, 1983).
[142]Davis, "Discussion—The Uses of the Past in Arbitration," Proceedings of the 8th Annual Meeting of NAA, 12–16 (BNA Books, 1955).

Successor Personnel

Arbitrators have ruled that the practices of prior administrators will bind their successors. In *St. Mary Corwin Hospital*,[143] the arbitrator ruled that a new administrator was bound by the past practices of management regarding who may be present in a grievance meeting. The arbitrator reasoned that it would be unfair and unjust to allow a new administrator to enforce a different interpretation of the grievance procedure than had been practiced in the past.

Similarly, in *Transit Management of Charlotte, Inc.*,[144] the arbitrator held that the actions of new management were insufficient to remove the grievant's impression of continued laxity in the enforcement of rules by the predecessor company. The arbitrator accordingly ruled that the employer did not have just cause to dismiss an employee who carried a weapon on the job, notwithstanding a rule calling for discharge for this conduct.[145]

Arbitrability

Questions may arise as to the arbitrability of a grievance based on a past practice where the agreement is silent.

In this respect the courts have established guidelines in determining whether a grievance is arbitrable under a collective bargaining agreement. In *Steelworkers v. Warrior & Gulf Navigation Co.*,[146] the Supreme Court stated that, given a valid agreement to arbitrate:

> An order to arbitrate the particular grievance should not be denied unless it may be said with positive assurance that the arbitration clause is not susceptible to an interpretation that covers the asserted dispute. Doubts should be resolved in favor of coverage.[147]

---

[143]76 LA 1142 (Aisenberg, 1981).

[144]77 LA 845 (Foster, 1981).

[145]See also LCP Chems.-W. Va., Inc., 81 LA 467, 469 (Ghiz, 1983); Republic Airlines, 80-2 ARB ¶8401 (Rchmus, 1980) (holding that employees could not be bound by a past practice they had not created and of which they had no knowledge). But see Maul Technology Corp., 83-1 ARB ¶8295 (Ipavec, 1983) (holding a past practice of allowing political postings on a union bulletin board inapplicable to the successor company).

[146]363 U.S. 574, 46 LRRM 2416 (1960).

[147]46 LRRM at 2419–20.

The court went on to state that absent an express provision excluding a particular grievance from arbitration, only the most forceful evidence to exclude a particular grievance from arbitration can defeat an arbitrability claim. The presumption is in favor of arbitrability.

Where the exclusion clause (if included in the agreement) is vague and the arbitrability provision broad, there would appear to be no difficulty concluding that a past practice grievance is arbitrable, even though the contract is silent on the matter involved in the practice.

Similarly, even where the agreement contains a clause providing that matters reserved to the employer's discretion are not grievable and that the employer retains all powers concerning matters not covered in the agreement, the better weight of authority holds that a past-practice grievance is subject to arbitration unless the subject matter of the practice is explicitly excluded from the arbitrator's jurisdiction by the parties' contract.[148]

Arbitrator Russell Smith, in a paper delivered at the 16th annual meeting of the National Academy of Arbitrators, provided the following thoughts where a party is asserting that an arbitrator lacks jurisdiction on the ground that the grievance relies, for its substantive basis, upon the alleged past practice rather than any provision of the agreement, or on an understanding reached outside the contract:

> If the contract specifically excludes such claims from the arbitration process, the arbitrator should dismiss the claim as non-arbitrable if he is satisfied, past practice again containing no indication to the contrary, that the parties meant what they said, and if he is convinced that a "past practice" relied upon does not in any way involve the interpretation or application of a provision, or an agglomeration of provisions, of the agreement. With respect to the matter, especially, of alleged understandings *dehors* the formal agreement, however, a distinction might well be taken, under certain circumstances, between those ante-dating and those post-dating the agreement. It is certainly not beyond the realm of rationality that the arbitrator could regard the latter as subsumed under and in effect a part of the labor agreement, and thus as commitments within his jurisdiction to enforce.[149]

---

[148]See, e.g., County of Allegheny v. Allegheny County Prison Employees Indep. Union, 476 Pa. 27, 381 A.2d 849, 96 LRRM 3396 (1977).

[149]Smith, "Arbitrators and Arbitrability," Proceedings of the 16th Annual Meeting of NAA, 75, 88 (BNA Books, 1963). See also Koppers Co., 73 LA 837 (Morgan, 1979).

Chapter 3

Plant Rules

Establishing Rules

Absent specific contractual language to the contrary, management has the right to establish and enforce work rules. Some agreements, to be safe, contain language reserving this right to management. BNA reports that 28 percent of contracts containing management rights clauses cite framing of company rules as a prerogative reserved to management.[1] This does not mean, however, that any and all rules established by management will pass muster once challenged through a grievance. Arbitrators have consistently held that valid work rules must meet three criteria: (1) they must be "published," in the sense that an employee must have some knowledge of the rules prior to their enforcement by management; (2) they must be reasonable; and (3) they must be applied in an evenhanded way. These standards, and other issues related to management's right to formulate and enforce rules, are discussed in this chapter.

Publication

Most arbitrators will hold that a rule or a policy cannot be applied retroactively because the employees were not aware, in the first instance, of what the rules are. Thus, one arbitrator stated the principle as follows:

> It is axiomatic that while an Employer has the right to establish reasonable rules to insure the effective functioning of its op-

---

[1]Basic Patterns in Union Contracts, 63 (BNA Books 1983).

eration, employers are entitled to adequate notice of the Company's regulations and the penalty that will be imposed for violation.[2]

However, one arbitrator stated that a rule may be considered published by virtue of its "long standing and long use" and accordingly held that a rule was published even though it was not in writing.[3]

New York Area Board Umpire Emanuel Stein, in reversing the dismissal of a fleet-service clerk for not adhering to company procedures for disposing of liquor left on aircraft, had this to say on the communication of rules to employees:

> It goes without saying that the Company has a right to promulgate rules for the handling of liquor and to enforce those rules by appropriate discipline. The difficulty in this case is that it appears virtually impossible to determine what those rules are. The employees, including at least some of the crew chiefs, indicate a view of the rules quite different from that expressed by the supervisors. To put it briefly, the procedures asserted by the supervisors do not seem to have been laid down with any definiteness. More to the point, there has not been any apparent program of communicating the procedures, such as they are, to the employees who are supposed to conform to them.[4]

Arbitrators, borrowing from the courts, have held that it is not always necessary that an employee have actual knowledge of the rules. Arbitrators have ruled that an employee may be charged with constructive knowledge of plant or work rules. For example, an employee who was given a copy of the plant rules upon being hired is generally charged with knowledge of the rules even though he may never have taken the time to read them. Indeed, once plant rules have been issued or posted, arbitrators have held that employees' knowledge of such rules may be presumed. As stated by Arbitrator Robert Howlett:

> The test with respect to a rule clearly communicated to employees must, of necessity, be determined by objective evidence. Unless strong reason is shown, every employee should be charged

---

[2]Lionel Leisure Co., 85-1 ARB ¶8229 (DiLauro, 1984), at 3958. See also Lima Register Co., 76 LA 935 (Heinsz, 1981), citing Trans World Airlines, Inc., 47 LA 1127 (Platt, 1967); Super Tire Eng'g. Co. v. Teamsters Local 676, 721 F.2d 121, 114 LRRM 3320, 3321 (CA 3, 1983) (reversing lower court decision vacating arbitration award that held that "[T]here must . . . be a clearly understood and uniform application of the rule against drinking prior to its strict implementation.")

[3]Hoover Co., 72 LA 297, 301 (Feldman, 1979).

[4]American Airlines, Inc., Maintenance Sys. Bd. of Adjustment, N.Y. Area Bd., Case No. M-444-81 (1982) (unpublished).

with knowledge of rules clearly communicated, whether he actually remembers them or not.[5]

Where an employee has personal knowledge of a rule change, the better weight of authority holds that the change is properly communicated even though the company has not made the rule known to the rest of its employees.[6]

Reasonableness

The most common ground for challenging a rule is asserted lack of reasonableness. However, arbitrators do not uniformly agree as to when a rule should be considered unreasonable. In *Hoover Co.*,[7] Arbitrator Marvin Feldman offered two tests: (1) whether the rule is too severe for the act committed, and (2) "whether or not the rule is overburdensome upon an employee employed at the facility." Arbitrator Feldman held that a "twenty-five-percent rule," which called for termination of employees who had been absent due to an illness for a period of 25 percent of their total working hours over a rolling year of employment, was unreasonable because the rule did not provide for "progressive discipline" as did the other rules.

Arbitrator Robert Foster, in *Transit Management of Charlotte, Inc.*,[8] considered the discharge of a bus driver for carrying a concealed weapon while on duty. The rule in effect provided that "Individuals violating that policy [no weapons while on duty] will be subject to immediate discharge." In reinstating the grievant on other grounds (the arbitrator found that management in the past had "closed its eyes" to violations), the arbitrator discussed the reasonableness criterion as follows:

> The basic standard of reasonableness of a Company rule is whether it is reasonably related to a legitimate interest of management, without imposing undue hardships on employees. No one can doubt that the safety of employees, the general public and the passengers who ride on buses operated by the Company is of critical concern to the Company. . . . There is no doubt that many of the drivers honestly believe that the hazard is reduced when they arm themselves with lethal weapons with which to

---

[5]Valley Steel Casting Co., 22 LA 520, 527 (Howlett, 1954), cited in Hill & Sinicropi, Evidence in Arbitration, 26 (BNA Books, 1980).
[6]See, e.g., General Cable Corp., 72 LA 975, 980 (Watkins, 1979).
[7]72 LA 297, 301 (1979).
[8]77 LA 845 (1981).

resist physical attack. Company management is equally convinced that to allow drivers to carry firearms serves only to compound the danger. The question is not necessarily who may be right, but rather whose judgment is paramount. Assuming that the question is a close one, and therefore either answer as to the better solution of the problem can be said to be reasonable, management who bears the ultimate responsibility must have the authority to make the decision.[9]

Arbitrator Adolph Koven, in *Union Sanitary District*,[10] reviewed further the tests of reasonableness. He stated:

> The tests of "reasonableness" which are most frequently invoked by arbitrators include whether the rule in question violates any part of the Contract; whether it materially changes a past practice or working condition; whether it is related to a legitimate business objective of management; whether it is arbitrary, capricious or discriminatory; and whether it is reasonably applied.[11]

Another arbitrator stated that a reasonable rule is one which the employees can understand and comply with and which "lend[s] itself to fair and equal application in all cases."[12]

In *Giant Foods, Inc.*,[13] the company implemented a new absenteeism control program that was based on the number of chargeable absences accumulated by an employee within a 12-month period. The union objected to the program, arguing that it was arbitrary and unreasonable in that it might result in the imposition of discipline on an employee who was ill for legitimate reasons. The program was also claimed to be discriminatory because some employees worked in refrigerated areas and thus were more likely to experience illness and other on-the-job injuries. The company argued that the program was reasonable because five other local unions had endorsed the same program. In addition, the company made a showing that the absenteeism rate of the employees who worked in the refrigeration department was no higher than that of other unit employees.

In holding that the attendance policy was reasonable, the arbitrator pointed out that the program was progressive in nature. Moreover, it took into account an employee's past

---

[9]Id. at 848.
[10]79 LA 193 (1982).
[11]Id. at 194 n.2 (citations omitted).
[12]Hoover Co., 77 LA 1287, 1290 (Strasshofer, 1982).
[13]79 LA 916 (Seibel, 1982).

work record and the reasons for absences. Finally, as evidence of the reasonableness of the absenteeism program, the arbitrator cited the existence of a review committee that was charged with examining all the facts and circumstances surrounding the case before discipline or discharge was imposed.

With respect to the reasonableness of "no-fault" absenteeism plans (plans that define "excessive" absence and trigger discipline automatically at fixed levels of absenteeism without regard to fault), Arbitrators Howard Block and Richard Mittenthal argue that most arbitrators find no-fault plans reasonable, but nevertheless believe that the principle conflicts with a "just cause" standard of discipline. They write:

> [T]he concept of "just cause" requires the arbitrator to make two essential inquiries. They are: (1) whether the employee is guilty of misconduct, and (2) assuming guilt, whether the discipline imposed is a reasonable penalty under the circumstances of the case. A no-fault plan precludes either inquiry. For the arbitrator who accepts such a plan is concerned with two entirely different questions: (1) whether the employee was absent, and (2) if so, whether the absence falls within any of the plan's express exclusions. Should these questions be answered in management's favor, the arbitrator has no choice but to affirm the penalty prescribed in the plan. The crucial issues of whether the employee's absence is misconduct and whether the penalty is reasonable are removed from the arbitrator's reach. All that is left is a hollow mechanical function, a mere reading of the plan's listed penalty for a numbered "absence occurrence." Thus, the plan seems inconsistent with the "just cause" standard.
>
> Most arbitrators, referring again to the reported decisions, have found no-fault plans to be reasonable in principle. They approach the problem from a highly pragmatic point of view. They stress the damage caused by absenteeism, the need for objective attendance standards, and the actual experience under the plan. They have given considerable weight to proof by the employer that the plan has been reasonable in operation or to the absence of proof by the union that the plan has worked a hardship in particular cases. This rationale is perhaps best summarized in the following words by Arbitrator James Duff:
>
>> "If a plan is fair on its face and its operation in the concrete cases at hand produces just results, and other common tests of reasonableness are satisfied, a plan ought not to be declared invalid based on the mere existence of some remote possibility that it could operate perversely in the indefinite future under hypo-

thetical circumstances which have not as yet materialized."[14]

Block and Mittenthal go on to assert that unqualified approval to a typical no-fault plan cannot be given because of the potential for inequitable results in exceptional cases and because such results cannot be harmonized with just cause concepts. They point out that arbitrators often temper these plans by imposing a de facto just cause requirement in the case before them. Block and Mittenthal comment:

> Such a compromise may not be aesthetically appealing, for it enables the arbitrator to introduce the foreign element of fault into a pure no-fault system whenever he feels it proper to do so. But the end result seems sound. A rule calling for automatic enforcement of penalties is modified by a provision for equitable exception to the rule as a safeguard against perverse applications.[15]

"No smoking" rules (a current subject of interest and increased grievance activity) have been challenged by unions on the basis that they are not a reasonable exercise of management's rights. When smoking will cause a clear safety hazard, as in highly explosive areas, management's rules have been upheld.[16] Arbitrator Edwin Teple stated the general proposition as follows:

> Unless it is clearly unreasonable and without foundation, the Company's judgment with reference to rules designed to increase safety . . . should not be disturbed.[17]

Arbitrators have also upheld no smoking rules in those jurisdictions that have passed clean air acts, even where the statutes are not directly applicable to factories.[18]

---

[14]"Arbitration and the Absent Employee," Proceedings of the 37th Annual Meeting of NAA, 77, 100–01 (BNA Books, 1984) (footnotes omitted), citing Robertshaw Controls Co., 69 LA 77, 79 (Duff, 1977). Cf. Iowa-Illinois Gas & Elec. Co., 85-1 ARB ¶8274 (Keefe, 1985) ("A management rule against theft which assigns *discharge* as the penalty on the occasion of the offense without regard to value of the purloined item, past record or seniority, has long been recognized as *reasonable* when properly ensconced and practiced." Id. at 4131 (emphasis in original).).

[15]Id. at 103–04.

[16]USM Corp., 71 LA 954 (Richman, 1978) (upholding discharge of employee smoking in area where flammable solvents were stored); Consolidation Coal Co., 82-2 ARB ¶8600 (Stoltenberg, 1982)(discharge for smoking in mine elevator); Schnadig Corp., 83-1 ARB ¶8267 (Keenan, 1983)(withdrawing restrooms from permissible smoking areas); Olin Corp., 81 LA 644 (Nicholas, 1983)(smoking in unauthorized area).

[17]United Fuel Gas Co., 68–2 ARB ¶8450 (1968) at 4537.

[18]Litton Indus., 75 LA 308 (Grabb, 1980); Department of Health, Educ. & Welfare, Soc. Sec. Admin., 79-2 ARB ¶8547 (Leventhal, 1979)(upholding HEW's smoking limitation to specified areas in break room). But see Burrell School Dist., 80-1 ARB

The harder cases are those where no direct safety hazard is present. In *Union Sanitary District*,[19] the union challenged the unilateral imposition of a no smoking rule that prohibited employees from smoking in their offices because smoking was prohibited in the administration building, an area sometimes used by the general public. The rule was challenged as being arbitrary in that there was no adequate basis for such a rule. Moreover, the union alleged that the rule was discriminatory since other employees were allowed to smoke in areas outside the administration building. The arbitrator, in ruling for the union, found that the grievant's smoking would not cause a health problem for other employees (only one nonsmoker worked in the same room with the grievant) and the public infrequently visited the restricted area. Also cited by the arbitrator was the company's policy in another building where a smoker and a nonsmoker occupying the same office could make their own arrangements.

In *Johns-Manville Sales Corp. v. Machinists Local 1609*,[20] the Fifth Circuit upheld an arbitration award that invalidated a rule prohibiting all smoking on company property and which provided escalating disciplinary sanctions, including discharge, for violations. Although the company could cite no statute or regulation prohibiting smoking in asbestos plants, it nevertheless argued that public policy favored the elimination of health hazards from the work environment. The appellate court refused to vacate the award, reasoning that public policy could not form the basis to overturn this award absent a specific statute or regulation.

In general the decisions indicate that a rule must be reasonably related to some legitimate business interest.[21] This is similar to the "rational basis" test applied by the courts when governmental action is challenged as unconstitutional under the Due Process and Equal Protection Clauses. Generally a company's power to regulate in a particular area will not be challenged. Rather, the union will more likely contend that the means used by the employer are not reasonably related to its objective, or that the rule was unilaterally promulgated by management.

¶8050 (Freeman, 1979)(school board's enforcement of no smoking ordinance improper in light of 23-year-old past practice of allowing smoking within school building).
[19]79 LA 193 (Koven, 1982).
[20]621 F.2d 756, 104 LRRM 2985 (CA 5, 1980).
[21]See, e.g., Robertshaw Controls Co., 55 LA 283 (Block, 1970).

Arbitrators have not hesitated to overturn discipline for rule infringements where the penalty was too harsh or out of proportion to the offense. There are a number of reported decisions where arbitrators have found a clear rule violation, but nonetheless have reversed the discipline imposed, stating that a "literal" interpretation is to be avoided,[22] or, alternatively, that "intent" must be weighted in deciding whether the rule was violated.[23]

A word of caution, however, is in order on the subject of reversing penalties. A holding that a rule is not reasonable because the penalty is out of proportion to the offense may be overturned if a reviewing court determines that the arbitrator dispensed his own brand of industrial justice and ignored the clear language of the contract.[24] In general, the courts have ruled that an arbitrator may under a just cause standard modify a disciplinary penalty so long as the parties' agreement does not proscribe any change in the penalty and does not set forth specific penalties for work-rule violations.[25]

A reviewing court is unlikely to reverse an arbitrator's determination as to reasonableness so long as the award in some way "draws its essence from the parties' collective bargaining agreement."[26] Where the rule involves some public

---

[22]Bethlehem Steel Corp., 79 LA 1185 (Sharnoff, 1982)(possession of marijuana).

[23]Atlantic Steel Co., 79 LA 163, 166 (Goodman, 1982)(possession of weapons).

[24]See, e.g., Teamsters Local 784 v. Ulry-Talbert Co., 330 F.2d 562, 55 LRRM 2979 (CA 8, 1964)(arbitrator without authority to change penalty where contract provided that employee may be discharged for proper cause, of which dishonesty was one, and that management's actions could only be reversed if complaint against employee was not supported by the facts or that management had acted arbitrarily and in bad faith or in violation of express terms of agreement); St. Louis Theatrical Co. v. Stage Employees Local 6, 715 F.2d 405, 114 LRRM 2097 (CA 8, 1983)(arbitrator exceeded authority under agreement in reducing penalty where contract provided that any employee violating no-strike clause may be disciplined or discharged and shall have "no recourse" to any other provisions of the agreement except as to "fact of participation").

[25]See Hill & Sinicropi, "Arbitral Authority to Reduce Discipline," Remedies in Arbitration, 97–105 (BNA Books, 1981); Physicians & Surgeons Community Hosp. v. Service Employees Local 597, 114 LRRM 2876, 2879 (N.D. Ga., 1983)(" 'just cause' encompasses not only whether the grievant in fact committed the alleged disciplinary rule violation, but also what range of penalties can fairly be meted out with respect to any violations found to have been committed").

[26]See, e.g., Parsons v. Lehigh Valley Indus., Inc., 517 F.Supp. 422, 111 LRRM 2643, 2644 (E.D. Pa., 1981)("the rule does not allow the employee's length of service or work record to affect the disciplinary action meted out by respondent or allow the employee to explain tardiness. The arbitrator concluded that the rule was reasonable and that respondent applied it consistently and fairly to petitioner. . . . The lack of a rational basis, not inflexibility or austerity, makes action impermissibly arbitrary or capricious. . . . Even if this court disagreed with the reasoning or conclusion of the arbitrator, the award cannot be set aside if it draws its essence from the parties' collective bargaining agreement."); Hospital Employees Dist. 1199 v. Tuomey Hosp.,

policy, however, a reviewing court may not accord the same degree of deference.[27] Thus, the Seventh Circuit, in *Meat Cutters Local P-1236 v. Jones Dairy Farm*,[28] considered an award upholding a rule prohibiting employees from dealing directly with the U.S. Department of Agriculture concerning any plant problems. In sustaining a lower court decision vacating the award, the appellate court reasoned that the rule affected not only the company and its employees but also the consuming public, which has an interest in insuring that meat and meat products are processed under sanitary conditions. It would not, therefore, uphold a rule forbidding employees from contacting inspectors regardless of the circumstances.

A rule may be reasonable under any of the above-cited tests, yet if the NLRB or a court concludes that the rule was motivated by the desire to discourage employee union activity, it will not be upheld. Thus in one case the NLRB found that the Taft-Hartley Act was violated when the employer promulgated rules prohibiting employees from smoking in a designated area, sitting down during working time, and playing video games, as well as requiring employees to remain at their work stations at all times, when these rules were motivated by the employees' union activities.[29]

A rule will not be judged unreasonable simply because it imposes a financial burden on employees.[30] Moreover, the possibility that the rule may in the future be subject to uneven application generally will not be sufficient grounds to invalidate a rule. The better view is that the reasonableness of a rule will be judged on past experience and not on a list of

---

112 LRRM 2336, 2336 (D.S.C., 1982)("The agreement further provides that arbitration of a grievance arising out of the enforcement of a work rule 'shall be limited to a finding of whether the rule was violated, and not as to the existence of the rules, or the reasonableness of the rules.' ").

[27]In Super Tire Eng'g. v. Teamsters Local 676, 721 F.2d 121, 114 LRRM 3320, 3323 n.6 (CA 3, 1983), the Third Circuit discussed the public policy exception for overturning an award, stating, "Public policy may be a ground for overturning awards 'only if upholding an award would amount to "judicial condonation" of illegal acts' and thus would conflict directly with federal or state law.' . . . The public policy must be 'well defined and dominant, and is to be ascertained "by reference to the laws and legal precedents." ' " (citations omitted).

[28]680 F.2d 1142, 110 LRRM 2805 (CA 7, 1982).

[29]Rambend Realty Corp., 268 NLRB 287, 115 LRRM 1005 (1983).

[30]See, e.g., Rohr Indus. Inc., 79 LA 900 (Richman, 1982)(replacement fee for lost production stamps); Mister A's Restaurant, 80 LA 1104 (Christopher, 1983)(requirement of blond wig for waitress).

potential abuses that a party may parade before an arbitrator.[31]

Even-Handedness of Enforcement

A finding by an arbitrator that an employer has been discriminatory or capricious in applying its work rules will likely preclude the imposition of discipline for violating that rule. Likewise, laxity in enforcement will have the same result. Applying this principle, one arbitrator stated:

> In addition to the requirement that the rule be reasonable in content, just cause for the discipline imposed requires the further finding that the rule was reasonably applied to the Grievant in a nondiscriminatory manner after the Grievant was made aware of the rule and the probable disciplinary consequences resulting from its violation. The fact that the rule expressly calls for termination upon the first occurrence of its breach, does not necessarily produce the required notice where lax enforcement over a period of time has served as a signal to employees that the Company condones the conduct.[32]

Concluding that the grievant had not been given sufficient notice to remove the impression of a permissive attitude of management, the arbitrator reversed the company's termination decision.

Similarly, in *Mobile Oil Corp.*,[33] the arbitrator, in considering a charge of discriminatory treatment in the application of a rule, declared:

> The same violation by one employee committed relatively close in time to that of another employee should not result in two kinds of justice under the collective bargaining agreement. . . . Thus, grievant should not suffer punishment any greater than that imposed upon any other employee under similar circumstances, rather, the issuance of unusual punishment must be justified by special circumstances or may be found to be discriminatory.[34]

When supervisors are given some discretion to apply rules,

---

[31]See, e.g., ARA Mfg. Co., 84 LA 856 (Lilly, 1985)(rejecting argument that rule prohibiting loud or abrasive comments or disrespectful attitude or actions towards any member of management will be used to throttle union's airing of complaints in grievance procedure).
[32]Transit Mgmt. of Charlotte, Inc., 77 LA 845, 848 (Foster, 1981).
[33]75 LA 143 (Herman, 1980).
[34]Id. at 147 (citations omitted).

a finding by an arbitrator that the rules are not being applied in an even-handed manner can be fatal to an employer's case.[35]

Courts have adopted a similar stand in the few instances where they have de novo considered the merits of a discharge. One court, sustaining a lower court's finding that an employee was improperly terminated for violating a policy requiring all employees to pay for food and beverages taken from the restaurant supplies, with violators subject to discharge and possible criminal action, stated the following principle:

> An employer's condonation of an employee's wrongful conduct is a mitigating factor which may cause the employer to waive its right to discharge the employee on the basis of such misconduct.... The jury was therefore entitled to consider the fact that [the employer] had never enforced the policy and that management had acquiesced in the violation of the express policy set forth in the 5-inch by 7-inch notice [posted by the time clock].
>
> In addition, discharge on the basis of alleged disobedience or insubordination is wrongful if the employer's policy or rule is vague and uncertain.... The rationale is that there can be no disobedience in the first instance if there is no clear prohibition of the conduct. In the present case the jury could consider the fact that [the company], through its management, engaged in activities that implicitly negated the express policy set forth in the 5-inch by 7-inch notice. [The employer] said one thing and did another.[36]

A union will often point to one or two instances involving allegedly uneven application of a rule and assert that the discipline at issue should be overturned because the employer has discriminated in applying its rules. Regarding discrimination charges Arbitrator Charles Short declared:

> The term "discrimination" connotes a distinction in treatment, especially an unfair distinction. The prohibition against discrimination requires like treatment under like circumstances. In the case of offenses the circumstances include the nature of the offense, the degree of fault and the mitigating and aggravating factors. There is no discrimination, or no departure from the consistent or uniform treatment of employees, merely because of variations in discipline reasonably appropriate to the variations in circumstances. Two employees may refuse a work assignment. For one it is his first offense, there being no prior warning or misconduct standing against his record. The other

---

[35]Central Tel. Co. of Va., 68 LA 957, 962 (Whyte, 1977).
[36]Bautch v. Red Owl Stores, 278 N.W.2d 328, 102 LRRM 2081, 2082 (Minn., 1979)(citations omitted).

has been warned and disciplined for the very same offense on numerous occasions. It cannot be seriously contended that discrimination results if identical penalties are not meted out.[37]

Another arbitrator had this to say on the issue of discriminatory treatment:

It is my opinion that management is not under an obligation to apply equal punishment to all transgressors, if to do so would cause injury to the operations. Discrimination may be validly charged only when there is either (a) a demonstrated inconsistency of posture towards the violations and the violators (such as is present when management tolerates, condones or ignores a series of mis-acts by some and then punishes others for committing the same improprieties); or (b) when the Employer is responding to an improper ulterior motive or animus, using the alleged wrongdoing as a pretext or subterfuge.[38]

Arbitrator Benjamin Aaron has stated what is regarded as the better rule on the issue of discriminatory treatment:

Absolute consistency in the handling of rule violations is, of course, an impossibility, but the fact should not excuse random and completely inconsistent disciplinary practices.[39]

Each case will depend on its own facts. Isolated instances of uneven treatment may not result in the reversal of discipline by an arbitrator, but a party that continually treats similarly situated employees differently, can look forward to having its penalties set aside. As stated by one arbitrator:

[W]here, by its conduct over a period of time, employees similarly situated are treated differently or where notices are posted which are unclear and ambiguous . . . discipline resulting therefrom, even a written confirmation of a verbal warning— must be set aside.[40]

In between the two extremes there is not much advice to give the practitioner other than to urge consistency in applying and enforcing rules.

---

[37]Alan Wood Steel Co., 21 LA 843, 849 (1954).
[38]Interchemical Corp., 48 LA 124, 131 (Yagoda, 1967).
[39]Aaron, "The Uses of the Past in Arbitration," Proceedings of the 8th Annual Meeting of NAA, 10 (BNA Books, 1955).
[40]Sprague Devices, Inc., 79 LA 543, 547 (Mulhall, 1982); see also the discussion by the Fourth Circuit in Norfolk Shipbuilding & Drydock Corp. v. Boilermakers Local 684, 671 F.2d 797, 109 LRRM 2329 (CA 4, 1982)(reversal of district court decision refusing to consider union's evidence of parties' custom and past practice as demonstrating disparate enforcement of rule).

Modifying Rules

Arbitrators are split on the issue of management's authority to unilaterally change rules once they have been established and enforced. Where the agreement specifically grants to management the right to make or change rules, arbitrators have generally held that management can amend or replace rules during the term of an agreement subject to a reasonableness test.[41] If, however, the rule affects a working condition, some arbitrators have required that the employer bargain the change with the union.[42]

Some arbitrators take the position that if the collective bargaining agreement specifically grants to the company the right to formulate and enforce rules, but is silent on the issue of changing rules, management still has the authority to unilaterally modify such rules.[43] Others hold that once a work rule has been promulgated and enforced over a number of years, it effectively becomes part of the agreement and, therefore, cannot be unilaterally changed during the term of a collective bargaining agreement.[44] Some agreements will explicitly provide that once a rule is promulgated, an employer cannot change it during the term of the agreement.[45] Under these contracts it will be difficult, if not impossible, for an employer to enforce a unilateral revision during the term of the agreement. In those cases that have allowed rule modifications, a showing of changed circumstances was required.

Arbitral rulings appear to track judicial holdings on the issue of effecting changes in rules.[46] Illustrative is a decision

---

[41]See, e.g., Union Tank Car Co., 77 LA 249 (Taylor, 1981)(no-fault absenteeism policy).

[42]See, e.g., Rohr Indus. Inc., 79 LA 900, 904 (Richman, 1982)("[W]here the right to promulgate rules is not retained as a management right, by specific language, and the rule promulgated places an additional burden upon the employee or deprives the employee of an existing benefit, the recognition clause may act as a bar to such unilateral action and require that the rule be negotiated between the parties.").

[43]See, e.g., Stroh Die Casting Co., 72 LA 1250 (Kerkman, 1979)(change in attendance policy); Litton Sys. Inc., 84 LA 688 (Bognanno, 1985).

[44]Mrs. Baird's Bakeries, Inc., 68 LA 773, 776 (Fox, 1977).

[45]Wolverine Aluminum Corp., 74 LA 252, 255 (Dorby, 1980).

[46]See, e.g., Production Plated Plastics, Inc., 254 NLRB 560, 106 LRRM 1143 (1981)(employer violated statute by failing to notify union before changing rule on tardiness, where new rule imposed different degree of punishment for repeated tardiness); La Mousse, Inc., 259 NLRB 37, 108 LRRM 1356 (1981)(no statutory violation in unilateral promulgation of rule changes, where change is not material, substantial, or significant); Continental Tel. Co., 274 NLRB No. 210, 118 LRRM 1598 (1985)(upholding unilateral change in tardiness and absence policy where union in past acquiesced in unilateral changes, and agreement contained broad management

reported by Arbitrator Mario Bognanno. In a grievance that was deferred by the NLRB to arbitration, Arbitrator Bognanno adopted a legal analysis in holding that an employer did not violate its duty to bargain rule changes under the LRMA. He stated:

> Clearly, most work rules are mandatory subjects of bargaining and thus a party is required to bargain in good faith over these items. Fibreboard Paper Products Corp. v. NLRB, 379 U.S. 203, 57 LRRM 2609 (1964). At the same time the National Labor Relations Board and the United States Supreme Court have consistently held that a Union may waive, through collective bargaining, some of the employee's [bargaining] rights. Magnavox Co. v. NLRB, 425 U.S. 322, 85 LRRM 2475 (1974). This waiver must be clear and specific and not involve a fundamental employee right such as the right to choose the bargaining representative. [citing Magnavox] Accordingly, the question is whether the Union did and could . . . waive its right to negotiate and bargain over work guidelines during the term of the present Collective Bargaining Agreement.[47]

Arbitrator Bognanno found that the union waived its right to bargain over work guidelines on absenteeism and tardiness when it negotiated a labor agreement containing a management rights clause that, in part, allowed the company the right to establish reasonable rules.

Arbitrator Dale Allen, Jr., summarized the thinking of most arbitrators in *U.S. Customs Service*.[48] After noting that "[t]he right to establish rules does not necessarily encompass the right to unilaterally significantly modify existing rules," Arbitrator Allen stated that "management should be permitted to change plant rules, where not contractually precluded, to meet changed circumstances."[49] He went on to state, however, that "'management must bargain with respect to such rules as affect conditions of employment. . . .'"[50] In the words of Allen:

---

rights clause); U.S. Postal Service, 275 NLRB No. 57, 119 LRRM 1057, 1058 (1985) (" . . . partial breach of an otherwise uniformly applied work rule inadequate basis to bar [company] from again applying the rule in a uniform manner to all its clerical employees."); Chef's Pantry, 274 NLRB No. 117, 119 LRRM 1096 (1985)(holding LMRA not violated where rule prohibiting employees from leaving jobs unless they had completed work or obtained permission of management did not change an established term or condition of employment).

[47]Litton Sys., 84 LA 688, 692 (1985).
[48]80 LA 777 (1983).
[49]Id. at 785.
[50]Id., quoting Elkouri & Elkouri, How Arbitration Works, 3d Ed., 519 (BNA Books, 1978) [repaginated at 556, 4th Ed., 1985].

In some cases, this bargaining requirement has been found to derive from the recognitional clause of the agreement. . . . Other arbitrators have simply stated that where revised rules affect wages, hours or working conditions of employees, including circumstances such as the present one where informal prior individual policies are consolidated into an overall written set of rules, 'they cannot be unilaterally adopted by the Company, but must be negotiated with the Union.' . . . This approach would also appear warranted here in light of analogous NLRB precedent. The Board has often indicated that work rules constitute a term or condition of employment and one over which an employee is statutorily compelled to bargain. . . . This is also true whenever existing rules are substantially altered or stricter penalties imposed.[51]

Accordingly, where an established plant or work rule involves a mandatory subject of bargaining, the better weight of authority holds that, absent permissive contractual language, an employer may not unilaterally institute a material change in a rule. This prohibition against unilateral changes extends past the expiration of the parties' contract until the parties negotiate a new agreement or bargain in good faith to impasse over the matter.

Conflicts With the Agreement

While management has the right to adopt and enforce rules of conduct and to apply reasonable penalties for their infraction, the terms of the bargaining agreement will always operate as a constraint on the discretion of the company. Even where the agreement recognizes the employer's right to promulgate rules, the better view is that the rules cannot conflict with the written agreement. To hold otherwise would mean that a company would have the power to unilaterally modify the contract.[52] For example, the Tenth Circuit, in *Campo Machining Co. v. Machinists Local 1926*,[53] held that an arbitrator confined himself to interpreting and applying the agreement when he ruled that an employer did not have just cause to discharge a grievant who left the plant without permission, even though discharge was prescribed for this offense. In re-

---

[51]80 LA at 785–86, quoting United Baking Co., 43 LA 337, 338 (Kreimer, 1964).
[52]See, e.g., Central Tel. Co. of Va., 68 LA 957, 961 (Whyte, 1977); Electrical Repair Serv. Co., 67 LA 173, 178 (Towers, 1976).
[53]536 F.2d 330, 92 LRRM 2513 (CA 10, 1976).

versing the district court's decision vacating the award, the court of appeals reasoned that the arbitrator took into account the "tension" between a literal application of the rule and a contract provision prescribing discharge only for "good and sufficient cause," and that the arbitrator's concern with this tension evidenced that he limited his efforts to interpretation of the contract. The court stated:

> The management rights clause of the agreement gives to management the right to promulgate rules and regulations so long as they are not "inconsistent or in conflict with the provisions of this agreement." In the light of this language, it becomes clear that when the arbitrator was determining whether mere violation of [the rule] was always cause of dismissal, he was engaged in interpretation of the agreement.[54]

This reasoning reflects the likely thinking of most arbitrators when confronted with a just cause provision and plant or work rules that outline specific penalties for their violation.[55]

Preenforcement Review by Arbitrator

Unions have sometimes encountered the argument that grievances over rules and their application should not be arbitrable until discipline for violating the rule is actually imposed. The better view is that an employee should not be forced to endure a penalty before the rule can be challenged in a grievance procedure. Illustrative is *Baltimore News American*,[56] where Arbitrator Richard Bloch posed the question and then answered it as follows:

> The Employer suggests the fairness of the rule is more properly tested in the context of a disciplinary proceeding. Here no discipline has yet been meted out. However, to respond that the employees' protection under this rule must be exercised only after its application is to promote an otherwise avoidable dispute. Additionally, perhaps more importantly, such deferred remedy overlooks the negative impact of a rule which, while obeyed, is nevertheless oppressive.[57]

---

[54]92 LRRM at 2515.
[55]The latitude of arbitrators in determining "just cause" and its relation to other contractual provisions is discussed in Chapter 4, notes 81–90, and accompanying text.
[56]65 LA 161 (Bloch, 1975).
[57]Id. at 163.

Whether a dispute is arbitrable because discipline has yet to be imposed is a question of ripeness and a procedural issue which, under current law, should be decided by the arbitrator.[58] Absent language to the contrary, if the subject matter of the rule is subject to the arbitration clause, the absence of a disciplined employee should not preclude arbitrability.

---

[58]John Wiley & Sons, Inc. v. Livingston, 376 U.S. 543, 55 LRRM 2769 (1964).

Chapter 4

Discipline and Discharge

Courts and labor arbitrators both recognize that management has a fundamental right to discipline the working force. Indeed, during the eighteenth and nineteenth centuries, an employer effectively had total discretion over its business. Under an 1877 legal principle, the employer-employee relationship existed "at will," meaning that employment could be terminated without penalty at the will of either party for a good reason, a bad reason, or no reason, absent a specific contract for a definite term.[1] Since few employees possessed the leverage to compel the employer to enter into a binding contract of employment for a specific duration, as a practical matter, the employment relationship existed solely at the will of the employer. The great latitude accorded employers was reinforced by the principle of mutuality of obligations, i.e., if an employee is free to quit at any time, then the employer must be free to dismiss at any time.[2]

Today, with protective labor legislation, unions, and collective bargaining, the at-will doctrine has been significantly modified. Moreover, the judiciary has increasingly limited management's discretion to discharge an employee by carving

---

[1]Part of this section is taken from Hill, "Arbitration as a Means of Protecting Employees From Unjust Dismissal: A Statutory Proposal," 3 N. Ill. U.L. Rev. 111 (1982). See generally Blades, "Employment at Will vs. Individual Freedom: On Limiting the Abusive Exercise of Employer Power," 67 Colum. L. Rev. 1404, 1405 (1967); Note, "Protecting At Will Employees Against Wrongful Discharge: The Duty to Terminate Only in Good Faith," 93 Harv. L. Rev. 1816 (1980).

[2]Smith v. Atlas Off-Shore Boat Serv., 643 F.2d 1057, 117 LRRM 2414, 2416 (CA 5, 1981), citing Summers, "Individual Protection Against Unjust Dismissal: Time for a Statute," 62 Va. L. Rev. 481, 484–85 (1976).

out "public policy," "whistle blowing," and "bad-faith" exceptions to the at-will doctrine.

Starting from the common law doctrine that absent an employment contract, management has the absolute right to effect a discharge, this chapter examines the three major exceptions to the at-will rule: (1) private- and public-sector employment statutory exceptions, (2) contractual limitations under a "just cause" provision of a collective bargaining agreement, and (3) court-created limitations mandated by the judiciary. Because of the wealth of literature devoted to the statutory area, only an overview of statutory limitations is provided here.

Statutory Limitations

Employment legislation during the last 50 years has gradually eroded the common law rule of employment at will. The once inflexible rule that an employer can discharge a worker at any time, for any reason, is no longer controlling. Ironically, statutes now limit the right of employers to terminate employees to such an extent that employers actually have less freedom than employees to terminate employment. Unlike the employer, a disgruntled employee can, with few exceptions, terminate the employment relationship whatever the reason.

National Labor Relations Act

The major governing statute in the area of private-sector labor relations is the National Labor Relations Act of 1935, or Wagner Act, as amended.[3] Since its inception, the Wagner Act has had as its primary concern the rights of employees. Section 1 of the Act, in relevant part, provides:

> It is declared to be the policy of the United States . . . [to protect] the exercise by workers of full freedom of association, self-organization, and designation of representatives of their own choosing, for the purpose of negotiating the terms and conditions of their employment or other mutual aid and protection.[4]

To effectuate this policy, Congress enacted Section 7, which

---

[3] 29 U.S.C. §§151–68 (1970), as amended (Supp. IV, 1980).
[4] 29 U.S.C. §151.

provides that employees covered under the statute have the right to "self-organization, to form, join, or assist labor organizations," and to engage in "other concerted activities for the purpose of collective bargaining or other mutual aid or protection."[5] Section 8 made it an unfair labor practice for an employer "to interfere with, restrain, or coerce employees" in the exercise of rights protected under Section 7.[6]

While the specific language of the Labor Management Relations Act of 1947, or Taft-Hartley Act, excludes supervisors from protection,[7] some courts have accorded them protection under the statute if their discharge has the effect of interfering, restraining, or coercing employees in the exercise of their Section 7 rights.[8]

The significance of the Act lies in its severe restriction of the common law at-will rule as applied to discharge because of union activity. Historically both the Board and the courts have accorded discharged employees significant protection under the Act in numerous situations, including the following:

- Complaining to the employer regarding breaches of the collective bargaining agreement[9]
- Drafting letters of complaint to a state occupational safety agency[10]
- Lobbying legislatures regarding changes in immigration laws[11]

---

[5]29 U.S.C. §157.

[6]Sec. 8(a)(1) of the Labor-Management Relations Act provides:

(a) It shall be an unfair labor practice for an employer—(1) to interfere with, restrain, or coerce employees in the exercise of the rights guaranteed in [§7] . . . .

Sec. 7 provides:

Employees shall have the right to self-organization, to form, join, or assist labor organizations, to bargain collectively through representatives of their own choosing, and to engage in other concerted activities for the purpose of collective bargaining or other mutual aid or protection, and shall also have the right to refrain from any or all of such activities except to the extent that such right may be affected by an agreement requiring membership in a labor organization as a condition of employment. . . .

In 1935, Congress created an administrative agency, the National Labor Relations Board (NLRB), to ensure that employees would, in fact, have the right to form, join, or assist labor organizations. The Board now consists of five members whose main function is to process representation cases and unfair labor practice cases. The Board also reviews unfair labor practice complaints after they are first heard by an administrative law judge at the regional level.

[7]29 U.S.C. §152(3).

[8]Management's right to discharge or discipline its own supervisors is examined in Chapter 17 infra.

[9]NLRB v. Interboro Contractors, Inc., 388 F.2d 495, 67 LRRM 2083 (CA 2, 1967).

[10]Indiana Gear Works v. NLRB, 371 F.2d 273, 64 LRRM 2253 (CA 7, 1967).

[11]Kaiser Eng'rs. v. NLRB, 538 F.2d 1379, 92 LRRM 3153 (CA 9, 1976).

- Insisting upon union representation in an investigatory interview conducted by the employer[12]
- Refusing to cross a picket line set up by a union that does not represent the employee[13]
- Participating in protests over the discharge of a supervisor[14]
- Walking off the job site without prior notice because of bitterly cold shop conditions[15]
- Spontaneously stopping work as a manifestation of disagreement with the employer's conduct[16] and
- Employees complaining separately about job-placed supervisors to company officials.[17]

The NLRB's view in 1984 of what constitutes "concerted activity" under Section 7 in a non-union setting is reflected in *Meyers Industries, Inc.*[18] An employee was dismissed for refusing to drive a truck he considered unsafe and for contacting the Tennessee Public Service Commission to arrange for an inspection of the vehicle. An administrative law judge (ALJ) held the employee's conduct protected. The ALJ reasoned that the employee's refusal was mandated by Department of Transportation regulations that reflected a concern for the safety of both drivers and the general public, and that "[a]n employee who complains about the safety of a particular truck speaks for the safety of any employee who may drive that truck." The Board, adopting an "objective" definition of "concerted," declared: "In general, to find an employee's activities to be 'concerted', we shall require that [they] be engaged in with or on the authority of other employees, and not solely by and on behalf of the employee himself." Applying this test, the Board upheld the discharge, finding that the employee had acted alone and "solely on his own behalf" when he refused to drive the vehicle and contacted the authorities.[19]

---

[12]NLRB v. J. Weingarten, Inc., 420 U.S. 251, 88 LRRM 2689 (1975).

[13]NLRB v. Southern Greyhound Lines, Inc., 426 F.2d 1299, 74 LRRM 2080 (CA 5, 1970); NLRB v. Difco Laboratories, Inc., 427 F.2d 170, 74 LRRM 2273 (CA 6, 1970).

[14]Puerto Rico Food Prods. Corp., 242 NLRB 899, 101 LRRM 1307 (1979).

[15]NLRB v. Washington Aluminum, 370 U.S. 9, 50 LRRM 2235 (1962).

[16]Vic Tanny Int'l, Inc. v. NLRB, 622 F.2d 237, 104 LRRM 2395 (CA 6, 1980).

[17]NLRB v. Guernsey-Muskingum Elec. Co-op, Inc., 285 F.2d 8, 47 LRRM 2260 (CA 6, 1960).

[18]268 NLRB 493, 115 LRRM 1025, 1029 (1984), remanded sub nom. Prill v. NLRB, 755 F.2d 941, 118 LRRM 2649 (CA DC, 1985).

[19]On appeal, the Court of Appeals for the District of Columbia Circuit concluded that the Board's interpretation of concerted activity was a new and restrictive stan-

Later in 1984, the Supreme Court, in *NLRB v. City Disposal Systems, Inc.*,[20] held that a single employee's invocation of a right derived from a collective bargaining agreement is concerted activity under the statute. In *City Disposal*, a worker refused to drive a truck based on his belief that the brakes were faulty. Although he did not refer to his collective bargaining agreement when he confronted his supervisors, he nevertheless explained to them that his refusal was based on safety considerations. The parties' agreement provided that "[t]he Employer shall not require employees to take out on the streets or highways any vehicle that is not in safe operating condition," and that "[i]t shall not be a violation of the Agreement where employees refuse to operate such equipment, unless such refusal is unjustified." Upholding the NLRB's position, the Court stated that "in the context of a workplace dispute, where the participants are likely to be unsophisticated in collective-bargaining matters, a requirement that the employee explicitly refer to the collective bargaining agreement is likely to serve as nothing more than a trap for the unwary."[21]

Particularly interesting in this decision is the Court's declaration with respect to an employee's duty to file a grievance when the employee believes that the agreement disagrees with a management directive. The Court stated:

> It is reasonable to expect that an employee's first response to a situation that he believes violates his collective-bargaining agreement will be a protest to his employer. Whether he files a grievance will depend in part on his employer's reaction and in part upon the nature of the right at issue. In addition, certain rights may not be susceptible of enforcement by the filing of a grievance. In such a case, the collective-bargaining agreement might provide for an alternative method of enforcement . . . . Thus, for a variety of reasons, an employee's initial statement to an employer to the effect that he believes a collectively bargained right is being violated, or that the employee's initial refusal to do that which he believes he is not obligated to do, might serve as both a natural prelude to, and an efficient substitute for, the filing of a formal grievance. As long as the employee's statement or action is based on a reasonable and honest belief that he is being, or has been, asked to perform a

---

dard that was not required by the statute. The case was remanded. Prill v. NLRB, supra note 18.

[20]465 U.S. 822, 115 LRRM 3193 (1984).

[21]115 LRRM at 3201.

task that he is not required to perform under his collective-bargaining agreement, and the statement or action is reasonably directed toward the enforcement of a collectively bargained right, there is no justification for overturning the Board's judgment that the employee is engaged in concerted activity, just as he would have been had he filed a formal grievance.[22]

The question of whether an employee was discharged for engaging in protected activity is a question of fact. The test to determine whether a discharge is an unfair labor practice is whether the employer's anti-union animus was a dominant motive. Where both a "good" and a "bad" reason for the discharge exist (a "dual motive" case), the burden is upon the General Counsel to establish a prima facie case that protected conduct was a motivating factor in the employer's decision. Once this is established, the employer has the burden of demonstrating the same action would have taken place notwithstanding the protected activity.[23]

The effect of the NLRA on managerial discretion is clear. Absent the statute, and without access to labor arbitration, most, if not all, of the above-cited situations would result in no protection for terminated employees under the common law at-will doctrine. Under the Act, relief to restore a terminated employee to his original status and seniority is available for an employee whose Section 7 rights have been violated.[24]

Title VII[25]

Title VII of the Civil Rights Act of 1964, as amended, explicitly prohibits discrimination in employment as to hiring, firing, compensation, and terms, conditions, or privileges of employment on the basis of race, color, religion, sex, or national origin.[26] Since 1972, the Act has applied to employers engaged in an industry affecting commerce who have 15 or more employees each working day in 20 or more calendar

---

[22]Id. at 3199–3200.
[23]NLRB v. Wright Line, Inc., 662 F.2d 899, 108 LRRM 2513 (CA 1, 1981); Peavey Co. v. NLRB, 648 F.2d 460, 107 LRRM 2359 (CA 7, 1981); NLRB v. Nevis Indus., Inc., 647 F.2d 905, 107 LRRM 2890 (CA 9, 1981); NLRB v. Consolidated Freightways Corp., 651 F.2d 436, 107 LRRM 3351 (CA 6, 1981).
[24]On the general subject of remedies in discharge and discipline cases, see Hill & Sinicropi, Remedies in Arbitration, 40–96 (BNA Books, 1981).
[25]Various Title VII issues and their effect upon managerial discretion are examined in parts of Chapters 5, 6, 7, 8, 9, and 10, infra.
[26]42 U.S.C. §§2000c to 2000e–17 (1982).

weeks of the current calendar year.[27] It also applies to employment agencies procuring employees for such an employer,[28] and to almost all labor organizations.[29] The 1972 amendments also extend coverage to all state and local governments; government agencies; political subdivisions, excluding elected officials, their personal assistants, and immediate advisors; and the District of Columbia departments and agencies, except where subject by law to the federal competitive service.[30] Any person claiming to be aggrieved under the statute may file a complaint with the Equal Employment Opportunity Commission (EEOC). The EEOC is vested with the authority to investigate individual charges of discrimination, to promote voluntary compliance with the statute, and to institute civil actions against parties named in a discrimination charge.[31] The EEOC cannot adjudicate claims or impose administrative sanctions. Rather, the EEOC prosecutes violations in the federal courts, which are authorized to issue injunctive relief and to order such affirmative action as may be appropriate.[32]

To effectuate the purposes and policies of the statute, Congress included Section 704(a), which essentially prohibits employers from retaliating against employees who initiate complaints under Title VII. This section has been held to afford protection even though the conditions and conduct complained of do not constitute a violation of Title VII.[33] Moreover, even relatives of persons who exercise rights under the statute are protected from employer retaliation.[34]

Title VII forbids discrimination only under specific circumstances. As outlined by Schlei and Grossman in their treatise on employment discrimination law,[35] discrimination is an unlawful employment practice only if: (1) committed by a "re-

---

[27] 42 U.S.C. §2000e(b), §2000e–2(a).

[28] 42 U.S.C. §2000e(c), §2000e–2(b).

[29] 42 U.S.C. §2000e(d), §2000e–2(c).

[30] Equal Employment Opportunity Act of 1972, §2 (amending 42 U.S.C. §2000e(a)). As originally enacted in 1964, Title VII did not cover employees of the federal government. In 1972, however, the statute was amended to include most federal employees. Equal Opportunity Act of 1972, §11, 42 U.S.C. §2000e–16 (1976 & Supp. III, 1979).

[31] 42 U.S.C. §2000e–5(b), (f)(1)(1976 & Supp. III, 1979).

[32] 42 U.S.C. §2000e–5(f), (g).

[33] See Novotny v. Great Am. Fed. Sav. & Loan Assn., 584 F.2d 1235, 17 FEP 1252 (CA 3, 1978), cert. granted, 439 U.S. 1066, vacated, 422 U.S. 366, 19 FEP 1482 (1979).

[34] Kornbluh v. Stearns & Foster Co., 73 F.R.D. 307, 14 FEP 847 (S.D. Ohio, 1976).

[35] Schlei & Grossman, Employment Discrimination Law, 1 (BNA Books, 1983) (hereinafter cited as Schlei & Grossman).

spondent"[36] cognizable under Title VII, (2) on a "basis"[37] cognizable under the Act, (3) with regard to an "issue"[38] cognizable under Title VII, and (4) where a causal connection, or nexus, exists between the basis and the issue.

Two theories by which the causal connection or nexus may be proved are "disparate treatment" and "disparate impact." The most easily understood type of discrimination is "disparate treatment," which involves treating an individual less favorably than others similarly situated because of race, color, religion, sex, or national origin.[39] Proof of a discriminatory motive is required, although it may be inferred from the mere fact of a difference in treatment. "Disparate impact" involves employment practices that are facially neutral but which have a discriminatory effect that cannot be justified by business necessity.[40] Proof of a discriminatory motive is not required under a disparate impact theory.

Thus, the reach of Title VII's prohibitions against employment discrimination has been expanded by the courts to include even neutrally stated and indiscriminately administered employment practices if, in the absence of demonstrable business necessity, a practice operates to favor an identifiable group of white employees over a protected class.[41]

Under Title VII, discrimination based on religion, sex, or national origin is regulated by a different statutory standard than that applied to race or color. Employment discrimination with respect to religion, sex, or national origin is tolerated only where religion, sex, or national origin is a bona fide occupational qualification (BFOQ) reasonably necessary to the normal operation of a particular business.[42] There is no statutory BFOQ for race or color.

---

[36]The respondent must be either an employer, 42 U.S.C. §2000e(b) (1976), an employment agency, id. §2000e(c), or a labor organization, id. §2000e(d).

[37]The statutory bases are race, color, religion, sex, and national origin. 42 U.S.C. §2000e-2(a)(1) (1976).

[38]The cognizable issues are: hiring, discharging, compensation, contract terms, conditions, or privileges of employment, 42 U.S.C. §2000e-2(a)(1) (1976); limitations, segregation or classification of employees or applicants for employment, id. §2000e-2(a)(2); unwillingness to refer, id. §2000e-2(b); exclusion or expulsion from membership, id. §2000e-2(c)(1); limitation, segregation, or classification of membership, id. §2000e-2(c)(2); retaliation, id. §2000e-3(a); printing or publishing a discriminatory employment notice or advertisement, id. §2000e-3(b).

[39]See, e.g., Teamsters v. United States, 431 U.S. 324, 335 n. 15, 14 FEP 1514 (1977).

[40]Id.

[41]Griggs v. Duke Power Co., 401 U.S. 424, 3 FEP 175 (1971).

[42]Sec. 703(e) provides: "Notwithstanding any other provision of this subchapter, (1) it shall not be an unlawful employment practice for an employer to hire and

Accordingly, the statute mandates a two-step analysis in employment discrimination cases. First, the court must find that the employer has engaged in discrimination under one of the prohibited classifications as outlined in the statute. Only after the court determines that a prohibited form of discrimination has occurred will the second step be considered. Thus, if discrimination is found, the employer still has the opportunity to demonstrate that the discrimination was justified as a BFOQ.

One of the notable applications of this statute, besides providing protection for minorities and women, has been its use in protecting whites. In *McDonald v. Sante Fe Trail Transportation Co.*,[43] the Supreme Court held that the terms of Title VII are not limited to discrimination against members of any particular race. To rule otherwise, the Court said, would "constitute a dereliction of the Congressional mandate to eliminate all practices which operate to disadvantage the employment opportunities of any group protected by Title VII, including Caucasians."[44]

Public-Sector Statutes

The most extensive statutory protections against dismissal at will are enjoyed by public-sector employees.[45] At the

---

employ employees, for an employment agency to classify, or refer for employment any individual, for a labor organization to classify its membership or to classify or refer for employment any individual, . . . on the basis of his religion, sex, or national origin in those certain instances where religion, sex, or national origin is a bona fide occupational qualification [BFOQ] reasonably necessary to the normal operation of that particular business enterprise. . . ."

[43]427 U.S. 273, 12 FEP 1577 (1976).

[44]12 FEP at 1580, citing EEOC Decision 74-31 (1973). The application of Title VII and its underlying color blindness has promoted two legal scholars to suggest that Title VII can be logically generalized to provide protection for all employees against unjustifiable employer discharge decisions without regard to race or sex. See Peck, "Unjust Discharges From Employment: A Necessary Change in the Law," 40 Ohio St. L.J. 1, 19–21 (1979); Blumrosen, "Strangers No More: All Workers Are Entitled to 'Just Cause' Protection Under Title VII," 2 Indus. Rel. L.J. 519 (1978). Peck and Blumrosen in combination assert that McDonnell-Douglas Corp. v. Green, 411 U.S. 792, 5 FEP 965 (1973), affords all employees protection by: (1) requiring the employer to articulate some legitimate, nondiscriminatory reason for discharge (McDonnell-Douglas); and (2) the application of Title VII to white employees (McDonald v. Santa Fe Trail). It is unclear whether this application has found acceptance in more than a handful of courts.

[45]See generally Lowy, "Constitutional Limitations on the Dismissal of Public Employees," 43 Brooklyn L. Rev. 1 (1976); Chaturvedi, "Legal Protection Available

federal level, a major statute governing labor relations is the Civil Service Reform Act of 1978.[46] Particularly noteworthy is a provision[47] in the statute which provides that, pursuant to regulations prescribed by the Office of Personnel Management, an employee subject to civil service can be disciplined for "misconduct, neglect of duty or malfeasance." The statute further provides that an employee against whom action is taken is entitled to:

(1) At least 30 days' advance written notice, unless there is reason to believe that the employee has committed a crime for which a sentence of imprisonment can be imposed

(2) Reasonable time, not less than seven days, to file an answer along with any supporting affidavits

(3) Representation by an attorney or other representative and

(4) A written decision and specific reasons at the earliest practicable date.[48]

Provision is also made for appeal to the Merit System Protection Board.[49]

Additional protection is afforded employees who make use of the statutory procedure. Section 7116(a) provides that it is an unfair labor practice for an agency "to discipline or otherwise discriminate against an employee because the employee has filed a complaint, affidavit or petition, or has given any information or testimony under this chapter."[50]

Protection afforded employees under state laws is typically not as complete as federal law, but nonetheless offers some safeguard from arbitrary dismissal. In most jurisdictions state employees are protected from discriminatory treatment because of union organization and Title VII-type criteria. State civil service laws and corresponding merit systems generally

---

to Federal Employees Against Wrongful Dismissal," 63 Nw. U.L. Rev. 287 (1968); Note, "Dismissal of Federal Employees—The Emerging Judicial Role," 66 Colum. L. Rev. 719 (1966); Rabin, "Job Security and Due Process: Monitoring Administrative Discretion Through a Reasons Requirement," 44 U. Chi. L. Rev. 60 (1976).
    [46]5 U.S.C. §§2101-8901 (1978).
    [47]5 U.S.C. §7543(a).
    [48]5 U.S.C. §7543(b).
    [49]5 U.S.C. §7543(d).
    [50]5 U.S.C. §7116(a)(4).

outline procedures for hiring, staffing, and promoting, rather than provide substantive protections against arbitrary discharges.

State statutes that grant and regulate collective bargaining rights provide a major source of protection against unjust dismissal, at least with respect to organizational activity. As of May, 1985, 39 states, the District of Columbia, and the Virgin Islands had statutes or executive orders providing collective bargaining rights to some or all of their employees. The importance of these statutes cannot be overlooked. Not only are state employees protected from dismissal for their union-related activity, but bargaining itself will generally result in the enactment and institution of employee grievance procedures. Other grounds for discipline and discharge will accordingly be subject to review by arbitrators or other bodies so designated in the bargaining agreement.

Other Legislation

There are a number of state and federal statutes that limit the freedom of employers to discharge employees at will. On the federal level, the following statutes are particularly of note:

(1) The Consumer Credit Protection Act,[51] which prohibits discharge because of wage garnishment for indebtedness

(2) The Age Discrimination in Employment Act,[52] which protects persons between the ages of 40 and 70 against discrimination in employment

(3) The Fair Labor Standards Act,[53] which prohibits a retaliatory discharge against those exercising rights under the statute

(4) The Occupational Safety and Health Act, which also prohibits the discharge of those exercising rights under the statute[54]

(5) The Selective Training and Service Act of 1940,[55] which essentially requires reinstatement of veterans

---

[51]15 U.S.C. §1674(a) (1982).
[52]29 U.S.C. §§621–34 (1976).
[53]29 U.S.C. §§201–219.
[54]29 U.S.C. §660(c).
[55]38 U.S.C. §§2021–26 (1974).

to their former positions of employment after discharge from military service and

(6) The Railway Labor Act, which prohibits discrimination on the basis of union activity and commands the parties to attempt to settle all minor disputes through grievance procedures (A minor dispute concerns the meaning and application of rules of working conditions under the collective bargaining agreement. If the parties' grievance procedures fail, compulsory arbitration is available before the National Railroad Adjustment Board.[56])

Individual states have passed legislation similar to the NLRA, Title VII,[57] and the Age Discrimination in Employment Act[58] which further limit management's freedom to discharge workers. In addition, state statutes have prohibited employer discrimination in such areas as: an employee's ac-

_____

[56]45 U.S.C. §§151–63; Hendley v. Central of Ga. R.R., 609 F.2d 1146, 103 LRRM 2509 (CA 5, 1980).

[57]Comprehensive fair employment legislation exists in the following (citations to the "Fair Employment Practices Manual" of BNA's Labor Relations Reporter): Alaska, 453:205; Arizona, 453:405; California, 453:805; Colorado, 453:1005; Connecticut, 453:1205; Delaware, 453:1405; District of Columbia, 453:1605, 1701; Florida, 453:1805; Georgia, 453:2015; Hawaii, 453:2205; Idaho, 453:2405, 2205; Illinois, 453:2605; Indiana, 453:2805; Iowa, 453:3005; Kansas, 453:3205; Kentucky, 455:5; Louisiana, 455:207; Maine, 455:405; Maryland, 455:605; Massachusetts, 455:805; Michigan 455:1005; Minnesota, 455:1205; Missouri, 455:1605; Montana, 455:1805; Nebraska, 455:2005, 2101; Nevada, 455:2205; New Hampshire, 455:2405; New Jersey, 455:2605; New Mexico, 455:2805; New York, 455:3005, 3037; North Carolina, 455:3205; North Dakota, 457:3; Ohio, 457:205; Oregon, 457:605; Pennsylvania, 457:805; Puerto Rico, 457:1005; Rhode Island, 457:1205; South Carolina, 457:1405; South Dakota, 457:1605, 1632; Tennessee, 457:1805; Utah, 457:2205; Vermont, 457:2405; Virgin Islands, 457:2705; Washington, 457:2805; West Virginia, 457:3005; Wisconsin, 457:3205; Wyoming, 457:3405.

[58]Age discrimination legislation exists in the following (citations to the "Fair Employment Practice Manual" of BNA's Labor Relations Reporter): Alaska, 453:205, 225; Arizona, 453:405; Arkansas, 453:605; California, 453:807, 831, 835, 836, 881; Colorado, 453:1025; Connecticut, 453:1210, 1225; Delaware, 453:1405; District of Columbia, 453:1605; Florida, 453:1805, 1845; Georgia, 453:2005, 2015; Hawaii, 453:2205; Idaho, 453:2405, 2519; Illinois, 453:2771; Indiana, 453:2835; Iowa, 453:3005, 3093; Kansas, 453:3223, 3229, 3265; Kentucky, 455:5, 71; Louisiana, 455:205; Maine, 455:405, 526; Maryland, 455:611; Massachusetts, 455:805, 831; Michigan, 455:1005, 1094, 1135; Minnesota, 455:1205, 1231; Mississippi, 455:1405; Montana, 455:1805, 1933, 1936; Nebraska, 455:2025, 2121; Nevada, 455:2205, 2225, 2245; New Hampshire, 455:2405, 2525; New Jersey, 455:2605; New Mexico, 455:2805; New York, 455:3005; North Carolina, 455:3205; North Dakota, 457:3, 15; Ohio, 457:205, 221, 231; Oregon, 457:605; Pennsylvania, 457:805; Puerto Rico, 457:1005; Rhode Island, 457:1205; South Carolina, 457:1405; South Dakota, 457:1631; Tennessee, 457:1805; Utah, 457:2205; Virgin Islands, 457:2705; Washington, 457:2805, 2825, 2835, 2935; West Virginia, 457:3005, 3026; Wisconsin, 457:3205.

ceptance of jury duty,[59] the exercise of political activities;[60] refusal to take a lie detector test;[61] filing of a worker's compensation claim;[62] "blowing the whistle" on employers;[63] and existence of a physical handicap.[64] Connecticut has even enacted a statute prohibiting an employer from disciplining an employee "on account of the exercise by such employee of rights guaranteed by the First Amendment to the U.S. Constitution. . . ."[65]

Contractual/Arbitral Limitations

Labor organizations have greatly limited employers' discretion to impose disciplinary sanctions on the work force. Collective bargaining agreements frequently outline standards and procedures which must be observed by an employer when assessing discipline. More important, in addition to the explicit limitations included in the agreement, arbitrators have developed both procedural and substantive guidelines that are operative under a just cause criterion. The effect is clear. Employees who are covered by a collective bargaining agreement with final and binding arbitration are protected from unjust dismissal under a just cause standard. Although the nuances of just cause cannot be quantified, the principles that have been articulated by arbitrators are sufficiently clear to afford significant protection from unjust discharge to a large portion of the labor force.

Contractual limitations on management's right to dis-

[59]See infra note 153 and accompanying text.
[60]Statutes concerning exercise of political activities exist in the following (citations to the "State Laws" (SLL) binders of BNA's Labor Relations Reporter): Arizona, 12:202; Arkansas, 13:202; California, 14:204; Colorado, 15:202; Connecticut, 16:202, 204; Delaware, 17:111; Florida, 19:203, 204; Idaho, 22:201; Indiana, 24:112, 113; Kentucky, 27:202; Louisiana, 28:201; Maryland, 30:201; Massachusetts, 31:202; Michigan, 32:201; Minnesota, 33:201; Mississippi, 34:201; Missouri, 35:201; Montana, 36:202; Nebraska, 37:201, 204; Nevada, 38:203; New Jersey, 40:201; Ohio, 45:201; Oklahoma, 46:201; Pennsylvania, 48:201; Puerto Rico, 49:201; Rhode Island, 50:201; South Carolina, 51:201; South Dakota, 52:201; Tennessee, 53:201; Utah, 55:201; West Virginia, 59:201; Wisconsin, 60:201; Wyoming, 61:201.
[61]See citations listed in Chapter 9, note 8.
[62]See infra note 140 and accompanying text.
[63]See infra note 166 and accompanying text.
[64]See, e.g., Cal. Lab. Code §1420(a) (1975) (repealed and merged into Cal. Gov. Code §12940 (West Supp., 1986)); Ill. Rev. Stat. Ch. 38, §65–23 (1977) (repealed in 1980 and merged into Ill. Rev. Stat. Ch. 68, §§1–101 to 9–102), which prohibits various types of discrimination.
[65]SLL 16:208.

charge employees are usually negotiated by a labor organization serving as exclusive bargaining representative for a specified unit of employees. The impact of collective bargaining agreements on the employer's absolute power of dismissal is magnified as a result of arbitral construction and interpretation, particularly of just cause principles, as discussed below.

Just Cause

A survey by The Bureau of National Affairs, Inc. revealed discharge and discipline provisions in 98 percent of a sample of 400 union contracts.[66] These contracts limit discharge and discipline by establishing "just cause" or "proper cause" provisions whereby employees cannot be discharged unless just cause exists.[67] Although specific grounds for discharge are found in many agreements,[68] few contracts contain a comprehensive definition of "just cause."[69] And while there is no uniform definition, a sampling of arbitral and judicial opinion indicates the following thinking on the subject:

> Although the contract is silent on criteria to be utilized in measuring the imposed discipline, just cause is not an ambiguous, amorphous concept. Tens of thousands of arbitration decisions have explicated standards by which to evaluate the degree of justifiable discipline. Under the facts of this case, the most important of these standards are those of mitigating factors that would excuse or extenuate the discipline.[70]

* * *

---

[66]Basic Patterns in Union Contracts, 6 (BNA Books, 1983).

[67]A study of published discharge grievances compiled in *Labor Arbitration Reports* (BNA), May 1971 through January 1974, reveals that management had its disciplinary action reduced or eliminated in approximately 58% (231 of 400 cases) of the awards. See Jennings & Wolters, "Discharge Cases Reconsidered," 31 Arb. J. 164 (1976). See also Stone, "Why Arbitrators Reinstate Discharged Employees," 92 Monthly Lab. Rev. 49; Summers, "Arbitration of Unjust Dismissal: A Preliminary Proposal," The Future of Labor Arbitration in America, 161 (AAA, 1976); Holly, "The Arbitration of Discharge Cases: A Case Study," Proceedings of the 10th Annual Meeting of NAA, 1 (BNA Books, 1957).

[68]BNA reports that specific grounds for discharge are found in 71% of the agreements sampled. Grounds most frequently referred to are: violation of the contract (35%), violation of leave provisions (32%), dishonesty or theft and intoxication (each 23%), violation of company rules (21%), unauthorized absence (20%), incompetence or failure to meet standards (19%), insubordination (18%), failure to obey safety rules (16%), misconduct (13%), and tardiness (9%). Basic Patterns in Union Contracts, supra note 66, at 6.

[69]See, e.g., Super Tire Eng'g. Co. v. Teamsters Local 676, 546 F.Supp. 547, 111 LRRM 2646, 2649 n.5 (D. N.J., 1982), where the parties' agreement listed "causes" for dismissal.

[70]Niagara Frontier Transit Sys., Inc., 61 LA 784, 791 (Ross, 1973).

The question of "just cause" is nothing less than the question of justice, placed in an industrial setting. True, it is not legal justice; it is not social justice—it is industrial justice.[71]

* * *

[Just cause mandates] not merely that the employer's action be free of capriciousness and arbitrariness but that the employee's performance be so faulty or indefensible as to leave the employer with no alternative except to discipline him.[72]

* * *

If the contract does not specify what constitutes "cause," it is obvious that the determination of what is "cause" must be made in light of the mores of the industrial community.[73]

* * *

There are many definitions of "just cause." All of them, however, sooner or later, get back to some evaluation of industrial punishment in the light of mores, those behavioral rules that structure a society, like it or not. And it is a very individual process, in arbitration, at least, because the determiner is, indeed, both single and final.

In years of exposure and study and thought, both to and of the bad as well as the good, some conclusions have inevitably emerged, and one of them is a definition of what "just cause" probably is, for here and now. It seems to be that cause which, to a presumably-reasonable determiner (is there one here?), appears to be (not necessarily is), fair and reasonable, when all of the applicable facts and circumstances are considered, and are viewed in the light of the ethic of the time and place. That's a mouthful, in words, but it really is only, bottom line, another expression of the now common expression, "fair shake."[74]

* * *

It is sufficient here to hold that in the context of teacher fault a "just cause" is one which directly or indirectly significantly and adversely affects what must be the ultimate goal of every school system: high quality education for the district's students. . . . It must include the concept that a school district is not married to mediocrity but may dismiss personnel who are neither performing high quality work nor improving in performance.[75]

---

[71]Lear Siegler, Inc., 63 LA 1157, 1160 (McBrearty, 1974).
[72]Platt, "Arbitral Standards in Discipline Cases," The Law and Labor-Management Relations, 223, 234 (U. of Mich., 1950).
[73]Smith, Merrifield, & Rothschild, Collective Bargaining and Labor Arbitration, 347 (Bobbs-Merill, 1970).
[74]Hiram Walker & Sons, Inc., 75 LA 899, 900 (Belshaw, 1980).
[75]Briggs v. Board of Directors, 282 N.W.2d 740, 743 (Iowa, 1979).

The thoughts of Arbitrator Raymond Roberts, in *Ritchie Industries, Inc.*,[76] are particularly noteworthy.

"Just cause" is a term of art as employed in Collective Bargaining Agreements. Attendant upon that term are established concepts of industrial fairness and due process of both a substantive and procedural nature.

Two aspects of these concepts are significant. . . .

The first of these aspects is that there must be some reasonable cause to justify disciplinary action or termination. Such cause is usually divided into two categories. The first and most frequently encountered category is where the employee is guilty of an industrial offense against Company rules actually or constructively known to the employee. An industrial offense involves wrong doing or culpability on the part of the employee, either of commission or omission. Some such industrial offenses are so serious that they are classified as industrial "felonies" which will justify discharge for a first offense. Others are less serious and are regarded as industrial "misdemeanors" which require progressive and corrective discipline before discharge will lie.

Under concepts of just cause, an employee may be subjected to disciplinary action only if he has committed an industrial offense, i.e., he is guilty of wrong doing or culpability. If an employee is not guilty of culpability or wrong doing, the employer has no "cause" to impose disciplinary penalties or sanctions upon that employee. . . .

The second class of reason or "cause" which will justify corrective action and, ultimately, termination of the employment relationship under the concepts of "just cause" is non-disciplinary in nature. Such cause is one that substantially impairs the essence of the employment relationship so that the employer cannot reasonably be expected to continue it, notwithstanding that the employee is guilty of no-fault [sic], wrong doing or culpability. Common examples of this class of "cause" for termination are where the employee, through no fault of his own, is simply unable to perform the work with reasonable efficiency to earn his wages, or where the employee, through no fault of his own, has excusable absenteeism that is so extensive that it impairs the employment relationship, or where the employee develops an irreconcilable [sic] conflict of interest with his employer even though he is not guilty of wrong doing.

Arbitrator Roberts outlined the usual standards for nondisciplinary discharge as follows:

1. That the cause or reason for non-disciplinary discharge substantially impairs the employment relationship.

---

[76]74 LA 650, 655 (1980).

2. That the cause has been chronic or, by its inherent nature, clearly will be so.

3. That there is no reasonable prognosis that the cause will be removed in a reasonable period of time.[77]

Perhaps the best (and the most often quoted) statement of the criteria used by arbitrators is in the form of a series of questions by Arbitrator Carroll Daugherty:

1. Did the company give to the employee forewarning or foreknowledge of the possible or probable disciplinary consequences of the employee's conduct?

2. Was the company's rule or managerial order reasonably related to (a) the orderly, efficient and safe operation of the company's business and (b) the performance that the company might properly expect of the employee?

3. Did the company, before administering discipline to an employee, make an effort to discover whether the employee did in fact violate or disobey a rule or order of management?

4. Was the company's investigation conducted fairly and objectively?

5. At the investigation did the "judge" obtain substantial evidence or proof that the employee was guilty as charged?

6. Has the company applied its rules, orders and penalties even-handedly and without discrimination to all employees?

7. Was the degree of discipline administered by the company in a particular case reasonably related to (a) the seriousness of the employee's proven offense and (b) the record of the employee in his service with the company?[78]

Arbitrator Daugherty states that a "no" answer to one or more of the above questions normally signifies that just and proper cause for discipline did not exist.

In evaluating any discharge case an arbitrator must first determine whether the grievant actually engaged in the conduct alleged. Thereafter, unless prohibited by the collective bargaining agreement, the arbitrator will make a determination whether termination was appropriate.[79] These are two separate but often interrelated issues. An arbitrator may, in a certain case, carry into his assessment of a penalty his feelings of uncertainty as to the facts at issue. Arbitrator Gabriel Alexander has observed:

---

[77]Id. at 655.

[78]Enterprise Wire Co., 46 LA 359, 363–64 (1966); Grief Bros. Cooperage Corp., 42 LA 555, 558 (1964). See also Sunshine Biscuits, Inc., 60 LA 197 (Roberts, 1973); McCall Printing Co., 64 LA 584, 588 (Lubic, 1975).

[79]See Hill & Sinicropi, supra note 24, at 97–105, where the authors discuss "Arbitral Authority to Reduce Discipline."

Traditionally it has been considered that the arbitrator was to execute the jury function, that is, determine guilt or innocence, before taking on the judicial function of determining the extent of penalty. I have no quarrel with this mode of approach. Indeed, in the present state of thinking of arbitrators and the parties to arbitration, I would be inclined to believe that the arbitrator who did not proceed in this matter was not meeting the expectations of the parties. I wonder, however, whether this is a realistic point of view in the light of experience in the lower steps of the grievance procedure. I suspect that, in many cases, companies and unions compromise disciplinary penalties as a means of circumventing the necessity for making a straight yes or no answer on questions of fact. If this be true, would it not be more realistic for the parties to permit, perhaps even to encourage, arbitrators to pursue the same line of reasoning.[80]

"Cause" or "Just Cause" as Legal or Arbitral Equivalents

The term "just cause" is generally held to be synonymous with "cause," "proper cause," or "reasonable cause." Rejecting an employer's contention that cause is a broader standard than just cause, one arbitrator stated:

It is common to include the right to suspend and discharge for "just cause", "justifiable cause", "proper cause", "obvious cause", or quite commonly simply for "cause". There is no significant difference between these various phrases. These exclude discharge for mere whim or caprice.[81]

The Eighth Circuit, in *Electrical Workers Local 53 (IBEW) v. Sho-Me Power Corp.*,[82] considered the meaning of the phrase "discharge for cause" in reviewing an arbitrator's award reinstating an employee found guilty of dishonesty. The appellate court stated that "interpreting this standard merely as requiring that the [employer] have some 'cause' for discharging an employee renders it superfluous; unless the [employer] randomly discharges its employees, it will always have some 'cause' as a reason for its discharge of an employee." It accordingly sustained the arbitrator's interpretation that cause was synonymous with just or reasonable cause and that these terms

[80]Alexander, "Concepts of Industrial Discipline," Proceedings of the 9th Annual Meeting of NAA, 79 (BNA Books, 1956).
[81]Keller Indus., Inc., 79 LA 807, 815 (1982), citing Arbitrator Joseph D. McGoldrick in Worthington Corp., 24 LA 1, 6–7 (1955) as quoted in Elkouri & Elkouri, How Arbitration Works, 3d Ed., 612 (BNA Books, 1973)(repaginated at 652 in 4th ed., 1985).
[82]715 F.2d 1322, 114 LRRM 2177 (1983).

imposed on management an obligation to refrain from unreasonable, arbitrary, or capricious actions.

Further, what is just cause is a question of fact, separate from the quantum of proof necessary to establish the fact.[83] And where the parties' agreement gives the employer the sole and exclusive right to discharge for just cause and also the right to determine what just cause means, a grievance alleging absence of just cause will, in all probability, be considered non-arbitrable.[84]

Latitude of Arbitrators

Under current law, an arbitrator is given wide, but not absolute, latitude by the courts in construing a collective bargaining agreement, including the just cause provision. Furthermore, where the grievance procedure declares that the arbitrator's decision is "final and binding," a discharged worker will be precluded from further adjudicating the claim absent a showing that the grievance process has been seriously flawed by the union's breach of its duty of fair representation.[85]

One federal court declared that it could not question an arbitrator's decision that the just cause provision of the contract controlled even specific provisions regarding discharges. The court stated that when the arbitrator held that the just cause provision controlled, he was authorized to apply all the surrounding facts and circumstances to determine whether a discharge was warranted. The court went on to note that in a proper case an arbitrator "may construe a 'just cause' provision of a labor contract to include a progressive discipline requirement and may determine that certain conduct is 'just cause' for discipline but not for discharge."[86]

Other courts have not been this receptive toward an arbitrator's determination of just cause. For example, in *DuPont*

[83]Simpson v. APA Transp. Corp., 108 LRRM 2754 (D.N.J., 1981).
[84]See, e.g., Johnston-Tombigbee Furniture Mfg. Co. v. Carpenters Local 2462, 596 F.2d 126, 101 LRRM 2486 (CA 5, 1979); Halstead & Mitchell Co. v. Steelworkers Local 7032, 421 F.2d 1191, 72 LRRM 2915 (CA 3, 1969)(contract excluding from arbitration all management functions listed in management rights clause, including sole and exclusive right to lay off employees for lack of work and sole and exclusive right to determine the fact of lack of work).
[85]Hines v. Anchor Motor Freight, Inc., 424 U.S. 554, 91 LRRM 2481 (1976).
[86]Super Tire Eng'g. Co. v. Teamsters Local 676, 546 F.Supp. 547, 111 LRRM 2646, 2648 (D.N.J., 1982); Mistletoe Express Serv. v. Motor Expressmen's Union, 566 F.2d 692, 695, 96 LRRM 3320 (CA 10, 1977).

v. Grasselli Employees Ass'n,[87] a federal court vacated an arbitrator's decision apparently because he premised his decision on the lack of fault of a grievant who had attacked another employee (the grievant was criminally charged, but was acquitted on the grounds of temporary insanity) "without an equally corresponding consideration of the extent of the violence involved and the employer's strong interests in maintaining a safe work place." Although the court conceded that the employee's degree of fault might be of some relevance, it nevertheless found that "the arbitrator's failure to balance this element against the other factors involved, especially the danger to other employees, shows that the decision does not 'draw its essence from the agreement.' " The court pointed out that just cause "creates an objective rather than a personal subjective test" and, in the instant case, the arbitrator was apparently attempting to enforce "his private notions of equity."[88]

The Fifth Circuit likewise found that an arbitrator dispensed his own brand of industrial justice in holding that an employee should be reinstated because of management's improper behavior. Two employees were discharged, the union filed grievances, and as a result of the grievances, one was rehired. Arbitration was evoked over the refusal to reinstate the other employee. In ordering the second employee's reinstatement, the arbitrator stated "that while there may have been adequate grounds to discharge both employees, [the employer] acted improperly" by rehiring one but not the other. The court of appeals rejected the argument that the award should be enforced "because disparate treatment of employees is disfavored in federal and arbitral law." In the words of the court, "Such industrial justice is unenforceable."[89]

Courts have recognized that arbitrators will often have to resolve the inherent tension between the management rights and just cause provisions of the collective bargaining agreement. It is possible that the parties' contract will reserve to management "the exclusive and unrestricted right to manage its business and its working forces including the sole right to discharge employees" and, at the same time, contain a tra-

---

[87]118 LRRM 3312 (N.D. Ind., 1985).
[88]118 LRRM at 3316.
[89]HMC Mgmt. Corp. v. Carpenters Dist. Council, 750 F.2d 1302, 118 LRRM 2425, 2426 (CA 5, 1985).

ditional just cause provision. Similarly, the agreement may contain just cause language while the employer's shop or plant rules declare that a single act by an employee will be punished by discharge. In both instances courts have recognized that where there is tension between two provisions of the contract, it is the arbitrator's obligation to resolve any conflicts in construction.[90]

Inferring Just Cause

While the traditional common law view is that absent a statutory or contractual declaration to the contrary, workers are employed at will, there is authority that when a collective bargaining agreement provides some measures regarding job security, a just cause provision will be inferred. The Court of Appeals for the Fifth Circuit, in *Smith v. Kerrville Bus Co.*,[91] held that a bus driver who was discharged for alleged dishonesty could maintain an action under Section 301 of the Labor Management Relations Act[92] for wrongful discharge, even though the collective bargaining contract was silent as to any formal grievance or arbitration procedures and corresponding just cause provisions. The courts of appeals reasoned that a collective bargaining agreement is designed to regulate all facets of the employment relationship and, accordingly, "the construction and application of its terms cannot be narrowly confined by ordinary principles of contract law." The court went on to state:

> In instances where the language of a collective contract does not explicitly prohibit dismissal except for just cause, arbitrators typically infer such prohibitions from seniority clauses or grievance and arbitration procedures. . . . Inherent in the body of arbitral common law which has evolved in this context

[90]See, e.g., Kewanee Mach. Div., Chromalloy Am. Corp. v. Teamsters Local 21, 593 F.2d 314, 100 LRRM 2845 (CA 8, 1979)(conflict between management rights provision and just cause language); Machinists Local 389 v. San Diego Marine Construc. Corp., 620 F.2d 736, 104 LRRM 2613, 2615 (CA 9, 1980)("[T]he arbitrator does have the power to determine *when* a matter is subject to Company discretion. When two possible interpretations of a clause of a collective bargaining agreement exist, an arbitrator's choice of one or the other ought to be honored.")(emphasis in original); Arco-Polymers, Inc. v. Oil Workers Local 8–74, 671 F.2d 752, 109 LRRM 3157 (CA 3, 1982)(conflict between absenteeism and just cause provisions); Campo Machining Co. v. Machinists Local Lodge 1926, 536 F.2d 330, 92 LRRM 2513 (CA 10, 1976)(conflict between just cause provision and plant rules).
[91]709 F.2d 914, 113 LRRM 3741 (CA 5, 1983).
[92]29 U.S.C. §185(a) (1978).

is a marked awareness of the harshness of discharge, and an adherence to the principle that seniority, grievance, arbitration, and other provisions that reflect the contracting parties' tacit acceptance of the employees' right to some measure of job security, pretermit discharge without good cause. . . . One arbiter summarizes this development as follows: "The weight of arbitral opinion is that a standard of just cause may be imposed upon disciplinary actions even though such a standard is not spelled out in the agreement."[93]

The court of appeals concluded by stating:

> To hold as a matter of law that management could, at its sole discretion, terminate an employee without cause would in effect allow it the unqualified power to avoid contractually mandated rights and benefits.[94]

In *Food & Commercial Workers Local 634 v. Gold Star Sausage Co.*,[95] a federal court, in holding that it was permissible for an arbitrator to imply a just cause provision in an agreement that provided for certain forms of job seniority, declared:

> If the [employer] had the power to fire employees at will, the seniority provisions and other benefits under the contract would be meaningless. Job security, a fundamental aspect of collective bargaining agreements, would be non-existent. By adhering to these principles, the arbitrator could reasonably infer that a just cause restriction was enmeshed in the fabric of the Agreement.[96]

This principle has been adopted by most arbitrators.[97] Arbitrator M. S. Ryder, in *B. F. Goodrich Tire Co.*,[98] rejected a company's argument that, since there was no provision in the parties' agreement with respect to the discharge of employees, management was free to discharge or suspend where it acted in good faith and was "motivated by sincere reasons." The arbitrator's reasoning, as follows, is especially instructive:

---

[93] 113 LRRM at 3743–44 (citations omitted).
[94] Id. at 3745. See also Lowe v. Pate Stevedoring Co., 558 F.2d 769, 96 LRRM 2205 (CA 5, 1977)(upholding district court's conclusion that, based on hiring hall arrangement, a just cause limitation should be implied); Young v. Southwestern Bell Tel. Co., 309 F.Supp. 475, 74 LRRM 2154, 2157 (E.D. Ark., 1969), aff'd, 424 F.2d 256, 74 LRRM 2256 (CA 8, 1970)(refusing to imply just cause provision for new employees where contract outlined distinctions between employees based on length of service).
[95] 487 F.Supp. 596, 104 LRRM 2252 (D. Colo., 1980).
[96] 104 LRRM at 2255.
[97] See the review of early case authority by Arbitrator Melvin Newmark in Pfizer, Inc., 79 LA 1225 (1982).
[98] 36 LA 552 (1961).

The fact that the applicable labor agreement does not deal with the subject matter of disciplinary discharge or suspension—which factual circumstance is hereby so found—does not give an employer the right to effect such kinds of severances from employment solely under the standards advanced here as correspondingly contractually proper by the Company. It is no modification of, or addition to the instant labor agreement, or a distortion of its meaning or misapplication of its mutual intent to require that beyond the bona fides, lack of arbitrariness or capriciousness and where there is sincerity of reason . . . the moving cause must also have the ingredient of justifiability. No labor agreement that purports to effect and maintain uninterrupted operations while at the same time promoting sound labor relations, as the instant agreement describes in its preamble, can eschew such a principled concept as that good or just cause should govern an employment severance bottomed on a disciplinary motivation.[99]

A Remedy Outside Arbitration: Section 301

Where the parties' agreement does not provide for arbitration (either because (1) an arbitration clause is absent in the contract, or (2) arbitration is unavailable because both parties could not agree to arbitrate the matter), but the contract nevertheless contains a just cause provision, employee recourse will be through the courts under Section 301 of the LMRA. Thus, the Seventh Circuit, in *Scott v. Riley Co.*,[100] observed that just cause was to be determined by the court on a case-by-case basis. The court of appeals noted that "good cause . . . means what a reasonable person would find sufficient; the phrase creates an objective rather than a personal subjective test."[101] Where the agreement does not provide for arbitration but explicitly preserves the right of "economic recourse," the better rule is that economic warfare will not be the parties' exclusive remedy, and that such language will not operate to divest the courts of their jurisdiction under Section 301 to resolve the contractual dispute.[102]

---

[99]Id. at 556. See also Corn Belt Elec. Coop., 79 LA 1045 (O'Grady, 1982)("[I]n the absence of language negating the need for a show of just cause in this disciplinary action, the Employer must show just cause for discharging the Grievant.").

[100]645 F.2d 565, 107 LRRM 2218 (CA 7, 1981).

[101]107 LRRM at 2220 n.4, citing Electrical Workers (UE) Local 205 v. General Elec. Co., 172 F.Supp. 53, 43 LRRM 2827 (D. Mass., 1959).

[102]Associated Gen. Contractors of Ill. v. Illinois Conference of Teamsters, 486 F.2d 972, 84 LRRM 2555 (CA 7, 1973); Machinists Local Lodge 1426 v. Wilson Trailer Co., 289 N.W.2d 608, 104 LRRM 2322 (Iowa Sup. Ct., 1980).

Group Discipline[103]

Not infrequently an employer knows that one or more employees has committed misconduct but, for whatever reason, is unable to identify the guilty party. A likely response might be to punish the entire group if the guilty person cannot be identified. However, most arbitrators have ruled that it is unfair to take such an overinclusive approach.

In *Quick Manufacturing Co.*[104] incidents of sabotage had resulted in considerable difficulties on an assembly line. Employees had closed carburetor mechanisms so that engines could not run, grease was placed upon starter cords, and toilet paper was stuffed into engines. The employees were warned that the incidents must stop and that continuation of this conduct would result in the line being shut down and the employees being sent home. Further, the foreman had requested that innocent members of the group be on the lookout for wrongdoers, but these requests were of no avail. When yet another act of sabotage occurred (14 bolts were discovered in a hex shaft), the employees were sent home one and one-half hours before the end of the first shift. While recognizing the seriousness of the conduct, the union maintained that management should have established who was guilty and applied the appropriate penalty to the guilty party only. According to the union, management did not check for fingerprints or otherwise conduct a professional investigation to establish the guilt of any individual.

Arbitrator Jerome Gross commented that the principle of punishing only the guilty must be upheld whether a mild or serious form of discipline is assessed. The arbitrator's reasoning, as follows, is noteworthy:

> While I am deeply sympathetic and concerned that the Company solve its problem, and I trust the problem can be solved, I cannot violate these basic principles of American justice even in the form of such mild discipline as one and one-half hours loss of wages. The monetary loss to these men is incidental and not worthy of much consideration. It is rather the establishment of a principle of group discipline which would not only use undesirable means to gain a desirable end, but would set a precedent that might well result in a greater dis-

---

[103]This section is, in part, taken from Hill & Beck, "Some Thoughts on Just Cause and Group Discipline," 41 Arb. J. No. 2 (1986).
[104]45 LA 53 (Gross, 1965).

ruption of relationships in this plant. These acts of sabotage should be punished when the guilty parties are apprehended, and certainly should be possible of detection through competent investigative methods, such as are used every hour and every day in the detection of crime.[105]

Similarly, in *Southern Ohio Coal Co.*,[106] Arbitrator Charles Ipavec considered the misconduct of nine miners who left the mine via a mantrip (a transport vehicle to the mine elevator), leaving their foreman alone in that section of the mine. The company suspended all nine miners for three days, contending that (1) the misconduct jeopardized the foreman's life, (2) the miners had been given notice that such misconduct would result in suspension, and (3) the foreman saw the mantrip begin to leave and his attempt to flag down the mantrip was acknowledged by several of the men. In reversing the discipline, the arbitrator reasoned that it could not be determined who was responsible for the early departure of the mantrip. Further, the entire group could not be disciplined because of misconduct by one or more men but, in all probability, fewer than all nine miners. The arbitrator commented, "Mass punishments against an entire group for wrongful conduct which may have been perpetrated by only one member of the group, is contrary to the American sense of fairplay, and should not be sustained."[107] According to the arbitrator, if each of the nine miners deliberately did nothing to prevent the mantrip from leaving without the foreman, then the entire group could properly be disciplined. However, since the evidence did not show that all of the grievants were guilty and the guilty members could not be singled out, the entire group must go unpunished.

When only two employees are disciplined and, in all probability, one is innocent, the employer is still left with the burden to demonstrate the guilt of the person responsible; it cannot shift that burden to a presumably innocent party to prove his or her innocence. In *Arizona Aluminum Co.*,[108] the company inserted disciplinary reports in the personnel files of two forklift drivers after substantial damage to an outside wall was discovered. The company had narrowed its search

[105]Id. at 57.
[106]76-2 ARB ¶8608 (1976).
[107]Id. at 7042.
[108]78 LA 766 (Sass, 1982).

for the wrongdoer to the two drivers, but the employer had no idea which was actually the guilty party. Both disciplinary reports ended by noting, " 'It is apparent one of these men did the damage . . . but neither one will own up to causing the damage.' "

In upholding the grievance, Arbitrator John Sass stated that "[j]ustice is not done when an innocent man is punished simply because a guilty man refuses to confess his guilt."[109] Before an employer may discipline a worker under the just cause standard, it must demonstrate a reasonable probability that the employee is guilty. In those few cases where it is impossible to prove that a particular individual was responsible, justice requires that the deed go unpunished, the arbitrator said. Arbitrator Sass added:

> The burden of proof means that whoever has it on a specific issue must be able to carry that issue by having the overall weight of the evidence in their favor. Anything less than that constitutes a failure to carry the burden of proof. And the fact that the discipline imposed is minor does not in any way reduce the burden of proof. Only after the infraction has been proved to the degree required does the extent of the penalty become relevant. Only then can the arbitrator reach the issue of whether the penalty is a just one in light of the infraction proved and all of the other surrounding circumstances. If no infraction has been proved, then no penalty is just. Any civilized system of justice requires proof of wrongdoing before discipline can be imposed and a "just cause" standard in a collective bargaining agreement is nothing if not the imposition of a civilized system of justice on the employer-employee relationship.[110]

Arbitrator Gerald McKay, in *Silva Harvesting, Inc.*,[111] likewise addressed the issue of group discipline when 19 broccoli pickers were dismissed for walking off the job after having worked an eight hour day. The arbitrator ruled the disciplinary treatment unjustified since it was not clear that every picker had been informed that overtime was required. In so ruling, the arbitrator stressed that all employees were not equally culpable:

> Some members of the Crew probably understood that they were required to work more than eight hours. Some of the Crew

---

[109]Id. at 770.
[110]Id. at 769.
[111]81-2 ARB ¶8575 (1981).

probably knew that by refusing to continue working on July 3, that they were doing something wrong. But the Employer has chosen to treat all of the employees in the same fashion. In doing this, the weakest link in the chain of proof will break the Employer's case. In the opinion of this arbitrator, not all of the Crew members who refused to work on July 3, 1981 knew that what they were doing was wrong and would lead to their discharge.[112]

As a remedy, the arbitrator ordered all 19 members of the group to be reinstated.

In addition to group discipline cases involving disruption of operations or safety issues, arbitrators have also considered situations in which an entire group has been admonished because an individual's poor performance resulted in faulty work or substandard production quality. These cases involve group punishment not for malicious wrongdoing, but for work one or more members have not done correctly. In *Marhoefer Packing Co.*,[113] Arbitrator John Sembower dismissed a grievance filed on behalf of six members of a boning crew who, as a result of poor workmanship, were suspended for three weeks. The company had originally discharged the crew, but later modified the discharges to three-week suspensions. According to management the employees all recognized that there was an unacceptable work product; however, each refused to claim any of the "dirty bones" (those bones which retained more than the allowable amount of residue meat). The union contended that as a function of management and a rational principle of justice, the wrongdoer should have been sought out, identified, and punished without the entire group having to suffer. However, in his decision, Arbitrator Sembower stated:

[T]here has to be a specific claim of invalidity of disciplinary action for any recovery to be granted. An arbitrator is at a greater handicap and disadvantage in singling out a wrongdoer from a group than either management or the employees. Yet he cannot grant a remedy without a basis for doing so.

Consequently, the Arbitrator has no choice but to dismiss the grievance in this instance, while at the same time he regrets that this allows a wrongdoer or wrongdoers to escape punishment and inflicts their wrong proportionately upon innocent individuals, both among his companions in the workforce and the Company for which he works.[114]

---

[112]Id. at 5522.
[113]54 LA 649 (1970).
[114]Id. at 653.

Other arbitrators have reasoned differently in similar situations. In an earlier case, *Westinghouse Electric Co.*,[115] Arbitrator Ralph Williams found management to be without just cause in imposing a disciplinary lay-off (for the remainder of one shift and the following shift) upon 21 employees in the company's distribution transformer division. The employees performed core-coil assembly work which was checked by inspectors in another bargaining unit. Originally the company had disciplined one employee for "deliberately creating defective work." However, in the two days following that action "a substantially higher than normal level of defective units" was produced in the core-coil assembly area. Further, the company noticed "loud shouting and noisemaking" in that work area. Noting that all 21 employees were disciplined for producing "defective apparatus," the arbitrator said:

> If deliberate production of defective work by any employee or group could have been sufficiently shown, disciplinary action against him or them would have been justified. But the work here involved is so complicated and diverse, and the opportunity for errors so broad, that I cannot in good conscience find that these 21 Grievants committed intentional acts of industrial sabotage by purposefully turning out defective transformers or other apparatus. . . .
> . . . To sustain disciplinary action against the group of employees, a concert of activity must be shown sufficient to implicate all members of the group; otherwise, group discipline cannot be justified. . . .
> The disciplining by the Company . . . was without just cause. There was no concerted effort by the employees to create defective work; however, the temporary reduction in production justified the furloughing of these 21 employees.[116]

Although arbitrators generally agree that the innocent cannot be disciplined along with the guilty, exceptions are recognized when the "innocent" cast their lot with the guilty employees by remaining silent. Arbitrator Frank Childs, in *Empire-Reeves Steel Corp.*,[117] upheld a company's one and one-half day suspension of six employees when they would not identify which of them had been throwing rocks at the plant building. The union maintained that the innocent could not be punished for failing to identify the guilty parties. Because

---

[115]48 LA 211 (1967).
[116]Id. at 212–13. See also Evinrude Motors Co., 36 LA 1302 (Marshall, 1961).
[117]64-2 ARB ¶8537 (1964).

of the danger involved and the breach of plant safety rules, the arbitrator, sustaining the discipline, reasoned as follows:

> By their silence in refusing to identify those guilty of rock throwing the "innocent" have chosen to not only stand with the guilty as a group but have also failed to follow [#]16 of the Safety Rules "Look out for the other man as well as yourself." . . . Safety is a joint responsibility and must be recognized as such. By their actions the six men disciplined by the Company have been guilty of infractions of the safety rules and both during and after the incident have chosen to remain silent rather than to act in the interest of safety for the plant.[118]

In another case an employer was upheld in sending all first shift employees home after a string of firecrackers was exploded in a toilet enclosure.[119] Arbitrator Charles Atwood found the action to be a reasonable exercise of the employer's right to deal with danger in the workplace and to maintain safe working conditions. His reasoning is noteworthy. Atwood noted:

> If legal and contractual managerial responsibility related to safety cannot be carried out because of a practical inability to establish the guilt of one or more persons and when that inability makes it impossible immediately to restrain wrongdoers from further wrongdoing, management should not be denied the right to deal with present danger in the manner in which this Company acted . . . .[120]

When weighing the appropriateness of a group discharge or disciplinary action, some common threads emerge. Arbitrators have agreed that the seriousness of the misconduct, in and of itself, does not warrant group discipline. Although the employer may be justified in penalizing a particular employee, management cannot retaliate and punish an entire group merely because the conduct is a gross transgression of the rules and imposes a hardship upon the company. In fact, many times in such cases there will be no union-management dispute concerning the seriousness of the misconduct or the underlying facts prompting the discipline. Rather, the dispute arises over procedural issues related to identifying who is responsible for the misconduct and limiting punishment to the specific individual(s) guilty of the misconduct.

---

[118]Id. at 4905.
[119]C. Schmidt Co., 62 LA 14 (Atwood, 1974).
[120]Id. at 16.

When confronted with group discipline cases, arbitrators have consistently adhered to an underlying principle of "justice and fair play." Arbitrator Jerome Gross comments:

> If the principle of group discipline against people who were punished because they were in close association or near the scene where acts of misconduct were committed is *upheld for mild discipline*, then the same principle could be established for *severe discipline* and soon the less difficult method of simply group disciplining employees could take place on a more stringent basis, thus upsetting all concepts of justice as we understand it.[121]

The issue of group discipline has also given rise to other noteworthy considerations. First, arbitrators should be more cognizant of the employer's disciplinary motive in cases involving group punishment when the guilty cannot be identified. Frequently the punishment is intended more as a warning to avoid future problems than as a penalty imposed upon the disciplined workers. Second, it is important for arbitrators to realize the impact of upholding a group discipline decision upon future labor-management relations. By allowing over-inclusive discipline, the arbitrator is arguably doing a disservice to the parties by creating a group method of discipline in which no "cause" is required. Third, arbitrators and practitioners should distinguish the situation where individual wrongdoers are purposely sheltered by group silence from those cases where employees simply cannot identify the guilty person. An employee who shelters a wrongdoer clearly casts his lot with the guilty, and, accordingly, should not complain when management concludes that he is a culpable party. Arbitrators are in agreement that employees have a duty to cooperate with management and that there is no privilege to withhold information concerning employee misconduct. Whether the employer disciplines the employee for engaging in the misconduct or for failing to cooperate, the result is the same: discipline is likely to be sustained.

There may be a significant cost to an employer who undertakes an overinclusive approach to discipline, even when the work force is not organized. Illustrative is *Agis v. Howard Johnson Co.*,[122] in which an employer notified all waitresses "that there was some stealing going on," but that the identity

---

[121]Quick Mfg. Co., 45 LA 53, 56 (1965)(emphasis in original).
[122]371 Mass. 140, 355 N.E.2d 315 (1976).

of the person or persons responsible was not known. Further, until the responsible person or persons were discovered, the employer indicated that it would begin firing all the present waitresses in alphabetical order. The first person fired commenced an action asking damages for mental anguish and emotional distress caused by her summary dismissal. The Supreme Court of Massachusetts held that she had a cause of action in tort for intentional infliction of emotional distress even though there was no resulting bodily injury. According to the court, "[p]laintiff has alleged facts and circumstances which reasonably could lead the trier of fact to conclude that defendant's conduct was extreme and outrageous, having a severe and traumatic effect upon plaintiff's emotional tranquility."[123]

In conclusion, arbitrators generally treat group discipline cases in the same manner as individual discipline cases. With few exceptions, innocent employees cannot be punished with the guilty merely because the guilty members of the group cannot be identified. Of course, group offenses, such as a wildcat strike, should be distinguished from an offense by an individual who, but for the group, cannot be identified. Where an employee has knowledge of a rule violation but, nevertheless, elects to remain silent, discipline would seem warranted, at least where management conducts an investigation and can demonstrate that the employee can identify the guilty party.[124]

Publication of Discharge Proceedings

A topic often overlooked by advocates and arbitrators alike is the communication of information by the parties in effecting the dismissal of an employee. In *General Motors Corp. v. Mendicki*,[125] the Tenth Circuit held that statements made during a conference or a proceeding relating to a grievance are privileged and so barred a damage suit based on a claim that the statements libeled an employee. The rationale, articulated as follows, was grounded on federal labor policy:

> We think Congress intended that the respective representatives of employer and employee at such conferences and bar-

---

[123]Id. at 319.
[124]See the discussion of an employee's duty of loyalty, notes 170–241 and accompanying text, in Chapter 8, infra.
[125]367 F.2d 66, 63 LRRM 2257 (CA 10, 1966).

gaining sessions should feel free to express their respective contentions as to the pertinent facts and the issues involved fully and frankly and to strongly support their positions with respect to the controversy, and—employing the words of Mr. Justice Fortas . . .—do so "untrammelled by fear of retribution for strong utterances." Otherwise, the chance for desirable fruitfulness from such conferences and bargaining sessions would be greatly lessened. Moreover, such actions for damages would create irritations between employer and employee, which would tend to impair the chance for a peaceful settlement of labor controversies between employer and employee in the future.[126]

The Tenth Circuit in 1981 extended the *Mendicki* holding in an action to recover libel damages where an employer, in a letter of discharge to the grievant, asserted dishonesty as the basis for dismissal. The court, in dictum, implied that the privilege applies only to those persons who are required to see the letter under the collective bargaining agreement. Publication of the letter to others not covered by the privilege would presumptively result in an adverse ruling against the disclosing party.[127]

Judicial Limitations

Judicial limitations establishing exceptions to the employment-at-will rule on the basis of public policy may generally be categorized into three major divisions: (1) statutorily established public policy, (2) whistle blowing, and (3) malice and bad faith exceptions. While admittedly these divisions overlap, it is useful to examine the cases within these categories.

Public Policy Exception

A widely adopted judicial theory that limits the employment-at-will rule is that employers should not be permitted to discipline or discharge employees for reasons violative of

---

[126]63 LRRM at 2261, quoting dissent by Justice Fortas in Linn v. Plant Guard Workers, 383 U.S. 53, 61 LRRM 2345, 2352 (1966).

[127]Hasten v. Phillips Petroleum Co., 640 F.2d 274, 106 LRRM 2547 (CA 10, 1981). See also Louisville & Nashville R.R. v. Marshall, 586 S.W.2d 274, 101 LRRM 2164 (Ky. Ct. App., 1979)(extending this same privilege to carriers under the Railway Labor Act).

public policy.[128] A rule to the contrary would mean that public policy could easily be defeated for retaliatory conduct on the part of employers.

Refusal to Violate a Criminal Statute

An employee may not be discharged for refusing to violate a criminal statute. The leading case in this category is *Petermann v. Teamsters Local 396*,[129] in which a union business agent was discharged for refusing to commit perjury for his employer. While recognizing that an employment contract without specified duration is generally terminable at the employer's will, the California Court of Appeals stated that "the right to discharge an employee under such a contract may be limited by statute . . . or by considerations of public policy."[130]

Similarly, in *Tameny v. Atlantic Richfield Co.*,[131] the Supreme Court of California found a cause of action in tort for an employee who was discharged for refusing to participate in an illegal price-fixing scheme. In so holding, the court declared:

> We hold that an employer's authority over its employee does not include the right to demand that the employee commit a criminal act to further its interests, and an employer may not coerce compliance with such unlawful directions by discharging an employee who refuses to follow such an order. An employer engaging in such conduct violates a basic duty imposed by law upon all employers, and thus an employee who has suffered damages as a result of such discharge may maintain a tort action for wrongful discharge against the employer.[132]

In the years following the *Petermann* decision, courts in a number of jurisdictions have allowed at-will employees to sue employers for wrongful discharge when fired for refusing to violate a criminal statute. For example, courts have allowed

---

[128]See generally Note "Protecting Employees At Will Against Wrongful Discharge: The Public Policy Exception," 96 Harv. L. Rev. 1931 (1983).

[129]174 Cal. App. 184, 344 P.2d 25, 44 LRRM 2968 (1959).

[130]44 LRRM at 2969.

[131]27 Cal. 3d 167, 610 P.2d 1330, 164 Cal. Rptr. 839, 115 LRRM 3119 (1980).

[132]115 LRRM at 3124. The Ninth Circuit, in Ostrofe v. H.S. Crocker Co., 740 F.2d 739, 117 LRRM 2105 (CA 9, 1984), held that a managerial employee, who allegedly was discharged for refusing to cooperate in his employer's price-fixing scheme and who was concertedly denied reemployment in the industry, had standing to sue his employer under §4 of the Clayton Act to recover treble damages for injuries resulting from violation of the Sherman Act.

a cause of action in tort for wrongful discharge in the following situations:

- When an X-ray technician was dismissed for refusing to perform catheterizations (New Jersey)[133]
- When an at-will railroad employee was discharged for refusing to alter state pollution control reports (Michigan)[134]
- When a boat deckhand was discharged for refusing to perform an illegal act of pumping bilges into water (Texas)[135]
- When an employee notified a customer that his employer had stolen salvaged property (Arizona)[136] and
- When a quality control inspector was discharged for informing his employer that packaged goods were mislabeled (Connecticut)[137]

The cases allowing claims by at-will employees for refusal to violate criminal statutes illustrate a limited application of the public policy exception. In general, where courts have found a cause of action based on a violation of public policy, they have cited a specific policy clearly mandated or implied in a state statute.

Exercising a Statutory Right

While recognizing that generally "an employee at will may be discharged without cause," in 1973 the Indiana Supreme Court, in *Frampton v. Central Indiana Gas Co.*,[138] carved out an exception to the at-will doctrine for employees discharged for exercising a statutorily conferred right to receive

---

[133]O'Sullivan v. Mallon, 160 N.J. Super. 416, 390 A.2d 149, 115 LRRM 5064 (1978).
   [134]Trombetta v. Detroit, Toledo & Ironton R.R., 81 Mich. App. 489, 265 N.W.2d 385, 115 LRRM 4361, 4364 (1978).
   [135]Sabine Pilot Serv. v. Hauck, 687 S.W.2d 733, 119 LRRM 2187 (1985).
   [136]Vermillion v. AAA Pro Moving & Storage, 146 Ariz. 215, 704 P.2d 1360, 119 LRRM 2337 (Ariz. Ct. App., 1985).
   [137]Sheets v. Teddy's Frosted Foods, Inc., 179 Conn. 471, 427 A.2d 385, 115 LRRM 4626, 4629 (1980). But see Phillips v. Goodyear Tire & Rubber Co., 651 F.2d 1051, 115 LRRM 4173 (CA 5, 1981)(denying cause of action for employee who testified truthfully in a deposition in a federal suit, holding neither Georgia nor Texas recognized cause of action for retaliatory discharge), and Buethe v. Britt Airlines, 749 F.2d 1235, 118 LRRM 2031 (CA 7, 1984)(disallowing federal cause of action for at-will employee who was dismissed for refusing to fly plane with inoperative items mandated by Federal Aviation Act).
   [138]260 Ind. 249, 297 N.E.2d 425, 115 LRRM 4611, 4612 (1973).

compensation. This was the first case allowing a tort action
for a discharge in retaliation for filing a workmen's compensation claim. The Indiana court reasoned that it would be
against public policy to prohibit a cause of action since the
language of the Indiana compensation statute prohibited any
"device" to circumvent the employer's liability. The court went
on to state:

> The Act creates a *duty* in the employer to compensate employees
> for work-related injuries (through insurance) and a *right* in the
> employee to receive such compensation. But in order for the
> goals of the Act to be realized and for public policy to be effec-
> tuated, the employee must be able to exercise his right in an
> unfettered fashion without being subject to reprisal.[139]

While some states have passed specific legislation prohibiting discharge of employees for filing workmen's compensation claims,[140] others have not and, accordingly, several courts
since *Frampton* have had to address the issue.[141]

---

[139]115 LRRM at 4612 (emphasis in original). In Vantine v. Elkhart Brass Mfg.
Co., 762 F.2d 511, 119 LRRM 2465, 2469 (CA 7, 1985), the Seventh Circuit held that
employees covered by workmen's compensation in Indiana who are covered by a
collective bargaining agreement may not rely on the tort exception for wrongful
discharge carved out for at-will employees in Frampton. The court declared that "the
termination of an employee [under a collective bargaining agreement] in retaliation
for filing a workmen's compensation claim would not be considered for 'just cause.'
Not all courts have adopted this position. See, e.g., Messenger v. Volkswagen of Am.,
585 F.Supp. 565, 117 LRRM 2368 (S.D. W.Va., 1984).

[140]See, e.g., Carnation Co. v. Borner, 610 S.W.2d 450 (Tex., 1981); Vaughn v.
Pacific N.W. Bell Tel. Co., 289 Or. 73, 611 P.2d 281, 106 LRRM 2063 (Or., 1980);
Smith v. Piezo Technology & Prof. Adm'rs, 427 So.2d 182, 117 LRRM 3378 (Fla.,
1983); Peabody Gallion Div., Peabody Int'l Corp. v. Dollar, 666 F.2d 1309, 109 LRRM
2068 (CA 10, 1981)(Oklahoma statute prohibiting retaliatory discharge for filing
workmen's compensation claim not preempted by federal labor laws; employee not
required to pursue matter under parties' grievance procedure).

[141]In addition to Frampton, decisions that have applied the public policy exception
to the at-will doctrine when an employee is discharged for filing a worker's compensation claim include: Hentzel v. Singer Co., 188 Cal. Rptr. 159, 115 LRRM 4036
(Calif. Ct. App., 1982); Kelsay v. Motorola, Inc., 74 Ill. 2d 172, 384 N.E.2d 353, 115
LRRM 4371 (1979); Sventko v. Kroger Co., 69 Mich. App. 644, 245 N.W.2d 151, 115
LRRM 4613, 4614 (1976)("Discouraging the fulfillment of the legislative policy by
use of the most powerful weapon at the disposal of the employer, termination of
employment, is obviously against the public policy of our state."); Lally v. Copy-
graphics, 85 N.J. 668, 428 A.2d 1317, 115 LRRM 6434 (1981); Brown v. Transcom
Lines, 284 Or. 597, 588 P.2d 1087, 115 LRRM 5072 (1978); Murphy v. City of Topeka-
Shawnee, 6 Kan. App. 2d. 488, 630 P.2d 186, 115 LRRM 4433 (1981); Firestone
Textile Co. Div. v. Meadows, 666 S.W.2d 730, 114 LRRM 3559 (Ky., 1984); Clanton
v. Cain-Sloan Co., 117 LRRM 2789 (Tenn., 1984); Hansen v. Harrah's, 675 P.2d 394,
115 LRRM 3024 (Nev., 1984); Shaw v. Doyle Milling Co., 683 P.2d 82, 116 LRRM
2773, 297 Or. 251 (1984). See also Smith v. Atlas Off-Shore Boat Serv., 653 F.2d
1057, 117 LRRM 2414 (CA 5, 1981)(discharge of an at-will seaman in retaliation for
exercising right under Jones Act to file personal injury suit against employer).

Cases that have denied the public policy exception when an employee is discharged for filing a claim include: Green v. Amerada-Hess Corp., 612 F.2d 212, 115
LRRM 4986 (CA 5, 1980)(applying Mississippi law); Wiley v. Missouri Pac. R.R., 115

Generally, those courts recognizing a cause of action have relied on the clear mandate of the law encouraging employees who sustain on-the-job injuries to seek disability benefits. Courts refusing to grant employees a cause of action under this type of claim typically insist that the legislature is best suited to create a new cause of action. Absent express legislative intent, these courts have been reluctant to imply cause of action for a retaliatory discharge.[142]

In *Darnell, Inc. v. Impact Industries*,[143] plaintiff Darnell was discharged on the second day of her job when her employer learned that she had filed a claim under the Illinois Workers' Compensation Act. Darnell, on her employment application, indicated that she had neither "had a serious illness or injury" nor "received compensation for injuries." The record indicated that she had been hurt and had received compensation for a former job-related injury. The appellate court held that the trial court should not have granted a directed verdict for the employer, but, rather, a jury should have been allowed to hear her evidence as to the reason she was discharged. The supreme court affirmed the appellate court and reasoned as follows:

> We perceive no distinction between the situation where an employee is discharged for filing a workers' compensation claim against the defendant employer and one where the employer discharges the employee upon discovering that the employee had filed a claim against another employer. In either situation a retaliatory discharge is equally offensive to the public policy of this State . . . .[144]

LRRM 5170 (La. Ct. App., 1982); Meeks v. OPP Cotton Mills, 459 So.2d 814, 117 LRRM 3160 (Ala., 1984); Christy v. Petrus, 365 Mo. 1187, 295 S.W.2d 122 (1956); Bottijliso v. Hutchison Fruit Co., 96 N.M. 789, 635 P.2d 992, 118 LRRM 3095 (N.M. Ct. App., 1981); Kelly v. Mississippi Valley Gas Co., 397 So.2d 874, 115 LRRM 4631 (Miss., 1981); Dockery v. Lambert Table Co., 36 N.C. App. 293, 244 S.E.2d 272, 115 LRRM 4307 (1978).

See generally Comment, "Kelsay v. Motorola, Inc.—A Remedy for the Abusively Discharged at-Will Employee, 1979 S. Ill. U.L.J. 563 (1979); Note, "Judicial Limitation of the Employment at-Will Doctrine," 54 St. John's L. Rev. 552 (1980); Note, "Protecting Employees at Will Against Wrongful Discharge: The Public Policy Exception," 96 Harv. L. Rev. 1931 (1983).

[142]Dockery v. Lampart Table Co., 36 N.C. App. 293, 244 S.E.2d 272, 115 LRRM 4307, 4308 (1978) ("[I]f the General Assembly of North Carolina had intended a cause of action be created, surely . . . it would have specifically addressed the problem."), cert. denied, 295 N.C. 465, 246 S.E.2d 215 (1978) and superseded by statute as stated in Buie v. Daniel Int'l Corp., 56 N.C. App. 445, 289 S.E.2d 118, petition denied, 292 S.E.2d 574 (N.C., 1982); Loucks v. Star Glass Co., 551 F.2d 745 (CA 7, 1977)(denying a cause of action for a retaliatory discharge in a workmen's compensation case where the Illinois legislature has not provided for a prohibition against retaliatory dismissals).

[143]105 Ill.2d 158, 473 N.E.2d 935, 117 LRRM 3371 (1984).

[144]117 LRRM at 3372.

More recently, the Illinois Supreme Court, in *Midgett v. Sackett-Chicago, Inc.*,[145] held that a union-represented employee could sue his employer in a state court on a claim of retaliatory discharge related to the filing of a Workers' Compensation Act claim, regardless of the availability of contractual grievance-arbitration procedure to adjudicate his discharge claim or his failure to proceed through such grievance procedure. It is of special note that prior to *Midgett*, the majority of courts in Illinois and, indeed, even the Seventh Circuit, had limited the availability of a tort remedy for such retaliatory discharges or for discharges for reporting criminal offenses to at-will employees not represented by a union or governed by a collective bargaining agreement.[146]

After *Midgett*, a union-represented employee would arguably have a parallel remedy in tort in addition to his contractual remedy under the collective bargaining agreement. More important to the parties, since punitive damages are available in tort but not generally in the arbitral forum, the *Midgett* court appears to sanction such a cause of action for an employee who has successfully pursued his grievance before an arbitrator. The court declined to rule on the issue of federal labor law preemption because that issue had not been raised in the lower court proceeding.

As of this writing the Ninth and Tenth Circuits have ruled that a suit alleging wrongful termination in violation of state public policy is not preempted by federal labor law, nor are such suits precluded by binding arbitration clauses of collective bargaining agreements.[147]

As was noted in the discussion of statutory limitations, laws designed to protect employees who seek union representation or who engage in union activities have provided courts with a public policy basis for finding exceptions to the at-will doctrine in cases where employees have been fired because of their union activities. In other contexts employees have like-

---

[145]105 Ill.2d 143, 473 N.E.2d 1280, 117 LRRM 2807 (1984).
[146]See, e.g., Lamb v. Briggs Mfg., 700 F.2d 1092, 115 LRRM 4824 (CA 7, 1983).
[147]Garibaldi v. Lucky Food Stores, Inc., 726 F.2d 1376, 115 LRRM 3089 (CA 9, 1984); Peabody Gallion Div., Peabody Int'l Corp. v. Dollar, 666 F.2d 1309, 109 LRRM 2068 (CA 10, 1981). Contra: Lamb v. Briggs Mfg., 700 F.2d 1092, 115 LRRM 4824 (CA 7, 1983)(state tort action for discharge in retaliation for exercise of Illinois statutory right available only to at-will employees and not to employees covered by a collective bargaining agreement).

wise invoked the policy expressed in various statutes in getting a court to carve out a public-policy exception to the at-will rule. Recent examples include an employee discharged for refusing to take a polygraph test[148] and a discharge for designating an attorney as a bargaining representative[149] where both areas of conduct had been protected by a statute. The court-created criteria for finding a public policy exception in all these cases has been: (1) a clear expression of public policy in a statute protecting employees within the employment relationship; and (2) protection by statute of the class within which the employee falls.

Perhaps the most expansive application of the public policy exception is *Novosel v. Nationwide Insurance Co.*[150] In that case the employer was lobbying for a no-fault insurance law in Pennsylvania. Novosel, an employee of Nationwide from December 1966 until November 1981, was a district claims manager. When Novosel refused to lobby and then in private said disparaging things about the campaign, his employment was terminated. Novosel sought damages, reinstatement, and declaratory relief. Following submission of briefs, the district court granted Nationwide's motion to dismiss the complaint.

On appeal, the Third Circuit ruled that Novosel's wrongful discharge claim was cognizable under Pennsylvania law since the "employment termination contravenes a significant and recognized public policy."[151] What is especially noteworthy is that the court relied on Novosel's First Amendment rights even though free speech protection had traditionally been interpreted as only protecting against governmental interference. The court found that concern for the rights of political expression and association of public employees was sufficient to state a public policy under Pennsylvania law.

As pointed out by Arbitrator Ted St. Antoine, Novosel may be regarded either as "one of those great landmark cases

---

[148]Perks v. Firestone Tire & Rubber Co., 611 F.2d 1363, 115 LRRM 4592 (CA 3, 1979). Contra: Jackson v. Kinark Corp., 282 Ark. 548, 669 S.W.2d 898, 117 LRRM 3374 (1984)(denying a cause of action in tort for refusing to take a polygraph examination in connection with the theft of a television set); Larsen v. Motor Supply Co., 117 Ariz. 507, 573 P.2d 907, 115 LRRM 4298 (1977)(no cause of action for two employees who were discharged for refusal to take psychological stress evaluation tests mandated for all employees).
[149]Montalvo v. Zamora, 7 Cal. App. 3d 69, 86 Cal. Rptr. 401, 403 (1970).
[150]721 F.2d 894, 114 LRRM 3105 (CA 3, 1983).
[151]114 LRRM at 3108.

that will change the landscape for the future" or as one that will be recognized as an aberration.[152] Either way, it is to date the most expansive judicial venture into the public policy exception to the at-will doctrine and a development that requires reflection on the part of practitioners.

Complying With a Statutory Duty

Courts have had to rule in cases involving discharge for compliance with a statutory duty. One statutory duty that has been the source of much litigation is jury duty.[153] In the lead case in this area, *Nees v. Hocks*,[154] the Supreme Court of Oregon held that an at-will employee may recover in tort for wrongful discharge when complying with this statutory duty, reasoning that the legislature and the courts regard the jury system as an important American institution and citizen obligation. It follows that if an employer were permitted with impunity to discharge an employee for serving on jury duty, the jury system would be adversely affected.[155]

Complying With Professional Codes[156]

In *Pierce v. Ortho Pharmaceutical Corp.*,[157] the Supreme Court of New Jersey considered whether a cause of action existed for a physician and research scientist employed at will

---

[152]Remarks of Ted St. Antoine, as cited in "Continuing Modification of Employment-At-Will Doctrine," 120 LRR 29, 30–31 (BNA, Sept. 9, 1985).

[153]As of May, 1985, 28 states had statutes protecting employees from discharge because of accepting jury duty (citations to the "State Laws" binders of BNA's Labor Relations Reporter): Alabama, 10:202; Arizona, 12:203; Arkansas, 13:203; California, 14:207; Connecticut, 16:206; Florida, 19:205; Idaho, 22:201; Illinois, 23:203; Indiana, 24:113; Kentucky, 27:202; Massachusetts, 31:201; Michigan, 32:202; Minnesota, 33:204; Nebraska, 37:203; New Mexico, 41:201; New York, 42:207; North Dakota, 44:202; Ohio, 45:203; Oregon, 47:203; Pennsylvania, 48:202; Puerto Rico, 49:202; South Dakota, 52:202; Tennessee, 53:202; Texas, 54:204; Vermont, 56:201; West Virginia, 59:202; Wisconsin, 60:202; Wyoming, 61:201.

[154]272 Or. 210, 536 P.2d 512, 115 LRRM 4571 (1975).

[155]See, e.g., Ruether v. Fowler & Williams, Inc., 255 Pa. Super. 28, 386 A.2d 119, 115 LRRM 4690, 4691 (1978)("[T]rial by jury in criminal cases is fundamental to the American scheme of justice."), citing Duncan v. Louisiana, 391 U.S. 145, 149 (1968); People v. Vitucci, 49 Ill. App. 2d 171, 199 N.E.2d 78 (1964) (contempt judgment against an employee reversed). But cf. Mallard v. Boring, 182 Cal. App. 2d 390, 6 Cal. Rptr. 171, 115 LRRM 4750, 4752 (1960) (protection for jurors, even if good public policy, should be given by legislature).

[156]See generally Note, "A Remedy for the Discharge of Professional Employees Who Refuse to Perform Unethical or Illegal Acts: A Proposal in Aid of Professional Ethics," 28 Vand. L. Rev. 805 (1975).

[157]84 N.J. 58, 417 A.2d 505, 115 LRRM 3044 (1980).

who was dismissed for refusing to continue a project she considered medically unethical (she opposed continued laboratory research, development, and testing of a drug containing saccharin, which Ortho intended to market for treatment of diarrhea). What is interesting in this case is the court's focus on the special considerations arising out of the right to fire an at-will employee who is a member of a recognized profession. The court stated:

> Employees who are professionals owe a special duty to abide not only by federal and state law, but also by the recognized codes of ethics of their professions. The duty may oblige them to decline to perform acts required by their employers. However, an employee should not have the right to prevent his or her employer from pursuing its business because the employee perceives that a particular business decision violates the employee's personal morals, as distinguished from the recognized code of ethics of the employee's profession.[158]

While the court made it clear that a cause of action would lie where the discharge is contrary to a clear mandate of public policy, it cautioned that not all professional codes of ethics express a clear mandate of public policy. Absent legislation, the court declared that the judiciary must define the cause of action in a case-by-case determination.

Pierce was followed by *Warthen v. Toms River Hospital*.[159] In that case a registered nurse employed in a hospital's kidney dialysis unit was assigned to dialyze a double-amputee patient who suffered from a number of maladies. On two occasions the nurse had to cease treatment because the patient suffered cardiac arrest and severe internal hemorrhaging during the dialysis procedure. When she was again scheduled to dialyze this patient, she informed management that "she had moral, medical, and philosophical objections" to performing this procedure because the patient was terminally ill and, according to the nurse, it was causing the patient additional complications. Her request for reassignment was initially granted but, approximately eight months later, she was again assigned to dialyze the patient. Once again she objected to the head nurse, who told her that if she continued to refuse to dialyze the patient, she would be dismissed.

In a trial on the pleadings, the lower court at first denied

---

[158]115 LRRM at 3049.
[159]199 N.J. Super. 18, 488 A.2d 229, 118 LRRM 3179 (1985).

the hospital's motion for summary judgment because it perceived "that there [was] . . . a question of fact as to whether or not there is a public policy as articulated in the nurses' code of ethics that would permit somebody in the nursing profession to refuse to participate in a course of treatment which is against her principles in good faith." However, upon reconsideration, the trial court granted the motion. The court concluded that "the nurses' code of ethics is a personal moral judgment . . . but it does not rise to a public policy in the face of the general public policies that patients must be cared for in hospitals and patients must be treated basically by doctors and doctors' orders must be carried out."[160] The appellate division of the superior court, upholding the lower court, ruled that "identifying the mandate of public policy is a question of law, analogous to interpreting a statute or defining a duty in a negligence case" and that the burden is on the employee "to identify a 'special expression' or 'a clear mandate' of public policy which might bar his or her dismissal."[161] The court accordingly held that the considerations cited by the nurse involving her own personal morals did not rise to the level of a public policy mandate.[162]

In *Geary v. United States Steel Corp.*,[163] the Supreme Court of Pennsylvania sustained the dismissal of an employee's complaint that public policy was violated when he was discharged after expressing his opinion to management that a new product was defective and dangerous. The record indicated that Geary, believing a product to be unsafe, by-passed his immediate supervisors and successfully persuaded higher management to withdraw the product from the market. The court sustained the dismissal of the employee's complaint because it revealed only "that there was a dispute over the merits of the new product," and because there was no evidence that Geary was discharged either for the specific purpose of causing him harm or for his refusal to break any law. The court found that "Geary had made a nuisance of himself, and the company discharged him to preserve administrative order in its own house." In so holding, the court dismissed as "speculative"

---

[160]118 LRRM at 3180.
[161]Id. at 3181, 3182.
[162]See also Kalman v. Grand Union Co., 183 N.J. Super. 153, 443 A.2d 728, 115 LRRM 4803 (1982)(holding that the Code of Ethics of the American Pharmaceutical Association redounded to the benefit of the public as a whole).
[163]456 Pa. 171, 319 A.2d 174, 115 LRRM 4665 (1974).

Geary's argument that the continued sale of the defective product might have entailed both criminal and civil liability.

Similarly, in *Campbell v. Eli Lilly & Co.*,[164] a former employee of Lilly brought an action for damages and reinstatement based on a retaliatory discharge. After a trial on the pleadings, the court held that a discharged at-will employee who disclosed to supervisors the lethal effects of various company-manufactured drugs had no cause of action where the employee cited no statutory source for the duty fulfilled. The court declared that a general expression of public policy embodied in federal drug regulatory laws is not sufficient to justify an exception to the at-will law in Indiana.

In a Colorado case, a court denied a nurse's cause of action for wrongful discharge after she refused a management order to reduce the overtime assignments of her staff. The court rejected the employee's contention that a cause of action should be allowed since she felt that the reduction of overtime would jeopardize the health of the patients. The court also held that a statute containing general principles pertaining to the licensing of nurses did not create a cause of action.[165]

Whistle Blowing

Related to the public policy exception are discharges or other disciplinary measures triggered by an employee's reporting of allegedly unlawful conduct.[166] In some cases the

---

[164]413 N.E.2d 1054, 115 LRRM 4417 (Ind. Ct. App., 1980).

[165]Lampe v. Presbyterian Medical Center, 41 Colo. App. 465, 590 P.2d 513, 115 LRRM 4313, 4315 (1979).

[166]A number of states have enacted statutes protecting whistle blowers, as follows (citations to the "State Laws" (SLL) binders of BNA's Labor Relations Reporter): California, 14:210c; Connecticut, 16:207; Delaware, 17:112; Illinois, 23:203; Iowa, 25:112; Kansas, 26:201; Louisiana, 28:203; Maine, 29:205; Maryland, 30:203; Michigan, 32:206; New York, 42:208a; Oklahoma, 46:203; Oregon, 47:205; Rhode Island, 50:203; Texas, 54:204; Utah, 55:202; Washington, 58:203; Wisconsin, 60:205.

In addition, Congress has acted to protect federal whistle blowers against retaliation. 5 U.S.C. §2302 provides in part:

(b) Any employee who has authority to take, direct others to take, recommend, or approve any personnel action, shall not with respect to such authority—

. . .

(8) take or fail to take a personnel action with respect to any employee or applicant for employment as a reprisal for—

(A) a disclosure of information by an employee or applicant which the employee or applicant reasonably believes evidences—

(i) a violation of any law, rule, or regulation, or

(ii) . . . a substantial and specific danger to public health or safety. . . .

See also §210(a) of the Energy Reorganization Act, 42 U.S.C. §5851(a), protecting from retaliation corporate whistle blowers who inform officials of corporate failings. Brown & Root v. Donovan, 747 F.2d 1029, 118 LRRM 2301 (CA 5, 1984).

reporting may be of a supervisor's conduct to upper management; in other cases the employee may report his company's
activities to a governmental authority. The fact pattern in
whistle blowing cases in often the same:

> The employee objects to work that the employee believes is
> violative of state or federal law or [conduct that is] otherwise
> improper; . . . the employee expresses his intention not to assist
> the employer in the furtherance of such work and/or engages
> in "self-help" activity outside the work place to halt the work;
> and the employer [finally] discharges the employee for refusal
> to work or incompatibility with management [or organizational
> goals.][167]

The courts have had little trouble in affording a cause of
action in tort to an employee who is urged by his or her employer to violate a criminal or civil statute as part of a company
pattern or practice. The more difficult situation involves those
cases where an employee reports conduct that the employee
believes is illegal or, because of professional considerations,
unethical.

For example, the Supreme Court of West Virginia, in
Harless v. First National Bank,[168] considered whether an employee who was discharged in retaliation for his efforts to
require his employer to comply with a state consumer credit
protection statute stated a cause of action in tort. Finding that
the legislature intended to establish a clear and unequivocal
public policy that consumers of credit were to be afforded protection, the court ruled that this "policy should not be frus-
trated by a holding that an employee of a lending institution
covered by the Act who seeks to ensure that compliance is
being made with the Act, can be discharged without being
furnished a cause of action."[169]

A similar result was reached by the Illinois Supreme Court
in *Palmateer v. International Harvester Co.*,[170] where the court,
in finding a cause of action in tort for an employee who was
discharged for supplying to local law enforcement agencies
information indicating that a fellow employee might be violating the criminal statutes, stated:

---

[167]Olsen, "Wrongful Discharge Claims Raised by at Will Employees: A New Legal
Concern for Employers," 32 Lab. L.J. 265, 276 (1981).
[168]246 S.E.2d 270, 115 LRRM 4380 (W. Va., 1978).
[169]115 LRRM at 4384.
[170]85 Ill. 2d 124, 421 N.E.2d 876, 115 LRRM 4165 (1981).

No specific constitutional or statutory provision requires a citizen to take an active part in the ferreting out and prosecution of crime, but public policy nevertheless favors citizen crime-fighters. "Public policy favors the exposure of crime, and the co-operation of citizens possessing knowledge thereof is essential to effective implementation of that policy. Persons acting in good faith who have probable cause to believe crimes have been committed should not be deterred from reporting them by the fear of unfounded suits by those accused."[171]

The court also noted that once Palmateer reported the crime, he was then under a statutory duty to further assist officials when requested to do so.

With few exceptions, before a court will allow a cause of action for whistle blowing, the conduct complained of must be clearly illegal. The burden in this regard is on the plaintiff-employee. A possibility of criminal activity will be insufficient to make out a cause of action. For example, in *Adler v. American Standard Corp.*,[172] an employee was discharged for revealing to higher management corporate conduct that supposedly included payments of commercial bribes and falsification of corporate records and financial statements. The court found that Adler's complaint was too vague and lacking in specifics to mount a prima facie showing that the claimed conduct contravened any criminal statute. Nor did the complaint demonstrate a clear violation of public policy. In the words of the court:

We have always been aware, however, that recognition of an otherwise undeclared public policy as a basis for a judicial decision involves the application of a very nebulous concept to the facts of a given case, and that declaration of public policy is normally the function of the legislative branch. ... As Mr. Justice Sutherland stated for the Supreme Court in *Patton v. United States*, ...:

"The truth is that the theory of public policy embodies a doctrine of vague and variable quality and, unless deducible in the given circumstances from constitutional or statutory provisions, should be accepted as the basis of a judicial determination, if at all, *only with the utmost circumspection*. The public policy of one generation may not, under changed conditions, be the public policy of another.[173]

---

[171]115 LRRM at 4168. (citations omittted).
[172]291 Md. 31, 432 A.2d 464, 115 LRRM 4130 (1981).
[173]115 LRRM at 4136 (emphasis added by Adler court). A sample of cases where courts have denied the public policy exception include: Crocker v. Chamber of Commerce of the U.S., ___ F.Supp. ___, 115 LRRM 4067 (D.D.C., 1983)(rejecting duty to adequately investigate charges of employee disloyalty before discharge as public

While the court admitted that Maryland recognizes a cause of action for discharge of an at-will employee where the motivation for the discharge is against public policy, Adler's complaint fell short of providing a "sufficient factual predicate for determining whether any declared mandate of public policy was violated."[174]

A review of whistle blowing cases indicates that, in finding a cause of action, the courts balance the competing interests. The employer's interest is to be permitted to efficiently operate a business; the employee's interest is security in earning a livelihood. At the same time the judiciary has recognized that society has an interest in making sure that its civil and criminal statutes are not violated.

Accordingly, where the conduct complained of clearly violates a criminal or civil statute, courts have little difficulty finding a cause of action in tort for a retaliatory discharge. These situations involve conduct that the legislature has clearly seen fit to address. Courts reason that to refuse a cause of action would effectively permit an employer to increase its chances of escaping liability for violating civil or criminal statutes. It is difficult to imagine any public policy that would

---

policy); Kavanaugh v. KLM Royal Dutch Airlines, 566 F.Supp. 242, 115 LRRM 4266 (D. Ill., 1983)(rejecting claim for wrongful discharge on theory that discharge violated public policy favoring right to counsel and free access to courts); Hinrichs v. Tranquilaire Hosp., 352 So.2d 1130, 115 LRRM 4385 (Ala., 1977)(denying cause of action for at-will nurse who refused to falsify medical records as directed by supervisor); Larsen v. Motor Supply Co., 573 P.2d 907, 115 LRRM 4298 (Ariz. Ct. App., 1977)(refusal to sign consent form to take psychological stress evaluation test required by company policy not protected by public policy to justify exception to at-will rule); Abrisz v. Pulley Freight Lines, Inc., 270 N.W.2d 454, 115 LRRM 4777 (Iowa, 1978)(denying cause of action to at-will employee who wrote letter in support of co-employee's application for unemployment compensation); Scrogham v. Kraftco Corp., 551 S.W.2d 881, 115 LRRM 4769 (Ky. Ct. App., 1977)(denying public policy protection for employee desiring to attend law school at night); Gil v. Metal Serv. Corp., 412 So.2d 706, 115 LRRM 4460 (La. Ct. App., 1982)(no cause of action for employee alleging dismissal for protesting employer's practice of shipping foreign steel to customers who specifically had ordered domestic steel); Ising v. Barnes Hosp., 674 S.W.2d 623, 116 LRRM 3140 (Mo. Ct. App., 1984)(rejecting cause of action for at-will employee who refused to sign release exonerating employer and polygrapher from negligent or intentional conduct arising out of polygraph examination); Howard v. Dorr Woolen Co., 120 N.H. 295, 414 A.2d 1273, 115 LRRM 4578 (1980)(rejecting discharge for sickness as violative of public policy where sickness remedied by medical insurance); Cisco v. United Parcel Serv., Inc., 328 Pa. Super. Ct. 300, 476 A.2d 1340, 116 LRRM 2514 (1984)(employer's refusal to rehire employee following acquittal not violative of public policy); Jones v. Keogh, 137 Vt. 562, 409 A.2d 581, 115 LRRM 4193 (1979)(upholding dismissal for asserting rights with respect to vacation time and sick leave); Ward v. Frito-Lay, Inc., 95 Wis. 2d 372, 290 N.W.2d 536, 115 LRRM 4320 (Wis. Ct. App., 1980)(denying public policy exception to at-will employee who was dismissed for living with another employee to whom he was not married).

[174]115 LRRM at 4137.

be served by preventing a remedy in those instances where a court determines that the employee's allegations are correct. As stated by one judge:

> A conscientious employee, albeit an employee at will, who, motivated by a sincere desire to further a clear and compelling public policy, either statutorily or judicially declared, calls to the attention of his employer or appropriate authorities facts revealing actual violations of such [public] policy for the purpose of carrying out that clear public policy should not be subjected to retaliatory discharge without being provided with a remedy. . . . Giving such a right of action for damages would serve as a deterrent to retaliatory discharge and would promote the very same strong and compelling public policy which the retaliatory discharge would violate.[175]

A more difficult problem arises where an employee reasonably but incorrectly concludes that his employer's conduct is illegal. Even though the disclosure is motivated by a good faith belief that the conduct was illegal, few courts will allow a cause of action for the so-called "good faith" whistle blower. Some states have passed legislation that prohibits employer reprisals or disciplinary action against an employee who reports to a public body an employer's violation or suspected violation of any federal, state, or municipal law or regulation.[176] There should be no difficulty in refusing a cause of action to an employee who, for vexatious reasons, falsely accuses his employer of violating statutes. No policy is served by affording protection in this case; indeed, an employer would likely have a cause of action in tort against such an employee.

Malice and Bad Faith

The malice and bad faith exception to the at-will doctrine operates in tandem with the public policy exception. The predominant cause in this area is *Monge v. Beebe Rubber Co.*[177] A married woman was discharged by her foreman because of her refusal to go out on a date with him. The New Hampshire Supreme Court held the discharge malicious and unlawful and

---

[175]Campbell v. Eli Lilly & Co., 413 N.E.2d 1054, 115 LRRM 4417, 4426 (Ind. Ct. App., 1980)(Ratcliff, J., concurring in part, dissenting in part, and concurring in result).
[176]Conn. Gen. Stat. Ann. §31–51m (West, 1985), Wash. Rev. Code Ann. 49.17.160 (West, 1986).
[177]114 N.H. 130, 316 A.2d 549, 115 LRRM 4755 (1974).

concluded that a termination by the employer of a contract of employment which is motivated by bad faith or malice or based on retaliation is not in the best interest of the economic system or the public good.

More recently, in *Lucas v. Brown & Root, Inc.*,[178] an employee was dismissed when she refused to sleep with her supervisor. Although the time for filing a sexual harassment claim had run out under Title VII, the Eighth Circuit reasoned that the decisions of the Arkansas Supreme Court established the proposition that there are exceptions to the at-will rule that come into play when the basis for the discharge is so extreme and outrageous as to render the discharge tortious for intentional infliction of emotional distress.[179] According to the court, "a woman invited to trade herself for a job is in effect being asked to become a prostitute," and "[p]laintiff should not be penalized for refusing to do what the law forbids."[180] The court, citing the decision in *Tameny*,[181] declared that "it is an implied term of every employment contract that neither party be required to do what the law forbids,"[182] and that if the plaintiff could prove that she was dismissed for refusing to sleep with her foreman, and that her employer was responsible for it, she could recover damages for breach of contract.

A related principle underlying the malice and bad faith exception is an implied covenant of good faith and fair dealing. According to this principle, in every contract there is an implied covenant that neither party shall do anything which will have the effect of destroying or injuring the right of the other

---

[178]736 F.2d 1202, 35 FEP 1855, 116 LRRM 2744 (CA 8, 1984).

[179]"The tort of intentional infliction of emotional distress is recognized in the employment context. . . . In order for the plaintiff to prevail in a case for liability under this tort, four elements must be established. It must be shown (1) that the actor intended to inflict emotional distress or that he knew or should have known that emotional distress was the result of his conduct; (2) that the conduct was extreme and outrageous; (3) that the defendant's conduct was the cause of the plaintiff's distress; and (4) that the emotional distress sustained by the plaintiff was severe." Murray v. Bridgeport Hosp., 40 Conn. Supp. 56, 480 A.2d 610, 117 LRRM 3111, 3113 (Conn. Super. Ct., 1984), citing 1 Restatement (Second) of Torts §46. "The general rule is that this tort, in essence, requires the defendant's conduct to be so extreme and outrageous as to go beyond all possible bounds of decency, and to be regarded as atrocious and utterly intolerable in a civilized community." Rulon-Miller v. IBM, 162 Cal. App. 3d 241, 208 Cal. Rptr. 524, 117 LRRM 3309 (1984). For an excellent review of this tort, see M.B.M. Co. v. Counce, 268 Ark. 269, 596 S.W.2d 681, 118 LRRM 2925 (1980).

[180]116 LRRM at 2746.

[181]See text at note 131 supra.

[182]116 LRRM at 2746–47.

party to receive the fruits of the agreement. Two decisions are of special note in this area. The first, *Fortune v. National Cash Register Co.*,[183] involved the discharge of a salesman with 25 years' service under a contract that reserved to the parties the explicit power to terminate the contract without notice. The record indicated that the salesman was discharged while on the verge of completing a transaction which would have resulted in a large commission. The Massachusetts Supreme Court refused to rule on the general question of whether a good faith requirement is implicit in every contract of employment at will. Nevertheless, it did declare that, on the record before it, the employer acted in bad faith when it sought to deprive the employee of commissions he otherwise would have earned. The court stated that this rule was necessary in order to prevent overreaching by employers and the forfeiture by employees of benefits almost earned.[184]

In *Pugh v. See's Candies, Inc.*,[185] a California appellate

---

[183]373 Mass. 96, 364 N.E.2d 1251, 115 LRRM 4658 (1977).

[184]115 LRRM at 4663. Subsequent to Fortune, the Supreme Court of Massachusetts decided Gram v. Liberty Mut. Ins. Co., 384 Mass. 659, 429 N.E.2d 21, 115 LRRM 4152 (1981), and Cort v. Bristol-Myers Co., 385 Mass. 300, 431 N.E.2d 908, 115 LRRM 5127 (1982). In Gram, the court allowed an insurance salesman, who would have been entitled to renewal commissions if not discharged, to recover for those commissions that were based on his past service. Unlike Fortune, an improper motive was not present in Gram. See Cort, 115 LRRM at 5129. At issue in Cort was a dismissal based on a refusal to provide the employer with certain biographical information, including data on "business experience, education, family, home ownership, physical data, activities, and [general goals] and aims." Id. at 5131. Finding that most of the questions were relevant to the employee's job qualifications and represented no invasion of privacy protected by the law, the court stated:

> We decline to impose liability on an employer simply because it gave a false reason or a pretext for the discharge of an employee at will. Such an employer has no duty to give any reason at the time of discharging an employee at will. Where no reason need be given, we impose no liability on an employer for concealing the real reason for an employee's discharge or giving a reason that is factually unsupportable.

Id. at 5129. The court did point out in a footnote, however, that if the employer was attempting to conceal the real reason for the discharge and the real reason was contrary to public policy, the fact that whatever reason was given to the employee was false could be relevant in establishing a cause of action. Id. at 5130 n.6. The court stressed that, on the facts of this case, public policy considerations did not justify the imposition of liability on the employer merely for falsely asserting that the employees were discharged for work reasons. Id. at 5130.

A fair reading of both cases is that, in Massachusetts, an at-will employee has two different possible causes of action for wrongful discharge:

> (1) where the discharge was motivated by a desire to retain financial benefits owed the employee (a public policy violation); . . . or (2) where the employee is discharged without good cause and without an improper motive yet is nonetheless deprived of ascertainable future financial benefits related to past services.

Magnan v. Anaconda Indus., 193 Conn. 558, 479 A.2d 781, 117 LRRM 2163, 2168 n.20 (1984).

[185]116 Cal. App. 3d 311, 171 Cal. Rptr. 917, 115 LRRM 4002 (1981).

court, reversing a lower court's granting of the defendant's
nonsuit motion, found that an employee demonstrated a prima
facie case of wrongful termination in violation of the employer's implied promise that it would not act arbitrarily in dealing
with the employee. The court stated that "[i]n determining
whether there exists an implied-in-fact promise for some form
of continued employment . . . a variety of factors in addition
to the existence of independent consideration" are relevant to
such a finding. These include: "the personnel policies or practices of the employer, the employee's longevity of service, actions or communications by the employer reflecting assurances
of continued employment, and the practices of the industry in
which the employee is engaged."[186] Given Pugh's 32 years of
employment, the commendations and promotions he received,
the apparent absence of any criticism of his work, the assurances he was given "that if you are loyal to [See's] and do a
good job, your future is secure," and the employer's acknowledged policies that administrative personnel would not be terminated except for good cause, the court had little trouble
concluding that there were facts in evidence from which a jury
could determine an implied promise of fair dealing with the
employee.

 Fortune and *Pugh* represent the minority view. Most courts
have adhered to the common law and have not adopted a
general requirement of good faith and fair dealing where employment contracts are of indefinite duration. The reasoning
is reflected in *Vandegrift v. American Brands Corp.*,[187] where
one federal court stated:

> [T]here exists in every contractual relationship an implied cov-
> enant that the parties will carry out their obligations in good
> faith. . . . The implied covenant, however, is dependent upon
> the contractual relationship of the parties, and does not itself
> create an independent tort duty. The claim that defendant owed
> to plaintiffs a duty of fairness is not that sort of positive legal
> duty, independent of the contract, upon which public policy
> rests.[188]

Moreover, even in the select jurisdictions that have ruled that
employment contracts are subject to an implied covenant that
the parties carry out their obligations in good faith, courts

---

[186]115 LRRM at 4009.
[187]572 F.Supp. 496, 115 LRRM 2317 (D. N.H., 1983).
[188]115 LRRM at 2320.

have declined to transform the requirement of good faith into an implied condition that an employee may be discharged only for good cause.[189]

Summary

The common law rule that an employer has an absolute right to discharge an at-will employee is, in many jurisdictions, now modified by the principle that where the employer's retaliatory action contravenes some substantial public policy principle, a cause of action will lie in contract or tort. In many jurisdictions, those employees who are discharged in retaliation for either having exercised a statutorily conferred personal right or having fulfilled a statutorily imposed duty will have a cause of action in tort. With few exceptions, the courts that have adopted this exception, however, have focused on a specific policy consideration rather than the general equities of the fact situation. Matters that are the subject of personal ethics which are not overlapped by legislative-type declarations have little, if any, chance of finding protection by the courts. While courts talk of the balancing of interests in arriving at a decision, unless an employee can point to a specific statutory right or duty, the balancing will inevitably result in a resolution adverse to the complainant.

Absent a cause of action in tort,[190] an employee challenging a discharge must rely on contract theory. The principle that every contract of employment, whatever its duration, is subject to an implied covenant of good faith and fair dealing (thereby making every employment relationship subject to a de facto standard of just cause) has not been

---

[189]In Magnan v. Anaconda Indus., 193 Conn. 558, 479 A.2d 781, 117 LRRM 2163, 2168 (1984), the Supreme Court of Connecticut stated: "While we see no reason to exempt employment contracts from the implication of a covenant of good faith and fair dealing in the contractual relationship, we do not believe that this principle should be applied to transform a contract of employment terminable at the will of either party into one terminable only at the will of the employee or for just cause." See also Gates v. Life of Montana Ins. Co., 196 Mont. 178, 638 P.2d 1063, 118 LRRM 2071, 2074 (1982) ("We hold that a covenant of good faith and fair dealing was implied in the employment contract of the appellant.") Gates, however, also involved a handbook of personnel policies that outlined procedural-type protections prior to termination.

[190]Many courts, of course, do not recognize the tort of bad faith breach of an employment contract. Brockmeyer v. Dun & Bradstreet, 113 Wis. 2d 561, 335 N.W.2d 834, 115 LRRM 4484 (1983).

adopted by the courts. Selected courts have enforced promises of job security in contracts of indefinite duration even
where there is no independent consideration and mutuality
of obligation,[191] but only in extreme cases where the employer created that dismissal would be for just cause only.

Similarly, most courts have rejected employee handbooks and personnel manuals as a basis per se for implying
a just cause standard for all at-will employees.[192] As stated
by one federal court, an employment manual is only a unilateral expression of company policy and is not bargained
for; accordingly, it cannot be the basis of an employment
contract.[193] Similar reasoning is frequently applied to oral
representations that were not mutually negotiated.[194]

The significance of the employment-at-will area is that
every employee is a potential member of a protected class.
More important, the cases are decided by juries, with large
punitive and compensatory damage verdicts possible. Employers should accordingly treat *any* discharge as a potential
liability event.[195]

---

[191]See, e.g., Toussaint v. Blue Cross & Blue Shield, 408 Mich. 579, 292 N.W.2d
880, 115 LRRM 4708 (1980)(employer's written or oral assertions can create contract
whereby employee cannot be terminated absent just cause), and Ariganello v. Scott
Paper Co., 588 F.Supp. 484, 117 LRRM 2064 (E.D. Mich., 1982)(extending Toussaint
to deprivation of severance pay in contravention to the understandings created by
the employer).
[192]See, e.g., Fletcher v. Wesley Medical Center, 585 F.Supp. 1260, 119 LRRM
2217 (D. Kan., 1984)(holding that employment handbook could be one of the relevant
circumstances from which the parties' intent to contract could be inferred); Sargent
v. Illinois Inst. of Tech., 78 Ill. App. 3d 117, 397 N.E.2d 443 (1979). But see Kaiser
v. Dixon, 127 Ill. App. 3d 251, 468 N.E.2d 822 (1984); Shaw v. S.S. Kresge Co., 167
Ind. App. 1, 328 N.E.2d 775, 115 LRRM 5030 (1975); Mau v. Omaha Nat'l Bank, 207
Neb. 308, 229 N.W.2d 147, 115 LRRM 4992 (1980); Chin v. American Tel. & Tel.
Co., 96 Misc. 2d 1070, 410 N.Y.S.2d 737, 115 LRRM 5066 (Sup. Ct., 1978), aff'd mem.,
70 A.D.2d 791, 416 N.Y.S.2d 160, 115 LRRM 5069 (1979); Edwards v. Citibank, N.A.,
100 Misc. 2d 59, 418 N.Y.S.2d 269, 115 LRRM 4624 (1979), aff'd mem., 74 A.D.2d
553, 425 N.Y.S.2d 327 (App. Div.), appeal dismissed, 51 N.Y.2d 875, 414 N.E.2d 400,
433 N.Y.S.2d 1020 (1980).
[193]Rouse v. Peoples Natural Gas Co., 605 F.Supp. 230, 119 LRRM 2220, 2222
(D. Kan., 1985). Accord: Garcia v. Aetna Fin. Co., 752 F.2d 488, 118 LRRM 2298 (CA
10, 1984). But see Toussaint v. Blue Cross & Blue Shield, 408 Mich. 579, 292 N.W.2d
880, 115 LRRM 4708 (1980); Gorrill v. Icelandair, 761 F.2d 847, 119 LRRM 2505
(CA 2, 1985)(holding that airline operations manual is express contractual limitation
on carrier's right to discharge, where manual provided that seniority be sole factor
in terminations stemming from the elimination or force reduction.); Wooley v. Hoff-
mann LaRoche, Inc., 99 N.J. 284, 491 A.2d 1257, 119 LRRM 2380, 2381 (1985)("We
hold that absent a clear and prominent disclaimer, an implied promise contained in
an employment manual that an employee will be fired only for cause may be enforceable against an employer even when the employment is for an indefinite term
and would otherwise be terminable at will.").
[194]Cederstrand v. Lutheran Bhd., 117 LRRM 2603, 2610 (Minn., 1962).
[195]The number of at-will suits has prompted management advocates to formulate

some guidelines for employers. One advocate has offered "ten commandments" to help employers to avoid wrongful discharge litigation, paraphrased below:

1) Review all written company documents that discuss termination or layoff to ensure that they are up-to-date and that they avoid conveying any impression that the employer guarantees long-term or permanent employment. One advocate suggests that this review should include all recruitment and pre-employment material, job advertisements, employment application forms, employment correspondence, letters used to offer employment, employee evaluation forms, handbooks, personnel manuals and guidelines, supervisory manuals, and collateral personnel documents such as employee benefit documents.

2) Employers should define their own standards of conduct and make them reasonable and attainable. These standards should be stated clearly and should be complied with by management. However, standards that deal with termination should avoid any inference that discharge will be for "just cause" only.

3) "Favorable documents" should be generated at key employee encounters. Moreover, after every such encounter—for example, hiring and exit interviews, disciplinary action, or advisement of benefits—management should take care to have employees sign documents stating that they received the information and understand it. Employers may want to consider a "Sears-type" disclaimer which, in relevant part, provides: "In consideration of my employment, I agree to conform to the rules and regulations of Sears, Roebuck and Co., and my employment and compensation can be terminated, with or without cause, and with or without notice, at any time, at the option of either the Company or myself. I understand that no store manager or representative of Sears, Roebuck and Co., other than the president or vice-president of the Company, has any authority to enter into any agreement for employment for any special period of time, or to make any agreement contrary to the foregoing." See "Reviewing Wrongful Discharge in Sunbelt," 118 LRR 292–94 (BNA, April 15, 1985).

4) Since performance evaluations are necessary to establish a pattern of employee behavior leading up to discharge, they should be handled very carefully. Few supervisors are completely candid in their appraisals and these documents may be the basis for a "wrongful evaluation" charge in a subsequent lawsuit.

5) Management in unorganized sectors should consider developing a written progressive discipline procedure which could help demonstrate fairness to a jury in a wrongful discharge suit.

6) Employers should appoint a "czar of discharge" to provide an objective review of all the factors relating to termination. Some employers may even obtain legal help to review discharges, especially ones involving middle-and upper-management employees.

7) All factors relating to the discharge should be reviewed before completing the discharge. Such factors include: the employee's age, the evidence against the employee, the consistency of the employer's application of its policies, and whether the employee has had an opportunity to tell his or her side of the story.

8) Employers should state candidly the reasons for the discharge, although management must take care not to defame the employee.

9) Management should make sure that the discharge is properly implemented so as to avoid charges of "pain and suffering" by employees. In all discharges, dignity and confidentiality are desirable. One advocate has suggested that employers restrict communications as to the reason for the employee's termination on a need-to-know basis. This would bring the communication under the qualified privilege and create a good chance that a common law defamation suit would fail.

10) Finally, employers may want to consider avoiding litigation altogether by "cutting a deal" with the discharged employee. Such an agreement could include submitting the dispute to arbitration. See "Conference on Proper Discharge Procedures," 119 LRR 75–77 (BNA) May 27, 1985.

Chapter 5

Legal Considerations in Negotiating Management Rights Clauses

Management rights generally are outlined in the contract and labeled accordingly, while union rights are usually found throughout the agreement according to subject matter. A management rights clause is one of the most common clauses in an agreement. In a study by The Bureau of National Affairs, Inc., management and union rights provisions were found in all 400 sample labor agreements surveyed, with statements regarding management rights included in 76 percent. Of the contracts containing management rights provisions, 79 percent reserved to management direction of the working force, 71 percent management of the business, and 38 percent control of production methods. Framing of company rules was cited 28 percent of the time; determining employees' duties, 25 percent of the time; closing or relocating the plant, 11 percent of the time; and changing of technology, 17 percent of the time.[1]

Restrictions on management rights were found in 88 percent of the sample. Subcontracting was mentioned in 50 percent; performance of bargaining-unit work by supervisors, in 54 percent; restrictions on technological changes, in 21 percent; and plant shutdown or relocation limitations, in 18 percent.[2]

While management rights provisions are common, there

---

[1]Basic Patterns in Union Contracts, 63 (BNA Books, 1983).
[2]Id. at 64–65.

134

are a number of legal considerations that should concern the practitioner (both private- and public-sector) when negotiating a management rights clause.

Management Rights and Taft-Hartley Concerns

Although the parties are free to bargain about any legal subject, the statutory duty imposed by the Taft-Hartley Act to bargain in good faith is limited to matters of "wages, hours, and other terms and conditions of employment," the so-called "mandatory subjects" of bargaining.[3] When the management rights clause contains a "nonmandatory" provision, however, an employer may not insist to impasse on that clause. For example, the NLRB has ruled that an unfair labor practice was committed when an employer insisted to impasse on a provision in a management rights clause allowing the company the right to make a stenographic transcription of bargaining sessions, since transcription is not a mandatory subject of bargaining.[4] Similarly, the Board has ruled that an em-

---

[3]Sec. 8(a)(5) of the National Labor Relations Act, 29 U.S.C. §158(a)(5), makes it an unfair labor practice for an employer to refuse to bargain collectively with its employees' representatives. Sec. 8(d) defines collective bargaining as follows: "[T]o bargain collectively is the performance of the mutual obligation of the employer and the representative of the employees to meet at reasonable times and confer in good faith with respect to wages, hours, and other terms and conditions of employment, or the negotiation of an agreement, or any question arising thereunder, and the execution of a written contract incorporating any agreement reached if requested by either party, but such obligation does not compel either party to agree to a proposal or require the making of a concession." 29 U.S.C. §158(d). In NLRB v. Wooster Div., Borg-Warner Corp., 356 U.S. 342, 42 LRRM 2034, 2036 (1958), the Supreme Court read these two provisions together as "establish[ing] the obligation of the employer and the representative of its employees to bargain with each other in good faith with respect to 'wages, hours, and other terms and conditions of employment. . . .' " The Court ruled that the "duty is limited to those subjects, and within that area neither party is legally obligated to yield. . . . As to other matters, however, each party is free to bargain or not to bargain, and to agree or not to agree." The parties may, under current law, bargain to impasse over these items and use economic weapons, including strikes and lockouts, to secure their inclusion in the agreement. Further, an employer may insist on a management rights clause to impasse without violating the statute. The Supreme Court, in NLRB v. American Nat'l Ins. Co., 343 U.S. 395, 30 LRRM 2147, 2152 (1952), held that an employer does not commit a per se unfair labor practice by bargaining for a management rights clause that gives management exclusive control over matters that would otherwise be subject to the duty to bargain. See also Struthers Wells Corp. v. NLRB, 721 F.2d 465, 114 LRRM 3553 (CA 3, 1983)(employer did not engage in unfair labor practice in insisting during contract negotiations that agreement provide company with sole discretion over grant of merit reviews and increases, unilateral control of promotional opportunities by elimination of posting and bidding provisions, and amendment of work jurisdiction language to recognize some bargaining unit work to be performed by supervisors).

[4]Quality Eng'g. Prods. Co., 267 NLRB 593, 114 LRRM 1100 (1983); NLRB v. Bartlett-Collins Co., 639 F.2d 652, 106 LRRM 2272 (CA 10, 1981).

ployer violated the statute when it insisted that the union agree to a clause stating that the union recognized the "religious mission" of the employer. This type of mission statement was considered nonmandatory even though the employer was involved in religious activities.[5]

If the management rights clause effectively precludes the union's statutory right to engage in meaningful negotiations, the employer commits an unfair labor practice. In one case where the employer insisted on exclusive control over discipline, discharge, layoff, and recall and, at the same time, excluded these subjects from the grievance and arbitration procedure, the Board ruled that the employer engaged in "surface bargaining"[6] and thus violated the Act.[7] The particular management rights clause at issue reserved exclusively to management "each and every right, power and privilege that it has ever enjoyed." As reported by the reviewing court, the agreement further provided that the company was authorized to:

1. Determine the qualifications and select its employees.
2. Determine the size and composition of its work forces.
3. Determine work schedules and all methods of production.
4. Assign overtime work.
5. Determine the number and types of equipment.
6. Hire, retire, promote, demote, evaluate, transfer, suspend, assign, direct, lay off and recall employees.
7. Reward, reprimand, discharge or otherwise discipline employees.
8. Determine job content and minimum training qualifications for job classifications and the amounts and types of work to be performed by employees.

---

[5]Salvation Army of Mass. Dorchester Day Care Center, 271 NLRB 195, 116 LRRM 1410 (1984).

[6]In North Coast Cleaning SVC, 272 NLRB 1343, 118 LRRM 1134 (1984), the Board stated: "Although the duty to bargain does not compel a party to make concessions or agree to any proposals, it does require certain affirmative actions such as entering 'into discussion with an open and fair mind, and a sincere purpose to find a basis of agreement.'" 118 LRRM at 1135, citing NLRB v. Herman Sausage Co., 275 F.2d 229, 231, 45 LRRM 2829 (CA 5, 1960). The Board went on to state that "a party's 'failure to do little more than reject (demands)' has been found 'indicative of a failure to comply with [the] statutory requirement to bargain in good faith.'" 118 LRRM at 1135, citing NLRB v. Century Cement Mfg. Co., 208 F.2d 84, 86, 33 LRRM 2061 (CA 2, 1954) and My Store, Inc., 147 NLRB 145, 155–56, 56 LRRM 1176 (1964), enforced, 345 F.2d 494, 58 LRRM 2775 (CA 7, 1965). Noting the Board's declarations in North Coast Cleaning, as well as the cited cases, one may define surface bargaining as meeting with the union but with no bona fide intention of ever reaching an agreement.

[7]A-1 King Size Sandwiches, Inc., 265 NLRB 850, 112 LRRM 1360 (1982), enforced, 732 F.2d 872, 116 LRRM 2658 (CA 11, 1984).

9. Establish and change working rules and regulations.
10. Establish new jobs and abolish or change existing jobs.
11. Increase or decrease the number of jobs or employees.
12. Determine whether and to what extent the work required in its operations should be performed by employees.
13. Have supervisors or other non-union employees perform work of the kind performed by employees of the Union.
14. Determine assignments of work.
15. Discontinue, transfer or assign all or any part of its functions, services, or production or other operations.
16. Subcontract any part of the Company's work.
17. Expand, reduce, alter, combine, transfer, assign, cease or create any job, job classification, department or operation for business purposes.
18. Alter or vary practices.
19. Otherwise generally manage the business, direct the work force and establish terms and conditions of employment.[8]

In upholding the Board, the Court of Appeals for the Eleventh Circuit stated that the NLRB correctly inferred bad faith from the insistence on proposals that were so unusually harsh and unreasonable that they were predictably unworkable. The court found that the company's proposals "would have left the Union and the employees with substantially fewer rights and less protection than they would have if they had relied solely upon the Union's certification."[9]

Whether a particular management rights provision has this effect is a question that frequently arises in an unfair labor practice proceeding where the union charges the employer with surface bargaining. In making a determination whether the duty to bargain has been breached, particularly in the context of a surface bargaining charge, the Board will examine the parties' conduct at bargaining to see if it evidences a real desire to reach an agreement.[10] In this respect it will examine the record as a whole, including the course of negotiations and the nature of the contract proposals themselves.[11] While the Board cannot "either directly or indirectly compel concessions or otherwise sit in judgment upon the substantive terms of a collective bargaining agreement,"[12] it can, under the Act, "consider the content of bargaining proposals

---

[8]116 LRRM at 2660.
[9]Id. at 2662.
[10]Rescar, Inc., 274 NLRB No. 1, 118 LRRM 1371 (1985).
[11]NLRB v. Insurance Agents' Int'l Union, 361 U.S. 477, 45 LRRM 2074, 2712 (1960).
[12]NLRB v. American Nat'l Ins. Co., 343 U.S. 395, 30 LRRM 2147, 2150 (1952).

as part of its review when making a determination as to the good faith of parties negotiating a contract."[13]

In one case the Board found that an employer did not commit an unfair labor practice when it proposed both a strong management rights clause and a no-strike clause, coupled with arbitration limited to matters involving discharge or discipline. Although the Board recognized that "unusually harsh, vindictive, or unreasonable proposals may be deemed so predictably unacceptable as to warrant the evidentiary conclusion that they have been proffered in bad faith," it nevertheless held that these proposals did not, in and of themselves, warrant such a finding.[14]

In *NLRB v. Tomco Communications, Inc.*,[15] the Ninth Circuit, stating that a bargaining proposal may contain terms "so hostile to the role of the other side's bargaining representative that it constitutes evidence of bad faith," nevertheless found that the following management rights clause did not "force the union into abandoning its statutory rights and duties":

> Section 1. All management rights, powers, authority and functions, whether heretofore or hereafter exercised, and regardless of the frequency or infrequency of their exercise, shall remain vested, exclusively in the Company. It is expressly recognized that such rights, powers, authority and functions include, but are by no means whatever limited to, the full and exclusive control, management and operation of its business and its plant; the determination of the scope of its activities, products to be processed or manufactured, and methods pertaining thereto, the location of such processing or manufacturing, the materials and products to be acquired or utilized, and the machinery and equipment to be utilized, and the layout thereof; the right to establish or change shifts, schedules of work and production schedules and standards; the right to establish, change, combine or eliminate jobs, positions, job classifications and descriptions; the right to establish wage rates for new or changed jobs or positions; the right to establish or change incentive or bonus compensation; the right to introduce new or improved procedures, methods, processes, facilities, machines and equipment or make technological changes; the right to maintain order and efficiency; the right to contract or subcontract any work; the determination of the number, size and location of its plant or

---

[13]Chevron Chem. Co., 261 NLRB 44, 110 LRRM 1005 (1982).
[14]110 LRRM at 1008 n.10. See also Miller Spring & Mfg. Co., 273 NLRB No. 72, 118 LRRM 1234 (1984).
[15]567 F.2d 871, 97 LRRM 2660, 2666 (CA 9, 1978).

plants or any part thereof, and the extent to which the means and manner by which its plant or plants, or any part thereof, shall be operated, relocated, shut down or abandoned; the right to terminate, merge, consolidate, sell or otherwise transfer its business or any part thereof; the right to make and enforce safety and security rules and rules of conduct; the determination of the number of employees, the assignment of duties thereto, and the right to change, increase or reduce the same, and the direction of the working forces, including but by no means limited to hiring, selecting and training of new employees, and suspending, scheduling, assigning, discharging, laying off, recalling, promoting, retiring, demoting, and transferring of its employees.
Section 2. It is the intention of the Company and the Union that the rights, powers, and authority and functions referred to herein shall remain exclusively vested in the Company except insofar as specifically surrendered or limited by express provision of this Agreement.[16]

In refusing to uphold the Board, the court of appeals stated that it would be a novel doctrine that the union has a duty of representation to its members which forbids it to concede certain prerogatives to management and which correspondingly forbids management to insist upon these prerogatives.[17]

The difficulty in this area is determining when a party has reached the "point where hard bargaining ends and obstructionist intransigence begins."[18] A company can insist to impasse on a management rights clause that outlines its prerogatives and, at the same time, take a hard line on other items, such as a "zipper" clause and a limited arbitration provision.[19] The test for finding an unfair labor practice has always been a "totality of circumstances" focus and the Board, in cases where bad faith bargaining is alleged, may properly take cognizance of the reasonableness of the positions advanced by the parties. Indeed, as stated by the Seventh Circuit, "sometimes, especially if the parties are sophisticated, the only indicia of bad faith may be the proposals advanced and adhered to."[20] It is rare, however, when the content of proposals advanced by a party are so egregious that an absence

---

[16]97 LRRM at 2664 n.4.
[17]97 LRRM at 2664.
[18]NLRB v. Big Three Indus., Inc., 497 F.2d 43, 86 LRRM 3031, 3035 (CA 5, 1974).
[19]The manner in which disputes are to be resolved during the term of an agreement is a mandatory subject of bargaining. NLRB v. Tomco Communications, Inc., 567 F.2d 871, 97 LRRM 2660, 2665 n.8 (CA 9, 1978).
[20]NLRB v. Wright Motors, Inc., 603 F.2d 604, 102 LRRM 2021, 2025 (CA 7, 1979); see also NLRB v. Billion Oldsmobile-Toyota, 700 F.2d 454, 112 LRRM 2873,

of good faith is inferred just from that alone. Under current law the parties are generally free to advance their proposals, including a hard-line management rights provision, so long as the substantive items within these proposals are mandatory subjects of bargaining.[21] The parties need only evidence a desire to reach agreement, and in this respect the best that can be said concerning the legal requirement for a showing of good faith is that the practitioner must enter bargaining with the right "state of mind."[22]

Public-Sector Concerns

State Restrictions

In those states that have passed collective bargaining statutes,[23] a variety of approaches have been adopted with

---

2874 (CA 8, 1983)("To find bad faith the Board looks to the employer's conduct in the totality of the circumstances in which the bargaining took place. . . . The Board not only looks to the employer's behavior at the bargaining table but also to its conduct away from the table that may affect the negotiations.").

[21]Under certain circumstances an employer may not be free to withdraw a proposal once it is on the table. Mead Corp. v. NLRB, 697 F.2d 1013, 112 LRRM 2797, 2803 (CA 11, 1983)("withdrawal of a proposal by an employer without good cause is evidence of a lack of good faith bargaining by the employer in violation of Section 8(a)(5) of the Act where the proposal has been tentatively agreed upon or acceptance by the Union appears to be imminent").

[22]"Determining whether parties have complied with the duty to bargain in good faith usually requires examination of their motive or state of mind during the bargaining process, and is generally based on circumstantial evidence, since a charged party is unlikely to admit overtly having acted with bad intent. Hence, in determining whether the duty to bargain in good faith has been breached, particularly in the context of a 'surface bargaining' allegation, we look to whether the parties' conduct evidences a real desire to reach an agreement—a determination made by examination of the record as a whole, including the course of negotiations as well as contract proposals." Chevron Chem. Co., 261 NLRB 44, 110 LRRM 1005, 1007 (1982).

[23]The following states have enacted legislation granting bargaining rights to public-sector employees (citations to the "State Laws" (SLL) binders of BNA's Labor Relations Reporter): Alabama, 10:215(firefighters); Alaska, 11:203, 224; California, 14:217, 220n; Connecticut, 16:253(municipal employees), 16:237(state employees), 16:261(teachers); Delaware, 17:127, 130; Florida, 19:209; Georgia, 20:115(firefighters); Hawaii, 21:224; Idaho, 22:223(teachers), 22:225(firefighters); Illinois, 23:215; Indiana, 24:113, 137; Iowa, 25:121; Kansas, 26:231; Kentucky, 27:215(firefighters), 27:222(teachers), 27:225(police officers); Louisiana, 28:225(public transit employees); Maine, 29:211, 222c; Maryland, 20:224(public school employees); Massachusetts, 31:244c, 245; Michigan, 32:263; Minnesota, 33:247; Missouri, 35:211; Montana, 36:219; Nebraska, 37:225, 235, 244a; Nevada, 38:226; New Hampshire, 39:221; New Jersey, 40:245; New Mexico, 41:208; New York, 42:251, 252t; North Dakota, 44:222a, 223; Ohio, 45:217; Oklahoma, 46:225, 232a; Oregon, 47:243(municipal employees), 47:233(state employees); Pennsylvania, 48:221, 240h; Rhode Island, 50:238; South Dakota, 52:205; Tennessee, 53:219(public transit employees), 53:220(education professional employees); Texas, 54:213(fire and police employees); Vermont, 56:219, 231, 233; Washington, 58:213, 237, 242c; Wisconsin, 60:242a, 243; Wyoming, 61:202(firefighters).

respect to the treatment of public-sector management rights. Some states have simply declared that certain rights are reserved to management. For example, the Iowa statute provides:

> Public Employer Rights. Public employers shall have, in addition to all powers, duties, and rights established by constitutional provision, statute, ordinance, charter, or special act, the exclusive power, duty, and the right to:
> 1. Direct the work of its [sic] public employees.
> 2. Hire, promote, demote, transfer, assign, and retain public employees in positions within the public agency.
> 3. Suspend or discharge public employees for proper cause.
> 4. Maintain the efficiency of governmental operations.
> 5. Relieve public employees from duties because of lack of work or for other legitimate reasons.
> 6. Determine and implement methods, means, assignments and personnel by which the public employer's operations are to be conducted.
> 7. Take such actions as may be necessary to carry out the mission of the public employer.
> 8. Initiate, prepare, certify, and administer its [sic] budget.
> 9. Exercise all powers and duties granted to the public employer by law.[24]

Similarly, the Montana statute declares:

> Management rights of public employers.—Public employees and their representatives shall recognize the prerogatives of public employers to operate and manage their affairs in such areas as, but not limited to:
> (1) direct employees;
> (2) hire, promote, transfer, assign, and retain employees;
> (3) relieve employees from duties because of lack of work or funds or under conditions where continuation of such work [would] be inefficient and nonproductive;
> (4) maintain the efficiency of government operations;
> (5) determine the methods, means, job classifications, and personnel by which government operations are to be conducted;

---

[24]Iowa Code Ann. §20.7 (West, 1974). See Saydel Educ. Ass'n v. Public Employment Relations Bd. (PERB), 333 N.W.2d 486, 117 LRRM 3134 (Iowa, 1983)(holding proposal that certain criteria other than seniority—including skill, ability, and experience—be considered by school district in connection with transfers or staff reductions, is mandatory subject of bargaining); Charles City Educ. Ass'n v. PERB, 291 N.W.2d 663, 109 LRRM 2249, (Iowa, 1980)(determination of job qualifications is exclusive right of employer under statute giving management right to hire, promote, demote, transfer, assign, and retain employees); Iowa City Community School Dist. v. Iowa City Educ. Ass'n, 343 N.W.2d 139, 116 LRRM 2832 (Iowa, 1983)(allowing arbitrator to determine what constitutes unsatisfactory teacher performance); City of Mason City v. PERB, 316 N.W.2d 851, 113 LRRM 3354 (Iowa, 1982)(benefit proposal that pertains to retirement systems is legally excluded subject of bargaining).

(6) take whatever actions may be necessary to carry out the missions of the agency in situations of emergency;
(7) establish the methods and processes by which work is performed.[25]

The right to select and evaluate employees, the right to administer the budget, and the right to determine the adequacy of the work force have frequently been cited as traditional management rights by numerous states.[26] These rights, and others considered as rights within management's domain, may be (and generally are) specifically referenced in the statute. Moreover, the statutes will usually provide that the public employer is not required to bargain over matters involving inherent management rights. The Pennsylvania act states:

> Public employers shall not be required to bargain over matters of inherent managerial policy, which shall include but shall not be limited to such areas of discretion or policy as the functions and programs of the public employer, standards of services, its overall budget, utilization of technology, the organizational structure and selection and direction of personnel.[27]

Likewise, the Illinois Public Labor Relations Act provides:

> Management Rights.—Employers shall not be required to bargain over matters of inherent managerial policy, which shall include such areas of discretion or policy as the functions of the

---

[25]Mont. Rev. Codes. Ann. §39-31-303 (1983); SLL (BNA) 36:219, 36:223. See Sorlie v. School Dist., 667 P.2d 400 (Mont. 1983)(holding reassignment, without reduction in salary, for legitimate financial constraints, permissible under board's power to financially manage school district); Butte Teachers' Union v. Board of Educ., 173 Mont. 215, 567 P.2d 51 (1977)(substitution of time clocks as more efficient method of recording attendance not managerial prerogative but subject to binding arbitration).

[26]Ramapo-Indian Hills Educ. Ass'n v. Board of Educ., 422 A.2d 90, 112 LRRM 2062 (N.J. Super. Ct. App. Div., 1980).

[27]Pa. Stat. Ann. tit. 43, §1101.702 (Purdon, 1974). See, Commonwealth v. Commonwealth Pa. Labor Rel. Bd., 74 Pa. Commw. 1, 459 A.2d 452, 113 LRRM 3052 (1983)(subject of whether employees may smoke at the workplace is unrelated to entrepreneurial or managerial judgments fundamental to the basic direction of enterprise); Pennsylvania Lab. Rel. Bd. v. Mars Area School Dist., 21 Pa. Commw. 230, 344 A.2d 285, 90 LRRM 2978 (1975)(elimination of paid teachers' aides for economic reasons is matter of inherent managerial policy not subject to bargaining); Borough of Wilkinsburg v. Sanitation Dept., 16 Pa. Commw. 640, 330 A.2d 306, 88 LRRM 2499, aff'd, 463 Pa. 521, 345 A.2d 641, 90 LRRM 2828 (1975)(decision to contract with private contractor for collection of refuse is one of inherent managerial policy, even though work had previously been performed by unit employees); State College Educ. Ass'n v. Pennsylvania Lab. Rel. Bd., 9 Pa. Commw. 229, 306 A.2d 404, 83 LRRM 3079 (1973), remanded, 337 A.2d 262, 461 Pa. 494, 90 LRRM 2081 (1974)(holding that even if a proposed item for bargaining involves wages, hours, and other terms and conditions of employment, if item also involves matters of inherent managerial policy, public employer is not required to bargain on policy matter, although employer is required to meet and discuss issue with union).

employer, standards of service, its overall budget, the organizational structure and selection of new employees, examination techniques and direction of employees. Employers, however, shall be required to bargain collectively with regard to policy matters directly affecting wages, hours and terms and conditions of employment as well as the impact thereon upon request by employee representatives.[28]

Other statutes have outlined some rights of management and, at the same time, have precluded the public employer from any bargaining over specific items.[29] The Minnesota law, for example, states that "[a] public employer is not required

---

[28]Ill. Ann. Stat. ch. 48, par. 1604, §4 (Smith-Hurd); SLL (BNA) 23:215, 23:217. See Jenkins, "Collective Bargaining for Public Employees," 10 So. Ill. L. J. 483 (1983).

[29]Besides the statutes discussed in this section, see, e.g., the following (citations are to the "State Laws" (SLL) binders of BNA's Labor Relations Reporter): Florida, 19:209, 19:214a ("It is the right of the public employer to determine unilaterally the purpose of each of its constituent agencies, set standards of services to be offered to the public, and exercise control and discretion over its organization and operations."); Hawaii, 21:224, 21:233 ("Excluded from the subjects of negotiations are matters of classification and reclassification, . . . retirement benefits and the salary ranges and the number of incremental and longevity steps now provided by law, provided that the . . . amount of wages to be paid in each range and step and the length of service necessary for the incremental and longevity steps shall be negotiable. . . . The employer and the exclusive representative shall not agree to any proposal which would be inconsistent with merit principles or the principle of equal pay for equal work . . . ."); Indiana, 24:137, 24:140 (allowing, but not compelling, bargaining on curriculum development and revision; textbook selection; teaching methods; selection, assignment, and promotion of personnel; student discipline; expulsion or suspension of students; pupil-teacher ratio; and class size or budget appropriations. The Indiana Public Employees Collective Bargaining Act was repealed by P.L. 3, L. 1982, effective September 1, 1982.); Maine, 29:211, 29:213 (". . . except that by such [bargaining] obligation neither party shall be compelled to agree to a proposal or be required to make a concession and except that public employers of teachers shall meet and consult but not negotiate with respect to educational policies; . . . ."); Maryland, 30:215, 30:218 ("Employer Rights. . . . [I]t is the exclusive right of the employer to determine the mission of each of its constituent agencies, set standards of services to be offered to the public, and exercise control and direction over its organization and operations. It is also the right of the employer to direct its employees, to hire, promote, transfer, assign or retain employees in positions within an agency and in that regard to establish reasonable work rules. It also retains the right to suspend, demote, discharge or take any other appropriate disciplinary action against its employees for just cause, ... The provisions of this section shall be deemed to be part of every memorandum of understanding reached by the employer and an employee organization, ..."); New Hampshire, 39:101, 39:223 (excluding from bargaining (state employees) "managerial policy within the exclusive prerogative of the public employer by statute or regulations adopted pursuant to statute."); New Jersey, 40:245, 40:249 (removing from bargaining obligation "standards or criteria for employee performance."); Ohio, 45:217, 45:227 ("The employer is not required to bargain on subjects reserved to the management and direction of the governmental unit except as affect wages, hours, terms and conditions of employment, and the continuation, modification, or deletion of an existing provision of a collective bargaining agreement."); Virginia, 57:217, 57:221 ("The school board shall retain its exclusive final authority over matters concerning employment and supervision of its personnel, including dismissals, suspensions and placing on probation."); Wisconsin, 60:243 ("The employer shall not be required to bargain on subjects reserved to management and direction of the governmental unit except insofar as the manner of exercise of such functions affects the wages, hours and conditions of employment of employees.").

to meet and negotiate on matters of inherent managerial policy," which include, but are not limited to, "such areas of discretion or policy as the functions and programs of the employer, its overall budget, utilization of technology, the organizational structure, selection of personnel, and direction and number of personnel."[30] The statute goes on to provide that "[n]o public employer shall sign an agreement which limits its right to select persons to serve as supervisory employees or state managers under [the statute] or require the use of seniority in their selection."[31]

Similar results may be expected in those states without a bargaining law. For example, prior to the passage of a bargaining law in Illinois, the courts had recognized the authority of a school board to bargain on a permissive basis.[32] Certain rights, however, were held discretionary and were not delegable by a board of education, making the rights incapable of being restricted by the terms of a collective bargaining agreement.[33] Such rights included the right to grant a permanent contract to a teacher, or the right to adopt a program of study.[34]

---

[30]Minn. Stat. Ann. §179A.07 (West, 1983); SLL (BNA) 33:247, 33:248e. See Arrowhead Pub. Serv. Union v. City of Duluth, 336 N.W.2d 68, 116 LRRM 2187 (Minn., 1983)(decisions concerning city budget, programs, and organizational structure not subject to arbitration); Ogilvie v. Independent School Dist. 341, 329 N.W.2d 555 (Minn., 1983)(assignment of vocational agricultural teacher to teach part time in adjacent school inherent managerial policy decision); Minneapolis Ass'n of Adm'rs & Consultants v. Minneapolis Special School Dist. 1, 311 N.W.2d 474, 110 LRRM 2802 (Minn., 1981)(procedure for determining which supervisor positions were to be divested of administrative functions matter of inherent managerial policy). But see State, Court & Municipal Employees, Minnesota Arrowhead Dist. Council 96 v. St. Louis County, 290 N.W.2d 608, 106 LRRM 2635 (Minn., 1980)(holding public employer, faced with labor agreement requiring negotiation on new job classifications and wages for employees, mandated to bargain on matters of inherent managerial policy where voluntarily made object of negotiation).

[31]Minn. Stat. Ann. §179A.07 (West, 1985); see also State, County & Municipal Employees, Minnesota Arrowhead Dist. Council 96 v. St. Louis County, 290 N.W.2d 608, 106 LRRM 2635 (Minn., 1980). The Supreme Court of Massachusetts, in Boston Teachers Union Local 66 v. School Comm., 368 Mass. 197, 434 N.E.2d 1258, 117 LRRM 2727 (1982), held that a provision in a collective bargaining agreement providing that, during the first two years of the agreement, "any teacher or nurse with tenure or permanently appointed shall continue to be employed," restricted the ability of the employer to determine on an annual basis the size of its teaching staff and, thus, intruded into the area of exclusive managerial prerogatives.

[32]Chicago Div. of Ill. Educ. Ass'n v. Board of Educ., 76 Ill. App. 2d 456, 222 N.E.2d 243 (1966).

[33]Board of Educ. v. Chicago Teachers Union Local 1, 88 Ill. 2d 63, 430 N.E.2d 1111 (1981).

[34]See also Moravek v. Davenport Community School Dist., 262 N.W.2d 797, 98 LRRM 2923 (Iowa, 1978)(decision whether to employ or terminate teacher exclusively the subject of school board and not properly the subject of arbitration), overturned in Shenandoah Educ. Ass'n. v. Shenandoah Community School Dist., 337 N.W.2d 477, 114 LRRM 2699 (Iowa, 1983); City of Covington v. Police, Lodge No. 1, 112

What results is that the public-sector practitioner cannot be guided by the private-sector model when negotiating a management rights clause. In many states the statute requiring bargaining will not only reserve to management certain rights but will preclude any bargaining on specific issues. Other states will outline specific management rights but will, at the same time, mandate bargaining over "terms and conditions of employment." However, virtually every decision of a public employer concerning its employees impacts upon or affects terms and conditions of employment. To permit bargaining whenever a term or condition of employment is affected could emasculate managerial prerogatives and the intent of the statute. In discussing the conflict between managerial prerogatives and the employer's obligation to bargain over conditions of employment, one court reasoned as follows:

> The two conflicting principles cannot be reconciled by focusing solely upon the impact or effect of a managerial decision, . . . but, instead, the nature of the terms and conditions of employment must be considered in relation to the extent of their interference with managerial prerogatives. . . . Although a weighing or balancing must still be made, the court has sanctioned an analysis which focuses on the impact of each principle on the other.[35]

Accordingly, the public-sector practitioner must take special care to research applicable statutes and court decisions when engaging in bargaining, especially when the bargaining is over rights traditionally reserved to management.

Federal Restrictions

Title VII of the Civil Service Reform Act of 1978, as amended,[36] contains the first statutory scheme governing labor relations between federal agencies and their employees. The statute accords federal employees the right "to engage in collective bargaining [through chosen representatives] with respect to conditions of employment." Federal agencies have a corresponding duty "[to] negotiate in good faith [with the

---

LRRM 3255 (Ky., 1981)(bargaining agreement invalid as unconstitutional delegation of legislative power where arbitration provision delegated "entire spectrum of police affairs" to neutral).
    [35]Ramapo-Indian Hills Educ. Ass'n. v. Board of Educ., 112 LRRM 2062, 2065 (N.J., 1980).
    [36]5 U.S.C. §7101 et seq. (Supp. V, 1981).

bargaining representative] for the purpose of arriving at a collective bargaining agreement." While an agency's obligation to bargain includes "matters which are the subject of . . . [an agency's] rule or regulation," there are specific exceptions outlined in the statute.[37] Included in the Act is a management rights section that enumerates specific rights to the agency-employer, but permits the agency to elect to bargain over certain of these rights. In relevant part the statute declares:

7106. Management rights
(a) Subject to subsection (b) of this section, nothing in this chapter shall affect the authority of any management official of any agency—
(1) to determine the mission, budget, organization, number of employees, and internal security practices of the agency; and
(2) in accordance with applicable laws—
(A) to hire, assign, direct, layoff, and retain employees in the agency, or to suspend, remove, reduce in grade or pay, or take other disciplinary action against such employees;
(B) to assign work, to make determinations with respect to contracting out, and to determine the personnel by which agency operations shall be conducted;
(C) with respect to filling positions, to make selections for appointments from—
(i) among properly ranked and certified candidates for promotion; or
(ii) any other appropriate source; and
(D) to take whatever actions may be necessary to carry out the agency mission during emergencies.
(b) Nothing in this section shall preclude any agency and any labor organization from negotiating—
(1) at the election of the agency, on the numbers, types and grades of employees or positions assigned to any organizational subdivision, work project, or tour of duty, or on the technology, methods, and means of performing work;
(2) procedures which management officials of the agency will observe in exercising any authority under this section; or
(3) appropriate arrangements for employees adversely affected by the exercise of any authority under this section by such management officials.[38]

In *Department of Justice v. FLRA*,[39] the Fifth Circuit ex-

---

[37] 5 U.S.C. §1703(a)(12) and §7106.
[38] 5 U.S.C. §7106.
[39] 727 F.2d 481, 115 LRRM 3499 (CA 5, 1984).

amined the scheme of management rights under the statute, stating:

> In analyzing the management rights set out in section 7106, it can be seen that these rights are to be placed in at least three general categories: first, in 7106(a), subjects which may not be negotiated and to which management's absolute right may not be diminished pursuant to any collective bargaining agreement; second, in 7106(b)(1), subjects which the agency may elect to negotiate or not to negotiate with a labor organization; and third, in 7106(b)(2) and (3), subjects which are negotiable.
>
> Generally, subsection (a) sets out management's rights which are absolute and non-negotiable *but* subject to some expressly limited exceptions carved out of these broad rights in subsection (b). For instance, although management has the absolute and unilateral authority to assign employees, to assign their work, and to direct this work, the agency may, pursuant to the provisions of subsection (b)(1), elect to negotiate on the "numbers, types and grades of employees" or "positions assigned" or "the methods of performing work," and may embody such an agreement reached by the parties in a collective bargaining agreement. If such an agreement were reached, management would have waived its right with respect to such matters for the duration of the collective bargaining agreement.[40]

The Ninth Circuit, in *Navy Public Works Center v. FLRA*,[41] stated that "application of section 7106 turns upon the elusive distinction between substantive and procedural proposals." Quoting the court:

> This distinction is always troublesome because each type extended unduly diminishes the scope of the other. In addition, the distinction frequently will not be clear. On the one hand, unions could use procedural language in framing proposals, the impact of which would be primarily substantive. . . . On the other hand, federal employers could assert as a management prerogative the authority to act in a manner totally inconsistent with proposals designed to provide bona fide procedural protections. In each case, the federal agencies and courts must attempt to fix the limits of "the range of proposals to be deemed 'procedural' " within the contemplation of the statute.[42]

One test often used to determine if a proposal constitutes a "procedure" under Section 7106(b)(2) is whether "implementation would 'directly interfere with the agency's basic

---

[40]115 LRRM at 3503 (emphasis in original).
[41]678 F.2d 97, 110 LRRM 2570 (CA 9, 1982).
[42]110 LRRM at 2571–72. See also the discussion of the D.C. Circuit in Department of Defense v. FLRA, 659 F.2d 1140, 107 LRRM 2901 (1981), cert denied, 455 U.S. 945, 109 LRRM 2779 (1982).

right [reserved] under section 7106(a).' "[43] Under this test, a proposal involves a nonnegotiable substantive right if it would "directly interfere" with management's ability to make the relevant determination.

A more common test to determine the validity of terming the proposal a "procedure" under the statute is whether it would prevent the agency from "acting at all" on the personnel limitation at issue. Thus, in *Veterans Administration Medical Center v. FLRA*,[44] the Eleventh Circuit held "procedural" a union proposal that would stay a proposed personnel action which had been made the subject of a grievance or arbitration, saying the proposal was a mandatory subject of bargaining since it did not preclude the agency from "acting at all." The Ninth Circuit has ruled that a proposal giving employees the right to remain silent during a disciplinary investigation was nonnegotiable. The court reasoned that a proposal which to a significant degree relieves an employee of a duty to account to his superiors does not make the government more efficient and accountable.[45]

A study of the legislative history and subsequent court decisions, as well as arbitrators' decisions,[46] interpreting the scheme of management rights under the statute indicates that

---

[43]Government Employees Local 2782 v. FLRA, 702 F.2d 1183, 112 LRRM 3112, 3114 (CA DC, 1983); Government Employees Local 32 v. FLRA, 728 F.2d 1526, 115 LRRM 3343 (CA DC, 1984).

[44]675 F.2d 260, 110 LRRM 2465 (CA 11, 1982).

[45]Navy Public Works Center v. FLRA, 678 F.2d 97, 110 LRRM 2570 (CA 9, 1982). See also Treasury Employees v. FLRA, 691 F.2d 553, 111 LRRM 2540 (CA DC, 1982)(promulgation of performance standards for federal civil service employees and identification of critical job elements nonmandatory subject of bargaining); Internal Revenue Serv. v. FLRA, 717 F.2d 1174, 114 LRRM 2795, 2796 (CA 7, 1983)(agency did not engage in unfair labor practice when it refused to bargain over design and location of office space); Department of Defense v. FLRA, 659 F.2d 1140, 107 LRRM 2901 (CA DC, 1981), cert. denied, 455 U.S. 945, 109 LRRM 2779 (1982)(proposal to stay removal or suspension of employee pending exhaustion of grievance procedure negotiable as "procedural" question); EEOC v. FLRA, 744 F.2d 842, 117 LRRM 2625 (CA DC, 1984)(agency required to bargain over union's proposal regarding agency's compliance with applicable laws and regulations concerning contracting out).

[46]See, e.g., Immigration & Naturalization Serv., 77 LA 638 (Weckstein, 1981)(applying §7106(b)(1); Department of Air Force, 82 LA 593 (Wann, 1984)(Applying Civil Service Reform Act (CSRA) to grievance involving separation of probationary employee); James A. Haley Veteran's Hosp., 82 LA 973 (Wahl, 1984)(probationary employees); U.S. Gov't Printing Office, 82 LA 78 (Feldesman, 1984)(applying exclusionary rule under CSRA); Department of the Army, 82 LA 1133 (Schubert, 1984)(applying §7106(a)(2)(B) in resolving subcontracting grievance); United States Penitentiary, 82 LA 939 (Yarowsky, 1984)(applying §7121(c)(4) which excludes from any negotiated grievance procedure disputes over "any examination, certification, or appointment"); U.S. Army III Corp., 80 LA 148 (Schedler, 1982)(holding agency may revise leave regulations without negotiating revisions); Department of Defense Dependents Schools, 78 LA 815 (Gilson, 1982)(right to assign or transfer employees).

Section 7106(b) clarifies rather than limits the scope of management rights under Section 7106(a).[47] The result is that reviewing courts have reflected a sensitivity to a need to "preserve the Federal Government's ability to operate in an effective and efficient manner."[48] Indeed, the statute itself mandates that the Act "should be interpreted in a manner consistent with the requirement of an effective and efficient government."[49] Public-sector labor organizations have, accordingly, been restrained in negotiating substantive limitations on the rights of management outlined in Section 7106(a).

---

[47]Government Employees Local 32 v. FLRA, 728 F.2d 1526, 115 LRRM 3343, 3344 (CA DC, 1984).

[48]For a discussion of the legislative history of the management rights provision, see Treasury Employees v. FLRA, 691 F.2d 553, 111 LRRM 2540 (CA DC, 1982).

[49]5 U.S.C. §7101(b).

Part II

Employee Privacy Concerns

Chapter 6

Dress and Grooming Codes

Arbitrator Clair Duff has pointed out that "there is no rule of dress that does not in some way inhibit the personal freedom of the employee."[1] Most arbitrators agree that even where the parties' agreement is silent on the matter management has the right to promulgate and enforce reasonable rules relating to employees' dress and grooming while at work.

Dress Codes

These rules may designate the type of clothing or uniform that must be worn by employees or, alternatively, types of clothing that may not be worn at work. When dress or grooming rules are challenged in a grievance, the arbitrator's task is to determine whether a particular restriction is necessary to serve a legitimate business interest of the employer. One arbitrator stated the general rule as follows:

> Ordinarily, while at work, employees have the right to dress as they choose, within the limits of common sense and decency, since choice of one's individual clothing is personal in nature. An employer cannot exercise its managerial rights in a manner which infringes upon or impairs the personal right of employees to select their clothing unless there is a controlling contract provision or past practice, or unless employee dress has an effect on the employer's business or health and safety.[2]

---

[1]Southern Bell Tel. & Tel. Co., 74 LA 1115, 1116 (1980).
[2]County of Cattaraugus, 77 LA 1027, 1029 (Denson, 1981) (upholding requirement of pink or combination of pink and white attire for nurse's aides). See also General Foods Corp., 76 LA 532 (Denson, 1981)(upholding rule prohibiting wearing of wedding rings).

Arbitrators have been particularly receptive to sustaining dress and grooming codes where employees are required to have contact with the general public. Arbitrator Duff, in *Southern Bell Telephone & Telegraph Co.*,[3] in upholding a rule prohibiting coin-telephone collectors from wearing shorts while on duty, recognized "company image" as a legitimate concern of management. Arbitrator Duff commented:

> Employers are not the censors of clothing fashions or preferences of [their] employees, and therefore, any dress and appearance regulations are not valid unless they are reasonably necessary to serve some legitimate business interest of the employer. The style of clothing that is worn by Company employees in their off-duty hours is of course a matter of their personal preference. Where any employee is frequently in direct contact with the public he represents the corporate entity in that business relationship. He is the personification of the Company to those persons who observe him and so it is essential that he project an appropriate image by maintaining a pleasing personal appearance.[4]

Duff went on to declare:

> Whimsical rules based strictly on caprice or the subjective preference of a supervisor are not reasonable but each such case must be determined on the totality of the circumstances.[5]

In another "image" case, Arbitrator Thomas Christopher, in *Mister A's Restaurant*,[6] recognized that "companies providing a service to the public have the right to protect their image." Upholding a rule that cocktail waitresses have blond hair or wear a blond wig "in the classical Roman or Grecian mode," the arbitrator applied the following balancing test:

> Any rule governing an employee's appearance must consider the impact the rule may have on the employee's freedom of expression. Such consideration balances the Company's desire to portray a special image against the employee's right to be free from unreasonable restrictions on her appearance. "If the nature of the business is such that its sales are highly sensitive to the image portrayed, the balance tends to weigh heavily in favor of the Employer."[7]

The arbitrator found that while the hair-color requirement

---

[3]74 LA 1115 (1980).
[4]Id. at 1116.
[5]Id. See also Allegheny County Port Auth., 58 LA 165 (Duff, 1971).
[6]80 LA 1104 (1983).
[7]Id. at 1105, citing Arrow Redi-Mix Concrete, Inc., 56 LA 597 (Fleischli, 1971).

was troublesome for employees, it did not affect the employee's appearance off the job since those employees who did not want to change the color of their hair could purchase a wig. The employer was not mandated, according to the arbitrator, to reimburse employees for the costs of wigs.

While management is accorded considerable discretion in its authority to designate dress codes, this power is not absolute. Many arbitrators will, in effect, substitute their judgment for that of management when it appears that the dress code is unreasonable. Arbitrator Sidney Wolff, in *Oxford Nursing Home*,[8] held unreasonable a 20-year old dress code requiring that female nursing personnel wear white dresses, white shoes, and stockings (male nursing personnel were required to wear white pants, white shirts, and black shoes). Saying that "an unreasonable exercise of Management's rights should not be enforced," Arbitrator Wolff declared that management "should have no difficulty in moving ahead with the times and relaxing its rules so as to grant its female nursing personnel the choice of pant-suits [or] dress uniforms while on duty."[9]

Arbitrator James Jones, Jr., in holding that a transit service could not prohibit bus operators from wearing reflecting or "mirror-type" sunglasses, clearly placed the burden on the employer to show that the prohibition against mirrored glasses was related to increased ridership. The arbitrator pointed out that the employer received no complaints, conducted no surveys, and gathered no data in support of its claim that maintenance of the rule was necessary to increased ridership and to facilitate the relationship between riders and operators. The arbitrator commented, "It is not enough for the Company to assert that a 'possible' negative impact on its business is sufficiently protected under the management rights clause to make the rule reasonable."[10]

Some collective bargaining agreements require employees to wear uniforms that are provided by the employer. The fact that an employer may impose dress and grooming requirements does not mean that it has unlimited discretion to require a particular type of uniform. Thus, where an employer required a lobby attendant to wear a uniform that was "re-

---

[8]75 LA 1300 (1980).
[9]Id. at 1301.
[10]Milwaukee Transp. Serv., Inc., 77 LA 807, 813 (1981).

vealing and sexually provocative" to the point that the attendant was subjected to sexual harassment, one federal court ruled that the discharge for refusal to continue to wear the uniform violated Title VII.[11]

Other contracts provide for partial or total reimbursement for uniform items and the issue will be whether a particular piece of clothing is part of a uniform. If the item of clothing is an article of usual street wear it is usually not considered part of a uniform subject to reimbursement.[12] Where the employer effects a change in the uniform, however, a usual "streetwear" item may be eligible for reimbursement. In *Cook United, Inc.*,[13] Arbitrator Orville Andrews ruled that a retail store was obligated to provide white shirts it required its male employees to wear in substitution for blue shirts where, in the past, the company had furnished all shirts required to be worn as part of a dress code. As to the remedy issue, the arbitrator had this to say:

> I have given considerable consideration as to whether those employees who purchased shirts at the employer's insistence should be reimbursed for the cost of such shirts. It is clear that under the facts of this case the employer was obligated to furnish the white shirts. Discipline and threats of discipline were applied to obtain compliance with the new dress code.
>
> This arbitrator, like most, has often said to employees that they have an obligation to comply with even questionable orders and then obtain relief through the grievance procedure and arbitration. These employees have complied with the comply now, grieve later doctrine, and they should not be penalized for having done so. I shall require the employer to reimburse those employees who purchased white shirts at the direction and insistence of supervision.[14]

As indicated by Arbitrator Andrews, with few exceptions[15] arbitrators have ruled that an employee who believes that a dress code is unreasonable will be required to pursue his or her complaint through the negotiated grievance pro-

---

[11]EEOC v. Sage Realty Corp., 507 F.Supp. 599, 24 FEP 1521 (S.D.N.Y., 1981); see also Marentette v. Michigan Host, Inc., 506 F.Supp. 909, 24 FEP 1665 (E.D. Mich., 1980)(dicta).

[12]Hotel Bancroft, 78 LA 819 (Wolff, 1982); Metropolitan Medical Center, 82 LA 538 (Miller, 1984)(uniform allowance not controlling where employer's policy required only that special attire be purchased and worn by employees). But see Riley Gear Corp., 69 LA 1186 (Goodman, 1977)(upholding uniform allowance for wearing of blue jeans as "work clothes" reimbursed by employer).

[13]74 LA 1136 (1980).

[14]Id. at 1139.

[15]Mitchell-Bentley Corp., 45 LA 1071 (Ryder, 1965).

cedure rather than simply defy management's rule. Failure to do so may result in denial of the grievance or a partial or total reduction in back pay.[16] Arbitrator James Duff stated the better rule as follows:

> When the Grievants chose to defy the instructions they were given [to remove T-shirts with letters spelling "THIS PLACE SUCKS"] on the day or days in question and to resort to unauthorized self-help to protest what they considered to be the unreasonableness of the instructions, they acted insubordinately and subjected themselves to appropriate penalties. This is so even though their underlying positions may well have some merit. Therefore, against this factual backdrop, the undersigned is powerless to disturb the suspensions Management imposed upon them.[17]

Identification Tags

Many employers have required their workers to display name or other identification tags while working. Illustrative is *Michigan Consolidated Gas Co.*,[18] a case reported by Arbitrator David Keefe. When a gas company required employees to display their surnames on their uniforms, Arbitrator Keefe held that it was a unilateral change in a term or condition of employment and thus improper. Notably, the arbitrator also found the requirement impermissible because it could expose an employee to abuse or ridicule. Although Arbitrator Keefe recognized management's right to require that employees carry proper identification, the wearing of a surname on a jacket and shirt was viewed as burdensome. The arbitrator noted:

> The protested surname display constitutes a recognizable and material change in the working conditions of employees which can believably be expected, under entirely plausible and predictable circumstances, to have adverse reactions on the peace-of-mind, personal security and family privacy of at least certain individuals, thereby subjecting them to unjustifiable and avoid-

---

[16]See Hill & Sinicropi, "Reductions for 'Self-Help,'" Remedies in Arbitration, 88–91 (BNA Books, 1981).

[17]True Temper Corp., 76 LA 1, 2–3 (1980); see also Arkansas Glass Container Corp., 76 LA 841 (Teple, 1981)(reinstatement without back pay); Lone Star Div., Day & Zimmerman, Inc., 44 LA 385 (Boles, 1965); Olin's, Inc., 41 LA 562, 565 (Black, 1963)("Grievants all deliberately refused to obey a direct order of their supervisor when they refused to wear the candy-striped dress. They continued unwilling to obey the order at the hearing. They should have protested by use of the grievance procedure rather than defying the order of their supervisor.").

[18]53 LA 525 (1969).

able hardship and inconvenience—if not outright personal hazard.[19]

A similar privacy argument was rejected by Arbitrator Robert Stutz in *City of Boston*.[20] The arbitrator ruled that the city did not violate the safety provisions of the agreement by requiring police officers to wear name tags on their uniforms. It was pointed out that in the 31 largest cities that had responded to an employer's survey, 29 departments were using name tags and planned to continue using them. Arbitrator Stutz also reasoned that the name tags aided in improving relations between the police and the public.

Arbitrator Robert Mueller, in *Briggs & Stratton Corp.*,[21] held that an employer had the right to institute an identification card program that required an employee's picture, social security number, and date of birth to be posted on a metal badge. Rejecting the argument that such information was an invasion of an employee's right to privacy, the arbitrator stated that "the matter of an employer requiring some form of identification of its employees, is one that is generally regarded as a unilateral management right in the first instance."[22]

This decision represents the better view on this subject. Where identification schemes have been challenged by unions as invasions of the privacy interests of the bargaining unit, the reported decisions reveal that arbitrators balance the interests of the employer against the privacy concerns of the employees. At a minimum, arbitrators uphold the employer's right to insist that employees carry information identifying them as members of the company's work force. Arbitrator David Keefe stated:

> [The issue] does not encompass a challenge to the Company's right to compel employees to carry official ID information, verifying their status as members of the Company's personnel. This is a right which Management generally (this company included) possesses inherently as a natural and necessary means for enforcing order in the work force, when, as is most common, rules are promulgated by the Company, rather than negotiated with the Union.[23]

---

[19]Id. at 529.
[20]55 LA 910 (1970).
[21]77 LA 233 (1981).
[22]Id. at 235.
[23]Michigan Consol. Gas Co., 53 LA 525, 529 (1969).

Beyond this, it is unclear to what extent an employer can require its work force to publicly display personal identification. Each case must be decided on its own facts.

Grooming Codes

As in the dress cases, the task for the arbitrator in most grooming cases is to strike a balance between the employer's desire for a particular grooming standard and the employees' preferences in this regard. Most arbitrators agree that employee preferences cannot be transgressed absent compelling reasons.[24] Arbitrators have not, however, accepted the argument that an employee's preference as to hair and beard styles should be considered as a constitutional or civil right of self-expression.[25]

In *Roskam Baking Co.*,[26] an arbitrator ruled that a bakery improperly discharged employees for refusing to cut their long hair after the employer had changed the grooming code, which previously had allowed employees to wear a hair net. The arbitrator found that no sanitary problems would result from wearing hair nets. Furthermore, the grievants were not dealing with customers and so the company's image was not adversely affected by the rule.

Where the concern of the employer is its "public image," arbitrators have generally accorded great deference to the employer's grooming standards. In this regard arbitrators have enforced prohibitions against facial hair for delivery personnel,[27] body-fender repairmen,[28] meter enforcement officers,[29] tank maintenance workers,[30] and grocery clerks.[31] This "deference" is especially likely in operations where legitimate safety and health concerns are involved[32] or in the private security

---

[24]Allied Chem. Corp., 74 LA 412, 416 (Eischen, 1980); International Minerals & Chem. Corp., 78 LA 682 (Jones, 1982).

[25]In this regard see Valtin, "Changing Life Styles and Problems of Authority in the Plant," Proceedings of the 25th Annual Meeting of NAA, 235–252 (BNA Books, 1972).

[26]79 LA 993 (Beitner, 1982).

[27]Albertsons, Inc., 77 LA 705 (Hulsey, 1981).

[28]Lloyd Ketcham Oldsmobile, 77 LA 953 (Hilgert, 1981).

[29]City of Cincinnati, 75 LA 1261 (Seifer, 1980).

[30]Arkansas Glass Container Corp., 76 LA 841 (Teple, 1981).

[31]Safeway Stores, Inc., 75 LA 798 (Madden, 1980).

[32]Kellogg Co., 55 LA 84 (Shearer, 1970); Pacific Sw. Airlines, 77 LA 320 (Jones, 1981)(airline had right to prohibit pilot from wearing beard where breathing device may not function properly).

industry, where "image" is considered important by management.

When grooming regulations are struck down by arbitrators, it is usually because the standard is unreasonable as applied to a particular employee (or group of employees), and not because the regulations are per se unreasonable. Thus Arbitrator E. J. Forsythe, in *Frito-Lay, Inc.*,[33] found "unreasonable" a no-beard rule for a route salesman operating in a rural community near a college where the wearing of beards was not unusual (salesmen were permitted to wear beards during the three-month deer season as an accommodation to local tradition). Another arbitrator expressed this principle as follows:

> [I]n rejecting the Grievants' claim for exemption, Management made its facial hair policy into . . . [a] sort of blanket rule . . . . But such blanket rules are arbitrary. A facial hair policy affects how a worker looks in his non-work activities as well as his on the job appearance. Where the health or safety of the worker, of others, or of property necessitates a rule, it is reasonable even if it has an impact on the worker's life outside the job. But where a rule has such an impact, administrative convenience alone is not an adequate justification for its existence if in fact it does not materially add to the protection of health or safety.[34]

Laxity in enforcing dress or grooming regulations may also preclude management from disciplining an employee for noncompliance. In one case an arbitrator found employer "acquiescence and acceptance of beards" where the union demonstrated non-enforcement of a grooming code. As a remedy the arbitrator allowed the employer the right to enforce its grooming code against all new employees but not against the grievant or any employee already wearing a beard.[35]

As in other cases where the reasonableness of rules is challenged in the grievance procedure,[36] arbitrators should be ever mindful of limiting provisions in the collective bargaining agreement. Illustrative is an award involving an employer's safety rule requiring employees to be clean shaven over

---

[33]81-2 ARB ¶8562 (1981).

[34]Union Carbide Corp., 82 LA 1084, 1089 (Goldman, 1984).

[35]Rosauer's, Inc., 82-2 ARB ¶8594 (LaCugna, 1982). See also Beatrice Foods Co., Butterkrust Bakeries Div., 77 LA 44 (Kulkis, 1981); United States Dep't of Justice, 81-2 ARB ¶8607 (Meiners, 1981).

[36]See "Reasonableness" in Chapter 3, supra, for a general discussion on the reasonableness criterion as it relates to the rule-making authority of management.

the facial area where a respirator would be worn. When four employees refused to shave, the company terminated their employment. Concluding that the employer did not establish that the rule was fair, reasonable, and contractual (the rule was formulated by a management directive), the arbitrator ordered reinstatement, although he found that the grievants had violated the "obey now, grieve later" principle and penalized each of them with one month's loss of pay. The Eighth Circuit, reversing the district court, vacated the award. It pointed out that the arbitrator expressly found that the grievants violated the agreement by refusing to obey the rule. Under the parties' contract the arbitrator was without authority to determine whether the discipline was appropriate. The appellate court said that "if the employees had obeyed the rule and followed the grievance procedure, it would be a different case," and in that situation "the central issue before the arbitrator would have been the reasonableness of the rule; there would not have been a question about the employees' behavior."[37]

Discriminatory Standards

When an employer applies a dress or grooming code to members of one sex and not the other, not only is the rule likely to be invalidated by an arbitrator but, more importantly, a violation of Title VII may result.[38] Similarly, where a dress or grooming code imposes a more "defined" standard of uniformity on female employees than male employees, a violation of the statute has been found.[39]

When confronted with claims by employees that distinctions in dress requirements are discriminatory, the better weight of arbitral and judicial authority holds that different standards of dress are not discriminatory so long as employment

[37]Riceland Foods, Inc. v. Carpenters Local 2381, 737 F.2d 758, 116 LRRM 2948, 2949–50 (CA 8, 1984), different results reached on reh'g en banc, 749 F.2d 1260, 117 LRRM 3397, cert. denied, 471 U.S. ___, 119 LRRM 2248 (1985).
[38]Laffey v. Northwest Airlines, 366 F.Supp. 763, 6 FEP 902 (CA DC, 1973) (requirement forbidding only female cabin attendants to wear eyeglasses violative of Title VII); EEOC v. Clayton Fed. Sav. & Loan Ass'n, 25 FEP 841 (E.D. Mo., 1981).
[39]Carroll v. Talman Fed. Sav. & Loan of Chicago, 604 F.2d 1028, 20 FEP 764 (CA 7, 1979), cert. denied, 445 U.S. 929, 22 FEP 315 (1980)(requirement of "career ensemble" for females and business suits for males discriminatory under Title VII); Gerdom v. Continental Airlines, 692 F.2d 602, 30 FEP 235 (CA 9, 1982)(policy of requiring only female category of flight attendants to comply with weight requirements violative of Title VII).

opportunities of one sex are not disadvantaged relative to the
other sex. Thus in *Fountain v. Safeway Stores, Inc.*,[40] the Ninth
Circuit ruled that there was no violation of Title VII, upholding the dismissal of a male employee for failure to wear a tie
even though no such requirement was made of females.[41] Other
circuits reason that grooming and dress requirements do not
violate Title VII unless the requirements are based on immutable sex characteristics or affect constitutionally protected
activities such as marriage or child-rearing, which present
insurmountable obstacles to one gender.[42] Under this standard it would not be impermissible for an employer to enforce
a no-beard regulation, although the rule clearly would have
a disparate impact upon male employees. A beard is not an
"immutable" trait of being male, nor is it a constitutionally
protected activity.[43]

Although a particular dress or grooming code may not be
discriminatory on the basis of sex, the employer must take
note that any regulations do not have a disparate impact on
the basis of religion[44] or race.[45]

Summary

Formulating and enforcing personal dress or grooming
standards for employees is a valid exercise of managerial pre-

[40]555 F.2d 753, 15 FEP 96 (CA 9, 1977).
[41]See also Barker v. Taft Broadcasting Co., 549 F.2d 400, 14 FEP 697 (CA 6,
1977)(grooming codes requiring different lengths of hair for men and women not
violative of statute); Knott v. Missouri Pac. Ry., 527 F.2d 1249, 11 FEP 1231 (CA 8,
1975)(permitting employer's limitation on hair length of male but not female employees); Rogers v. American Airlines, 527 F.Supp. 229, 27 FEP 694 (S.D.N.Y.,
1981)(restriction on wearing "all-braided" hairstyle not violative of prohibitions on
the basis of sex or race); Carswell v. Peachford Hosp., 27 FEP 698 (N.D. Ga.,
1981)(employee dismissed for wearing "corn row" hair style in violation of hospital
policy not entitled to relief under Title VII's proscriptions against race and sex discrimination).
[42]See, e.g., Sprogis v. United Air Lines, 444 F.2d 1194, 3 FEP 621 (CA 7), cert.
denied, 404 U.S. 991, 4 FEP 37 (1971)(unlawful to restrict employment of married
females but not married males, even though most flight attendants female); Wil-
lingham v. Macon Tel. Pub. Co., 507 F.2d 1084, 9 FEP 189 (CA 5, 1975)(grooming
regulation applicable to males with long hair not sex-based discrimination since
employer applied personal grooming code to all employees); Earwood v. Continental
S.E. Lines, Inc., 539 F.2d 1349 (CA 4, 1976)(dicta).
[43]Kelley v. Johnson, 425 U.S. 238 (1976)(upholding hair-grooming regulation for
police officers against constitutional challenge of deprivation of "liberty" interest).
[44]EEOC v. Electronic Data Sys., 31 FEP 588 (W.D. Wash., 1983). See also Louisville Water Co., 80 LA 957 (Hunter, 1983)(upholding discharge for refusing to wear
"man's apparel"; Alameda-Contra Costa Transit Dist., 75 LA 1273 (Randall,
1980)(discharging bus driver for wearing turban).
[45]Haynes v. E.I. DuPont de Nemours & Co., 33 FEP 496 (S.D. Texas, 1983).

rogatives so long as the rules are reasonably related to a legitimate business objective. In determining whether a particular dress or grooming standard is reasonable, arbitrators engage in a balancing process that takes into account the standards of the particular business and industry, as well as the parties' past practice.[46]

Where the employer's rule is based on health or safety considerations, or some other legitimate business interest proven by specific evidence of customer complaints or lost business, and is administered in a nondiscriminatory manner, the regulation can be expected to be affirmed if challenged as an improper exercise of managerial discretion in an arbitral proceeding. A dress or grooming standard that is based only on the personal preference of a particular individual within the organization will, in all probability, not survive a "reasonableness" challenge in the grievance procedure.[47] Perhaps the best summary of current arbitral standards is provided by Arbitrator Peter Maniscalco where he observed:

> The prevailing theory is that the Company has a right to require its employees to cut their hair and shave, when long hair and beards can reasonably threaten the Company's relations with its customers or other employees, or a real question of safety is involved, and an employer should be able to expect that his employees will practice personal hygiene and will clothe themselves in a neat manner, at least where the employees meet the public.
>
> However, there must be a showing of a reasonable relationship between the Company's image or health and safety considerations and the need to regulate employee appearance. Therefore, management's right to regulate in this area is not absolute. Its exercise in any specific manner may be challenged as arbitrary, capricious or inconsistent with the objective for which the right is being exercised.[48]

With respect to Title VII considerations, the courts have taken a "common sense" approach and have recognized man-

---

[46]Meat Cutters Local 494 v. Rosauer's Super Mkts., Inc., 29 Wash. App. 150, 627 P.2d 1330, 107 LRRM 2338 (Wash. Ct. App., 1981)(holding that an employer's adoption of an appearance rule 30 days after execution of collective bargaining agreement was arbitrable where parties' past practice had been to allow meat cutters to wear beards).

[47]See, e.g., the discussion by Arbitrator George Fleischli in Arrow Redi-Mix Concrete, Inc., 56 LA 597 (1971)("The arbitrator does not consider such personal likes or dislikes to be a legitimate basis for the establishment of a rule that impinges on the conduct of employees both on and off the job.").

[48]Missouri Pub. Serv. Co., 77 LA 973, 976 (1981).

agement's right to formulate and enforce dress and grooming codes, even where the employer's only interest is enhancing its image with the public. The D.C. Circuit stated:

> Perhaps no facet of business life is more important than a company's place in public estimation. That the image created by its employees dealing with the public when on company assignment affects its relations is so well known that we may take judicial notice of an employer's proper desire to achieve favorable acceptance. Good grooming regulations reflect a company's policy in our highly competitive business environment. Reasonable requirements in furtherance of that policy are an aspect of managerial responsibility.[49]

The statute was never intended to interfere in the promulgation and enforcement of nondiscriminatory personal appearance regulations by employers.[50] An employer may require male employees to adhere to different modes of dress and grooming than those required of female employees and not run afoul of the statute.

---

[49]Fagan v. National Cash Register Co., 481 F.2d 1115, 5 FEP 1335, 1341–42 (D.C. Cir., 1973); Lanigan v. Bartlett & Co. Grain, 466 F.Supp. 1388, 19 FEP 1039, 1041 (W.D. Mo., 1979)("The decision to project a certain image as one aspect of company policy is the employer's prerogative which employees may accept or reject. If they choose to reject the policy, they are subject to such sanctions as deemed appropriate by the company. An employer is simply not required to account for personal preferences with respect to dress and grooming standards.").
[50]Craft v. Metromedia, Inc., 572 F.Supp. 868, 33 FEP 153, 160 (W.D. Mo., 1983).

Chapter 7

Medical Screening

There is rising interest on the part of management in the use of screening, testing, and security programs[1] to identify medically unfit and drug-using employees.[2] The impact of worker's compensation claims and the epidemic-like spread of Acquired Immune Deficiency Syndrome (AIDS) has resulted in a realization on the part of employers (and their insurance companies) of the importance of medical screening. At the same time, more employers believe that behavioral and psychological factors may affect an individual's ability to function in a particular job and, accordingly, many employees are periodically required to undergo psychological or personality testing. Moreover, drug use and drug testing are on the increase.[3] With respect to testing, no occupation or group seems immune from managerial scrutiny. Professional baseball players have been invited by the Commissioner to submit to periodic drug testing (so far, they have declined the invita-

---

[1]Common security measures include interrogation; polygraph examinations; surveillance; and auto, locker, desk, or personal searches. These are discussed in Chapter 9, infra.

[2]See Rothstein, Medical Screening of Workers (BNA Books, 1984); Denenberg & Denenberg, Alcohol and Drugs: Issues in the Workplace (BNA Books, 1983); Williamson, "The Arbitration of Drug Abuse Cases: An Industrial Relations Perspective," Proceedings of the 36th Annual Meeting of NAA, 120 (BNA Books, 1984).

[3]In his article "Legal Issues Raised by Drugs in the Workplace," 36 Lab. L. J. No. 1, 42–54 (1985), Peter Susser points out that the National Institute on Drug Abuse reported in 1982 that 33 percent of Americans over the age of 12 have used marijuana, cocaine, heroin, hallucinogens, or psychotherapeutic drugs for nonmedical purposes at some time, compared to 4% in 1962. Also, in the three-year period between 1979 and 1982, cocaine use by those over the age of 26 had doubled. Id. at 43, citing N.Y. Times, March 21, 1983, at A-1. See also "Some Federal Agencies Given Broad New Powers to Screen Employees for Suspected Drug Use," 23 Gov't Empl. Rel. Rep. 615 (BNA), (April 29, 1985).

tion). Even a New Jersey school board has voted to subject students to urinalysis testing in a search for drug users.[4]

Three types of medical screening are considered in this section: (1) physical examinations, (2) psychological testing, and (3) drug and alcohol testing. The major focus is management's right to compel an employee to undergo some type of medical or psychological screening process, although attention is also directed to dissemination of medical information obtained from employee examinations.

Physical Examinations

Absent specific contractual language to the contrary, there is no serious dispute that management has the inherent right to use reasonable tests in determining the qualifications of an employee for a job. The better rule has been stated by one arbitrator as follows:

> [I]t is implicit that Management may use tests to assist in determining the qualifications of an employee for a job if the responsibility for making the determination of qualifications is Management's, if the tests are reasonably adapted to the measurement of the requirements of a given job, and if they are used fairly and reasonably for this purpose.[5]

In this respect most arbitrators hold that management has the power to require its employees, as a condition of initial or continued employment, to submit to a physical examination. Management assumes contractual and, in certain cases, even statutory or common-law tort liability for the injuries caused by its work force; an employer's right to request a medical examination is therefore rarely questioned. Many agreements will specifically declare that management has the right to require an employee to undergo a physical examination,[6] but where the agreement is silent, labor arbitrators have ruled that the right is held by management as either a

---

[4]"Putting Them All to the Test," Time, October 21, 1985, at 61. "Sniffer dogs" have also been used in the war against drug abuse by students. See, e.g., Jones v. Latexo Indep. School Dist., 499 F.Supp. 223 (E.D. Texas, 1980)(holding unconstitutional "sweeping, undifferentiated, and indiscriminate" scope of "sniffer dog" search of students, noting that dog replaced, rather than enhanced, the perceptive abilities of school officials).
[5]Caradco, Inc., 35 LA 169, 172 (Graff, 1960).
[6]See, e.g., Welshhons v. Sivyer Steel Corp., 674 F.2d 748, 110 LRRM 2311 (CA 8, 1982) Birmingham-Jefferson County Transit, 84 LA 1272, 1273 (Statham, 1985).

residual management prerogative or as an adjunct to the right to ensure the overall safety of the work force. Arbitrators have accordingly ruled that an employee who refuses, without good cause, to undergo a physical examination can be disciplined or discharged.

Management's right to require a physical examination is not without limits however. Most arbitrators have required that there be some reasonable, nondiscriminatory basis to impose a requirement that an employee submit to a physical examination. For instance, Arbitrator Roy Ray commented as follows in ruling that management could not suspend an employee for refusing to take a physical:

> Practically all the cases holding that the Company may require an employee to take a physical examination deal with the situation of employees returning from layoff after illness or injury or extended layoff; or the situation where an employee is being assigned to a new job. In most of the cases the contract specifically provided for examination in such instances. . . . In the absence of such specific authorization we must look to the Management Rights Clause. It gives the Company the right to determine ability and this must be assumed to include physical ability. One way of determining such ability is through an examination by a doctor. Under some circumstances the Company must have the right to require a physical examination. But this right is not an absolute one exercisable at the whim of the Company. It cannot be arbitrarily insisted upon without reasonable grounds. The Company must have some reasonable basis for believing that the employee has a physical disability which prevents him from performing his job or endangers his safety or that of other employees.[7]

In the case cited the arbitrator reasoned that the company acted upon the hearsay statements of an insurance investigator that the grievant had filed a claim for a back injury, without itself investigating to see if there was such claim. Arbitrator Ray also pointed out that the company was unable to demonstrate the existence of any uniform and consistent past practice requiring employees to take a physical examination when hired.

Likewise, Arbitrator Robert McIntosh declared:

> Absent such a prohibition or clause of some kind [in the parties' agreement], the Company would have the right to require the medical examination but the general rule seems to have been

---

[7]Conchemco, Inc., 55 LA 54, 57 (1970).

modified by the general opinion of arbitrators that such request
must be based upon reasonable grounds and not be purely capricious.[8]

Arbitrator McIntosh rules that management acted reasonably
in requesting a physical examination for one of its truck drivers who had had a fainting spell approximately six months
before a driving accident. In the words of the arbitrator, the
company "acted fairly upon [a] reasonable basis to protect both
the health and life of the grievant as well as others on the
highway . . . ."[9] The fact that the examination and tests took
approximately three weeks did not, in the arbitrator's view,
warrant reimbursement for the grievant's time lost from work
as a result of the examination.

Disclosure of Medical History

At common law, private-sector employees may not refuse
to disclose past medical history[10] to a prospective employer.
Illustrative of the common law in this area is *Cort v. Bristol
Myers Co.*[11] In that case three long-time employees of a pharmaceutical company were required to complete a biographical
summary, including questions on "business experience, education, family, home ownership, physical data, activities, and
[general goals] and aims." The employer required answers to
a medical history section, which included many questions that
the employees considered personal (operations, serious illnesses, nervous disorders, medication taken) and, accordingly,
they refused to answer. The court found that most of the questions were relevant to the employees' job qualifications and
represented no invasion of privacy protected by law.

One can expect a similar result in the arbitral forum with

---

[8]Chatfield Paper Corp., 46 LA 530, 532 (1966).
[9]Id. at 532.
[10]One commentator has properly noted that health *history* records should be
considered separately from health *condition* records. A health history reveals the
past status of the worker's medical condition. This history may, for example, include
past incidents of alcoholism, venereal disease, drug dependencies, or nervous conditions, and other sensitive items that the prospective employee desires to remain
secret. Medical condition, on the other hand, deals with the employee's present health
condition, i.e., his "present status of mind and body." Of the two types of records,
medical history is arguably the more sensitive since it often documents conditions,
some embarrassing, that are not part of the employee's present capacity to perform
work-related tasks. See O'Reilly, "Unions' Rights to Company Information," 116–18
(Indus. Res. Unit, The Wharton School, U. of Pa. Lab. Rel. & Pub. Policy Series No.
21, 1981).
[11]385 Mass. 300, 431 N.E.2d 908, 115 LRRM 5127 (1982).

respect to disclosure of medical history by applicants for employment. When disclosure is required of current employees, however, arbitrators require that management demonstrate that the requested information be job-related. Illustrative of the problems in this area is a decision reported by Arbitrator William Coburn. In *Bondtex Corp.*,[12] an individual applied for a job and executed the necessary medical forms, including a medical history questionnaire. On his form he stated that he was in good health, had no physical handicaps, and that he had no prior operations. He also stated that he had never been treated with X-rays and had never suffered from stomach ulcers. The form contained a statement that false answers were grounds for discharge. The applicant was given a physical examination and found physically and psychologically qualified for work. When the grievant was hospitalized and operated on for a peptic ulcer condition two years after he was hired, it was discovered that he had been hospitalized twice for the same condition before being employed with this company. The employer then attempted to obtain additional medical data on the grievant but, lacking a release from the employee, was unsuccessful. It then requested the grievant to sign the following release form:

> I authorize any physician, hospital, insurer or other organization or person having any records, data or information concerning me or my dependents to furnish such records, data or information as may be requested by BONDTEX, INC. or their duly authorized representative. I understand that in executing this authorization I waive the right for such information to be privileged.[13]

The grievant refused to sign, claiming that he had answered the medical questionnaire properly when hired and that an investigation of his medical history was an invasion of his privacy. He was terminated for refusing to sign the release.

The arbitrator held that the company's discharge of the grievant for his refusal to sign this authorization form was an abuse of managerial discretion and, thus, the dismissal was not for proper cause. Arbitrator Coburn reasoned:

---

[12]68 LA 476 (1977).
[13]Id. at 477.

The foregoing procedure, it appears to me, was entirely proper in terms of the Company's need to develop all the facts before reaching a decision involving so serious a charge against an employee as falsification of records with its attendant liability of termination of service if proven. What is troubling, however, is the wording of the authorization form allegedly constituting an invasion of the privacy not only of the involved employee, but also his family. Examination of the language of the form reveals that it goes far beyond the scope of its stated purpose: to authorize the release of hospital and medical records to the Company. For example, it covers not only physicians and hospitals but any *"insurer or other organization*—having any records, data or information concerning me or my dependents as may be requested ... " by the Company or its authorized representative. (Emphasis supplied) And, finally, it requires the employee to waive his right that the information so obtained be treated as privileged, meaning that any information so obtained would not be subject to the bar against disclosure of a privileged communication in an action at law or in equity.[14]

In *Western Airlines*,[15] an employee returning from a medical leave of absence after a non-work-related shoulder and back injury was required by management to be examined by the company's physician. Although the grievant agreed to release all his medical records to the company's doctor, he refused to sign a general release to the company as a precondition to the examination (it was the practice of the company's doctor to have all records released jointly to the company doctor and to the company since the company doctor feared some potential liability if information from medical records released to him personally was subsequently released by the company). The company and the union agreed to have the grievant examined by a neutral doctor; however, the company denied any liability for any interim pay on the grounds of the grievant's refusal to cooperate with the company's medical evaluation. The grievant was subsequently examined by a neutral doctor and found able to return to work without restrictions.

Arbitrator Fredric Richman ruled that management did not have the power to order an employee to release all of his medical records to the company as a condition of being allowed to return to work after a medical leave of absence. Although the agreement provided that the company may request that an employee submit to a physical examination after a leave

---

[14]Id. at 478.
[15]74 LA 923 (Richman, 1980).

of absence, the arbitrator nevertheless found no contractual justification to require an employee to release all of his medical records to the company as a prerequisite to a physical examination. The grievant in fact agreed to release his records to the doctor and this was sufficient under the contract. The arbitrator accordingly held that the company violated the agreement in not returning the grievant to work when he was physically able.

Similarly, another arbitrator discussed as follows the requirement that each employee furnish the company broad authority to obtain medical information in order to determine whether medical excuses are valid:

> Management is not authorized by management's inherent managerial rights to infringe upon employees' right to privacy with regard to medical information which does not relate to the employees' employment. While it is unquestionably true that management does not intend to utilize the Authorizations to obtain medical information which is unrelated to the employee's employment, the Company's right to have access to medical information does not extend to allow the Company access to medical information which is unrelated to the employment relationship, and the employees have the right to avoid the potential use of broader authority than is needed to obtain information which management has no right to obtain.[16]

Designation of Examining Physician

Where the agreement is silent as to who performs the examination, the better weight of authority holds that the employer can mandate that employees be examined by a company-designated physician.[17] Arbitrator Raymond Roberts, in *National Steel Corp.*,[18] recognized the company's right to force employees to submit to an examination by a company-designated doctor. Expressing the better rule, Arbitrator Roberts declared:

> The Company's requirement that the examination be administered by the Company physician rather than another is not unreasonable. It is the Company that is responsible for safety in the plant and it is the Company who needs to be satisfied

---

[16]AAA Case No. 294-14, Cannelton Indus., Inc. (Cannelton, Va.) and Mine Workers Local 1961 (July 7, 1983)(Williams), as cited in Wilson, "Medical Evidence in Arbitration: Aspects and Dilemmas," 39 Arb. J. No. 3, at 16 (1984).
[17]See, e.g., Gravely Tractors, Inc., 31 LA 132 (Stouffer, 1958).
[18]76 LA 103 (1981).

with the results of the examination. Grievant need not rely upon the examination as a mark of his own health. If Grievant is not satisfied with the examination he is in no way deprived of the right to use his own physician as he sees fit and he is not prejudiced by being examined by the Company physician. It is immaterial whether or not Grievant would be satisfied with such an examination since the examination is to be relied upon and used by the Company and not the Grievant. The Company does have a right and need to use its own physician to insure that consistent standards are applied. Using a multitude of physicians would result in a chaotic situation.[19]

Another arbitrator expressed this principle as follows:

There is no question that an employer acts reasonably, when it questions the physical condition of an employee and seeks to have such an employee examined by a doctor of its own choosing. Sometimes, such provisions are negotiated and appear in the Contract. If they do not appear in the Contract, ... it is a matter of proper industrial relations or "common law of the shop", which permits an employer to have an employee examined by its own doctor, if it doubts the report of the attending physician of the employee.[20]

Under a rule that stated only that refusal to submit to a physical examination as may be required from time to time by the company is an offense that may be cause for immediate dismissal, Arbitrator Peter Kelliher, in *Aetna Bearing Co.*,[21] held that it was permissible for management to insist that the examination be performed by its physician. The reasoning of the arbitrator is particularly instructive:

[I]t should be remembered that among the prerogatives of a Company has been the right to direct its working forces and to establish a safe and efficient plant operation and that as the Labor Agreement had no provision limiting or otherwise restricting the Company's right to require physical examinations of employees, as herein involved, it must follow that said right was neither abridged nor bargained away.[22]

In another case Arbitrator V. P. Daniel cautioned against "over examination" by the company's doctor:

It is noted that this submission of employees to examination by company physicians may result in an "over examination" and development of medical facts clearly unrelated to the pri-

---

[19]Id. at 108.
[20]West Carrollton Parchment Co., 80-1 ARB ¶8001, at 3008–09 (Chalfie, 1979).
[21]50 LA 351, 352 (1968).
[22]Id. at 352.

mary question. This was somewhat evident in the case of (K) and should cause concern since it may unintentionally violate the employee's right to privacy and provide to the company knowledge of facts and circumstances, not only of a medical nature but of a personal nature, of which it was previously unaware and which might, in the future, be used adversely to the employee. It stands to reason, then, that any examination by the company physician based upon a specified medical condition should be narrowly conducted and limited both as to examination and as to report to the company.[23]

If there is a conflict between the opinion of the employee's physician and the company's doctor, arbitrators have held that it is permissible for management to rely on the opinion of its physicians. The better weight of arbitral authority is summarized by Arbitrator James Doyle as follows:

> It is axiomatic that the initial judgment in matters of this kind belongs to management. The judgment of the plant physician is entitled to great weight. He is conversant with the requirements of the occupation involved and the risks inherent in such work. It is generally held that where there is a conflict in the views of qualified physicians, whose veracity there is no reason to question, the Company is entitled to rely on the views of its own medical advisers.[24]

Instead of relying on the company's physician, other arbitrators will remand conflicts in medical opinion to the parties for further analysis by an impartial physician. One arbitration board, faced with a conflict in medical opinion as to whether an employee was qualified to work (the carrier's physician concluded that the employee was no longer physically qualified to work as a locomotive engineer because his "heart was in such condition that he would be likely to suffer an acute coronary episode"), appointed a committee of three physicians to examine the grievant, one chosen by the employer, one selected by the employee, and the third chosen by the two so selected. The medical issue was to be decided by majority vote of the physicians. Reversing the district and appeals courts, the Supreme Court, in *Gunther v. San Diego & Arizona Eastern Railway Co.*,[25] held that the arbitration board did not exceed its jurisdiction in appointing a medical

[23]AAA Case No. 288–5, Alofs Mfg. Co. and CLA Local 55 (July 16, 1982), as cited in Wilson, supra note 16, at 16.
[24]Hughes Aircraft Co., 49 LA 535, 539 (1967). See also Hill & Sinicropi, Evidence in Arbitration, 30–34 (BNA Books, 1980).
[25]382 U.S. 257, 60 LRRM 2496 (1965).

board to decide the question of fact relating to the employee's fitness.

Dissemination of Exam Results

Management Access

Another issue involving physical examinations concerns management's right to view and disseminate the results. A union may recognize management's right to require a physical but may nevertheless object to its having access to the entire spectrum of the results of the examination. This concern was evident in *Williams Pipe Line Co.*,[26] where the arbitrator considered the scope of company access to the exam results of employees who had been required to take physical exams because of exposure to chemicals. The union had insisted that only aggregate information should be furnished to the company and that the company should have no right to personal medical data that was not job related. The arbitrator held that medical problems which were discovered in the course of the physical examination which were not job-related should be communicated to the employee only. Moreover, the arbitrator discussed confidentiality issues.

> Aggregate information and all information as required by law may be supplied to the Company. Individual medical data will only be available to (1) the Company physician and his staff, (2) the industrial hygienist for the Company, and that for the sole purpose of communication with the physician regarding present or imminent danger to the employee or his fellow workers in regard to any action required by law. In the event there is a job related medical problem which affects the work performance of the employee or presents a present or imminent danger to the employee or his fellow workers, the Employer is entitled to counsel about the medical fitness of the employee in relationship to work and to the fellow employees, but the Company is not entitled to a diagnosis or details of a specific nature.[27]

Employee/Union Access

A related issue is whether the employee has a right to review and challenge medical records possessed by the employer.

---

[26]78 LA 617 (Moore, 1982).
[27]Id. at 620.

Some states have enacted statutes that permit an employee to examine any medical records retained by the employer.[28] Other jurisdictions[29] prohibit releasing medical information to the employee's union, employer, or prospective employer without authorization from the employee.

In those states that have passed legislation limiting access to, and dissemination of, information contained in employees' personnel files,[30] an employee may be protected from an employer's improper use or dissemination of his medical records.[31] An employee may also be protected from disclosing to management medical information that is not job-related. For example, in Maryland employers are prohibited from asking a job applicant any question about his physical, psychological, or psychiatric illnesses or treatments that do not bear a direct relationship to the applicant's fitness for a particular position.[32]

Most collective bargaining agreements do not provide for employee or union access to medical records. Where a statute mandating access does not exist or is not applicable, an employee who believes that he or she has been adversely affected by an employer's use of inaccurate medical records may grieve the employer's adverse action and, as part of the remedy, request that the incorrect data be purged from the employee's file.

In preparing for an arbitration hearing, unions frequently request the personnel records of selected employees in order to determine whether the contested discipline was discriminatory. A union may also request the results of physical examinations in order to obtain information on employee exposure to hazardous chemical substances. In such cases, employers commonly raise either a blanket or limited confidentiality

---

[28]Conn. Gen. Stat. Ann. §31–128(c) (West, 1985); Ohio Rev. Code Ann. §4113.23 (Page, 1980); Wis. Stat. Ann. §103.13 (West, Supp. 1985).

[29]Cal. [Civil] Code §56.10 (West, 1985).

[30]Access or dissemination legislation exists in the following states (citations to the "Fair Employment Practices Manual" of BNA's Labor Relations Reporter): California, 453:842; Connecticut, 453:1253; District of Columbia, 453:1647; Maine, 455:461; Michigan, 455:1027; Oregon, 457:652; Pennsylvania, 457:825; Utah, 457:2217; Wisconsin, 457:3227.

[31]An interesting aside to the development of state legislation dealing with access and dissemination of information contained in an employee's personnel file is that this area may be preempted by federal law.

[32]Md. Ann. Code art. 100, §95A (1978). At the federal level, the Occupational Safety and Health Act provides limited access by employees to the records in the employer's possession. 45 Fed. Reg. 35,212 (1980), codified at 29 C.F.R. Part 1910.20 (1985).

defense when these files contain references to medical problems. The NLRB has consistently found that the identity of individuals who suffer from medical disorders is confidential, especially where the employer had informed employees that their files were confidential or where the employees requested confidentiality.[33] When the records are relevant but nevertheless contain references to medical problems, a common practice is to make the information available to the union with the individual names deleted.[34]

Federal Employee Statutes

In the federal sector two statutes govern issues concerning access to and dissemination of medical information: the Freedom of Information Act (FOIA)[35] and the Privacy Act of 1974.[36] While a detailed analysis is beyond the scope of this inquiry, passing reference should be noted since both statutes limit some disclosure of personnel information.[37]

The FOIA, which has replaced the Public Information section of the Administrative Procedure Act of 1946,[38] exempts from public disclosure "personnel and medical files and similar files the disclosure of which would constitute a clearly unwarranted invasion of personal privacy."[39] To qualify under this exemption, the requested information must consist of "personnel, medical, or similar files" held by a governmental agency, and the disclosure of the material must constitute a "clearly unwarranted invasion of personal privacy." This is a two-part test and the better rule is that a balancing test is to be used when privacy interests collide with the public's right to government information.[40]

Under the Privacy Act an individual covered by the statute is entitled to determine what information is maintained, as well as how and by whom it is used. Subject to 11 exceptions, no records maintained on an individual may be released with-

---

[33]Johns-Manville Sales Corp., 252 NLRB 368, 105 LRRM 1379 (1980).
[34]Washington Gas Light Co., 273 NLRB No. 20, 118 LRRM 1001 (1984); Plough, Inc., 262 NLRB 1095, 111 LRRM 1013 (1982)(ordering employer to supply union with results of employee physicals with identifying data removed).
[35]Public Law 89-487, 80 Stat. 250, 5 U.S.C. §552 (Supp., 1980).
[36]Public Law 93-579, 88 Stat. 1896, codified at 5 U.S.C. §552a (Supp., 1980).
[37]See O'Reilly, supra note 10, at 81–94, 143–59.
[38]Public Law 79-404, 60 Stat. 237, 5 U.S.C. §1001–11 (1964).
[39]5 U.S.C. §552(b)(6).
[40]Department of Air Force v. Rose, 425 U.S. 352 (1976).

out consent of the individual. The Act also mandates that the employing agency is to collect "only such information about the individual as is relevant and necessary to accomplish a purpose of the agency required to be accomplished by statute or by executive order of the President." Further, the statute directs the agency to "collect information to the greatest extent practicable directly from the subject individual where the information may result in adverse determinations about an individual's rights, benefits, and privileges under Federal programs."[41]

Psychological Testing

There are few reported decisions involving the employer's right to force an employee to submit to a psychological evaluation. In *Southern Indiana Gas & Electric Co.*,[42] the employer required that an employee, as a condition precedent to returning to work, obtain a psychological evaluation following a gunshot injury to his leg. The arbitrator pointed out that there was no credible evidence that the employee presented a danger to any of his co-employees, to any management personnel, or to any company property by reason of his mental condition, nor was there any evidence that the grievant was incapable of performing his job. Having concluded that the gunshot wound was accidental, the arbitrator held that it was improper for the company to require a psychological evaluation as a condition of returning to work. As a remedy, Arbitrator Katz ordered that the grievant be reimbursed for the expense of the psychological evaluation and that he be made whole for the work days lost as a result of the company's action in requiring a psychological evaluation.

Arbitrator Sidney Cahn, in *Standard-Knapp Division, Emhart Corp.*,[43] recognized that under certain circumstances management has the inherent right to require a psychiatric examination, even when the bargaining agreement contains no provision concerning the company's right to have one of its employees submit to a psychiatric examination. According to the arbitrator,

---

[41]5 U.S.C. §552a(e).
[42]79 LA 590 (Katz, 1982).
[43]68-2 ARB ¶8563 (1968).

implicit in every Collective Bargaining Agreement is the right
on the part of the Company not to employ or continue in employment a worker who presents a danger to co-workers or to
management personnel or property, or who is by reason of mental impairment incapable of properly performing his job.

As a concomitant of this right, it must be said that when
a substantial basis exists for concluding that an employee presents such a danger or by reason of mental impairment cannot
properly perform his work, the Company may well be warranted
in requiring the employee to submit to a psychiatric examination as a condition of his continued employment. However,
before such psychiatric examination can be required of an employee, some cogent showing that the employee presents such
a danger or is so incapable of performing his job must be made.[44]

The arbitrator found that the company did not have cause to
require a psychiatric examination of an employee who had
"red eyes," appeared "very angry," and gave his foreman "tre-
mendous dirty looks" after a "nose-to-nose" confrontation with
him. The employer requested the exam in part because of a
prior incident in which the grievant had produced a knife and
stabbed it into a table, telling a co-worker words to the effect,
"Why don't you use this to stab me in the back." The arbitrator
noted that the grievant had adequately performed his job and
had never physically attacked or injured co-workers or management personnel.

In *Caterpillar Tractor Co.*,[45] Arbitrator Carroll Daugherty
likewise held that an employer must have good and sufficient
cause in order to mandate that an employee submit to a psychiatric examination. Daugherty commented:

[T]he Arbitrator finds the Company lacked just cause for the
removal of B— and for asking him to pay for psychiatric con-
sultations. It may have been a fact that B— was mentally
deranged; that his religious beliefs were a major cause or effect
of such derangement; that the quantity and quality of his work
output was below standard because of said disability; that his
condition threatened his own safety and/or other employees'
safety; and that his score on the psychological tests and his
interview with [the company physician] strongly suggested
mental difficulties. But, as already suggested . . . , the Company
chose to introduce very little evidence on these matters. The
Arbitrator is not criticizing or upbraiding the Company for said
choice; the Company doubtless had good reasons for its decision
on what evidence to present. The fact remains, however, that

---

[44]Id. at 4939.
[45]36 LA 104 (1961).

in a case like this an arbitrator's determination on whether or not to uphold a company must rest on the record. . . . The record is devoid of testimony of probative value from Company witnesses as to *why* this Company attitude developed and this course of Company action was taken.[46]

Where the parties' agreement declared that the company could "arrange at its own expense for medical examinations of any employee at any time for the purpose of determining the fitness of an employee to continue in his position," Arbitrator James McBrearty found that an employee could not be compelled to submit to psychological testing by a clinical psychologist with a Ph.D as a condition to continued employment. The arbitrator said a "psychological" exam was not a "medical" exam if administered by a person without a medical degree, as in this case. In dictum McBrearty reflected the thinking of most arbitrators when he stated:

> [T]he Employer has the right to require medical examinations (including psychiatric examinations) of any employee at any time to determine if the employee is fit for work, so long as there is reasonable or substantial basis to question fitness, such as Grievant presenting a danger to any of his fellow employees, to any management personnel, or to any machinery, equipment, or other Company property by reason of his physical or mental condition, or because Grievant was incapable of properly performing his job. . . . Any doubts the Employer might legitimately have as to an employee's mental condition cannot be taken as showing that the employee's mental condition adversely affects his ability to perform his job or indicates a danger to others.[47]

Alcohol and Drug Testing

When faced with the question whether an employee was under the influence of alcohol or other stimulants, arbitrators have concluded that it is not necessary that physiological testing (blood-alcohol, urine, or "breathalizer" testing) be performed in order for the company to conclude that an employee was in fact under the influence. Nor is it necessary that there be witnesses to the act of consuming alcohol or ingesting drugs before it can be deduced that the conduct took place, arbitra-

---

[46]Id. at 105–06.
[47]Public Serv. Co. of N.M., 82-2 ARB ¶8494 (1982), at 5220. See also Jamestown Tel. Corp., 61 LA 121 (France, 1973).

tors have held. The standard that has been developed is that employees who exhibit the "classic" signs associated with intoxication or drug use may properly be considered "under the influence." Arbitrator Julius Rezler noted:

> Several arbitrators have concluded, however, that supervisors who have no medical training nevertheless are capable of recognizing when an employee is intoxicated or being under the influence of an intoxicant "if they objectively compare an employee's normal demeanor and work habits with those at the time his sobriety is questioned". A further requirement of presenting evidence in cases involving problems with intoxicants is that the testimony of the witnesses should be "sufficiently specific in describing various details of appearance and conduct."[48]

Similarly, another arbitrator declared:

> It is not necessary for the ordinary observer to see someone in the act of drinking before he can deduce drunkenness, for example. By the same token, a similar conclusion can be reached respecting drug symptoms whether or not an individual is observed in the act of ingesting [drugs] in some manner.[49]

Mandatory Testing

Where there is reason to suspect that an employee is under the influence, most arbitrators hold that management has the right to require that the employee submit to an alcohol or drug test. The rationale supporting this rule has been stated by Arbitrator Raymond Roberts in *Porcelain Metals Corp.*:[50]

---

[48]Sherwin-Williams Co., 66 LA 273, 275 (1976), citing Grievance Guide, 54 (BNA Books, 1972)(repaginated at 85 in 1982 edition).

[49]Structurlite Plastics Corp., 73 LA 691, 696 (Leach, 1979). See also United Parcel Serv., 72 LA 1069 (White, 1979)(grievant observed by management as "uncharacteristically sloppy and disheveled in appearance, loud, somewhat incoherent, and slurred in his speech, and with a smell of alcohol about his person"); Okonite Co., 74 LA 664 (Ghiz, 1980)(foreman's observations were that the grievant was "staggering and his speech was slurred"); Hiram Walker & Sons, Inc., 75 LA 899 (Belshaw, 1980)(grievant was "staggering, with slurred speech; he had at least two collisions"); General Tel. Co. of Calif., 77 LA 1052, 1054 (Schuster, 1981)(sustaining suspension where employee's performance "was not of the type of performance that [she] would normally give"); Dayton-Walther Co., 77 LA 1064 (Traynor, 1981)(discharge upheld after showing that grievant uncoordinated, leaning; rambled on when normally a quiet person; eyes bloodshot; jumping from one subject to another; swayed while walking); Cities Serv. Co., 77 LA 1180 (Brisco, 1982)(employee observed talking loudly and shielding mouth with hands; walking slowly while holding stair railing with both hands); Baumfolder Corp., 78 LA 1060 (Modjeska, 1982)(smelled of alcohol and looked and acted drunk; speech slurred and walk wobbly); American Airlines and Transport Workers Local 502 (Case No. S-41-78-LAX) (Eaton, 1979)(strong smell of alcohol, eyes reddish, tried to throw up in trash can, bouncing off aisle sides).

[50]73 LA 1133, (1979).

Being under the influence of drugs or alcohol renders an employee incapable of properly performing his work. In the industrial environment, it also renders the employee a hazard to himself and others. The prohibition is clearly designed with a two-fold purpose. First and foremost, it is a safety rule to protect both the employee who might be under the influence of drugs and his fellow employees from harm or injury. Secondly, it is designed to protect the Company against paying wages to an employee who is incapable of performing productively with reasonable efficiency. Given these two clear purposes of the rule, it is immaterial whether the drug is prescriptive and its possession is legal or illegal.[51]

Some arbitrators hold that refusal to submit to such a test is a fact that can properly be used by the employer as evidence that the employee was under the influence.[52] Others declare that no adverse inference may be drawn from such a refusal.[53] Still another approach is to deny back pay on the theory that the employee, while not subject to discipline for refusing to submit to the test, failed to mitigate damages by declining an opportunity to clear himself of the charges.[54]

In *Springfield Mass Transit District*,[55] the arbitrator held that, under its power to make and enforce reasonable rules, a company could require any bus operator who was involved in a serious accident, or suspected of being influenced by liquor or drugs or who, for reasonable cause, was suspected of having an alcohol or drug problem, to submit to a breathalizer test. The test was to be administered by a trained individual on a standard device used by law enforcement agencies. While the test could be given without prior notice, it has to be given "at a time bearing a logical and reasonable relationship to the operator's work schedules."

Similarly, in *Griffin Pipe Products Co.*,[56] the arbitrator held that, as part of a program to eliminate plant accidents, an employer was within its rights to make and implement a rule requiring a drug-screen urine test of anyone injured on the job or applying for employment. The arbitrator found unpersuasive the union's argument that the rule should be de-

---

[51]Id. at 1139.
[52]See, e.g., American Standard, 77 LA 1085 (Katz, 1981), discussed infra note 57.
[53]American Airlines and Transport Workers Local 512 (Case No. M-476-80) (Luskin).
[54]Bi-State Dev. Agency, 72 LA 198 (Newmark, 1979).
[55]80 LA 193 (Guenther, 1983).
[56]82-2 ARB ¶8616 (Daly, 1982).

clared invalid since the company had no breathalizer or equivalent test for alcohol. Arbitrator J. Harvey Daly reasoned that, unlike drug use, alcohol abuse is immediately apparent by a number of symptoms including heightened facial color, slurred speech, faulty coordination, unsteady movements, uncertain steps, and alcoholic breath. On the other hand, physical appearance and independent evidence would not suffice in drug-related cases.

Where the parties' agreement declared that the company "may require a medical examination . . . at any time during his employment for the purpose of determining whether or not [the employee] is fit for employment," Arbitrator Jonas Katz held that an employee was properly discharged for refusing to submit to a drug-screen test. The arbitrator found "probable cause" where the grievant's speech was slow and slurred and she was observed "wobbling down the aisles."[57]

In *Birmingham-Jefferson County Transit*,[58] Arbitrator C. Gordon Statham, under an agreement that provided that management could require medical examinations at any time, ruled that included within this power was the right to require a drug-screen test. The arbitrator also held that such a test did not violate the employee's Fourth and Fifth Amendment rights, since there was no evidence that the results of the exams would be made available for criminal prosecution purposes.

Stating that "asking an employee to take blood test is clearly as much for his protection as for the company's" Arbitrator Lamont Stallworth upheld a five-day suspension under a rule providing that an employee who while at the workplace was discovered to be under the influence of alcohol or controlled substances would be given a direct order to take an ambulance to the hospital for testing. Under the rule any employee refusing to take such tests would be suspended with intent to discharge.[59]

National Railroad Adjustment Board Referee Robert O'Brien, in *Southern Pacific Transportation Co.*,[60] ruled that the carrier did not have the right unilaterally to randomly "spot check" employees with a breathalizer-type device. Ref-

---

[57]American Standard, 77 LA 1085 (Katz, 1981).
[58]84 LA 1272 (Statham, 1985).
[59]Zeigler Coal Co., Mine No. 5 and Mine Workers Dist. 12, Local 1870 (unpub., 1984), citing Tennessee River Pulp & Paper Co., 68 LA 421 (Simon, 1976).
[60]79 LA 618 (1982).

eree O'Brien pointed out that at least for the past 50 years, the practice has always been that evidence of intoxication was based on visual observation, surmise, and other outward manifestations (flushed face, slurred speech, unsteady gait, and glassy eyes, among others). The practice had accordingly become a binding condition of employment even though it was not expressed in the agreement.

Public-Sector Considerations

The entire area of medical screening for drugs has been subject to litigation, especially where there is no collective bargaining agreement in effect. Where there is a bargaining agreement, however, state tort claims will likely be held preempted. As noted by the Fifth Circuit, "These cases are grist for the mill of grievance procedures and arbitration."[61] Although there appear to be no legal constraints on pre-employment medical screening (employees are routinely given pre-employment physical examinations in which blood and urine tests are administered), a different result may apply for employees already on the payroll in the public sector. Especially interesting are decisions where public-sector employees have argued that compulsory blood or urine tests violate Fourth Amendment rights.[62]

As one court explained, "The Fourth Amendment is intended to protect the privacy of individuals from invasion by unreasonable searches of the person and those places and things wherein the individual has a reasonable expectation of privacy."[63] The amendment does not prohibit all searches, but only unreasonable searches.[64] The test in a Fourth Amendment case is whether the search was reasonable, and in determining reasonableness, courts balance the intrusiveness of the search as regards the individual's privacy interests against its promotion of legitimate governmental interests.[65] As stated by the Supreme Court,

---

[61]Strachan v. Union Oil Co., 768 F.2d 703, 120 LRRM 2001, 2002 (CA 5, 1985).
[62]The Fourth Amendment provides as follows:
   The right of the people to be secure in their persons . . . against unreasonable searches and seizures, shall not be violated, and no Warrants shall issue, but upon probable cause, supported by Oath or affirmation, and particularly describing the place to be searched, and the persons or things to be searched.
[63]McDonnell v. Hunter, 612 F.Supp. 1122, 1127 (S.D. Iowa, 1985).
[64]Carroll v. United States, 267 U.S. 132, 147 (1925).
[65]State County Employees AFSCME, Security and Law Enforcement Employees Dist. Council 82 v. Carey, 737 F.2d 187, 201 (CA 2, 1984).

The test of reasonableness under the Fourth Amendment is not capable of precise definition or mechanical application. In each case it requires a balancing of the need for the particular search against the invasion of personal rights that the search entails. Courts must consider the scope of the particular intrusion, the manner in which it is conducted, the justification for initiating it, and the place in which it is conducted.[66]

In *Transit Union Division 241 v. Suscy,*[67] the Seventh Circuit upheld rules by the Chicago Transit Authority (CTA) requiring that CTA bus and train operators submit to blood and urine tests when they are involved in a "serious" accident,[68] or when they are suspected of being intoxicated or under the influence of narcotics while on duty.

The union argued that the rules were facially invalid under the Fourth and Fourteenth Amendments. The court, applying a balancing test,[69] outlined the approach to take where employees' rights under the Fourth Amendment are in conflict with the rights of public management, as follows:

> The Fourth Amendment protects an individual's reasonable expectation of privacy from unreasonable intrusions by the state. Whether the individual has a reasonable expectation of privacy and whether the intrusion is reasonable are determined by balancing the claims of the public against the interests of the individual. . . . It is clear that a governmental agency can place reasonable conditions on public employment. . . . In this case, the CTA has a paramount interest in protecting the public by insuring that bus and train operators are fit to perform their jobs. In view of this interest, members of plaintiff Union can have no reasonable expectation of privacy with regard to submitting to blood and urine tests.[70]

In reaching this conclusion the court pointed out that the conditions under which the intrusion would take place (following a "serious" accident involving a specific bus driver was required, and no medical testing would be conducted unless

---

[66]Bell v. Wolfish, 441 U.S. 520, 559 (1979).

[67]538 F.2d 1264 (CA 7), cert. denied, 429 U.S. 1029 (1976).

[68]CTA General Bulletin G2-75 provides: "Operating employees directly involved in any serious accident such as a collision of trains, collision of buses, derailment, [collision of] bus and person or serious collision with vehicle or fixed object, may be required to be hospitalized for medical attention, a physical examination and/or a blood and urinalysis test." 538 F.2d at 1266.

[69]According to the court, "where the employee asserts that his right is protected by the general ambit of the Fourteenth Amendment, the state need show only that the rule is reasonable. . . . Therefore, if there is no invasion of Fourth Amendment rights, it follows that there is also no violation of the Fourteenth Amendment." Id. (citation omitted).

[70]Id. at 1267 (citations omitted).

two supervisory employees concurred), and the manner of taking the samples (the tests would be performed in a hospital) were reasonable.

In *McDonnell v. Hunter*,[71] a federal court ruled that the Iowa Department of Corrections may not require prison employees to submit to urine and blood tests for evidence of illegal drug use without reasonable suspicion that employees are using such substances. *McDonnell* was a class action on behalf of some 1,750 individuals employed by the department at various prison facilities. The record indicates that McDonnell was dismissed after refusing to undergo urinalysis, requested by prison officials on the basis of reports that he had been seen the previous weekend with individuals suspected of drug activity. He was later reinstated and transferred to another institution, but nevertheless lost ten days' pay. McDonnell had signed a consent-to-search form when he was hired that required submission to urine or blood testing "when requested by the administration of the Reformatory." The court found that since it was not clear who had the authority to request samples from an employee, the consent policy was defective. According to the court, "without any standards, it appears that any institutional officer may authorize or make a search or demand for blood or urine at his or her own unfettered discretion, and that the procedures followed will be another matter within the unfettered discretion of the officer implementing the Department's policy."[72]

Of special note is the court's reasoning that the taking of blood is a "search and seizure" because it must be extracted from the body. The taking of urine, according to the court, is a "seizure" within the meaning of the Fourth Amendment, even though it is routinely discharged from the body and no governmental intrusion into the body is required to seize urine. The court stated, "One does not reasonably expect to discharge urine under circumstances making it available to others to collect and analyze in order to discover the personal physiological secrets it holds, except as part of a medical examination."[73] Therefore, blood and urine tests may be made only on the basis of a reasonable suspicion that the employee "is then

---

[71]612 F.Supp. 1122 (S.D. Iowa, 1985).
[72]Id. at 1128 n.4.
[73]Id. at 1127.

under the influence of alcoholic beverages or controlled substances."[74]

As to blood and urine samples that are obtained as part of a pre-employment examination, or as part of a routine, periodic physical examination, the court further explained that

> the Fourth Amendment does not preclude taking a body fluid specimen as part of a pre-employment examination or as part of any routine periodic physical examination that may be required of employees, nor does it prohibit taking a specimen of blood, urine, or breath on a periodic basis as a condition of continued employment under a disciplinary disposition if such a condition is reasonably related to the underlying basis for the disciplinary action and the duration of the condition is specified and is reasonable in length.[75]

The analysis of the federal courts in *Suscy* and *Hunter* represent the approach taken by the judiciary in the publi sector. Under the Fourth Amendment, individuals have a right to be free from unreasonable government intrusions into their legitimate expectations of privacy. Absent reasonable suspicion that is based on specific objective inferences of wrongdoing by a particular employee, public-sector management may not require that an employee submit to blood and urine testing.[76] Blood and urine tests represent a significant governmental intrusion into the privacy interests of employees and, absent some type of probable cause, courts have struck the balance of rights in favor of employees. Even when management obtains advance consent to conduct tests, courts still hold in favor of employees. "Public employees cannot be bound by unreasonable conditions of employment" and "[a]dvance consent to future *unreasonable* searches is not a reasonable condition of employment."[77]

---

[74]Id. at 1130.

[75]Id. n.6. See also State County Employees AFCSME, Security and Law Enforcement Employees Dist. Council 82 v. Carey, 737 F.2d 187 (CA 2, 1984)(court-approved warrant based on probable cause required for body-cavity searches of prison guards).

[76]Under the Fourth Amendment, it is important to distinguish (1) performing a blood and urine test as part of pre-employment or routine physical examinations, and (2) selective blood and urine testing that is conducted without reasonable suspicion. As the authors read the cases, in the first situation management may properly conduct a blood and urine test for drugs on a routine basis. See discussion of McDonnell v. Hunter, supra notes 71–75 and accompanying text. In the second situation, however, some type of probable cause is required before an individual can be selectively compelled to submit a blood and urine specimen.

[77]612 F.Supp. at 1131, citing Pickering v. Board of Educ., 391 U.S. 563, 568 (1968) (emphasis in original).

Maintenance Programs and Title VII

In *New York City Transit Authority v. Beazer*,[78] the Supreme Court considered the Transit Authority policy of not employing persons who use narcotic drugs. In relevant part, the Authority's rule provided:

> Employees must not use, or have in their possession, narcotics, tranquilizers, drugs of the Amphetamine group or barbiturate derivatives or paraphernalia used to administer narcotics or barbiturate derivatives, except with the written permission of the Medical Director—Chief Surgeon of the System.[79]

The Supreme Court, reversing both the district court and the court of appeals, found that the Authority's blanket policy under this rule of refusing to employ persons who are on a methadone maintenance program was not violative of Title VII and the Equal Protection Clause of the Constitution. Mr. Justice Stevens, writing for the majority, stated that a *prima facie* violation of Title VII could be established by statistical evidence showing that the practice has the adverse effect of denying the members of one race equal access to employment opportunities. Even assuming that the employees established the necessary disparate effect upon blacks, the Court ruled that the Authority rebutted the *prima facie* case by demonstrating that its narcotics rule, and its application to methadone users, was "job related." The majority found that the Authority's legitimate employment goals of safety and efficiency required the exclusion of all users of illegal narcotics, and that the record demonstrated that the Authority's rule bore a " 'manifest relationship to the employment in question.' "[80]

Rejecting a claim that the drug policy as relating to methadone users violated equal protection, the Court approved the employer's rule that postpones eligibility until the methadone treatment program is completed. In the words of the Court, "[i]t is neither unprincipled nor invidious in the sense that it implies disrespect for the excluded subclass."[81] The closing comment of Justice Stevens is noteworthy:

---

[78]440 U.S. 568, 19 FEP 149 (1979).
[79]19 FEP at 150.
[80]Id. at 156 n. 31, quoting Griggs v. Duke Power Co., 401 U.S 424, 3 FEP 175, 178 (1971).
[81]Id. at 158.

No matter how unwise it may be for [the employer] to refuse employment to individual car cleaners, track repairmen, or bus drivers simply because they are receiving methadone treatment, the Constitution does not authorize a Federal Court to interfere in that policy decision.[82]

Summary

The most intrusive level of medical screening, an employer procedure requiring that an individual produce a complete medical history and at the same time submit to a physical examination by the employer's doctor,[83] has been consistently upheld. The reported decisions indicate that management has the inherent right to require compliance with such procedures, not only as a condition of initial employment but whenever there is a bona fide reason to believe that the employee's capacity to perform the job is in question. This right derives from management's rule-making authority or, alternatively, from management's statutory obligation to provide a safe working environment for its employees.[84] As a corollary to this principle, absent a contractual provision to the contrary, an employer that suspects that an employee is "under the influence" is clearly within its rights when it compels the

---

[82]Id.

[83]Virtually nonexistent in the private sector, in the public sector visual body-cavity searches " 'represent one of the most grievous offenses against personal dignity and common decency.' " State County Employees AFSCME, Security and Law Enforcement Employees Dist. Council 82 v. Carey, 737 F.2d 187, 207 (CA 2, 1984), quoting Justice Marshall's dissent in Bell v. Wolfish, 441 U.S. 520, 576–77 (1979). In the words of Justice Stevens, such searches " '—clearly the greatest personal indignity—may be the least justifiable measure of all.' " Id., quoting Justice Stevens' dissent in Bell, 441 U.S. at 594.

[84]In E.I. DuPont v. Grasselli Employees Ass'n, _____ F.Supp. _____, 118 LRRM 3312, 3316 (N.D. Ind., 1985), a federal court, in vacating an arbitrator's award, recognized management's duty to maintain a safe working environment. The court pointed out that

This duty arises by statute as well as by common law. For example, 29 U.S.C. sec. 654(a)(1) states:

Each employer shall furnish to each of his employees employment and a place of employment which are free from recognized hazards that are causing or are likely to cause death or physical harm to his employees.

Moreover,

[E]mployees have an inherent obligation to protect their own safety and to cooperate in promoting safety.

118 LRRM at 3316. Grasselli was a case involving the dismissal of an employee who assaulted two employees and destroyed company property. It is of special note that the federal court, in overturning an arbitration award ordering reinstatement (the arbitrator, crediting the testimony of two psychiatrists, found that the employee was not at fault for his actions due to a temporary "psychotic episode"), applied the cited statute to an employee's violent behavior.

employee to submit to a blood-alcohol or drug-screen test for detection of alcohol or drug use.[85] Most, but not all, arbitrators hold that an employee's refusal to submit to such a test may properly result in the imposition of a disciplinary sanction.[86]

More troublesome is the question of whether management should have access to all the results of the employee's physical examination. Although there is no strict physician-patient relationship in the situation where the employee is examined by the company's doctor,[87] the authors believe that the better rule is that the employer should have access only to information regarding employment-related medical conditions and not to the total spectrum of information regarding an employee's medical condition. Accordingly, if the company's doc-

---

[85]Whatever management's right may be under the bargaining agreement to disqualify employees for medical reasons, there is evidence that, in certain circumstances, it may have to first bargain the matter with the union. In Lockheed Shipbldg & Constr. Co., 237 NLRB 213, 118 LRRM 1283 (1984), a three-member Board ruled that an employer violated its bargaining obligation under §8(a)(5) of the LMRA by unilaterally implementing a pulmonary function and audiometric medical screening program for the purpose of denying employment to new employees who could not pass the tests, without bargaining about the utilization of the results with the union.

[86]On this topic Susser argues as follows:

As might be imagined, employees covered by collective bargaining agreements that do not establish such explicit testing rights on the part of employers (and presumptions of intoxication if such screens are refused) have sometimes been unwilling to submit to drug testing; in many of these instances, those workers have been discharged by their employers. Such actions have been most commonly reviewed by arbitrators from the perspective of whether the employee's refusal to submit to an exam, viewed independently or together with eyewitness testimony and other available evidence of drug involvement, constitutes the "just cause" required for discharge under most union contracts. Questions of privacy and self-incrimination, as well as implicit versus explicit consent, are also invariably raised in connection with drug testing. There is some support in arbitrators' rulings for the view that an employee's refusal to take a test would *not*, in and of itself, justify disciplining or removing him from employment, even where the collective bargaining agreement or company policy specifically requires the test. On the other hand, some cases uphold employee dismissal where the policy to dismiss for refusing to take a screening test is clearly stated in advance. Not suprisingly, arbitrators have been more comfortable in reaching such conclusions where the substantive offense, i.e., the drug infraction, is also established through fairly convincing proof or is corroborated by witnesses.

Susser, supra note 3, at 48 (footnote omitted)(emphasis in original).

The authors believe that most arbitrators will uphold discipline or even dismissal when an employee refuses to take an examination so long as management can establish a reasonable basis in fact (probable cause in the public sector) for believing that the employee was under the influence. Alternatively, when a test is refused, an arbitrator may simply conclude that the employee was under the influence and not bother to rule on the question of whether discipline was proper for refusing the examination. Whichever alternative is chosen, the end result is the same. The suspected drug user is disciplined or terminated from employment.

[87]See Rothstein, supra note 2, at 90–92; Ahnert v. Wildman, 176 Ind. App. 630, 376 N.E.2d 1182 (1978); Lotspeich v. Chance Vought Aircraft, 369 S.W.2d 705 (Tex. Civ. App., 1963); Mrachek v. Sunshine Biscuit, Inc., 308 N.Y. 116, 123 N.E.2d 801 (1954).

tor, for example, were to discover that the employee at one time experienced an incident of venereal disease, insofar as this condition is not job-related the employer's physician should treat as confidential what is learned in this regard from the examination. Moreover, medical findings and records that are job-related should be accessible to individuals in the company only on a bona-fide "need to know" basis.[88]

---

[88]In this respect see Cal. [Civil] Code §56.20 (West, 1985) (Use and Disclosure of Medical Information by Employers).

Chapter 8

Residency, Off-Duty Conduct, and Loyalty

Residency Requirements

A residency or distance requirement is frequently imposed by public employers and more occasionally by private employers. Generally a person's residence is the place where he or she resides (the domicile or abode) and where he or she intends to stay. For example, Arbitrator George Roumell, Jr., concluded that although a grievant may from time to time sleep at the home of one of his three female friends, and even keep clothes there, this does not indicate that one of the three addresses is his "residence." Arbitrator Roumell accordingly found that this arrangement reflected the grievant's lifestyle, rather than his residence.[1] In determining a person's true residence arbitrators' decisions mirror those of the courts.[2] Thus, physical presence for a long period of time is not dispositive of "residence;" other factors include: where one votes; where one receives mail; the address on one's drivers' license; where one keeps clothes; whether one owns property in the claimed area of residence; and where one pays rent.

Arbitrators have held that residency requirements, if nec-

---

[1]City of Sterling Heights, 78-2 ARB ¶8400 (Roumell, 1978).

[2]Courts have upheld residency requirements in the face of challenges based on the right to interstate travel and due process-equal protection under the Fourteenth Amendment. McCarthy v. Philadelphia Civil Serv. Comm'n, 424 U.S. 645 (1976); Detroit Police Officers Ass'n v. City of Detroit, 385 Mich. 519, 190 N.W.2d 97, 78 LRRM 2267 (1971). The Seventh Circuit has held that once it is determined that a public employee is in violation of a residence rule, the employee's job status is that of an "at-will" employee. Brockert v. Skornicka, 711 F.2d 1376, 1387 (CA 7, 1983).

essary to serve some legitimate business interest, are a valid and legitimate exercise of management's authority.[3] For example, in *City of Monmouth*,[4] the arbitrator considered a rule that required all employees in the electrical division of the city's public works department to live within three miles of city hall. While the contract recognized the right of the employer to establish reasonable rules and regulations for the safe and efficient conduct of the city's business, the arbitrator nevertheless held that the rule was unreasonable because the city did not specifically justify a three-mile range. The city had documented the need for a short response time for the electrical department to report in the case of an emergency. As such, the arbitrator remanded to the parties the task of bargaining an acceptable "residency" rule.[5]

In *City of Cincinnati*,[6] the employer enacted an ordinance requiring new employees to be residents of the city. The prior ordinance, secured by the political and bargaining efforts of the police and firefighters unions, provided for a county residency requirement. According to Arbitrator William Richard, the city was bound by the old ordinance since it was "part of the labor-management relationship." He explained that "as a subsisting law at the time the contract was made, it was incorporated into that contract as surely as if it had been expressly written therein." The city therefore could not unilaterally legislate on the matter without the consent of the unions.

A Wisconsin Supreme Court case, *WERC v. Teamsters Local No. 563*,[7] illustrates the tension between a just cause provision and a statutory residency requirement. The parties negotiated a standard just cause provision at a time when the city had a statutory residency requirement that provided for dismissal for any employee moving out of the city. There was no indication in the parties' agreement as to how the just cause provision would relate to the pre-existing ordinance. When a street and sanitation employee moved out of the city, his em-

---

[3]See, e.g., Volunteer Elec. Coop., 84-1 ARB ¶8079 (Rayson, 1983); Stearns Coop. Elec. Ass'n, 78 LA 331 (Jacobs, 1982).
[4]79 LA 345 (Harter, 1982).
[5]See also PLRB v. School Dist., 102 LRRM 2341 (Pa. Ct. Comm. Pleas, 1979) (residency requirement mandatory subject of bargaining and unilateral implementation of residency requirement constitutes unfair labor practice).
[6]83 LA 89, 97–98 (1984).
[7]75 Wis.2d 602, 250 N.W.2d 696, 94 LRRM 2840 (1977).

ployment was terminated. An arbitrator, finding that the ordinance in question was not contained in the contract, reasoned that it was a work rule which was not reasonably related to the job performed. Therefore, the discharge was not for just cause, and the grievant was ordered reinstated. The city ignored the award, and the union appealed the decision to the Wisconsin Employment Relations Commission (WERC). WERC held that the city committed a prohibited practice by refusing to abide by the award. The trial court ruled that the arbitrator exceeded his powers in determining that the discharge was not for just cause. In upholding the lower court, the Wisconsin Supreme Court found that in arbitrating whether the discharge pursuant to the ordinance was for just cause, the parties used a contractual provision as a means for violating the law, and a contract provision that violates the law is void.

Off-Duty Conduct[8]

Discharge of an employee for misconduct committed while at work is a well-grounded management right and will usually be upheld by arbitrators as long as "just cause" is demonstrated. If, however, the misconduct occurs away from the workplace while the employee is off duty, management's right to impose discipline under a just cause provision is less clear. The late dean of the Yale Law School, Harry Shulman, pointing to the nature of the problem, observed:

> We can start with the basic premise that the Company is not entitled to its disciplinary power for the purpose of regulating the lives and conduct of its employees outside of their employment relation. . . . What the employee does outside of the plant after working hours is normally no concern of the employer. If the employee commits no misconduct in the plant or during his working hours he is not subject to disciplinary penalty, though he may beat his wife, spend his money foolishly, or otherwise behave like an undesirable citizen.
>
> But the jurisdictional line which separates the cases with which the employer may be concerned from those with which he may not, is not always the physical line which bounds his property on which his plant is located. In most cases, to be sure,

---

[8]This section is taken, in part, from an article by one of the authors and Donald Dawson. See Hill & Dawson, "Discharge for Off-Duty Misconduct in the Private and Public Sector," 40 Arb. J. No. 2, 24–44, (1985).

the boundaries of the plant fix also the boundaries of the employer's concern.[9]

Certain instances arise, however, where the employer may properly demonstrate concern. For example, an off-premises fight during non-working hours over a purely personal matter would not normally be subject to management's disciplinary power. Alternatively, if the fight has its roots in the employment relationship and has a demonstrable effect on the work environment, management's concern is legitimate. As Dean Shulman noted, "the jurisdictional line which limits the Company's power of discipline is a functional, not a physical line. It has power to discipline for misconduct directly related to the employment."[10] The difficulty is determining when an employee's "privacy" interests must give way to the legitimate business interests of the employer.

Just Cause Criteria

An examination of awards reveals a number of standards arbitrators use to evaluate discharge or discipline for off-duty misconduct. These include injury to the employer's business, inability to report for work or unsuitability for continued employment as a result of the misconduct, co-employee refusal to work with the off-duty offender or danger to other employees, and adverse effect of the misconduct upon the employer-employee relationship. While there is frequently overlap within these categories, it is nevertheless useful to examine the cases under these headings.

Injury to Employer's Business

A common argument presented by management is that the employee's off-duty conduct has caused an actual business loss or injured the company's reputation. Arbitrator D. Emmett Ferguson summarized the standard as follows:

> The general rule is that an employee upon being employed by a company, places himself under the jurisdiction of the employer so far as their joint relationship is concerned. While it is true that the employer does not thereby become the guardian of the

---

[9]Opinion A-132, Ford Motor Co. and UAW-CIO (N.Y. State Sch. Indus. & Lab. Rels., 1944).
[10]Id.

employee's every personal action and does not exercise parental control, it is equally true that in those areas having to do with the employer's business, the employer has the right to terminate the relationship if the employee's wrongful actions injuriously affect the business.[11]

Discharge for an employee's off-duty misconduct is most likely to be upheld where an employer can link the conduct to an actual business loss. For example, Arbitrator Joseph Sharnoff ruled that an employee's 30-day jail term justified discharge because of lost production encountered as a result of the employee's incarceration.[12] Similarly, under a rule that an employee could be dismissed for absence without reasonable cause, Arbitrator Robert Boyd found that a company having a huge backlog of orders was "injured" when a skilled employee failed to report for work due to a short stay in jail. According to the arbitrator, management was not obligated to grant the employee a leave of absence to serve out his jail term.[13] The employee could not obtain a work release from jail and no other employees were qualified to replace him. The arbitrator upheld discharge because of the resulting harm to the company. Alternatively, in *Quick Manufacturing, Inc.*,[14] Arbitrator Edwin Teple ruled that discharge was too severe for an employee who missed eight working days while serving a jail sentence for operating a vehicle under a suspended license. The record showed no loss or inconvenience to the company as a result of the employee's absence, the employee's job was found not critical to plant operations, and management had stipulated that production was not affected. Although there was a contract provision stating that seniority rights would be terminated if an employee was absent for three consecutive days without permission, the arbitrator pointed out that termination of seniority rights is not the same thing as the termination of the employment relationship.[15]

In a few cases a discharge has even been upheld where a business loss was only a possibility. In *Baltimore Transit Co.*,[16] a bus operator was publicly identified as the acting grand dragon of the state branch of the Ku Klux Klan. In upholding

[11]Inland Container Corp., 28 LA 312, 314 (1957).
[12]Bethlehem Steel Corp., 72 LA 210 (Sharnoff, 1979).
[13]Oren Roanoke Corp., 70 LA 942 (Boyd, 1978).
[14]43 LA 54 (Teple, 1964).
[15]Id. at 60.
[16]47 LA 62 (Duff, 1966).

the discharge, Arbitrator Clair Duff acknowledged that, unless the discharge was sustained, there existed a clear and present danger of physical violence and an inevitable economic boycott against the company. In finding that there was just cause for dismissal, the arbitrator also noted that there was considerable support for a wildcat strike by the grievant's fellow employees. The arbitrator pointed out that the grievant's activities, not his beliefs, were at issue in the case:

> While an employee's right to be protected from an unjust discharge needs to be vigilantly guarded lest the subjective judgment of employers becomes the criteria for regulating the morals of the community, yet even traditional individual rights must be restricted when upon considered reflection, they are found to seriously conflict with the vital rights of the community. By X____'s zealous espousal of racial intolerance and bigotry he became a public leader in a movement of intolerance and hate. His activities, not his beliefs, are the issue. . . .
> Whether or not membership in the Klan is prohibited by statute is not determinative. Some activities are *malum in se.* X____ was not discharged because of his beliefs or membership in any organization. His public utterances were widely publicized and the admitted aims and objectives of the Klan made it eminently clear that the target of his activities was not mere words but action contrary to the rights of a large segment of the population of the City of Baltimore which included at least 50% of patrons of the Company's bus lines.[17]

Likewise, a criminal conviction, coupled with numerous arrests, a known habit of consorting with criminals and prostitutes, and a job requiring the employee to work alone in customer homes reading meters amounted to enough "potential" harm to a company that an arbitrator upheld a discharge even though no actual business loss was demonstrated.[18]

Where an injurious effect upon a company's reputation is argued, arbitrators look at the source and degree of adverse publicity,[19] the type of misconduct,[20] and the position held by the employee[21] in determining the extent of "injured reputation."

---

[17]Id. at 66.

[18]Gas Serv. Co., 39 LA 1025 (Granoff, 1962).

[19]See, e.g., Fairmont Gen. Hosp., 58 LA 1293 (Dybeck, 1972); Baltimore Transit Co., 47 LA 62 (Duff, 1966); and Martin Oil Co., 29 LA 54 (Brown, 1957).

[20]See, e.g., Quaker Oats Co., 15 LA 42 (Abrahams, 1950); Gas Serv. Co., 39 LA 1025 (Granoff, 1962); and Consolidated Badger Coop., 36 LA 965 (Mueller, 1961).

[21]See, e.g., Fairmont Gen. Hosp., 58 LA 1293 (Dybeck, 1972); Gas Serv. Co., 39 LA 1025 (Granoff, 1962); and Consolidated Badger Coop., 36 LA 965 (Mueller, 1961).

At times, the employer's plant or work rules will address the issue. For example, American Airlines' Rule No. 34 provides in part, "Any action constituting a criminal offense, whether committed on duty or off duty, will be grounds for dismissal."[22] In *Trailways Southeastern Lines, Inc.*,[23] Arbitrator Robert Gibson considered the discharge of a driver for violating the following rule: "Words or acts hostile to the Company, or words or acts which result in damage to the Company's reputation, property or service, are cause for disciplinary action." The grievant had entered a guilty plea to breaking and entering his estranged wife's house with intent to commit murder, as well as trying to burn down another house belonging to his wife. In sustaining the discharge, the arbitrator reasoned that the employee's conduct "could not help but result in damage to the reputation of the Company . . . because of the notoriety Grievant received in the newspaper reports."[24]

In recognizing the difficulty in determining injury or harm to company reputation, one arbitrator commented:

> In some situations the impact upon the employer's affairs of the employee's misconduct off the premises may be immediate and/or obvious; short of this, there is no objective standard by which it may be determined whether or not the misconduct WILL HAVE any effect or impact and consequently any conclusion thereon lies wholly within the realm of prediction. . . . Where there is no evident immediate effect upon the affairs of the employer, the best that can be done is to seek an answer to the question: Does the employee's misconduct exhibit such a defect of character as makes it likely, in the light of human experience, either that others will be caused thereby to be unfavorably disposed toward the employer or that the same type of misconduct will recur with deleterious effect upon the affairs of the employer?[25]

To illustrate, in *Cashton Cooperative Creamery*,[26] Arbitrator Robert Mueller considered the discharge of an employee who had entered a plea of *nolo contendere* to taking indecent

---

[22]See, e.g., American Airlines and Association of Flight Attendants, Case No. SS-165-80-LAX (Kagel, 1981) (unpublished).
[23]81 LA 712 (1983).
[24]Id. at 716. See also Air Canada, 75 LA 301, 302 (Brown, 1980) (rule prohibiting "violations of a public law or commission of a criminal offence"); Allied Materials Corp., 78 LA 1049 (Allen, 1982) (rule prohibiting "conduct that violates common decency or morality"); Eastern Air Lines, 76 LA 961, 963 (Turkus, 1981) ("Conduct on or off the job which was in conflict with the Company's interest").
[25]Hyman-Michaels Co., 62-1 ARB ¶8334, 4274 (Townsend, 1962).
[26]61-1 ARB ¶8008 (Mueller, 1960).

liberties with a female (his 14-year-old daughter). In sustaining the discharge, the arbitrator noted that the conviction resulted in widespread publicity throughout the small community in which the employer operated in a highly competitive industry. Although this is not related to the reputation issue, the arbitrator also recognized the importance of the views of the grievant's colleagues by pointing out that, at the hearing, the employer presented a signed statement by 13 out of 18 employees to the effect that they did not want the grievant back as a coworker.

Where actual business loss or injury to reputation is not established or, alternatively, is not apparent from the misconduct itself, arbitrators are reluctant to sustain a discharge. In *Quaker Oats Co.*,[27] discharge was not sustained for an employee who pleaded guilty to contributing to the delinquency of a minor. The arbitrator noted that the employee's position did not place him in direct contact with the public and no complaints were received as a result of the incident. Similarly, another arbitrator refused to allow discharge of an employee with 19 years' seniority who faced an assault charge for shooting his wife.[28] Even though adverse publicity resulted from the incident, the arbitrator commented: "If [the employee] has lost his acceptability to customers that fact, too, will quickly appear and the Company will have concrete evidence, rather than speculation, on which to base its decision."[29]

Likewise, in *Vulcan Asphalt Refining Co.*,[30] Arbitrator Henry Welch reversed the discharge of an employee for selling a former classmate (working as an undercover narcotics agent) a small amount of marijuana. The arbitrator pointed out: (1) that while the incident was common knowledge in the small town and had been the subject of newspaper reports, it did not in any noticeable degree harm the company's reputation or product; (2) that the misconduct did not render the employee unable to perform his duties; and (3) that his arrest and conviction could not be expected to cause refusal, reluctance, or inability on the part of other employees to work with him.

Proving injury to the company's reputation is more difficult than demonstrating that the employer's business suf-

---

[27]15 LA 42 (Abrahams, 1950).
[28]Martin Oil Co., 29 LA 54 (Brown, 1957).
[29]Id. at 56.
[30]78 LA 1311 (Welch, 1982).

fered a financial loss due to the grievant's conduct. Indeed, some arbitrators have viewed "business reputation" as too nebulous a concept to be useful.[31] When confronted with arguments that a grievant's off-duty misconduct damaged a company's reputation, arbitrators have required a clear showing before sustaining discharges. This may be accomplished by reference to adverse media coverage or, in selected cases, by direct reference to the conduct itself. As a note of caution to employers, it may be difficult for an employer to argue that the off-duty criminal conduct of a grievant adversely affects its reputation where the company has in the past hired ex-convicts who have proved to be able and trustworthy employees.

Inability to Report for Work

Employees may absent themselves from work for a variety of reasons having to do with off-duty misconduct. An arrest or jail term usually requires that an employee be away from work. In this respect, arbitrators generally look for a violation of a specific provision of the collective bargaining agreement before sustaining discharge. In *Dorsey Trailers, Inc.*,[32] an employee was detained in jail for armed robbery. The company had a plant rule that any employee failing to report for work without giving notice to the employer within three days lost all employment rights under the agreement. The arbitrator sustained the discharge.

In *Rite-Way, Inc.*,[33] however, Arbitrator Myron Roomkin held discharge too severe for an incarcerated employee who failed to give notification of his absence as required under the collective bargaining agreement. The arbitrator reasoned that the company failed to apply its practice of progressive discipline and to issue a reprimand as it had done with a previous employee.

In another incarceration case the arbitrator stated the rule as follows:

[W]hen an employee is incarcerated, a company has the right to discharge him since he is, for the period of time, unable to work. The reason a discharge is proper in such cases is not

---

[31]Movielab, Inc., 50 LA 632 (McMahon, 1968).
[32]73 LA 196 (Hamby, 1979).
[33]63 LA 783 (1974).

because of the crime the employee has committed but rather it is simply that through the employee's own actions, he has made it impossible to fulfill his obligation to report to work. Therefore, in such cases, a company has "just cause" to terminate the employee since he is of no benefit to the company.[34]

The arbitrator went on to point out that while a number of arbitrators have made it clear that management's decision to grant an employee a leave of absence to serve a jail term is within the sole discretion of the employer, some arbitrators have held that this discretion must be exercised in a reasonable manner.[35]

Arbitrator John Murphy summarized the better weight of authority in this area as follows:

> Whether or not confinement of an employee in jail will authorize his employer to take some sort of disciplinary action depends upon all the circumstances, including, among other things:
> a. The language of their contract.
> b. The length of confinement.
> c. The nature of the cause for confinement; i.e., whether as the result of an arrest and inability to post bond, or as the result of a sentence.
> d. The nature of the conduct resulting in confinement, i.e., its degree of seriousness and impropriety.
> e. The nature of the disciplinary action to be taken or which results.
> f. The employee's previous work and disciplinary record.
> g. The extent to which the absence affected the employer's production, etc.
> h. The effect upon plant morale.
> i. Whether or not the conduct occurred on plant property or during working hours.[36]

Unsuitability for Continued Employment

An individual may possess the physical capacity to perform a job but, because of the nature of the off-duty misconduct, may be considered unsuitable for continued

---

[34]Ralphs-Pugh Co., 79 LA 6, 9–10 (McKay, 1982), citing McInerney Spring & Wire Co., 72 LA 1262, 1265 (Roumell, 1979); accord, Boeing Servs. Int'l, 75 LA 967 (Kramer, 1980). See also Ampco Pittsburgh Corp., 75 LA 363, 366 (Seinsheimer, 1980) (just cause for dismissal of employee convicted of voluntary manslaughter and absent from work for extended period of time.

[35]79 LA at 10 (citations omitted).

[36]Sperry Rand Corp., 60 LA 220, 222–23 (1973); see also Bethlehem Steel Co., 32 LA 543, 544–45 (Seward, 1959).

employment. Arbitrator Alfred Dybeck, in *Fairmont General Hospital*,[37] considered the discharge of a hospital maid for shoplifting at a local department store. Because the hospital had experienced a recent problem of theft, and even though the maid was not accused of stealing from the hospital, the arbitrator upheld discharge because her actions created a serious doubt as to her trustworthiness as an employee.

In another case, an employee was discharged after pleading guilty to falsely reporting that his car had been stolen.[38] The employer's business involved confidential processes and designs, and this, coupled with the employee's known associations with persons engaging in illegal activities, prompted the arbitrator to sustain the employee's discharge. According to the arbitrator, the "risk attendant upon his retention would have been a major one."

The question of an employee's honesty in dealing with his employer forced the arbitrator, in *Southern California Edison Co.*,[39] to sustain a discharge. The employee failed to give notice of his absence and lied to the employer about his off-duty arrest for possession of marijuana (the employee said that he had been arrested for drunk driving). The employee did not attempt to make alternate arrangements and was away from work for several days to take care of legal matters. His failure to state the truth led the arbitrator to comment:

> [The company] must evaluate an employee's breach of the law to determine if the employee has disqualified himself for employment with the Company and it is entitled to accurate information from the employee in order to make that evaluation.[40]

Similarly, in *Safeway Stores, Inc.*,[41] Arbitrator James Doyle ruled the company had just cause to discharge an employee for "proven dishonesty" after he was convicted for stealing a vacuum cleaner at another store. In so ruling, the arbitrator rejected the argument that the words "proven dishonesty" in

---

[37]58 LA 1293 (Dybeck, 1972).
[38]NRM Corp., 51 LA 177, 181 (Teple, 1968).
[39]59 LA 529 (Helbling, 1972).
[40]Id. at 533.
[41]74 LA 1293 (1980).

the contract[42] meant only dishonesty relating to the grievant's employment.[43]

In *American Airlines*,[44] however, an employee was given a "second chance" after being convicted of shoplifting while off duty and not in uniform. The arbitrator reasoned that the employee had not given the employer any reason to question her honesty during her previous four years of employment and should be given the benefit of the doubt. No publicity was given the incident.[45]

Summary

Where off-duty misconduct results in the physical inability of an employee to properly perform work duties, arbitrators examine whether such conduct violates a specific provision of the agreement. If it does, discharge will normally be upheld, especially where the company can also demonstrate injury to its operations. When it is argued that an employee's off-duty misconduct renders the employee unsuitable for employment, arbitrators in sustaining dismissals have focused on considerations of honesty and the overall character of the grievant as these traits relate to a specific job. Other considerations being equal, it will be difficult for an employer to sustain a discharge based merely upon the fact of a criminal conviction. In the "inability" and "unsuitability" cases, however, arbitrators may properly take into consideration mitigating circumstances such as the employee's prior work record

---

[42]The agreement stated, "Employer shall not discharge any employee without just cause." The contract further stated, "An employee shall have at least two (2) written warning notices of the specific complaint against the employee before discharge except in cases of proven dishonesty,. . ." Id. at 1294.

[43]See Southern Bell Tel. & Tel. Co., 75 LA 409 (Seibel, 1980)(upholding discharge of outside repair technician for making obscene telephone calls); Corn Belt Elec. Coop., 79 LA 1045 (O'Grady, 1982)(discharge by electric cooperative of journeyman-lineman for "theft" of electricity); Hilton Hawaiian Village, 76 LA 347 (Tanaka, 1981)(discharge of bellman for sale of stolen handgun).

[44]68 LA 1245 (Harkless, 1977).

[45]See also Means Servs. Co., 81 LA 1213, 1216 (Slade, 1983) ("connection between the facts of this case [off-duty theft] and the extent to which the business is affected must be reasonable and discernible"); Maust Transfer Co., 78 LA 780 (LaCugna, 1982) (discharge of truck driver for dishonesty after entering guilty plea of theft reversed absent showing of causal link between conduct and ability to perform job); Ralphs Grocery Co., 77 LA 867 (Kaufman, 1981) (reversing discharge of employees who hosted party where "lesbian show" had taken place); Nugent Sand Co., 81 LA 988, 989 (Daniel, 1983) (reinstating employee who entered guilty plea for growing marijuana notwithstanding rule subjecting employees to discharge for "[c]onviction of a felony involving honesty, death other than negligent homicide, morals, drugs or narcotics").

and whether in similar situations progressive discipline had been applied.

Objectionability or Danger to Other Employees

In some cases an employee's off-duty misconduct will cause co-employees to refuse to work with the grievant. When confronted with such a claim, arbitrators generally require a clear demonstration that this is true. Otherwise, discharge may be viewed as too harsh.

Refusal to work with a fellow employee may stem from an employee's conviction of a serious crime. This was the case in *Robertshaw Controls Co.*,[46] where an employee pleaded guilty to sodomy and corrupting the morals of children. The employee was a scoutmaster in the community where he worked with parents, friends, and relatives of the victimized children. In analyzing this case, Arbitrator Clair Duff restated the principle set forth in the often-quoted *Chicago Pneumatic Tool Co.*,[47] decision.

> Arbitrators are reluctant to sustain discharges based on off-duty conduct of employees unless a direct relationship between off-duty conduct and employment is proved. Discretion must be exercised lest Employers become censors of community morals. However, where socially reprehensible conduct and employment duties and risks are substantially related, conviction for certain types of crimes may justify discharge.[48]

Arbitrator Duff, in sustaining the discharge, noted that the misconduct could not be kept separate from the activities of the workplace because so many families were involved. As the arbitrator stated, "A business enterprise by its nature requires collaboration, accord and reasonable harmony among employees. The technical and administrative sides of an enterprise cannot function correctly if the human side of the business is disrupted with conflict."[49] Arbitrator Duff reasoned that families do not want their sons to seek or retain employment in a company where they would be subjected to the possible influence of a convicted sodomist. It is of note that the arbitrator made this finding notwithstanding the fact that

---

[46]64-2 ARB ¶8748 (1964).
[47]38 LA 891, 893 (Duff, 1961).
[48]Robertshaw Controls Co., supra note 46, at 5613.
[49]Id.

25 employees signed a statement that they had no objection
to working with the grievant.

In *Lone Star Gas Co.*,[50] an employee of a public utility
was indicted and later found guilty of incest. The arbitrator
found it was impossible to reinstate the employee when there
was testimony by the grievant's fellow workers that they were
reluctant to continue working with him.

The same reasoning in *Robertshaw Controls Co.*, however,
was not controlling in *Kentile Floors, Inc.*,[51] where an employee was convicted of possession of narcotics (amphetamines). Even though the company had a rule stating that
employees convicted of crimes were subject to discharge, the
arbitrator held that the discharge was inappropriate because
the conviction had no discernible effect upon the employee's
relationship with fellow workers. It is of special note that
Arbitrator Howard Block reasoned that the employer's rule
was overbroad since it failed to take into account the relationship between the crime and the employment situation.
The discharge was thus seen as arbitrary and capricious. Similarly, in *International Paper Co.*,[52] discharge was reversed for
an employee convicted of an off-duty assault and battery against
his foreman. (The employee, in an apparent argument over a
woman in a tavern, had slashed his foreman with a knife.)
Though the arbitrator viewed the knifing as a serious act of
misconduct, he believed that it would not disrupt plant operations by creating fear among fellow employees.

In another case,[53] an employee was offered $20 by co-
employees to "streak" in front of a baggage terminal at the
airport where he worked. The employee accepted the offer and
later, wearing nothing but a ski mask, tee shirt, and cowboy
boots, streaked in front of the terminal. When news of the
incident reached management, the employee was discharged
for irresponsibility. In overturning the discharge, the arbitrator reasoned, in part, that the misconduct was not viewed
negatively by co-workers. In fact, because some had even en-
couraged it, they had little, if any, reluctance to work with
the grievant.

When it is believed that the off-duty misconduct poses a

---

[50]56 LA 1221 (Johannes, 1971).
[51]57 LA 919 (1971).
[52]52 LA 1266 (Jenkins, 1969).
[53]Air Cal., 63 LA 350 (Kaufman, 1974).

threat to the safety of fellow workers, however, arbitrators are not reluctant to sustain discharge. In one case, an employee's conviction for aggravated assault for attacking an elderly man prompted the company to terminate his employment. The company successfully argued that the employee was dangerous and continued employment would endanger the safety of his fellow workers. Similarly, in *Central Packing Co.*,[54] an employee convicted for attacking his wife and mother-in-law with a knife was subsequently discharged. At work, the employee had easy access to knives, cleavers, and other instruments. Even though the employee's numerous arrests and convictions were all unrelated to work, the board of arbitration upheld discharge for the protection of other employees.

Even when the off-duty conduct does not involve acts of violence, discharges have been sustained where a showing has been made that the safety or health of workers would be threatened by reinstating the grievant. In *Martin-Marietta Aerospace, Baltimore Division*,[55] Arbitrator Louis Aronin, in sustaining a discharge upon the employer's discovery that an employee had been convicted of selling cocaine to an undercover agent, found that this conduct had an impact on the employer's product, reputation, employee safety, plant security, production, and discipline. The company established that the grievant had a history of drug abuse and, at times, was even under the influence of cocaine while at work. The arbitrator, concluding that the employee was a "pusher," found that the evidence established more than mere "social use" of drugs by the grievant and determined that the employer could conclude that the grievant might attempt to sell drugs to other employees.[56]

On the other hand, discharge may be inappropriate despite serious misconduct. Thus, in *Certain-Teed Products Corp.*,[57] an employee was discharged after serving 10 weeks

---

[54]24 LA 603 (Granoff, 1955).
[55]81 LA 695 (1983).
[56]Id. at 698–99. See also Chicago Pneumatic Tool Co., 38 LA 891 (Duff, 1961) ("Degeneration of the addict could at any time reach a point where it would seriously endanger the health and safety of fellow employees."); New York City Health & Hosps. Corp., 76 LA 387 (Simons, 1981) (discharge of probationary ambulance corpsman for sale of cocaine); Eastern Air Lines, 76 LA 961 (Turkus, 1981) (discharge sustained when stewardess while at airport and in uniform sold marijuana to co-employee.
[57]24 LA 606 (Simkin, 1955).

of a six-month sentence for assault. The company argued unsuccessfully that reinstatement posed a serious threat to other workers. Absent clear evidence that reinstatement would endanger the safety of other employees, the arbitrator found that the grievant's good work record, coupled with 30 years of service, more than offset any potential danger to the other employees.

In general, where co-employee concerns are at issue arbitrators will uphold discharge if management demonstrates that the safety of other workers is endangered by reinstatement. While there are exceptions in this regard, a clear showing that co-employees have refused to work with the grievant will generally be sufficient to sustain a discharge. Evidence that employees will not work with the grievant if reinstated has also been credited by arbitrators.

Adverse Effect on Employer-Employee Relationship

Of the several standards, demonstrating that the employee's off-duty conduct has an adverse effect upon the employer-employee "relationship" is probably the most difficult to establish. This standard appears so far-reaching that it arguably encompasses just about every facet of the workplace. Indeed, it is fair to say that, at times, this standard is a catch-all used by arbitrators when the conduct does not neatly fit into the other categories.

The guiding principle was acknowledged by Arbitrator George Bowles in *General Telephone Co. of Kentucky*:[58]

> In many of the incidents involving events outside a plant the nexus or connection between that which has occurred within the employment relationship and outside the plant cannot be established. The Company cannot dictate the private lives of employees, and each employee has a right of privacy outside the employment relationship. However, if outside the plant an incident occurs that is related to and connected with that which has happened within the employer-employee relationship, then the Company under established principles of industrial jurisprudence, and so-called management rights, may take disciplinary action.[59]

As in all off-duty cases the key, therefore, is to establish

---

[58]69 LA 351 (Bowles, 1977).
[59]Id. at 357.

the so-called "nexus" between the misconduct and the employment relationship. In the cited case, Arbitrator Bowles sustained the discharge of an employee who verbally and physically assaulted his supervisor at a restaurant while both were off-duty. The arbitrator reasoned the assault would be detrimental to the supervisor's ability to handle employees and the employee's bitterness and hostility toward company supervision would carry over into the employment relationship.

In another case involving a company supervisor, Arbitrator David Beckman, in *Heaven Hill Distilleries, Inc.*,[60] sustained the discharge of an employee who, unprovoked, assaulted his supervisor and threatened the plant manager at a local restaurant. The arbitrator's reasoning is noteworthy:

> The commission of an unprovoked assault and battery on one's immediate supervisor is in and of itself harmful to the employment relationship and to the supervisor. The harm need not be measured in medical bills or blood. The harm is even more lasting and pervasive than superficial cuts or injuries. The very existence of the commission of the act against the supervisor alters the supervisor's fundamental ability to supervise the perpetrator in the future. The existence of the act sets up a barrier to future direction which unreasonably hampers the supervisor in his task of directing the work force. The essence of wrong here is that the negotiators have specifically agreed that the supervisor has the right to direct the work force. The [employee] by his actions, however, has unreasonably blunted the exercise of that right in the future. His actions thus amount to a serious and fundamental violation of the negotiated agreement, for which discharge is not an unreasonable or unjust remedy.[61]

Arbitrator Joe Kerkman, in *Murray Machinery, Inc.*,[62] considered whether a suspension was proper for employees who prevented other persons from coming to the aid of a foreman who was being assaulted by the employees' guest at a party. In upholding the suspension the arbitrator reasoned that even though the altercation occurred off duty and away from company premises, it was "so inextricably connected with the work place setting and supervisor-subordinate relationships, that it properly falls within recognized exceptions to

[60]74 LA 42 (Beckman, 1980).
[61]Id. at 46. See also Simmons Co. USA, 78 LA 347, 351 (Yarowsky, 1982) ("The simple test is whether the act is so inconsistent with the employer-employee relation as to be just cause for the discharge.")
[62]75 LA 284 (1980).

the ... principle that the company may not control off duty employee conduct via disciplinary methods."[63]

Adverse effect on the employer-employee relationship is not solely illustrated in cases involving altercations between supervisors and employees. In *Joy Manufacturing Co.*,[64] for example, Arbitrator Charles Freeman concluded that an adverse effect would result from the reinstatement of an employee who was convicted of selling marijuana. The arbitrator, noting that the company had recently implemented a drug rehabilitation program with the assistance of the union, ruled that the grievant's continued employment would undermine the program's purpose.

The continued ability of the employer to direct the work force after an employee engaged in questionable off-duty conduct was one consideration cited by the arbitrator in *Hughes Air Corp.*[65] In this case, a male flight attendant made a "sexual offering" to a male employee of the hotel where the attendant was staying on layover. The arbitrator held the discharge unjust because the incident was isolated in nature and did not undermine the employer's ability to manage other employees. Similarly, in *Vulcan Materials Co.*,[66] discharge was not allowed for an employee who received a suspended sentence after pleading guilty to possession of marijuana. The arbitrator reasoned, in part, that absent any evidence of disruption of employee relations, discharge cannot be allowed. In making his award, the arbitrator took pains to point out that the grievance must be viewed in light of the law and the court proceedings with respect to the grievant. The arbitrator noted that it was the intent of the court *not* to brand the grievant a convicted criminal if he successfully met the terms and conditions of his probation. The arbitrator concluded that the court was trying to protect the grievant against the stigma and its consequences, such as reduced employment opportunities. Likewise, Arbitrator Sam Nicholas, Jr., in *Union Oil Co. of California*,[67] stated that "one point that runs in Grievant's favor is the fact that she received an unadjudicated probation,

[63]Id. at 287.
[64]68 LA 697 (Freeman, 1977).
[65]73 LA 148 (Barsamian, 1979).
[66]56 LA 469 (Shearer, 1971).
[67]85-1 ARB ¶8161 (1985).

with heavy penalties facing her should she become involved in further possession or delivery of narcotics."[68]

Where the off-duty "harassment" of a supervisor by an employee is not vindictive in nature, but simply amounts to a series of pranks that do not have an impact on a supervisor's ability to manage, discharge has been overturned. Thus in *Gould, Inc.*,[69] the arbitrator found that discharge was too severe for an employee who allegedly placed a supervisor's home with an agent for him to sell and who had a load of black dirt dumped on the supervisor's driveway.

Application to Public Sector

In the public sector, discharge for off-duty misconduct may be restricted by contractual, statutory,[70] or even Constitutional mandates.[71] Constitutional considerations are discussed separately below. Contractual limitations, as in the private sector, are imposed by just cause provisions in collective bargaining agreements. In general, just cause precedents and standards established by private-sector labor arbitrators have also been applied in the public sector, although in off-duty cases there appears to be a greater sensitivity to the criteria of the reputation and mission of the agency on the part of both arbitrators and courts.

As in the private sector, the overriding principle in the public sector is that discipline for off-duty misconduct is appropriate only when such misconduct has a demonstrable ad-

---

[68]Id. at 3674.

[69]76 LA 1187 (Boyer, 1981).

[70]5 U.S.C. §7513(a) of the Civil Service Reform Act of 1978 permits removal of an employee "only for such cause as will promote the efficiency of the service." To dismiss a federal employee for off-duty conduct the government must make at least two separate determinations: (1) did the employee commit the act(s) allegedly responsible for his removal; and (2) is there a nexus between the employee's misconduct and the efficiency of the service. Cooper v. United States, 639 F.2d 727, 729 (Ct. Cl., 1980). The Merit Systems Protection Board (MSPB) has, at times, interpreted §7513(a) to mean that, where the misconduct is egregious, a nexus is presumed. Abrams v. Department of the Navy, 714 F.2d 1219, 1221 (CA 3, 1983)("employee may rebut this presumption by showing an absence of adverse effect upon the efficiency of the service, thereby shifting the burden of going forward with evidence to the agency to establish, by a preponderance of the evidence, a nexus between the off-duty misconduct and the efficiency of the service"); Borsari v. FAA, 699 F.2d 106 (CA 2, 1983), cert. denied, 464 U.S. 833 (1983); Masino v. United States, 589 F.2d 1048 (Ct. Cl., 1978). Note, however, that not all courts have embraced the MSPB's application of a "presumption of a nexus."

[71]See, infra notes 98–169 and accompanying text.

verse effect upon the employer's business or the overall employment relationship. Illustrative is *U.S. Internal Revenue Service*,[72] in which two male employees were suspended for "mooning" a woman in a parking garage. While discharge was not involved, the reasoning and analysis articulated by Arbitrator Samuel Edes are consistent with holdings of arbitrators in private-sector discharge cases.

> [The] applicable standard to be applied in judging the conduct of employees in public service takes into realistic account the fallible nature of the human condition which results, with substantial frequency, in conduct which is less than exemplary by commandment of both moral and legal codes. It recognizes, quite properly, that, however much an employer may be wont to enforce such codes and condemn their transgression, [the employer] is entitled to do so only to the degree that there is a direct and demonstrable relationship between the illicit conduct and the performance of the employee's job or the job of others.[73]

Arbitrator Edes further noted that because one employee's off-duty actions may be subject to disciplinary penalty and another's may not, determination of the propriety of disciplinary penalty can only be made on a case-by-case basis. Furthermore, an employer's power to discipline is restricted even where misconduct results in substantial embarrassment to the employer. In discussing this aspect, he commented:

> It is not unworthy of an employer to hope that all of his employees conduct themselves in a manner which . . . is above suspicion. Failing the realization of such goals, [the employer] can only exercise his authority in respect to conduct which affects the work of his employees and, accordingly, the efficiency of his enterprise.[74]

The declarations by Arbitrator Edes highlight a principle used by many arbitrators in regard to off-duty misconduct. Again, arbitrators generally look for a nexus between the conduct of the employee and the employment setting.

A paradigm case in the public sector is *United States Customs Service*,[75] in which Arbitrator Joseph Rocha considered the discharge of a customs inspector for homosexual behavior. In holding that the agency did not have just cause to effect the termination, the arbitrator reasoned that:

---

[72]77 LA 19 (Edes, 1981).
[73]Id. at 21–22.
[74]Id. at 22.
[75]77 LA 1113 (1981).

If any fact has been firmly established by the evidence, it is that the grievant separated his homosexual practices from his activities as a Customs Inspector. He succeeded so well in this respect that no one associated with his employment knew of his homosexuality until he was discharged. Also critical is the fact that no traveler ever complained about [grievant] for any valid reason. Certainly, [grievant's] homosexual behavior did not manifest itself in any way that resulted in notoriety or public censure which would reflect unfavorably on Customs. . . .

Customs relied for precedent on a 1970 "sanitized" case arising in Buffalo in which a Customs Inspector was discharged because he had been arrested and convicted for engaging in homosexual conduct in a public toilet. That case is easily distinguished from the instant case. In the 1970 case, the homosexual activity occurred in a public place; the arrest and conviction became a matter of public record. As a consequence, Customs was identified with notoriety and public censure and was exposed to an erosion of public confidence. These elements are absent from the present proceeding.[76]

This nexus requirement was again applied in *Social Security Administration*,[77] where an arbitrator was forced to determine if a nexus existed between an employee's conviction for sexual offenses against a minor, for which he served a six-month sentence, and his employment with satisfactory performance as a clerk-typist. The arbitrator was particularly concerned with possible adverse public reaction, for which the employer offered no supporting evidence. In overturning the discharge, the arbitrator held that, absent any demonstrable loss of public confidence in the employer, there could be no impairment in the efficiency of the agency. His reasoning is cited at length:

> Under 5 U.S.C. 7701(c)(1)(B) [of the Civil Service Reform Act], Management has the burden of proof under the preponderance of evidence test. In this respect, the Agency has a twofold burden. It must first prove that a wrongful act has occurred and then that the discharge for the wrongful act would promote the Agency's efficiency. Since the Grievant's removal, as stated aforesaid, was based upon two actions, the sexual offense and impeding the operations of the SSA, they will be discussed separately. The sexual offense will be considered first.
>
> Although H____ denied in his testimony that he committed the sexual offense as charged, a copy of his conviction was entered into the record. Copies of court records are acceptable evidence and may be received by an arbitrator as such. Maroon

---

[76]Id. at 1117 (footnote omitted).
[77]80 LA 725 (Lubic, 1983).

v. Immigration and Naturalization Service, 364 F.2d 982 (8th Cir. 1966), U.S. v. Verlinsky, 459 F.2d 1085 (5th Cir. 1972). Thus Management has met its burden in proving the commission of a wrongful act by the Grievant.

It next must be determined whether, due to the Grievant's wrongful act, his removal from employment will promote efficiency of the SSA. This must be accomplished by proving a logical connection (nexus) between H＿＿＿'s off-duty misconduct and his employment with SSA. As stated in Doe v. Hampton, 566 F.2d 265, 272 (D.C. Cir. 1977),

> * * * there must be a clear and direct relationship demonstrated between the articulated grounds for an adverse personnel action and either the employee's ability to accomplish his or her duties satisfactorily or some other legitimate government interest promoting the efficiency of the service."

Although, in the case of "certain egregious circumstances * * * a presumption of nexus may arise from the nature and gravity of the misconduct" [Merritt v. Department of Justice, MSPB Docket No. PH075209058 (1981)] the Agency specifically states that it does not intend to rely upon any such presumption. Thus the SSA must directly prove by a preponderance of evidence the nexus between the Grievant's off-duty sexual activities and [their effect] upon the efficiency of the service.

The testimony by various supervisors of H＿＿ upon which the Agency relies for this purpose, involved the concern for disabled employees, as well as student aides, working around the Grievant, the effect of disclosure and possible contact work with the public and the possibility that H＿＿ could become a physical threat. All of this is speculative. In order to engage in public contact work the Grievant would have to be transferred to a field office which under the circumstances appears highly unlikely. The fact that H＿＿ has made sexual advances to minors does not necessarily imply that he would while on duty attempt to engage in similar activities with disabled employees or student aides, especially since nothing even slightly similar to this has occurred over the past eight years. There was also no evidence that the public was even aware of H＿＿'s conviction. Thus the foregoing evidence is not sufficient to prove the necessary nexus.

Referring further to federal law, the arbitrator concluded:

> As reprehensible as H＿＿'s misconduct is to this Arbitrator, I must hold that the recent decision of the Court of Appeals in Bonet v. United States Postal Service [661 F.2d 1071, 108 LRRM 3158 (CA 5, 1981)] is controlling in this matter. The employee in that case appealed from a decision of the Merit Systems Protection Board affirming his discharge from his job

with the Post Office for alleged grossly immoral and indecent off-duty conduct with a child. As stated therein:

> "The Agency cannot satisfy the statutory requirement that an employee's removal promote the efficiency of the service by use of unsupported, general assertions that such action is necessary to maintain the public confidence. To permit otherwise would be to render nugatory the protections afforded the federal employee by the imposition of a standard for removal which requires a connection between employee misconduct (especially when off-duty and non-work related) and the job. The agency must demonstrate, therefore, a relationship between this employee's misconduct and the spectre that *public confidence will be undermined.*" (emphasis added)

> * * * "Despite our reflective revulsion for the type of off-duty misconduct in question, whether resulting from a now-cured mental disability or not, the 1978 (Civil Service Reform) Act does not permit this court nor an employing agency to characterize off-duty conduct as so obnoxious as to show, per se, a nexus between it and the efficiency of the service. The 1978 Act prohibits the discharge of a federal employee for conduct that does not adversely affect the performance of that employee or his co-employees, * * * ."

Although the Agency attempts to differentiate Bonet on the grounds that the employee in that matter was not actually convicted of a crime as here and that the employer therein relied solely upon the grossly immoral nature of the off-duty conduct as establishing a nexus per se, this argument is specious to say the least. The Bonet decision appears to be on all fours with the facts in the present matter and just because the criminal indictment against the employee therein was dismissed due to the unwillingness of the mother of the child to prosecute, this should not control the reliance thereon. Other than proof of the commission of the subject sexual act, the Agency here has failed to prove any relationship between that act and the undermining of public confidence.[78]

Similarly, the arbitrator in *City of Wilkes-Barre*,[79] refused to allow discharge of a blue-collar employee who pleaded guilty to possession of drugs. In so ruling, the arbitrator examined the employee's job performance, possible injury to the city's image and reputation, and the existence of a drug problem among other city employees. In all three instances, the arbi-

---

[78]Id. at 728–29 (footnotes omitted).
[79]74 LA 33 (Dunn, 1980).

trator concluded there was no evidence that indicated any injury to the employer.[80]

However, in *Commonwealth of Pennsylvania*,[81] discharge was sustained for a state liquor store employee for "conduct unbecoming a State employee." In that case, the employee fatally injured a 71-year-old woman who asked him to stop beating his wife. News of the incident was widely reported in the media, which prompted his termination. In recognizing that an employer may take appropriate disciplinary action when off-duty misconduct affects or is likely to affect the employment relationship, the arbitrator concluded that the publicity would cause fellow workers to fear the grievant and make customers hesitant to deal with him.[82]

Discharge was also justified for a police officer in *City of Taylor*.[83] The officer gave drugs to a female citizen who was also an informer for the city. The arbitrator determined that the incident would negatively reflect upon the police force and would further give rise to the distinct possibility of adverse publicity against the city and lowered police force morale.

Alternatively, in *United States Postal Service*,[84] discharge was held improper for an employee who was convicted of violating a federal firearms statute. The employer argued that because of widespread publicity, employee morale was lowered and public trust in the Postal Service was lessened. Furthermore, the employer argued that the grievant's character and trustworthiness as an employee was seriously questioned because of the possibility he might be required to handle firearms through the mail. Despite contractual language suggesting disciplinary action was appropriate for criminal convictions, the arbitrator failed to find a nexus between the employee's conviction and his employment. The arbitrator held that even

---

[80]See also County of Cass, 79 LA 686 (Gallagher, 1982)(discharge of deputy sheriffs after their illegal taking of game fish held improper absent showing of direct threat to security of employer); Cuyahoga County Welfare Dep't, 76 LA 729 (Siegel, 1981)(discharge improper for county clerical worker who, while away from work on her own time, swore and threatened assistant supervisor).

[81]65 LA 280 (Stonehouse, 1975).

[82]See also Polk County, Iowa, 80 LA 639 (Madden, 1983) (suspension proper for correctional facility counselor whose duties included administering breathalyzer tests after grievant entered guilty plea to charge of operating vehicle while intoxicated); N.Y. Div. of Criminal Justice Servs., 79 LA 65 (Sabghir, 1982)(upholding discharge of senior identification clerk in division of criminal justice services for sale of methadone to undercover police officer).

[83]65 LA 147 (Keefe, 1975).

[84]72 LA 522 (Krimsley, 1979).

though the public knew of the employee's crime, it did not affect anyone else, and his nine years of faithful service suggested no impairment to his character or trustworthiness.

These cases suggest that public-sector arbitrators examine off-duty misconduct discharges in a fashion similar to private-sector arbitrators. In determining whether a nexus exists between misconduct and the employment relationship, public-sector arbitrators examine any actual or potential adverse publicity and its potential to damage the agency's image or "product," possible co-employee refusals to work with the offending employee, and an employee's ability and "suitability" to perform job functions properly. These standards are analogous to those used by private-sector arbitrators. While specific factual situations might lead arbitrators to rule differently, there appears to be consistency among arbitrators in both sectors.

Summary

In evaluating arbitral response to off-duty conduct, this much is clear: The better view is that arbitrators examine both the alleged misconduct of the employee and the effect of that misconduct on the employer's business. These are two separate, although interrelated, considerations. At times, however, the conduct itself is of such a nature that the mere occurrence of the act will give rise to a presumption that the employer's business interests are adversely affected by the employee's off-duty conduct.

An excellent example is the case in which an employee, currently performing a job that requires contact with the public and work in private homes, is found guilty of theft in a criminal proceeding. The employee is discharged and, in a subsequent arbitration proceeding, the employer asserts that the off-duty conduct warrants discharge because of the nature of the employee's work and the competitive nature of the employer's business. The arbitrator, applying concepts of issue preclusion,[85] will most likely not permit the grievant to "re-

---

[85]See Vestal and Hill, "Preclusion in Labor Controversies," 35 Okla. L. Rev. 281 (1982). See also Bethlehem Steel Corp., 72 LA 210, 211 (Sharnoff, 1979)("The Parties' arbitration procedures cannot be used as a forum to reevaluate the criminal proceeding by which an employee is convicted and incarcerated. A grievant may avail himself of whatever appeals procedures exist to contest the validity and justness of his conviction and incarceration, but until such conviction is overturned on appeal, it must be assumed by the Umpire to have been correct.").

litigate" the finding of guilt in the criminal forum. At the same time, the result in the criminal forum will not be dispositive of the merits of the grievance (i.e., "claim preclusion" will not be applied by most arbitrators). The employer will still be required to prove that the conduct of the employee, in this case the off-duty theft, is significantly related to on-the-job considerations. Given the nature of the employee's position in this example, however, it is submitted that, in the eyes of some arbitrators and courts, the employer's burden would simply be to demonstrate to the arbitrator that the conduct took place by an employee working in a sensitive position.[86] For example, in *Borsari v. Federal Aviation Administration*,[87] the Second Circuit, in sustaining the discharge of an air traffic controller for an off-duty marijuana offense, stated:

> The phrase "promote the efficiency of the service" cannot be so limited as to require the Agency to wait for an on-the-job violation before dismissing an offending employee. Indeed, it has repeatedly been held that where an employee's misconduct is in conflict with the mission of the agency, dismissal without proof of a direct effect on the individual's job performance is permissible under the "efficiency of the service" standard.[88]

The nexus requirement has also figured prominently in other cases involving judicial review of adverse actions against employees for engaging in alleged "immoral" or "disgraceful" behavior. In *Doe v. Hampton*,[89] the District of Columbia Circuit outlined the law as follows:

> In law as well as logic, there must be a clear and direct relationship demonstrated between the articulated grounds for an adverse personnel action and either the employee's ability to accomplish his or her duties satisfactorily or some other legitimate governmental interest promoting the "efficiency of the service." Absent a nexus between the "cause" asserted—here mental disability—and "promotion of the efficiency of the service," the adverse action must be condemned as arbitrary and capricious for want of a discernible rational basis.[90]

---

[86]The legal parallel here is *res ipsa loquitur* where, in an action in tort claiming negligence, as a matter of law negligence is presumed simply from the fact that the conduct took place, leaving the amount of damages as the only issue for the jury.

[87]699 F.2d 106 (CA 2, 1983), cert. denied, 464 U.S. 833 (1983).

[88]Id. at 110.

[89]566 F.2d 265 (CA DC, 1977).

[90]Id. at 272 (footnotes omitted). See also Bonet v. United States Postal Service, 661 F.2d 1071, 1074 (CA 5, 1981) ("agency [must] establish what has been termed a 'vital nexus' between the misconduct—whether it be criminal, immoral, or both—and the efficiency of the service"); Norton v. Macy, 417 F.2d 1161, 1167 (CA DC,

As noted by Judge Harry Edwards, a former arbitrator, employee discharge cases in the federal sector indicate that the required nexus between discharging the employee and promoting the efficiency of the service must be greater where the discharge is based on conduct that is not work-related.[91]

There are situations in which arbitrators will place a heavy burden on the employer to demonstrate that the conduct complained of does have an adverse effect on its business. For example, it is not at all clear that a marijuana conviction has any adverse effect on the employer's operations when the employee works as a boiler helper.[92] Before such a discharge is sustained, most arbitrators will require the demonstration of a clear nexus between the conduct complained of and some legitimate facet of the employer's business. Moreover, this "nexus" must be reasonable and discernible. Evidence in this regard that the conduct noticeably harmed the employer's reputation or product (demonstrated, for example, by notoriety in the local press or a decline in business), or that the incident rendered the employee unable to perform his or her job with the same degree of competency as before the misconduct, will maximize the employer's probability of success in the arbitral forum.

Title VII Considerations

There is an additional consideration that the practitioner should keep in mind when faced with off-duty misconduct by an employee. While litigation in this regard has concerned applicants for employment rather than individuals who already are employees, it is conceivable that similar arguments could be raised in the course of judicial review of arbitration decisions concerning terminations of employment.

In *Green v. Missouri Pacific Railroad*,[93] the Eighth Circuit held that an employer violated Title VII of the Civil Rights

---

1969)("reviewing court must at least be able to discern some reasonably forseeable, specific connection between an employee's potentially embarrassing [homosexual] conduct and the efficiency of the service"); Hoska v. Department of the Army, 677 F.2d 131, 136–37 (CA DC, 1982)("[I]t is well established that an adverse personnel action [revocation of security clearance] cannot withstand judicial scrutiny unless there is some rational nexus between the adverse action taken and the government's articulated reasons for the action.").

[91]*Hoska*, supra note 90, at 144 n.22.
[92]Vulcan Asphalt Ref. Co., 78 LA 1311 (Welch, 1982).
[93]523 F.2d 1290 (CA 8, 1975).

Act of 1964 by using a conviction record as an absolute bar to employment. The court found that since blacks are convicted at a higher rate than whites, the employer's practice of summarily rejecting all applicants with a conviction record (minor traffic offenses were excluded) had an adverse impact on a protected class under the statute.

While an individual's criminal record may well have an impact on his suitability for continued employment in a particular job, the Equal Employment Opportunity Commission has similarly consistently taken the position that reasonable cause exists to believe that the statute is violated when employees are automatically eliminated from job consideration because of their off-duty conduct.[94] According to the Commission, automatic disqualifications because of a conviction have a disproportionate adverse impact on blacks and therefore violate Title VII absent a showing by the employer of a "business necessity." The business necessity showing would effectively mandate that the employer demonstrate the nexus between the off-duty misconduct and the employer's business interests. Among the factors that the EEOC suggests should be considered by an employer who has concluded that a conviction is "job related" are (1) the number of offenses and the circumstances of each offense for which the individual was convicted; (2) the length of time intervening between the offense and the employment decision; (3) the individual's employment history; and (4) the individual's efforts at rehabilitation.[95] The EEOC has declared that this last factor is particularly important. As stated by the Commission,

> [A]n individual who has paid his debt to society must be able to earn a living if he is to be able to avoid further offenses. Efforts by an individual to improve his/her education, successful performance on the jobs which the individual has held subsequent to the convictions, satisfactory probation or parole records, community work, etc., and/or the fact that the conviction occurred several years in the past are factors which indicate efforts at rehabilitation and should serve to mitigate the adverse effect of a job related conviction.[96]

Consistent with the better weight of arbitral authority, the

---

[94]EEOC Decision 80-16, 26 FEP 1799 (1980); EEOC Decision 80-8, 26 FEP 1790 (1980).
[95]EEOC Decision 78-35, 26 FEP 1755 (1978).
[96]26 FEP at 1757.

EEOC has taken the position that for an employer to justify the rejection of an individual for employment it must appear reasonable, based upon a careful evaluation, that the conviction renders the individual unable to perform the job consistent with the safe and efficient operation of the employer's business. Accordingly, arbitrators should proceed with caution in ruling on a discharge where the employer merely offers the proof of a conviction and argues that this alone establishes a nexus between the conduct and the job, especially where the grievant is a protected minority under the statute.

Public-Sector Constitutional Considerations

A public-sector employee dismissed because of off-duty conduct may be protected under the Constitution. Specifically, at the state level the Fourteenth Amendment prohibits deprivations of life, liberty, or property without due process of law. Application of this prohibition requires a two-stage analysis: a court will first determine whether the asserted individual interests are encompassed within the Fourteenth Amendment's protection of "life, liberty, or property"; if protected interests are implicated, the court then decides what procedures constitute "due process of law" or, stated differently, the type of notice and hearing to which the individual is entitled under the Fourteenth Amendment.[97] As the Su-

---

[97]Robb v. City of Philadelphia, 733 F.2d 286, 116 LRRM 3081, 3085 (CA 3, 1984).

The Fourteenth Amendment provides in part that "[no state] shall . . . deprive any person of life, liberty, or property, without due process of law; nor deny to any person within its jurisdiction equal protection of the laws." The Fifth Amendment is a limitation only upon the actions of the federal government, Public Util. Comm'n v. Pollak, 343 U.S. 451 (1952), and in part provides that "no person shall . . . be deprived of life, liberty, or property, without due process of law." It is settled that although not explicitly drafted in the language of the Fifth Amendment, the Due Process Clause of the Fifth Amendment contains an equal protection component prohibiting the United States from invidiously discriminating among individuals or groups. Bolling v. Sharpe, 347 U.S. 497 (1954).

While most case law regarding off-duty conduct involves a state as employer, the discussion in this section has applicability to the federal government as employer although, in many instances, the forum for resolving federal employee constitutional claims will be not the courts but arbitration under a collective bargaining agreement. See 5 U.S.C. §7121 (providing that all collective bargaining agreements in the federal sector contain a procedure for settlement of grievances, including questions of arbitrability). Moreover, arbitration decisions involving employee removals, suspensions for more than 14 days, reductions in grade or pay, or furloughs of 30 days or less ("Category II" claims), are subject to review by the U.S. Court of Appeals for the Federal Circuit. 28 U.S.C. §1295(a)(9); 5 U.S.C. §7121(f). Alternatively, a federal employee may elect to process a grievance through the Merit Systems Protection Board (MSPB), with appeal to the Federal Circuit. For Category II issues, the arbitrator is governed by the same criteria and standards that would govern the MSPB. See, Elkouri & Elkouri, How Arbitration Works, 4th Ed., 54–55 (BNA Books, 1985).

preme Court has noted, "The question is not merely the 'weight' of the individual's interest, but whether the nature of the interest is one within the contemplation of the 'liberty or property language of the Fourteenth Amendment.' "[98]

The significance for the public-sector advocate of concluding that an individual has a protected property or liberty interest in some aspect of his employment is this: an individual cannot be denied a property or liberty interest without "due process of law." From a procedural standpoint, an employee facing discipline or discharge for off-duty conduct who has some property or liberty interest in continued employment is entitled to "procedural due process." Equally important, substantive guarantees are also inherent in the Due Process Clause. The late Justice John Harlan, rejecting the view that the Due Process Clause is a guarantee only of procedural fairness, declared that the Due Process Clause contains both a substantive and a procedural component. As stated by Justice Harlan,

> Were due process merely a procedural safeguard it would fail to reach those situations where the deprivation of life, liberty or property was accomplished by legislation which by operating in the future could, given even the fairest possible procedure in application to individuals, nevertheless destroy the enjoyment of all three. . . . Thus the guarantees of due process, through having their roots in Magna Carta's "per legem terrae" and considered as procedural safeguards "against executive usurpation and tyranny," have in this country "become bulwarks also against arbitrary legislation."[99]

The test applied for finding a violation of substantive due process, the Ninth Circuit has said,

> involves a case-by-case balancing of the nature of the individual interest allegedly infringed, the importance of the government interests furthered, the degree of infringement, and the sensitivity of the government entity responsible for the regulation to more carefully tailored alternative means of achieving its goals.[100]

In both the arbitral and the MSPB forum, as well as on appeal to the Federal Circuit, employees may argue that the federal government is precluded by the Fifth Amendment's Due Process Clause from adversely affecting an individual's employment status.

[98]Morrissey v. Brewer, 408 U.S. 471, 481 (1972).

[99]Poe v. Ullman, 367 U.S. 497, 541, citing Hurtado v. California, 110 U.S. 516, 532 (1884).

[100]Beller v. Middendorf, 632 F.2d 788, 807 (CA 9, 1980).

Property Interests

In a 1985 case the Supreme Court declared that property interests "are not created by the Constitution, 'they are created and their dimensions are defined by existing rules or understandings that stem from an independent source such as state law'. . . ."[101] The leading case in this area is *Board of Regents v. Roth*,[102] where the Supreme Court discussed the basis for a public employee's claim of a property right in continued employment. In that case a university professor argued that his employer's failure to provide any reason or hearing for his nonrenewal violated procedural due process. The Court reasoned that, prior to determining what form of hearing is required under the Due Process Clause, it must first be ascertained whether a liberty or property interest has been denied. Although the Court recognized that the re-employment of Roth by the university was of major concern to him, the Court nevertheless held that the nonrenewal decision violated neither a liberty nor a property interest where the state did not make any charge that might seriously damage Roth's standing in the community or impose on him a stigma or other disability that foreclosed his freedom to take advantage of other employment. The Court further stated that in order to have a property interest in a benefit one must have more than an abstract demand for it; a legitimate claim of entitlement is mandated.[103] Roth's property interest in employment, the Court reasoned, was created and defined in the terms of his employment, and since the university made no provisions whatsoever for renewal, no procedural infirmity existed in the denial of a hearing.

In *Perry v. Sindermann*,[104] a companion case to *Roth*, the Court made it clear that implied promises may give rise to a property interest under the Due Process Clause. *Sindermann* involved another professor serving on a year-to-year basis whose employment was not renewed and who had not been granted a hearing. The Court ruled that a potential property interest in continued employment existed where the university had a

---

[101]Cleveland Bd. of Educ. v. Loudermill, 470 U.S. ____, 118 LRRM 3041 (1985), citing Board of Regents v. Roth, 408 U.S. 564, 577 (1972).
[102]408 U.S. 564 (1972).
[103]Id. at 577.
[104]408 U.S. 593 (1972).

de facto tenure system for professors after seven or more years of service. In remanding the case to the district court, the Court found that Sindermann, who had taught at a state college for 10 years, must be accorded the opportunity to establish that his property interest was secured by explicit rules and understandings of the institution.[105]

The Court, in *Bishop v. Wood*,[106] stated that where a property interest is created by state law, the issue of what satisfies due process is determined by reference to the appropriate state statute creating that right. Of particular note in the employment area, the Court declared that the Due Process Clause "is not a guarantee against ill-advised personnel decisions."[107] More recently, however, the Court said in 1985 that "[w]hile the legislature may elect not to confer a property interest in [public] employment, it may not constitutionally authorize the deprivation of such an interest, once conferred, without appropriate procedural safeguards."[108]

Liberty Interests

In *Meyer v. Nebraska*,[109] the Supreme Court stated:

[Liberty] denotes not merely freedom from bodily restraint but also the right of the individual to contract, to engage in any of the common occupations of life, to acquire useful knowledge, to marry, establish a home and bring up children, to worship God according to the dictates of his own conscience, and generally to enjoy those privileges long recognized . . . as essential to the orderly pursuit of happiness by free men.[110]

The Supreme Court, in a series of cases, has placed several limitations upon a public employee's ability to prove a deprivation of liberty under the Constitution.[111] The Court has held

---

[105]Id. at 602–03.

[106]426 U.S. 341 (1976).

[107]Id. at 349–50.

[108]Cleveland Bd. of Educ. v. Loudermill, 470 U.S. _____, 118 LRRM 3041, 3044 (1985).

[109]262 U.S. 390 (1923).

[110]Id. at 399.

[111]In Robb v. City of Philadelphia, supra note 97, the Third Circuit stated that "[a]n employment action implicates a Fourteenth Amendment liberty interest only if it (1) is based on a 'charge against [the individual] that might seriously damage his standing and associations in the community . . . , for example, that he had been guilty of dishonesty, or immorality' or (2) 'impose[s] on him a stigma or other disability that forecloses his freedom to take advantage of other employment opportunities.'" 116 LRRM at 3087, quoting Board of Regents v. Roth, 408 U.S. 564, 573.

that in order to make a successful claim of liberty deprivation, an employee must demonstrate that the dismissal resulted in the publication[112] of information that was both false[113] and stigmatizing.[114] The information must have the general effect of curtailing the employee's future freedom of choice or action.[115] A liberty interest is not implicated merely because nonretention on one job, taken alone, might make an individual somewhat less attractive to other employers.[116] As pointed out by one commentator, "To rise to the level of a deprivation of liberty, the foreclosure of other employment opportunities [has] to be more severe, like the foreclosure achieved through regulations barring an employee from future employment in a particular jurisdiction."[117] Simply stated, "the mere fact of discharge from a government position does not deprive a person of a liberty interest,"[118] although it may deprive an individual of a property interest, as in the case of a tenured public employee.

In *Paul v. Davis*,[119] the Court held that reputation alone is not a protected liberty interest when the action is not accompanied by an alteration of the individual's legal status. As such, a defamation unaccompanied by an adverse personnel action or, alternatively, minor personnel actions such as reprimands, internal transfers, and investigatory reports now escape procedural scrutiny under *Paul v. Davis*.[120]

What Process Is Due?

Once an individual proves that his or her property or liberty interest has been impermissibly infringed upon by the state, a determination must be made as to what procedural process is due. It is often the case that a state statute, an

---

[112]Bishop v. Wood, 426 U.S. 341, 348 (1976).
[113]Codd v. Velger, 429 U.S. 624, 638 n.11 (1977).
[114]Board of Regents v. Roth, 408 U.S. 564, 573 (1971).
[115]Sipes v. United States, 744 F.2d 1418, 1422 (CA 10, 1984)("a liberty interest may be impinged if the Government 'imposed on him a stigma or disability that foreclosed his freedom to take advantage of other employment opportunities.' "), quoting Board of Regents v. Roth, 408 U.S. 564; Asbill v. Choctaw Housing Auth., 726 F.2d 1499, 115 LRRM 3559, 3562 (CA 10, 1984)(no denial of liberty interest where intra-government dissemination of reasons for employee's dismissal not "published").
[116]Roth, supra note 102, 408 U.S. at 574 n.13.
[117]"Developments in the Law—Public Employment," 97 Harv. L. Rev. 1611, 1788 (1984).
[118]Beller v. Middendorf, 632 F.2d 788, 806 (CA 9, 1980).
[119]424 U.S. 693 (1976).
[120]"Developments in the Law—Public Employment," supra note 117, at 1790.

ordinance, or even a collective bargaining agreement[121] sets out the specific procedures to be followed where an individual has been adversely affected. In this situation the procedures must be substantially followed and must not be less restrictive than the minimal constitutional constraints of due process.[122] With respect to the minimal constitutional guarantees, the Court, as early as 1855, made it clear that a government entity is not free to make any process "due process," and that the courts, in effecting the due process guarantee, must examine "not [the] particular forms of procedure, but the very substance of individual rights to life, liberty, and property."[123] In this respect, due process does not necessarily mandate a court proceeding in every case where property or liberty interests are affected. The late Justice Felix Frankfurter, in suggesting a balancing test, stated that every case must be considered by itself:

> The precise nature of the interest that has been adversely affected, the manner in which this was done, the reasons for doing it, the available alternatives to the procedure that was followed, the protection implicit in the office of the functionary whose conduct is challenged, the balance of hurt complained of and good accomplished—these are some of the considerations that must enter into the judicial judgment.[124]

More recently, the Court stated that "the root requirement" of the Due Process Clause is "that an individual be given an opportunity for a hearing *before* he is deprived of any significant property interest";[125] however, the Court, in a footnote, did recognize that there are some situations in which a post-deprivation hearing will satisfy due process require-

---

[121]See, e.g., Hamilton v. Adult Educ. Dist., _____ F.Supp. _____, 118 LRRM 3197 (E.D. Wis., 1985)(holding that plaintiff-janitors' collective bargaining agreement "provided all the process that was due them"), and Parrett v. City of Connersville, 737 F.2d 690, 696 (CA 7, 1984)(indicating in dictum that grievance procedure providing for arbitration might be procedurally adequate).

[122]See the discussion by Justice White, writing for the majority, in Cleveland Bd. of Educ. v. Loudermill, 470 U.S. _____, 118 LRRM 3041, 3044 (1985)(rejecting the argument that where the legislature which confers the substantive right also sets out the procedural mechanism for enforcing that right the individual "must take the bitter with the sweet").

[123]Hurtado v. California, 110 U.S. 516, 532 (1884).

[124]Joint Anti-Fascist Refugee Comm. v. McGrath, 341 U.S. 123, 163 (1951) (concurring).

[125]Cleveland Bd. of Educ. v. Loudermill, 470 U.S. _____, 118 LRRM 3041, 3045 (1985)(emphasis in original).

ments,[126] commenting, "In general, 'something less' than a full evidentiary hearing is sufficient prior to adverse administrative action." What is particularly interesting is that, in balancing the competing interests, the Court appeared to accord more than passing note to "the significance of the [employee's] private interest in retaining employment."[127] With respect to the government's interests in immediate termination, the Court said:

> [A]ffording the employee an opportunity to respond prior to termination would impose neither a significant administrative burden nor intolerable delays. Furthermore, the employer shares the employee's interest in avoiding disruption and erroneous decisions; and until the matter is settled, the employer would continue to receive the benefit of the employee's labors. It is preferable to keep a qualified employee on than to train a new one. A governmental employer also has an interest in keeping citizens usefully employed rather than taking the possibly erroneous and counter-productive step of forcing its employees onto the welfare rolls. Finally, in those situations where the employer perceives a significant hazard in keeping the employee on the job, it can avoid the problem by suspending with pay.[128]

Case law clearly suggests that a public employer, in dismissing a nonprobationary employee for off-duty conduct, should provide either oral or written notice of the charges and an opportunity for a pretermination hearing *of some kind*. The hearing need not be a full adversarial evidentiary hearing prior to governmental action,[129] but may simply be a request that the employee provide his or her side of the story in person or in writing to management. While the pretermination hearing "need not definitively resolve the propriety of the discharge," it should be constructed as an initial check against incorrect decisions. As stated by the Court, it should be "essentially, a determination of whether there are reasonable grounds to believe that the charges against the employee are true and support the proposed action."[130]

---

[126]118 LRRM at 3045 n.7.
[127]Id. at 3045.
[128]Id. at 3046 (footnotes omitted).
[129]The Court, in Loudermill, supra note 125, at 3046, noted that in only one case, Goldberg v. Kelly, 397 U.S. 254 (1970), has the Court required a hearing of this type.
[130]118 LRRM at 3046.

Deprivation of Protected Interests

One federal court stated the black-letter rule regarding the deprivation of constitutionally protected interests as follows:

> It is well established that terminable-at-will government employees, while they may generally be discharged for any number of reasons or for no reason at all, may not be discharged for exercising their constitutional rights.[131]

At the same time, the courts have indicated that the state may have a greater interest in regulating the conduct of its employees than the activities of the population at large.[132] Although there is overlap between them, three areas are of particular interest in the off-duty area: (1) political affiliation or patronage, (2) privacy, and (3) association and speech.

Political Affiliation

The Court of Appeals for the Seventh Circuit has stated the law regarding limitations on a public employee's political affiliations as follows: "A public agency that fires an employee because of his political beliefs or political affiliations infringes his freedom of speech, . . . but there are exceptions to this principle, carved out to minimize its adverse impact on the effective functioning of government."[133] Employees at the policy-making level of government can therefore be fired on political grounds.[134] The Seventh Circuit, for example, has recognized that a public employer cannot run a government with officials who are forced to keep political enemies as their confidential secretaries.[135] In *Branti v. Finkel*,[136] the Supreme Court stated that "the ultimate inquiry is not whether the label 'policymaker' or 'confidential' fits a particular position; rather, the question is whether the hiring authority can demonstrate that party affiliation is an appropriate requirement

---

[131]McMullen v. Carson, 568 F.Supp. 937, 943, 115 LRRM 2051, 2056 (M.D. Fla., 1983)(upholding dismissal of clerk typist for active membership in Ku Klux Klan).
[132]Kelley v. Johnson, 425 U.S. 238 (1976).
[133]Soderbeck v. Burnett County, 752 F.2d 285, 288 (CA 7, 1985). See Elrod v. Burns, 427 U.S. 347 (1976)(patronage dismissals prohibited by First Amendment).
[134]Shakman v. Democratic Org. of Cook County, 722 F.2d 1307 (CA 7, 1983).
[135]Soderbeck v. Burnett County, supra note 133. See also De La Cruz v. Pruitt, 590 F.Supp. 1296, 116 LRRM 3334 (N.D. Ind., 1984)(reversing dismissal of government nonpolicymaking and nonconfidential employee for political beliefs).
[136]445 U.S. 507 (1980).

for the effective performance of the public office involved."[137] Applying this test, the Court concluded that the continued employment of an assistant public defender could not properly be conditioned upon his allegiance to the political party in control of the county government.

Privacy

Although the Constitution does not explicitly mention any right of privacy, in a line of decisions going back to 1891, the Supreme Court has recognized a right of personal privacy, or a guarantee of certain areas or "zones of privacy" that exist under the First, Fourth, Fifth, and Ninth Amendments, or in the concept of liberty granted by the Fourteenth Amendment.[138] "[O]nly rights that are 'fundamental' or 'implicit in the concept of ordered liberty' " are included in the right to privacy.[139]

Many public employees disciplined for off-duty conduct have successfully argued that the regulation of off-duty behavior by the state, unaccompanied by any nexus to the job, is an unconstitutional invasion of privacy. A review of the cases reveals that public management can discipline employees for off-duty conduct if that conduct does not involve a "fundamental" right. If it is determined that an employee's conduct involves a "fundamental right," it can only be abridged to the extent necessary to achieve a strong, clearly articulated state interest. The Supreme Court has not exhaustively articulated those rights that are "fundamental" or the kinds of interests that are within the "zone of privacy" protected against unwarranted government intrusion. Instead, the Court has taken a case-by-case approach. The Court has extended a guarantee of privacy to marriage, procreation, contraception, family relationships, child rearing and education, abortion,[140] and the private possession of obscene matter.[141]

It is interesting to note the decisions that have denied public employees a privacy interest for certain types of off-

---

[137]Id. at 518.

[138]Roe v. Wade, 410 U.S. 113, 152–53 (1973).

[139]Dronenburg v. Zech, 741 F.2d 1388, 1396 (CA DC, 1984)(Navy's policy of discharge for homosexual conduct not violative of any constitutional right to privacy or equal protection).

[140]See Roe v. Wade, 410 U.S. 113, 152 (1973), and citations within the decision.

[141]Stanley v. Georgia, 394 U.S. 557 (1969).

duty conduct. In the sexual area, for example, several courts have refused to recognize homosexual conduct as a privacy interest, although the better view is that a public employee cannot be dismissed from employment merely because he or she is a homosexual.[142] One federal court correctly noted that the rationale for these decisions is that dismissal solely because of one's status as a homosexual is "so arbitrary and capricious as to violate due process."[143] Where dismissals have been upheld, there has generally been a showing that the homosexual conduct was open and notorious, or a finding that the state's interest in discipline, morale, or efficiency outweighed the employee's privacy interests.[144] Similarly, extramarital heterosexual cohabitation has sometimes been accorded constitutional protection but, more often, courts have denied this activity protected status.[145] Some public-sector employers,

---

[142]Saal v. Middendorf, 427 F.Supp. 192 (N.D. Cal., 1977)(military service); Society for Indiv. Rights, Inc. v. Hampton, 63 F.R.D. 399 (N.D. Cal., 1973), aff'd on other grounds, 528 F.2d 905 (CA 9, 1975)(Civil Serv. Comm'n); Norton v. Macy, 417 F.2d 1161, 1164, 9 FEP 1382 (CA DC, 1969)(prohibiting discharge on basis of sexual preference absent proven connection between homosexual conduct and disruption of agency efficiency); benShalom v. Secretary of the Army, 489 F.Supp. 964, 977, 22 FEP 1396 (E.D. Wis., 1980)(no "nexus" between homosexuality and military capability); Baker v. Wade, 553 F.Supp. 1121, 1148 (N.D. Tex., 1982)(right of privacy extends to private sexual conduct between consenting adults—whether husband and wife, unmarried males and females, or homosexuals).

[143]Shuman v. City of Philadelphia, 470 F.Supp. 449, 459 n.8 (E.D. Pa., 1979).

[144]Singer v. Civil Serv. Comm'n, 530 F.2d 247 (CA 9, 1976), vacated, 429 U.S. 1034 (1977); McConnell v. Anderson, 451 F.2d 193 (CA 8, 1971), cert. denied, 405 U.S. 1046 (1972)(denial of university employment because of "activist" role concerning the social status to be accorded homosexuals); Rich v. Secretary of the Army, 735 F.2d 1220, 37 FEP 598, 603 (CA 10, 1984)("even if privacy interests were implicated in this case, they are outweighed by the Government's interest in preventing armed service members from engaging in homosexual conduct.").

[145]See, e.g., Briggs v. North Muskegon Police Dep't, 563 F.Supp. 585 (W.D. Mich., 1983)(upholding constitutional right to sexual privacy); Mindel v. Civil Serv. Comm'n, 312 F.Supp. 485 (N.D. Cal., 1970)(postal clerk's extramarital cohabitation protected); Shuman v. City of Philadelphia, 470 F.Supp. 449, 459 (E.D. Pa., 1979)("a party's private sexual activities are within the 'zone of privacy' protected from unwarranted government intrusion"); Hollenbaugh v. Carnegie Free Library, 436 F.Supp. 1328, 1332–33 (W.D. Pa., 1977), aff'd, 578 F.2d 1374 (CA 3), cert. denied, 439 U.S. 1052 (1978)(sustaining dismissal of public employees who were living together in a state of "open adultery," applying minimum rationality test); Fabio v. Civil Serv. Comm'n, 489 Pa. 309, 414 A.2d 82 (1980)(upholding discharge); Suddarth v. Slane, 539 F.Supp. 612 (W.D. Va., 1982)(dismissal of police officer for adultery permissible); Johnson v. San Jacinto Junior College, 498 F.Supp. 555 (S.D. Tex., 1980)(extramarital affair not protected within scope of privacy). The Supreme Court has yet to answer the question whether and to what extent the Constitution prohibits state statutes from regulating private consensual sexual behavior among adults. In addition, "no Supreme Court case has held that married persons have a constitutional right to engage in adultery." Andrade v. City of Phoenix, 692 F.2d 557, 563 (CA 9, 1982). See generally Karst, "The Freedom of Intimate Association," 89 Yale L.J. 624 (1980); Note, "Public Employees or Private Citizens: The Off-Duty Sexual Activities of Police Officers and the Constitutional Right of Privacy," 18 U. Mich. J.L. Ref. 195, 211 (1984).

with concurrence from selected courts, have asserted that extramarital off-duty relationships are permissible so long as the affair is "clandestine" rather than "open." When the affair is exposed or, for whatever reason, becomes "unconventional" in the eyes of society (practicing polygamy, for example),[146] the employee's privacy interest is often outweighed (in the eyes of the courts) by the public employer's interest in "conventional" employees. In *Shuman v. City of Philadelphia*,[147] for example, the district court recognized that even though activities may be within the protected "zone of privacy," this protection is by no means absolute. It commented, "For example, if the sexual activities of a public employee were open and notorious, or if such activities took place in a small town, the public employer might very well have an interest in investigating such activities and possibly terminating an employee." According to the court, "[i]n such a case, the actions of the public employee with respect to his or her private life could be deemed to have a substantial impact upon his or her ability to perform on the job."[148] Likewise, an individual may give up any reasonable expectation of privacy when he or she makes public the conduct that is arguably protected.[149]

In *Swope v. Bratton*,[150] a federal court stated that a police department has an interest in and may investigate some areas of the personal sexual activities of its employees "*if* the activities have an impact upon job performance." The court noted, however, that "in the absence of a nexus between the personal, off-duty activities and poor job performance, inquiry into these activities violates the Constitutionally protected right of privacy; a party's private sexual activities are within the 'zone of privacy' and protected from unwarranted governmental intrusion."[151] In this case the court concluded that a police chief did not have the right to order a policeman to refrain from developing a "more than casual relationship" with a police

---

[146]In Potter v. Murray City, 760 F.2d 1065, 37 FEP 1652, 1655–56 (CA 10, 1985), the court of appeals rejected the argument that a constitutional right of privacy prevented the State of Utah from discharging a police officer for entering into a polygamous marriage.

[147]470 F.Supp. 449 (E.D. Pa., 1979).

[148]Id. at 459.

[149]See, e.g., Johnson v. San Jacinto Junior College, 498 F.Supp. 555, 576 n.5 (S.D. Tex., 1980)(admitting extramarital affair to several persons); Lovisi v. Slayton, 539 F.2d 349 (CA 4, 1976), cert. denied, 429 U.S. 977 (1977)(presence of onlooker in bedroom of married couple defeated couple's reasonable expectation of privacy).

[150]541 F.Supp. 99 (W.D. Ark., 1982).

[151]Id. at 108 (emphasis in original).

dispatcher, at least where the relationship was not "open and notorious" and there was no "public outcry" or complaints by any citizen.

Association and Speech[152]

It has long been held that mere membership in an organization without specific advocacy of any illegal conduct by the organization is protected by the Constitution.[153] As stated by the District of Columbia Circuit,

> The first amendment protects the rights of all citizens, including government employees, to hold political beliefs and belong to lawful political parties and associations. . . . Like other citizens, government employees also have a constitutional right to form political beliefs and lawful associations without governmental intrusion or compelled disclosure. . . . Significant impairments of these first amendment rights must withstand exacting scrutiny and may not be justified on a showing of a mere legitimate state interest.[154]

At the same time, however, not all public employees can rely on this "safe harbor." For example, the courts have been consistent in holding that law enforcement agencies are qualitatively different from other branches of government. In *McMullen v. Carson*,[155] the Eleventh Circuit stated:

> The First Amendment does not protect personal behavior in the law enforcement context to the same extent that it does in other areas of Governmental concern. The need for high morale and internal discipline in a police force led this Court to hold that "a reasonable likelihood of harm generally is . . . enough

---

[152]Speech within an employment context is discussed in another section. See infra notes 218–40, and accompanying text.

[153]United States v. Robel, 389 U.S. 258 (1967); Elfbrandt v. Russell, 384 U.S. 11 (1966); Hess v. Indiana, 414 U.S. 105, 109 (1973)(advocating illegal conduct at some indefinite future time protected by First Amendment); Brandenburg v. Ohio, 395 U.S. 444, 447 (1969)(First Amendment protects advocacy of illegal conduct except where conduct is "directed to inciting or producing imminent lawless action"). The legal standards by which First Amendment claims are judged has been outlined by the Supreme Court in Mt. Healthy City Bd. of Educ. v. Doyle, 429 U.S. 274 (1977). First the court must determine whether the employee's activity was protected by the First Amendment. If so, the employee still has the burden of showing that the activity was a substantial or motivating factor in the public employer's decision to take adverse employment action against the employee. Having done so, the burden then shifts to the employer to demonstrate that the same action would have taken place absent the protected conduct. Id. at 287.

[154]Clark v. Library of Congress, 750 F.2d 89, 94 (CA DC, 1984).

[155]754 F.2d 936 (CA 11, 1985).

to support full consideration of the police department's asserted interests in restricting its employees' speech."[156]

Illustrating the extent to which a public employer can discipline a protective service employee for off-duty behavior is *Shawgo v. Spradlin*,[157] a decision by the Fifth Circuit. In that case a patrolwoman and a police sergeant were suspended from their jobs, and the sergeant demoted to patrolman, because they dated and spent several nights together. These punishments were imposed even though the department failed to provide any notice that their conduct was prohibited. The district court ruled that the officers did not have a protected property or privacy interest. The court of appeals affirmed and the Supreme Court, declining to review,[158] let the ruling stand. In rejecting the officers' argument that the state could not regulate their off-duty association, the appeals court reasoned that "this argument fails to take into account the fact that the right to privacy is not unqualified, . . . and that the state has 'more interest in regulating the activities of its employees than the activities of the population at large.' "[159] The court went on to point out that the burden on the police officer is compelling:

> To sustain the attack on these police personnel regulations, the plaintiff officers must 'demonstrate that there is no rational connection between the regulation, based as it is on the county's method of organizing its police force, and the promotion of safety of persons and property.' . . . In this case we do not attempt to outline all the contours of a police department's scope of regulation of the off-duty activities of its employees, for we can ascertain a rational connection between the exigencies of Department discipline and forbidding members of a quasi-military

---

[156]Id. at 939–40. See also Baron v. Meloni, 556 F.Supp. 796, 800 (W.D. N.Y., 1983) ("An individual joining a police agency must recognize that acceptance of such an important and sensitive position requires the individual to forego certain privileges and even some rights that an ordinary citizen often exercises without restrictions or thoughts of sanctions, because a police force is a para-military organization with all the attendant requirements and circumstances.").
[157]701 F.2d 470 (CA 5, 1983).
[158] 464 U.S. 965, 104 S.Ct. 404 (1983). Justice Brennan, in a dissent to the denial of a writ of certiorari, joined by Justices Marshall and Blackmun, was of the view that petitioners' conduct involved a fundamental right. Brennan commented: "The intimate, consensual, and private relationship between petitioners involved both the 'interest in avoiding disclosure of personal matters [and] the interest in independence in making certain kinds of important decisions,' . . . that our cases have recognized as fundamental." 104 S.Ct. at 409, quoting Whalen v. Roe, 429 U.S. 589, 599–600.
[159]701 F.2d at 482–83, citing Kelley v. Johnson, 425 U.S. 238, 245 (1976).

unit, especially those different in rank, to share an apartment or to cohabit.[160]

There are limits, however, even in the protective services. The Fifth Circuit, in *Wilson v. Taylor*,[161] overturned a decision of a lower court that had ruled in favor of a police department that had fired an officer because of his association with the daughter of a convicted felon and reputed crime figure. The court of appeals pointed out that the fact that the individual is a policeman does not obviate the need to balance the interests of the employee against the interests of the governmental employer: "[P]olicemen, like teachers and lawyers, are not relegated to a watered-down version of constitutional rights."[162] Still, the court noted that several courts have read into the balance "more deference to the state interest in preserving the morale and integrity of police departments than might be appropriate in other contexts."[163]

The courts have similarly held that while a state has an interest in regulating the speech of its teachers that differs from its interest in regulating the speech of the general citizenry, a teacher's First Amendment rights may be restricted only if "the employer shows that some restriction is necessary to prevent the disruption of official functions or to insure effective performance by the employee."[164] Thus, in *National Gay Task Force v. Board of Education*,[165] the Tenth Circuit declared unconstitutional a portion of a statute that allowed punishment of teachers for "public homosexual conduct," which was defined as "advocating, soliciting, imposing, encouraging or promoting public or private homosexual activity in a manner that creates a substantial risk that such conduct will come to the attention of school children or school employees." According to the court, although a teacher could properly be dismissed for public homosexual conduct, discipline for mere "advocacy" would be barred since this does not necessarily imply incitement to immediate action.

---

[160]Id. See also Baron v. Meloni, 556 F.Supp. 796 (W.D. N.Y., 1983) (sheriff's order that deputy sheriff cease associating with wife of reputed mobster not violative of deputy's constitutional right of privacy.).

[161]658 F.2d 1021 (CA 5, 1981).

[162]Id. at 1027.

[163]658 F.2d at 1027.

[164]National Gay Task Force v. Board of Educ., 729 F.2d 1270, 34 FEP 459, 462 (CA 10, 1984), citing Childers v. Independent School Dist. No. 1, 676 F.2d 1338, 1341 (CA 10, 1982).

[165]727 F.2d 1270 (1984), aff'd, 470 U.S. ____, 37 FEP 505 (1985).

In another education case, a school board dismissed a middle-aged female teacher who allowed a 26-year-old male visitor to stay at her apartment overnight for engaging in "social misbehavior that is not conducive to the maintenance of the integrity of the public school system."[166] The Eighth Circuit, declining to consider the dismissal on the basis of association or privacy, instead reversed the termination on substantive due process grounds. Applying a *de facto* nexus requirement, the court of appeals found that the teacher could successfully argue that her dismissal was arbitrary and capricious if she could prove "that each of the stated reasons [underlying [her] dismissal] is trivial, or is unrelated to the educational process or to working relationships within the educational institution, or is wholly unsupported by a basis in fact."[167]

Morality Standards

When considering the issue of public employers' promulgation of rules and regulations relating to an employee's off-duty conduct, two additional considerations should be addressed. The first is whether a public employer possesses the power to enact a morality standard for its employees. The second issue, applicable only if the employer is found to have this power, is whether the power has been exercised consistently with the mandates of due process. The courts considering the validity of enacting standards of morality have consistently held that the state may indeed enact rules prescribing the moral standards of its employees, especially in teaching and the protective services.[168] The Supreme Court,

---

[166]Fisher v. Snyder, 476 F.2d 375, 377 (CA 8, 1973).

[167]Id. at 377, citing McEnteggart v. Cataldo, 451 F.2d 1109, 1111 (CA 1, 1971), cert. denied, 408 U.S. 943 (1972).

[168]See, e.g., Beilan v. Board of Pub. Educ., 357 U.S. 399, 405, 408–09 (1958); Andrews v. Drew Mun. Separate School Dist., 371 F.Supp. 27 (N.D. Miss., 1973), aff'd, 507 F.2d 611 (CA 5, 1975); Velasquez v. City of Colorado Springs, 23 FEP 621 (D. Colo., 1980)(noting that "lack of sufficient moral character" defense is suspect on its face because it is highly subjective); Dolter v. Wahlert High School, 483 F.Supp. 266, 21 FEP 1413 (N.D. Iowa, 1980)(rejecting argument that Catholic Church cannot be held liable for sex discrimination where standards of morality for teachers were not in accord with moral and religious precepts of church concerning unwed pregnancy); Hoska v. United States Dep't of the Army, 677 F.2d 131 (CA DC, 1982)(stating that "a pronouncement of 'immorality' tends to discourage careful analysis because it unavoidably connotes a violation of divine, Olympian, or otherwise universal standards of rectitude," and holding that Army failed to provide any "careful analysis" of connection between incidents of alleged immoral or improper behavior and employee's

however, has stated that if a state designates some form of moral character as a criterion for bestowing a benefit or imposing a burden, it must be based on *present* moral character.[169]

Summary

Case law indicates that when a public employer regulates the off-duty conduct of employees, it must do so consistent with the mandates of procedural and substantive due process. At a minimum, this means that there must be some rational connection between the off-duty behavior and the employee's job. An employer will not be able to effect the dismissal of an employee for off-duty conduct if management can articulate no interest whatsoever for its action. If the employee's conduct involves a fundamental right such as speech or is within an individual's recognized "zone of privacy" such as heterosexual intercourse, a public employer will have to show more than a *de minimis* interest before it can justify a discharge for engaging in protected conduct. At times the employer's interest must be "compelling," depending upon the particular occupation at issue and the degree of the infringement on the protected conduct. Finally, if a court finds that the employee has a property interest in continued employment, or that the discharge affects a "liberty" interest, certain procedural guarantees must be accorded the individual.

Employee Loyalty

The right of an employer to demand loyalty from the work force represents an undefined and nebulous area of management rights.[170] The thoughts of Arbitrator Edgar Jones, Jr., reflect the complexity of formulating a useful definition of this concept:

---

ability to execute responsibilities). See also Smith v. Price, 616 F.2d 1371 (CA 5, 1980)(providing for dismissal of employee for failure to meet prescribed standards of work, morality, and ethics, to an extent that makes employee unsuitable for any kind of employment in city's service); Johnson v. Uncle Ben's Inc., 17 FEP 1247 (S.D. Tex., 1978)(dismissal for violating established policy that employees conduct themselves in accordance with standards of common decency and morality).

[169]Schware v. Board of Bar Examiners, 353 U.S. 232 (1957).

[170]See generally Foster, "Disloyalty to the Employer: A Study of Arbitration Awards," 20 Arb. J. 157 ("any attempt to fit disloyalty cases into a unified theoretical framework is destined for futility." Id. at 167.)

"Loyalty" is indeed a nebulous psychological phenomenon. As a state of mind, it varies widely both among individuals, in their capacity to experience it, and again, in relation to the nature of the various groups with which a particular individual has significant contact—his family, his country, his community, his church, his schools, his friends, his employer, his clubs and professional associations. Because it is so individual a matter it would be impossible to exhaust all of the various clusters of interests and people with which in some way each of us forms social contact and generates aspects of attachment and support which may properly be describable as "loyalty."[171]

Of course, loyalty is more than a state of mind. Similar to the legal concept of negligence, as used here loyalty concerns conduct. Arbitrator Jones recognized this when he went on to argue that a "legally cognizable duty" to act in a loyal fashion may arise in the employer-employee relationship. Jones commented:

As part of the complex of rights and duties comprising the employment relationship, the duty of loyalty of an employee to an employer must certainly be reckoned as an important aspect of the common enterprise. As difficult as it is to speak with any precision about the dimensions of that duty, it is not a vague sentiment to which pious hypocrisy must give lip service at the cost of employment. As marked out in decisions in cases in which an employee has been disciplined or terminated for allegedly violating it, it is a practical command subject to a rule of reason.[172]

Although loyalty defies precise definition, its parameters may be revealed through a look at the following problem areas: (1) competing with the company; (2) maintaining or failing to disclose a conflict of interest; (3) releasing negative information about an employer; and (4) failing to report wrongdoing by co-employees.

Competing With the Company

Holding another job while working for an employer, commonly known as "moonlighting," does not by itself breach the duty of loyalty. In fact, many collective bargaining agreements specifically provide unit employees with the right to hold a second job free from punishment. However, when the

---

[171]Los Angeles Herald-Examiner, 49 LA 453, 464 (1967).
[172]Id. at 464.

nature of an employee's outside interests closely resembles the work done by the primary employer, an employee's loyalty can be questioned. Perhaps the element that arbitrators find most significant is the moonlighting's economic impact on the primary employer. For example, Arbitrator James Stern, in *Phillips Brothers, Inc.*,[173] upheld the discharge of a cigarette salesman who, while working for a cigarette wholesaler on a commission basis, had been running his own vending machine company that also supplied cigarettes. Arbitrator Stern found that so long as the grievant refused to terminate his closely related activities that caused economic harm to the company, the legitimate business interests of the employer compelled dismissal.[174]

Similarly, in *Jacksonville Shipyards, Inc.*,[175] Arbitrator Richard Taylor upheld the discharge of two hourly-paid supervisors who had started a company to do ship-decking work. The employees were found to have violated a rule that prohibited "[d]isloyalty to the Government or law, the Company, the foreman or other supervisor."[176] The grievants apparently formed a company in competition with the employer and contracted to perform work for a competitor that had been the successful bidder on work their employer had lost in the bidding process. Further, the grievants were actively soliciting decking jobs from among the employer's customers.[177]

In *City of Rockville*,[178] a city plumber, who had been doing plumbing work on his own time (but without a required license), was reinstated by an arbitrator, despite work rules prohibiting outside work. Arbitrator Levitan found that the employee had not been warned and, furthermore, other employees who had violated the city's rules regarding outside employment and working without licenses were reinstated after a period of suspension.

One issue frequently litigated in the arbitration forum is the ability of an employee to keep working a second part-time or full-time job when the job is interfering with the employee's performance of, or attendance at, his primary job. In *Mercoid*

---

[173]63 LA 328 (1974).
[174]Id. at 331.
[175]74 LA 1066 (1980).
[176]Id. at 1067.
[177]But see Heinrich Motors, Inc., 68 LA 1224 (Hildebrand, 1977)(soliciting business in employer's paint shop on employee's own behalf).
[178]76 LA 140 (Levitan, 1981).

Corp.,[179] an employee was charged with working a second job during his sick leave. The grievant had been working this job weekends for several years with the employer's knowledge. Arbitrator Sinclair Kossoff stated the general proposition on moonlighting as follows:

> Where, however, there is no rule against dual employment and the employee involved has held the second job for many years without its interfering with production or efficiency in any way, there is no reason to fear that an employee on a legitimate leave of absence, obtained without deceit, is abusing that leave by continuing on his second job during the period of his leave. This is especially true where the second job is a part time job, performed only on weekends, and during hours when the employee would not be scheduled to work on his regular job.[180]

In *Aluminum Foundries, Inc.*,[181] an employee, while making an emergency trip to pick up a part, went out of his way to stop by a competitive foundry to inquire about position openings. In sustaining the discharge, Arbitrator Marshall Seidman focused, in part, on the lack of loyalty of the grievant:

> It seems to me that an employee who believes that he can take paid premium time off from his employer's business to engage in personal business, particularly when the main purpose of that business is to seek employment from a competitor of his employer, does not have either that sense of loyalty or understanding of the American economic system to continue in the employ of his employer.[182]

A final consideration in the area of competition and moonlighting concerns employees who solicit business from among the employer's customers. In *Dispatch Services, Inc.*,[183] Arbitrator Arthur Matten sustained the discharge of an employee who was charged with giving his employer's customers proposals dealing with the costs and viability of setting up their own dispatching offices. The purpose of this proposal was to enable these customers to cease using the grievant's employer. Further, the grievant had apparently recommended himself for the position of department head of the new office for one customer. While recognizing that it is perfectly acceptable for an employee to seek other employment, Arbitrator Matten

---

[179]63 LA 941 (1974).
[180]Id. at 945.
[181]82 LA 1259 (1984).
[182]Id. at 1261.
[183]67 LA 632, 76-2 ARB ¶8543 (1976).

found that the grievant had gone beyond this. His reasoning is particularly instructive:

> In every contractual relationship, and employment is a contractual relationship, there is a "reasonable person" understanding as to what each party may expect from the other party. . . .
> When an individual agrees to accept employment, he knows there will be rewards in wages and fringe benefits in return for his properly carrying out his job duties. His efforts are necessary so the employer can meet its business responsibilities to customers and clients. If the employee does not perform well, he *indirectly* can cause the employer to fail.
> An employee is also responsible for his actions which may *directly* harm the employer. When an employee has contacts with a customer or customers, proposing that they can do without the services of the employer, his actions are a *direct* threat and detriment.[184]

In a similar case, *Arroyo Foods*,[185] an arbitrator upheld the discharge of a grievant who had been soliciting business for a competitor. The grievant had taken a trip to San Diego, which he claimed to be for pleasure only. Management later discovered that he went with a friend, a sales manager for a competitive firm, and visited several long-standing customers of Arroyo, arguably to solicit business. In sustaining the discharge Arbitrator Melvin Darrow concluded that the grievant has been disloyal to his employer by soliciting for his friend business that normally would have gone to his employer. The arbitrator commented that "such an act tends to injure the interests of the employer and cannot be excused as an act of friendship."[186]

In *Quality Building Maintenance*,[187] an employee began seeking other employment following an incident that he believed resulted in his discharge. In the course of his search he solicited customers of his soon-to-be ex-employer. When the original incident, a meeting concerning his performance, did

---

[184]Id. at 634 (emphasis in original). See also Monarch Mach. Tool Co., 82 LA 880, 883 (1984), where Arbitrator Edmund Schedler upheld the 20-day suspension of a grievant who wrote "America Builds Junk" on the bottom of a newspaper clipping displayed on a company bulletin board. Arbitrator Schedler stated: "The Grievant had a duty to do his job well and support the Company's efforts to remain a competitor in the machine tool industry. . . . In my opinion, the disparaging comment was malicious and almost reached the point of a disloyal act."

[185]67 LA 985 (1976).

[186]Id. at 988.

[187]80 LA 302 (Heliker, 1983).

not result in discharge, the employer nevertheless discharged him for an act of disloyalty—recruiting customers from among the employer's customers. Arbitrator George Heliker found that the grievant had every reason to believe that he had been discharged, and therefore "was justified in seeking work anyplace he could find it, including with customers of his about-to-be ex-employer."[188]

Conflicts of Interest

Conflict of interest cases concern an employee's duty to avoid or disclose any actual or possible conflict of interest with the employer. Often arbitrators find that it is not the conflict itself that results in discipline. Rather, it is the failure to disclose the conflict of interest, or to divest the interest when warned that gives rise to some form of punishment.

In an illustrative case, *University of California*,[189] Arbitrator Marshall Ross held that discharge was "reasonable" for an employee who had failed to disclose a conflict of interest to the university. The grievant, in charge of arranging video taping of workshops at the university, contracted with a firm in which her husband (under a fictitious name) had a substantial financial interest. At no time did she reveal this relationship to management. In upholding the discharge, Arbitrator Ross stated that it was not unreasonable for management to conclude that the employee knew her conduct was improper and that her failure to disclose her husband's involvement constituted an act of disloyalty to her employer. The arbitrator rejected the grievant's argument that she should not be disciplined because she had no prior notice of rules or policy on the matter at issue.

> Common sense dictates knowledge [that] there is "something improper about an employee participating in an action that makes it possible for an outside concern to do business with an employer and for an employee to obtain personal gain from that transaction without the employer's knowledge."[190]

---

[188]Id. at 315.

[189]78 LA 1032 (1982).

[190]Id. at 1037 (quoting the grievant). See also United States Medical Center, 80-1 ARB ¶8134 (1980), where Arbitrator Wilbur Bothwell found that a correctional officer violated prison rules regarding contact with the families of inmates when he failed to inform management that he was renting a house to the divorced wife and son of an inmate.

The conflict of interest problem surfaced in *New York Post Corp.*,[191] a decision involving a sportswriter whose job was to pick favorites for horse races. The sportswriter, through an arrangement with one of the stable owners, became part-owner of a horse. Although the employee refrained from picking favorites when his horse was racing, management still believed that a substantial conflict of interest was present since horses of the same stable ran in other races. Arbitrator Milton Friedman rejected the writer's argument that he was above being influenced towards picking horses from his horse's stable. Arbitrator Friedman reasoned that conflicts of interest, or apparent conflicts of interest, should be judged using a "reasonable person" standard, that is, a "standard of conduct which may properly be demanded of *everyone*, those of weaker moral fiber—or potentially weaker moral fiber—as well as those who may be generally regarded as possessing unimpeachable virtue."[192]

Arbitrator Richard Calhoon, in *Great Atlantic & Pacific Tea Co.*,[193] found that a conflict of interest must be proven before discipline can be sustained. The grievant, a butcher for A&P, was suspended following the discovery that he was teaching his son how to cut meat in the son's butcher shop. Since his son's shop also sold meat on a retail basis, management believed that a conflict of interest existed. Arbitrator Calhoon found otherwise:

> Conflict of interest in itself is difficult to determine, contingent as it is on both the nature and volume of outside activities in relation to the principle occupation. Factors to be considered in this case are competition and job performance.[194]

Finding no effect on either job performance or competition with A&P, Arbitrator Calhoon sustained the grievance.[195]

Denigrating the Company

The basic issue involved in an employee's releasing negative information about the company was summarized by Ar-

[191]62 LA 225 (Friedman, 1973).
[192]Id. at 226–27 (emphasis in original).
[193]75 LA 640 (1980).
[194]Id. at 641–42.
[195]See also Airport Ground Transp., 58 LA 1296 (Rohman, 1972); Albertsons, Inc., 65 LA 1042 (Christopher, 1975); Department of Justice, 72 LA 1095 (Kossoff, 1979).

bitrator Calvin McCoy, who asked, "Can you bite the hand that feeds you, and insist on staying for future banquets?"[196] Reflecting the better weight of arbitral authority, Arbitrator McCoy answered this question in the negative. A review of some of the published cases in this area demonstrates the standards applied by arbitrators.

Arbitrator Robert Johnston, in *San Diego Gas & Electric Co.*,[197] upheld a utility's issuance of a written reprimand for an employee who had written a letter, containing substantial falsehoods, to a local newspaper opposed to the use of nuclear power. Arbitrator Johnston reaffirmed that the employment relationship imposes responsibilities on both the employer and employee. One obligation of the employee is loyalty to his place of employment. It is of note that the arbitrator found inapplicable the grievant's argument that his conduct was protected by the First Amendment, correctly stating that "the right to be free from government interference does not extend to a private company."[198] Similarly, Arbitrator Edgar Jones, in *Los Angeles Herald-Examiner*,[199] upheld the discharge of a general assignment reporter for what Jones termed a "breach of his duty of loyalty to his employer." The facts are especially interesting. The grievant resigned due to an action of the newspaper that he believed to be unethical. For modesty's sake the paper had airbrushed the penis off the Infant Jesus in a reprint of a painting, Veronese's *Holy Family*, that was to be shown on the front page. In seeking other employment, the employee explained his reasons for leaving the *Herald* to a competitor, which then made a headline story of the disclosure. As a consequence, the *Herald* discharged him immediately, before the end of his two-week notice period. The grievant then attempted to rescind his resignation. Arbitrator Jones let stand the original resignation and, further, ruled that during this two-week period the grievant was not released from his duty of loyalty to the company. Arbitrator Jones reasoned as follows:

> When Grievant tendered his written resignation on December 27 he gave two weeks' notice, agreeably to his employer,

---

[196]Forest City Publishing Co., 58 LA 773, 783 (1972).
[197]82 LA 1039 (1983).
[198]Id. at 1041. See discussion under "Public Employee Constitutional Rights" in Chapter 9, infra.
[199]49 LA 453 (1967).

assuring himself a financial cushion while he found another job. During that time, he remained on the payroll, was entitled to all of the benefits of an employee, and was subject to the normal duties of any employee. Included in that latter category throughout his employment, in those last few days as much as in his first days on the job, was his obligation to do his best to act or refrain from acting so as to enhance rather than to endanger the best interests of his employer. This is the duty of loyalty.[200]

An interesting aspect of releasing negative information is whether arbitrators recognize constitutional-type rights of employees to speak freely about their employers.[201] In *Washoe County*,[202] a county employee made public to the local elected board of health his views concerning public management and his employer's venereal disease program. He was subsequently dismissed, allegedly for making these statements to the board and to the media. Arbitrator Patrick Boner, stating that the resolution of the grievance depended upon the balancing of the "free speech" rights of the employee and the right of the employer to conduct its business in an orderly fashion, ruled that the public statements were not sufficient to sustain a discharge under a just-cause standard.

In *Town of Plainville, Connecticut*,[203] a public works employee was discharged for writing an anonymous letter to a town councilman. The grievant, who had admitted authorship, had charged the town with misappropriating tools, in this case a "rototiller." Arbitrator Howard Sacks, acting as a panel chairman, defined the issue as "whether a public sector employee can be disciplined if his whistle-blowing proves to be mistaken." Balancing the interests of a whistleblower against the interests of the employer, Arbitrator Sacks applied the following noteworthy standards:

> [W]e have formulated a set of standards for judging whistle-blowing in the public sector. Our aim has been to balance the competing interests of employee and employer, and to give appropriate attention to the public's interest in bringing to light instances of suspected official wrongdoing or mismanagement.

---

[200]Id. at 463–64. See also Forest City Publishing Co., 58 LA 773 (McCoy, 1972); General Elec. Co., 40 LA 1126 (Davy, 1963)(union business agent guilty of "indisputable disloyalty" for publishing article stating that employer was "insisting on bad parts" in production of military orders).

[201]See notes 218–41, infra, and accompanying text.

[202]75 LA 1033 (Boner, 1980).

[203]77 LA 161 (1981).

1. The significance of the activity exposed by the act of whistle-blowing. The more important such interest, the greater the protection that ought to be afforded the whistleblower. Compare the communication of information about (1) illegal acts; (2) the investment of municipal pension funds in corporations doing business in South Africa; and (3) a projected reorganization of a six-person clerical unit in a recreation department that would reduce the whistleblower's responsibilities.

2. The employee's motives in becoming a whistleblower. Are they purely personal, e.g., to protect or advance his own career, or to damage someone else's career? Or are they directed toward vindicating the public's interest in preventing fraud, waste or criminal activity?

3. Whether the information given by the employee is true, and if not, the employee's "state of mind" regarding the truth of such information. Thus, if it turns out that the employee is mistaken, did he have reasonable grounds for believing the truth of his charges? Or was he guilty of knowing use of false information or of reckless indifference to the truth of such information? In this regard, we prefer the standard established by the Civil Service Reform Act, "reasonable belief," to the somewhat lower standard enunciated in *Pickering* [*Pickering v. Board of Education*, 391 U.S. 563 (1968)], any state of mind other than "knowledge of falsity or reckless disregard for truth or falsity of the information."

4. The means chosen by the employee to communicate his information or allegations. Ordinarily, internal channels should first be used, unless there are good reasons for not using them, such as a reasonable belief that his superiors will do a poor or dishonest job of investigating the matter. If special channels for whistleblowers are established, . . . the employee should use this channel. If the circumstances justify going outside of regular channels, does the employee write his legislator or the prosecutor, or does he arrange a media event? If he attempts to maintain his anonymity, is there good reason for it, such as a legitimate fear of employer reprisal?

5. The potential or actual harm to the employer caused by the whistleblowing. Harm can take several forms: creation of disharmony within the enterprise; impairment of discipline of the whistleblower and others; other interference with efficiency; damage to the employer's relations with other government agencies, persons it services, taxpayers, or citizens generally. The employer's ability to defend itself must also be considered, such as its ability promptly and effectively to refute false charges of wrongdoing. . . .

6. The employee's right to engage in self-expression, that is, his freedom, as a citizen, to exercise his rights of free speech and the right to petition.[204]

---

[204]Id. at 166–67.

In reinstating the employee the arbitrator declared that while the award vindicated the right of whistleblowing by a public-sector employee, it did not decide whether there is a duty on the part of employees to "blow the whistle" when wrongdoing or mismanagement is suspected.[205]

Tolerating Co-Employee Wrongdoing

The issue whether an employee has a duty to expose wrongdoing as part of his "duty of loyalty" to the company most often surfaces where an employee knows, or has reason to believe, that theft of company property has taken place or is currently taking place but, for whatever reason, elects to remain silent. Illustrative of the thinking of many arbitrators is a decision by Arbitrator Laurence Seibel. In *C&P Telephone*,[206] management discharged an employee because he had either actual or implied knowledge that materials were being stolen from a store room over which he exercised responsibility, and he failed to inform the company of this fact. The arbitrator's reasoning is noteworthy:

> That the Grievant did not benefit, directly or indirectly, from the theft of Company property is of no significance, in my opinion. While his failure to act was not motivated by material gains, it was equally inexcusable for him to be acting out of a misguided sense of loyalty to fellow employees engaged in stealing from the Company. If he desired not to be a "stool pigeon" (despite his obligation to report the misconduct of which he was aware) he undertook a course of action for which he had to be prepared to meet the consequences.[207]

In making his ruling, the arbitrator mentioned the size of the loss involved and also pointed out that the grievant was a storekeeper in charge of the stolen materials. Moreover, the grievant knew of the theft for a considerable time before reporting the matter to his supervisor. Although the grievant had privately discussed the theft with a supervisor who worked at another location, this was not considered a mitigating factor by the arbitrator.

Some arbitrators have taken a different view, especially

---

[205]See also City of Detroit, 83-2 ARB ¶8562 (McCormick, 1983)(upholding five-day suspension of city auditor for violating rule against discussing work-related matters with media).
[206]51 LA 457 (1968).
[207]Id. at 459.

when the employee has no supervisory duties whatsoever. Arbitrator John Sembower approached the problem as follows:

> [T]he Company's case rests largely upon its belief that the Grievant knew of the "climate" which existed in the plant, and should have taken steps to dispel it. Yet there is grave doubt as to whether it is feasible for a rank and file employee to perform as a vigilante, even if he knows first hand of large-scale wrongdoing. . . .
>
> Whose responsibility is it to ensure an honest climate in the shop? One employee? When a Company cannot count on its own foreman to be honest, it admittedly is in a precarious position. One honest foreman in this situation would have been worth a dozen of the Company's excellent security personnel. Even under the old common law, with the onerous burden of the "fellow servant doctrine," the premise was accepted that it was an obligation of the employer to his employees that he hire fellow employees who were reasonably capable and trustworthy. If the Grievant found himself in, to use a figure of speech, a "den of thieves," on whom must the blame rest; upon him for not launching a one-man crusade to clean it up, or upon his employer to ensure him a safe, wholesome, law-abiding place to work? The conclusion is inescapable[;] the duty to provide a "climate" of the work place principally is the employer's.[208]

A more difficult case is when the employee voluntarily supplies management with information about a theft but declines to name the thieves because of fear for the safety of his family and himself. Arbitrator Stanford Madden, in *Eisen Mercantile, Inc.*,[209] ruled that management was justified in suspending an individual who, for a fee, volunteered information about a theft and then declined to name the persons responsible. Although the grievant alleged that his refusal to name the guilty was based on his own and his family's personal safety, the arbitrator rejected this defense since the employee offered no objective evidence to support these fears. Arbitrator Madden ruled that the grievant was not entitled to reinstatement until he revealed the names to management. As a protective-type remedy, the arbitrator further provided that the grievant was entitled to an agreement from the company that he would be indemnified in the event that man-

---

[208]Spiegel, Inc., 44 LA 405, 411, 65-1 ARB ¶8213 (1965); Scott & Fetzer Co., 83-1 ARB ¶8184 (Kossoff, 1983)(discharge too severe for non-supervisory employees who concealed from management knowledge that theft was occurring in service department).
[209]58 LA 340 (1972).

agement were to use the information in a manner that would subject him to liability.

Summary

The reported cases indicate that loyalty, however nebulous the concept, is an integral part of the employment relationship. Arbitrator Edgar Jones listed some of the many elements that arbitrators consider when management is attempting to justify discipline or discharge on the basis of "disloyalty":

> [T]he type of business; the nature of the employment; the degree of public visibility; the extent of the responsibility for the offensive acts of the person allegedly disloyal; the significance of any public policy affected by the conduct; the foreseeability of adverse economic impact on the employer; actual impact; whether, and to what degree, malice or carelessness motivated the conduct; the privilege of the employee to engage in self-expression or in the pursuit of economic or psychological self-interest; the confidentiality of the material disclosed; the relevance of the disclosure to the expected job functions of the employee; the extent of authority or confidence reposed in the employee by the employer.[210]

Most arbitrators have upheld the dismissal of employees who engage in activity that is directly competitive with the employer's business. In this regard, Arbitrator Gary Axon has reflected the better weight of arbitral authority by stating the following proposition:

> It is an established rule of employment law that an employee may not use for his own benefit, and contrary to the interest of his employer, information obtained in the course of the employment.[211]

It would be a difficult burden for a grievant, engaging in the same type of business as his employer, albeit during the grievant's private time, to prove that he or she did not use any information gained through this primary employment that would otherwise undermine the primary employer.[212]

On the other hand, arbitrators reason differently when an employee is disciplined or discharged for exercising con-

---

[210]Los Angeles Herald-Examiner, 49 LA 453, 464 (1967).
[211]Alaska Sales & Serv. Co., 73 LA 164, 166 (1979).
[212]But see Northwest Tank Serv., 82-1 ARB ¶8051 (Jackson, 1981) (employee bidding against employer at auction to obtain special equipment).

stitutional-type rights, such as "going public" with information that reflects negatively on the employer. Although most employers would like to believe that they have a right to discipline their employees for publicly creating embarrassing situations, arbitrators' decisions have depended on the public or private nature of the employment and, to an even larger extent, the many considerations outlined by Arbitrator Sacks in *Town of Plainville*.[213] Simply stated, no *per se* rules are operative in this area.

With respect to the duty to come forward with information when an employee knows or suspects wrongdoing, arbitrators generally avoid a result that discourages employees from coming forward with information which would inhibit crime.[214] Further, arbitrators have recognized that employers should not be hindered in their efforts to safeguard the company's property.[215] With few exceptions, arbitrators have rejected the argument that there is no obligation on the part of the employee to make disclosures. The reported cases indicate that management is entitled to expect that its employees will act in a manner that does not directly or indirectly harm the company,[216] and in this regard, the better rule is that there is no constitutional- or industrial-type privilege to remain silent. Arbitrator John McGury aptly remarked:

> The grievant may have acted as he did [claiming Fifth Amendment protection in a trial of a fellow employee for theft of company property] to avoid being an informer. This again is a human and understandable motive, but is also inconsistent with his status as a trusted employee. The assumed desire not to help convict a fellow-employee of wrongdoing, which had already adversely affected all concerned, is not to be given precedence over the grievant's duty to his employer who was not guilty of wrongdoing and who was making a legitimate and necessary inquiry.
>
> The position of a person who observes a crime committed on the streets by a friend, and is reluctant to come forward with evidence, is different from the position of an employee who was

---

[213]77 LA 161, 166–67 (1981).
[214]Eisen Mercantile, Inc., 58 LA 340, 342 (Madden, 1972).
[215]Id.
[216]One commentator has correctly pointed out that "[t]o say that an employee must refrain from activity which harms his employer would be too broad, since this would make participation in a strike an act of disloyalty. . . . It is probably more accurate to say that an employee's action is disloyal if the harm it produces is directed at the employer primarily *in his capacity as a producer of goods and services*, rather than in his capacity as an employer of people." Foster, "Disloyalty to the Employer: A Study of Arbitration Awards," 20 Arb. J. No. 3, 157, 167 (1965)(emphasis in original).

placed in a position of trust and responsibility on the assumption that he would not either engage in dishonesty, or abet, condone, or cover up the dishonesty of fellow-employees.[217]

Public-Sector Considerations

In *Pickering v. Board of Education*,[218] the Supreme Court again rejected the theory that public employment, which may be denied altogether, can be subject to any conditions, regardless of how unreasonable they are.[219] This does not imply that public management cannot demand some semblance of loyalty from its employees by requiring that they not "air their dirty laundry" in public. As stated by the *Pickering* Court,

> [I]t cannot be gainsaid that the State has interests as an employer in regulating the speech of its employees that differ significantly from those it possesses in connection with regulation of the speech of the citizenry in general. The problem in any case is to arrive at a balance between the interests of the [employee] as a citizen, in commenting upon matters of public concern and the interest of the State, as an employer, in promoting the efficiency of the public services it performs through its employees.[220]

Of special note in *Pickering* is that the employer argued that a teacher, by virtue of his public employment, "has a duty of loyalty to support his superiors . . . and that, if he must speak out publicly, he should do so factually and accurately." The Court stated that absent proof of false statements knowingly or recklessly made, "a teacher's exercise of his right to speak on issues of public importance may not furnish the basis for his dismissal from public employment."[221] The Court declared that it was not appropriate or feasible to lay down a general

---

[217]Simoniz Co., 44 LA 658, 663 (1964).

[218]391 U.S. 563 (1964).

[219]Id. at 568, citing Keyishian v. Board of Regents, 385 U.S. 589, 605–06 (1967). One federal court, commenting on the First Amendment rights of employees, stated: "The interest in holding a job with a government agency is not itself a First Amendment interest. . . . Instead, the protections of the First Amendment come into play when a government employer makes the decision to deprive a public employee of the benefit of government employment on a basis that infringes his interest in freedom of speech or association, since 'if the government could deny a benefit to a person because of his constitutionally protected speech or associations, his exercise of those freedoms would in effect be penalized or inhibited.'" Rose v. Eastern Neb. Human Servs. Agency, 510 F.Supp. 1343, 115 LRRM 5105, 5114 (D. Neb., 1981), quoting Board of Regents v. Roth, 408 U.S. 564 (1971), and Perry v. Sindermann, 408 U.S. 593, 597 (1971).

[220]391 U.S. at 568.

[221]Id. at 574.

standard by which employees' statements may be judged. It did, however, point out that the employment relationship at issue did not involve "the kind of close working relationships for which it can persuasively be claimed that personal loyalty and confidence are necessary to [the employees'] proper functioning."[222] In a footnote the Court stated further:

> It is possible to conceive of some positions in public employment in which the need for confidentiality is so great that even completely correct public statements might furnish a permissible ground for dismissal. Likewise, positions in public employment in which the relationship between the superior and subordinate is of such a personal and intimate nature that certain forms of public criticism of the superior by the subordinate would seriously undermine the effectiveness of the working relationship between them can also be imagined.[223]

In a 1983 decision, *Connick v. Myers*,[224] the Supreme Court considered the discharge of a state employee for circulating a questionnaire concerning internal office matters. The plaintiff, Sheila Myers, as assistant district attorney, circulated a questionnaire soliciting the views of her fellow staff members concerning office transfer policy, office morale, the need for a grievance committee, the level of confidence in supervisors, and whether employees felt pressured to work in political campaigns. After distributing the questionnaire to 15 assistant district attorneys, Myers was terminated. The Supreme Court, reversing the district[225] and appellate courts,[226] pointed out that "the repeated emphasis in *Pickering* on the right of a public employee 'as a citizen, in commenting on matters of public concern,' was not accidental." Justice Byron White, writing for the majority, noted that, unlike the issues that *Myers* addressed, the subject matter in *Pickering* was "a matter of legitimate public concern" upon which "free and open debate is vital to informed decision-making by the electorate." White wrote:

> We hold only that when a public employee speaks not as a citizen upon matters of public concern, but instead as an employee upon matters only of personal interest, absent the most unusual circumstances, a federal court is not the appropriate

---

[222]Id. at 570.
[223]Id. n.3.
[224]461 U.S. 138 (1983).
[225]507 F.Supp. 752 (E.D. La., 1981).
[226]654 F.2d 719 (CA 5, 1981).

> forum in which to review the wisdom of a personnel decision taken by a public agency allegedly in reaction to the employee's behavior. . . . Our responsibility is to ensure that citizens are not deprived of fundamental rights by virtue of working for the government; this does not require a grant of immunity for employee grievances not afforded by the First Amendment to those who do not work for the state.[227]

According to the majority, Myers' questionnaire touched upon matters of public concern in only a limited sense. The Court concluded that the survey "is most accurately characterized as an employee grievance concerning internal office policy."[228] The dissent argued that the manner in which a government agency operates is a matter of public concern and that *Pickering* had established that discussion about how government agencies function is vital to informed decision-making by the public.

More recently, in *Rowland v. Mad River Local School District*,[229] the Supreme Court in 1985 let stand the Sixth Circuit's holding that it was permissible for a school district not to renew the contract of a high school guidance counselor because she was bisexual and revealed her sexual preference.[230] Although a jury had found that the employee's mention of her bisexuality did not in any way "interfere with the proper performance of [her or other school staff members'] duties or with the operation of the school generally," the Sixth Circuit nevertheless reasoned that the nonrenewal based on her workplace statements was unobjectionable under the First Amendment because, under *Connick*, her speech was not "a matter of public concern."[231]

Brown v. Department of Transportation,[232] a decision by the Court of Appeals for the Federal Circuit, applied both *Pickering* and *Connick*, and recognized loyalty as a valid managerial interest. Brown, a supervisory air traffic control spe-

---

[227]461 U.S. at 147.
[228]See also Davis v. West Community Hosp., 755 F.2d 455, 461 (CA 5, 1985)(letters to superiors at hospital involving "personal grievances"); Yoggerst v. Hedges, 739 F.2d 293 (CA 7, 1984)(state employee's comment, "Did you hear the good news?", upon hearing that supervisor had been dismissed, protected under First Amendment); Boehm v. Foster, 670 F.2d 111, 110 LRRM 2097 (CA 9, 1982)(letter sent by employee to supervisor, which was parody of notice normally sent by management to employees, not protected).
[229]470 U.S. ____, (1985).
[230]730 F.2d 444, 37 FEP 175 (CA 6, 1984).
[231]730 F.2d at 449.
[232]735 F.2d 543, 116 LRRM 2523 (CA Fed., 1984).

cialist with the Federal Aviation Administration, was removed from his position for making comments to striking air traffic controllers. Although Brown did not participate in the nationwide air controllers' strike (indeed, he worked a 12-hour shift the first day of the strike), during his off-duty hours Brown went to the local union hall and advised his controllers that he was still working. He also stated: "I wish you'd all come back, 'cause I'm too tired and too old to be working these long hours." He further stated: "I'm so happy that you're together. Stay together, please, because if you do, you'll win."[233] The remarks of Brown were picked up by the media and broadcast nationwide that same evening. Brown was subsequently removed from his position by the agency, and this action was upheld by the Merit Systems Protection Board (MSPB). On appeal, the court addressed whether Brown's speech was constitutionally protected and, if not, whether a nexus existed between Brown's off-duty remark and the efficiency of the agency's operations.

With respect to the constitutional question the court, citing *Pickering*, stated that the test to be applied was "(1) whether Brown's speech addressed a matter of public concern and, if so, (2) whether the interest of the agency in promoting the efficiency of the public service it performs (air traffic control) outweighed Brown's interests as a citizen."[234] In deciding whether the employee's remarks addressed a matter of public concern, the court, applying *Connick*, looked to the "content, form, and context" of the statements. It concluded that Brown's comments "extended well beyond the local union hall and his friends, the controllers, to rise to the level of speech on a matter of urgent public concern."[235]

More interesting is the court's analysis with regard to the second part of the test. Again citing *Pickering* and *Connick*, the court reasoned that, on the agency's side of the balance was the seriousness of the general situation: a nationwide strike that was illegal and a criminal offense. The court went on to focus on Brown's "duty of loyalty," holding that his remarks were not constitutionally protected:

Brown's position as a supervisor not only to whom nine con-

---

[233]116 LRRM at 2525.
[234]Id.
[235]Id. at 2526.

trollers reported but who reported himself to higher-level agency management, weighs heavily on the agency's side. As was stated by a predecessor court in a first amendment context:

Management cannot function effectively unless it operates "with one voice" *vis-a-vis others* [emphasis in original]. Cohesive operation of management is dependent on the loyalty of inferior management to superior management. This loyalty must be maintained in situations involving management's relations with nonmanagerial employees. For management to countenance disloyalty in such situations would be for management to render itself impotent.[236]

The implications of *Pickering* and *Connick* for public management are clear: the Constitution, while protecting the speech of public employees, does not give an employee *carte blanche* to castigate his employer or supervisors in a public forum.[237] As so well put by the Seventh Circuit, "public employers do not lose their ability to control behavior and speech in the work-place merely because they are governmental bodies subject to the restraints of the First Amendment."[238] No hard and fast rules exist other than to stress that the key is whether the employee's speech touches a matter of "public concern," and according to the *Connick* Court, this is determined by the content, form, and context of a given statement. Case law indicates that when the employee's speech deals with personnel disputes or individual grievances with management, it will not be protected under the Constitution. Such information, however meritorious, adds little to the public's evaluation of the performance of government, and, accordingly, is not a matter of concern by the public.[239] Moreover, even when the

---

[236]Id., citing Brousseau v. United States, 640 F.2d 1235, 1249 (Ct. Cl., 1981). It is of note that the court also found that the necessary nexus existed between Brown's conduct and his job responsibilities in a supervisory position. The court remarked: "Brown's 'common sense should have forewarned him' that appearing before a union hall full of strikers, even though those strikers were his friends, could easily turn into a situation where his loyalty to management could be cast in doubt—as indeed it was." 116 LRRM at 2527 (footnote omitted). Still, the court found the penalty of removal too severe and remanded the case for mitigation of that penalty. Id. at 2528.

[237]In Bush v. Lucas, 462 U.S. 367 (1983), the Supreme Court considered the legal remedies available to a federal employee who is the victim of a retaliatory demotion or discharge. The Court held that a federal employee's First Amendment claim is fully cognizable under the provisions of the Civil Service Reform Act of 1978, whereby a federal employee may be removed or demoted "only for such cause as will promote the efficiency of the service." See supra note 70.

[238]Yoggerst v. Hedges, 739 F.2d 293, 295 (CA 7, 1984).

[239]The Ninth Circuit, citing and quoting *Connick*, has formulated the inquiry as follows: "Speech by public employees may be characterized as not of 'public concern' when it is clear that such speech deals with individual personnel disputes and grievances and that the information would be of no relevance to the public's evaluation of the performance of governmental agencies." The court further stated: "On the

speech does touch a matter of public concern, if the speech or activity adversely affects the efficiency, discipline, or administration of the public employer, the employee's conduct may

---

other hand, speech that concerns 'issues about which information is needed or appropriate to enable the members of society' to make informed decisions about the operation of their government merits the highest degree of first amendment protection." McKinley v. City of Eloy, 705 F.2d 1110, 1114 (CA 9, 1983). See also O'Brien v. Town of Caledonia, 748 F.2d 403, 407 (CA 7, 1984)(officer was entitled to injunction against institution of disciplinary proceedings against him for disclosing potential police graft; "public's interest in being informed of serious governmental misconduct is very great"); Anderson v. Central Point School Dist. No. 6, 746 F.2d 505, 507 (CA 9, 1984)(teacher-coach's letter to school board concerning structure of athletic program was protected speech), citing Pickering and Connick ("Connick does not require every word of a communication to be of interest to the public"); Zook v. Brown, 748 F.2d 1161 (CA 7, 1984)(endorsement for particular ambulance service by deputy sheriff protected).

A case that outlines with clarity the law in this area is Roberts v. Van Buren Pub. Schools, 773 F.2d 949, 120 LRRM 2377 (CA 8, 1985). Two elementary teachers filed three grievances against a school district on forms developed by the union. Two of the grievances related to a fifth-grade class trip, the first expressing dissatisfaction with the manner in which parental complaints concerning seating arrangements for the bus had been handled, and the second criticizing the failure of the school to provide monetary support for the trip. The third grievance pertained to the inadequacy of teaching supplies. The teachers' contracts were not renewed. At trial the teachers argued that by not renewing their contracts the board acted in retaliation for their protected speech activities, depriving them of their rights under the First and Fourteenth Amendments. The judge submitted to the jury the following instruction:

> Do you find that [teacher's name] was engaged in activity protected by the First Amendment and that the protected activity was a substantial or motivating factor *in any of the defendants*[*] decisions not to renew her teaching contract?

120 LRRM at 2378 (emphasis in original). The jury answered "no" to this interrogatory. The Eighth Circuit ruled that the use of the jury instruction to determine whether the teachers' speech was protected was improper. "The inquiry into the protected status of speech is one of law, not fact." Id. at 2379, citing Connick v. Myers, 461 U.S. 138, 148 n.7 (1983).

Particularly interesting is the court's declarations of law with respect to the First Amendment claims of the teachers:

> [The teachers'] constitutional claims invoke the holding in Pickering that "[p]ublic employee[s do] not relinquish First Amendment rights to comment on matters of public interest by virtue of government employment." Consideration of such claims involves a three-step-analysis. First, plaintiffs must demonstrate that their conduct was protected; second, plaintiffs must demonstrate that such protected conduct was a substantial or motivating factor in the adverse employment decision; and third, the employer may show that the employment action would have been taken even in the absence of the protected conduct.
>
> Identification of protected activity since Connick is a two-step process in itself. As a threshold matter, the speech must have addressed a "matter of public concern,"; then, the interest of the employee in so speaking must be balanced against "the interest of the State, as an employer, in promoting the efficiency of the public services it performs through its employees."

Id. at 2379 (citations omitted), quoting Pickering v. Board of Educ., 391 U.S. 563, 568 (1968). The court further stated that the Pickering balance looks to the following factors:

> (1) the need for harmony in the office or work place; (2) whether the government's responsibilities require a close working relationship to exist between the plaintiff and co-workers when the speech in question has caused or could cause the relationship to deteriorate; (3) the time, manner, and place of the speech; (4) the context in which the dispute arose; (5) the degree of public interest in the speech; and (6) whether the speech impeded the employee's ability to perform his or her duties.

still be subject to regulation.[240] Arbitrators who either apply or look to the law in deciding loyalty cases should take a similar approach.[241]

Id., citing *Bowman v. Pulaski County Special School Dist.*, 723 F.2d 640, 644 (CA 8, 1933). In determining whether the teachers' speech addressed a matter of "public concern," the court stated that:

> We need not proceed to the Pickering balance when the employee spoke not as a citizen but as an employee expressing a personal grievance as to internal office policy.... The state has a greater interest in regulating the speech of its employees than it has in regulating the speech of its citizenry in general, ... and respect for fundamental rights does not require that the first amendment be read to afford to state employees a grant of immunity for job-related grievances not afforded to those who do not work for the state.

Id. at 2380, citing *Connick*, supra at 147. Although the court declared that "[t]he public nature of the subject of the speech . . . is not negated by the fact that, as here, the employees chose to communicate their concerns privately," it pointed out that the teachers' grievances went more to the relationship between employee and employer than to the discharge by the school administration of its public educational function. The court also found that the time and manner of the employees' speech "implicate to a great degree legitimate concerns of the government, as an employer, with insubordination versus respect for proper authority and decision-making procedures . . . ." Id. at 2381.

[240]See, e.g., the analysis of the Fourth Circuit in *Jurgensen v. Fairfax County*, 745 F.2d 868 (CA 4, 1984), where the court observed: "Where personal or employee grievances are more the subject-matter of the speech than matters of public interest it is the rule that 'a wide degree of deference to the employer's judgment is appropriate.' . . . In fact, it has been said that 'under Connick, employment issues are not of a public concern. . . .' Similarly, the judgment of the employer is generally to be deferred to where, even if there is public concern, there is such concern 'in only a most limited sense.' " Id. at 879–80 (footnotes and citations omitted).

[241]See, e.g., *City of Detroit*, 83-2 ARB ¶8562 (McCormick, 1983), where an arbitrator, citing Pickering, sustained the suspension of a city auditor who, during an interview on a network television station, implicated city officials in a coverup of improprieties in a contract with an oil company; *Town of Plainville*, 77 LA 161 (Sacks, 1981)(finding *Pickering* "and the host of decisions which have followed it" relevant); *Douglas County*, 79-2 ARB ¶8522 (Doyle, 1979)(upholding suspension of employee for making public statements that care provided by hospital-employer was inadequate; *Pickering* distinguished). See also *Department of the Navy*, 75 LA 889 (Aronin, 1980)(holding employees' use of media to resolve grievance disputes was permitted, reasoning, in part, that the activity was protected under the First Amendment); *Los Angeles Harbor Dep't*, 84 LA 860 (Weiss, 1985)(holding city employer properly suspended employee for writing letter to newspaper referring to department head as "head inquisitor," and applying both *Pickering* and *Connick*, stating "[h]ere, it is the interest 'of the State, as an employer, in promoting efficiency of the public services it performs through its employees' which must take precedence." Id. at 862, quoting *Pickering*, 391 U.S. at 568.)

Chapter 9

Polygraphs, Searches, and Surveillance

Polygraph Examinations

A polygraph examination, or "lie detector" test, is a test that measures and records on a paper tape certain physiological changes: blood pressure, rate of respiration, and galvanic skin response or conductivity. To measure these responses, a sphygmograph (arm cuff) similar to that used to take blood pressure is placed around the individual's arm, pneumograph tubes are placed around the chest and abdomen, and electrodes are attached to two fingers on the hand. Each of the attachments drives a pin which, in turn, produces a line on a paper chart. Four graphs are generated: two showing respiration; one (from the sphygmograph cuff) for heart beat, blood pressure, and pulse rate; and one (from the electrodes) indicating increase or decrease in perspiration.[1]

The theory behind the test is that the act of not telling the truth causes psychological distress or conflict, conflict causes fear, and fear will bring about measurable physiological changes which, in turn, will be detected and recorded by the polygraph machine. The procedure usually involves a polygraph examiner asking a series of questions whose answers the examiner knows are true, and another series whose answers are known to be false. Physiological variations are recorded and com-

---

[1]See "Polygraphs and Employment: A BNA Special Report," BNA Employee Relations Weekly, Daily Labor Report, and Government Employee Relations Reporter (September 1985), 3–7.

pared. The examiner renders an opinion as to the truthfulness of the individual based on these prior test measurements and the measurements obtained during subsequent questioning.

Most accounts suggest the polygraph machine was first used in the 1920s. While primarily used in law enforcement in its early years, the test is now becoming a relied-upon method of screening applicants for employment and a security device for determining the truthfulness of employees suspected of misbehavior.

One arbitrator explained as follows why an employer may require that an employee, suspected of wrongdoing, submit to a polygraph examination:

> First, there is always the chance that the test may exonerate the grievant. Although that is principally a concern of the grievant, the Company has a legitimate interest in establishing the honesty of its employees.
>
> . . .
>
> Second, if the result of the test should be adverse to grievant it might induce him to confess. It has been recognized that one of the values of polygraph testing is the inducing of confessions. . . .
>
> Third, even if the result of the test has no evidential value in a subsequent proceeding it might provide the employer with an argument to justify its own action in taking disciplinary action, particularly in an otherwise close case. The arbitrator officially notices that administrative decisions to proceed with a matter are sometimes based upon evidence which would be inadmissible in a subsequent proceeding. There is a circumstantial case against grievant. If the test further indicated guilt, employer might be motivated to discharge grievant, at the risk of another grievance proceeding, even if the results of the test would be without value in the subsequent proceeding.
>
> Fourth, if the result of the test should prove adverse to the grievant, even if of little value in a subsequent proceeding, the Company's supervisors even if they chose not to discipline grievant, would have reason to keep him under a legitimate surveillance, to guard against such further acts.
>
> Finally, in view of the developing change of attitude, an arbitrator, in a grievance proceeding based upon a discharge, might accept and credit the result of the polygraph test. Thus, if the tests can be accepted as reliable, and not barred because of policy objections, the employer has legitimate reasons for desiring to know the results of a polygraph test.[2]

The admissibility and weight of evidence obtained from

---

[2]Bowman Transp., Inc., 61 LA 549, 557 (Laughlin, 1973).

the use of the polygraph has occupied the attention of both arbitrators and advocates.[3] The authors in 1980 reported a split among arbitrators over the admissibility of evidence obtained from polygraph exams, with the overwhelming majority holding that such evidence should not be credited.[4] In 1983 Owen Fairweather issued a similar finding, commenting:

> The attitudes of labor arbitrators are in sharp conflict with respect to the acceptability of and—if accepted—the weight to be given to, the testimony of a polygrapher reporting his views as to the credibility of other witnesses. Some arbitrators accept such testimony, believing that polygraphy is in general use and that the views of a qualified polygrapher acting as an expert witness will provide additional information which will assist the arbitrator in resolving the credibility problems with which he or she is confronted. Other arbitrators refuse to listen to the polygrapher's views, believing that judges in criminal and civil courts do not listen to such views and hence, as a matter of policy, an arbitrator should also refuse to do so. . . . And some arbitrators accept the testimony but then straddle the conflicting views by announcing in their awards that they have given little weight to the testimony.[5]

One arbitrator, concluding that polygraph testing's 70 percent accuracy rate is high enough to make the tests useful to an arbitrator in resolving close cases of credibility, nevertheless pointed out that admitting the tests would "substantially change" the arbitration process:

> Admission of such evidence by the arbitrator would substantially change the dispute-resolution procedure to which the parties have agreed in their contract. If, as here, one party offers polygraph evidence to bolster the credibility of its witness, the other party is put in the position of having to rely solely on cross-examination of the "adverse" polygrapher or of having its witness also tested by a polygrapher. In other words, the offer of polygraph evidence by one party could convert the arbitration into a contest of polygraphers.[6]

The arbitrator accordingly found that the evidence should not be used except by agreement of the parties.

---

[3]See, e.g., Jones, " 'Truth' When the Polygraph Operator Sits as Arbitrator (or Judge): The Deception of 'Detection' in the Diagnosis of Truth and Deception," Proceedings of the 31st Annual Meeting of NAA, 75 (BNA Books, 1979); "Polygraph Control and Civil Liberties Protection Act," Hearings on S. 1845 Before the Subcomm. on the Constitution of the Senate Comm. on the Judiciary, 95th Cong., 1st & 2d Sess. (1977–78).

[4]Hill & Sinicropi, Evidence in Arbitration, 69–74 (BNA Books, 1980).

[5]Fairweather, Practice and Procedure in Labor Arbitration, 357 (BNA Books, 1983).

[6]Kisco Co., 75 LA 574, 582 (Stix, 1980).

There is no agreement among arbitrators that polygraph results will be credited even when an employee voluntarily takes the examination. Where one employee voluntarily took a polygraph and "flunked" it, Arbitrator David Dolnick, in *Purolator Armored, Inc.*,[7] held that it was not conclusive evidence that the employee was unfit to work, especially as there was no independent basis to charge the grievant with any wrongdoing.

Aside from the issue of what weight arbitrators accord polygraph evidence, in those jurisdictions where it is permissible to require that employees submit to a polygraph test,[8]

---

[7]75 LA 331 (1980).

[8]As of this writing, 25 states and the District of Columbia have legislation either prohibiting altogether or otherwise regulating the use of the polygraph in employment. Many states provide fines, but most specifically exempt the use of the polygraph by law enforcement agencies. These statutes are listed with citations to the "Fair Employment Practices Manual" of BNA's Labor Relations Reporter: Alaska, 453:225; California, 453:843 ("No employer shall demand or require any applicant for employment . . . or any employee to submit to or take a polygraph . . . as a condition of employment or continued employment."); Connecticut, 453:1236 (providing fines for violation of prohibition against polygraph as condition of employment); Delaware, 453:1445; District of Columbia, 453:1685 ("No employer or prospective employer shall administer, accept or use the results of any lie detector test in connection with the employment, application or consideration of any individual . . . ."); Hawaii, 453:2209; Idaho, 453:2446; Iowa, 453:3016 (misdemeanor to require polygraph as condition of employment); Maine, 455:437; Maryland, 455:635; Massachusetts, 455:865 (fine not to exceed $200); Michigan, 455:1043 (permissible for employee or applicant for employment to request polygraph); Minnesota, 455:1234 (prohibiting polygraph, voice stress test, "or any test purporting to test the honesty of any employee or prospective employee"); Montana, 455:1826; Nebraska, 455:2051; Nevada, 455:2235; New Jersey, 455:2626; New York, 455:3045 (prohibiting use of "psychological stress evaluator examination" used to determine truth or falsity of statements); Oregon, 457:652; Pennsylvania, 457:823; Rhode Island, 457:1236; Utah, 457:2217; Virginia, 457:2625; Washington, 457:2836; West Virginia, 457:3033; Wisconsin, 457:3211 (prohibiting use of "polygraph, voice stress analysis, psychological stress evaluator or any other similar test purporting to test the honesty of any employee or prospective employee"). In Illinois, it is unlawful to administer lie detector tests without a license issued by the Illinois Department of Registration. See Illinois Polygraph Soc'y v. Pellicano, 414 N.E.2d 458 (Ill., 1980). At the federal level, Rep. Pat Williams (D., Mont.) has introduced legislation (H.R. 1524) that would prohibit the use of lie detectors in employment settings. The measure is reported to have 42 sponsors. See "Use of Pre-employment Polygraph Examinations," 118 LRR 311–13 (April 22, 1985).
The proposed Polygraph Protection Act of 1985 provides that
[n]o employer or other person engaged in any business in or affecting interstate commerce, . . . shall—
   (1) directly or indirectly require, request, suggest, permit or cause any employee, agent, prospective employee or prospective agent to take or submit to any lie detector test or examination for any purpose whatsoever;
   (2) use, accept, or refer to the results of any lie detector test or examination of any employee, agent, prospective employee or prospective agent for any purpose whatsoever; or
   (3) discharge, dismiss, discipline in any manner, or deny employment or promotion, or threaten to do so, to any employee, agent, prospective employee or prospective agent who refuses, declines, or fails to take or submit to any lie detector test or examination.
   . . .

arbitrators sharply disagree whether management can discipline an employee for refusing to take such a test.

Decisions Upholding Management Requirements

Only a few decisions uphold management's right to require that an employee submit to a polygraph examination. In *Grocers Supply Co.*,[9] Arbitrator Ralph Roger Williams upheld the dismissal of an employee for refusing to take a lie detector test where the employee, upon being hired, signed the following statement:

> I, [grievant], do hereby agree to submit to a Polygraph Test during my employment for Grocers Supply Company at any time the company may request. I fully understand that refusal to do so will be sufficient cause for dismissal.[10]

When the company was notified by the local police that a vehicle registered in the name of an employee had been found containing some $5,000 worth of the company's merchandise, the employer asked him to take a polygraph. The grievant first agreed, but after talking to the polygraph examiner decided not to take the test. Arbitrator Williams commented:

> Employees may be required by their employer to undergo polygraph tests as a part of an investigation, and may be disciplined or discharged for refusal to submit to such a test. This is especially true when the employees sign a statement at the time they are hired agreeing to submit to a polygraph test during their employment at any time the employer may request. The eventual use of the test results, and whether or not they would be admissible in an arbitration hearing, are not involved in the present grievance.
>
> The Grievant refused to follow instructions, and failed to do what he had agreed to do when he was hired. The guilt or innocence of the Grievant, with respect to the merchandise found by the police in a motor vehicle registered in the Grievant's name, is not at issue and is immaterial to the present

---

As used in this Act—

. . .

(2) The term "lie detector" includes but is not limited to any polygraph, deceptograph, voice stress analyzer, psychological stress evaluator, or any other device (whether mechanical, electrical, or chemical) which is used, or the results of which are used, for the purpose of detecting deception or verifying the truth of statements.

[9]75 LA 27 (1980).

[10]Id. at 28.

grievance. The issue concerns whether or not the Company may require an employee to honor a written promise—made at the time of employment—to submit to a polygraph test if requested to do so by the Company at any time during the term of employment.

> The Company acted properly and within its rights in requiring the Grievant to submit to the polygraph test, and discharged him for proper cause when he failed to take it.[11]

In an early case discussing an employee's duty to cooperate with management, *Allen Industries, Inc.*,[12] after a supervisor found company materials in two cars parked next to the company's warehouse, the police were called to the scene in order to question the cars' owners. Both of the employee-owners were taken to the police station and asked to submit to a polygraph. One employee submitted to the test and admitted participating in the theft. The grievant denied knowing how the materials came to be in his car and refused a polygraph examination. He was subsequently suspended by the company. A grievance was filed requesting that he be reinstated. Arbitrator Joseph Klamon, in denying the grievance, focused on the employee's duty to cooperate with management, rather than his guilt or innocence. The arbitrator remarked:

> The refusal on the part of [grievant] to take a lie detector test even after the Arbitrator has afforded an opportunity to take such a test at any time within ten days of the hearing does not indicate guilt or innocence in any way; it does indicate a complete failure to respond affirmatively to requests that appear to use to be reasonable to cooperate with the Company in its effort to find out who was responsible for what happened.

The arbitrator went on to state:

> We do not hold that the Company has every right, out of a clear sky to walk out into the plant and to demand that any employees of its selection serve as a spy or as an informer upon fellow employees. Certainly, the circumstances in this case are entirely different. [Grievant] himself said that the Company had every right to be suspicious since valuable material admittedly the property of the Company was found in two cars, one of which was his car, and up to the present time there is no satisfactory explanation as to how the material got there. This clearly does not mean that [grievant] is guilty of anything. He testified that he had no enemies in the plant and no one who might be interested in "framing" him. Conceivably whoever

---

[11]Id. at 29.
[12]26 LA 363 (Klamon, 1956).

was the thief may have had a car parked close by on the lot and may have intended to effect a quick transfer to his own car to accomplish the theft. If this were so, then perhaps all the more reason why [grievant] who may be entirely innocent of any wrongdoing, and who also may have no knowledge at all of who may have engineered the theft, should be more than eager to take a lie detector test in order to clear himself emphatically of the suspicious circumstance of having this material found in his car. While the Company may not require any employee at random or selected in a capricious manner to serve as an informer upon other employees, under pain of discharge, nevertheless it is the duty of every employee to assist the Company in every way to prevent theft of its property or material used in manufacture.[13]

Arbitrator Charles Laughlin, in *Bowman Transportation, Inc.*,[14] rejected the argument that forcing an employee to submit to a polygraph test has constitutional-type infirmities:

At the hearing the Union representative stated that the Union objected to the Company's practice of requiring polygraph tests of its employees because the practice violated their constitutional rights. The Company representative answered, in part, that the limitations of the federal constitution apply only to governmental activity and not to private endeavors.

If the Union position be taken literally the Company's argument is sound. Without question the first ten amendments to the United States Constitution serve as limitations only upon the federal government. Most of those amendments are extended as limitations upon state action by the Fourteenth Amendment. These constitutional principles, as such, do not limit the activity of non-governmental organizations.[15]

Decisions Upholding Employee Refusals

The majority of arbitrators are in accord that in the absence of a voluntary or agreed right to administer an examination, employers cannot discharge or discipline an employee for failure to submit to a test.[16] Although arbitrators agree

---

[13]Id. at 369.
[14]61 LA 549 (1973).
[15]Id. at 552.
[16]Besides the cases discussed in this section, see Glen Manor Home for the Jewish Aged, 81 LA 1178 (Katz, 1983)(rule requiring employees to undergo polygraph was improper, since results of test would not be admissible in court or arbitration hearing); Cardinal Servs., Inc., 77 LA 213, 215 (Millious, 1981)("overwhelming weight of arbitral authority is that employees are not to be penalized for refusing to take polygraph tests due to the reasonable doubt as to the reliability of such tests"); Bisbee Hosp. Ass'n, 79 LA 977, 986 (Weizenbaum, 1982)("[u]nder the overwhelming weight of arbitral authority, employees are not to be penalized for refusal to take lie detector

that an employee has a duty to cooperate in the employer's investigations of wrongdoing, they have nevertheless taken a stand against management on this particular issue. The reasoning may vary from arbitrator to arbitrator, but the result is the same. If management wants the right to discipline an employee for refusing to take a polygraph exam, the company will have to secure that right in bargaining. Absent clear contract language, the right to require that employees submit to a polygraph is not an "inherent" right reserved to management. One arbitrator stated:

> Absent any language in the Agreement on the subject, prohibitory or permissive, we cannot agree that a requirement that employees submit to lie detector tests is a retained right of management to be exercised at will.[17]

Even if an employer had the unrestricted right to require that an employee must submit to polygraph exams, Arbitrator David Dolnick stated, in dictum, that the right would have to be reasonably exercised and "the circumstances would need to show that the employee in question had committed some act of moral turpitude which adversely reflected upon his honesty and integrity."[18] Arbitrator Dolnick ruled that although the employer in this instance was in the security business, the nature of the company's business did not give management an inherent right to subject its employees to a polygraph exam.

Holding that an employee's refusal to submit to a polygraph examination can be given no negative import relative to guilt or innocence, Arbitrator Edgar Jones, Jr., in *World Airways*,[19] focused on the inherent unreliability of the polygraph machine:

> The invalidity of the polygraph test ("lie detector") as a scientific determinant of deception or truth has been conclusively demonstrated in recent impartial studies by persons whose livelihood is not dependent upon the perpetuation of the myth that a polygraph examiner can reliably separate the innocent

---

tests"); Bowman Transportation, Inc., 60 LA 837 (Hardy, 1973); Publishers' Ass'n of New York City, 32 LA 44 (Simkin, 1959); Town & Country Food Co., 39 LA 332 (Lewis, 1962); Chapman Harbor Convalescent Hosp., 64 LA 27 (Neblett, 1975); National Elec. Coil, 46 LA 756 (Gross, 1966); Transit Mgmt. of Tucson, Inc., 81-2 ARB ¶8334 (Hildebrand, 1981); Smitty's Super Valu, Inc., 81-1 ARB ¶8209 (Eckhardt, 1980)(employee handbook stating that employees were expected to submit to voluntary polygraph of no effect).
   [17]Temtex Prods., Inc., 75 LA 233, 236 (Rimer, 1980).
   [18]Purolator Armored, Inc., 75 LA 331, 335 (1980).
   [19]78 LA 454 (1982).

from the guilty. The simplistic machine which the polygrapher operates can *"only"* ask and answer a single question without any qualifiers: "Has there, or has there not, been an emotional arousal in response to a particular question?" The conclusion that there has been a meaningful arousal or a "no-deception" phlegmatic response is left to the operator who must, in the light of the person's demeanor and remarks, interpret the record of arousal or no-arousal seen in the machine recordings as "deception" or "truth." That is precisely what the polygraph schools teach their students. ... The significance of reactions is necessarily left to the personal judgment of that individual operating the machine. It is a judgment which that person educationally, vocationally and experientially is simply not qualified to make.[20]

Arbitrator Ralph Hon, in *Bunker Ramo Corp*,[21] considered the dismissal of four employees for allegedly not cooperating with an employer's investigation of a theft of some silver bars. The contract at issue contained a standard just-cause provision. Moreover, the work rules declared that discharge would ordinarily be the penalty for any "major violation." Listed as a major violation was a rule prohibiting employees from "refusing to cooperate with Security-Safety personnel in the performance of their duties, or refusal to cooperate in any accident investigation or other legitimate inquiry." Although the employees submitted to a polygraph examination, they were, according to the examiner, deceptive and withholding information regarding the missing bars. Ruling that the employer did not have just cause to terminate the grievants, Arbitrator Hon reasoned that arbitrators should follow the lead of the federal courts in this area and hold inadmissible evidence obtained from polygraph examinations. The view of the courts, according to the arbitrator, was best represented by a 1975 decision of the Eighth Circuit when it spoke on the question of the scientific reliability and acceptability of the polygraph. The arbitrator quoted the court as follows:

"While the polygraphic science and its instruments have advanced significantly since the *Frye* case [*Frye v. United States*, 293 F.1013 (CA DC, 1923)], we are still unable to conclude that there is sufficient scientific acceptability and reliability to warrant the admission of the results of such tests in evidence. There is an insufficient degree of assurance that polygraph machines and operators are capable of discovering and controlling the

[20]Id. at 462–63 (citation omitted; emphasis in original).
[21]76 LA 857 (1981).

many subtle abnormalities and factors which affect test results."[22]

Arbitrator Jay Murphy has also advanced the idea that arbitrators should follow the thinking of the courts, commenting:

> It is my judgment that arbitration hearings, as in our present grievance, will do well to follow the policies of the courts as arbitration boards are confronted with the exceedingly technical field of evaluating the uses of the polygraph. Until the courts have established the admissibility of the results of such tests through the extensive resources available in judicial proceedings of specialized counsel and scientific experts converging on the whole problem of the prediction of falsehood through mechanical and chemical tests and reactions, the arbitrator feels he should tread warily in this field where the overwhelming weight of judicial expertise has itself "feared to tread."[23]

Constitutional-Type Considerations

Arbitrator J. Thomas Rimer, Jr., in *Temtex Products, Inc.,*[24] found that an order to submit to a polygraph examination exposed the employee to the danger of self-incrimination. In holding that an employee could not be disciplined for refusing to take a polygraph, the arbitrator stated:

> The precept of "obey now, grieve later," while universally accepted as the theory under which a contractual grievance procedure functions, is not applicable under circumstances where the employee has a good faith (and demonstrable) belief that to carry out a supervisor's instructions would place him in imminent danger to his health and safety. His refusal to follow those instructions under the circumstances would be justified and discipline for this "insubordination" set aside.
>
> We find an order to submit to a polygraph test to be analogous. It exposes the employee to another sort of danger, that of self-incrimination, by forcing the revelation of information which may be placed in the hands of the employer to his future detriment, whether accurate or not, and whether or not material to the investigation at hand. The examiner of employees of Plant No. 2 in this case, for example, included questions relating to personal habits, arrest records, and the probing for answers on other matters which the employee must have the right to hold within himself. While it was said that these ques-

---

[22]Id. at 865, quoting United States v. Alexander, 526 F.2d 161 (CA 8, 1975).
[23]Bowman Transp. Co., 59 LA 283, 289 (1972).
[24]75 LA 233 (1980).

tions were asked as a "warm-up" before questions were asked pertinent to the theft of the discs and the answers not recorded, the strong threat remains to destroy the confidentiality of personal information by forcing participation in the test on pain of discipline for refusal.[25]

Similarly, in *Illinois Bell Telephone Co.*,[26] Arbitrator Meyer Ryder focused on constitutional-type considerations in holding that an individual should not be disciplined for refusing a test. Arbitrator Ryder declared that assessing discipline for insubordination due to a lack of cooperation is compelled self-incrimination, "a proposition repugnant to Anglo-Saxon legal codes."

Public Employee Constitutional Rights

The better weight of arbitral authority recognizes that arguments based on rights secured to individuals by the U.S. Constitution are misplaced when asserted against a private employer in an arbitration proceeding. Simply stated, the Constitution does not apply to an employee-employer relationship at the workplace. As stated by one arbitrator:

> As a general rule in the area of labor relations, an employee cannot refuse to meet with an employer or to cooperate with the employer regarding legitimate work-related conduct. To do so is an act of insubordination, subject to disciplinary action up to and including discharge. . . .
> In this case, the Company sought information regarding the Grievant's conduct during work hours on Company assignment. While the Constitution protects an accused in criminal proceedings, it does not guarantee that an employee who invokes the Fifth Amendment during the investigation of infractions of Company rules and policies will continue to be employed. Probably the best summary of the application of the Fifth Amendment to the employer-employee relationship is given by Arbitrator McGury is Simoniz Company (44 LA 658, 663) when he states that:
> > Employers properly have a certain criteria of employee qualifications than mere freedom from a criminal conviction. Employers have a right to absolute honesty, as well as a reasonable amount of cooperation, from their employees.
> > The Fifth Amendment does not guarantee that a person who invokes it will not be subject to any unfavorable

---
[25]Id. at 237.
[26]39 LA 470, 479 (1962).

inference and does not guarantee that a person who invokes it shall be continued in employment.[27]

When the employer is a public employer, however, additional parameters must be considered. The Supreme Court has made it clear that a public employee cannot be dismissed from employment merely for exercising a constitutional right.[28] Moreover, the Court has held that the government cannot condition a benefit, including employment, upon the surrender of otherwise constitutionally protected conduct.[29] As stated by the Court in *Perry v. Sindermann*, "if the government could deny a benefit to a person because of his constitutionally protected speech or associations, his exercise of those freedoms would in effect be penalized and inhibited. . . . Such interference with constitutional rights is impermissible."[30] More recently, the Supreme Court has indicated that the constitutional rights of individuals as government employees may be subject to some reasonable constraints. In 1983 in *Connick v. Myers*,[31] the Court stated that when a public employee speaks "not as a citizen upon matters of public concern, but instead as an employee upon matters only of personal interest," the wisdom of a personnel decision taken by a public agency allegedly in reaction to the employee's behavior should not be reviewed in the federal courts.

A public employee's constitutional rights do not extend to a refusal to cooperate with a public employer's investigation of wrongdoing at the workplace, so long as the employee's responses are not used against the employee in a subsequent criminal proceeding. The District of Columbia Circuit addressed this issue in *Devine v. Goodstein*,[32] in which the Immigration and Naturalization Service requested an employee to respond to a complaint it received from a British citizen at a border checkpoint. When the employee refused, he was charged

---

[27]Illinois Power Co., 84 LA 586, 590 (Penfield, 1985).
[28]Shelton v. Tucker, 364 U.S. 479 (1960); Keyishian v. Board of Regents, 385 U.S. 589 (1967); Mt. Healthy City Dist. Bd. of Educ. v. Doyle, 429 U.S. 274 (1977).
[29]See generally Van Alstyne, "The Demise of the Right-Privilege Distinction in Constitutional Law," 81 Harv. L. Rev. 1439 (1968); O'Neil, "Unconstitutional Conditions: Welfare Benefits With Strings Attached," 54 Calif. L. Rev. 443 (1966); Western, "Incredible Dilemmas: Conditioning One Constitutional Right on the Forfeiture of Another," 66 Iowa L. Rev. 741 (1981).
[30]408 U.S. 593, 597 (1972).
[31]461 U.S. 138 (1983). *Connick* is discussed further in Chapter 8, supra, notes 224–228, and accompanying text.
[32]680 F.2d 243, 110 LRRM 2887 (CA DC, 1982).

with insubordination and suspended for 15 days. An arbitrator reversed the suspension, holding that INS could not order a report without first giving complete immunity because "under the Constitution of the United States, no citizen is required to testify against himself." The Office of Personnel Management intervened and sought reconsideration of the decision. Upon reconsideration, the arbitrator held that both the Self-Incrimination and the Double Jeopardy Clause of the Fifth Amendment protected the employee and also that equal protection principles extended the same protection to citizens not charged with criminal violations. The OPM then sought review in the courts.

In reversing the arbitration decision, the D.C. Circuit commented on the applicable law with respect to public employees asserting constitutional rights in an employment setting:

> "[P]ublic employees are entitled, like all other persons, to the benefit of the Constitution, including the privilege against self-incrimination." . . . Thus testimony elicited from an employer at an administrative hearing under a threat of discharge cannot be used against him in a criminal prosecution. . . . Conversely, the state cannot discharge an employee who refuses to sign a waiver of immunity. . . . Nor can an employee be discharged for refusing to testify at an administrative hearing when the state threatens use of the testimony in criminal proceedings. . . . At the same time, if an employee is informed that his responses and their fruits cannot be employed against him in a criminal case, the state may insist that the employee answer questions directed specifically and narrowly at the performance of his job or else suffer loss of employment.[33]

As of this writing the Supreme Court has not addressed the question of requiring public employees to take polygraphs.[34] The lower courts that have considered the issue have upheld the use of the polygraph so long as the questions are specifically, directly, and narrowly related to the performance

---

[33]110 LRRM at 2888 (citations omitted), quoting Uniformed Sanitation Men Ass'n, Inc. v. Commissioner of Sanitation of City of New York, 392 U.S. 280, 284–85 (1968). See also the discussion by Arbitrator Marvin Feldman in U.S. Air Force Logistics Command, 78 LA 1092, 1102 (1982).

[34]Cf. Gardner v. Broderick, 392 U.S. 273 (1968)(holding unconstitutional police officer's dismissal for refusing to sign waiver of immunity prior to testifying before grand jury investigating departmental corruption and bribery); Uniformed Sanitation Men Ass'n, Inc. v. Commissioner of Sanitation of City of New York, 392 U.S. 280 (1968)(holding unconstitutional dismissal of sanitation employees for refusing to answer questions after informed that answers could be used against them in subsequent proceeding).

of official job duties, and the public employee is not required to waive any constitutional rights.[35]

Effect of Prior Consent

Even where an employee, upon his initial employment, agrees to submit to a polygraph examination from time-to-time, there is a risk that the agreement will be invalidated by an arbitrator. Arbitrator David Dolnick, in *Buy-Low, Inc.*,[36] ruled that employees were improperly suspended for refusing to take a polygraph examination which they individually agreed to take from time-to-time upon signing an application for employment. The arbitrator reasoned that the agreement became invalid and unenforceable when each employee continued to work beyond the probationary period provided in the agreement. In reasoning that is particularly noteworthy, Arbitrator Dolnick commented:

> [The parties' contract] states that no such individual agreement is valid "which is in violation and in conflict with an express and specific provision in the Agreement." While there is no language in the Agreement expressly and specifically prohibiting an individual agreement to submit to polygraph tests, public policy, as established by law and arbitral decisions, denies an employer the right to compel an employee to submit to such a test. In view of the overwhelming authority rejecting the results of such tests as proof of guilt, a decision sustaining the employer's right to expect the grievants to take polygraph

---

[35]See, e.g., Szmaciarz v. California State Personnel Bd., 79 Cal. App. 3d 904, 145 Cal. Rptr. 396 (1978)(Department of Corrections justified in advising prison guard that refusal to answer questions or submission to polygraph would result in dismissal); Civil Serv. Ass'n v. Civil Serv. Comm'n, 139 Cal. App. 3d 449, 188 Cal. Rptr. 806 (1983)(termination of police clerk-stenographer for refusing to take polygraph); Rivera v. City of Douglas, 644 P.2d 271 (Ariz., 1982)(reversing lower court injunction and holding that employees may be required to take polygraph); Gulden v. McCorkle, 680 F.2d 1070 (CA 5), reh'g denied, 685 F.2d 157, cert. denied, 459 U.S. 1206 (1982) (holding public works employees properly discharged for refusing to take polygraph on employment-related matter); McGingle v. Town of Greenburgh, 48 N.Y.2d 949, 425 N.Y.S.2d 61, 401 N.E.2d 184 (1979)(rejecting public works employee's constitutional right to refuse polygraph examination); Baker v. City of Lawrence, 379 Mass. 332, 409 N.E.2d 710 (1979)(requiring officer to take polygraph in connection with citizen's accusation); Sorbello v. Maplewood, 610 S.W.2d 375 (Mo. App., 1980)(upholding dismissal of officer for refusing polygraph). But see, Kaske v. City of Rockford, 96 Ill.2d 298, 450 N.E.2d 314, cert. denied, 464 U.S. 960 (1983)(police officer may refuse polygraph examination); City of Sioux City, Iowa v. Fairbanks, 287 N.W.2d 579 (Iowa, 1980)(stating that order to take polygraph "bore no relationship to advancement or improvement of the public service.") See generally, "Refusal to Submit to Polygraph Examination as Ground for Discharge or Suspension of Public Employees or Officers," 15 A.L.R.4th 1207, §4.
[36]77 LA 380 (1981).

tests as they agreed in their employment applications would be an exercise in futility.[37]

In the often-quoted *Lag Drug Co.* decision, Arbitrator Peter Kelliher considered the dismissal of an employee who similarly refused to submit to a polygraph examination after a burglary on the employer's premises where a narcotics vault was penetrated. The grievant's employment application provided the following: "I also agree to take a Lie Detector Test at any time that the Company may request." A release was also executed that stated:

> I also grant my employer the right to dismiss me at any time I refuse to take a Lie Detector Test, if I am hired or fail to be cleared by said Tests.

In holding that the discharge was improper, Arbitrator Kelliher declared:

> The principle question that is before this Board is whether the Company, as the result of an attempted individual contract with the employee at the time of his hire, may continue to impose as a working condition the requirement that he may be dismissed if he refuses to take a lie detector test. If such an unlimited contractual device were to be upheld, then presumably a Company could set forth a long list of offenses that would grant to the Company the right to dismiss an employee for any listed violation. Such a procedure would circumvent the Collective Bargaining rights of this Union and would constitute individual bargaining with employees.
>
> . . . .
> The Board is mindful of the serious financial problem confronting this Company as a result of pilferage. In view, however, of the overwhelming weight of impartial scientific authority that these lie detector tests are not accurate and legal authority that they do not constitute competent evidence and invade the right of privacy and the constitutional rights against self incrimination, this Board cannot uphold such a requirement in this case.[38]

Most arbitrators are unreceptive to arguments that if the employee at one time consents to the test, polygraph evidence should be credited. Arbitrator Edgar Jones, Jr., in an address before the National Academy of Arbitrators, addressed the consent issue as follows:

> Oddly, my research disclosed that there are arbitrators who

---

[37]Id. at 383.
[38]Lag Drug Co., 39 LA 1121, 1122–23 (1962).

reason to exclusion or no-weight conclusions based on "unreliability," yet whose concerns in this regard would be wholly dissipated if an employee were to "consent" to be tested. But that is surely an unworldly view on at least two grounds. First, and obviously, unreliability is not altered simply because some workers, succumbing to employer appeals to motivations of fear or favor express or implicit in the situation, have been conned into submitting to it. Second, and less obviously but no less realistically, the "consent" of an innocent employee, fearful of the loss of livelihood or reputation, over whom looms the possibility of criminal proceedings brought by a presumed influential employer in the community who is angered by the refusal of a suspected employee to "cooperate," is no real consent. It falls within those instances of contractual relationships in which disparate bargaining power nullifies any prospect of negotiation and consent to be bound—situations of "adhesion," as the courts use the term.

Thus the conclusion is compelling that it would be improper for a court or an arbitrator to relax the determination to assure fair procedures that are protective of ignorant or misled persons solely because they have "consented" to a polygraph examination or, by "stipulation," to the admission in evidence of test results.[39]

Arbitrator Meyer Ryder concluded that polygraph evidence can be one factor in the search for truth, but it could not by itself establish guilt. With respect to the consent issue, he remarked:

The implicit social threat to an employee in the setting of a plant community were he to refuse to submit to lie detector testing where crimes have concededly been committed so compels consent that a guiltless but emotionally fearful employee has practically no choice but to consent to a testing procedure where infallibility is not fully present. The point should be made here that consent should not operate as a waiver to proof beyond the polygraph of culpable knowledge.[40]

After noting the " '[u]nder the overwhelming weight of arbitral authority, employees are not to be penalized for refusal to take lie detector tests,' "[41] Arbitrator Timothy Heinsz noted that one instance where arbitrators have upheld a polygraph requirement is where the union specifically agrees to such an examination. As such, when the union agreed as part of a strike settlement agreement that employees would submit

---

[39]Jones, supra note 3, at 101–02 (footnotes omitted).
[40]B. F. Goodrich Tire Co., 36 LA 552, 558 (1961).
[41]Leggett & Platt, Inc., 85-1 ARB ¶8288 (Heinsz, 1985) at 4188, citing Bisbee Hosp. Ass'n, 70 LA 977, 986 (Weizenbaum, 1982).

to a polygraph examination regarding sabotage of company machinery during a strike (if no employees admitted to the actions by quitting their jobs), the arbitrator ruled that the union created on the part of the bargaining unit a contractual agreement to submit to a polygraph examination. Arbitrator Heinsz did rule, however, that the company could not dismiss those employees who refused to sign an overly broad waiver (the union never agreed that all employees would sign a release as a condition of administering the polygraph tests) which released the company from " 'any and all' legal actions as a result of the polygraph" and released the polygraph examiner "from any claim [the grievant] might otherwise have against [the examiner] for any damage or liability . . . resulting from the taking of the test and the disclosure of the results . . ."[42] The arbitrator pointed out that the release would cover even improper questions not relevant to the sabotage investigation, and that there was no limit placed on the examiner's disclosure of material. According to the arbitrator, once the company had made the requirement to take the polygraph test reasonable by eliminating the overly broad waiver form, the employees were under a contractual obligation to take the examination.[43]

The issue of consent may even surface in those states that have enacted statutes prohibiting employers from conditioning initial or continued employment on taking a polygraph examination. In *Smith v. Greyhound Lines, Inc.*,[44] a Pennsylvania district court considered an employee's wrongful discharge and invasion of privacy claim based on his taking and failing a polygraph examination. The employer moved for summary judgment on the ground that plaintiff-employee executed a waiver and release when, pursuant to a company investigation of how the employee handled a cash transaction, he submitted to the polygraph. Since the employee was not an at-will employee, the court held that he did not have a cause of action in tort for wrongful discharge (there was a collective bargaining agreement with a mandatory grievance-arbitration procedure in existence and, although now time-

---

[42]Id. at 4189.
[43]See also Warwick Elec., Inc., 46 LA 95, 98 (Daugherty, 1966)(holding that plant guards had no right to refuse to take a polygraph examination once the union agreed to give the company the right to require its guards to take a polygraph).
[44]614 F.Supp. 558, 117 LRRM 2253 (W.D. Pa., 1984).

barred, he would have had a claim under Taft-Hartley's Section 301). With respect to the privacy claim, however, the court denied the motion to dismiss. It reasoned that there was a genuine issue of fact as to whether the employee's release and waiver was a condition of continued employment which, under Pennsylvania law, was arguably proscribed.[45]

In *Cordle v. General Hugh Mercer Corp.*,[46] the West Virginia Supreme Court held that an employee had a cause of action in tort when an employer effected a termination of three employees for refusing to submit to a polygraph test. Although the employees had signed a consent form under protest, the court reasoned that the public policy of the state, as expressed in a statute restricting the employer's right to utilize a polygraph, precluded the discharge even though the statute did not become effective until nine months after the discharge. The court reasoned that the public policy against polygraph testing is grounded upon an individual's right of privacy, and that the company's termination for refusal to submit to a polygraph violated the policy of the state.

Cordle may be an aberration. As noted by the dissent, most courts have rejected suits for polygraph discharges where there is no statutory prohibition on polygraph tests.[47]

Requiring a Polygraph as "Outrageous" Conduct

In one case an employee who was required to take a polygraph examination sued her employer under the common law tort of intentional infliction of emotional distress. When audits revealed shortages at a store, management, announcing that "heads were going to roll," required full-time employees to submit to a polygraph. One employee sued for intentional

---

[45]117 LRRM at 2256, citing Polsky v. Radio Shack, 666 F.2d 824 (CA 3, 1981).

[46]325 S.E.2d 111, 116 LRRM 3447 (W. Va., 1984). See also Swolsky Enters. v. Halterman, 12 Ohio App. 3d 23, 465 N.E.2d 894 (1983), where the Ohio Court of Appeals ruled that an employee who signed a pre-employment contract stating that he agreed to take a polygraph exam at the employee's request, was not entitled to unemployment benefits when he was dismissed for refusing to submit to an examination. But see Douthitt v. Kentucky Unemployment Ins. Comm'n, 676 S.W.2d 472 (Ky. App., 1984)(allowing unemployment compensation for an employee dismissed for refusing to submit to a polygraph, stating that "[a]n employer's requirement that employees submit to polygraph examination is an unreasonable rule."); Everitt Lumber Co., Inc. v. Industrial Comm'n, 39 Colo. App. 336, 565 P.2d 967 (1977)(employees entitled to compensation if even fired for refusing polygraph examination); Valley Vendors, Inc. v. Jamieson, 129 Ariz. 238, 630 P.2d 61 (1981)(awarding compensation).

[47]116 LRRM at 3453, citing Green v. American Cast Iron Pipe Co., 446 So.2d 16 (Ala., 1984); Larsen v. Motor Supply Co., 117 Ariz. 507, 573 P.2d 907 (1977).

infliction of emotional distress when she was discharged after a polygrapher reported the test was "inconclusive with signs of deception" and that the employee had confessed to taking approximately $100 worth of merchandise during her employment. A Missouri court, reversing a lower court decision, ruled that there was insufficient evidence to show that the employer's conduct in requiring the polygraph, and dismissing the employee, went "beyond all possible bounds of decency."[48] In another case, however, the Supreme Court of Arkansas held that the conduct of an employer was actionable when, after an at-will employee was terminated, management (1) forced the employee to take a polygraph, (2) withheld part of the employee's paycheck to cover part of a cash shortage even though she had passed the test, and (3) lied to unemployment compensation authorities.[49]

Summary

One commentator has observed that the commonplace use of the polygraph in employment presents serious privacy questions, not only because of the work-related questions that are asked the subject, but because the polygraph examiner often probes areas of an employee's life which the employee prefers to remain personal.[50] The overwhelming weight of arbitral authority is that polygraph evidence is not admissible to establish the guilt or innocence of a grievant because of the inherent unreliability of the test, and for this reason most arbitrators rule that an individual cannot be disciplined for refusing to submit to a polygraph examination. Although employees have a duty to cooperate with management's work-related investigations, most neutrals have held that this duty does not include submitting to a polygraph. Even when the parties' agreement contains a specific provision requiring that employees submit to a polygraph examination, there is no guarantee that an arbitrator will credit the evidence obtained

---

[48]Gibson v. Hummel, 688 S.W.2d 4, 118 LRRM 2943 (Mo. App., 1985). See also Martin v. Citibank, N.A., 762 F.2d 212, 37 FEP 1580 (CA 2, 1985)(employee's allegation that she was polygraphed because of race, even if established, not legally adequate for claim of intentional infliction of emotional distress under New York law).
[49]M.B.M. Co. v. Counce, 596 S.W.2d 681, 118 LRRM 2925 (Ark., 1980).
[50]Comment, "Privacy: The Polygraph in Employment," 30 Ark. L. Rev. 35 (1976).

from the test, or sustain discipline imposed for an employee's refusal to cooperate with this type of testing.

The reported decisions indicate that the best hope that management has in getting an arbitrator to credit polygraph evidence occurs where both parties stipulate to its reliability, and where the evidence is used to verify the truthfulness of testimony rather than to detect unreliability.[51] One arbitrator suggested that the following guidelines should be observed if the testimony of a polygrapher is to be heard by an arbitrator:

1. The adverse party should have advance notice [of the test.];
2. The polygrapher should tape record his entire interview and interrogation of the subject.
3. The polygrapher should not use deception . . . to induce the subject to believe that the machine will detect any untruth.
4. The polygrapher should reach his opinion without any resort to observation of behavior and verbal "cues."
5. The polygrapher should use a recognized scoring system.
6. The opposing party should have access, before and during the arbitration hearing, to the chart and tape of the polygraph test and interview.
7. The polygrapher should be qualified.[52]

Searches and Investigations

Body Searches

There is a split of authority whether an employer can force an employee, under threat of discharge or other discipline, to submit to a search of his or her person.

The decisions upholding management's right to search an employee, with few exceptions, focus on the reasonableness of the order. "Reasonableness" usually requires some showing that the employer had good cause to suspect illegal activity on the part of the employee. When arbitrators have ruled that management could not search employees, they have usually reasoned that the search violated the individual's privacy or a constitutional-type right.

In *Kraft, Inc.*,[53] three employees suspected of smoking

---

[51]Bethlehem Steel Corp., Burns Harbor Plant, 68 LA 581 (Seward, 1977); Dayton Steel Foundry Co., 39 LA 745 (Porter, 1962); Nettle Creek Indus., 70 LA 100 (High, 1978); Brink's, Inc., 70 LA 909 (Pinkus, 1978).
[52]Kisco Co., 75 LA 574, 582 (Stix, 1980).
[53]82 LA 360 (1984).

marijuana while on duty were asked to submit to a search of their personal possessions and lockers. While the grievants agreed to a locker search, they refused a personal search. They were dismissed for insubordination. Arbitrator Fred Denson found no infirmity in asking the employees to submit to a search.

> Whether the grievants' conduct was insubordinate involves an examination of whether a supervisory order was given, whether the grievants understood the order and whether it was reasonable. . . .
> The Company's request was reasonable since the Company in my opinion had probable cause to believe that there had been an infraction of its drug rule by the grievants. My determination that there was probable cause is based on the information the Company had available to it at the time it made the request and not on information that was forthcoming over the following five (5) days. This information included the grievants location in a secluded area of the warehouse near where the odor of marijuana smoke had been detected, the substance found on the floor and the ash mark on the wall found by [management] in this same area, the grievants suspicious conduct, and the acknowledgments made by T—— and L—— to [supervisor] Diehl.[54]

The discharges were overturned nonetheless, because the employer would not permit the grievants' union steward to be present while they were being questioned by management.

Similarly, in *Associated Grocers of Colorado, Inc.*,[55] an employee was ordered to remove all the contents from his pockets after the company had received an anonymous phone call indicating that the grievant had been using narcotics or controlled substances at the plant. When summoned to the office, the employee removed his coveralls, rolling up his trousers and pushing down his socks, and then, according to the company, emptied all of his pockets except one (the grievant alleged that he emptied all of his pockets once). The arbitrator concluded that the company was justified in imposing a severe penalty for the grievant's insubordination in refusing to empty all his pockets.

Arbitrator J. Earl Williams, in *Mobil Oil Corp.*,[56] considered the dismissal of an employee for refusing to submit to a

---

[54]Id. at 365.
[55]80 LA 611 (Sartain, 1983).
[56]84-1 ARB ¶8229 (1983).

drug search. The company had in effect a two-year policy which indicated that there would be searches conducted by authorized management representatives. Moreover, the policy, mailed to each employee and posted on a bulletin board, stated:

> Any company employee who refuses to submit to a search or if found using, distributing, selling or in possession of any such illegal unauthorized items without an explanation satisfactory to [the company] will be subject to disciplinary action up to and including immediate discharge.[57]

Subsequently the company conducted a search of 28 employees, including supervisors. Each employee, each employee's locker, and each employee's personal vehicle were searched. The grievant was dismissed after declining to submit to the search.

While the arbitrator commended the company for trying to control the drug problem, he nevertheless reinstated the grievant, in part because the grievant believed that he would be strip-searched, and also because of a prior award between these same parties holding that an employee should not be terminated for a first violation of a plant rule.

Arbitrator Nathan Lipson, in *Dow Chemical Co.*,[58] declared that management has the inherent right to institute a rule, reasonably and impartially enforced, providing for searches of employee effects upon entering or leaving the plant. The arbitrator pointed out that the Fourth Amendment did not create a problem since it does not altogether bar searches, but only unreasonable and unlawful searches. Still, the arbitrator said that constitutional-type limitations should be given consideration by arbitrators.

> [W]hile constitutional limitations on unlawful searches are normally construed as restraints on government authorities, and are not usually applicable to contractual disputes between private parties, nevertheless the rights to privacy and personal dignity are so fundamentally a part of the American tradition that they should at least be given consideration by a labor arbitrator in passing on search problems in plants. This is because plant rules and their application must meet the test of fundamental fairness if they are to be sustained. . . .[59]

Even where there was not a previously promulgated rule

[57]Id. at 4026.
[58]65 LA 1295 (1976).
[59]Id. at 1298.

requiring employees to submit to searches, Arbitrator Lipson found that the traditional management rights clause conferred sufficient authority on management to support an *ad hoc* search by plant security "limited to clear circumstances of wrong doing such as were indicated in this case."[60] He accordingly held that a plant protection officer was within his rights in requesting that the grievants open their jackets while leaving the plant.

Another arbitrator, in *Champion Spark Plug Co.*,[61] likewise held that it was permissible for management to require that an employee, suspected of drinking on the job, unbutton his sweater beneath which he had concealed a flat glass bottle. In rejecting the argument that the grievant had a constitutional right to refuse a search, the arbitrator said:

> The real issue is, did Management have the right to order Grievant to unbutton his sweater, exposing his undershirt?
>
> In criminal cases, an officer who has probable cause to believe a felony has been committed and probable cause to believe that a specific individual committed such a felony, may arrest the individual and search him in connection with the arrest. There is *no* constitutional protection against such a search.
>
> It is quite inappropriate to attempt to establish an exact parallel between rights of citizens on the street and employees in the plant. When employees take an employment, they do so subject to normal restrictions inherent in a crowded industrial setting. The right of Management to fairly operate its business without undue impediment must be balanced against the right of the employees to continue to enjoy their civil rights to the fullest. However the two will clash and in the factual setting of this case, it is not inappropriate to treat a supervisor by analogy to a peace officer in the plant setting.[62]

Where a plant rule only provided that it was management's "privilege to examine the contents of any and all packages and bundles being taken into or out of the plant by any employees," Arbitrator Ralph Roger Williams held that a company could not discharge an employee, suspected of carrying a gun, for refusing an order to empty his pockets. The arbitrator found that the rule did not give the company the right to search an employee, other than when he enters or leaves the plant.[63]

---

[60]Id. at 1298 n.2.
[61]68 LA 702 (Casselman, 1977).
[62]Id. at 705.
[63]Scott Paper Co., 52 LA 57 (1969).

Lockers or Personal Effects

In certain fact situations arbitrators have recognized privacy-type rights of unit employees where employers have conducted searches in areas where the individual has some legitimate expectation of privacy. In such instances the usual remedy is to resolve the grievance in favor of the employee whose rights have been violated. Another remedy is simply to exclude the evidence, which in many cases will result in overturning the discipline meted out by management.

Most arbitrators have ruled that an employer can search company-owned property such as lockers, vehicles, and desks even if the property is temporarily in the control of the employee. For example, in *International Nickel Co.*,[64] the company conducted a search of all lockers in order to find some company-owned clipboards. Although the agreement was silent on management's right to search employees' lockers, Arbitrator Joseph Shister ruled that the particular search was permissible under the management rights provision. The arbitrator pointed out the circumstances that made this search reasonable:

1. There was no "sweeping, indiscriminate search lacking in reasonable and specific foundation." Management unlocked the lockers in response to the particular problem of the missing clipboards.
2. The lockers were unlocked by the janitor, a bargaining unit employee.
3. A union official was present when the unlocking and search was conducted.
4. No property of any employee was removed or examined.
5. No disciplinary action was taken against any employee found with company property in his locker.

Many arbitrators have allowed searches of employees' personal effects, such as a purse, briefcase, or lunch box, when the search was carried out pursuant to an existing rule or an

---

[64]50 LA 65 (1967).

established past practice.[65] A few labor arbitrators have even held that an employer can break and enter an employee's home or the employee's personal property, such as a car or lunchbox, when there is probable cause to suspect wrongdoing.[66] Completely random searches, conducted without warning and prior notice to employees, are suspect,[67] although a few arbitrators have sanctioned this conduct and have credited the evidence obtained through such measures.[68]

General Paint & Chemical Co. involved both a blanket search and a random search of an employee's possessions.[69]

---

[65] AMF/Harley-Davidson Motor Co., 68 LA 811 (Martin, 1977)(employee properly suspended for refusing order to open purse for inspection on leaving plant); Aldens, Inc., 51 LA 469, 68-2 ARB ¶8814 (Kelliher, 1968)(upholding discharge for refusing to open purse where rule reserved to management right to request that employees open purses and display contents); Fruehauf Corp., 49 LA 89 (Daugherty, 1967)(past practice of searching lunch baskets for possible pilfered property). But see Orgill Bros. & Co., 66 LA 307 (Ross, 1976)(probable cause required to support search of employees). Shell Oil Co., 84 LA 562, 564 (Milentz, 1985)(upholding dismissal of employee for refusing order to permit search of car in company parking lot after marijuana "roaches" seen in ashtray and on dashboard, stating: "Several arbiters have upheld discharge when an employee, under similar suspicious circumstances, refused to comply with Company requests to submit to a search," and citing Prestige Stamping Co., 74 LA 163 (Keefe, 1980)(refusal to open newspaper management thought contained narcotics); Michigan Consol. Gas Co., 80 LA 693 (Keefe, 1983)(upholding discharge of employee who flushed toilet when told not to do so at time he was suspected of dropping drugs into toilet); Alden's Inc., 73 LA 396 (Martin, 1980)(upholding dismissal of employee who refused to lift pant leg when instructed to do so by guard when bulge showed under pant leg); WABO—Div. of American Standard, 82-1 ARB ¶8090 (Katz, 1981)(upholding discharge for refusing to take drug-screen test).

In Safeway Stores, Inc., 84 LA 1193 (Gentile, 1985), Arbitrator Joseph Gentile ruled that management had the right to inspect any vehicles that entered its premises under the following management rights clause: "All rights of the Employer not specifically limited by the terms of this Agreement are hereby reserved to the Employer. Furthermore, it is understood by the parties that the negotiations resulting in this Agreement provided ample opportunity for all matters to be considered and this Agreement shall not be construed to contain any matter not specifically set forth." Id. The arbitrator stated that "[a]bsent contractual prohibitions and restrictions, and there were none, such a right is a reasonable exercise of [the above provision]." Id. at 1194.

[66] Weirton Steel Co., 68-1 ARB ¶8249 (Kates, 1968)(evidence obtained as a result of search of employee's garage credited); Lockheed Aircraft Corp., 27 LA 709 (Maggs, 1956)(personal vehicle). See also Smith's Food King, 66 LA 619 (Ross, 1976)(amphetamines found after grievant handcuffed and searched by employer's security officer); New York Tel. Co., 66 LA 1037 (Markowitz, 1976)(blood sample from employee while unconscious). Contra: Campbell Soup Co., 2 LA 27 (Lohman, 1946)(locker opened and contents of employee's purse examined by employer); Imperial Glass Corp., 61 LA 1180 (Gibson, 1973)(search of grievant's apartment held improper).

[67] Anchor Hocking Corp., 66 LA 480 (Emerson, 1976)(employer, without prior notice, lined up 75 employees and searched lunch boxes, discharging those employees who were removing company property).

[68] Mare Island Naval Shipyard, 78 LA 1147 (Staudohar, 1982)(marijuana "roaches" discovered in routine search of personal vehicles).

[69] 80 LA 413, 415 (Kossoff, 1983).

A company installed a metal detector to screen all employees entering and leaving the plant for possession of metal objects. The apparatus, similar to those used at airports, consisted of a framework containing a sensitive alarm system that would go off when a person passed through it with metal in his or her possession. A supervisor, on a random basis, assisted by a guard stationed next to the metal detector, inspected the contents of purses, lunchboxes, parcels, and similar items that employees placed on the table next to the detector. An employee who tripped the machine would be asked to remove metal objects from his or her pockets, such as coins or keys, and then re-enter the detector. If the alarm continued to be set off after two tries, the employee would be taken to the supervisor's office and asked to submit to a "pat" search. Any employee who refused to be searched would be informed that he or she would be discharged for insubordination.

The day after the detection procedure was introduced, the union filed a grievance alleging that it constituted an undue intrusion on the privacy and dignity of the employees. In addition, the union argued that in the absence of an agreement by the parties, the employer could not properly establish a random search procedure where there was no reasonable ground for suspecting theft.

Arbitrator Sinclair Kossoff stated that from a legal standpoint, an employer unquestionably has the right to institute a metal detection and bag or purse inspection system for its employees. He noted that the Fourth Amendment grants the individual a right of privacy vis-a-vis the federal government; it does not apply to private individuals in their relations with their employer. Moreover, "there is no law which prohibits an employer from screening its employees for metal objects in their possession or conducting spot inspections of bags or parcels which they may carry into or out of the plant."

In discussing the privacy argument from a collective bargaining perspective, Arbitrator Kossoff applied a balancing test and determined that the company's screening-inspection program was not unusual (the arbitrator pointed out that he was forced to open his briefcase when he leaves the library of the Chicago Bar Association) and was not unduly intrusive of employees' privacy. No stigma was attached to being searched since every employee, salaried or otherwise, was searched, and anyone might be selected for a bag or purse inspection.

McGraw-Edison Co., National Electric Coil Division[70] illustrates the discrimination problem. Without prior consultation with the union, McGraw-Edison instituted a policy that required all items such as lunchboxes, briefcases, and packages to be checked at the plant gate. Certain supervisory and administrative personnel who exited through the front were not subject to the rule. Although the union did not object to the inspection of briefcases as a means of tightening plant security, it argued that the application of the rule was discriminatory because, in effect, only union officers' briefcases were inspected. Rejecting this argument, Arbitrator Stanley Sergent reasoned that the employer was responding to an increase in theft of articles found and used in the plant area. Accordingly, it was reasonable for the employer to direct its efforts toward increasing security at the main gate through which almost all of the employees who work in that area departed.

In his comprehensive research on the subject, Professor R.W. Fleming found that arbitrators generally agree that a company may impose reasonable rules calling for searches of one's person and property where such rules are made a condition of employment. Furthermore, Professor Fleming found that arbitrators would permit employers to use evidence obtained without the knowledge or consent of the employee if obtained from company property, even if the property were momentarily under the control of the employee. Although exclusionary rules are not automatically applicable in labor arbitration, Professor Fleming reported that few arbitrators would permit the employer to use evidence obtained by breaking and entering an employee's personal property, even when the property is located on plant premises. According to Professor Fleming, there is a difference of opinion as to the use of evidence of this type when the employee's personal property is searched without his consent, but without the necessity for entering by force.[71]

---

[70]76 LA 249 (Sergent, 1981).
[71]Fleming, The Labor Relations Process, 189 (Univ. of Ill. Press, 1967) as cited in Hill & Sinicropi, supra note 4, at 83.

Airline Industry Guidelines

The airline industry has frequently insisted on a right to conduct searches of employees. In one case[72] a carrier issued a regulation that called for a search of lockers and personal property "which might serve to conceal evidence of violation of [the company's regulations]." Pursuant to this regulation, the company stated that searches would be of two types, those involved with the investigation of particular incidents (such as a theft) and general searches of lockers. Crew kit inspections were also randomly made. The declarations made by System Board Chairman John Kagel are particularly noteworthy, especially for the practitioner looking for specific guidelines as to what constitutes a reasonable search. Umpire Kagel declared:

1. The industry has a legitimate interest in having its employees subject themselves to a search in light of the substantial theft problem that plagues the industry.
2. The solution required is a joint one of the parties.
3. An invasion of privacy under appropriate guidelines is the price that an employee must pay, under certain circumstances, to maintain the employer as a viable organization.
4. The company must be afforded the right to search the personal effects of employees who are handling the company's or the public's property.
5. The right to conduct searches cannot become a vehicle of intimidation or employee belittlement.

Certain restrictions are necessary to accomplish the latter criterion, Kagel noted:

1. Completely random searches must be banned.
2. If called upon, the company must demonstrate that there was a basis for its action. (In this regard the umpire stated that "no attempt should here be made to spell out the parameters of what constitutes a rea-

---

[72]Association of Professional Flight Attendants and American Airlines, Inc., Case No. SS-165-800 (Kagel, 1981)(unpublished). See also Transport Workers Local 502 and American Airlines, Case No. M-779-79 (Eaton, 1980)(unpublished)(search of employee lunch box).

sonable basis for engaging in an inspection, but clearly the Company should be in a position to state that one was deemed necessary and such statement, and explanation if requested, should be one that is acceptable to reasonable men and women.")

3. When there is an inspection of an employee's private effects, it should occur in a private room and if other management employees are available rather than a supervisor, they should conduct the search.

4. The right of representation should be afforded if desired by the employee.

Notably, the arbitrator did not require the posting of specific rules for the conduct of searches.

Applying the above criteria, Umpire Kagel ruled that the carrier was justified in discharging a flight attendant of 19 years who refused to allow the company to conduct a search of her two suitcases, where management had reasonable cause to believe that she had been involved in a theft (an employee had informed a flight service supervisor he had seen the grievant walk to the front of the first class section to a credenza on which were a round of cheese and some grapes and place them in her tote bag). Umpire Kagel also found that the employee knew by the time of her ultimate refusal to open her bags that she would be discharged if she refused to do so.

Search/Surveillance as Employment Term or Condition

There is authority to suggest that a search and surveillance program may be a term or condition of employment that cannot be implemented absent notice and, in selected cases, agreement from the union. In *Locomotive Engineers v. Burlington Northern Railroad*,[73] the carrier unilaterally implemented a surveillance and search program that was designed to prevent the on-duty use of alcohol and controlled substances by its employees. The program involved the use of dogs trained to detect the presence of drugs or controlled substances. Se-

---

[73]117 LRRM 2739 (D. Mont., 1984), later proceedings, 620 F.Supp. 163, 120 LRRM 3047 and 620 F.Supp. 173, 120 LRRM 3054 (D. Mont., 1985)(holding unilateral implementation of urine-testing policy "arguably justified" under parties' agreement where urinalysis is not done on random basis).

curity personnel of the carrier would subject employees and their belongings to searches by such dogs on a random basis. If the security personnel received a positive indication that there were drugs or controlled substances on the employee's person, or in the employee's possession, the employee would be subjected to further procedures designed to determine whether, in fact, he or she was in possession of any prohibited substances.

The federal court's discussion of the issue in the case is of particular interest because it outlined the thinking of most courts and arbitrators on the issue:

> The B.N., as a private entity, is entitled to maintain its business premises in any manner acceptable under the law. The use of dogs trained to detect the presence of any illicit substance is a matter within the prerogative of any private property owner. The issue in the matter *sub judice* is not the legality of the use of such dogs *pro se*, since such is valid under the law. In that vein, I find nothing prohibiting a private entity from requiring any person, including an employee, to submit to a "search" by such dog as a condition of entering that entity's premises, or refusing entry to any person believed to be in possession of an illicit substance.
>
> The issues before the court in this matter are (i) the use to which the B.N. may put the information obtained from the "search" of an employee incident to that employee's entry upon B.N. premises; and (ii) the propriety of allowing "searches" of "on-duty" employees.[74]

The court held that the union demonstrated a strong likelihood that it would prevail on the merits in its claim that the carrier's program represented a change in working conditions within the meaning of Section 6 of the Railway Labor Act.[75] A preliminary injunction enjoining the carrier from implementing its surveillance and search program was accordingly granted. The court remarked:

> The subjection of an "on-duty" employee to at random "searches," the result of which may be suspension or discharge from employment, appears to be more arguably than not, a change in working conditions. Likewise, the utilization of information obtained from a search, conducted incident to entry upon B.N.'s premises, to alter an employee's status would also appear to be a change in working conditions.[76]

---

[74]117 LRRM at 2740.
[75]45 U.S.C. §156.
[76]117 LRRM at 2741.

Surveillance

Arbitrator Hugo Black, Jr., in an address before the National Academy of Arbitrators, discussed three separate categories of employee surveillance: surveillance by observation, surveillance by extraction, and surveillance by reproduction.[77] In the employment setting observational surveillance simply involves observing an employee at work, although the employee may not be aware he or she is being observed at the time. Surveillance by extraction, where most of the problems in labor arbitration have arisen, is discussed earlier in this chapter in the context of polygraph and psychological testing. Finally, surveillance by reproduction, or "reproductibility of communications," concerns surveillance by recording or other mechanical devices.

This scheme is a useful way to consider the respective rights of management and employees when it is argued that the company's surveillance tactics are impermissible under the parties' collective bargaining agreement.

Tape and Video Recordings

Arbitrators have generally held that management has the right to install video-tape equipment in order to monitor employees on the job site. A good example in this area is *FMC Corp.*,[78] in which the union argued that the installation of closed-circuit television equipment violated the agreement. The employees' ability to work "without cameras focusing on their every move" was a beneficial "working condition," the union said, and the company's actions interfered with the employees' right of privacy. The union also argued that use of the camera violated the parties' past practice. Arbitrator Richard Mittenthal's reasoning is worth repeating at length:

> The Union seems to say that if a given course of conduct qualifies as a practice, it must automatically be considered a binding condition of employment. That is not so. For a practice, to be enforceable, must be supported by the *mutual agreement* of the parties. Its binding quality is due not to the fact that it is a

---

[77]Black, "Surveillance and the Labor Arbitration Process," Proceedings of the 23rd Annual Meeting of NAA, 1–14 (BNA Books, 1970), citing Westin, Privacy and Freedom (Atheneum, 1967).

[78]46 LA 335 (1966).

past practice but rather to the agreement on which it is based. Yet, there are many practices which are not the result of joint determination at all. . . .

. . . To treat all practices as binding conditions of employment, without regard to the matter of mutuality, would be to place past practice on an equal footing with the written Agreement, a result which these parties could hardly have contemplated. There is, after all, no provision in this Agreement which specifically requires the continuance of existing practices. And the arbitrator certainly has no authority to write a "past practice" clause into the Agreement under the guise of contract interpretation.

It is true that there had been no closed-circuit television in this plant in the past. But nothing in the evidence indicates that this practice—this absence of television—was in any way based upon the mutual agreement of the parties. Management had never agreed not to install such a television system. The matter had never been discussed prior to 1965. The fact that television had not been used to watch employees was not the result of design or deliberation. Nowhere does the record suggest that Management had ever before considered installing closed-circuit television. Traditional methods of supervision had been followed in the receiving room for years. Nowhere does it appear that these methods were the subject of Union-Management discussion or negotiation. . . . Clearly, the claimed practice lacks the requisite mutual agreement. The Union's position therefore must be rejected.[79]

Arbitrator Mittenthal also rejected the Union's argument that management had an obligation to secure the union's agreement prior to installing the television system. The arbitrator explained:

The use of television to watch employees concerns the subject of supervision. A decision as to how employees are to be supervised and what are the proper methods of supervision is a normal function of Management.[80]

Arbitrator J. Marcus, in *Sun Drug Co.*,[81] sustained an employee's discharge for conducting a "bookmaking" business at work, based on evidence obtained by a listening and recording device the employer hooked up to a telephone booth. While the union objected to the method by which the employer

---

[79]Id. at 336–37 (emphasis in original).
[80]Id. at 337. See also United States Customs Serv., 77 LA 1001 (Merrifield, 1981)(video-taping of alleged drug transaction); Casting Eng'rs, 76 LA 939 (Petersen, 1981)(video-taping of time clock area); Pennzoil Co., 76 LA 587 (Duff, 1981)(video-taping of strike misconduct).
[81]31 LA 191 (1958).

gathered its evidence, labeling it entrapment, Arbitrator Marcus reasoned that the legality of the means by which information is gathered is for other authorities to determine. Similarly, in *A. B. Chance Co.*,[82] an arbitrator credited evidence obtained as a result of a "pen register" (a mechanical device placed on a telephone line that registers where a call originates) to prove that an employee was responsible for making anonymous phone calls to the homes of some supervisors.

When an employee claimed to have made a secret tape recording of an investigatory meeting concerning a grievance, Arbitrator James Vadakin, in *VRN International*,[83] reflected the better weight of authority by ruling that this was, in part, just cause for her dismissal. The arbitrator stated that his major concern was not that the secret recording was a felony under state law, but that engaging in such conduct with impunity would have a chilling effect on sound industrial procedures.[84]

The NLRB has taken a similar approach to the use of tape recordings. In *Carpenter Sprinkler Corp. v. NLRB*,[85] the Second Circuit held that the NLRB was within its discretion in fashioning a rule making surreptitiously prepared tape recordings inadmissible as evidence in an unfair labor practice proceeding. In reaching this decision, the Second Circuit stated:

> Negotiations in the labor relations field are often a delicate matter. Courts must balance the interests of an employer against the possibility of coercing or intimidating employees in their exercise of rights under the Act, and harming the collective bargaining process.... The ruling of the Board in this case specifically referred to the "significant problems" which might result [inhibiting the expression of the parties] from allowing tape recordings of contract negotiations into evidence....[86]

Undercover Surveillance

Arbitrators have, with few exceptions, recognized management's right to conduct reasonable surveillance to inves-

---

[82]57 LA 725 (Florey, 1971).
[83]75 LA 243 (1980).
[84]See also Needham Packing Co., 44 LA 1057 (Davey, 1965)(recordings of phone conversations between attorney and union officers not admissible in arbitration proceeding where recorded without officers' knowledge).
[85]605 F.2d 60, 102 LRRM 2199 (CA 2, 1979).
[86]102 LRRM at 2202. See also NLRB v. Plasterers Local 90, 606 F.2d 189, 102 LRRM 2482 (CA 7, 1979)(NLRB did not err in admitting into evidence telephone conversations between job applicant and union official).

tigate employee absenteeism or moonlighting.[87] Less common instances of employers' surveillance include dispatching "undercover" personnel in order to investigate theft,[88] or the use of dogs to detect possession of drugs.[89] In the area of observational surveillance, most disputes concern not management's right to find out "what is going on" but, rather, whether management's observations, if correct, justify the discipline meted out. Often management's undercover spotters generate written reports of their findings that are subsequently introduced at the arbitration hearing as evidence. This presents hearsay concerns if the spotter is not present at the hearing to testify and be cross-examined by the party against whom the evidence is offered. While the strict rules of evidence do not apply in an arbitration proceeding, it is expected that an arbitrator will not accept the reports into the record. If the material is accepted, it will not be accorded any significant weight.[90]

State Laws

Many states have limited the ability of management to engage in certain types of surveillance.[91] California, for example, makes it unlawful for any public service corporation to discipline or discharge an employee based on information or a report generated by a "special agent, detective, or person commonly known as a 'spotter' " involving a question of honesty or integrity of the employee, unless the employee has the right to a hearing and the opportunity to present defense testimony.[92] Connecticut has perhaps the most protective safeguards of an employee's privacy rights. State law forbids private

---

[87]Los Angeles Transit Lines, 25 LA 740 (Hildebrand, 1955)(reports of "spotters" credited, notwithstanding hearsay objections). But see Keystone Asphalt Prods. Co., 3 LA 789 (Hampton, 1946).

[88]Lockheed Eng'g and Mgmt. Servs. Co., 75 LA 1147 (Overman, 1980)(employment of paid undercover agents to detect theft); Associated Grocers of Colorado, Inc., 81 LA 974 (Smith, 1983)(use of undercover police agents to investigate theft and vandalism).

[89]United States Air Force Logistics Command, 78 LA 1092 (Feldman, 1982).

[90]See the discussion of hearsay in arbitration proceedings in Hill & Sinicropi, supra note 4, at 42–50.

[91]Besides the statutes discussed in this section, see the following laws (citations to the "State Laws" (SLL) binders of BNA's Labor Relations Reporter): Hawaii, 21:219; Kansas, 26:218; Michigan, 32:201 (railroad employees and spotters); New York, 42:232a (unfair labor practice to spy on employees with respect to organizational activities); Rhode Island, 50:230 (organizational activities).

[92]California, SLL 14:205.

and public employers, upon penalty of graduated fines and even imprisonment for a third offense, from conducting surveillance activities "in areas designed for the health or personal comfort of the employees or for the safeguarding of their possessions, such as rest rooms, locker rooms or lounges."[93] Wisconsin's Employment Peace Act contains a provision that makes it an unfair labor practice for an employer to spy on employees with respect to their bargaining rights.[94]

---

[93]Connecticut, SLL 16:203. See also Nevada, SLL 38:202.
[94]Wisconsin, SLL 60:230.

Part III

Management's Right to Manage the Business

Chapter 10

The Hiring Process

Probationary Employees

In a sample taken by BNA, probationary periods were found in 78 percent of the collective bargaining agreements. Further, of the contracts requiring a probationary period, in 76 percent the employer retained full authority to discipline or discharge probationary employees. At the end of the trial period, usually from one to three months, the employee's seniority would typically date back to the original date of hire.[1]

The primary purpose of a trial or probationary period is to allow management to determine if an employee satisfies the employer's job requirements. Since a probationary period is a matter of contract, a company cannot unilaterally create a probationary class of employment during the term of a collective bargaining agreement. Moreover, an employee's acquiescence in a probationary period as a condition of employment would have no effect absent the agreement of the union.[2]

Some contracts provide that employees shall be given a trial period of a specified number of days, "during which period [an employee] may be discharged without recourse."[3] Other contracts allow a probationary employee to be dismissed at

---

[1]Basic Patterns in Union Contracts, 74 (BNA Books, 1983).
[2]MAC Coal Co., 52 LA 1125 (Krimsly, 1969).
[3]American Stevedoring Corp., 72 LA 559, 560 (Ables, 1979); Allen Indus., Inc., 52 LA 1131, 1133 (Altrock, 1969).

any time "at the discretion of the employer."[4] Under these provisions many arbitrators hold that a dismissal during the probationary period is not arbitrable.

Another possibility is illustrated by *Murphy Oil USA, Inc.*,[5] a case reported by Arbitrator Mario Bognanno. In that case the agreement provided that upon the completion of 90 days of service, an employee would assume the status of regular employee. The contract further provided that all employees having less than 90 days of service "shall be considered as temporary employees and may be terminated at the discretion of the Company." Arbitrator Bognanno ruled arbitrable the dismissal of a 75-day employee, but held that the parties created two classes of employees, temporary and regular, with respect to whether terminations had to be "for cause." He remarked:

> [T]emporary, as opposed to regular, employees are subject to the doctrine of "at will" employment. This doctrine allows the Company to discharge temporary employees without having to prove or provide a work-related reason for its decision.[6]

Where a party alleges that a probationary employee's dismissal was intended to evade the collective bargaining agreement, or motivated by race, sex, or union activities, most arbitrators will hold the dispute arbitrable, especially if the contract has a broad no-discrimination clause.[7]

Where grievances during probationary periods have been considered on the merits or, alternatively, where arbitrators have ruled a dispute non-arbitrable but have spoken *in dictum*, most arbitrators conclude that management has great discretion to effect a discharge during a trial period, at least in the sense that it will not have to justify its action under a just-cause standard.[8] This does not mean, however, that the

---

[4]See, e.g., Flint Bd. of Educ., 76 LA 1080 (Roumell, 1981); State of Alaska, 75 LA 635 (Jackson, 1980); Bucyrus-Erie Co., 69 LA 93, 96 (Lipson, 1977); Canadian Johns Manville Co., 58 LA 1054 (Weatherill, 1972).

[5]83 LA 935 (1984).

[6]Id. at 938.

[7]Amoco Oil Co., 70 LA 979 (Britton, 1978)(employer's power to discharge probationary employee limited by contract's prohibition of discrimination); Keystone Consol. Indus., Inc., 71 LA 574 (Cohen, 1978)(grievance claiming sex discrimination arbitrable and alternative right to proceed in court did not prevent arbitration); Texas Int'l Airlines, 68 LA 244 (Gruenberg, 1976) (union activities); Basic Vegetable Prods., Inc., 64 LA 620 (Gould, 1975). But see American Stevedoring Corp., 72 LA 559 (Ables, 1979); MJB Co., 77 LA 1294 (Burns, 1982).

[8]See, e.g., the discussion of case authority by Arbitrator J.F.W. Weatherill in John Inglis Co., 58 LA 430, 431–32 (1972).

employees or their bargaining representative are not entitled to any information concerning the dismissal of probationary employees. Some arbitrators, while holding that management need not show just cause, still require management to exercise its discretion in a reasonable manner which, at the very least, may imply that the employees are given reasons for the employer's actions.[9]

Federal Sector Mandate

Citing the Federal Service Labor-Management Relations Act,[10] arbitrators have uniformly found that dismissals of probationary employees in the federal sector are not arbitrable. The reasoning is reflected by Arbitrator Sol Yarowsky in *United States Penitentiary*:[11]

> Section 7121(c)(4) of LMRA excludes from any negotiated grievance procedure disputes over "any examination, certification, or appointment." This even includes bargaining over probationary employees' termination rights because the probationary period is part and parcel of the appointment and examination process. It also conflicts with Sections 3321 and 4303 of the [Civil Service Reform Act], which authorizes the probationary period and denies probationary employees . . . the right to challenge their removal for unacceptable performance. . . .[12]

As stated by the arbitrator, "the rationale for this exclusion is said to be that it would be inappropriate 'to restrict an agency's authority to separate an employee who does not perform acceptably during this period.' "[13] Similarly, another arbitrator summarized the law in this area as follows:

> Probationary employees, working under Federal laws, are afforded little protection in their jobs. They do not have expectations of continued employment to give rise to a property interest within the protection of the Fifth Amendment of the U.S. Constitution. . . . Nor do they have sufficient statutory safeguards. As the court stated in *U.S. Department of Justice, Immigration and Naturalization Service v. Federal Labor Relations Authority*, . . . Congress, in the Civil Service Reform Act of 1978,

---

[9]See, e.g., Pan Am. World Airways, 50 LA 722 (Galenson, 1968)(contract giving management right to dismiss probationary employees "at its option").
[10]5 U.S.C. §7101 et seq. (Supp. V, 1981).
[11]82 LA 939 (1984).
[12]Id. at 940.
[13]Id. at 941, quoting Senate report accompanying LMRA.

"reaffirmed its unwillingness to provide statutory protections for probationary employees being terminated for unacceptable performance," but rather "expressly perceived an agency's discretion to remove [them] summarily" . . . .[14]

In *Department of Air Force*,[15] the agreement provided that the agency must raise any issue of nongrievability or nonarbitrability within specified time limits. Although the agency did not raise an arbitrability issue concerning the dismissal of a probationary employee prior to arbitration, it nevertheless argued that the grievance was not arbitrable. Citing the INS case mentioned in the quotation supra,[16] it argued that the prior decision handed down by the District of Columbia Circuit held that the separation of a probationary employee is not negotiable and, thus, probationary employees do not have the right to have their separation considered under the negotiated grievance and arbitration procedures during their probationary period. The arbitrator, in ruling for the agency, noted that ordinarily arbitrators are duty bound to follow the terms of the agreement. However, the contract at issue also provided:

> In the administration of all matters covered by this Agreement, officials of the Employer and the Union and employees of the bargaining unit are governed by Title VII of the Civil Service Reform Act of 1978.[17]

The arbitrator accordingly found himself "duty bound" by the decision of the D.C. Circuit, even though the decision had not been issued at the time the grievance was processed.[18]

Outside Hires

Many bargaining agreements restrict management from hiring "outsiders" (employees who are not in the bargaining

---

[14]James A. Haley Veteran's Hosp., 82 LA 973, 975 (Wahl, 1984)(citation omitted).
[15]82 LA 593 (Wann, 1984).
[16]Immigration & Naturalization Serv. v. FLRA, 709 F.2d 724, 113 LRRM 3488 (CA DC, 1983). In *INS* the court held that it was impermissible for the FLRA to require the agency to bargain over a union proposal to bring probationary employees within the mandatory grievance procedure of the collective bargaining agreement. Stating that "[t]he concept of a probationary term is of congressional, not administrative, creation," the appellate court declared: "The right to summary termination, . . . assures management that it alone can assess an individual's skills and determine whether those skills satisfy the requirements of the service. Ordering INS to negotiate about a proposal that would diminish management's authority over employment decisions undermines the discretion that Congress (and OPM) intended management to have." 113 LRRM at 3492.
[17]82 LA at 596.
[18]See also Veterans Admin. Center, 81 LA 325 (Gentile, 1983).

unit) by including a provision limiting the number of employees management can hire from the outside in filling vacancies.[19] Similarly, if the employer has agreed to train employees pursuant to a seniority system, there is authority that management has negotiated away its right to hire new employees to fill skilled positions.[20] Weaker restrictions are found in those agreements mandating that management give "simultaneous consideration" to both inside and outside applicants,[21] or provisions declaring that it is the intent of management to fill vacancies by promoting qualified employees from within the bargaining unit.[22] Under certain circumstances a job-posting requirement may have the same effect as a provision limiting the number of outside hires, by ensuring that consideration is given to unit employees.[23] At times, the parties' recognition and seniority provision may even be a limiting factor on managerial discretion to hire from the outside, especially if there is a past practice of filling vacancies from within the unit.[24]

Most disputes in this area involve management's right to fill a position from outside the unit where employees working in other classifications are by-passed,[25] or where employees on layoff are not recalled to work.[26] The major issue for the parties is the appropriate standard of selection for a particular vacancy. If the selection or hiring standard is a "sufficient ability" criterion, management will find it more difficult to hire from the outside than if a "relative ability" test is used.[27] When questions are raised concerning the ability of competing employees, arbitrators generally rule that management has the right to make the initial determination subject to challenge by the union that the employer's decision was unreasonable.[28]

---

[19]Rohm & Haas Tex., Inc., 82 LA 271 (Taylor, 1984).
[20]American Can Co., 73 LA 1218 (Denson, 1979).
[21]Internal Revenue Serv., 71 LA 1018 (Harkless, 1978).
[22]West Mifflin Area School Dist., 74 LA 627 (Hays, 1980); Walker Mfg. Co., 62 LA 1283 (Kelliher, 1974).
[23]Geuder, Paeschke & Frey Co., 69 LA 871 (Wyman, 1977).
[24]City of Milwaukee, 65 LA 833 (Rauch, 1975).
[25]Zenith Elecs. Corp., 80 LA 525 (Belshaw, 1983).
[26]Tucson Unified School Dist., 80 LA 1010 (Roberts, 1983); Elliott Packing Co., 80 LA 1118 (Rotenberg, 1983); School Dist. of Superior, 72 LA 719 (Pieroni, 1979).
[27]See, e.g., United States Steel Corp., 75 LA 511 (Beilstein, 1980)("relative ability" is proper criterion for selection to apprentice-training program); Franklin Elec. Co., 68 LA 823 (Bothwell, 1977); Community Health Care Center Plan, Inc., 66 LA 1329 (McKone, 1976); Forest Home Cemetery, 66 LA 1239 (Schoenfeld, 1976).
[28]Rotek, Inc., 73 LA 937, 940 (Rybolt, 1979).

In this same respect, unless otherwise provided for in the labor agreement, arbitrators have ruled that management is not required to establish a trainee position or trial period for a by-passed employee who is presently unqualified for the job at issue.[29] If, however, the by-passed employee's qualifications are such as to lead to reasonable expectations that the employee can learn, within a reasonable time, to perform the work in a competent manner, with no danger to the employee, the public, or co-employees, a trial period may be in order.[30]

Falsification of Applications

In the selection and appointment process management has consistently asserted its right to truthful and accurate information from a prospective employee. Arbitrators have regularly found that a fraudulent entry of a material fact is grounds for discharge, although no hard and fast rules are applied.[31] The reported decisions indicate that the following

---

[29]General Battery Corp., 82 LA 478 (Hearne, 1984); Oshkosh Truck Corp., 66 LA 1057 (Torosian, 1976). Trial periods are discussed further under "Trial and Training Periods" in Chapter 11, infra.

[30]Kerns DeSoto, Inc., 64 LA 1125 (Conant, 1975).

[31]See, e.g., Owens-Illinois Forest Prods., 83 LA 1265 (Cantor, 1984)(sustaining dismissal of employee for failing to "fully disclose" to physician at time of pre-employment physical exam past medical history relating to back injury); Wine Cellar, 81 LA 158 (Ray, 1983)(dismissal of waiter for failure to disclose most recent employment on job application was proper); I.E. Prods., Inc., 72 LA 351 (Brooks, 1979)(upholding discharge of employee for intentionally failing to disclose on employment application workman's compensation award for back injury suffered in prior employment, reasoning that the agreement does not limit management's right to determine criteria for hiring, including establishment of health standards for employment applicants); Indianapolis Power & Light Co., 73 LA 512, 516 (Kossoff, 1979)(sustaining discharge for employee who answered "no" to question whether she had relatives employed by employer, where rule provided for discipline or discharge for dishonesty, including falsification of employment application, and "management rights clause expressly reserved to the Company the right to 'manage and operate its property and business according to its best judgment.' "); United States Steel Corp., 74 LA 354 (Dybeck, 1980)(upholding termination for falsification of employment application regarding psychiatric problems although grievant was permitted to work for one month after examination by company medical director); Armco Composites, 79 LA 1157 (House, 1982)(falsification of grievant's identity); Gardner-Denver Co., 71 LA 1126 (Dunn, 1978)(criminal record); Huntington Alloys, Inc., 74 LA 176 (Katz, 1980)(criminal conviction); I.E. Prods., Inc., 72 LA 351 (Brooks, 1979); Brink's, Inc., 79 LA 816 (Briggs, 1982); Eaton Corp., 73 LA 367 (Atwood, 1979); Farmland Foods, Inc., 64 LA 1260 (McKenna, 1975)(withholding information on medical condition); Chanslor-Western Oil Co., 61 LA 1113 (Meiners, 1973)(back injury); Price Bros. Co., 62 LA 389 (High, 1974)(prior employer). But see United States Postal Serv., 71 LA 100 (Krimsly, 1978)(discharge improper where employee held belief that criminal charges had been expunged); Kaiser Steel Corp., 64 LA 194 (Roberts, 1975)(discharge improper where grievant told that misdemeanor was dismissed); Commonwealth of Pa., 66 LA 96 (LeWinter, 1976)(12-year-old criminal indictment); Gold Kist, Inc., 77 LA 569 (Statham, 1981)(employee reinstated where evidence established that individual in personnel department helped grievant fill out employment application).

factors may be considered by arbitrators in deciding whether just cause exists for the dismissal of an employee: (1) the nature of the fact or item falsified; (2) the number of items concealed; (3) the time between the occurrence and falsification; (4) whether disclosure would have precluded hiring; (5) the time between falsification and disclosure; (6) the employee's overall job performance; (7) the reason or factor that triggered the discharge; (8) the employer's motivation (was it punitive in nature?); (9) special safety or security considerations; and (10) mitigating factors, such as the employee's marital status or age.[32]

When an employee is found to have falsified relevant information on an employment application, some arbitrators have not sustained discharge, especially when a long period of time has elapsed since the hiring and the employee's work record is good. The leading and perhaps most-often quoted decision in favor of a limitations period was reported by the late Dean Shulman while an umpire for Ford Motor Company. Dean Shulman stated that some time limitation should be implied, even if the falsification was deliberate and material:

> The question remains, however, of how long an employee's false statement in securing employment can continue to hang over him as a ground for discharge. Is he subject to discharge for time without limit so long as he remains in the employ of the Company? That would surely be a harsh and unjust rule. The notions of waiver and conditions are as well established in law and morals as is that of rescission for fraud. If, after learning of the false statement, the employer does not promptly discharge the employee but continues his employment, the continuance after knowledge may properly be considered as employment in the first instance with knowledge, and the falsification of itself cannot thereafter be deemed a proper ground for discharge.
>
> But a rule that the employee guilty of such falsification is subject to discharge for a reasonable period after the employer first learns of the falsification, whenever that may be, would also be unduly harsh and capricious. It, too, would provide for no definite time limit. In addition, it would put a premium on the employer's failure to ascertain the truth. And the fate of employees similarly situated would depend entirely upon the pure chance of when the employer happened to learn of the falsification.
>
> Again, in law and morals generally, the principle of a stat-

---

[32]See Brink's, Inc., 79 LA 816 (Briggs, 1982), which applied the criteria outlined by Arbitrator Burton Turkus in Kraft Foods, 50 LA 161 (1967).

ute of limitations is well recognized, even though it means that the mere lapse of time thus enables a guilty person to escape what otherwise would be regarded as just punishment. The principle is recognized not merely in order to encourage diligence on the part of the aggrieved persons and to direct energies to the relative present rather than to the remote past, but also as a measure of justice to the guilty person whose offense, it is believed, should not render him permanently insecure.[33]

The concept of a "statute of limitations," apparently introduced by Dean Shulman, has not found a great deal of support in the reported decisions,[34] particularly when the parties' agreement or the employer's work rules provide that falsification of an application or dishonesty shall be grounds for discharge.[35] Arbitrator Jonas Katz, in *Huntington Alloys, Inc.*,[36] rejected the "statute of limitations" theory, and reasoned as follows:

> This Board of Arbitration is not willing to conclude that an employer who is deliberately misled by an employee loses its right to invoke reasonable disciplinary actions simply because it had not discovered the employee's fraud for a period of time, provided the falsification would have borne on the employee's initial employment.
>   . . . [T]here is a substantial line of cases which uphold the discharge of persons filing false employment applications even

---

[33]Case No. A-184 (1945), cited in Opinions of the Umpire (New York State School of Indus. and Labor Relations).

[34]But cf. Labor Mgmt. Servs. Admin., 80 LA 250 (Dworkin, 1983); I.E. Prods., Inc., 72 LA 351 (Brooks, 1979).

In Wine Cellar, 81 LA 158 (Ray, 1983), Arbitrator Douglas Ray had this to say on the issue of false statements on employment applications and time limits:

> The published arbitration reports contain dozens, if not hundreds, of cases involving alleged false statements on employment application forms. Most such cases involve alleged misrepresentation on questions involving physical condition and prior injuries, arrest records and, as in the instant case, employment history. Numerous cases have recognized that an employee may be discharged for his failure to mention prior employment in [an] application where such information is material for the assessment of qualifications. Here, however, there has been a lapse of time between the misrepresentation and the discharge. In such cases, many arbitrators will not automatically uphold a discharge, but rather apply safeguards in the form of a four point test. The test consists of the following questions:
>   (1) was the misrepresentation willful?;
>   (2) was the misrepresentation material to the hiring?[;]
>   (3) was it material at the time of discharge?;
>   (4) has the employer acted promptly upon discovery?

Id. at 163 (citations omitted).

[35]See, e.g., the lengthy discussion of case authority by Arbitrators Burton Turkus in Kraft Foods, 50 LA 161, 165–66 (1967), and Jonas Katz in Huntington Alloys, Inc., 74 LA 176, 179 (1980). See also United States Steel Corp., 74 LA 354 (Simpkins, 1980).

[36]74 LA 176 (1980).

after a substantial period of time under certain facts and circumstances. . . . These cases upholding discharges are based upon one of two theories: the punishment theory and the annulment theory. The first theory is that, where certain facts exist, a penalty of discharge is appropriate even where several years elapse prior to discovery of the falsification of the employment application. The annulment theory holds that where the employment contract is obtained by the applicant upon the basis of a misrepresentation of a material fact, there is a voidable contract which the employer may void at its option upon learning of the material misrepresentation which was part of the basis of the employer's decision to hire the applicant.[37]

Where individuals have failed to disclose prior convictions, courts have upheld dismissals for falsification of applications against charges that these policies violate Title VII.[38] In *NLRB v. Florida Steel Corp.*,[39] the Fifth Circuit stated:

"Any employer has the right to demand that its employees be honest and truthful in every facet of their employment. Absent an antiunion motivation, any employer has the right to discipline an employee for his dishonesty or untruthfulness."[40]

One arbitrator correctly observed that "[t]he problem with falsification of employment application cases is that discovery often occurs weeks, months or years after the event. By that time, the employee has established a work record and has a stake in the job."[41] This is an area where arbitrators are somewhat split, although more appear to subscribe to the "annulment" as opposed to the "punishment" theory in upholding discharges for falsification of employment applications. The better rule in falsification cases is simply to avoid absolutes and to give consideration to all the ten factors noted above.

---

[37]Id. at 179 (citations omitted).
[38]Avant v. South Cent. Bell Tel. Co., 716 F.2d 1083, 32 FEP 1853 (CA 5, 1983); Trapp v. State Univ. College at Buffalo, 30 FEP 1499 (W.D.N.Y., 1983); Jimerson v. Kisco Co., Inc., 542 F.2d 1008, 13 FEP 977, 978 (CA 8, 1976)(noting that "black persons are indisputably more likely to suffer arrest than white persons," but holding that plaintiff-employee was not discharged for having an arrest record, but for falsifying this record when applying for employment. In the words of the court, "To establish a prima facie case of disproportionate racial impact under Green [Green v. Missouri Pacific Railroad Co., 523 F.2d 1290, 10 FEP 1409 (CA 8, 1975)], it was necessary for [plaintiff] to show that blacks as a class were excluded for falsifying their arrest records at a higher rate than whites.").
[39]586 F.2d 436, 100 LRRM 2102 (1978).
[40]100 LRRM at 2107, quoting NLRB v. Mueller Brass Co., 509 F.2d 704, 713, 88 LRRM 3236, 3243 (CA 5, 1975).
[41]Wine Cellar, 81 LA 158, 164 (Ray, 1983).

Fair Employment Considerations

The effect of fair employment legislation, particularly Title VII, on managerial discretion has been discussed.[42] Again, any recruiting, hiring, promotion, or retention criterion that has a disparate impact on a protected class must be shown to be job-related if liability under the statute is to be avoided. Under Title VII an employment practice must first be shown to have a disparate impact before the employer's obligation to demonstrate job-relatedness comes into play. Title VII does not mandate that all selection criteria be job related, but only those criteria that have an adverse impact on the employment opportunities of members of a race, color, religion, sex, or national origin. In theory, a selection criterion could be invalid in that it is not job related, yet if the impact on both non-minorities and minorities is the same, Title VII is not violated. In other words, an employer is entitled to use a job criterion that does not predict performance on the job, so long as the criterion does not have a disparate impact on a member of a protected minority. One can, of course, question why an employer would ever use a selection device that has no predictive utility whatsoever. Nevertheless, the law does not require rationality, but only that the criteria used be nondiscriminatory.

In a nutshell, Title VII imposes substantial limitations on managerial discretion within the entire employment context. At the same time arbitrators continue to apply fair employment law when resolving grievances alleging prohibited race- or sex-based discrimination.[43] For this reason, it is im-

---

[42]See discussion under "Title VII" in Chapter 4, supra.

[43]See "External Law as a Remedy in Labor Arbitration," in Hill & Sinicropi, Remedies in Arbitration, 207–25 (BNA Books, 1981), where the issue is discussed at length. Hill & Sinicropi write: "Frequently the parties will explicitly incorporate legal standards into the agreement or, alternatively, will by submission empower the arbitrator to rule on a legal issue. In such cases, arbitrators, with few exceptions, have not hesitated to 'apply the law' when interpreting the agreement." Id. at 211. The authors go on to point out that "[w]hen the contract is silent concerning incorporation of external law in formulating awards and remedies, most arbitrators, while not announcing that their decision is based upon legal doctrine, will not ignore the mandates of law, but rather will issue an award consistent with the law." Id. at 213. With respect to the situation where there is a conflict between the agreement and the law, the authors note that the reported cases indicate divergent views whether the contract or the law should prevail. Of course, in the federal sector arbitrators are required to deal with external law. See also Fairweather, Practice and Procedure in Labor Arbitration, 2d Ed., 436–68 (BNA Books, 1983)(discussing external law and its impact on arbitration); Elkouri & Elkouri, How Arbitration Works, 4th ed., 369–92 (BNA Books, 1985).

perative that practitioners have some insight into specific statutory limitations as applied by the courts in the hiring area.

Standards Limited by Law

There are any number of factors that may work to disqualify an individual from consideration for a job vacancy. Subjective-type considerations by the person doing the evaluating and personal-appearance criteria are discussed in other sections.[44] Although management has great discretion in designating job qualifications, the courts have applied fair employment laws so as to limit an employer's consideration and use of certain factors that might otherwise be used in screening job applicants. Of special note are the following: (1) police records; (2) height and weight requirements; (3) educational standards; (4) anti-nepotism policies; and (5) garnishment and credit history.

Police Records

Common to many employment applications are questions relating to an applicant's arrest or conviction record. Both the EEOC and the courts have distinguished inquiries concerning pre-employment arrests from inquiries concerning convictions. Inquiries into an employee's arrest records have been struck down unless shown to be job-related; courts have taken judicial notice of the fact that blacks, in disproportionate numbers, are subject to arrest for serious crime.[45] On the other

---

[44]See discussion under "Use of Subjective Criteria" in Chapter 11, infra, and Chapter 6, supra.
[45]Perhaps the most-often-cited case in this area is Gregory v. Litton Sys., Inc., 316 F.Supp. 401, 2 FEP 842 (C.D. Cal., 1970), aff'd, 472 F.2d 631, 5 FEP 267 (CA 9, 1972), in which the court held that the use of arrest records in private employment decisions violates Title VII where such use has a disparate impact against black applicants and is not related to a reasonable business purpose. See also Richardson v. Hotel Corp. of Am., 332 F.Supp. 519, 3 FEP 1031 (D. La., 1971)(upholding practice of inquiring into arrest records of applicants for position of bellboy where employees have access to rooms and luggage of hotel guests); McCray v. Alexander, 29 FEP 653 (D. Colo., 1982)(taking judicial notice of the disproportionate number of blacks in the United States subjected to arrest for serious crimes, but holding that plaintiff-employee's removal from employment was for an off-duty act of shooting motorist; fact of arrest irrelevant to final decision to suspend and ultimately remove plaintiff from employment); Smith v. American Serv. Co. of Atlanta, Inc., 611 F.Supp. 321, 35 FEP 1552 (N.D. Ga., 1984)(refusing to overturn practice of use of polygraph examination, which in this case reflected deception in response to inquiries about arrest record, where employer did not have policy of excluding applicants with arrest records); Batiste v. Burke, 746 F.2d 257, 261 (CA 5, 1984)(upholding use of arrest

hand, with few exceptions, conviction inquiries have been held to constitute a legitimate employer concern.[46] Still, employers are advised not to adopt a blanket policy of excluding any employee with a conviction record.[47] The EEOC has consistently taken the position that reasonable cause exists to believe that Title VII is violated when employees are automatically eliminated from job consideration because of a conviction. The following comments typify the reasoning of the Commission:

> Blacks are convicted at a rate significantly in excess of their percentage in the population. Thus, an employment practice of discharging persons from employment because of their conviction records can be expected to have a disproportionate adverse impact upon Blacks and would therefore be unlawful under Title VII in the absence of a justifying business necessity. To establish business necessity, the employer must demonstrate that the nature of a particular criminal conviction disqualifies the individual job applicant from performing the particular job in an acceptable, business-like manner. The most important factor in this determination is the job-relatedness of the conviction. If it is established that the conviction is not job-related, it is unlawful under Title VII to disqualify the individual because of the conviction.[48]

Most courts, however, have not found that a policy of rejecting applicants with a conviction record has a *per se* disparate impact on minorities.[49] Rather, to establish a *prima facie* case of discrimination, courts require the rejected applicant to show that the conviction rate for blacks is higher than that for nonminorities in the relevant labor market. Again,

records by United States Postal Service as not invalidated by the Due Process Clause, stating that "a mere applicant may properly be refused initial employment on the basis of a record which showed four arrests."); Webster v. Redmond, 599 F.2d 793 (CA 7, 1979)(state school board did not impair teacher's liberty interest in considering prior arrest in declining to promote him to principal); Reynolds v. Sheet Metal Workers Local 102, 498 F.Supp. 952, 24 FEP 648 (D.D.C., 1980).

[46]But see Green v. Missouri Pac. R.R., 523 F.2d 1290, 10 FEP 1409 (CA 8, 1975), injunctive order aff'd, 549 F.2d 1158, 14 FEP 878 (1977)(practice of refusing to consider for employment any person convicted of a crime other than minor traffic offense violated Title VII, where blacks disqualified at higher rate than whites).

[47]See, e.g., the policy of the Postal Service in Hill v. United States Postal Serv., 522 F.Supp. 1283, 26 FEP 1426, 1428 (S.D.N.Y., 1981).

[48]EEOC Decision No. 80–12, 26 FEP 1794, 1795 (1980), citing Commission Decision No. 78–35, 26 FEP 1755 (1978). See also the authors' discussion of discharge for off-duty misconduct in Chapter 8, supra.

[49]Craig v. HEW, 508 F.Supp. 1055, 25 FEP 560, 562 (W.D. Mo., 1981)(rejecting argument that courts should take judicial notice of probable disparate impact of a rule against employing persons with felony conviction).

an employer need not demonstrate that its policy is job-related absent a showing of discriminatory impact.

As of this writing 17 states have enacted legislation addressing the use and dissemination of information concerning a job applicant's arrest or conviction record in an employment setting.[50] The effect of this legislation is, in most cases, a mandate that management not consider arrests that have not resulted in convictions or, alternatively, convictions that have been expunged from the applicant's record. Some states even provide that an applicant may answer falsely if asked about an arrest that was expunged and that management may not use this as grounds for an employment-related decision.[51]

---

[50]California, SLL (BNA) 14:210, 210a (providing limited exception to financial institutions and public utilities); Colorado, SLL 15:204; Connecticut, SLL 16:204 (arrest information shall not be available to any member of the firm interviewing the applicant except the job personnel department or the person in charge of employment); Georgia, SLL 20:112 (Crime Information Center permitted to make available to employers records of employees whose duties involve: (1) working in or near private dwellings without immediate supervision; (2) custody or control over or access to cash or valuable items; (3) knowledge of or access to trade processes, trade secrets, or other confidential business information; or (4) insuring the security or safety of other employees, customers, or property of the employer); Hawaii, SLL 21:204 (limiting types of criminal records that may be considered); Illinois, SLL 23:203 ("It is a civil rights violation for any employer . . . to inquire on a written application whether a job applicant has ever been arrested."); Maryland, SLL 30:203 ("An employer or educational institution may not, in any application, interview, or otherwise, require an applicant for employment or admission to disclose information concerning criminal charges against him, that have been expunged."); Massachusetts, SLL 31:205 ("An applicant for employment with a sealed record on file may answer 'no record' with respect to an inquiry herein relative to prior arrests."); Michigan, SLL 32:208 ("An employer . . . shall not in connection with an application for employment . . . make, or maintain a record of information regarding an arrest, detention, or disposition of a violation of law in which a conviction did not result."); Minnesota, SLL 33:204 (public employer limitation); New York, SLL 42:208 ("unlawful discriminatory practice . . . to make any inquiry about, . . . any arrest or criminal accusation of such individual not then pending"); Ohio, SLL 45:202; Oregon, SLL 47:204 (providing for notice to applicant when arrest and conviction information requested from state); Pennsylvania, SLL 48:204 ("Convictions for felonies, as well as misdemeanor convictions and arrests for offenses, which relate to an applicant's suitability for employment in the position for which he has applied, may be considered by the employer. . . . The employer shall notify in writing the applicant if the decision not to hire is based in whole or part on criminal history record information."); Rhode Island, SLL 50:203 ("unlawful employment practice" to "inquire whether the applicant has ever been arrested or charged with a crime; provided however that nothing herein shall prevent an employer from inquiring whether the applicant has ever been convicted of any crime"); Texas, SLL 54:205 (allowing institution of higher education to obtain from any law enforcement agency "criminal history information" to evaluate applicants for security-sensitive positions); Virginia, SLL 57:203 (limiting use of expunged records).

[51]Ohio, SLL (BNA) 45:202 ("In any application for employment, . . . a person may not be questioned with respect to any arrest for which the records were expunged. If an inquiry is made in violation of this division, the person may respond as if the expunged arrest did not occur, and the person shall not be subject to any adverse action because of the arrest or the response.").

Height and Weight Requirements

Height and weight requirements that have a disproportionate effect upon women are impermissible under Title VII unless shown to be job-related.[52] The more difficult case occurs where the pool of job applicants is limited to women and, at the same time, the employer maintains a height or weight restriction that eliminates some women for consideration. In light of the Supreme Court's rejection of a "bottom line" defense to discrimination in *Connecticut v. Teal*,[53] employers are advised to undertake a self-examination of their height and weight requirements and discard those that have an illegal discriminatory effect. Even though there may be no discrimination in the process of selecting women for positions when the "bottom line" or end result is examined, one view of *Teal* suggests that the proper stage at which to evaluate a Title VII claim is at the point at which the employer's neutral criteria impact a protected class.[54] If the criteria have an impermissible disparate impact that cannot be justified under a business necessity test, they violate Title VII.

Education Requirements

Most Americans, regardless of sex, race, or national origin, obtain a high school diploma.[55] A growing minority now obtain college degrees. Many employers specify high school or college degrees as minimum qualifications for jobs. In *Griggs v. Duke Power Co.*,[56] a high school diploma requirement was found to have a disparate impact because 34 percent of the white males in the state had completed high school, while only 12 percent of black males had graduated. College-degree requirements have also operated to exclude women in a number disproportionate to men.[57] Under Title VII, educational

---

[52]Dothard v. Rawlinson, 433 U.S. 321, 15 FEP 10 (1977).
[53]457 U.S. 440, 29 FEP 1 (1982).
[54]Costa v. Markey (*Costa II*), 694 F.2d 876 (withdrawn from bound volume after reh'g en banc granted), 30 FEP 593 (CA 1, 1982), rev'd (reaff'g *Costa I*, 677 F.2d 158, 28 FEP 1347 (1982)) in reh'g en banc (*Costa III*), 706 F.2d 1, 11, 31 FEP 1324 (CA 1, 1983), cert. denied, 461 U.S. 920, 33 FEP 656 (1983). See also "The 'Bottom Line' Approach," infra.
[55]Vulcan Soc'y v. Fire Dep't, 505 F.Supp. 955, 28 FEP 893, 902 (S.D.N.Y., 1981).
[56]401 U.S. 424, 3 FEP 175 (1971).
[57]Hawkins v. Anheuser-Busch, Inc., 697 F.2d 810, 30 FEP 1170, 1175 (CA 8, 1983).

requirements that have a disparate impact which are not found to be job related will be struck down by a court if challenged by women or a protected minority. In this respect, the EEOC and the courts have found disparate impact by using: (1) actual applicant flows (i.e., the effect that the educational requirement has on the actual number of black applicants vis-a-vis white applicants); (2) potential applicant flows (i.e., a comparison between potential white and black applicants in the same area);[58] and (3) a mixture of the above, for example, where a court compares the percentage of whites in the employer's work force who meet the educational requirement and the percentage of blacks in the general areawide population who meet the same requirement.

One federal court has declared that educational requirements for employment are less suspect than requirements such as height or weight. Further, the reported cases indicate that the burden of proving job-relatedness may be lighter when the job involved requires a high degree of skill and substantial risk to the public.[59]

No-Spouse Rules

The courts have held anti-nepotism policies precluding the employment of relatives to be a reasonable method of eliminating possible employee conflicts. The federal courts have generally upheld no-spouse rules against charges that they violate Title VII because they have a disparate impact on account of sex.[60] Employees may fare better at the state

---

[58]See, e.g., Carpenter v. Stephen F. Austin State Univ., 706 F.2d 608, 31 FEP 1758 (CA 5, 1983)(47% of whites versus 24.8% of blacks with high school degree over age of 25 in population of locality surrounding the university).

[59]Vulcan Soc'y v. Fire Dep't, 505 F.Supp. 955, 28 FEP 893, 902 n.3 (S.D.N.Y., 1981), citing Spurlock v. United Airlines, 475 F.2d 216, 5 FEP 17 (CA 10, 1972) (upholding college degree requirements for airline pilots). See also Bartholet, "Application of Title VII to Jobs in High Places," 95 Harv. L. Rev. 945 (1982); Note, "Relative Qualifications and the Prima Facie Case in Title VII Litigation," 82 Colum. L. Rev. 553 (1982).

[60]George v. Farmers Elec. Coop., Inc., 32 FEP 1801 (CA 5, 1983); Klanseck v. Prudential Ins. Co., 509 F.Supp. 13, 23 FEP 163 (E.D. Mich., 1980); Vuyanich v. Republic Nat'l Bank, 505 F.Supp. 224, 24 FEP 128 (N.D. Texas, 1980); Harper v., Trans World Airlines, 525 F.2d 409, 11 FEP 1074 (CA 8, 1975); Yuhas v. Libbey-Owens-Ford Co., 562 F.2d 496, 16 FEP 891, 893–94 (CA 7, 1977)(rule against hiring hourly employee at plants where applicant's spouse already employed discriminatory but job related); Meier v. Evansville School Corp., 416 F.Supp. 748, 16 FEP 1713 (S.D. Ind., 1975)(upholding transfer of female teacher to another school under policy of prohibiting spouses from teaching in same school). Contra: EEOC Decision No. 75–239, 21 FEP 1777 (1975).

level, where legislation prohibiting discrimination on account
of "marital status" may be held to encompass an employer's
policy against hiring spouses of current employees. No state,
however, has extended protection to employee "live-in" relationships under a statute prohibiting discrimination on the
basis of the existence or non-existence of a spouse.[61]

Garnishment and Credit History

In the often-quoted *Johnson v. Pike Corp.*,[62] a California
federal court, relying on articles and census data showing that
blacks and other racial minorities have their wages garnished
more frequently than nonminorities, held that a company policy of discharging employees after several garnishments violated Title VII. Since *Pike*, both the courts[63] and the EEOC
have taken this position,[64] although some courts will require
that the plaintiff use the debt-paying characteristics of the
employer's work force rather than the population at large in
establishing disparate impact.[65]

A similar rule under which employees could be discharged
for not paying their "just debts" was challenged in *Robinson
v. City of Dallas*.[66] Where only a few employees had been
disciplined under the "just debts" rule, the Fifth Circuit held
that the plaintiff had failed to prove that the rule had a discriminatory racial effect.[67]

Also of note is the Consumer Credit Protection Act,[68] which
provides that no employer may discharge any employee by
reason of the fact that the employee's earnings have been
subjected to garnishment for any one indebtedness. In *Las*

[61]Sears v. Ryder Truck Rental, Inc., 596 F.Supp. 1001, 117 LRRM 3237 (E.D.
Mich., 1984)(prohibition against marital status discrimination not extended to employer rule prohibiting co-employee dating). Cf. Espinoza v. Thoma, 580 F.2d 346,
17 FEP 1362 (CA 8, 1978)(city's inclusion under no-spouse policy of female job applicant living with company bus driver not violative of Equal Protection Clause).
[62]332 F.Supp. 490, 3 FEP 1025 (C.D. Cal., 1971).
[63]Keenan v. American Cast Iron Pipe Co., 707 F.2d 1274, 32 FEP 142 (CA 11,
1983).
[64]EEOC Decision No. 74–27, 6 FEP 1248 (1973).
[65]EEOC v. Georgia Hwy. Express, Inc., 26 FEP 198 (N.D. Ga., 1981).
[66]514 F.2d 1271, 10 FEP 1235 (CA 5, 1975).
[67]See also Paxton v. Union Nat'l Bank, 519 F.Supp. 136, 25 FEP 1651 (E.D. Ark.,
1981)(bad credit history); United States v. Commonwealth of Va., 454 F.Supp. 1077,
20 FEP 209, 228 n.14 (E.D. Va., 1978)(upholding background investigation of prospective state troopers).
[68]15 U.S.C. §1674 (1968).

Vegas Building Materials, Inc.,[69] Arbitrator Lionel Richman sustained a discharge of an employee who had his wages garnished by the Internal Revenue Service. The employee, who was unmarried, as part of an organized tax protest submitted a tax form showing 14 dependents. In rejecting the relevance of the Consumer Credit Protection Act, the arbitrator, citing case law, reasoned that enforcement of the statute rests with the Secretary of Labor and it was not clear whether there is a private cause of action. "If a court lacks jurisdiction to grant the relief at the behest of a private individual," he stated, "what authority does an arbitrator have?"[70]

Finally, at the state level, employer discretion to use garnishments or credit history as an employment criterion may be limited in some respects but, more often than not, the statutes specifically permit employers to use credit information for employment purposes.[71]

Quota Hiring and Title VII

When considering quota hiring and Title VII it is important to distinguish between compensatory and affirmative relief. Compensatory relief is designed to "make whole" victims of discrimination. Examples include back pay, payment of the

[69]83 LA 998 (Richman, 1984).
[70]Id. at 1001. See also BBC Mfgd. Buildings, Inc., 77 LA 1132 (Bell, 1981)(holding that Consumer Credit Protection Act does not prohibit discharge for multiple garnishments, even when there is a significant interval between first and second garnishment); Shawnee Plastics, Inc., 71 LA 832 (Goldstein, 1978)(sustaining discharge for two instances of garnishments, holding that Act not applicable where state exempted); Delta Concrete Prod. Co., 71 LA 538 (Bailey, 1978)(ordering reinstatement where garnishments resulted from debts that grievant co-signed).
[71]All states have laws concerning garnishments. Seven states have addressed the use of credit references: Arizona, SLL (BNA) 12:204 ("[A] consumer reporting agency may furnish a consumer report . . . to a person which it has reason to believe: intends to use the information for employment purposes. . . . An employer who denies a consumer employment, a promotion, retention as an employee . . . shall, upon written request, disclose to such consumer the name and address of any consumer reporting agency which has furnished such employer with a consumer report on such consumer which was considered by the employer in making the determination."); California, SLL 14:209, 14:210 ("An investigative consumer reporting agency shall only furnish an investigative consumer report . . . to a person which it has reason to believe: (1) intends to use the information for employment purposes. . . ."); Maine, SLL 29:205 ("A consumer reporting agency may furnish a consumer report . . . to a person who it has reason to believe: . . . intends to use the information for employment purposes."); Massachusetts, SLL 31:204 (allowing use for employment purposes); New Hampshire, SLL 39:202 (precluding use of selected information); New Mexico, SLL 41:202 ("inquiries shall be made only for the purposes of granting credit or other bona fide business transactions, such as evaluation of present or prospective credit risks or evaluation of the qualifications of present or prospective employees"); New York, SLL 42:203 (permitting use for employment purposes).

value of fringe benefits, and retroactive seniority credits. Affirmative relief is designed to remedy the effects of discrimination that may not be cured by compensatory relief. It may include the setting of long-term hiring targets or, alternatively, the imposition of a requirement that the employer actually hire a specified number of women or minorities. As stated by one federal court, such relief may be (and generally is) required where the employer is found to have egregiously engaged in a practice of discrimination that is likely to have discouraged members of the protected group from becoming members of the applicant pool. Affirmative relief is normally justified only if the defendant's discrimination has been intentional, or there has been a continuous pattern of egregious discrimination.[72] Accordingly, quota-type relief, including orders to hire or promote a specific number of blacks or women, is expected where a court determines that the employer engaged in intentional discrimination.[73] Further, a court-ordered quota, as part of a remedy for intentional employment discrimination, will take preference over a conflicting collective bargaining agreement.[74]

Unless under court order or, under a consent decree, employers may not adopt a strict "quota" hiring system that is based on race or sex. Employers may, of course, adopt affirmative action plans whereby hiring "goals" are implemented. But where a court does not mandate any particular percentage of minority-group employees in particular positions, no employer is required by Title VII to adopt an affirmative action program in which minorities or women are granted preference in hiring.[75]

---

[72]Berkman v. City of New York, 705 F.2d 584, 31 FEP 767, 775 (CA 2, 1983)(ordering city to restore 45 positions for women).

[73]Bentley v. City of Thomaston, 32 FEP 1476 (M.D. Ga., 1983)(order to fill one-half of all new vacancies with blacks until proportion of total black employees to total white employees, viewed by job classification, department, and rate of pay, is equal to proportion of blacks to whites in working age population in available labor pool).

[74]Arthur v. Nyquist, 712 F.2d 816, 32 FEP 822, (CA 2, 1983)(upholding one-for-one hiring and promotional goal as remedy for intentional employment discrimination).

[75]See, e.g., §703(j), 42 U.S.C. 2000e-2 (1982), which in relevant part, provides: "Nothing contained in this subchapter shall be interpreted to require any employer, employment agency, labor organization, or joint labor-management committee subject to this subchapter to grant preferential treatment to any individual or to any group because of the race, color, religion, sex, or national origin of such individual or group on account of an imbalance which may exist with respect to the total number or percentage of persons of any race, color, religion, sex, or national origin employed by any employer, ... in comparison with the total number or percentage of persons

To what extent may an employer grant a racial preference? The leading case in the area of preferences is *Steelworkers v. Weber*,[76] the first Supreme Court decision on the
issue with a majority opinion.[77] In *Weber* the parties, in an
effort to increase the number of minority workers in craft
positions, entered into a collective bargaining agreement that
removed the requirement of prior craft experience for on-the-
job training and established an entrance ratio of one minority
worker to one white worker until the percentage of minority
workers roughly equaled the percentage of minority population in the locality surrounding each plant. To implement
their affirmative action goal it was necessary to establish dual
seniority lists: for each two training vacancies, one black and
one white employee would be selected on the basis of seniority
within their racial groups. Brian Weber, a white employee
who was passed over for a vacancy in favor of a black with
less seniority, alleged that by preferring black employees with
less seniority for admission to on-the-job training programs,
Kaiser and the Steelworkers were guilty of unlawful discrimination in violation of Title VII. The district court agreed and
enjoined the use of the training eligibility quota.[78] The Fifth
Circuit held that the training quota adopted by Kaiser was
"flatly and literally prohibited by Title VII, §703(d),[79] which
makes it unlawful to limit access to on-the-job training programs on the basis of race. The court of appeals stated that
"quotas imposed to achieve the 'make whole' objective of Title
VII rest on a presumption of some prior discrimination. There
can be no basis for preferring minority workers if there has
been no discriminatory act that displaced them from their

---

of such race, color, religion, sex, or national origin in any community, State, section,
or other area, or in the available work force in any community, State, section, or
other area."

[76]443 U.S. 193, 20 FEP 1 (1979).

[77]Compare Weber with the plurality decision in Regents v. Bakke, 438 U.S. 265,
17 FEP 1000 (1978), where the Court split into a four-one-four grouping with Justice
Powell providing the swing vote for both sides. The District Court for the District of
Columbia in 1985 read Bakke as holding that "an affirmative action plan containing
classifications based on race must be regarded as suspect. A government can employ
race-based classifications only when they serve a compelling governmental interest. . . . One such compelling interest is the 'interest in ameliorating, or eliminating
where feasible, the disabling effects of identified discrimination.' " Hammon v. Barry,
606 F.Supp. 1082, 37 FEP 609, 619 (D.D.C., 1985), quoting Bakke, supra, 438 U.S.
at 307.

[78]Weber v. Kaiser Alum. & Chem. Corp., 415 F.Supp. 761, 12 FEP 1615 (E.D.
La., 1976).

[79]Weber v. Kaiser Alum. & Chem. Corp., 563 F.2d 216, 16 FEP 1, 2 (CA 5, 1977).

'rightful place' in the employment scheme."[80] The appellate court focused on the absence of prior discrimination by Kaiser and stated that in the absence of prior discrimination a racial quota must be banned as an unlawful racial preference.

The Supreme Court, with Justice Brennan writing for the majority, held that Title VII does not forbid private employers and unions from voluntarily agreeing upon a *bona fide* affirmative action plan that accords racial preferences in the manner designated by the Kaiser-Steelworkers plan. Joined by Justices Stewart, White, Marshall, and Blackmun, Justice Brennan noted several significant aspects of the plan: (1) the purpose of the plan, to break down old patterns of racial segregation, mirrored the statute;[81] (2) at the same time, "[T]he plan does not unnecessarily trammel the interests of the white employees. The plan does not require the discharge of white workers and their replacement with new black hires";[82] (3) the plan did not create an absolute bar to the advancement of white employees, as half of those trained in the program would be white; (4) the plan was a temporary measure; it was not intended to maintain racial balance, but simply to eliminate a manifest racial imbalance; and (5) the preference scheme would end as soon as the percentage of black craft workers in a plant approximated the percentage of blacks in the local labor force.[83]

The *Weber* Court observed that it was not "defin[ing] in detail the line of demarcation between permissible and impermissible affirmative action plans."[84] One appellate court has stated that in *Weber* "the Court has thus made clear that recitation of a benign purpose for disparate treatment based on race will not necessarily immunize a private employer from liability to the disadvantaged class of employees."[85] An affirmative action plan may still be unlawful even though it does not require an employee's discharge, permanently bar possible employment advancement, or intentionally constitute a racial balance.[86]

---

[80]Id. at 4.
[81]20 FEP at 7.
[82]Id.
[83]Id.
[84]Id.
[85]Parker v. Baltimore & Ohio R.R., 652 F.2d 1012, 25 FEP 889, 891 (CA DC, 1981).
[86]Id.

The post-*Weber* courts have consistently ruled that the substantive and procedural safeguards discussed in *Weber* must be part of the affirmative action process. At a minimum, practitioners who desire to implement an aggressive affirmative action program are advised to first determine a specific need level. Furthermore, the plan must be "temporary and remedial rather than permanent and designed to maintain a particular balance."[87] In this respect the words of the Seventh Circuit in *Lehman v. Yellow Freight System, Inc.*[88] are especially appropriate:

> Thus, *Weber* sets forth certain procedural and substantive commands for affirmative action programs. First, there must be some need—remedying some past discrimination—for a plan. Of course, this past discrimination need not be proof of *de jure* discrimination. At the least, however, some type of statistical disparity between the local labor force and the minority composition of the employer's work force is the first step in assessing whether that employer decides properly to institute an affirmative action plan.

The court of appeals in *Lehman* ruled that an employer was guilty of reverse discrimination in hiring a black applicant because of race instead of a white, where the company had no clear idea about the percentage of blacks in the labor force. The court reasoned that the employer had acted "without any idea of a goal for which minority hiring should reach nor with any idea of when such a level was reached." The Seventh Circuit remarked:

> We believe that such a system is fraught with dangers. If the individual making the hiring decisions is unaware of the goal (such as the local labor force) he may unfairly discriminate against non-minority employees beyond a reasonable goal.[89]

More recently, the Seventh Circuit, applying *Weber*, held that a disparity between the percentage of minorities employed and the percentage of minorities within the community is not enough to justify an employer's implementation of an affirmative action plan. There must be, the court said, some finding of past discrimination, and this determination cannot

---

[87]Johnson v. Transp. Agency, 748 F.2d 1308, 36 FEP 725 (CA 9, 1984).
[88]651 F.2d 520, 26 FEP 75, 80–81 (CA 7, 1981)(footnotes omitted).
[89]26 FEP at 81 (footnotes omitted).

be based solely upon a showing of statistical disparity.[90] Not all circuits, however, have read *Weber* this restrictively.[91]

The state of the law after *Weber* is still unsettled. Although it is impossible to provide an outline of the legally permissible methods that the parties can adopt to prefer one race over another, this much is clear: the employer defending a reverse discrimination suit will have to produce some evidence that its affirmative action program is a remedial response to a conspicuous racial imbalance. Further, in some jurisdictions a showing that this imbalance was caused by discrimination will be required. An additional burden in a reverse discrimination suit is the company's need to produce some evidence that its affirmative action plan is reasonably related to the plan's remedial purpose. As stated in the EEOC's Affirmative Action Guidelines,[92] the plan should be tailored to solve the problems that were identified in the self-analysis and to ensure that employment systems operate fairly in the future, while avoiding unnecessary restrictions on opportunities for the work force as a whole.[93] The race-, sex-, or national origin-conscious provisions of the plan or program should be maintained only so long as necessary to achieve these objectives.

Public-Sector Affirmative Action

Title VII does not prohibit affirmative action by governmental employers. Indeed, although the holding in *Weber* was limited to employers in the private sector, the *Weber* Title VII analysis has been applied to public-sector employers.[94] In *Detroit Police Officers' Association v. Young*,[95] the Sixth Circuit extended the *Weber* holding to public-sector employers. In *Young*, the Detroit police department, after an internal determination that blacks were underrepresented in the de-

---

[90]Janowiak v. City of South Bend, 750 F.2d 557, 36 FEP 737 (CA 7, 1984).

[91]Johnson v. Transportation Agency, 748 F.2d 1308, 36 FEP 725 (CA 9, 1984); Setser v. Novak Inv. Co., 657 F.2d 962, 26 FEP 513, 516 (CA 8, 1981)("A showing of a conspicuous racial imbalance by statistics is sufficient, even if the statistics employed would not be sufficient to show a prima facie violation of [T]itle VII.").

[92]29 C.F.R. §1608, et seq.

[93]29 C.F.R. §1608.4(c)(2).

[94]See Hammon v. Barry, 606 F.Supp. 1082, 37 FEP 609, 615 (D.D.C., 1985); Williams v. City of New Orleans, 729 F.2d 1554, 34 FEP 1009, 1023 n.4 (CA 5, 1984)(Wisdom, concurring opinion).

[95]608 F.2d 671, 20 FEP 1728 (CA 6, 1979), cert. denied, 452 U.S. 938, 25 FEP 1683 (1981).

partment, voluntarily adopted an affirmative action program that promoted blacks to sergeant ahead of white patrolmen ranked higher on the eligibility list. The white officers challenged the promotion plan as being violative of Title VII and the Equal Protection Clause of the Constitution. Even though there had been no prior finding of discrimination, the Sixth Circuit, relying on *Weber*, reasoned that the internal determination of racial disparities justified the voluntary plan. Further, the court of appeals specifically rejected the lower court's holding that there must be a judicial determination of racial discrimination before a state can undertake a race-conscious remedy.[96]

An example of a permissible affirmative action hiring plan "designed to break down an old pattern of racial segregation and hierarchy" is provided by *Hammon v. Barry*,[97] a 1985 decision by the District Court for the District of Columbia. To reduce the disparate impact of a 1984 entrance examination, the Washington, D.C. Fire Department set the pass point at a level that met the 80 percent rule of thumb for determining adverse impact.[98] The record indicated that a total of 1,626 persons took the 1984 test, of whom 1,050 (64.6 percent) were black, 492 (30.3 percent) were white, and 84 (5.1 percent) were Hispanic or others. Of the 1,626 individuals who took the examination, 1,384 passed, of whom 830 (60 percent) were black, 486 (35.1 percent) were white, 33 (2.4 percent) were Hispanic, and 35 (2.5 percent) were others. Of those who passed, 1,287 (93 percent) were males and 96 (6.9 percent) were females. The test had not been validated, and there was no evidence that applicants who scored higher on the test were likely to perform better on the job than applicants who scored lower.

---

[96]See also Wygant v. Jackson Bd. of Educ., 746 F.2d 1152, 36 FEP 153 (CA 6, 1984)(upholding affirmative action plan adopted by employer and union under which minority group teachers were retained during layoffs); Deveraux v. Geary, 596 F.Supp. 1481, 36 FEP 415 (D. Mass., 1984)(declining to hold that affirmative action program was precluded by Firefighters Local 1784 v. Stotts, 467 U.S. 561, 34 FEP 1702 (1984)).
[97]606 F.Supp. 1082, 37 FEP 609, 615 (D.D.C., 1985).
[98]See EEOC Uniform Guidelines on Employee Selection Procedures, 29 C.F.R. §1607.4(D). The Guidelines provide that an adverse impact exists when the selection rate for a particular group is less than ⅘ (the "four-fifths rule") or 80% of the selection rate for other groups. For example, if 70% of the male applicants are selected and 60% of the female applicants are selected, no adverse effect exists because 60%, the female selection rate, is 86% of 70%, the male selection rate. However, if 60% of the male applicants and 40% of the female applicants are selected, an adverse impact does exist under the four-fifths rule because 40% is only 67% of 60%.

If the applicants had been rank-ordered, the following selection would have resulted for the first 100 passing candidates: 79 white males, 12 black males, 3 white females, 4 Hispanic males, 1 Hispanic female, and 1 unspecified male.[99] Because rank order resulted in an adverse impact, a procedure for proportional appointment of passing applicants was adopted. Under the plan, candidates were placed on 12 certificates (lists), each consisting of approximately 120 candidates. The certificates derived from separate lists of white males, white females, black males, black females, and so on. The plan at issue directed that each certificate approximate the pass rate for blacks, whites, Hispanics, and others. Finally, candidates were selected from the certificates in a manner which assured that the composition of each academy class would be 60 percent black and 5 percent female.

In upholding the hiring plan, the court pointed out that according to applicant flow data, approximately 65 percent of the test-takers were black. In light of these figures, the court found that the plan's hiring goal of 60 percent blacks was reasonable, particularly for the short period that the plan was in effect (approximately 18 months). What is particularly interesting, and especially relevant for public-sector advocates, is that the court applied all of the *Weber* criteria[100] in concluding that the hiring portion of the plan was permissible under Title VII. The promotion aspect of the plan, which in part required "advancement of black firefighters over white firefighters solely on race rather than on merit,"[101] was struck down. The court pointed out that, "[u]nlike the entry-level examinations and the entire hiring process in the District's Fire Department, there has never been an administrative, legislative, or judicial finding of discrimination in the promotion process." Citing *Weber* and other decisions,[102] the court stated the law in this area as follows:

The teaching of these cases taken together is that before an

---

[99]37 FEP at 614. Similar disparate effects would result for selection of successive applicants in groupings of 100.
[100]See supra notes 76–86 and accompanying text.
[101]37 FEP at 621.
[102]Regents v. Bakke, 438 U.S. 265, 17 FEP 1000 (1978); Janowiak v. City of South Bend, 750 F.2d 557, 36 FEP 737 (CA 7, 1984); Bushey v. New York State Civil Serv. Comm'n, 733 F.2d 220, 34 FEP 1065 (CA 2, 1984), cert. denied, 469 U.S. ____, 36 FEP 1166 (1985); Vanguards v. City of Cleveland, 753 F.2d 479, 36 FEP 1431 (CA 6, 1985); Van Aken v. Young, 750 F.2d 43, 36 FEP 777 (CA 6, 1984); EEOC v. Sheet Metal Workers Local 638, 753 F.2d 1172, 36 FEP 1466 (CA 2, 1985).

employer, public or private, can utilize race-conscious quotas, there must be a prior determination of discrimination in the area the remedy is designed to effect. This determination can be made based on either statistical evidence or an official finding.[103]

The "Bottom Line" Approach

An employer may attempt to compensate for a discriminatory hiring process (or discriminatory selection process, which can include procedures for promotion, assignment, etc.) by hiring a sufficient number of minorities so that its overall hiring meets the 80 percent rule of thumb. Even though an employer's "bottom line" reflects a racial balance consistent with the relevant labor force, a discriminatory selection practice is not saved under Title VII. In *Connecticut v. Teal*,[104] plaintiff Teal failed a nonvalidated promotion examination that had a disparate impact on minorities. The employer argued that the adoption of a remedial selection procedure which ensured that significant numbers of minorities would be promoted precluded a finding that Title VII was violated. In rejecting the "bottom line" approach in favor of an "individual approach," the Supreme Court reasoned as follows:

> The suggestion that disparate impact should be measured only at the bottom line ignores the fact that Title VII guarantees these individual respondents the *opportunity* to compete equally with white workers on the basis of job-related criteria. Title VII strives to achieve equality of opportunity by rooting out "artificial, arbitrary and unnecessary" employer-created barriers to professional development that have a discriminatory impact upon individuals. Therefore, respondents' rights under [the act] have been violated, unless petitioners can demonstrate that the examination given was not an artificial, arbitrary, or unnecessary barrier, because it measured skills related to effective performance . . . .
> In sum, respondents' claim of disparate impact from the examination, a pass-fail barrier to employment opportunity, states a prima facie case of employment discrimination under [the statute], despite their employer's nondiscriminatory "bottom line," and that "bottom line" is no defense to this prima facie case under [the act].[105]

---

[103]37 FEP at 621.
[104]457 U.S. 440, 29 FEP 1 (1982).
[105]29 FEP at 6–7 (emphasis in original).

Chapter 11

Ability Assessments

Management's Right to Evaluate

In an address before the National Academy of Arbitrators, James Healy asserted that in the early days of collective bargaining management could use the word "ability" without fear that it would be watered down by grievance arbitrators. Management was the "master" of the term and the word meant just what management chose it to mean. Healy went on to argue that "more and more the parties jointly determine the meaning of 'ability,' and if the parties' relationship is one of cooperation, disputes will be infrequent." Professor Healy also pointed out that a major difficulty encountered by management in its attempt to preserve the ability criterion is the inherent vagueness of any contractual expression describing the term. Healy remarked:

> The isolated terms of "ability", "qualifications", "qualified to do the work", "satisfactory experience" and the many others now used in layoff and promotion clauses mean many things to many people. The relatively precise meaning of seniority, by comparison, gives it an immediate advantage.[1]

In a similar fashion, Arbitrator Gabriel Alexander has argued that the terms "ability" or "ability, merit, and capacity" are much less specific in their meaning than the word "seniority." According to Arbitrator Alexander,

> "Ability", in the terms of the semanticists is a term of high

---

[1]Healy, "The Factor of Ability in Labor Relations," Proceedings of the 8th Annual Meeting of NAA, 45, 48 (BNA Books, 1955).

abstraction. Its meaning in customary usage is loose, vague, and resists exact definition. Among the more specific concepts included in it are these: Physical strength, physical coordination, intellectual capacity, formal education, work experience and personality and character traits. I know of no formula by which these or other components included in the broad concept "ability" may be synthesized into a positive and reliable concept applicable as a uniform standard of reference for use in a given set of circumstances. Efforts have been made to objectify the concept of "ability" in terms of a formalized system of measurement. But I know of none that has been incorporated into collective bargaining agreements.[2]

Even without a uniform definition of "ability," the right of management to use a written, oral, performance, or aptitude test in evaluating an employee's ability has long been recognized by arbitrators.

Testing

Most arbitrators have held that, unless otherwise stated in the labor agreement, "ability" means the ability present in the employee at the time that he or she is being considered for a job vacancy. Nevertheless, reported cases sometimes refer to "ability" as the expected job performance of an employee. For example, an employee may not be able to operate a forklift truck or a word-processor, but could master the requirements of either machine after a reasonable break-in and training period. This latter notion of ability refers to the potential of the employee to perform, as opposed to the present capacity to do a job. Arbitrators sometimes use the term "ability" in both senses; for this reason, it is important to keep this difference in mind, especially when testing concepts are at issue.

Perhaps the most difficult problem encountered by management in this area is developing a device or a set of criteria that will provide a valid measure of an employee's ability to perform a job.[3] *Capital Manufacturing Co.*[4] typifies the think-

---

[2]Alexander, Discussion, "The Factor of Ability in Labor Relations," supra note 1, at 59.

[3]For two notable articles by Arbitrator Wayne Howard on management's determination of ability, see "Criteria of Ability," 13 Arb. J. No. 4, 179 (1958), and "The Role of the Arbitrator in Determination of Ability," 12 Arb. J. 14 (1957). Elkouri & Elkouri discuss factors considered by management in determining fitness and ability in their text, How Arbitration Works, 4th Ed. (BNA Books, 1985), at 617–49. See also discussion under "Is There a Presumption Favoring Management?" in Chapter 12, infra.

[4]45 LA 1003 (Gibson, 1965).

ing of arbitrators on the subject of testing as a measure of ability. Rejecting the union's argument that the employer could not unilaterally utilize written job tests because the subject of tests had never been raised in bargaining, Arbitrator Rankin Gibson declared:

> The determination of employee ability is by no means susceptible to any set formula applicable to any and all circumstances. Reported arbitration awards generally show that in the absence of contract prescription of the method to be used or the factors to be considered in determining employee qualifications, management may utilize a variety of methods including, in proper circumstances, use of written or oral performance or aptitude tests, trial periods on the job, reliance on a merit rating plan or upon the opinion of supervision, consideration of production records, attendance or disciplinary records, formal education, experience, physical fitness and the like. . . .
>
> Where the contract is silent with respect to the use of tests, many arbitrators have held that management is entitled to give reasonable and appropriate written tests as an aid in determining the ability of competing employees.[5]

Arbitrator Robert Wagner, in *Equitable Gas Co.*,[6] reviewed in depth a number of early arbitration awards on the subject of management's right to use written tests and concluded as follows:

> It appears clear that the evidence is overwhelming that arbitration authorities have found that, absent anything to the contrary in the Agreement between the parties, an employer has the right to make tests a part of the minimum requirements or qualifications of job applicants.[7]

Jacobs and Biddle report similar findings. In a study of 100 arbitration awards relating to management's right to use tests to measure an employee's ability to perform a job, they conclude:

> If the contract language states that seniority is the sole governing factor of promotion then management has clearly bargained away its prerogative to evaluate qualifications via written or non-written tests. If, however, management has bar-

---

[5]Id. at 1005, citing Bethlehem Steel Co., 29 LA 710 (Seward, 1957); Wallingford Steel Co., 29 LA 597 (Cahn, 1957); Kuhlman Elec. Co., 26 LA 885 (Howlett, 1956); M.A. Hanna Co., 25 LA 480 (Marshall, 1955); Standard Oil Co., 11 LA 810 (Updegraff, 1948); Kaiser Aluminum & Chem. Corp., 33 LA 951 (McCoy, 1959); Avco Mfg. Corp., 34 LA 71 (Gill, 1959); Mead Containers, Inc., 35 LA 349 (Dworkin, 1960); Advanced Structures, 37 LA 49 (Roberts, 1961).
[6]46 LA 81 (1965).
[7]Id. at 90.

gained to examine qualifications, then management has the right to test unless there is: (1) a letter of agreement that written tests will not be used to evaluate qualifications, (2) a mutual understanding that qualifications will not be evaluated by written tests, or (3) expressly forbidding contract language. If the contract language is silent on the subject of testing and qualifications are mentioned, then management has the right to test.[8]

Arbitrator J. Fred Holly reasoned similarly in *Atlantic Richfield Co.* Rejecting an argument that a company was prohibited by the recognition clause from making a unilateral determination to administer tests, Arbitrator Holly stated the following principle:

> The Recognition Clause does establish the Union as the exclusive representative of the employees on matters within the scope of collective bargaining. This does not mean, however, that Management has therein been deprived of any of its rights. The other portions of the Agreement deal with such substantive matters, and there is no mention made of testing.
> Section 7 of Article IX of the Agreement provides that in cases of promotion "Plant seniority and sufficient fitness and ability to perform the job will be the determining factors." These determinations must be made by Management since there is no restriction set forth in the clause.[9]

Nevertheless, when presented with the question whether management may unilaterally require an employee to submit to a written test, a few arbitrators have ruled that management must first bargain the matter with the union, at least where the test did not predate the parties' labor agreement, since it affects a term and condition of employment.[10] This position appears consistent with the thinking of the National Labor Relations Board.[11]

Arbitrator Marvin Feldman, in *Rockwell International*

---

[8]Jacobs and Biddle, "Testing Candidates for Promotion," 2 Collective Bargaining & Negotiating Contracts (BNA) 17:301 (1967), quoted in I-T-E Imperial Corp., 68 LA 1, 6 (Johnson, 1976). Besides the cases discussed in this Chapter, see Rollins Environmental Servs., Inc., 75 LA 655 (Mann, 1980); Milwaukee Metro. Sewerage Dist., 76 LA 657 (Pieroni, 1981); Menasha Corp., 64 LA 307 (Kabaker, 1975); Robertshaw Controls, Inc., 67 LA 678, 682 (Wagner, 1976); United States Steel Corp. (Eastern Steel Div.), 67 LA 1172 (Garrett, 1976); Union Camp Corp., 68 LA 708, 712 (Morgan, 1977).

[9]69-2 ARB ¶8476 (1968), at 4617.

[10]Hussmann Refrigerator Co., 62 LA 554 (Yarowsky, 1974). See also County of Los Angeles, 68 LA 85 (Tamoush, 1976). Contra: Armstrong Cork Co., 42 LA 349, 351–52 (Handsaker, 1964).

[11]See, e.g., American Gilsonite Co., 122 NLRB No. 127, 43 LRRM 1242 (1959) (unilateral institution of aptitude tests violative of Taft-Hartley).

Corp.,[12] reflected the thinking of most arbitrators of management's use of written tests. Under an agreement that contained no prohibition against testing, Arbitrator Feldman ruled that management had the right to test under a provision that reserved to management all matters not covered by the agreement. Feldman said that the use of a test is nothing more than a perpetuation of the right of management to operate its business efficiently. The arbitrator commented:

> The Union is seeking from this Arbitrator by this protest an indication that tests are prohibited under the language of the Agreement. No such language of prohibition exists. Nor, does the fact that seniority provisions exist in the contract or posting and bidding provisions exist in the contract deny to the company the right to administer testing as it has in this particular case. That testing of the bargaining unit, if it be reasonable, evenhandedly administered and if the test bears a meaningful and substantial relationship to the classification sought, then in that event the Company may continue their use.[13]

Test Standards

While arbitrators have recognized management's right to rely upon written tests in assessing the qualifications of employees, this right has generally been subject to a reasonableness requirement. Arbitrators have uniformly held that a test must be both reasonably adapted to the measurement of the requirements of a given job and used fairly and reasonably for this purpose. Accordingly, for jobs where the work is routine, or where an employee learns the work as a helper, an employer may not be able to administer a test that "measures the person in the abstract."[14] Indeed, some arbitrators have applied the law under Title VII to determine whether an ability test will pass muster under a labor agreement. This standard is not unreasonable, especially where the parties have contractually agreed to comply with all applicable fair employment laws.[15]

Arbitrator Raymond Hilgert, in *Star Manufacturing Co.,*[16]

---

[12]82 LA 232 (1984).
[13]Id. at 234.
[14]Martin Co., 46 LA 1116, 1123 (Gorsuch, 1966); American Oil Co., 50 LA 1227 (Simon, 1968); Vulcan Materials Co., 49 LA 577 (Duff, 1967); Caradco, Inc., 35 LA 169 (Gaff, 1960); Independent School Dist. No. 279 (Osseo, Minn.), 71 LA 116, 118 (Fogelberg, 1978); Lancaster School Dist., 72 LA 693, 695 (Raymond, (undated)).
[15]See, e.g., Sterling Drug, Inc., 79 LA 1255 (Gibson, 1982).
[16]79 LA 868 (1982).

exemplifying the thinking of most arbitrators when ruling on a claim that a test is unreasonable, commented:

> [T]ests can and should be used in determining employee qualifications and abilities provided that such tests are:
> 1. Related to the specific requirements of the job;
> 2. Fair and reasonable;
> 3. Administered in good faith and without discrimination;
> 4. Properly evaluated.

> It appears to the Arbitrator that in the instant case before him the use of the tests met all of the above criteria. For example, it was uncontested that the Company tests given to [the grievant] and the other job bidders were quite job-related involving the kinds of tasks that would be expected of a Model Maker. The tests did not appear to be extraordinarily difficult given the history of the various employees who had taken them before. The same tests or versions of the same tests had been given to job bidders for many years, and both the development and evaluation of the test results were accomplished by . . . a professional engineer . . . .[17]

Likewise, where an appendix to a collective bargaining agreement provided that the company's examinations and tests should be limited to testing procedures which were (a) job-related, (b) fair in both make-up and administration, and (c) free of cultural, racial, or ethnic bias, Arbitrator Sylvester Garrett, concluding that the tests were not job-related, remarked:

> The tests which the Company now uses to select Apprentices are marketed by the Psychological Corporation and may be purchased by anyone interested in measuring the particular characteristics of individuals which each test originally was designed to measure. There is no suggestion that any of these tests was prepared with the "specific requirements" of any given U.S. Steel trade or craft job in mind. There now are 26 separate trade or craft jobs listed in [the basic agreement.] . . .

> Nonetheless the Company now urges that its imported battery of commercially available tests may be applied, with uniform minimum cutting scores, so as to determine basic qualifications for apprentice training for all 26 of the separate trade or craft jobs. No prolonged discussion of this proposition is warranted. It simply cannot be squared with the controlling definition of "job-related" in Appendix G. On its face this requires that *any* test used to determine basic qualifications for admission to the apprentice training program for a given craft job must be developed in light of the specific requirements of

---

[17]Id. at 877, quoting Elkouri & Elkouri, How Arbitration Works, 3d Ed., 578 (BNA Books, 1973)(repaginated at 620, 4th Ed., 1985).

the given craft. This precludes use of a test battery developed for the world at large, without reference to the content of specific trade or craft jobs in the bargaining unit at U.S. Steel.[18]

Not only must tests be job-related, but management must also take care that they are administered in an even-handed manner. No individual should receive an advantage of any kind, e.g., advanced knowledge of test questions, having the test waived, or having points added to test results.[19] Moreover, arbitrators have required that prior to implementing its testing procedure, an employer discuss with the union its intention to administer tests, explaining what the examination will cover and what constitutes a passing grade.[20]

Ability Tests Distinguished From Aptitude Tests

Some arbitrators have properly distinguished an aptitude test from an ability test. For instance, in *Butler Manufacturing Co.*,[21] the employer unilaterally introduced a general aptitude test prepared by an outside psychologist (U.S. Employment Service GATB test) and used it to disqualify a senior employee from entering a training program. Arbitrator John Larkin noted that while arbitrators generally sustain management's right to use job-specific tests, the use of generalized tests to disqualify employees with established seniority could undermine the entire seniority system. The arbitrator noted that aptitude tests not directly related to the work in question may be properly used by management only in the selection of new employees, in counseling, or in other general uses. As Arbitrator Larkin said, "such general tests may not be used as a proper guide for denying a senior employee promotion."[22]

---

[18]United States Steel Corp. (Eastern Steel Operations), 70 LA 1235, 1242 (1978)(emphasis in original).

[19]See, e.g., Equitable Gas Co., 57 LA 834 (Altrock, 1971)(supervisors adding points); John Strange Paper Co., 43 LA 1184, 1187 (Larkin, 1965)("So long as the system of selection is fair, uniform and without deliberate discrimination against any individual or group, the Company may establish standards of qualification, or competency, apart from seniority. From the record before us, we must conclude that the grievant was given equal consideration with the others who took the same test.").

[20]Martin Co., 46 LA 1116, 1123 (Gorsuch, 1966)("[T]he Company was in error in not discussing with the Union, in advance, its intention to give a written test and to explain what the examination was to cover, what was to be a passing grade and to assure the Union that the job would be given to the worker who would be entitled, under [the contract], to the job subject only to his receiving a passing, not the best, grade on the test.").

[21]52 LA 633 (Larkin, 1969).

[22]Id. at 638. See also Armstrong Cork Co., 42 LA 349 (Handsaker, 1964)(allowing employer to give Wonderlic Personnel Test for "mental alertness").

Physical Ability Tests[23]

Some agreements explicitly allow management to consider an employee's physical condition in awarding a position.[24] Other contracts may outline the physical requirements of the job in the agreement itself, specifying criteria such as height, weight, or lifting qualifications.[25] Where the agreement is silent, arbitrators have consistently held that management has the right, either as a reasonable management prerogative or as a necessary adjunct to its right to manage and direct the work force, to consider an employee's physical fitness for a position.[26] Arbitrators have ruled that in assessing an employee's physical ability, management may properly take into account (1) the nature of any physical limitation, (2) the diagnosis of both the company's and the grievant's physician, and (3) even the possibility of increased workmen's compensation liability.[27] Furthermore, arbitrators have held that management need not tailor a job to accommodate the physical limitations of an employee.[28]

Where job related, the use of a test designed to measure the physical abilities of employees has been sustained even where the test is the sole criterion in determining employees' qualifications.[29]

Physical Qualifications: Vocational Rehabilitation Act

In rejecting individuals for a position on the basis of physical or mental infirmities, covered employers must take care

---

[23]See the discussion of physical and psychological examinations in Chapter 7, supra.

[24]Verniton Corp., 77 LA 349 (Shipman, 1981); General Tel. Co. of Calif., 72 LA 1026 (Rule, 1979); Hercules, Inc., 61 LA 621 (Murphy, 1973); Celanese Fibers Co., 51 LA 1143 (Altrock, 1969).

[25]B.F. Goodrich Co., 63 LA 216 (Volz, 1974).

[26]Metropolitan Atlanta Rapid Transit Auth., 79 LA 357 (Aronin, 1982).

[27]McCreary Tire & Rubber Co., 72 LA 1279 (Rollo, 1979); Owens-Corning Fiberglas Corp., 51 LA 27 (Jaffee, 1968); Consolidated Gas Supply Corp., 51 LA 152 (Altrock, 1968); Delta Match Corp., 53 LA 1282 (Marshall, 1969)(failure to grant a trial period because of lack of physical dexterity and coordination).

[28]In this respect see the discussion of case authority by Dale Allen in Jesco Lubricants Co., 62 LA 1294 (1974).

[29]Northwestern Bell Tel. Co., 75 LA 148 (Karlins, 1980); Illinois Bell Tel. Co., 76 LA 432 (Erbs, 1981); United States Steel Corp., 65 LA 626 (Friedman, 1975)(upholding "personal observation" of supervisor that grievant was too small in size and stature to handle work).

not to violate the Vocational Rehabilitation Act of 1973,[30] or any applicable state law protecting the handicapped.[31]

Section 503 of the Act requires that any federal contract in excess of $2,500 for the procurement of personal property and nonpersonal services (including construction) include a provision requiring contractors to seek to employ handicapped individuals. Further, contractors with federal contracts that exceed $50,000 and who employ 50 or more employees must establish a written affirmative action program within 120 days after receiving the contract, and must update the program annually. Although Section 503 requires affirmative action programs to hire and advance qualified handicapped employees, these programs do not require goals and timetables. It is important to note that Section 503 does not outlaw discrimination but, rather, requires affirmative action covenants in government contracts. Current regulations specify that a complaint may be filed with the director of the Office of Federal Contract Compliance Programs (OFCCP) and that the director is primarily responsible for investigating the complaints.[32]

Section 504 of the amended statute prohibits discrimination against any individual on the basis of handicap in any program receiving federal financial assistance. Specifically, the statute provides:

> No otherwise qualified handicapped individual . . . shall, solely by reason of his handicap, be excluded from the participation in, be denied the benefits of, or be subjected to discrimination under any program or activity receiving Federal financial assistance or under any program or activity conducted by any Executive agency or by the United States Postal Service.[33]

A handicapped individual is defined as "any person who (i) has a physical or mental impairment which substantially limits one or more of such person's major life activities, (ii) has a record of such an impairment, or (iii) is regarded as having such an impairment."[34] The definition includes persons who

---

[30]29 U.S.C. §701 (Supp. V 1982), as amended by Pub. L. No. 95-602, Title I, §122(a)(1), 92 Stat. 2984 (1978).
[31]See, e.g., Cessna Aircraft Co., 72 LA 367, 369 (Laybourne, 1979)(refusing to apply Rehabilitation Act in arbitration proceeding).
[32]41 C.F.R. Part 60-741.25, 741.26(a). See, e.g., Moon v. Secretary, U.S. Department of Labor, 747 F.2d 599, 36 FEP 477 (CA 11, 1984).
[33]29 U.S.C. §794 (1982).
[34]29 U.S.C. §706 (7)(B) (1982).

have a record indicating an impairment (e.g., recovered mental, cancer, or heart attack patients) or who are perceived as having such an impairment. The term "handicap" does not include any individual who is an alcoholic or drug abuser whose current use of alcohol or drugs prevents such individual from performing the duties of the job in question, or whose employment, by reason of such alcohol or drug abuse, would constitute a direct threat to the property or safety of others.[35] There is no affirmative action requirement in Section 504.[36] The Supreme Court in 1984 held that a handicapped individual may bring a court action on his or her own behalf where a violation of Section 504 is claimed, regardless of whether the primary objective of the federal funds is to provide employment opportunities.[37] The burden of proof in Rehabilitation Act cases follows the scheme under Title VII case law.[38]

The significance of this statute for labor and management

---

[35]The Department of Health and Human Services has advised recipients of financial assistance under §504 of the Rehabilitation Act as follows: "With respect to the employment of a drug addict or alcoholic, if it can be shown that the addiction or alcoholism prevents successful performance of the job, the person need not be provided the employment opportunity in question. For example, in making employment decisions, a recipient may judge addicts and alcoholics on the same basis it judges all other applicants and employees. Thus, a recipient may consider—for all applicants including drug addicts and alcoholics—past personnel records, absenteeism, disruptive, abusive or dangerous behavior, violations of rules, and unsatisfactory work performance. Moreover, employers may enforce rules prohibiting the possession or use of alcohol or drugs in the work place, provided that such rules are enforced against all employees." See Susser, "Legal Issues Raised by Drugs in the Workplace," 36 Lab. L. J. No. 1, 42–51 (1985), quoting 45 C.F.R. Part 84, App. A, Subpart A-4.

In McCleod v. City of Detroit, ___ F.Supp. ___, 39 FEP 225, 228 (E.D. Mich., 1985), a federal court held that individuals who were rejected for firefighter jobs after drug screening tests detected marijuana were not handicapped under the Rehabilitation Act. The court stated in dictum:

Assuming that drug use is a handicap and that plaintiffs are drug users, the Act excluded them from its benefits. 29 U.S.C. sec. 706 reads:

For purposes of sections 793 and 794 of this title as such sections relate to employment, such term (handicapped individuals) does not include an individual who is an alcoholic or drug abuser whose current *use of alcohol or drugs prevents such individual from performing the duties of the job in question or whose employment, by reason of such current alcohol or drug abuse, would constitute a direct threat to property or the safety of others.* (emphasis added by the court).

[36]Southeastern Community College v. Davis, 442 U.S. 397 (1979).

[37]Consolidated Rail Corp. v. Darrone, 465 U.S. 624, 34 FEP 79 (1984).

[38]See, e.g., Whiting v. Jackson State Univ., 616 F.2d 116, 22 FEP 1296 (CA 5, 1980), and Guinn v. Bolger, 598 F.Supp. 196, 36 FEP 506 (D.D.C. 1984), applying McDonnell Douglas Corp. v. Green, 411 U.S. 792, 802–05, 5 FEP 965 (1973). The scheme for allocating the burden of proof in a disparate treatment case was articulated by the Supreme Court in *McDonnell Douglas*, where it stated that "the complainant in a Title VII trial must carry the initial burden under the statute of establishing a prima facie case of racial discrimination. This may be done by showing (i) that he belongs to a racial minority; (ii) that he applied and was qualified for a job for which the employer was seeking applicants; (iii) that, despite his qualifications, he was

is illustrated by *Southeastern Community College v. Davis*.[39] During the initial interview of an applicant to a nursing program, the interviewer became aware that the individual was having trouble hearing the questions being asked of her. Upon further investigation, the applicant (Davis) was found to have a severe hearing impairment. An adjustment of her hearing aid was made, but even this allowed only the hearing of "gross sound" occurrences—Davis would need to learn lip reading to understand fully what was being said. The admission committee subsequently rejected Davis' application to the program, reasoning that it would endanger patients to allow Davis to become a nurse. Davis then filed a complaint in federal court alleging both a violation of Section 504 and a denial of equal protection and due process.

The district court upheld the college's action, citing examples, such as in the operating room, where the wearing of surgical masks would prevent any possibility of lip reading.[40] Because Davis would be unable to function as a nurse in such circumstances and, therefore, was held not to be "an otherwise qualified handicapped individual" within the meaning of the Act, the district court held that there was no violation of Section 504. The Fourth Circuit reversed, holding that the college should have reviewed the plaintiff's application based on her "academic and technical qualifications" and not with regard to her hearing disability.[41]

The Supreme Court, reversing the Fourth Circuit, held "otherwise qualified" to mean "qualified in spite of the handicap" rather than "qualified except for the handicap." Therefore, it said, "an otherwise qualified person is one who is able

---

rejected; and (iv) that, after his rejection, the position remained open and the employer continued to seek applicants from persons of complainant's qualifications." 411 U.S. at 802 (footnote omitted).

After plaintiff establishes a prima facie case, the respondent, in order to avoid liability, is required to "articulate a legitimate non-discriminatory reason for the employee's rejection." Finally, should the defendant carry this burden, the claimant could challenge it on the basis that the reason given was a pretext for discrimination. Texas Dept. of Community Affairs v. Burdine, 450 U.S. 248, 252–53, 25 FEP 113 (1981).

It has been recognized that *McDonnell Douglas* "did not purport to create an inflexible formulation." Teamsters v. United States, 431 U.S. 324, 358, 14 FEP 1514 (1977). See also Bell v. Birmingham Linen Service, 715 F.2d 1552, 1556, 32 FEP 1673 (CA 11, 1983)(*McDonnell Douglas* "is not intended to be a Procrustean bed within which all disparate treatment cases must be forced to lie.").

[39]442 U.S. 397 (1979).

[40]Davis v. Southeastern Community College, 424 F.Supp. 1341 (E.D.N.C., 1976).

[41]574 F.2d 1158 (CA 4, 1978).

to meet all of a program's requirements in spite of his handicap."[42] Federally assisted programs could therefore require "legitimate physical qualifications" as prerequisites to admission.

The implications of *Davis* for federal contractors and employers receiving federal assistance are clear. Management may properly take into account the physical requirements of a job in all phases of employment. Where an applicant faces what might be termed "insurmountable impairment barrier," i.e., where the handicap itself prevents the individual from fulfilling the essential requirements of the position, the applicant is not "otherwise qualified" for the job under Section 504. Moreover, a fair reading of *Davis* is that an individual facing a "surmountable employment barrier," a barrier to job performance that can be overcome with accommodation, is not otherwise qualified if the accommodation would require a substantial modification in the job requirements, or would result in an undue administrative and financial burden to the employer.[43]

The burden of proving inability to accommodate rests with the employer.[44] Factors considered in assessing hardship include the size of the program, the type and duration of the program, and the nature and cost of accommodation.[45] A business-necessity test is used to determine whether accommodation of a handicapped individual is required.[46] Accordingly, an employer may not deny any employment or training opportunity to a qualified handicapped employee, applicant, or participant if the basis for the denial is the need to reasonably accommodate the physical or mental limitations of the employee.

---

[42]442 U.S. at 406.

[43]Nelson v. Thornburgh, 567 F.Supp. 369, 32 FEP 1640, 1647 (E.D. Pa. 1983), citing Note, "Accommodating the Handicapped: The Meaning of Discrimination under Section 504 of the Rehabilitation Act," 55 N.Y.U. L. Rev. 881 (1980).

[44]Prewitt v. United States Postal Serv., 662 F.2d 292, 27 FEP 1043 (CA 5, 1981). The secretary's regulations provide that job qualifications "which would tend to exclude handicapped individuals because of their handicap . . . shall be related to the specific job or jobs for which the individual is being considered and shall be consistent with business necessity and safe performance."

[45]Nelson v. Thornburgh, 567 F.Supp. 369, 32 FEP 1640 (1983)(half-time readers or mechanical equivalent for blind income maintenance workers); Smith v. Administrator of Veterans Affairs, 32 FEP 986 (C.D. Cal., 1983)(dismissal of epileptic violative of §504 absent evidence that he caused injury to himself or others or that he caused additional costs to hospital-employer).

[46]Bentivegna v. Department of Labor, 694 F.2d 619, 30 FEP 875 (CA 9, 1982), citing 29 C.F.R. Part 32.14.

Disclosure of Test Scores

Disclosure and privacy issues exist where the union requests that the employer make available the scores of all employees taking a written test. One arbitrator, considering a company's refusal to disclose scores from a mechanical assembly test, ruled that absent any provision in the bargaining agreement stating that management could keep the scores secret, the results must be made available to both the union and the affected employees.[47] Similarly, another arbitrator, offering some fundamentals on testing, declared that "the union is entitled to know 'the method of scoring the tests, the manner in which passing grades are set, and the scores of the individual applicants.' "[48]

Where the reasons against disclosures are legitimate and substantial, both the Board and the courts have held that a party need not disclose, even though the requested information may be relevant. Thus, in *Detroit Edison Co. v. NLRB*,[49] the Supreme Court upheld an employer's claim of privilege against disclosure of psychological testing information and reversed a Board order to make available directly to the union the aptitude tests, answer sheets, and employee-linked scores that had been used in making disputed promotion decisions. The Court rejected the proposition that the union's interests in arguably relevant information must always predominate over all other interests, however legitimate. Rather, the Court indicated that determining the employer's duty to supply such information when it is assertedly confidential requires a balancing of the union's need for the information against the confidentiality interests of the employer. Stressing the sensitive nature of testing information, the Court found no evidence that the employer had fabricated concern for employee confidentiality (the employer had promised the employees that the information requested would remain private) only to frustrate the union in the discharge of its responsibilities. The practitioner can expect an arbitrator to adopt a similar position when a party requests disclosure of sensitive information.

---

[47]General Elec. Co., 72 LA 1307, 1310 (Marcus, 1979).
[48]Martin Co., 46 LA 1116, 1123 (Gorsuch, 1966), citing Fansteel Metallurgical Corp., 36 LA 570, 573 (Marshall).
[49]440 U.S. 301, 100 LRRM 2728 (1979).

Testing and Fair Employment

Fair employment decisions of the courts have influenced the thinking of both practitioners and arbitrators on the issue of testing. In the leading case, *Griggs v. Duke Power Co.*,[50] prior to the effective date of Title VII an employer openly discriminated on the basis of race in the hiring and assigning of employees. The plant was organized into five operating departments: (1) Labor, (2) Coal Handling, (3) Operations, (4) Maintenance, and (5) Laboratory and Testing. Blacks were employed only in the Labor Department, where the highest paying jobs paid less than the lowest paying jobs in the other four operating departments. Promotions were normally made within each department on the basis of seniority. Transferees into a department usually began in the lowest position.

In 1955 the company instituted a policy of requiring a high school education for initial assignment to any department except Labor, and for transfer from Coal Handling to any inside department (Operations, Maintenance, or Laboratory). When the company abandoned its policy of restricting blacks to the Labor Department in 1965, completion of high school was also made a prerequisite to transfer from Labor to any other department.

The company added a further requirement for new employees on the effective date of Title VII. To qualify for placement anywhere but the labor department it became necessary to register satisfactory scores on two professionally developed aptitude tests, as well as to have a high school degree. Completion of high school alone continued to render employees eligible for transfer to the four desirable departments from which blacks had been excluded if the incumbent had been employed prior to the time of the new requirement. Subsequently, the company began to permit incumbent employees who lacked a high school education to qualify for transfer from labor or coal to an "inside" job by passing two other tests—the Wonderlic Personnel Test and the Bennett Mechanical Aptitude Test. Since a smaller percentage of blacks relative to whites had received a high school degree (12 percent vs. 34 percent in North Carolina), and because whites fared better on the tests than blacks (a pass rate of 58 percent vs. 6 percent),

---

[50]401 U.S. 424, 3 FEP 175 (1971).

the Supreme Court found the requirement had an adverse impact on blacks.

More important, no relationship was shown between possession of a high school degree and successful job performance (a large percentage of whites without a high school degree had performed successfully in the cited jobs). The *Griggs* court made it clear that Title VII proscribes not only overt discrimination, but also employment practices that are fair in form but discriminatory in operation. If a test or other practice that operates to exclude a protected class cannot be shown to be related to job performance, the practice is prohibited. The Court stated that "any tests used must measure the person for the job and not the person in the abstract."

The issue of whether a test is a valid predictor of job performance arises in employment discrimination cases only after the plaintiff has demonstrated that the challenged tests exert a disparate impact on a protected class. The requirement that a plaintiff must first prove adverse impact was reaffirmed in *Albemarle Paper Co. v. Moody*.[51] In that case the Supreme Court again considered the issue of job-relatedness of a test-oriented selection process. Albemarle had required applicants for the skilled lines of progression to have a high school diploma and to pass two tests, the Revised Beta Examination (allegedly a measure of nonverbal intelligence) and the Wonderlic Test (verbal facility). Approximately four months before the case went to trial, the employer engaged an expert industrial psychologist to validate the "job relatedness" of its testing program. A "concurrent validation study" was devised. The study dealt with 10 job groupings selected from near the top of nine lines of progression. Within each job grouping the study compared the test scores of each employee with an independent ranking of the employee, relative to each of his coworkers, made by the employee's supervisor.

The Court found the validation methods of the company "materially defective" in several respects. First, the Court said that even if the study had been otherwise adequate, the tests still would not be valid for all the skilled lines of progression for which the tests were then required (the study demonstrated statistical significance for only three of the eight lines). Second, in applying the federal employee selection Guidelines

---

[51]422 U.S. 405, 432, 10 FEP 1181 (1975).

discussed below, the Court pointed out that the study compared test scores with subjective supervisorial rankings, noting that "while [the Guidelines] allow use of supervisorial rankings in test validation, the Guidelines quite plainly contemplate that the rankings will be elicited with far more care than was demonstrated [in this case]." Third, the Court also noted that the study focused on job groupings near the top of the various lines of progressions. Where job progression is not automatic, it said, a candidate should have been considered as being measured for a job at or near the entry level. Fourth, the Court stated that the validation study dealt only with job-experienced white workers. The tests, however, were given to new job applicants who were younger, largely inexperienced, and, in many instances, non-white. There was no showing that differential validation (validation studies for different groups or categories of employees) was not feasible for lower-level jobs.

   Under the current status of the law, any test that has an "adverse impact" on the members of a protected class is unlawful unless (1) it is validated as being related to job performance, and (2) alternative selection procedures which have a lesser adverse impact are unavailable. An employer is not compelled to demonstrate that its testing program is job-related unless it is first found to have a discriminatory impact. The current Uniform Guidelines on Employee Selection Procedures[52] define "adverse impact" as "a substantially different rate of selection in hiring, promotion or other employment decision which works to the disadvantage of members of a race, sex, or ethnic group." Although they do not include a legal definition of discrimination, the Guidelines provide that an adverse impact exists when the selection rate for a particular group is less than 80 percent of the selection rate for other groups. For example, if 70 percent of the male applicants are selected and 60 percent of the female applicants are selected, no adverse effect exists because 60 percent, the female selection rate, is 86 percent of 70 percent, the male selection rate. However, if 60 percent of the male applicants and 40 percent of the female applicants are selected, an adverse impact exists because 40 percent is only 67 percent of 60 percent. Smaller differences in selection rates may still constitute ad-

---

[52]See Fair Employment Practices Manual 401:2268 (BNA).

verse impact, where they are significant in both statistical and practical terms or where an employer's actions have discouraged applicants disproportionately. It should be noted that the number of candidates may be so small that the statistical results do not reflect the reality of the employment situation, or that the statistical universe is so small that the results achieved are due mainly to chance or random distribution.[53]

Once the test is shown to have an adverse impact, the employer, in order to escape liability under Title VII, must demonstrate that the test is valid. Validation consists of a showing that the test predicts job-performance. In this regard, the first step in the validation process is for the employer to formulate a proper definition of the job. The Guidelines do not specify specific procedures for analyzing a job, but state that any professional method of job analysis is acceptable if it is comprehensive and otherwise appropriate for the specific validation strategy used. A validation-type study is then performed. The Guidelines cite three validity strategies for showing that a test is job related: (1) Criterion-related validity requires a statistical demonstration of a relationship (correlation) between scores on a test and actual job performance. (2) Content validity requires a demonstration that the content of a test is representative of important aspects of the job,[54] as, for example, a typing test given to an applicant for a secretarial position, or a driving test given an applicant for a fork-lift job. Content validity is present to the extent that the actual content of a test contains samples of job performance. (3) Construct validity is present where there is a relationship between a "construct" or "trait" and successful job performance. To validate a test through this method it is first necessary to determine through job analysis that a particular trait or construct (honesty, for example) is actually related to job performance (cashier). Second, it must be demonstrated that the test used does in fact measure the specific trait. Finally, it must be demonstrated that success on the test is a predictor or measure of success on the job.

It is, of course, possible that a test may predict job performance in a different manner for a minority sample than

---

[53]See Commonwealth v. Rizzo, 466 F.Supp. 1219, 20 FEP 130 (E.D. Pa., 1979)(statistical universe too small to be probative where 154 whites and only nine blacks took test).
[54]29 C.F.R. Part 1607.5B (1985).

for the majority sample. Moreover, because of differences in work behavior, criterion measures, study samples, or other factors, a test or selection procedure that is valid in one situation may not be valid in another. For this reason, the Guidelines encourage cooperative and multi-unit studies.

Rank-Ordering Employees

Frequently employers will rank-order employees on the basis of their test scores or other selection devices. The Guidelines provide that if an employer bases its selection procedure on a ranking, and that method has a greater adverse impact than an appropriate pass/fail method, the employer should have sufficient evidence of validity to support its system.[55] The Sixth Circuit in 1983 declared that ranking of employees is a valid job-related selection technique only where the test scores vary directly with job performance.[56] Other courts are in accord with this view.[57]

Arbitral Authority

Where tests are shown to have a discriminatory impact on the basis of race or sex, arbitrators, along with the courts and the EEOC, have required that tests be job-related.[58] Even where tests have not been shown to be discriminatory, neutrals have imposed a reasonableness or job-related requirement.[59] In a case where a general aptitude test (which included verbal, numerical, mechanical, and oral-directions sections) was required by the parties' contract, Arbitrator Robert Foster upheld management's right to discontinue using a specific test where the employer's action was based on the belief that the

---

[55] 29 C.F.R. Part 1607.5G (1985).

[56] Williams v. Vukovich, 720 F.2d 909, 33 FEP 238, 250 (CA 6, 1983).

[57] See, e.g., Walls v. Mississippi Dept. of Public Welfare, 31 FEP 1795, 1821 (N.D. Miss., 1982), citing Ensley Branch of NAACP v. Seibels, 616 F.2d 812, 822, 22 FEP 1207 (CA 5, 1980)("[T]here is inadequate evidence to show that the tests were valid for purposes of ranking, as opposed to screening out applicants, since there is nothing to indicate 'that those with a higher test score do better on the job than those with a lower test score.'").

[58] See the discussion by Arbitrator Arnold Karlins in Northwestern Bell Tel. Co., 75 LA 148, 151 (1980). See also Gulf States Utilities Co., 62 LA 1061, 1071 (Williams, 1974); Joy Mfg. Co., 70 LA 4 (Mathews, 1977).

[59] Industrial Garment Mfg. Co., 74 LA 1248 (Griffin, 1980).

test was not valid under the Uniform Guidelines, discussed above.[60] Foster's analysis is particularly instructive:

> The sole issue raised by the grievances in this dispute and presented to this Arbitrator is whether the Company was justified in failing to observe the terms of the agreement to employ a general aptitude test as a factor in the selection of applicants . . . to the Apprenticeship Program. Based on the likely violation of federal law and the consequences that could result from such performance of the contract in the face of a direction from appropriate federal authorities, it is the decision of this Arbitrator that the company is excused from its contract obligation. Beyond this, no opinion is expressed as to whether the selection of black applicants into the Apprenticeship Program constituted discrimination against other employees, based on some other factors not appearing in the record in this case. . . . Suffice it to say that this Arbitrator is in accord with and bound by the statement in *Griggs v. Duke Power Company* . . . that "Congress has not commanded that the less qualified be preferred over the better qualified, simply because of minority origins [but] . . . only . . . that race, religion, nationality, and sex become irrelevant. What Congress has commanded is that any test used must measure the person for the job and not the person in the abstract."[61]

Trial and Training Periods

One method of evaluating an applicant for a position is to grant a "trial" or "training" period. Arbitrator Wayne Howard observed that a trial period has several basic purposes: (1) it replaces subjective estimates of ability with an objective test of job performance; (2) it familiarizes the employee with the general requirements of the job; and (3) it can resolve reasonable doubt concerning an employee's ability in cases where other criteria have not resolved the issue. A trial period is thus used as the final measure of ability only after other criteria have indicated the employee has the requisite ability.[62]

---

[60]ASG Indus., Inc., 62 LA 849 (Foster, 1974).

[61]Id. at 853–54, quoting Griggs v. Duke Power Co., 401 U.S. 424, 3 FEP 175, 180 (1971). See also Mountain States Tel. & Tel. Co., 64 LA 316 (Platt, 1974); Day & Zimmermann, Inc., 60 LA 495 (Marcus, 1973)(rejecting argument that employer had right to unilaterally eliminate qualifying test because it determined that test could not be validated under fair employment laws). See generally Stone & Banderschneider, Arbitration of Discrimination Grievances (American Arbitration Association, 1974).

[62]Howard, "Seniority Rights and Trial Periods," 15 Arb. J. 51 (1960). See also Zack & Bloch, Labor Agreement in Negotiation and Arbitration, 130 (BNA, 1983); Gulf States Utilities Co., 62 LA 1061, 1077 (Williams, 1974).

Some agreements specifically provide for a trial or training period when an employee is initially promoted.[63] Other provisions may provide for a trial period when there is a bona fide dispute regarding the qualifications of an employee to perform the job for which he has applied.[64] When the contract is silent, most arbitrators hold the view that there is no right to a trial or probationary period in order to demonstrate "ability."[65] To rule otherwise would mean, in effect, that management must give a trial period to an employee it has already reasonably and justifiably determined to be unqualified.[66] Situations arise, however, where arbitrators will impose a trial or break-in period to resolve disputes over ability even in the absence of a contractual provision. Arbitrator Howard points out that, while dependent on the facts of each case, the imposition of a trial period by an arbitrator is related to several factors in each situation, namely, the degree of seniority afforded by the labor contract, the nature of the particular job, and, most important, the inability of other criteria to resolve the issue of ability.[67]

With regard to seniority considerations, arbitrators' awards suggest that a trial period may be appropriate under a "sufficient-ability" clause where the applicant is evaluated in relation to the job requirements, and not to another employee.[68] The rationale is that the parties, by their language favoring the allocation of promotions by seniority, evidence a preference for seniority and that a trial period will resolve any ambiguity in cases where a senior employee's ability is contested. Senior employees have sometimes been given a trial or break-in period on the basis of having had some experience, even though the junior employee has more experience.[69]

---

[63]Olympic Stain Co., 72 LA 1038, 1040 (Fitch, 1979); Emerson Elec. Co., 54 LA 683, 684 (Williams, 1970); Central Soya Co., 41 LA 1027, 1028 (Tatum, 1963); Purex Corp., 39 LA 336 (Miller, 1962); Trans World Airlines, 45 LA 267 (Beatty, 1965).

[64]Beatrice Foods, Inc., 54 LA 998 (McKenna, 1970).

[65]Tennessee Casting Co., 82 LA 1247 (Hart, 1984); Semling-Menke Co., 62 LA 1184, 1188 (Bilder, 1974); Greif Bros. Corp., 64 LA 1219, 1221 (Butler, 1975); Delta Match Corp., 53 LA 1282, 1287 (Marshall, 1969); Vulcan Materials Co., 54 LA 460, 466 (Block, 1970); American Cyanamid Co., 52 LA 247 (Cahn, 1969); U.S. Indus., Inc., 44 LA 1193, 1195 (Singletary, 1965).

[66]Judson Steel Corp., 76 LA 825, 827 (Griffin, 1981).

[67]Howard, "Seniority Rights and Trial Periods," supra note 62, at 54.

[68]Chromalloy Am. Corp., 62 LA 84, 88 (Fox, 1974); Perfect Circle Corp., 43 LA 817, 823 (Dworkin, 1964).

[69]See, e.g., the discussions by Arbitrator William Hart in Tennessee Casting Co., 82 LA 1247, 1250 (1984), and Milden Fox in Chromalloy American Corp., 62 LA 84, 88–90 (1974).

If the test results or other criteria used in determining ability are inconclusive, or where ability to perform can only be determined by performance on the job, arbitrators have ruled that the senior employee should be granted a trial period, as opposed to a training period, to demonstrate ability.[70] Absent clear language stating that a "trial period" is meant for training, most arbitrators will not infer such a right or impose this obligation on the parties. As stated by Arbitrator Marlin Volz in *Reynolds Metals Co.*:[71]

> [A] significant difference is recognized between a trial and a training period. The purpose of a trial period is to determine whether an employee who possesses the basic qualifications can satisfactorily do a job which she does not regularly perform. It is assumed that she will not have to be trained in all aspects of the job; for a trial period is not a training period, but simply an opportunity to demonstrate ability to do the job. A trial period, in effect, is a lengthened familiarization or orientation period in which the employee is acquainted with the nature and techniques of the job. It presupposes that the employee will be given instruction and assistance and that she will not simply be turned loose to "sink or swim". But, it also assumes that she brings with her to the trial period by virtue of prior experience or education considerable knowledge, background, and skill for performing the duties of the new position.[72]

The authors believe that the better rule is that arbitrators should not grant trial periods on a contested job unless (1) a bona fide dispute exists over an employee's ability to perform the job, (2) there are reasonable grounds to believe that the grievant has the ability to perform the job, and (3) a party requests a trial period as a remedy under a sufficient-ability clause. Further, when a particular job is critical to the safety of the public or the economic health of the organization, a trial period should not be ordered.[73]

---

[70]See, e.g., Dearborn Fabricating & Eng'g, Co., 64 LA 271 (Kallenbach, 1975); Southwest Airmotive Co., 41 LA 353 (Elliott, 1963); Zack & Bloch, Labor Agreement in Negotiation and Arbitration, supra note 62.
[71]66 LA 1276 (1976).
[72]Id. at 1280.
[73]For a related note on trial periods see Hill, "Summary—Seniority and Ability," Proceedings of the 9th Annual Meeting of NAA 44, 47 (BNA Books, 1956).

Performance and Merit Evaluations[74]

It is well established that merit increases are an appropriate subject for collective bargaining,[75] and that, under most circumstances, a union may properly demand a copy of the merit or performance evaluation of an employee.[76] Labor agreements frequently contain provisions establishing objective standards for merit increases, or fixing a regular review period, or making such increases subject to review or negotiation by the union.[77] One arbitrator correctly pointed out that "a merit-rating system is concerned with *how* an individual performs his job and *not* with what the duties of that job entail. Therefore, under that kind of system, of necessity, some employees may be receiving a higher [wage] rate than other employees [even though] both employees are doing substantially the same work."[78] A merit rating assumes that, within an established wage rate, the rates of individual employees will vary according to their individual effort, initiative, and demonstrative efficiency. As such, the fact that two employees doing the same kind of work and placed in the same job classification receive different merit increases does not imply arbitrary or discriminatory treatment by management.[79]

Arbitrators have also held that any contract that provides for merit increases also contemplates that management will periodically evaluate the performance of employees.[80] In determining whether an employee is eligible for a merit increase, the rule followed by arbitrators is that there is no presumption of progress or improvement due only to the pas-

---

[74]See generally Holley, "Performance Ratings in Arbitration," 32 Arb. J., No. 1, 8, 16–18 (1977).

[75]Frito-Lay, Inc., 42 LA 426, 429 (Lee, 1964)("The Employer's contention that merit rates are not proper subjects of bargaining is not well taken. Wages, including gratuitous wage increases such as those unilaterally granted the grievants, and termed, *for merit*, are made subject to bargaining by [Taft-Hartley]."(emphasis in original)).

[76]See, e.g., New York Times Co., 270 NLRB 1235 (1984), where a three-member Board held that an employer had to make available to a union copies of all an employee's performance evaluations where the information was necessary for the union's administration of the labor agreement with respect to promotion and non-discrimination).

[77]Sommers & Adams Co., 6 LA 283 (Whiting, 1947).

[78]C.F. Mueller Co., 75 LA 135 (Light, 1980)(emphasis in original).

[79]International Harvester Co., 14 LA 77 (Seward, 1950).

[80]Wisconsin Dep't of Industry, 64 LA 663, 668 (Marshall, 1975).

sage of time.[81] Arbitrator Thomas Coyne expressed this principle when he declared:

> A "merit" pay raise means just that. It is something awarded a person for meritorious service. It is not a right to which one is entitled by virtue of his presence on the payroll.[82]

Most reported decisions involve claims that an employee has a contractual right to a merit increase,[83] or that an employee's merit evaluation was arbitrary, biased, or otherwise discriminatory.[84] With few exceptions, arbitrators have held that unless otherwise limited by the collective bargaining agreement, management retains the sole right to determine whether an employee's job performance warrants a merit increase. The better view is that the management's evaluation will not be overturned merely because the union or the arbitrator would have judged an employee's job performance differently. In this regard, one arbitrator stated:

> The ultimate question to be decided here is whether the review of [the grievant's] work was fair and just. This calls into play the rule stated many times and with seeming unanimity, that unless it is shown that management has been arbitrary or capricious, or has been motivated by discrimination or bias or some similarly improper purpose, decisions in this area are not overturned in arbitration proceedings.[85]

Likewise, Arbitrator Edgar Warren expressed this principle as follows:

> It is almost impossible for an outsider, who has not studied the work being performed by different men in a particular department in detail, to determine what the level of pay should be for individual workers within their appropriate rate ranges. The arbitrator cannot substitute his judgment for that of [management] unless there is some showing that the decision of the [management] was arbitrary and capricious.[86]

---

[81]Ralph C. Coxhead Corp., 21 LA 480 (Cahn, 1953); General Elec. Co., 64 LA 765 (Schmertz, 1975).

[82]Koehring Co., 65 LA 638, 640 (1975).

[83]VS Evansville State Hosp., 74 LA 1091 (Deitsch, 1980)(merit increase while employee was on leave); H.K. Porter Co., 55 LA 593 (McDermott, 1970); Singer Co., 57 LA 1261 (Cahn, 1972).

[84]Federal Aviation Admin., 64 LA 289 (Amis, 1975)(consideration of impermissible criterion); Kent State Univ., 59 LA 1007 (Kindig, 1972)(lower performance evaluation because of appointment as union steward); Kansas City Power & Light, 60 LA 852 (Allen, 1973); A.O. Smith Corp., 48 LA 752 (Gundermann, 1967).

[85]Koppers Co., 50 LA 296, 298 (Cayton, 1968).

[86]Pacific Airmotive Corp., 16 LA 508, 509 (1951). See also Cerro Copper & Brass Co., 47 LA 126, 128 (Altrock, 1966).

The question whether a merit evaluation is arbitrary or capricious relates not only to the reasons for that action, but also the procedure followed. Arbitrator Ralph Seward commented:

> If a merit increase system is not to operate arbitrarily, then, there must be some regular system for the periodic review of the employee's merit—some means of ensuring that the timing of increases depends upon orderly, fair and impartial operation of the system rather than on the complaints of employees, or the willingness of a busy foreman to take the time to consider those complaints.[87]

There are a number of reported decisions involving the arbitrability of performance-evaluation or merit grievances.[88] Absent clear evidence that the parties intended to remove matters pertaining to merit adjustments from the purview of arbitrators, performance-evaluation or merit grievances are considered arbitrable.[89]

Use of Subjective Criteria[90]

While arbitrators and courts have recognized management's need to apply criteria involving elements of judgment or discretion in some employment decisions, managers must be wary of fair employment constraints. Subjective evaluations as measures of employee ability and potential have been challenged as discriminatory in a variety of contexts including hiring,[91] promotion,[92] compensation,[93] discharge, or a combination of these and other areas.[94]

---

[87]Bethlehem Steel Co., 26 LA 824, 826 (1956).

[88]Social Sec. Admin., 77 LA 136 (Atleson, 1981).

[89]Washington Aluminum Co., 41 LA 314, 315 (Seidenberg, 1963); National Cash Register Co., 48 LA 421, 424 (Gilden, 1967)("[The] employee has no cause for complaint until some affirmative action, adversely affecting his employment relationship, is taken against him. That is to say, on the allegation that a particular discipline imposed, or a certain promotion that is denied, is in violation of the terms of the labor contract, the employee, unquestionably has a right to grieve.").

[90]See generally Stacy, "Subjective Criteria in Employment Decisions Under Title VII," 10 Ga. L. Rev. 737 (1976); Bartholet, "Application of Title VII to Jobs in High Places," 95 Harv. L. Rev. 947, 973–78 (1982); Comment, "Subjective Employment Criteria and the Future of Title VII in Professional Jobs," 54 U. Det. J. Urb. L. 165 (1976).

[91]Nanty v. Barrows Co., 660 F.2d 1327 (CA 9, 1981).

[92]Page v. U.S. Indus., Inc., 726 F.2d 1038 (CA 5, 1984); Grano v. Department of Development, 699 F.2d 836 (CA 6, 1983); Hung Ping Wang v. Hoffman, 694 F.2d 1146, 30 FEP 703 (CA 9, 1982); Watkins v. Scott Paper Co., 530 F.2d 1159, 12 FEP 1191 (CA 5, 1976).

[93]Heagney v. University of Wash., 642 F.2d 1157 (CA 9, 1981).

[94]Carroll v. Sears, Roebuck & Co., 708 F.2d 183, 32 FEP 286 (CA 5, 1983)(hiring,

Legal Considerations

Title VII of the 1964 Civil Rights Act, which forbids discrimination in employment because of race, color, sex, religion, or national origin, provides the basis for most challenges to subjective evaluations. Violation of Title VII's provisions may be established in one of two ways: (1) under the "disparate treatment" theory, by showing that persons of one race, sex, or ethnic group are treated different from persons of another race, sex, or ethnic group and this difference is not justified by a bona fide occupational qualification, or (2) under the "disparate impact" theory, by demonstrating that a facially neutral employment practice has a significantly discriminatory impact that is not justified by business necessity.

A plaintiff need not prove intentional discrimination under a disparate impact theory, but must show that the employment or selection practice has a substantial adverse impact on a group protected by Title VII. Once a plaintiff establishes a *prima facie* case of disparate impact, the employer must prove either that no disparity exists, or that the practice is necessary to the efficient operation of the business. A *prima facie* case of disparate treatment is established by proof of facts supporting an inference of intentional discrimination.[95] There is disagreement as to which of these theories should be applied in subjectivity cases; however, the later decisions seem to indicate acceptance of either disparate treatment or disparate impact theory.

A distinction has emerged with respect to the permissibility of using subjective criteria, depending on the type of worker involved. The majority of cases lost by companies have involved subjective evaluations of employees in hourly-rate jobs.[96] In such cases a court may enjoin the use of the criteria and require that detailed affirmative steps be taken to eliminate past abuses.[97] When employees are being evaluated for lower-classified jobs, courts presume workers need only pos-

---

job assignment, training, promotion, compensation, termination); Williams v. Anderson, 562 F.2d 1081, 17 FEP 1772 (CA 8, 1977)(assignment, salary, promotion, hiring); United States v. Sheet Metal Workers Local 36, 416 F.2d 123, 2 FEP 127 (CA 8, 1969)(admission to union).

[95]McDonnell Douglas Corp. v. Green, 411 U.S. 792, 5 FEP 965 (1973).

[96]See Schlei & Grossman, Employment Discrimination Law, 192 (BNA Books, 1983).

[97]Baxter v. Savannah Sugar Ref., 495 F.2d 437, 8 FEP 84 (CA 5), cert. denied, 419 U.S. 1033, 8 FEP 1142 (1974).

sess certain minimum physical or mechanical skills to qualify and, thus, are more likely to dismiss subjective criteria as pretexts for discrimination.

The leading "blue collar" case is *Rowe v. General Motors.*[98] In *Rowe*, a black production worker alleged he had been discriminatorily denied promotion to a salaried foreman or clerk position. At the time of his lawsuit, two promotion methods were utilized by management—one whereby an hourly employee's immediate supervisor submitted a recommendation to the general foreman or salaried personnel administrator, who in turn gave it to a 10-person management development committee for majority approval, and the other whereby the employee initiated the process by applying directly to the salaried personnel administrator, who, upon receiving a recommendation from the employee's foreman, submitted the employee's name to the committee. Under either method the foreman's recommendation, which was based in part on a subjective evaluation of "ability, merit, and capacity," and (indirectly) experience, but not seniority, was the key step in the process.

The appellate court found a violation of Title VII because (1) the foremen were given no written instructions pertaining to qualifications necessary for promotion, (2) controlling standards were vague and subjective, (3) hourly employees were not notified of either promotion opportunities or necessary qualifications, (4) there were no procedural safeguards designed to avert discriminatory practices, and (5) the foreman's recommendation was the indispensable single most important factor in the promotion process.[99]

Similarly, the Supreme Court, in *Albemarle Paper Co. v. Moody*,[100] commented as follows about supervisors' subjective ratings as a method validating a discriminatory pencil-and-paper test:

> Albemarle's supervisors were asked to rank employees by a "standard" that was extremely vague and fatally open to divergent interpretations. Each "job grouping" contained a number of different jobs, and the supervisors were asked, in each grouping, to
>
> "determine which ones [employees] they felt irrespective

---

[98]457 F.2d 348, 4 FEP 445 (CA 5, 1972).
[99]4 FEP at 452.
[100]422 U.S. 405, 10 FEP 1181 (1975).

of the job that they were actually doing, but in their respective jobs, did a better job than the person they were rating against. . . ."

There is no way of knowing precisely what criteria of job performance the supervisors were considering, whether each of the supervisors was considering the same criteria or whether, indeed, any of the supervisors actually applied a focused and stable body of criteria of any kind. There is, in short, simply no way to determine whether the criteria *actually* considered were sufficiently related to the Company's legitimate interest in job-specific ability to justify a testing system with a racially discriminatory impact.[101]

Although post-*Rowe* courts have frequently noted that subjective evaluation processes provide ready mechanisms for both race and sex discrimination,[102] they have been reluctant to treat them as unlawful per se,[103] preferring instead a case-by-case determination. The First Circuit has observed that "judicial tolerance of subjective criteria seems to increase with the complexity of the work involved."[104] While at lower levels of white collar employment courts may apply standards similar to those used for blue collar workers, generally "in the white collar context, courts are less likely to insist on the elimination of subjectivity than they are to require that the evaluation procedure be fair and safeguarded."[105] In this regard one commentator has advanced the following argument:

On the upper level, courts have applied a far more lenient standard. Often they simply assert that subjective decision-making is appropriate, and that is the end of the matter: an employer has no burden to demonstrate the job-relatedness, validity, or business necessity of any particular subjective system. . . .

The contrast in judicial attitudes toward subjective systems on the two levels is striking. The discrepancy cannot be explained by differences in the subjective systems at issue. Upper level systems typically involve white decisionmakers passing judgment on black candidates. These decisionmakers typically use criteria so vague that they allow the expression of conscious

---

[101]10 FEP at 1193 (footnotes omitted)(emphasis in original).

[102]Johnson v. Uncle Ben's, Inc., 628 F.2d 419, 426, 24 FEP 1 (CA 5, 1980); Shack v. Southworth, 521 F.2d 51, 55–56, 11 FEP 273 (CA 6, 1975); Royal v. Missouri Highway & Transp. Comm'n., 655 F.2d 159, 164, 26 FEP 587 (CA 8, 1981); Conner v. Fort Gordon Bus Co., 761 F.2d 1495, 37 FEP 1574 (CA 11, 1985)(sex).

[103]Page v. U.S. Indus., Inc., 726 F.2d 1038, 1046, 34 FEP 430 (CA 5, 1984); Hung Ping Wang v. Hoffman, 694 F.2d 1146, 1148, 30 FEP 703 (CA 9, 1982).

[104]Sweeney v. Board of Trustees, 569 F.2d 169, 176 n.14 (CA 1, 1978).

[105]See Waintroob, "The Developing Law of Equal Employment Opportunity at the White Collar and Professional Level," 21 Wm. & Mary L. Rev. 45, 49 (1979).

and unconscious bias—the kind of criteria condemned by the *Albemarle* Court as "fatally open to divergent interpretations." Upper level systems typically grant decisionmakers significant discretion in determining which candidates should ever be considered for selection. But although these features are sufficiently suspect on the lower level to call for condemnation of the subjective process, they are viewed with benign approval on the upper level.[106]

Subjective Evaluations: Practitioner Guide

The use of subjective criteria alone is not prohibited by Title VII and the mere fact that an employer uses subjective considerations in evaluating employees is not sufficient to shift the burden on the company to show job-relatedness. A plaintiff must still demonstrate the discriminatory effect of the subjective criteria.[107] Employers that desire to use subjective evaluative criteria should observe the following guidelines.

1. Management should be conscious of differences in the race and sex of decision makers and applicants. White supervisors and foremen, especially, have been viewed as ready discriminators.[108] While numerous courts have expressed concern that selection procedures that depend almost entirely upon subjective evaluations may be a ready mechanism for discrimination, as stated by the Ninth Circuit, however, "The law does not infer that an individual will exercise or has exercised subjective, discretionary responsibilities in an intentionally discriminatory manner merely from the color of his skin."[109] The point to stress is that practitioners must be ever aware that a subjective evaluation that forms the basis of an adverse employment decision will be subject to particularly close scrutiny wherever the evaluators themselves are not members of the protected class, especially when the job at issue is an unskilled blue collar position.[110]

[106]Bartholet, "Application of Title VII to Jobs in High Places," 95 Harv. L. Rev. 947, 976–78 (1982).
[107]Peters v. Lieuallen, 693 F.2d 966, 968, 30 FEP 706 (CA 9, 1982).
[108]Williams v. City of Montgomery, 550 F.Supp. 662, 33 FEP 1801, 1806 (N.D. Ala., 1982)("the board members relied on such secondary and extremely subjective evidence as the opinion of the two white firepersons' fellow employees . . . ."); Swint v. Pullman Standard, 539 F.2d 77, 105 n.72 (CA 5, 1976), citing numerous decisions.
[109]Gay v. Waiters & Dairy Lunchmen's Union, 694 F.2d 531, 554 n.18, 30 FEP 605 (CA 9, 1982).
[110]Bell v. Bolger, 708 F.2d 1312, 32 FEP 32, 38 (CA 8, 1983)("subjective promotion procedures are to be closely scrutinized because of their susceptibility to discriminatory abuse"); Grano v. Department of Development, 699 F.2d 836, 837 (CA 6, 1983).

2. Management should develop clear, written criteria and instructions for use by supervisors in making employment evaluations. The importance of established, measurable criteria is illustrated by the Fifth Circuit's statement that an "employer may not utilize wholly subjective standards by which to judge its employees' qualifications and then plead lack of qualifications when its promotion process . . . is challenged as discriminatory."[111] Still another appellate court declared that "the failure to establish 'fixed or reasonably objective standards and procedures for hiring' is discriminatory practice."[112]

The Fifth Circuit, in *Carroll v. Sears, Roebuck & Co.,*[113] noted the infirmities in Sears' promotion policies:

> The promotional practices at Sears warrant strict scrutiny by this Court. Sears's promotion criteria are predominately subjective. In the pretrial order, Sears stipulated that its criteria for promotion include fitness and demonstrated ability, employees' past work histories and abilities to produce, annual evaluations, and the opinions of supervisors. Sears has no written criteria or guidelines for promotion, and does not post notices concerning specific job openings or promotion opportunities. It is undisputed that a majority of the supervisors are white. Given the importance of supervisory ratings and opinions and the presence of unwritten, subjective criteria for promotion, black employees face a greater risk of discrimination at Sears.[114]

In *Bell v. Bolger,*[115] the Eighth Circuit ruled that the form used by a promotional review committee was a subjective rating device. The form included nine characteristics for evaluation: (1) appearance, bearing, and manner; (2) ability in oral expression; (3) stability and social adjustment; (4) mental qualities; (5) vitality; (6) maturity; (7) work attitudes; (8) motivation and interest; and (9) subject-matter knowledge. Below each characteristic, the form contained boxes for ratings ranging from "outstanding" to "below average." The appellate court noted that the form had not been validated and, more important, that the use of such a subjective rating device, coupled with statistical evidence of a pattern of discrimination, might be probative evidence of pretext in a disparate treatment case.[116]

---

[111]Crawford v. Western Elec. Co., 614 F.2d 1300, 1315, 22 FEP 819 (CA 5, 1980).
[112]Watson v. National Linen Serv., 686 F.2d 877, 30 FEP 107 (CA 11, 1982).
[113]708 F.2d 183, 32 FEP 286 (CA 5, 1983).
[114]32 FEP at 293.
[115]708 F.2d 1312, 32 FEP 32 (CA 8, 1983).
[116]32 FEP at 38.

Where subjective evaluations are used to assess ability, management should identify those characteristics associated with successful employees and then develop clear guidelines for the exercise of the subjective judgment by the persons evaluating the characteristics of the applicant. If criteria such as "appearance," "bearing," and "attitude" cannot be validly measured, they should be excluded from the evaluation scheme.

3. *Management should provide some type of due process with respect to employment decisions.* Posting of notices of job vacancies, necessary qualifications, and deadlines for application; discussion of supervisory ratings with the employee and opportunity for review by at least two other supervisors; and some mechanism for appeal to top management present possible procedures that management should consider in order to provide some type of due process. In this regard one federal court found that the disparate impact inherent in subjective criteria was reduced by the institution of procedures and standards to control and review subjective judgments.[117] Within the context of an admission interview for an apprentice program in the sheet metal trades, the district court for the District of Columbia, in *Reynolds v. Sheet Metal Workers Local 102*,[118] discussed the use of subjective evaluations and the absence of review procedures:

> Subjective evaluations have been condemned, whether as a means of admitting applicants into unions or determining those employees qualified for promotions. . . . The interview procedure at issue in this case has many of the undesirable characteristics associated with subjective evaluations: categories such as "attitude," "interest in trade," "work experience" are likely to reflect the subjective judgments of the interviewers; no guidelines exist elaborating upon or narrowing the criteria, e.g. what work experience might be important in predicting an applicant's success in the program; the interviewers' judgments are unreviewable.[119]

4. *To the extent possible, lower-level supervisors should seek to build informal contacts with minority employees.* In *Rowe*, testimony of a foreman as to his complete absence of

---

[117]EEOC v. E.I. du Pont de Nemours & Co., 445 F.Supp. 223, 16 FEP 847, 869 (D. Del., 1977).
[118]498 F.Supp. 952, 24 FEP 648, 666–67 (D.D.C., 1980).
[119]24 FEP at 666. See also Dearborn Fabricating & Eng'g Co., 64 LA 271, 275 (Kallenbach, 1975)(rejecting "initiative" and "ambition" as measures of an employee's ability to perform a job).

familial or social association with blacks was accepted as evidence of an enhanced likelihood of discrimination. Accordingly, lower-level management should establish and maintain informal contact in order to bridge this gap.

Management as Sole Judge of Ability

Some agreements provide that management is the sole judge of an employee's ability and qualifications.[120] In *Teamsters Local 89 v. Hays & Nicoulin, Inc.*,[121] the bargaining agreement stated that "the [employer] shall be the sole judge of the qualifications, capability, number, purpose and tenure of the employees." When an arbitrator concluded, on the basis of expert medical testimony, that an employee's bad health did not render him unfit for work, the Sixth Circuit ruled that under the above-cited language the arbitrator could not contradict the company's determination that an employee was unfit.

In a similar case, an employer claimed that a discharge was not arbitrable because the contract provided: "The Employer shall be the sole judge of the employee's capabilities to perform work in a workmanlike manner." The agreement also compelled arbitration of all disputes, unless the arbitration clause "was in conflict with some other portion of the agreement." The Fifth Circuit, in holding the dispute arbitrable, reasoned that the contract contained a no-strike clause and concluded that some *quid pro quo* was required from management. The court stated:

> Without some accountability under the bargaining agreements, [the employer] could discharge any employee and could avoid arbitration by merely phrasing the discharge in terms of the employee's failure to perform properly. To avoid this interpretation of the otherwise clear language of the "sole discretion" clause before us, but, at the same time to protect a party's right to withhold certain issues from the scope of arbitration, the accountability required on these facts must be limited to determining whether the employer acted in good faith, and not arbitrarily, in making the discharges.[122]

---

[120]See, e.g., Ivers & Pond Piano Co., 42 LA 88, 89 (Autrey, 1964); John Strange Paper Co., 43 LA 1184, 1186 (Larkin, 1965).

[121]594 F.2d 1093, 100 LRRM 2998 (CA 6, 1979).

[122]Plumbers & Steamfitters Local 52 v. Daniel of Alabama, 479 F.2d 342, 343, 83 LRRM 2522 (CA 5, 1973). See also Klochko Equip. Rental Co. v. Operating Eng'rs Local 324, 110 LRRM 2875 (E.D. Mich., 1982).

Notwithstanding the view of the Sixth Circuit, most arbitrators hold that provisions of this type do not accord management the absolute right to determine qualifications merely by asserting that an employee is unqualified. The better view, as expressed by the Fifth Circuit, is that management must provide some rational basis for its action.

Chapter 12

Seniority: Promotion and Demotion

Promotions

A BNA study found that seniority was assigned some role in promotion decisions in 72 percent of the contracts surveyed and was the sole factor in 5 percent of the agreements. Under this latter system the most senior employee will be promoted without regard to qualifications. In the 40 percent of the contracts with "sufficient ability" clauses, seniority was the determining criterion when the employee was qualified for the job. It was a secondary factor to be considered when other factors were equal in the 24 percent of the contracts with "relative ability" clauses. Two percent of the agreements provided that seniority would be given "equal" weight with other criteria in making promotion decisions.[1]

Management has traditionally argued that, absent any limitation in the parties' contract, it has the inherent right to direct and manage the operations of the business and that this includes the right to evaluate and select employees for jobs within the organization. Unions, on the other hand, deny that employers have an inherent, absolute right to evaluate and select employees. Instead, they argue that even when the agreement is silent this power is subject to a reasonableness requirement and therefore cannot be exercised in an arbitrary, capricious, or unreasonable manner. This philosophical

---

[1]Basic Patterns in Union Contracts, 75 (BNA Books, 1983).

clash is most sharply displayed where "competitive status" seniority issues are raised.[2]

Contractual Basis for Seniority

The idea of allocating benefits or status by a longevity criterion is not unique to collective bargaining in the United States. Carl Gersuny, investigating the origins of seniority provisions in collective bargaining, writes that over 1000 years ago in the Sung dynasty, allocation of promotion in the Chinese civil service was governed by time in grade. Moreover, from the end of the 18th century the principle of seniority had been applied in matters of reward and promotion in the Prussian bureaucracy. The British civil service adopted seniority principles in 1854. Gersuny notes that in the private sector, the American railroads were the first to allocate job benefits according to length of service.[3]

Traditionally, unions consider seniority both as a useful method of preventing arbitrary action by management and as an organizational tool. Gersuny explains:

> Unions, as organizations formed to give coherent voice to the interests of their members, seek due process in the workplace not only through establishment of grievance machinery but also by means of seniority rules. Seniority is germane to due process because its implementation serves to restrict management's capacity for applying arbitrary and capricious criteria in making invidious distinctions among employees. Invidious distinctions may be unavoidable when one person is promoted while another is passed over and when one is retained while another is laid off. Seniority rights provide an element of due process by limiting nepotism and unfairness in personnel decisions.
>
> Seniority also serves to buttress the bargaining power of unions by curbing competitive and aggressive behavior that pits one worker against another. Instead of fighting among

---

[2]"Competitive status" seniority is concerned with layoff, rehire, promotion, demotion, transfer, and other items in which employees are in competition with each other. It is different from "benefits" seniority, which depends solely on an employee's length of service and is used for allocation of contractual benefits such as vacation, retirement pay, and severance pay. Both of these concepts should be distinguished from the use of seniority as a mitigating factor in discipline cases. See Slichter, Healy, and Livernash, The Impact of Collective Bargaining on Management, 106 (Brookings Institution, 1960).

[3]Gersuny, "Origins of Seniority Provisions in Collective Bargaining," Proceedings of the Industrial Relations Research Association (IRRA), 518 (Spring Meeting, 1982).

themselves over scarce opportunities and currying favor with supervisors—behavior which enhances employers' capacity to divide and rule—employees submit to a hierarchic principle based on institutional age. Within limits, seniority provides an objective criterion of time priority for making distinctions. Thus, seniority reinforces the bargaining strength of unions, a strength that would vanish if the shop floor became the scene of cutthroat competition for preferment.[4]

In a paper delivered to the National Academy of Arbitrators, Jay Kramer argued that seniority rights are a form of property, but that just as private property rights are not absolute, seniority rights are limited in various ways.

I would suggest to you that seniority is job security. Thus, as generally understood, can it not be said, at least provocatively and to stimulate discussion and analysis, that seniority rights are the wage earner's equivalent of the right which we all call the right to private property? But private property is not an absolute right. It is limited in various ways, and so, too, with seniority rights. . . .

Just as our private property may be large at one moment and then subject to contraction or diminution by governmental taxation, so too is seniority a mountain of support for "layoff" purposes and a mere hillock of protection as against "bumping." . . . Private property may be lessened in capital gains fashion or by the greater inroads of ordinary income tax, dependent upon the nature of the transaction involved. So also with seniority. It may be greater in retaining one's job and mean much less if promotion is involved and "ability" or "adaptability" or "competence" come into play. Finally, just as the non-wage earner's private property or, if you will, the wage earner's private property in his "non-industrial life" is subject to elimination by "eminent domain" and "condemnation" or business failure, so too may seniority be eliminated by merger or technological displacement—both factors hardly within the control of the individual wage earner.[5]

With few exceptions[6] seniority rights derive their scope and significance exclusively from union contracts. As such, employees have no inherent, constitutional, or natural right

---

[4]Id. at 519 (emphasis omitted).

[5]Kramer, "Seniority and Ability," Proceedings of the 9th Annual Meeting of NAA, 41–42 (BNA Books, 1956).

[6]See, e.g., Aeronautical Indus. Dist. Lodge 727 v. Campbell, 337 U.S. 521, 24 LRRM 2173 (1949); Ford Motor Co. v. Huffman, 345 U.S. 330, 31 LRRM 2548 (1953)(upholding contract giving seniority credits for pre-employment military service as not violating Selective Training and Service Act of 1940); Teamsters v. United States, 431 U.S. 324, 14 FEP 1514 (1977)(awarding seniority credits to identifiable victims of race discrimination as a Title VII remedy).

to seniority. Arbitrators and courts have uniformly held that seniority does not exist in the abstract and an employee acquires no seniority rights apart from the collective bargaining agreement. This doctrine was best expressed by one arbitrator as follows:

> [W]hatever seniority rights employees have exist only by virtue of the collective bargaining agreement that is in existence between the union and the employer. Such seniority rights depend wholly upon the contract. . . . Before a collective bargaining contract is in existence, there are no seniority rights. . . .
> How does this situation change when a collective bargaining agreement is in existence? It changes to the extent that these rights are given up by the employer and given to the workers under the terms of the contract. Therefore, whatever the employer has yielded in his absolute time-established rights of hiring, firing, promoting, and demoting and whatever the workers have gained in the way of seniority rights with respect to these matters must be measured entirely by the contract.[7]

Further, employees' seniority rights may be changed by a subsequent contract without their consent, absent arbitrary, capricious, or discriminatory action by the parties. One arbitrator, reviewing case law, stated the principle as follows:

> "As a general rule, courts have stated that absent bad faith, arbitrary action, fraud, or racial discrimination, a collective bargaining agreement altering or even extinguishing seniority rights of an employee is valid, since it is usually recognized that if a union has the power to enter into a contract creating seniority rights, it likewise has the power to enter into a contract which modifies those rights in the interest of all its members."[8]

"Straight" Seniority Provisions

Unmodified or "straight" seniority provisions are rarely found in collective bargaining agreements. Instead, most contracts provide for a combined consideration of seniority and ability in promotion or demotion decisions. Where unmodified provisions exist, managerial discretion is limited (at least in theory) to selecting the most senior employee without regard to qualifications.

Does this mean that management is obligated to select

---

[7]Alan Wood Steel Co., 4 LA 52, 54 (Brandschain, 1946).
[8]Washington County, Or., 78 LA 1081, 1086 (Tilbury, 1982), quoting 90 ALR 2d 1004.

an employee who clearly is not qualified for the position? Probably not. Unless there is evidence that the parties intended such an absurd result, the better rule is that the senior employee will be promoted if he can perform the job at some bare minimum level of competency. This, in turn, may mandate a trial or even a training period[9] if it appears that the employee, while not presently qualified, has the potential ability to perform the job.

"Sufficient Ability" Provisions

"Sufficient ability" clauses require management to assign, promote, or retain the employee with the longest continuous service if the employee is qualified to perform the job. The fact that a junior employee is more qualified is of no effect. In cases involving sufficient-ability clauses, most arbitrators place the burden on the employer to show that the by-passed senior employee is not competent. As pointed out by former arbitrator and now Judge Harry Edwards, where work is of a semi-skilled or low-skilled nature, a sufficient-ability standard is virtually the same as a straight seniority approach.[10]

"Relative Ability" Provisions

Under a "relative ability" type of seniority provision, seniority is the determining factor only if the qualifications of competing employees are "relatively" equal. The question of "relative ability" involves comparing competing employees on all the qualities that indicate capacity to perform a job. Management is responsible for making the initial determination as to which employee is better qualified and awarding that employee the position. Unless otherwise limited by the parties' agreement, management's decision is subject to challenge through the grievance-arbitration procedure.

When comparing two employees under a relative-ability clause, Arbitrator D. L. Howell reflected the thinking of most arbitrators when he stated:

---

[9]Trial and training periods are discussed in Chapter 11, supra notes, 62–73, and accompanying text.

[10]Edwards, "Seniority Systems in Collective Bargaining," Arbitration in Practice, 126 (ILR Press, New York State School of Industrial & Labor Relations, Cornell Univ., Zack ed., 1984).

[E]ven with the use of tests, one must be mindful that a seniority clause is being construed, which is intended to grant certain preferences to the senior employee. This comparison is at best inexact. Human beings are different and cannot be inspected and measured as finished products from the assembly line. Doubt must be resolved in favor of the senior employee. The words "relative ability" do not suggest exactness or absolute equality. An approximate or near equality is sufficient. Since the nod is to be given to the senior in close cases, it is usually held by arbitrators that the junior must demonstrate more than slight superiority. His greater ability should be clearly discernible to outweigh the factor of seniority.[11]

This principle is also termed the "head and shoulders rule." That is, other considerations being equal, unless a junior is proved by management to be "head and shoulders" above the senior employee in ability, the junior is not entitled to a promotion under a relative-ability clause. Similar standards include "substantially and demonstrably superior," "significantly, measurably, and demonstrably greater," and "measurably and substantially superior."[12] Even under a "head and shoulders" rule, the nature of the job is probably the key variable that influences the thinking of many arbitrators. Comparative ability plays a greater role in the higher-skilled jobs, and in these disputes a "slight" edge in a junior employee's ability may normally suffice.

Similarly, when a seniority provision uses the terms "equal" or "relatively equal," in comparing competing employees' ability, ability need not be exactly equal in order for the seniority factor to predominate.[13] Still, absent qualifying language in the parties' agreement, arbitrators have applied the ability factor differently to promotion cases than to movements down the scale. Harry Edwards points out that there may be a presumption that employees in the upper-level jobs can always perform the lower-classified work:

[I]t is important to recall that seniority does not always apply comparably in all kinds of job movements. Thus, for example, seniority may be a more weighty factor in job movements downward than in promotion situations. If the employing enterprise

---

[11]Screw Conveyor Corp., 72 LA 434, 436–37 (1979). See also Lancaster School Dist., 72 LA 693 (Raymond, undated); British Overseas Airways, 61 LA 768, 769 (Turkus, 1973).
[12]Mountain States Tel. & Tel. Co., 70 LA 729, 741 (Goodman, 1978).
[13]See the review of case authority by Arbitrator Roger Tilbury in Washington County, Or., 78 LA 1081, 1085 (1982).

has a relatively narrow upward path of jobs and employees at the upper end of the job progression generally are able to perform the work in jobs below them, the parties may rely on seniority alone for regression and layoffs. In other words, there is a convenient presumption that employees in the upper level jobs can always perform lower level work.[14]

Another well-known arbitrator, James Hill, notes that "[i]t was a general viewpoint and experience that the competitive standard applies to promotions, while capacity to do the work applies in down-grading and transfers associated with layoff," but again, "it all depends on the particular agreement at issue."[15]

Standard and Burden of Proof

Harry Edwards has argued that "arbitrators continue to differ on the nature of the evidence required and the burden of proof in seniority cases involving an application of the relatively equal test."[16] The Eighth Circuit's decision in *Teamsters Local 120 v. Sears, Roebuck & Co,*[17] provides an interesting illustration of the deference accorded arbitrators in decisions where the standard of proof is not spelled out in the parties' contract. The agreement provided that "length of service will be recognized in filling vacancies and making promotions when, in the opinion of the Company, merit and ability are substantially equal."[18] A grievance was filed when management awarded a junior employee a carpenter's position. A tripartite arbitration panel, chaired by Arbitrator John Flagler, ruled that the senior employee should have received the position, and that the burden of proof rested on the company to establish that the two employees were not substantially equal in terms of their ability to perform the carpenter's job. Further, the arbitration panel held that it was necessary for the company to sustain its burden by "clear and convincing evidence" in order to justify the decision to pass over an employee with substantially more seniority (13 years). According to the court

---

[14]Edwards, supra note 10, at 129.
[15]Hill, Summary, "Seniority and Ability," supra note 5, at 46.
[16]Edwards, supra note 10, at 127.
[17]535 F.2d 1072, 92 LRRM 2980 (CA 8, 1976).
[18]92 LRRM at 2981.

of appeals, the following reasons underlay the arbitration panel's determination of the standard of proof:

> (1) seniority rights have been considered under law as fundamental constitutional rights; (2) length of service has been recognized in industrial relations as a property right; and (3) the burden of proof is placed on the party best able to improve the employee evaluation process.[19]

In refusing to enforce the award, the district court disagreed with the arbitration panel's conclusion that the company was required to sustain its burden by "clear and convincing evidence." The lower court emphasized that the parties' agreement and its history were devoid of any basis for holding the company to a "clear and convincing standard" when, in a civil case, a party need only sustain a burden of proof by a "preponderance of the evidence." The appellate court reversed. Holding that the district court "erroneously substituted its judgment for that of the arbitration panel" with respect to the content of the burden of proof, the court reasoned that the agreement did not define the standard of proof, and neither "the language in the contract nor the bargaining history expressly or specifically prohibits [the] panel from articulating a standard."[20] The court went on to point out that its function, as a reviewing court, is limited, but even assuming that a review of the merits was proper, "the arbitration panel's ostensible reliance on a 'clear and convincing' burden of proof was not necessarily improper." The court explained:

> It is not clear whether the language "clear and convincing" in the arbitration panel majority opinion, written by a non-attorney, was utilized as a legal term of art distinct from "preponderance of the evidence" or "greater weight of the evidence." Furthermore, the imposition of a "clear and convincing" standard is not unique in the field of industrial relations.[21]

Seniority Provision Guideline

Many of the problems involving employee seniority and promotion or demotion can be avoided by careful drafting of

---

[19]Id. at 2981 n.2.
[20]Id. at 2982, citing Meat Cutters Dist. 540 v. Neuhoff Bros. Packers, Inc., 481 F.2d 817, 819, 83 LRRM 2652 (CA 5, 1973).
[21]Id. at 2983, citing Norton & Son, Inc., 49 LA 275 (Jones, 1967); Interlake Steel Corp., 46 LA 23 (Luskin, 1965); Darin & Armstrong, 13 LA 843 (Platt, 1950).

the seniority provision. Perhaps the best checklist is offered by Rothschild, Merrifield, and Edwards:

(1) For what purposes is seniority to be recognized? Reductions in force (layoffs)? Re-employment after layoff? Promotions? Transfers? Shift preferences? Work assignments?

(2) What *kind* of seniority is to be recognized? Company length of service? Plant length of service? Department length of service? Occupational group length of service? Job classification length of service? Some combination of these? May this depend in part on the degree of complexity of the plant and the variety of different occupational skills required in the operation? How does the type of seniority comply with the anti-discrimination proscriptions of federal law?

(3) To what degree shall seniority be made the controlling factor? Entirely controlling? Controlling if the employee has the necessary job competence? Controlling if relative merit and ability are relatively equal? Not controlling at all, but only a factor to be "considered," along with others?

(4) How shall an employee's seniority standing be determined? Credit, if any, to be given for non-working time (sick leave, layoffs, leave of absence, etc.)? Credit, if any, to be given for time spent outside the bargaining unit (prior to initial agreement, subsequent to initial agreement)? "Super-seniority" for union officers or others?

(5) Under what circumstances shall seniority be lost or forfeited? Resignation? Discharge? Extended layoff or other absence from work? Transfers to jobs outside the bargaining unit? Change in employer status (merger, consolidation, abandonment of facilities, relocation of plant)?[22]

Is There a Presumption Favoring Management?

While many arbitrators have placed the burden of proof upon management to demonstrate that a junior employee is more qualified when a senior employee is by-passed, the cases indicate that arbitrators have accorded a presumption in favor of management's assessment of an employee's ability. Arbitrator Jerome Klein stated in *Shenango Furnace Co.*:[23]

It is a well established principle of Arbitration Law that the determination of whether or not an employee is qualified to perform the duties of a particular job is initially a judgment of Management . . . and Management's decision in this regard will

---

[22]Rothschild, Merrifield, and Edwards, Collective Bargaining and Labor Arbitration, 583–84 (Bobbs-Merrill, 1979)(emphasis in original).
[23]46 LA 203 (1966).

not be upset unless found to be unreasonable, arbitrary, capricious, discriminatory or made in bad faith.[24]

Arbitrator William Belshaw pointed out that there are two schools of thought, regardless of whether an arbitrator is dealing with a "comparative ability" or "sufficient ability" situation:

> The first of these calls for a decider to review an employer determination with the understanding that it can be set aside only upon satisfactory proof that it was not *bona fide*, but was, instead, the result of bias, prejudice or mistake. The second (and probably the better) calls for a trial of the company's determination "in terms of reasonable, demonstrable and objective standards." (It is never the function of an arbitrator to rework the company's decision, but is, rather, to examine its manner, without judgment substitution).[25]

Arbitrator James Hill, in a discussion before the National Academy of Arbitrators, summarized arbitrators' views on this subject when he reported the consensus of a workshop devoted to seniority and ability considerations.

> A fairly basic proposition was made, which seemed to command general support. This was that the determination of ability must be made by the management, and the issue should not be one of the arbitrator's judgment versus that of the management but whether the company's determination was arbitrary, capricious (the proponent's adjective was "whimsical"), or discriminatory. If not, this should end the matter. While each side musk seek to persuade the arbitrator of his position, it was recognized that it is a managerial responsibility to make the determination and initiate the action, that there is an area of latitude for judgment and discretion, and that within this area, bound as it were by the adjectives suggested, the employer's decision should not be overruled on grounds that the arbitrator might have reached a different conclusion.[26]

In this respect the interpretation of "arbitrary," "capricious," or "discriminatory" is especially important. One arbitrator, in determining that an evaluation was not arbitrary,

---

[24]Id. at 208. See also Reynolds Metals Co., 66 LA 1276, 1280 (Volz, 1976); Anaconda Aluminum Co., 63-2 ARB ¶8583 (Peck, 1963); Marathon Elec. Mfg. Corp., 31 LA 656 (O'Rourke, 1958); Sandia Corp., 31 LA 338 (Hayes, 1958); Youngstown Hosp. Ass'n, 79 LA 324 (Duff, 1982)(demonstration of discriminatory animus by asking female what she would do with painter's wages, with which a man could support a family); Computing & Software, Inc., 61 LA 261, 264 (Shieber, 1973).

[25]Zenith Elec. Corp., 80 LA 525, 527 (1983)(footnotes omitted).

[26]Hill, Summary, "Seniority and Ability," supra note 5, at 45–46.

capricious, or discriminatory, listed the following considerations in support of his decision:

(*1*) The evaluation of the grievant was fair.

(a) The length of the training period was sufficient and applied to all promotions contractually.

(b) The preferred standard of observed performance was used.

(c) There was sufficient instruction, assistance, and full cooperation of the mechanics.

(d) There was no specific evidence that the standard was not the same as had been applied to previous helpers under actual day-to-day conditions.

(e) There was no evidence of a past practice of company-wide policy for all evaluations to be in written form.

. . .

2. There were numerous formal and informal sessions with the grievant in regard to his failure to meet job requirements.

3. It cannot be concluded that there was a conspiracy to get the grievant.[27]

The distinguished arbitrator Harry Platt elaborated further on the meaning of "arbitrary action" in the general area of evaluating employees:

"Arbitrary Action" has acquired a fairly clear meaning. . . . [T]he term has been defined as a "failure of the Company's supervisory personnel to follow the Company's various instructions and procedures pertaining to any phase of the selection process. It is the failure to properly weigh the various factors which are considered in the selection determination. (This of course, includes the error of allowing one factor being evaluated to become controlling.) It is the failure to properly and fairly investigate all factors. It is the failure to afford each candidate a full, fair and impartial opportunity to have his qualifications considered. And, in regard to testing, it is the failure to be reasonable and fair in light of that which is known or prudently ascertainable at the time of crucial decisions." In general, it may be added, action is arbitrary when it is without consideration and in disregard of facts and circumstances of a case, without rational basis, justification or excuse.[28]

Demotions

There are times when an employee is prevented from exercising his seniority rights. Demotions (downgrades) for med-

---

[27] Gulf State Utilities Co., 62 LA 1061, 1090 (Williams, 1974)(emphasis omitted).
[28] South Cent. Bell Tel. Co. (Meridan, Miss.), 52 LA 1104, 1108–09 (1969)(quoting from union's brief).

ical reasons, unacceptable job performance, or for disciplinary purposes are often imposed by management. In this regard, an employee's unsatisfactory job performance may result from factors within the control of the employee (inattentiveness, carelessness, negligence, indifference, poor attitude, for example), or it may result from factors beyond his control, such as physical or mental disorder. Management is free to respond to either situation. If, as noted by one arbitrator, it is responding to willful or blameworthy misconduct that can be corrected, then the response is considered to be disciplinary; if management is responding to innocent or involuntary conduct, then the response is nondisciplinary.[29] This distinction is especially important when considering management's right to demote or downgrade an employee.

Demotion for Medical Reasons[30]

Where for mental, physical, or emotional reasons an employee can no longer competently perform a particular job, arbitrators have not hesitated to sustain a management decision to demote an employee to a lower-rated position. For instance, Arbitrator Ira Jaffe, describing a grievant as a danger to himself and others, in *Roper Corp.*[31] sustained his transfer from expeditor/material handler to the lower-rated classification of production laborer where the evidence showed that the employee was sickness- or accident-prone (no other employee had reported to the first aid office with the same degree of frequency as the grievant).

Similarly, in *United Parcel Service, Inc.*,[32] Arbitrator H. Ellsworth Steele reflected the thinking of most arbitrators in stating that a company can maintain and enforce minimum medical standards for its employees. The arbitrator accordingly ruled that it was permissible to remove a diabetic on insulin from a driver position and to assign him a lower-rated position of car washer.

Arbitrators have even sustained a demotion where the employee was unable to perform only a small portion of the

---

[29]Libby, McNeill & Libby of Canada, Ltd., 74 LA 991, 996–97 (O'Shea, 1980).

[30]For a related discussion, see Marlin Volz, "Medical and Health Issues in Labor Arbitration," Proceedings of the 31st Annual Meeting of NAA, 156–86 (BNA Books, 1979).

[31]78 LA 1160 (1982).

[32]61 LA 765 (1973).

work due to a medical condition or disability. They reason that an employer is not required to keep an employee on the job who cannot perform 100 percent of a job's duties.[33]

Hughes Aircraft Co.,[34] a decision reported by Arbitrator Howard Block, reflects the better weight of arbitral authority on this subject:

> When an employee has a physical disability which endangers his own safety or that of other employees, the Company has the responsibility of taking corrective action. . . . The Union has the right to challenge Management's decision when it believes that the Agreement has been violated. If the Company's decision is based upon a full and fair consideration of all relevant factors and its action is reasonable, its determination should be sustained.[35]

Incapacity to Work Overtime

Arbitrators are split over whether an employee can be demoted for a refusal to work overtime based on bona fide medical reasons. In *National Vendors*,[36] Arbitrator Leo Brown addressed the issue as follows:

> How should the situation be handled in the future when an employee assigned to work overtime produces a doctor's certificate that says he can't work the overtime?

Arbitrator Brown concluded:

> When an employee presents a doctor's certificate to the effect that he or she is unable to work the overtime scheduled on his or her job, the employer may require such employee to take a leave of absence until such time as he or she presents a doctor's certificate stating that the employee is able to work the overtime scheduled for his or her job.[37]

Arbitrator Marlin Volz suggested that a distinction must be made between a bona fide illness which constitutes an excuse for refusing a particular overtime assignment and a

---

[33]See, e.g., Crucible, Inc., 80 LA 28 (Strongin, 1982); Midland-Ross Corp., 76 LA 1161 (Falcone, 1981)(demotion of maintenance and production electrician for injury to wrist); Handy & Harman, 60 LA 1184 (James, 1973)(demotion of employee for being overweight).
[34]41 LA 535 (1963).
[35]Id. at 541.
[36]72-1 ARB ¶8272 (1972).
[37]Id. at 3920, 3922.

blanket medical restriction which prevents the employee from working any overtime:

> [I]t must be concluded that [the grievant] was willing and physically able to work normal workdays of eight hours five days per week for a normal workweek of 40 hours. The question for decision is whether the Company violated the contract and abused its managerial discretion by not permitting her to work under work restrictions which prevented her from working any overtime. Unless the total contractual relationship between the parties provides otherwise no different standard as to physical fitness to perform the full duties of the job exists where an employee returns to work after layoff or after illness or injury. Just as when he or she is originally hired or at any other time, an employee in the above mentioned situations must possess the physical ability, except as the contract specifies differently, to perform the normal and unusual duties of the job throughout the workday and workweek, including reasonable amounts of overtime work. What is reasonable depends on the circumstances. . . . A distinction must be made between a situation where bona fide illness or physical disorders is offered as an excuse for refusing a particular overtime assignment and one where a blanket medical restriction prevents the employee from working any overtime. In the latter situation it is generally held that management does not abuse its inherent managerial discretion in directing the work force if it determines that the employee is not qualified to perform the work.[38]

On this same issue, Arbitrator Thomas Christopher, in *General Telephone Co. of California*,[39] held that an employer could not demote an employee who, for medical reasons, could not work one and one-half to two hours of overtime on a daily basis. The contract provided for final "decisions" by the employer, including the right to establish job requirements. However, these decisions cannot be arbitrary, capricious, or unreasonable when they affect the employment relationship since, the arbitrator said, "In every contract there exists an implied covenant of good faith and fair dealing . . . ."[40] The employer was wrong, according to the arbitrator, to insist that the grievant work overtime on a continuous basis.

Demotion for Unsatisfactory Performance

Arbitrators have declared that an employee's obligation to perform his or her job on a satisfactory basis is a continuous

---

[38] Anaconda Aluminum Co., 66 LA 269, 271–72 (1976).
[39] 79 LA 399 (1982).
[40] Id. at 402.

one. The late Harry Shulman, speaking of demotions in a reduction-in-force case, declared:

[I]n the interest of achieving optimum performance, the Company may make periodic or sporadic appraisals of its employees and demote those whose performance falls below standard. We may assume further that the obligation to perform satisfactorily is a continuous condition of the maintenance of the better job, and that an employee's performance, though once adequate, may fall below standard and merit demotion, either because his own performance has deteriorated or, though it has not deteriorated, because the standard in his occupation has been raised by the greater ability of those around him. Such a demotion would be an instance of the Company's continuing interest in the satisfactory performance of each of its jobs.[41]

Arbitrator Thomas McDermott has recognized management's right to effect a demotion even after the employee's performance has been satisfactory for a long period of time.

[I]t is possible that an employee through the years may perform his job in a satisfactory manner, but at a later time his performance may deteriorate to the point of becoming unsatisfactory. If the basis for the deterioration is beyond the control of the employee, and keeping him on his present job creates a safety hazard or results in below standard output, then it is within the authority of the employer to demote the employee down to the next highest ranking job that is within his capabilities. In such case it is not a disciplinary matter, but one of incompetence. On the other hand if the deterioration grows out of personal misconduct, then disciplinary measures are in order with the object of correcting the misbehavior and of trying to make the employee once again a fully productive person on his job.[42]

Similarly, Arbitrator Whitley McCoy said:

[T]he Union argues that "when an employee takes a job, he retains the job until he quits or is fired." I know of no such principle. The books are full of decisions justifying actions of companies in disqualifying employees who are not able to perform the job they are on, even though they had previously qualified on the job. There is such a thing as an employee losing his skill with age, ill-health, or infirmity.[43]

Most reported demotion cases are based on an employee's alleged incompetency or defective job performance. In this

---

[41]Ford Motor Co., Case No. 53 (1943) (400-Highland Park), as cited in Opinions of the Umpire, 1943–46 (New York State School of Industrial Relations).
[42]Duquesne Light Co., 48 LA 1108, 1112 (1967).
[43]H.K. Porter Co., 44 LA 1180, 1182 (1965).

respect many arbitrators have ruled that, unless the agreement provides otherwise, an employee should not be demoted without first having been warned that his or her performance was not satisfactory.[44] Other arbitrators have declared that the company, in effecting a demotion, must demonstrate that the employee was unqualified and that the employee received the training and orientation necessary to satisfy the stated job requirements. This includes, but is not limited to, according the employee the full trial period provided in the agreement or by the parties' past practice.[45] Some arbitrators have even required management, in effecting a permanent demotion, to subject the employee to a medical examination to determine whether there was some deterioration in mental, physical, or emotional abilities that affected job performance.[46]

The reported decisions indicate that arbitrators accord management more discretion in deciding to demote an employee in a supervisory or leadership position than in demoting an ordinary worker.[47]

Punitive Demotions

Many companies have argued that even though the labor agreement does not expressly confer the right to demote for disciplinary reasons, management retains this right as a residual power or reserved right.[48] While this is not the majority view, some arbitrators recognize that a company may demote an employee pursuant to the management rights clause, but require that such disciplinary demotions be for just cause. For example, in *Ameron Corrosion Control Division*,[49] Arbitrator W. Albert Rill held that management could demote a "leadman" to a shipper position where it was shown that he left work under false pretense. The contract provided that once

---

[44]San Antonio Air Logistics Center, 74 LA 486 (Coffey, 1979); Parkin Printing & Stationery Co., 76 LA 1075 (Robinson, 1981).

[45]Hayes Int'l Corp., 61 LA 1295 (Nicholas, 1973); Timex Corp., 63 LA 758 (Gruenberg, 1974).

[46]Scott Paper Co., 61 LA 617 (Somers, 1973).

[47]See, e.g., Von's Grocery Co., 61 LA 347 (Gentile, 1973); Dixie Elec. Mfg. Co., 63 LA 392 (Crane, 1974). Selection and removal of supervisors is discussed in Chapter 17.

[48]See, e.g., the discussion by Arbitrator Burton Turkus in Trans World Airlines, 66 LA 1193, 1197 (1976).

[49]66 LA 588 (1976).

selected to the leadman position, the employee was to be retained in that capacity so long as his performance remained acceptable. The arbitrator found the demotion "morally justified" in that the employee's conduct breached the trust that the company had placed in him.

Nevertheless, the majority of arbitrators take the position that demotion is not a proper form of discipline because it abridges seniority rights[50] and is for an indefinite period of time. Arbitrator Thomas McDermott expressed what is believed to be the better view as follows:

> The Union position that demotion may not be used as a form of discipline is consistent with the findings of most arbitrators. The most generally held principle is that absent a specific contractual provision permitting such, demotion is an improper form of penalty in discipline cases. The particular reason given in support of this finding is that the use of demotion is an indeterminate sentence, which has no terminal point and may go far beyond the extent of the penalty warranted by the infraction committed. Also the use of a demotion encompasses more than a simple penalty for an infraction. It may violate the employee's seniority rights under the contract or adversely affect pension or other individual benefits guaranteed him by the labor agreement.[51]

Additionally, one arbitrator reasoned that by demoting an employee without any measurable limitation on the duration of the discipline, the company not only secured the same result as a discharge but also circumvented the burden of proof necessary to sustain a discharge action.[52]

Elkouri and Elkouri cite still another rationale for not permitting an employer to demote for disciplinary reasons:

> Management has also been denied the right to discipline an employee by demotion where the contract gave the employer the right to discipline employees by various specified means which did not include demotion, on the theory of "expressio unius est exclusio alterius" [to express one thing is to exclude others]. Management likewise has not been upheld in demoting an employee for occasional carelessness or failure to obey in-

---

[50]Metromedia v. Stage Employees Local 819, 105 LRRM 2908 (CA DC, 1980)(upholding award that overturned disciplinary demotion as violative of seniority rights).

[51]Duquesne Light Co., 48 LA 1108, 1111 (1967), citing Republic Steel Corp., 25 LA 733 (Platt, 1955); Kroger Co., 61-3 ARB ¶8844 [37 LA 345] (Barrett, 1961); Lukens Steel Co., 42 LA 252 (Crawford, 1963); National Carbide Co., 47 LA 154 (Kesselman, 1966).

[52]Trans World Airlines, 66 LA 1193, 1197 (Turkus, 1976).

structions, the arbitrator distinguishing between a lack of ability and temporary poor performance, but recognizing that some form of discipline should be imposed in such a case.[53]

Demotion for lack of ability to perform a job properly, however, is upheld by the majority of arbitrators where the action is not explained as being taken for disciplinary reasons. Arbitrator David Keefe, in *City of River Rouge*,[54] argued that a distinction must be made between a careless or indifferent worker and an incompetent worker. A careless worker is capable of performing his job but chooses not to fulfill this obligation, he said. Accordingly, he can be disciplined not by demotion but with time off and even discharge under appropriate circumstances. In contrast, an incompetent employee is one who delivers to the best of his ability but with substandard results. This person cannot be disciplined, but can be demoted from a position properly demonstrated to be beyond his capacity. Arbitrator Keefe submitted that there is no rationalization to support a demotion, with reduced earnings, as a corrective form of discipline for an incompetent employee. Arbitrator Marlin Volz, in an address before the National Academy of Arbitrators, expanded on this principle as follows:

> [I]t is understood that discipline cannot induce a person consistently to work beyond his or her capability. An employee must have sufficient ability to get the job done in an acceptable manner. Discipline cannot overcome a deficiency in ability where the employee is doing his or her best to succeed. Nevertheless, discharge or termination is permissible where the employee demonstrates physical or mental inability to do the work in an acceptable manner and where demotion or transfer is not possible.[55]

Most arbitrators are in accord with this view.[56]

---

[53]Elkouri & Elkouri, How Arbitration Works, 4th Ed., 568–69 (BNA Books, 1985), citing Reynolds Alloys Co., 2 LA 554, 555 (McCoy, 1943); and Republic Steel Corp., 25 LA 733, 735 (Platt, 1955).

[54]62 LA 121, 123–24 (1974).

[55]Volz, "Medical and Health Issues in Labor Arbitration," Proceedings of the 31st Annual Meeting of NAA, 157 (BNA Books, 1979).

[56]Besides the cases discussed in this Chapter, see Naval Amphibious Base, 74 LA 1131 (Gregg, 1980)(demotion for refusing Sunday work because of religious reasons); Phillips Petroleum Co., 80 LA 1257 (Yarowsky, 1983)(reversing decision to demote for incompetence); Lukens Steel Co., 42 LA 252 (Crawford, 1963)(under contract stating that employer may "demote for just cause," employer may not use demotion for discipline); Riverside Book Bindery, Inc., 38 LA 586, 592 (McKelvey, 1962).

In summary, unless otherwise stated in the parties' contract, management can demote an employee who is not capable of performing a particular job. According to arbitral authority, however, management must not use demotion as a form of discipline when the employee's failure to perform satisfactorily is due to incompetence or other factors beyond the employee's control. Moreover, even when the reason for the poor performance is within the employee's control, such as negligence, carelessness, or a poor work attitude, many arbitrators still hold that management cannot demote an employee unless the agreement specifically so provides, because to do so would abridge seniority rights granted by the collective bargaining agreement. Even where some form of discipline is warranted, most arbitrators are reluctant to sustain a demotion or transfer *as a penalty* absent clear contractual authority.[57]

Layoff in Lieu of Demotion

For many employees, the existence of unemployment compensation and supplementary unemployment benefits may make layoff more attractive than being demoted to a lower-paying job. Some labor agreements grant an employee the right to choose between layoff or demotion when reductions in force are effected.[58] When the contract is silent, an issue arises as to whether an employee can choose layoff rather than demotion.[59] Aside from the problem of whether a state would pay unemployment benefits to an individual who had the option of working, although in a lower-paid or "unsuitable" job, arbitrators have not been receptive to an employee's request to take a layoff to draw unemployment benefits.[60] In such a case Arbitrator Adolph Koven ruled that a company did not breach any duty owed the grievant when it notified state authorities that the grievant had elected to take a layoff rather than bump into a lower-rated position (the state, in turn, dis-

---

[57]See the discussion by Arbitrator Peter Kelliher in Allied Tube & Conduit Corp., 48 LA 454, 456 (1967), citing Boeing Airplane Co., 23 LA 252 (Kelliher, 1954), and Elkouri & Elkouri, How Arbitration Works, 2d Ed., 365 (BNA Books, 1960)(repaginated at 568–69, 4th Ed., 1985).

[58]See, e.g., Tappan Co., 40 LA 149, 150 (Dworkin, 1962).

[59]See, e.g., Karnish Instruments, Inc., 45 LA 545 (Bender, 1965).

[60]United States Steel Corp., 31 LA 988 (Garrett, 1959). But see United Eng'g & Foundry Co., 47 LA 164 (McCoy, 1966)(employee entitled to choose layoff rather than demotion where right to elect layoff supported by past practice and uniform interpretation of agreement).

qualified the employee from benefits). Arbitrator Koven found unpersuasive the grievant's argument that the company had profited by the denial of unemployment compensation. The grievant's decision, Arbitrator Koven said, "was not made so much on the basis that he would be entitled to unemployment benefits, but because he did not wish to accept another position with its lower wage rates and because he might be exposed to discharge."[61]

Where an employee has a good faith belief that he is not qualified to perform the new assignment, however, a layoff may be a permissible alternative. Arbitrator David Dolnick stated this principle as follows:

> An employe may not arbitrarily refuse to perform a task properly assigned to him. If propriety is questioned, the employe should comply and grieve under the Agreement. Similarly, the Company should not insist that an employe accept an assignment where there is reasonable doubt that the employe is capable of performing the work under normal physical and other working conditions; or where, because of demonstrable evidence, there is good reason for the employe to refuse to accept the job.[62]

[61]Western Steel Council, 66 LA 1046, 1050 (1976).

[62]Standard Brands, Inc., 59 LA 596, 598 (1972). See also Kimberly-Clark Corp., 40 LA 586 (McNaughton, 1963)(upholding discharge for demoted employee who refused work assignment and failed to challenge company's action in grievance procedure).

Chapter 13

Layoffs, Reductions in Force, and Mandatory Retirement

Layoffs and Reductions in Force

Unless restricted by a labor agreement, arbitrators consistently rule that management has the right to determine the number of employees to be used at any given time and to effect layoffs, reductions in force (RIFs) or possibly involuntary retirements in order to achieve that number.[1] The following declaration by Arbitrator Erwin Ellmann reflects the thinking of most arbitrators on management's right to effect layoffs:

> Guarantees of continued employment, irrespective of the employer's need for the work or ability to pay for it, are still unusual in both the private and public sectors. Managements generally are regarded as having the inherent right to direct the working force and determine the jobs to be performed and the number of employees needed to fill them. Before requiring an employer to continue employment he does not need or which he cannot afford, the contractual obligation should be seen to be clear, unequivocal and mandatory. Inferences and implications, no matter how imaginative, do not justify the imposition of so drastic a curtailment upon managerial authority.[2]

What Constitutes a Layoff?

A "layoff" is usually defined as the placing of an employee "on leave" together with the employee's severance from the

---

[1]See, e.g., Associated Mechanical Contractors, 80 LA 1337, 1340 (Hall, 1983), citing National Biscuit Co., 55 LA 312, 324 (Blair, 1970).
[2]City of Pontiac, 73 LA 1083, 1086 (Ellmann, 1979)(footnote omitted).

payroll. Layoffs are distinguished from "suspensions" in that the former may result from a wide variety of reasons, including plant closings or relocations, reductions in force, or furloughs, while a suspension implies a disciplinary break in an employee's continuous service. A layoff can be temporary, indefinite, or even permanent,[3] although the term inherently anticipates an employee's recall.[4] Suspensions are usually for a definite length of time. Layoffs and suspensions, however, must be distinguished from a "discharge," which is a permanent dissolution of the employer-employee relationship, often for reasons other than discipline.

Layoffs should also be distinguished from an "early quit" or "short workweek" situation. For instance, when employees were sent home because of lack of work, Arbitrator John Larkin ruled that this did not violate the agreement by refusing to allow the grievants to bump into other departments.[5] Cases likewise arise when the workweek is reduced and employees allege that they have been laid off merely because their hours have been decreased. The better view holds that a layoff and a reduction in hours are two different things. Unless otherwise defined in the parties' labor agreement, there must be a temporary severance or interruption in the employment relationship for an employee to claim layoff status.[6] Arbitrator Henri Mangeot stated the general view as follows:

> Virtually without exception arbitrators have construed the term "layoff" to require an actual severance, interruption or break in service, whether temporary or indefinite, to trigger "bumping" or other related seniority rights. A reduction of work hours based on legitimate business management considerations is not considered a layoff.[7]

Arbitrators have similarly ruled that an inventory shutdown, for a specific, limited, short period of time, is not a

---

[3]Continental Can Co., 23 LA 137 (Platt, 1954).

[4]CBS, Inc. v. Stage Employees Local 644, 603 F.2d 1061, 102 LRRM 2026 (CA 2, 1979).

[5]Jenn-Air Corp., 80 LA 931 (Larkin, 1983). See also Allen Group, Inc., 66 LA 909 (Young, 1976).

[6]J.R. Simplot Co., 68 LA 1167 (Flagler, 1977); Wayne State Univ., 76 LA 368 (Cole, 1981).

[7]Madison Mut. Ins. Co., 81 LA 519, 522 (1983). See also Oscar Mayer & Co., 75 LA 555 (Eischen, 1980); O'Neal Steel, Inc., 66 LA 118, 125 (Grooms, 1976)("It has been held that a reduction in the work week is not a layoff, but rather, rescheduling of the work."); Rex Chainbelt, Inc., 52 LA 852, 856 (Murphy, 1969)("A layoff and a reduction in hours are clearly two different things.").

"layoff," at least where no employee is removed or displaced from a job classification as a result of the action.[8]

Where severance pay is available for discharged employees, arbitrators have ruled that an employee is "terminated" where there is no reasonable expectancy of employment in the future, even though the employee is "laid off" with a contractual right to be recalled to his or her former position.[9] A " 'mere statement by the Company of its future plans and expectations' " is not controlling as to whether the employee is considered laid off or discharged.[10]

One issue that arises is whether employees who are subject to permanent layoff may resist termination in order to "creep" toward retirement eligibility. Most arbitrators who have considered this issue have ruled that such employees are not privileged to resist termination, unless the parties' agreement provides otherwise.[11]

Disciplinary Layoffs

With few exceptions,[12] arbitrators have ruled that an employer has the inherent right (subject to the grievance procedure) to impose a disciplinary layoff or suspension, unless specifically prohibited by the agreement. Arbitrator Don Sears, in *Denver Post, Inc.*,[13] in ruling that management could impose disciplinary suspensions under a discharge-for-just-cause provision, reflected the thinking of most arbitrators as follows:

> Obviously, discharge may be too severe a penalty for the offense under the circumstances of a particular case. Moreover, arbitrators agree that a "no discharge save for just cause" type of clause is a *restriction* on management's right. It cannot be viewed as conferring a *right* upon management by any stretch of the imagination. As a practical matter, a view that the Company would not have the right to suspend for cause absent a

---

[8]Olin Corp., 81 LA 585 (Mikrut, 1983).

[9]Radio Station WFDF, 79 LA 424 (Ellmann, 1982).

[10]Blaw-Know Co., 52 LA 773, 780 (Bradley, 1969), quoting Republic Steel Corp., Spaulding Mines (Platt, 1957).

[11]See, e.g., Fitzsimons Steel Co., Youngstown, Ohio, 81-2 ARB ¶8408 (Ruben, 1981), and citations at 4773.

[12]Reynolds Elec. & Eng'g, Co., 50 LA 760 (Abernethy, 1968)(accepted practice in construction industry did not permit disciplinary suspensions); National Lead Co., 39 LA 1231 (Sembower, 1962)(parties by their conduct indicated that disciplinary suspensions not sanctioned under labor agreement).

[13]41 LA 33 (1963). Besides the cases discussed in this section, see Sequoia Rock Co., 76 LA 114 (Lennard, 1981); Koppers Co., 11 LA 334 (McCoy, 1948); Malo, Inc., 81 LA 497 (Roberts, 1983).

specific reference to it in a labor agreement would not be to the benefit of the employees covered by the Contract. The Company, in a case justifying some kind of discipline, would always be compelled to use the *harshest penalty possible—discharge*. This would be to the advantage of neither party and would make it difficult in the extreme for an employer to operate any establishment efficiently and maintain proper discipline.[14]

Arbitrator Marshall Ross similarly declared:

If the parties mutually agree, for their own reasons, to forego suspension, they should expressly declare this intent. The fact the contract discusses discharges and is silent as to suspensions is not enough to indicate compliance on the part of the Employer with the Union's intent to impose this restriction. There have been unions, who, for other policy considerations, desired to impose this restriction and have expressed this policy in their labor agreement. However, in the absence of such explicit language, the rationale of these several cases supporting the right to suspend must be given weight. The few cases opposed to this conclusion are either distinguishable or unpersuasive.[15]

Notice or Consultation Requirements

In a sample taken by The Bureau of National Affairs, Inc. (BNA), advance notice of layoff was required in 47 percent of the agreements. Of the contracts so specifying, 46 percent specified notification to the employee, 19 percent mandated notification to the union, and 35 percent specified notification to both.[16]

When notice is mandated, arbitrators have held that the notice, to have effect, must specify a date certain on which employment will be terminated, at least where the arbitrator finds that the purpose of the notice provision is to assist employees by assuring a source of income while they seek alternative employment opportunities.[17] General statements by management that a layoff may take place in the near future are considered insufficient.[18] Similarly, a layoff notice to all employees at a time when the employer anticipates laying off

---

[14]41 LA at 38 (emphasis in original).

[15]Albertson's, Inc., 71 LA 632 (1978)(citations omitted).

[16]Basic Patterns in Union Contracts, 53 (BNA Books, 1983).

[17]Wilson Foods Corp., 83 LA 405 (Sinicropi, 1984); Oregon Steel Mills, Inc., 66 LA 79 (Hedges, 1976); Washington Star Co., 78 LA 555 (Gamser, 1982); Phillip's Waste Oil Pick-up Serv., 24 LA 136 (Kahn, 1955); Kretschmar Brands, Inc., 83-2 ARB ¶8556 (Madden, 1983).

[18]C. Schmidt Co., 69 LA 80 (Albrechta, 1977); Anaconda Aluminum Co., 65 LA 498 (Goldman, 1975).

only a portion of the employee group is arguably without any effect when the labor agreement calls for timely notice.[19]

Layoff Criteria

In the BNA sample, seniority was a factor in selecting employees for layoff in 89 percent of the contracts.[20] Few arbitrators allow employers to deviate from a seniority criterion where layoffs are governed only by seniority. Under "sufficient ability" clauses, where layoff procedures make seniority a consideration if employees are qualified for available jobs, arbitrators have required management to adhere to this procedure even when the junior employee is clearly more qualified. Under "relative ability" clauses, which make seniority a consideration only where physical ability and qualifications are equal, many arbitrators require that the junior employee be clearly more qualified in order for management to lay off a senior employee.[21] Management is accorded considerable discretion in judging ability,[22] but this discretion is not absolute and may be challenged by a union on the basis that the evaluation was incorrect, arbitrary, or discriminatory.

Exceptions to Seniority Criterion

Some exceptions to using seniority as a criterion for layoff were allowed in 41 percent of the labor agreements sampled by BNA. For example, seniority rules could be waived during temporary layoffs of less than two weeks or during emergency layoffs in 36 percent of the layoff clauses sampled.[23]

Even when the agreement does not contain an emergency-type exception, a few arbitrators have granted employers "leeway" in selecting employees for layoff status during emergencies. Arbitrator Louis Kesselman, in the often-quoted *Virginia-Carolina Chemical Co.* decision,[24] offered this statement:

---

[19]County of Santa Clara, 71 LA 909 (Levy, 1978).
[20]Basic Patterns in Union Contracts, supra note 16, at 52.
[21]See the review of case authority by Arbitrator Sinclair Kossoff in Hyster Co., 66 LA 522, 531 (1976).
[22]See "Is There a Presumption Favoring Management?" notes 23–28, and accompanying text in Chapter 12, supra.
[23]Basic Patterns in Union Contracts, supra note 16 at 52–53.
[24]42 LA 237 (1964).

Common sense and the entire pattern of American industrial experience make it necessary to acknowledge that emergencies do develop as a result of factors beyond the control of even the best of Managements and that a company should not be penalized for taking steps to cope with such unforeseen developments even if it necessitates failure to observe all provisions of the contract. However, there are limits and standards which must be observed:

1) Management must not be directly responsible for the emergency

2) The emergency must involve a situation which threatens to impair operations materially

3) The emergency must be of limited time duration

4) Any violation or suspension of contractual agreements must be unavoidable and limited only to the duration of the emergency[25]

One arbitrator defined an emergency as "an unforeseen combination of circumstances which calls for immediate action."[26] Still another arbitrator said that a "condition beyond the Company's control" must be interpreted to be "a condition which could not be reasonably expected and prepared for by the Company."[27] In effecting "layoffs" or "reductions in force" of short duration, management has been permitted to by-pass seniority provisions in situations involving unforeseen breakdowns in equipment, shortages in parts, or shutdowns due to severe weather conditions.[28] *International Association of Machinists*[29] illustrates the thinking of many arbitrators when confronted with a clause requiring advance notice of a layoff. In this decision, Arbitrator Martin Zimring held that a union-employer did not violate the contract when it laid off employees without giving the contractually required two-weeks' notice, where a contractor had not completed a new building to which the union-employer was moving. The arbitrator rea-

---

[25]Id. at 240.

[26]Canadian Porcelain Co., 41 LA 417, 418 (Hanrahan, 1963).

[27]Gould Nat'l Batteries, Inc., 42 LA 609, 611 (Linn, 1964). See also Pennsylvania State Univ., 67 LA 33 (Stonehouse, 1976)(closing of campus because of rock concert held at adjacent public park was "unforeseen circumstance" permitting shorter layoff notice).

[28]Lennox Indus., Inc., 70 LA 417 (Seifer, 1978)(shortage of parts); International Paper Co., 65 LA 620 (Dunn, 1975)(repair of power equipment); Stupp Bros. Bridge & Iron Co., 80 LA 499 (Westbrook, 1983)(heavy snowfall). But see Sims Cab, Inc., 74 LA 844 (Millious, 1980)(shortage of inventory parts caused by fire not "emergency" for purposes of denying seniority rights of laid-off employees); Nashua Corp., 64 LA 256 (Edes, 1975)(relief from seniority rules during emergency-type situations does not apply to layoffs due to lack of business).

[29]73 LA 1127 (Zimring, 1979).

soned that the notice provision was intended to apply solely to a normal layoff situation where, for economic or business reasons, it is necessary to reduce the working force. Arbitrator Robert Moran, in *Continental Metal Products, Inc.*,[30] similarly concluded that management was not bound by a 48-hour notice provision when it closed its plant early because of a heavy snowstorm.[31]

Reducing the Workweek

At times management may elect to reduce the workweek and distribute remaining work within the unit rather than lay off junior employees. When the parties's agreement is silent on worksharing and, at the same time, makes seniority the determining factor in layoff decisions (i.e., the more senior employees are retained during a reduction in force only if they are qualified for available jobs), many arbitrators are reluctant to allow management to reduce the workweek instead of laying off junior employees.[32] Some arbitrators, however, have upheld worksharing as an alternative to layoff where the contract states that the employer has no responsibility to employ workers any minimum number of hours.[33]

Other arbitrators have ruled that where the agreement does not bar a reduced workweek, such action by management is permissible notwithstanding seniority provisions in the contract.[34] The theory most often expressed is that restrictions and limitations to the exercise of the right to schedule work must be contracted for and should not be lightly inferred.[35]

Similarly, arbitrators have not required that management resort to layoffs, rather than reduce the workweek, where the agreement specifically recognizes management's right to

---

[30]50 LA 290 (1968).
[31]See also San Francisco Theatre Owners Ass'n, 51 LA 1151 (Koven, 1969); Burgermeister Brewing Corp., 44 LA 1028 (Updegraff, 1965)(notice not applicable for strike-related layoffs); Village of Coal Grove, 67 LA 699 (McIntosh, 1976)(notice not required where effect would be to require city to pay money it did not have); Norris Indus., Inc., 70 LA 936 (Gentile, 1978).
[32]Arkansas-Missouri Power Co., 74 LA 1254 (McKenna, 1980); Ambridge Borough, 73 LA 810 (Dean, 1979)(no right to reduce workweek as alternative to laying off employees, under contract providing that work schedules would not be changed unless agreed upon by union and employer).
[33]Dixie Container Co., 65 LA 1089 (Wolff, 1975); Southwest Forest Indus., Inc., 80 LA 553 (Traynor, 1983).
[34]O'Neal Steel, Inc., 66 LA 118 (Grooms, 1976).
[35]St. Regis Paper Co., 51 LA 1102, 1107 (Solomon, 1968).

shorten or lengthen employees' hours,[36] or where the contract provides for a specified level of worksharing before layoff is to be undertaken.[37] Where the agreement provides only that the regular workweek consists of a specified number of hours, most arbitrators have held that such a clause alone does not preclude management from cutting the workweek. Arbitrator Steven Briggs, in *Ampco-Pittsburgh Corp.*,[38] summarized the typical arbitral variations concerning management's right to reduce the workweek:

1. *If the agreement defines the "normal work week", the employer must have sound business reasons to make unilateral changes in that work week.* Among the sound business reasons accepted by arbitrators were plant efficiency, product quality, and economic considerations . . . . Among those reasons not accepted by arbitrators were a preference on the part of the employer for work sharing over layoffs and the employers' wish to reduce overtime costs . . . .

2. *If the agreement defines the "normal work week", the employer cannot make unilateral changes in it for indefinite periods.* Where the parties have contractually defined a normal work week or a work day, arbitrators have viewed such language as an indication that such definitions were meant to apply to normal conditions. Employers can make unilateral changes to meet abnormal conditions, but such changes cannot be indefinite. Indeed, allowing employers to do so would be tantamount to letting them unilaterally redefine the term "normal work week" . . . .

3. *If specific language in the agreement is construed as a guarantee of eight hours per day or forty hours per week, the employer cannot unilaterally tamper with it.* Obviously, such a guarantee is an indication of the parties' mutual intent that bargaining unit employees would be provided with a certain amount of work. One of the parties cannot, on its own, take an action repugnant to that mutual intent. For such a guarantee to be construed, however, arbitrators have held that the language must expressly state that such was the parties' intent. Specifications of a "normal work week" without such express language have not been construed as guarantees that employees will receive a specific amount of work . . . .

4. *Unilateral reductions in hours do not automatically violate seniority provisions.* Seniority clauses for layoff purposes provide employees with a relative claim to available work. Such a clause is obviously violated if the employer lays off employees by some standard other than the one specified, but arbitrators

---

[36]Rochester Monotype Composition Co., 77 LA 474 (Miller, 1981).
[37]Industrial Garment Mfg. Co., 65 LA 875 (Hall, 1975).
[38]80 LA 472 (1982).

have held that in the absence of a layoff employers may reduce hours of work as long as such reduction does not favor junior employees over senior employees .... Arbitrators have also held that agreements with seniority provisions for layoff purposes do not automatically mean that employers must resort to layoffs in periods of slack demand for their product or service ....

5. *An employer may not unilaterally change hours of work where specific agreement language prohibits it.* Some agreements indicate that hours of work may not be changed except by mutual agreement with the union. Where such language exists, employers are clearly prohibited from taking such action unilaterally .... Also, if an agreement contains language specifying the only reasons for which hours of work may be changed, employers cannot unilaterally make such changes for any other reasons .... [39]

Superseniority

A major exception to the strict application of seniority in layoffs involves "superseniority" for union representatives.[40] A superseniority clause usually accords protection to certain union officers in layoff or recall situations, although some superseniority-type provisions allow management the right to select key employees for retention during a layoff without regard to contractual seniority procedures. Still other superseniority-type clauses permit management to lay off probationary employees without regard to their hiring dates, thus allowing management considerable discretion in retention decisions.

NLRB Steward Function Limitation

Decisions by the NLRB and courts since the mid-1970s bring into question the legality of many clauses according superseniority rights to union officers.

---

[39]Id. at 476–77 (citations omitted)(emphasis in original).

[40]See, e.g., Crucible, Inc., 79 LA 1188 (Strongin, 1982)(appointment of laid-off employee as union treasurer); American Precision Indus., Inc., 78 LA 247 (Cook, 1982)(union president entitled to use superseniority to remain on job during vacation shutdown); Mohawk Rubber Co., 81 LA 1242 (Groshong, 1983)(union division chairman exercising superseniority in bumping onto day shift); Davis Cabinet Co., 80 LA 1055 (Williams, 1983)(gaining extended recall rights by election as assistant business agent); Hobart Corp., 67 LA 741 (Ipavec, 1976)(upholding grievance protesting employee with greater seniority to bump shift employee-steward with superseniority); Litton Bus. Sys., Inc., 78 LA 1145 (Gruenberg, 1982)(extending superseniority to temporary layoff of employees).

In *Dairylea Cooperative, Inc.*,[41] the Board considered the lawfulness of a superseniority clause that accorded union stewards top seniority with respect to all contractual benefits where seniority was considered, such as preference in recall, layoff, overtime assignments, vacations, driver routes, shifts, and days off. The Board held that superseniority clauses that are not on their face limited to layoff and recall are presumptively unlawful, and that the burden of rebutting that presumption rests on the party asserting their legality. The Board stated the policy reasons for its holding as follows:

> The lawfulness of [superseniority clauses] is, however, based on the ground that it furthers the effective administration of bargaining agreements on the plant level by encouraging the continued presence of the steward on the job. It thereby not only serves a legitimate statutory purpose but also rebounds in its effects to the benefit of all unit employees. Thus, super seniority for layoff and recall has a proper aim and such discrimination as it may create is simply an incidental side effect of a more general benefit accorded all employees.[42]

Two years later, in *Electrical Workers (UE) Local 623 (Limpco Manufacturing Co.)*,[43] the Board addressed the broader issue of superseniority not just for union stewards but for "functional union officers." At issue in *Limpco* was whether a union recording secretary, the only union representative at the affected plant, could benefit from superseniority in case of a layoff where it was shown that the officer participated informally in grievance processing by advising stewards and shop foremen in contract interpretation matters. A sharply divided Board ruled that, upon a showing that the official responsibilities of the union officer "bear a direct relationship to the effective and efficient representation of unit employees," the officer is entitled to the benefit of the same presumption afforded to union stewards. The majority thus found that the NLRB General Counsel has the burden of showing that application of superseniority provisions to a "functional union officer" in a layoff situation is invalid. The dissent concluded that the only proper objective of superseniority is to retain those union officers responsible for the processing of griev-

---

[41]219 NLRB 656, 89 LRRM 1737 (1975), enforced, NLRB v. Teamsters Local 338, 531 F.2d 1162, 91 LLRM 2929 (CA 2, 1976).
[42]89 LRRM at 1738 (footnote omitted).
[43]230 NLRB 406, 95 LRRM 1343 (1977), enforced, D'Amico v. NLRB, 582 F.2d 820, 99 LRRM 2350 (CA 3, 1978).

ances on the job and whose presence on the job is therefore required for the proper performance of this function.[44]

In *American Can Co.*,[45] a Board majority found unlawful the application of retention and recall superseniority provisions to a union trustee and a union guard whose respective duties were "to have charge of the hall and all property of the Local Union," and "to take charge of the door and see that no one enters who is not entitled to do so."

More recently, the Board in 1983 in *Gulton Electro-Voice*,[46] returned to its position announced in *Dairylea* and held that the presumption of validity for layoff and recall superseniority clauses is limited to union stewards and those officers with steward-like functions. The Board rejected the *Limpco* principle that superseniority was justified for representatives other than stewards because it helped to maintain an effective and efficient bargaining relationship. The Board commented:

> [The] "Board should not be in the business of assuring that a union has an efficient and effective organization to conduct collective bargaining where this results in the linkage of job rights and benefits to union activities. . . ."
> Further, an officer's continued employment within the unit is not determinative of a union's ability to administer a collective-bargaining agreement. Merely because an officer is laid off does not compel his or her renunciation of union responsibilities. Further, changes in union officers are not so disruptive to unit representation as to warrant a blanket conveyance of superseniority. Unions can and do routinely replace their officers through constitutional procedures without undue disruption to their ability to administer their collective-bargaining agreements.[47]

The Board has consistently applied the standards set forth in *Gulton Electro-Voice* when superseniority clauses have been challenged as violative of Taft-Hartley.[48]

---

[44]95 LRRM at 1346–47 (Jenkins & Penello, dissenting).

[45]244 NLRB 736, 102 LRRM 1071 (1979), enforced, 658 F.2d 746, 108 LRRM 2192 (CA 10, 1981).

[46]266 NLRB 406, 112 LRRM 1361 (1983), enforced, Electrical Workers (IUE) Local 900 v. NLRB, 727 F.2d 1184, 115 LRRM 2760 (CA DC, 1984). See also Auto Workers Local 1384 v. NLRB, 756 F.2d 482, 118 LRRM 2753 (CA 7, 1985).

[47]112 LRRM at 1364, quoting the dissent in *Limpco*, 95 LRRM at 1343.

[48]Inmont Corp., 268 NLRB 1442, 116 LRRM 1009 (1984)(superseniority provision violative of statute where duties performed by trustees and sergeant-at-arms did not constitute day-to-day administration of contracts or involve steward-like duties); Wayne Corp., 270 NLRB 162, 116 LRRM 1049 (1984)(intermittent, occasional performance of steward-like duty on a substitute basis insufficient to warrant grant of superseniority under *Gulton* standards); International Harvester Co., 270 NLRB 1342, 116 LRRM 1343 (1984)(union and employer jointly and severally liable for

Strike Replacement Limitations

The Supreme Court has held that preferential seniority credits for strike replacements and strikers who elect to abandon a strike violate Taft-Hartley.[49] Similarly, an employer violates its bargaining obligation under Taft-Hartley by insisting to impasse on a contract proposal for superseniority for strike replacements.[50]

Title VII Issues

With increasing frequency, layoffs brought about by budget cuts and a recessionary economy have a disproportionate impact on minority employment under a "last hired, first fired" layoff criterion. One study estimates that the reduction-in-force rate for minorities working for the federal government is about 50 percent greater than for nonminorities.[51] These layoffs have been challenged as violative of fair employment laws where prior acts of discrimination prevented minorities from being hired earlier and thereby barred them from accruing sufficient seniority to withstand the layoffs.[52]

The Supreme Court, in *Firefighters Local 1784 v. Stotts*,[53] addressed the issue within the context of a consent decree. In 1977 Carl Stotts, a black fire-fighting captain working for the city of Memphis, filed a class action complaint alleging that the city engaged in a pattern or practice of making hiring and promotion decisions on the basis of race in violation of Title VII. In settlement of the lawsuit, the city entered into a consent decree to remedy the hiring and promotion practices of the department with respect to blacks. The settlement agreement provided promotions and back pay to specified firefight-

---

back pay due employees who were laid off because of improper grant of superseniority to union officers); Electrical Workers (IUE) Local 664, 271 NLRB 607, 116 LRRM 1423 (1984)(grant of superseniority to financial secretary, trustees, sergeant-at-arms, and executive board members-at-large improper where no on-the-job contract administration functions performed).

[49]NLRB v. Erie Resistor Corp., 373 U.S. 221, 53 LRRM 2121 (1963).
[50]Philip Carey Mfg. Co. v. NLRB, 331 F.2d 720, 55 LRRM 2821 (CA 6, 1964).
[51]"Layoffs, RIFs, and EEO in the Public Sector: A BNA Special Report," 5 (Supplement 439)(1982).
[52]For background information on the problem and early case law, see Note, "Last Hired, First Fired Layoffs and Title VII," 88 Harv. L. Rev. 1544 (1975); Edwards, "Seniority Systems in Collective Bargaining," in Arbitration in Practice, 130–138 (Zack, ed., ILR Press, New York State School of Indus. & Labor Relations, Cornell Univ., 1984).
[53]467 U.S. 561, 34 FEP 1702, 1711 (1984).

ers and, further, contained goals for increasing the proportion of minority-group representation in each job classification in the fire department. However, the city did not, by agreeing to the decree, admit any violations of law alleged in the complaint.

Approximately one year later, the city announced that projected budget deficits required a reduction of non-essential personnel. Layoffs were to be based on a "last hired, first fired" basis under which citywide seniority, determined by each employee's length of continuous service from the latest date of permanent employment, was the basis for deciding who would be laid off. At Stotts' request, a federal district court enjoined the layoff of any black employee within a certain job classification. A modified layoff scheme was presented and approved. In certain instances, to comply with the injunction, nonminority employees with more seniority than minority employees were laid off or demoted.

The Supreme Court, with Justice White writing for the majority, held that the order entered by the district court was an impermissible Title VII remedy. The appellate court had concluded that the injunction could be entered notwithstanding its conflict with the seniority system. Explaining the Court's reason for reversing, Justice White commented:

> The difficulty with this approach is that it overstates the authority of the trial court to disregard a seniority system in fashioning a remedy after a plaintiff has successfully proved that an employer has followed a pattern or practice having a discriminatory effect on black applicants or employees. If individual members of a plaintiff class demonstrate that they have been actual victims of the discriminatory practice, they may be awarded competitive seniority and given their rightful place on the seniority roster. This much is clear from Franks v. Bowman Transportation Co., 424 U.S. 747, 12 FEP Cases 549 (1976) and Teamsters v. United States, 431 U.S. 324, 14 FEP Cases 1514 (1977). Teamsters, however, also made clear that mere membership in the disadvantaged class is insufficient to warrant a seniority award; each individual must prove that the discriminatory practice had an impact on him.

Explaining the Court's ruling that the lower court had no authority to order the department to maintain its current racial balance or to provide preferential treatment to blacks, Justice White stated that even where an individual demonstrates that the discriminatory practice has an impact on him, he is not automatically entitled to have a nonminority employee laid off to make room for him. Indeed, the employee may have to wait until a vacancy occurs, and if there are nonminority employees on layoff, the court must balance the equities in determining who is entitled to the job.

One federal court stated that while *Stotts* prohibits a court from preferring minority rights over seniority rights, it does not prohibit the parties themselves from reaching an accommodation between those rights. Moreover, the court declared that "nothing in the Supreme Court decision prevents sharing the work week in order to prevent layoffs, rotating promotions, providing by agreement for minority and female hiring, training and recruitment, or finding other creative means to protect and advance the rights of women and minorities."[54]

A cautionary note is in order: *Stotts* involved a consent decree that specifically disclaimed any liability for past discrimination and also failed to contain any provision relating to seniority or layoff procedures. More important, the decision was based on Title VII, which contains a clause specifically exempting a bona fide seniority system from attack.[55]

One federal court, in a post-*Stotts* decision, has already rejected the argument that Title VII law regarding seniority is controlling in constitutional litigation.[56] As such, the general applicability of *Stotts* to last-hired, first-fired layoff situations is unclear in fact situations different from *Stotts*.

Mandatory Retirement

Legal Authority: Age Discrimination in Employment Act

Forced retirement is essentially a question of age discrimination. In 1967 Congress acted to bar discrimination against workers between the ages of 40 and 65 (now 70) by

---

[54]Vulcan Pioneers, Inc. v. New Jersey Dep't of Civil Serv., 588 F.Supp. 732, 35 FEP 24 (D. N.J., 1984).
[55]Sec. 703(h), 42 U.S.C. §2000e–2h (1982).
[56]NAACP v. Detroit Police Officers Ass'n, 591 F.Supp. 1194, 35 FEP 630 (E.D. Mich., 1984).

passing the Age Discrimination in Employment Act (ADEA).[57] In 1974 the statute was amended to apply to state and local governments. Although the federal government is not a defined "employer," under the Act it is required to take personnel actions "free from any discrimination based on age."[58] As amended in 1978, the statute prohibits discrimination in the hiring or firing of employees between ages 40 and 70 by public and private employers having 20 or more employees, labor unions, and employment agencies. In addition, the 1978 amendments removed the upper age limit for federal employees. The Act also prohibits employers, employment agencies, and labor organizations from advertising or indicating a preference as to age. On July 1, 1979, enforcement of the ADEA was transferred from the secretary of labor to the Equal Employment Opportunity Commission (EEOC).

Although enacted separately from Title VII, the statute is closely aligned legislatively with Title VII, as much of the substantive language of the ADEA is drawn from Title VII. Because of this similarity, the courts have indicated that, as a general proposition, Title VII and ADEA litigation should parallel each other, with the procedural steps and burden of proof in Title VII and ADEA cases being similar.

The statute, with limited exceptions, forbids management to involuntarily retire an employee under 70 because of the individual's age. One exception in the Act does permit compulsory retirement for certain executives and individuals in policy-making positions, provided that certain conditions are satisfied. Further, the statute allows an employer to discriminate on the basis of age where it can be proven that "age is a bona fide occupational qualification [BFOQ] reasonably necessary to the normal operation of the particular business." Since the BFOQ is a defense under which an employer would be allowed to discriminate against all members having a particular characteristic, most BFOQ cases under the ADEA involve maximum hiring ages and mandatory retirement ages.

The Seventh Circuit has pointed out that the BFOQ exception frees an employer from making individual judgments regarding the ability of older workers and, accordingly, overuse of the exception involves the risk of reintroducing on a

---

[57]Pub. L. No. 90-202, 81 Stat. 602 (codified as amended at 29 U.S.C. §§621–634 (1982).
[58]29 U.S.C. §633a (1982).

broad scale the very age stereotypes the Act was designed to prevent.[59] Adopting this reasoning, courts have consistently narrowly construed the BFOQ as applied to age, and placed the burden on the employer to demonstrate its applicability to a particular situation.

An employer trying to establish or implement a mandatory retirement age of less than 70 should be prepared to show how the limitation is necessary to the normal operation of the particular business as it pertains to the specific job in question. Most courts will require management to show that some part of that job cannot be performed safely or efficiently by all or substantially all persons in the excluded age group. In the authors' view, the easiest way to do this is to demonstrate a danger to the public or other employees if the job were filled by someone with questionable health, or to demonstrate that such person could not function in that position regardless of the safety factor. In some jurisdictions an employer should be prepared to prove that testing members of the excluded group for the cited inadequacies would not reliably reveal those inadequacies or that this sort of test would place an unreasonable burden on the employer. At times this is a difficult, if not impossible, task.[60]

Arbitral Authority

Prior to the ADEA many arbitrators held that management had the right to promulgate mandatory retirement policies, either pursuant to a management rights clause or as an adjunct to its rule-making authority.[61] The following decision by Arbitrator Joseph Shister typified most arbitrators' reasoning in upholding management's right to promulgate mandatory retirement rules absent restrictive contract provisions:

> It is well established that layoff, discharge, and retirement are completely different methods of employment termination. And that crystal-clear fact leads to these propositions. (a) The contractual provisions on layoff and discharge have absolutely no bearing on the matter of retirement. (b) Where the contract is

---

[59]Orzel v. City of Wauwatosa Fire Dep't, 697 F.2d 743, 30 FEP 1070 (CA 7, 1983).
[60]See Hill & Bishop, "Aging and Employment: The BFOQ under the ADEA," 34 Lab. L. J. 763, 771–72 (1983).
[61]See the reviews of case authority by Arbitrator John Gorsuch in Cummins Power, Inc., 51 LA 909, 913–14 (1968), and Arbitrator William Ferguson in H.D. Lee Co., 70 LA 245, 247–48 (1978).

silent on the question of retirement—as it is here—the silence barrier must be pierced without the use of the contractual provisions on layoff and discharge.

... The Company does have the right to establish a compulsory retirement age for its employees, *provided* that it can demonstrate that such a policy is not unreasonable, arbitrary, or discriminatory.[62]

Whatever effect the ADEA has had upon the thinking of arbitrators, the reported decisions reveal that most neutrals are reluctant to permit management to effect the involuntary retirement of an individual, absent some rational or defined basis comparable to the "bona fide occupational qualification" exception contained in the statute.[63] Some arbitrators have ruled that requiring employees to accept a mandatory retirement age amounts to an attempt to impose a new condition of employment.[64] Others have barred management from retiring employees against their will where the agreement contains a provision proscribing age discrimination,[65] even when the employee is beyond the retirement age covered by the federal statute.[66]

Still other arbitrators, in ruling on the validity of forced retirements, find state and federal law controlling.[67] In these

---

[62]General Aniline & Film Corp., 25 LA 50, 52 (1955)(emphasis in original). See also International Minerals & Chem. Corp., 22 LA 732, 735–36 (Gilden, 1954); Swift & Co., 9 LA 560, 561 (Gregory, 1946); Cook & Brown Lime Co., 50 LA 597, 600 (Rice, 1968)("Employer has the unilateral right to establish and administer a compulsory retirement policy. This unilateral right continues until it is restricted as a result of collective bargaining. In the absence of contractual restriction, the only limitation on the unilateral establishment by the Employer of a compulsory retirement policy is that the policy must not be unreasonable, arbitrary or capricious.").

[63]Pepsi-Cola Gen. Bottlers, Inc., 80 LA 752, 756 (Leiberman, 1983)(prohibiting involuntary retirement of employee upon reaching age 70 where retirement policy not disseminated to employees not uniformly applied); Simpson Bldg. Supply Co., 73 LA 59 (Chiesa, 1979)(employer improperly forced employee to retire, where union and employee did not have actual knowledge of policy of requiring employees to retire upon reaching age 65); Connecticut Limousine Serv., Inc., 78-1 ARB ¶8238 (Johnson, 1978); Safety Elec. Equip. Corp., 82-2 ARB ¶8351 (Blum, 1982)(involuntary retirement "not a reasonable use of the management prerogative, in this particular matter, to make rules and regulations governing the conduct and safety of the bargaining unit employees").

[64]Chicago Zoological Soc'y, 61 LA 387, 388 (Kelliher, 1973).

[65]Waterbury Hosp., 62 LA 113, 117 (Jaffee, 1974).

[66]MaGee-Women's Hosp., 62 LA 987 (Joseph, 1974); Air Cal., 67 LA 1115 (Roberts, 1976).

[67]Alta Bates Hosp., 74 LA 278 (Barsamian, 1980)(applying state law); Armour Agricultural Chem. Co., 47 LA 513 (Larkin, 1966)(citing Exec. Order No. 11141); Jackson Pub. Schools, 79-1 ARB ¶8065 (Keefe, 1978)(applying federal and state law); World Airways, 83 LA 401 (Concepcion, 1984)(applying federal law including 1978 amendments to ADEA); MAC Tools, Inc., 79-1 ARB ¶8044 (Kindig, 1978)(citing 1978 amendments to ADEA); Reynolds Metals Co., 74 LA 1121 (Welch, 1980)(rejecting claim of ADEA violation and upholding forced retirement at age 65 under provisions of pension plan).

cases, however, the arbitrator must take pains not to base the decision on the requirements of enacted legislation, but rather to base it on an interpretation of the collective bargaining agreement. Illustrative of the consequences of invoking the law rather than the agreement is *Wilmington Typographical Union No. 123 v. News-Journal Co.*,[68] where the parties' agreement provided for a mandatory retirement age of 65. Arbitration was invoked when an employee was terminated upon reaching age 65. The arbitrator concluded that the language of the agreement which would otherwise justify the forced retirement was contrary to the terms of the ADEA and directed that the grievant be reinstated. The union brought an action to enforce the award when the company refused to comply with the arbitrator's decision.

The federal court, in vacating the award, quoted the words of the Supreme Court in *Alexander v. Gardner-Denver Co.*:

> "As the proctor of the bargain, the arbitrator's task is to effectuate the intent of the parties. His source of authority is the collective-bargaining agreement, and he must interpret and apply that agreement in accordance with the "industrial common law of the shop" and the various needs and desires of the parties. The arbitrator, however, has no general authority to invoke public laws that conflict with the bargain between the parties .... If an arbitral decision is based 'solely upon the arbitrator's view of the requirements of enacted legislation,' rather than on an interpretation of the collective bargaining agreement, the arbitrator has 'exceeded the scope of the submission,' and the award will not be enforced."[69]

The court accordingly ruled that the award was not enforceable because the arbitrator based his decision on the requirements of the law rather than the agreement.

Finally, arbitrators have also held that it is improper for an employer unilaterally to institute a new retirement age when the former retirement policy was considered part of an established past practice.[70]

Absent a provision in the parties' agreement, management appears most likely to have its mandatory retirement policy upheld by an arbitrator where the policy is clearly dis-

---

[68]513 F.Supp. 987, 108 LRRM 2793 (D. Del., 1981).
[69]108 LRRM at 2794, quoting Alexander v. Gardner-Denver Co., 415 U.S. 36, 53, 7 FEP 81 (1974), which in turn quotes Steelworkers v. Enterprise Wheel & Car Corp., 363 U.S. 593, 597, 46 LRRM 2423, 2425 (1960).
[70]Jefferson County Bd. of Educ., 69 LA 890 (Render, 1977); Ingersoll-Rand Co., 42 LA 483 (Scheiber, 1964).

seminated to the employees and the information and plan predates the collective bargaining agreement.[71] If an arbitrator is convinced, however, that on its face the policy is violative of state or federal fair employment laws regarding age discrimination, or is applied discriminatorily, the mandatory retirement plan is unlikely to be upheld, although, as mentioned above, in order to avoid vacation of the award by a court, arbitrators may state that the basis for such a decision comes from the contract itself rather than from law outside the contract.[72] The least favored situation occurs where management unilaterally implements a retirement policy during the term of the collective bargaining agreement without prior notice or consultation with the union.[73] Where the union does not object to the unilateral promulgation of a forced retirement policy, however, and the policy survives subsequent contract negotiations, arbitrators have ruled the policy effective due to the union's acquiescence.[74]

---

[71]Illinois-California Express, Inc., 63 LA 805 (Gentile, 1974); H.D. Lee Co., 70 LA 245 (Ferguson, 1978); Beatrice Foods, Inc., 71-1 ARB ¶8073 (Young, 1970).
[72]Safeway Stores, Inc., 77-1 ARB ¶8189 (Bothwell, 1975)("A compulsory retirement policy established unilaterally by the Company must be administered equally with regard to all employees, and without discrimination. It must apply equally to employees regardless of which bargaining unit they are in, or whether they are non-bargaining unit employees." Id. at 3828).
[73]Grancolombiana, Inc., 42 LA 559 (Altieri, 1964).
[74]Todd Shipyards Corp., 27 LA 153 (Prasow, 1956); International Minerals & Chem. Corp., 22 LA 732 (Gilden, 1954).

Chapter 14

Job Classification and Evaluation

It has been observed that it is difficult to analyze the area of "jobs" and "job classification" because of problems in terminology.[1] Arbitrator Charles Livengood discussed this problem in *Golden Belt Manufacturing Co.*:[2]

[T]he word "job" is used in several different senses, both on the street and in industrial relations. It can mean an individual task, or it can be used in a broader sense to mean a job classification or type of occupation or kind of work. This is reflected in the arbitration awards dealing with job bidding for vacancies. Some of the decisions tend to support the view that "job" means a particular assignment and that a senior employee is therefore entitled to preferred work in the same classification. . . . Other decisions indicate that in a given situation, "job" may mean a classification, so that an employee cannot bid just to get a different machine. . . . The problem is one of interpreting the particular contract clause in the light of the circumstances which clarify its meaning.[3]

In a 1946 decision, Arbitrator Whitley McCoy, in *Fulton-Sylphon Co.*,[4] remarked:

There is no question that the word "job" may have a different meaning from the word "classification." Two men may have the same classification, for example, "painter" but one may have the job of keeping certain rooms painted while the

---

[1]See Elkouri & Elkouri, How Arbitration Works, 4th Ed., 494–95 (BNA Books, 1985).
[2]20 LA 19 (1953).
[3]Id. at 21 (citations omitted).
[4]2 LA 116 (1946).

389

other has the job of keeping certain equipment painted. On the other hand the two words are sometimes used synonymously. The question is in what sense did the parties use the word job. . . . The intent of the parties is to be gathered from the whole contract and from past practice under the similar wording of previous contracts.[5]

Compounding the difficulty is that arbitrators and practitioners often use the terms interchangeably. Still, because of the overlap between the concepts of "job" and "job classification," arbitral authority on establishing, changing, and eliminating jobs is often applicable[6] when considering rulings by arbitrators on job classification schemes.

Establishing Jobs and Job Classifications

With few exceptions, arbitrators have recognized management's right to establish new jobs, eliminate obsolete jobs, or combine jobs and job classifications.[7] In this regard, there is arbitral authority for the proposition that absent a clear contractual waiver, in establishing a new job classification management must bargain to impasse with the union since a job classification affects wages, hours, and working conditions.[8] Further, the Board, under numerous fact patterns, has similarly maintained that a job evaluation/job classification system is a mandatory subject of bargaining.[9]

---

[5]Id. at 117–18.
[6]But not always. See, e.g., Sealright Co., 82-2 ARB ¶8533 (Yarowsky, 1982), where the arbitrator, citing Esso Standard Oil Co., 19 LA 569 (McCoy, 1952), observed that "[j]obs can be changed and duties combined within classifications but not for distinct or separate classifications or wage scales." 82-2 ARB at 5382.
[7]Besides the cases discussed in this section, see Success Village Apartments, Inc., 84-1 ARB ¶8096 (Davis, 1983)("residual rights theory includes the right to establish new classifications." Id. at 3440). Georgia-Pacific Corp., 82-1 ARB ¶8161 (Ruiz, 1982)(reassignment of expanded job to newly created classification permissible where job not removed from bargaining unit and change dictated by operational requirements).
[8]General Motors Corp., 7 LA 368 (Griffin, 1947); Emge Packing Co., 15 LA 603 (Hampton, 1948). But see the discussion by Arbitrator Ronald Talarico in Penn Cambria School Dist., 81 LA 1040 (1983).
[9]See, e.g., Thurston Motor Lines, Inc., 257 NLRB 1262, 108 LRRM 1087 (1981) (failing to notify newly certified union before unilaterally establishing new job classification of part-time warehouseman and reducing employees' workweek); Jensen's Motorcycle, Inc., 254 NLRB 1248, 107 LRRM 1095 (1981)(unilateral adoption of classification system for mechanics). Cf. E.I. du Pont de Nemours & Co., 276 NLRB No. 34, 120 LRRM 1108 (1985)(employer that proposed restructuring of jobs violated LMRA by denying request for copies of feasibility studies, intercompany and intracompany correspondence relating to restructuring proposals, and labor cost data). See also infra notes 44–45 and accompanying text.

Some labor agreements explicitly recognize management's right to establish or add job classifications and rates. As long as the new rates are consistent with the former job classification/evaluation system, unilateral additions are likely to be upheld.[10] For example, where a collective bargaining agreement expressly empowered management to add to the negotiated classifications and rates, and stipulated that changes might be required "to maintain appropriate job classifications and equitable rates of pay," Arbitrator Patrick Hardin ruled that the employer could establish new job classifications for those employees involved with new production functions.[11] The union argued that by unilaterally creating the new classifications with a higher rate of pay the company violated the agreement, since the new classification did not require significantly greater skill than the former classification. If a wage increase was to be given, the union believed it should be given to all employees and not just those who were involved with new production functions. In holding for the employer, the arbitrator found that the new pay rates bore "a proper and equitable relationship" to the former rates in the plant and, therefore, the company's action was not a proscribed alteration or modification of the contract. The arbitrator also found that the job tasks required "a new level of complexity" and, thus, the protested job classifications were appropriate. Notably, the arbitrator ruled that the employer was not required to adhere to seniority in making shift assignments within the new classification since, under the contract, seniority was defined as length of service with the company, and not length of service within a job classification.

Some agreements, however, expressly "freeze" classifications and, in that case, management may not be able to effect unilateral changes.[12]

---

[10]See, e.g., City of Cedar Rapids, 78-2 ARB ¶8427 (Sinicropi, 1978)(holding that by changing some job duties, management in effect abolished the old job and established a new position, and as such was obligated to post the newly established job).

[11]T.N.S., Inc., 76 LA 278 (1981).

[12]See the discussion by Arbitrator Sol Yarowsky in Sealright Co., 82-2 ARB ¶8533 (1982).

Supervisory Classifications

While an employer is entitled to decide alone how best to supervise its operations,[13] this power is not absolute, especially where new supervisory job or work classifications are created and the bargaining unit loses work. In a case where an employer promoted an employee out of the bargaining unit and established a new supervisory job classification that caused the bargaining unit to lose work, a three-member Board held that the employer violated Taft-Hartley by not bargaining the matter to impasse with the union.[14] The Board stated that when an employer promotes an employee out of the unit into a supervisory position, and the unit does not lose that employee's work, the employer has no duty to bargain over the selection. However, where an employer wishes to create a new supervisory position and the several unit employees whom the employer wishes to place in the new supervisory jobs will continue to perform duties that they had performed as unit employees, the matter must be bargained, the Board stated. The loss of work is considered a change in a term or condition of employment under Section 8(d) and the employer is obligated to bargain with the union.[15]

Arbitrators have likewise implied limitations in the collective bargaining agreement when management has "promoted" employees out of the unit to supervisory classifications with essentially the same job duties. Thus, when a hospital promoted a chemistry technician out of the bargaining unit to a supervisory position as chief lab technician and subsequently eliminated the position of chemistry technician, Arbitrator William LeWinter found a violation of the labor agreement when the employee continued to perform most of the former job duties. As a remedy the arbitrator directed the hospital to reinstate the former position.[16]

In general, while the creation of new supervisory positions and the selection of the individuals to fill these positions is not a mandatory subject of bargaining, an employer may have

---

[13]See Chapter 17, infra, notes 1–8 and accompanying text for a discussion of managerial discretion in selecting supervisors.
[14]Lutheran Home of Kendallville, Ind., 264 NLRB 525, 111 LRRM 1654 (1982).
[15]111 LRRM at 1655 n.2. See also Oil Workers v. NLRB, 547 F.2d 575, 92 LRRM 3059 (CA DC, 1976), cert. denied, 431 U.S. 966, 95 LRRM 2642 (1977).
[16]Monongehela Valley Hosp., 76-2 ARB ¶8368 (1976).

an obligation to bargain with the union if it reduces bargain-ing-unit work. This would be the situation if an individual promoted to a supervisory position continues to perform bar-gaining-unit work.[17]

Workload and Job-Content Changes

Upgrading Jobs

Arbitrators frequently consider claims that an increase in job assignments or duties amounts to a change in a job classification that must be followed by a corresponding change in a pay grade or a rate of pay. Many agreements specifically outline the circumstances under which an employee is entitled to have a job upgraded or reclassified.[18] A decision reported by Arbitrator Richard Miller illustrates the thinking of many arbitrators in this area. In *Minnesota Mining & Manufactur-ing Co.,*[19] employees classified as utility stockpersons were required to assume additional responsibilities for adapting themselves to new equipment and, accordingly, the union re-quested a job-grade increase. Arbitrator Miller, in denying the grievance, held that before a change in a job grade can be made, the job's content must change substantially, with skill, responsibility, effort and working conditions being the criteria used to measure whether the job has changed enough to war-rant upgrading. Significantly, the arbitrator recognized that a substantial change may be composed of many minor changes.

Similarly, in *Household Manufacturing Co.,*[20] manage-ment introduced work-content changes by requiring caster employees, working at piecework rates, to carry their slip buckets and to clean their workbenches. Arbitrator Ronald Talarico, in holding that the company had not affected the integrity of the job classification, stated as follows:

---

[17]St. Louis Tel. Employees Credit Union, 273 NLRB No. 90, 118 LRRM 1079 (1984)(holding that company did not violate its bargaining obligation in promoting 21 employees to newly created supervisory positions even though some unit work was still being performed, where employer immediately began to hire replacements to fill vacancies and more unit jobs would be created.).

[18]See, e.g., Ducommun Metals Co., 74 LA 272 (Weiss, 1980)(requiring reclassi-fication where employee performed new work operations for more than 50 percent of his time).

[19]80 LA 1078 (1983).

[20]80 LA 1111 (Talarico, 1983).

In general, arbitrators have recognized broad authority in management, (absent clear limitations in the agreement), to determine methods of operation. Unless restricted by the agreement, management has the right to determine what work shall be done, to determine what kinds of services and business activity to engage in, and to determine the techniques, tools, and equipment by which work in its behalf shall be performed. . . . As a corollary, it follows that the employer has the right to have the employees operate improved machines and perform changed operation methods in good faith to up the level of their productive capacity. . . .

The Management Rights Clause in Section VII of the collective bargaining agreement clearly grants the Company broad authority over the management of its business, without limitation on its right to direct the working forces. These same broad powers are also reflected in the Wage Incentive Agreement which contemplates that the Company has the power to make changes "in the work content of the operation because of a change in the method of performance, materials, tools, fixtures, equipment, speeds, feeds, quality requirements, product, process or other similar factors". The issue then becomes whether requiring the casters to carry their slip buckets and to clean their benches is a proper change in the work content of the operation.

The combination of the management rights clause of the collective bargaining agreement and Section VII of the Wage Incentive Agreement clearly gives the Company the right to establish new jobs or job classifications, or job duties. Arbitrators often have recognized the right of management, unless restricted by the agreement, to eliminate jobs or re-allocate duties where improved methods or other production justification exists and management otherwise acts in good faith. . . .

. . .

The only real limitation on the Company's right to make work content changes is the duty to act fairly, reasonably and for proper objectives and purposes. Comparison of the minor additional duties (carrying slip buckets and cleaning their benches) to the more significant eliminated duties clearly rebuts any argument that the Company acted arbitrarily or capriciously.[21]

The arbitrator further noted that the new duties were merely incidental to the main job and had not "substantially or fundamentally changed the nature of the casters function."[22]

---

[21]Id. at 1113–14.

[22]Id. at 1114. See also May Dep't Stores, 76 LA 254 (Hannan, 1981)(employer had right to require furniture sales personnel to perform light dusting of furniture where nonselling work was de minimis in nature); Powder Metal Prods., Inc., 77 LA 499 (Gootnick, 1981)(upholding employer's decision to require molding operators to train new employees); Sperry Corp., 80 LA 166 (Taylor, 1983)(upgrading of storeroom

In the public sector, Arbitrator George Heliker, in *Department of Army,*[23] rejected an argument that management's decision to add unrelated janitorial duties to job descriptions of white-collar employees constituted a change in working conditions inconsistent with the parties' agreement. The arbitrator stated that it is clear from Federal Labor Relations Authority decisions that the law has been interpreted consistently in support of management's right to control the substance of work assignments without the need to invite or tolerate the union's participation. While procedural questions relating to work assignments are negotiable, Arbitrator Heliker ruled that in this case there was no genuine procedural issue that the agreement required management to negotiate.

In general, minimal changes in job content will not justify upgrading an established job classification; rather, only major or significant alterations in job duties will suffice. Further, changes in one job cannot be considered alone but must be weighed against changes in other jobs. As pointed out by one arbitrator, "the essence of job evaluation is to determine the *relative* wage scale of a particular job in comparison to all other jobs in the plant."[24]

Downgrading Employees

Arbitrators have likewise sustained management's decision to downgrade an employee where there is a showing that the individual is performing lower-rated duties or, alternatively, is not performing assigned duties adequately.[25] Even

---

classification not warranted following introduction of CRTs where use of computer terminals did not require mastering of computer programming); Acme Elec. Corp., 76-2 ARB ¶8416 (Liebowitz, 1976)(holding job should be upgraded: "It seems to me that the issue is not whether the Company's action was arbitrary or capricious, but rather, whether it was correct." Id. at 6316); Trust Fund Computer Servicing, Inc., 67 LA 1016 (Juvinall, 1976)(holding employee entitled to higher rate of pay while performing work of higher classification); Fisher Scientific Co., 79-1 ARB ¶8122 (Gottlieb, 1979)(upgrading ordinance for wiring-assembler classification where greater skill and knowledge required); Sealright Co., 82-2 ARB ¶8533 (Yarowsky, 1982)("Job content or duties are not to be considered totally insulated from change for otherwise there would be no room for any production innovation in the form of new skills and technological advancement, materials or design of product." Id. at 5382.); Pratt & Lambert, Inc., 83-1 ARB ¶8101 (Denson, 1983)(directing parties to negotiate new pay rate).

[23]77 LA 918 (1981).

[24]Minnesota Mining & Mfg. Co., 77-1 ARB ¶8244 (Cohen, 1977), at 4056 (emphasis in original).

[25]See, e.g., Delphi Body Works, Inc., 83 LA 276 (Roomkin, 1984); Sanyo Mfg. Corp., 80-1 ARB ¶8150 (Sinicropi, 1979)(downgrading of TV-chassis transfer position

though the employee may possess the skill required in the higher classification, the criterion is the work actually performed. An employer is not required to pay for "talent" that is not used.[26] For example, in *Electronic Communications, Inc.*,[27] an electronics firm changed the job of testing one of the company's products (a wafer circuit chip) from grade 13 to grade 2 after the testing procedure was computerized and it was no longer necessary that the testor be able to read or comprehend any electronic device, or make any value judgments. The parties' agreement contained a management-functions clause that granted to the company the right to "introduce new or improved production methods or equipment" and, further, granted to management the exclusive responsibility to determine the manner in which the work should be done. The agreement also stated that "[a]ll new or re-created jobs shall be classified and slotted into an existing labor grade by mutual agreement." In denying the grievance, the arbitrator noted that the job at issue differed from the job that existed before the introduction of the computerized testing process, and that a high school graduate with a short training course could perform the function. He reasoned that if the parties cannot agree on the job description and the slotting, as in this case, then it is permissible for management to take a unilateral step and have that decision tested in the grievance procedure. The arbitrator, after observing the testing procedure, concluded that grade 2 was a reasonable classification for the work.

Before effecting a downgrade, management may have to provide the employee with sufficient training[28] in situations where, because of technological changes in the equipment used,

---

from labor grade 3 to labor grade 1 improper where only change in content of position was reduction in weight of TV chassis; initiative, inventiveness, product responsibility, and hazards associated with position not diminished); Lindsay Wire Weaving Co., 78-2 ARB ¶8518 (Van Pelt, 1978)(downgrading of six loom operators to helper classification in response to drop in customer orders permissible where agreement, while providing for job classifications and the amount of compensation within a classification, placed no limitation on the number of employees required in any classification). Demotion as part of the general evaluative process is discussed in Chapter 12, supra, notes 41–47, and accompanying text.

[26]In this regard see the discussion by Arbitrator Stanford Madden in Gill Studios, Inc., 52 LA 506, 511 (1969).

[27]77-2 ARB ¶8457 (Manson, 1977).

[28]Trial and training periods are discussed in Chapter 11, supra, notes 62–73, and accompanying text.

the employee no longer is able to perform a part of a job's functions.[29]

There is authority for the position that when an employee is assigned to the wrong classification for a long period of time, management may be precluded from effecting a change to the detriment of the employee.[30] Similarly, an employer must not be discriminatory or capricious in downgrading (or upgrading) employees, nor can it effect a downgrade based on union animus.

Eliminating Jobs or Job Classifications[31]

Abolishing or combining a job classification outlined in the parties' contract is different from altering the duties or job content within a classification, or even abolishing a job within a job classification. Accordingly, arbitrators' decisions relating to management's prerogative to abolish, change, or combine jobs may not always be relevant where the issue is management's right to change job classification schemes.

Arbitrators have recognized that there is a difference between (1) eliminating job classifications and jobs because of lack of work due to changing economic or technological conditions and (2) transferring work to a different classification and then eliminating the former job classification. Arbitrators have also distinguished between (3) eliminating a job and the duties associated with that job, and (4) eliminating a job and reassigning the duties to other classifications or to non-unit positions. The latter case is not a bona fide elimination of a job and, depending upon the particular factual situation, an employer may be precluded from effecting such a transfer. This principle was stated by one arbitrator as follows:

> Unless it involves the most minor of minor functions a company can eliminate a job classification only if it likewise

---

[29]See, e.g., Rooney Optical Co., 83-2 ARB ¶8473 (Curry, 1983)(management's decision to downgrade journeyman to laborer overturned where 50 hours of intermittent training that employee received was below apprenticeship standard).

[30]National Tube Co., 7 LA 575 (Blumer, 1945). Compare McGill Mfg. Co., 83-1 ARB ¶8231 (Ratner, 1983)(stating that a job could be reclassified even though there was "no essential change" in the job where there was an error in the company's initial evaluation).

[31]See Chapter 15, infra, notes 78–94, and accompanying text for a discussion of management's right to sell or liquidate the business where the contract is silent.

eliminates the function served by that classification. It is the function of the classification that is important, not the classification itself. . . .

The issue deals with the Company's contention that [it] [sic] has a right to abolish a function (classification). It does have such a right if in fact the function is abolished. In this case they did not abolish the function, [therefore] they are committed to it and the higher rate of pay associated with it for the duration of the existing agreement.[32]

And in *Gisholt Machine Co.*,[33] Arbitrator Thomas McDermott held that an employer violated the parties' contract by eliminating a bargaining-unit job classification and assigning the duties to a newly created department outside the unit. The reasoning of the arbitrator is especially noteworthy.

It is correct that the above cited provisions [stating that employees not covered by the contract will not perform production and maintenance work] do not freeze jobs or "job content." The Company does have the right to combine jobs or to remove specific duties from particular jobs, but this does not mean that the Company, in the absence of such changed conditions as technological change or elimination of the need for particular job duties, can take a bargaining unit job, abolish it, and assign all the duties to another job that is created outside of the bargaining unit.[34]

Arbitrator Bernard Cantor outlined the rule this way in a case involving the elimination of the job of "assistant operator" after management installed new equipment so that most of the operator's job could be carried out through the push of a button:

The power of a lever and the precision of an electron can eliminate the need for a job that is limited to the work which the new equipment can perform. The job might then continue as a name in the contract document, but it also might not be filled. Nothing in this agreement requires any particular job to be filled, but that does not mean that, if the work content of the job continues to be performed, it can be spelled off anywhere Management wishes. That would permit a specified job to be destroyed, and, since we are [working] on the proposition that this contract recognizes and delineates the jobs in this plant as such, the job may not be destroyed if the work is being done. Job and work are equivalent entities.[35]

---

[32]Sonoco Prods. Co., 77 LA 266, 269 (Coyne, 1981).
[33]44 LA 840 (1965).
[34]Id. at 846.
[35]Tennessee Am. Water Co., 77-2 ARB ¶8477 (1977) at 5070.

Maintenance-of-Standards Provisions

A maintenance-of-standards provision may have little utility in preventing management from abolishing, changing, or combining jobs. For example, in *Mead Corp.*,[36] the parties' contract contained a maintenance-of-standards provision whereby the employer promised to "continue present working conditions providing it is consistent with sound economic operations." When management eliminated a press-department classification, changed the size of the press crew, and increased the wages of the remaining press-crew employees, the union filed a grievance alleging that crew size was a working condition which was entitled to be continued under the above provision. In rejecting this argument the arbitrator reasoned that the change was based on sound economic reasons (lowering of production costs and a change in the product mix) and, furthermore, the management-prerogatives clause reserved to the company the authority to "determine the working force necessary for efficient operations."

Likewise, Arbitrator Jonas Silver, in *Hoboken Board of Education*,[37] ruled that a school board did not violate the following contractual provision when it increased cafeteria duty for teachers because the student population necessitated an increase in the number of lunch periods:

> "Existing practices that have been changed as a result of negotiations for this Agreement shall be null and void. However, those practices which were not specifically changed shall remain in full force and effect."[38]

The arbitrator reasoned that a past practice represents a settled way of responding to a continuing condition so long as that same condition persists. In view of the additional students, management could not be held to the former operating method.[39]

---

[36]81-2 ARB ¶8507 (Edelman, 1981).
[37]75 LA 988 (1980).
[38]Id. at 991.
[39]See also Department of Army, 77 LA 918, 919 (Heliker, 1981)(rejecting union's argument that the following language precluded the employer from adding janitorial duties to white-collar jobs: "All working conditions and negotiable policies already in effect and consistent with the provisions of this agreement are hereby adopted. Changes must be agreeable to both parties.").

Negotiated Rate or Classification Structures

In upholding the right of management to eliminate jobs or job classifications, Arbitrator Howard Block, in the often-quoted *American Cement Corp.* decision,[40] reflected the two lines of authority as regards the effect of a negotiated rate structure:

> The impact of a changing technology upon the work force has posed problems to both management and labor not easy of solution. That this issue has been a persistent and vexing one over the years is indicated by the significant number of arbitration proceedings on this subject dating back to the earliest reported decisions. A review of these decisions reveals that they fall into two fairly distinct categories which seem noteworthy here: (1) One line of cases emphasizes that where a Collective Bargaining Agreement sets forth a comprehensive rate structure, the wage rate established for each classification evidences an agreement between the parties as to the wage rate, as well as [to] the classification; these cases then go on to provide that, in general, the terms of this bargained for exchange may not be unilaterally altered. To the extent that some of these decisions regard the classification structure as being unalterably frozen during the life of the Agreement, they do not represent the weight of arbitration authority. (2) A second group of cases holds that the existence in the Agreement of a negotiated rate structure does not guarantee that the classifications will remain unchanged during the term of the Agreement. The reason[] advanced for this interpretation is that economic necessity in a competitive market makes it essential that management have the degree of flexibility necessary to adapt the work force to changed conditions. Where arbitrators have upheld management's right to eliminate jobs or classifications and reallocate residual job duties, they have stressed that such changes must be made in good faith, based upon factors such as a change in operations, technological improvements, substantially diminished production requirements, established past practice, etc. It is this second line of cases which appears to reflect the present weight of authority on this issue.[41]

In an unpublished decision, Arbitrator Jim Hill stated the governing principle as follows:

> "Many arbitrators have construed the labor agreement to presume or imply that, in the absence of significant changes in

---

[40]48 LA 72 (1967).

[41]Id. at 76. For an excellent review of the minority position, see the discussion by Arbitrator James Doyle in Omaha Cold Storage Terminals, Inc., 48 LA 24 (1967).

materials, methods or equipment, and so long as work is available, work assignments among job classifications and plant units will continue unchanged. But the agreement does not freeze the status quo in the face of technological change. Where new methods and equipment resulting from technological change make it more efficient to alter work assignments, arbitrators frequently hold that Management retains the right to make such changes, unless it has waived such right by some explicit provision of the agreement.

"Arbitrators have frequently stressed the point that changes in work assignments are subject to the basic test of good faith, or, conversely, the absence of any purpose of injury or loss to bargaining unit employees or the Union."[42]

The most extensive and comprehensive analysis of the subject is contained in a decision reported by Arbitrator James Doyle. Arbitrator Doyle's research led him to the following conclusion:

[T]he strong and prevailing trend of authority is to the effect that for economic or other reasons an employer may eliminate a classification, designated in an agreement and for which a wage rate has been negotiated, in the absence of a clear limitation in the Agreement limiting its authority to do so. The mere enumeration of the job classifications in the Agreement will not support an implied limitation on the employer's residual management power to reorganize the work load in the interests of efficiency and economy even if such redistribution of duties results in the elimination of a classified occupation. The displaced employee or employees may or may not be subject to layoff depending upon their seniority rights under the contract. The prevailing rule is based on the premise that a freezing of classifications by implication would unduly restrict and hamper the Company in making decisions that would improve the economy and productivity of the plant. Such a limitation should not be lightly inferred. One arbitrator said the limitation must be express . . . . Others have said it must be specific . . . . Still another said that the limitation must be a clear and forceful statement . . . .[43]

In the above case Arbitrator Doyle ruled that, in the absence of an express or specific limitation, the company could assign the duties of a fireman classification to an engineer,

---

[42]Bell Tel. Co. (Case 14-30-1000-72)(unpublished), quoted in Bell Tel Co., 75 LA 750, 755 (Garrett, 1980).
[43]Omaha Cold Storage Terminals, Inc., 48 LA 24, 31 (1967) (citations omitted). See also the discussion by Arbitrators Shister in Philips ECG, 79 LA 123 (1982); Volz in Mobile Chem. Co., 73-1 ARB ¶8025 (1973); Seinsheimer in Olin Corp., 71-2 ARB ¶8445 (1971); Abrams in Anchor Hocking Corp., 80 LA 1267 (1983).

where the duties were within the competence of the engineer and were not overly burdensome. The arbitrator reached this conclusion even though the company's action resulted in the layoff of its remaining firemen.

Effect of a Strong Management-Rights Clause

A union may waive its statutory right to bargain over an employer's elimination of a job classification[44] and this waiver may be found in the management-rights clause. For example, where under a management-rights clause the employer expressly retains the sole right to "establish new job classifications," as well as to "organize, discontinue, enlarge or reduce a department, function or division," the NLRB's Office of the General Counsel has taken the position that, although the elimination of a job classification is not literally covered by this clause, the right to discontinue a function or division covers the right to eliminate a job classification. In this respect there is authority for the position that the inclusion of the words "exclusively" and "sole" in a management-rights clause has been held by the Board to afford an employer the right to make unilateral changes with respect to the matters covered.[45]

One arbitrator held that the following language was sufficient to allow management to consolidate three jobs into one in the interest of economy and efficiency:

> "The COMPANY shall have the right at all times, during the existence of this Agreement and subject to the provisions thereof, to operate its property according to its best judgment and the order of lawful authority."[46]

A similar approach was taken in *Formosa Plastics Corp.*,[47] where Arbitrator Jay Taylor held that the company, as part

---

[44]See, e.g., International Harvester Co., 227 NLRB 85 (1976)(holding that management must bargain removal of job classification). But see National Fresh Fruit & Veg. Co., 227 NLRB 2014 (1977), enforcement denied, 565 F.2d 1331 (CA 5, 1978) (removal of classification held non-mandatory subject of bargaining).

[45]Hahneman Medical Center & Hosp., Case No. 4-CA-13140, 112 LRRM 1418 (1982)(advisory memorandum), citing Consolidated Foods Corp., 183 NLRB 832, 833 and n.6, 74 LRRM 1374 (1970). See also General Tel. Co. of Ohio, 80 LA 111 (Tharp, 1983)(prohibiting displaced employee from bumping into higher classification, except at sole discretion of management); Fort Cherry School Dist., 82-1 ARB ¶8197 (Hannan, 1982)(school district's failure to fill seven extracurricular positions upheld where schoolboard retained right not to maintain participation in any activity or program).

[46]Southeastern Trailways, Inc., 78-1 ARB ¶8042 (Mulhall, 1978), at 3203.

[47]83 LA 792 (Taylor, 1984).

of its inherent reserved managerial rights, could eliminate a field-clerk job and assign the duties to a foreman:

> A threshold question, then, is whether the Company, after having agreed to a Contract containing classifications, [can] abolish a classification in midterm of the Agreement? . . . The answer to this question must be that there is no Contractual language precluding the Company's action. This Company prerogative is based not only on its Management rights not ceded in the Contract but also on the right and obligation to manage its business efficiently in the absence of language limiting that right. The right of an Employer to eliminate a classification or even to institute a new classification, when acting in good faith and in the interest of promoting efficiency, has been upheld in a veritable legion of arbitration cases. The Contract simply does not require frozen classifications for the life of that Agreement.[48]

Summary

Unless the labor agreement expressly provides otherwise, management's right to eliminate a job or a job classification is usually recognized where (1) there are changed economic or technological conditions that have eliminated the need for most of the duties performed, or (2) the duties that are eliminated or transferred are "residual" or "de minimis" in nature.[49] The mere listing of job classifications and their corresponding wage rates in the parties' contract does not

---

[48]Id. at 796.

[49]Besides the cases discussed in this section, decisions dealing with changed economic or technological conditions include: Kroger Co., 85-1 ARB ¶8174 (Seidman, 1985); Quaker Oats Co., 84 LA 390 (Edelman, 1985)(elimination of driver classification where duties had diminished to point of nonexistence; seniority provisions did not guarantee continuation of specific job classification); Southeastern Trailways, Inc., 78-1 ARB ¶8042 (Mulhall, 1978)(consolidation of three jobs by bus company); United States Steel Corp., 84-2 ARB ¶8321 (Dybeck, 1984)(elimination of diesel-operator position after installation of remote control device capable of performing duties); Babcock & Wilcox, 83-2 ARB ¶8482 (McDermott, 1983)(change in equipment and production methods justified elimination of jobs); Hooker Chem. Corp., 71-1 ARB ¶8235 (Oppenheim, 1971)(elimination of furnace operator's helper following technological improvement); Bethlehem Steel Corp., 77 LA 372 (Seward, 1981)(position eliminated where basis for original practice had been removed by changes in equipment); Dravo Corp., 75 LA 1042 (Hannan, 1980) (elimination of dispatcher where physical relay of messages unnecessary); Leavenworth Times, 71 LA 396 (Bothwell, 1978)(publisher-employer had right to reduce classifications following conversion of hot metal process to cold metal process); Freeport Kaolin Co., 72 LA 738 (Vadakin, 1979)(combining job classifications following structural change); Western Kraft Paper Group, Willamette Indus., Inc., 76 LA 1129 (Curry, 1981)(assistant-operator position properly eliminated although position remained listed in wage schedules); GAF Corp., 75 LA 1016 (Wolff, 1980)(employer could eliminate clerical jobs due to the cessation of production lines for which those jobs performed clerical functions).

preclude management from changing or eliminating the classifications, unless as otherwise specifically provided by the
agreement. The better rule is that classifications are not "frozen" so long as there is some rational basis for effecting the
changes. Where no specific provisions proscribe the performance of bargaining-unit work by non-unit personnel, some
arbitrators hold that management may even transfer the work
to non-unit employees; it is likely in this case, however, that
most arbitrators would imply such a proscription from the
mere existence of a recognition-and-seniority provision in the
agreement, especially where there is no sound economic reason for the employer to effect such a change.

Out-of-Classification Assignments

Most grievances arising from out-of-classification assignments involve the temporary assignment of out-of-classification work to an employee or, alternatively, the assignment of
an employee to another classification on a temporary basis.
Cases in this area involving non-unit personnel (supervisors)
performing bargaining-unit work are addressed in a later
chapter.[50]

As a general proposition it may be said that management
cannot eliminate a bargaining-unit job and transfer the duties
to supervisory personnel where the agreement restricts management from assigning unit work to supervisory employees.[51]
Even when the agreement is silent regarding supervisors performing bargaining-unit work, the majority of arbitrators will
find a violation when management unilaterally effects such
a transfer.

Under an agreement that reserved to management the
right to determine the size of its work force and to assign
work, one arbitrator concluded that an employer had the right
to eliminate one on-and-off classification and one relief on-
and-off classification, and to assign another employee holding
a different classification the duties of the eliminated position

---

[50]See "Supervisors Performing Bargaining-Unit Work," in Chapter 17, infra, and
accompanying notes 31–83.

[51]Welsh Foods, Inc., 79-2 ARB ¶8605 (Denson, 1979); Litton Microwave Cooking
Prods., 78-2 ARB ¶8339 (Lipson, 1978); Phoenix Closures, Inc., 68-1 ARB ¶8307
(Sembower, 1967).

on a temporary basis. The arbitrator pointed out that no work was lost to the bargaining unit, no overtime was lost, and that any intent by the parties to keep classifications and duties separated did not prohibit temporary assignments outside of the classification on a temporary basis.[52]

Where the agreement was completely silent on the issue, another arbitrator held that management had the right to transfer employees in a paint-line classification to other classifications and to pay them the prevailing rate in their newly assigned classifications after the company determined that decreased production requirements did not justify the employees' retention in their regular classifications. The arbitrator reasoned that "the employer has an absolute right to establish or change working conditions for which the collective bargaining agreement makes no provisions."[53]

Other arbitrators, in ruling on the issue of assigning work to the "wrong" classification, have focused on the amount of work at issue and the likely effect that a ruling for the union would have on the employer's competitive position. In *Reliance Electric & Engineering Co.,*[54] the contractual provision at issue provided as follows:

> "Overtime work shall be distributed as equally as practicable among employees in the same occupational classification in the department where the overtime work is available."[55]

An employer scheduled a skeleton work crew on Saturday overtime and the crew obtained all tools it expected to need from a tool crib attendant on the preceding Friday. During Saturday work, however, it became necessary for the crew to obtain additional tools from the tool crib. The union alleged that the attendant should have been scheduled for Saturday overtime since the tool crib was open for part of the time that day (about 30 minutes). In rejecting the grievance, Arbitrator Jerome Klein held that the "de minimis" doctrine applied:

> The "de minimis doctrine" is a rule based on sound economic logic, and, therefore, a principle of practical necessity. A Collective Bargaining Agreement with its attendant job classification structure cannot be interpreted in an economic vacuum devoid of all common sense. It would be absurd to compel

---

[52]Tennessee Am. Water Co., 80 LA 265, 267 (Flannagan, 1983).
[53]Wall Tube & Metal Prods. Co., 77 LA 857 (Eyraud, 1981).
[54]41 LA 1045 (1963).
[55]Id. at 1046.

a Company to give a Tool Crib Attendant eight (8) hours pay at time and one-half merely because a fraction of an hour tool crib work may have to be performed on a particular overtime day. To impose such a requirement on a Company, would be to grease the skids on its path to competition oblivion. Stating it another way, it would be illogical to conclude that a Company must have a Tool Crib Attendant on duty for eight (8) hours on a Saturday at overtime rates merely because a tool might break and a replacement [might be] required or because there may be an isolated instance or two of production employees failing to anticipate on a Friday that a particular tool will be needed on Saturday.[56]

Reassignment of Unit Work to Non-Unit Personnel

Arbitrators are divided concerning management's right to transfer work out of the bargaining unit absent any express restrictions or limitations in the labor agreement. One line of cases holds that under such circumstances management can transfer work out of the unit under its reserved rights. In contrast, other arbitrators hold that the existence of the recognition, seniority, or classification provisions in a contract by implication restrict the right to unilaterally transfer work out of the unit. These arbitrators reason that the transfer of work customarily performed by unit employees to others outside the unit in effect attacks one of the labor agreement's basic purposes, employee job security. In one of the leading decisions in this area, *New Britain Machine Co.*,[57] Arbitrator Saul Wallen stated as follows:

> The transfer of work customarily performed by employees in the bargaining unit to others outside the unit must . . . be regarded as an attack on the job security of the employees whom the agreement covers and therefore on one of the contract's basic purposes.[58]

Still other arbitrators reject the alternative positions described above and hold that absent contractual restrictions management is neither altogether free to transfer unit work nor prohibited under all circumstances from transferring unit work. This line of authority represents an attempt to balance the needs of the employer for flexibility in managing the com-

---

[56]Id. at 1049.
[57]8 LA 720 (1947).
[58]Id. at 722.

pany with the right of the union to be protected against the erosion of the bargaining unit by transfers of unit work.[59]

Adopting this "balancing" test, Arbitrator Harry MacLean, in *Eastern Slope Rural Telephone Association, Inc.*,[60] ruled that an employer could assign supervisory personnel to assume a portion (25 percent) of duties formerly performed by bargaining-unit employees. His reasoning is especially noteworthy and can be summarized as follows:

1. The parties' agreement, specifically the management rights clause, reserved to the company the right to assign work, modify job duties, and introduce improved or different operation methods.
2. There were legitimate business reasons, evidenced by technological efficiency, for assigning non-unit personnel the work.
3. The employer evidenced no intent to undermine or erode the bargaining unit.
4. The amount of the bargaining unit work actually transferred did not include substantial segments of production work.
5. The effect on the bargaining unit as a whole was not great.
6. The past practice of the parties, although favoring the union, was not sufficient to overcome the other considerations.

Numerous arbitrators have applied the above criteria in deciding whether management is permitted to transfer unit work to non-unit supervisors or other personnel.[61]

Arbitrator Wayne Howard provided perhaps the best summary of arbitral authority on this issue, declaring:

> "It is reasonably well-established by arbitral precedent that permanent re-assignments of bargaining unit duties to non-bar-

---

[59]Ben Secours Hosp., Inc., 79-2 ARB ¶8594 (Matthews, 1979)("basic problem is to balance the rights of management to direct its operations and to discharge effectively its responsibilities for the success of the Hospital with the right of the Union to protect the job security of its members and the basic integrity of the bargaining unit." Id. at 5658.).
[60]80 LA 986 (1983).
[61]See, e.g., Western Craft Paper Group, 74 LA 13 (Allen, 1980); Citterio U.S.A. Corp., 80 LA 1027 (DiLauro, 1983)(intent, clarity of language, bargaining history, and past practice relevant factors); Teledyne Monarch Rubber, 75 LA 963 (Feldman, 1980)(past practice of management in programming of microprocessing equipment); E.W. Bliss Co., 40 LA 1032 (Klein, 1963)(past practice of taking inventory).

gaining unit employees represent a dilution of the bargaining unit and a loss of representation rights over work formerly under the bargaining agent's control. *Even in the absence of express provisions in the collective bargaining agreement limiting such transfers of duties, a constructive obligation exists on the part of the employer by reason of the recognition and seniority provisions, among others, to prevent the invasion of bargaining unit work by non-bargaining unit personnel.* The problem of balancing the legitimate interests of the employees and the union in work opportunity within the bargaining unit against the legitimate interests of the employer in efficient operation of the business becomes more difficult when, in the course of a comprehensive technological change, job duties become significantly changed or modified. Notwithstanding these difficulties, the employer has a clear obligation to respect the integrity of the bargaining unit.

"*What constitutes 'bargaining unit work' and what constitutes 'maintaining the integrity of the bargaining unit' cannot be defined in broad legal or philosophical principles. Rather, it is a factual question uniquely dependent on the particular characteristics of the job duties which have undergone change and have been reassigned.* Where the job duties within the bargaining unit have been eliminated, where the job duties have been significantly changed to encompass duties historically excluded from the bargaining unit, or where the changed duties embrace significantly different skills from those normally possessed by the bargaining unit, there can be little quarrel with the conclusion that there has been no invasion of the bargaining unit or the conclusion that the integrity of the bargaining unit has been maintained."[62]

The better weight of authority may be represented by the decision quoted above. That is, the permanent reassignment or transfer of bargaining-unit work to non-unit personnel represents a dilution of the unit and, accordingly, before a company can effect such a transfer, "good cause" must be demonstrated. In view of the trend in case law dealing with transfers of unit work during the term of a collective bargaining agreement,[63] however, it is unclear whether arbitrators will continue to imply any limitations on the discretion of management to transfer work. One federal court, for example, vacated an arbitrator's award which had held that even though the contract was silent on the subject of work transfers, management could not transfer work outside the jurisdiction

---

[62]Bell Tel. Co. (Case 14-30-1000-72)(unpublished), quoted in Bell Tel. Co., 75 LA 750, 759 (Garrett, 1980) (emphasis added in 75 LA 750).
[63]See Chapter 15, infra, notes 45–70, and accompanying text.

of the unit. The arbitrator had stated that "[t]he general rule to be applied here [when the agreement is silent] is that by entering into a collective bargaining agreement an employer implicitly agrees to perform the work covered by the agreement in accordance with the terms of that agreement."[64] The court, citing decisions by the courts and NLRB, concluded as follows:

> When the contract is silent regarding transfers of work outside the bargaining unit the rule to be applied is clear: . . . "unless transfers are specifically prohibited by the bargaining agreement, an employer is free to transfer work out of the bargaining unit if: (1) the employer . . . bargain[s] in good faith to impasse; and (2) the employer is not motivated by anti-union animus."[65]

The court pointed out that the arbitrator, "[i]nstead of applying this rule to the facts of the present case," formulated a "general rule" that allowed no unilateral changes by a contract signatory. The federal court considered this the "wrong legal standard in manifest disregard of the proper authority."[66]

Disclosing Classification/Evaluation Schemes

Where two employees filed grievances alleging that their duties and job descriptions were the same as higher job classifications but both were classified in lower salary ranges, the Eighth Circuit, upholding the NLRB, ruled that a union was entitled to detailed information concerning how a company evaluated certain job classifications. The court found that the company's job evaluation scheme was a complicated, highly sophisticated plan to determine job classifications and salaries, and that the union needed this information to determine whether the grievants were placed into the proper grade. The rationale of the court is of special note.

---

[64]Lone Star Indus. v. Teamsters Local 291, ___ F. Supp. ___, 119 LRRM 2121, 2122 (N.D. Cal., 1985).
[65]119 LRRM at 2122, citing Boeing Co. v. NLRB, 581 F.2d 793, 797, 99 LRRM 2847 (CA 9, 1978); University of Chicago v. NLRB, 514 F.2d 942, 89 LRRM 2113 (CA 7, 1976); Newport News Shipbldg. & Dry Dock Co. v. NLRB, 602 F.2d 73, 77, 101 LRRM 2998 (CA 4, 1979); Newspaper Printing Corp. v. NLRB, 625 F.2d 956, 964, 104 LRRM 2432 (CA 10, 1980); Milwaukee Spring II, 268 NLRB 601 at 11, 115 LRRM 1065 (1984).
[66]119 LRRM at 2123.

Information pertaining to the wages, hours and working conditions of employees in the bargaining unit is so intrinsic to the core of the employer-employee relationship that it is considered presumptively relevant. . . .

. . .

[T]he sole purpose of the Company's job evaluation plan is to determine the salary range for each clerical position by placing each position into one of seven lettered categories. The placement of a clerical position into a lower instead of a higher lettered category causes a salary differential. When the two grievants filed grievances contending that their positions were improperly placed in a lower lettered category than each employee thought appropriate, in effect they were contending that the Company was not paying them enough money for the work they were performing. To determine whether to submit these grievances to arbitration, the Union needed the requested information to determine whether, as the grievants contended, the duties they performed were similar to other clerk positions which were placed into a higher grade.

The job evaluation manual is relevant because it explains the operation of the job evaluation plan, including the factors used to evaluate clerical positions, the definition of these factors, and the weight assigned to each factor. The current job descriptions for departmental clerks are needed to compare duties with those duties performed by the grievants.[67]

The authors believe that the Eighth Circuit was correct in finding that the employer has an obligation to provide a union with information on its job-evaluation and/or job-classification scheme.[68]

---

[67]Procter & Gamble Mfg. Co. v. NLRB, 603 F.2d 1310, 102 LRRM 2128, 2130–31 (CA 8, 1979).

[68]See, e.g., Washington Hosp. Center, 270 NLRB 396, 116 LRRM 1459 (1984) (holding that management must make available a job-classification and salary-review study even though outside recommendations had not been fully implemented); New York Times, 270 NLRB 1267, 117 LRRM 1117 (1984)(holding employer must furnish union with names, job classifications, and functions of employees performing editing and formatting work). See also General Motors Corp. v. NLRB, 700 F.2d 1083, 112 LRRM 2976 (CA 6, 1983), where the Sixth Circuit, upholding the Board, ruled that original time study worksheets upon which the employer relied in establishing production standards were relevant and necessary to the union's bargaining and grievance evaluation function, even though the production-standard grievances were resolved in the past without original time study worksheets.

Chapter 15

Material Changes in Business Operations

Legal Authority

Plant sales, liquidations, partial closings, plant relocations, and subcontracting bring the employer's interest in entrepreneurial control of the business into direct conflict with labor's interest in job security and work preservation. Unions have traditionally sought protection from business closings by arguing that employers should be compelled to bargain such decisions under Section 8(a)(5) of Taft-Hartley.[1] Unfortunately, both the National Labor Relations Board and the appellate courts have ruled inconsistently regarding plant closings and relocations. Moreover, recent decisions by the NLRB have left a number of questions unanswered.

This section examines management's obligations to bargain about the decision and effects of a partial or total business closing. The right of an employer to transfer bargaining-unit work is also analyzed. Arbitrators' awards frequently track NLRB and court decisions in plant- and work-relocation cases. As such, an advocate or arbitrator must have a working knowledge of the law involving changes in business operations in order to determine which management prerogatives may be unilaterally implemented and which are restricted by law.

---

[1] 29 U.S.C. §158(a)(5).

Management's Duty to Bargain
About Operational Changes

A closing or liquidation may be total, as in the case where an employer simply sells or transfers its assets and stops doing business altogether. Partial closings or liquidations may be effected by (a) liquidating a part of the assets, (b) transferring work from one plant to another—usually non-union—plant, or (c) subcontracting work from one plant to a bona fide outside contractor. A third situation, referred to as a "runaway shop," involves a business relocation where the employer, in order to circumvent the labor agreement, closes a business at one location and reopens at another. It is a sham transaction and the employer's action is frequently challenged under an "alter ego" theory, as discussed later in this chapter.

"Decision" and "Effects" Bargaining

The obligation to bargain over a decision to make a material business change simply requires an employer to notify its employees' representative that an operational change which will affect employee tenure is planned and to discuss and consider in good faith any suggestions the union might offer concerning alternative courses. This duty to "decision bargain" is designed to accommodate the employees' security interest in continued employment and the business interests of the employer. The employer's obligation to bargain "does not include the obligation to agree, but solely to engage in a full and frank discussion with the union."[2] However, a bona fide effort to explore alternatives that would mutually satisfy and accommodate both the employer and the employees must be made. If such efforts fail, the employer is free to unilaterally make its decision. Compelling an employer to decision bargain does not preempt its freedom to manage a business. In this respect the Third Circuit has declared that the statute's purpose, and the NLRB's sole function, is to assure that each party has the opportunity to influence the final decision, irrespective of whether the final decision is actually influenced by "full and frank" discussion.[3]

---

[2]Ozark Trailers, Inc., 161 NLRB 561, 63 LRRM 1264, 1268 (1966).
[3]Brockway Motor Trucks v. NLRB, 582 F.2d 720, 99 LRRM 2013 (CA 3, 1978).

Decision bargaining does not encompass including union representatives in management decision making concerning such areas as investments, advertising, operation strategies, or product design. The duty does not give employees an equal voice in corporate decision making.[4] Rather, the duty to decision bargain requires that the employer, upon deciding to make an operational change having a direct impact on employment, notify the union of the plan, confer in good faith, and discuss any alternatives the union may formulate before implementing the modification.

In contrast to decision bargaining, "effects bargaining" focuses not on ways that the contemplated change might be avoided, but instead on the terms under which it will be effectuated.[5] The NLRB first outlined its position on effects bargaining in *Brown Truck and Trailer Manufacturing Co.*,[6] holding that an employer violated its duty to bargain about the impact of an otherwise lawful plant closing and transfer. While the Board did not declare that the decision to transfer operations was a mandatory subject of bargaining, it ruled that the company had a good faith obligation "at least, to advise the union of the contemplated move and to give the union the opportunity to bargain with respect to the contemplated move as it affected the employees."[7]

The purpose of the duty to bargain over the effects of a decision has been described as to provide the union with "an opportunity to bargain over the rights of the employees whose employment status will be altered by the managerial decision."[8] Effects bargaining also provides an opportunity to moderate the decision's impact on the work force.

The courts have not limited the scope of effects bargaining to a specific list of subjects. All aspects related to the decision may be encompassed in the broad scope of effects bargaining.[9] Such bargaining topics may include severance pay, pension

---

[4]First Nat'l Maintenance Corp. v. NLRB, 452 U.S. 666, 107 LRRM 2705, 2709 (1981).
[5]See, e.g., Soule Glass & Glazing Co. v. NLRB, 652 F.2d 1055, 107 LRRM 2781, 2796 (CA 1, 1981).
[6]106 NLRB 999, 32 LRRM 1580 (1953).
[7]32 LRRM at 1582.
[8]Ozark Trailers, Inc., 161 NLRB 561, 63 LRRM 1264, 1266 (1966), quoting NLRB v. Royal Plating & Polishing Co., 350 F.2d 191, 196, 60 LRRM 2033 (CA 3, 1965).
[9]NLRB v. Acme Indus. Prods., 439 F.2d 40, 76 LRRM 2697, 2699 (CA 6, 1971).

eligibility, and recognition of seniority in any subsequent re-opening or rehiring.

While many courts continue to view the distinction be-tween decision and effects bargaining as a "real one,"[10] others have argued that the distinction is "more apparent than real,"[11] or "may be one which in actuality barely exists."[12] In this regard one commentator has observed:

> The goals of decision and effects bargaining are essentially identical: to afford the affected employees' bargaining repre-sentative notice sufficiently in advance of the implementation of an operational change to permit the union the opportunity, through bargaining, to preserve jobs and otherwise protect the interests of employees. Further, their mechanical features are alike. Within their respective spheres, the scope of bargaining is equally broad, and in both, the union has the right to secure information under the employer's control which the union needs in order to bargain intelligently. Finally, and most critically, the duties attach at virtually the same time, i.e., sufficiently in advance of the implementation of a change as to permit the union a "meaningful opportunity" to bargain.[13]

Further, the Board has recognized that, at times, the "effects" are inextricably interwoven with the "decision" so that there is no way to prevent bargaining on the former from having an impact on the decision itself. As stated by the Board,

> while meaningful bargaining over the *effects* of a decision to close one plant may in the circumstances of a particular case be all that the employees' representative can actually achieve, especially where the economic factors guiding the management decision to close or to move or to subcontract are so compelling that employee concessions cannot possibly alter the cost situ-ation, nevertheless in other cases the effects are so inextricably interwoven with the decision itself that bargaining limited to effects will not be meaningful if it must be carried on within a framework of a decision which cannot be revised. An interpre-tation of the law which carries the obligation to "effects", there-

---

[10]NLRB v. North Carolina Coastal Motor Lines, 542 F.2d 637, 93 LRRM 2411 (CA 4, 1976).

[11]Miscimarra, "The NLRB and Managerial Discretion: Plant Closings, Reloca-tions, Subcontracting, and Automation," Labor Rels. and Pub. Policy Series, No. 24, (Indus. Research Unit, The Wharton School, Univ. of Pa., 1980). See generally Swift, "The NLRB and Management Decision Making," Labor Rels. and Pub. Policy Series, No. 9, 4–42 (Indus. Research Unit, The Wharton School, Univ. of Pa., 1980).

[12]Kohler, "Distinctions Without Differences: Effects Bargaining in Light of First National Maintenance," 5 Ind. Rel. L. J. 402, 420 (1983).

[13]Id. at 421.

fore, cannot well stop short of the decision itself which directly affects "terms and conditions of employment".[14]

Plant Closings and Liquidations

In an early subcontracting case, the Supreme Court, in dictum, referred to management's right to make business decisions such as to close or relocate a plant. In *Fibreboard Paper Products Corp. v. NLRB*,[15] the Court ruled that an employer's decision to subcontract plant maintenance work formerly performed by the bargaining unit was a mandatory subject of bargaining. Writing for the majority, Chief Justice Warren stated:

> The subject matter of the present dispute is well within the literal meaning of the phrase "terms and conditions of employment."... A stipulation with respect to the contracting out of work performed by members of the bargaining unit might appropriately be called a "condition of employment." The words even more plainly cover termination of employment which, as the facts of this case indicate, necessarily results from the contracting out of work performed by members of the established bargaining unit.[16]

The Court reasoned that the decision did not alter the firm's basic operation, and therefore requiring the company to bargain would not unreasonably burden the employer:

> The Company's decision to contract out the maintenance work did not alter the Company's basic operation. The maintenance work still had to be performed in the plant. No capital investment was contemplated; the Company merely replaced existing employees with those of an independent contractor to do the same work under similar conditions of employment. Therefore, to require the employer to bargain about the matter would not significantly abridge his freedom to manage the business.[17]

Furthermore, labor costs were a motivating factor behind the decision, which suggested that the decision was amenable to collective bargaining. The Court accordingly held that the type of subcontracting at issue in *Fibreboard*—the replacement of employees in the existing bargaining unit with those

---

[14]Ozark Trailers, Inc., 161 NLRB 561, 570, 63 LRRM 1264, 1269 (1966)(emphasis in original).
[15]379 U.S. 203, 57 LRRM 2609 (1964).
[16]57 LRRM at 2612 (citation omitted).
[17]Id. at 2613.

of an independent contractor to do the same work under similar conditions of employment—was a mandatory subject of bargaining.

Of special note is the often-cited concurring opinion of Justice Stewart, who sought to limit the scope of the decision. Taking a "middle-of-the-road" approach between the two extreme positions concerning reductions in employment as triggering the duty to decision bargain, Stewart stated:

> [T]here are . . . areas where decisions by management may quite clearly imperil job security, or indeed terminate employment entirely. An enterprise may decide to invest in labor-saving machinery. Another may resolve to liquidate its assets and go out of business. Nothing the Court holds today should be understood as imposing a duty to bargain collectively regarding such managerial decisions, which lie at the core of entrepreneurial control. Decisions concerning the commitment of investment capital and the basic scope of the enterprise are not in themselves primarily about conditions of employment, though the effect of the decision may be necessarily to terminate employment.[18]

Stewart also noted that it is up to Congress to change the balance between labor and management with respect to operating the business:

> Congress may eventually decide to give organized labor or government a far heavier hand in controlling what until now have been considered the prerogatives of private business management. That path would mark a sharp departure from the traditional principles of a free enterprise economy. Whether we should follow it is, within constitutional limitations, for Congress to choose. But it is a path which Congress certainly did not choose when it enacted the Taft-Hartley Act.[19]

In the following term, the Court, in *Textile Workers UTWA v. Darlington Manufacturing Co.*,[20] ruled that management has the absolute right to close an entire business, even if the liquidation is motivated by anti-union animus. In *Darlington*, the company threatened to close a textile mill if the union won a representation election. When the union won, the board of directors voted to liquidate the corporation. The action was approved by the stockholders and the plant ceased operations

---

[18]Id. at 2617.
[19]Id. at 2618.
[20]380 U.S. 263, 58 LRRM 2657 (1965).

entirely. All plant machinery and equipment was sold piece-meal at auction.

The NLRB found that *Darlington* had been closed because of anti-union animus.[21] The Board, finding Darlington to be part of a single integrated employer group controlled through Deering-Milliken, concluded that Darlington violated Sections 8(a)(3) and 8(a)(5) of Taft-Hartley.

On review, the court of appeals held that even if the Board was correct in determining that Deering-Milliken had the status of a single employer, a company has the absolute right to close out a part or all of its business regardless of anti-union motives.[22] The Supreme Court held that "an employer has the absolute right to terminate his entire business for any reason he pleases." But the Court disagreed with the lower court's finding that "such right includes the ability to close part of a business no matter what the reason." The Court reasoned that a complete plant closing, albeit discriminatory, in effect ends the employer-employee relationship. Rejecting the argument that a closing motivated by anti-union animus was analogous to a discriminatory lockout, the Court concluded:

> One of the purposes of the Labor Act is to prohibit discriminatory use of economic weapons in an effort to obtain future benefits. The discriminatory lockout designed to destroy a union, like a "runaway shop," is a lever which has been used to discourage collective employee activities in the future. But a complete liquidation of a business yields no such future benefit for the employer, if the termination is bona fide. . . .
>
> We are not presented here with the case of a "runaway shop," whereby Darlington would transfer its work to another plant or open a new plant in another locality to replace its closed plant. . . . Such [a case] would involve discriminatory employer action for the purpose of obtaining some benefit in the future from the new employees. We hold here only that when an employer closes his entire business, even if the liquidation is motivated by vindictiveness towards the union, such action is not an unfair labor practice.[23]

The majority pointed out that a total closing must be distinguished from a closing of one or more facilities by an employer having an interest in other facilities. A discriminatory partial closing may affect the remaining business op-

---

[21] 139 NLRB 241, 51 LRRM 1278 (1965).
[22] 325 F.2d 682, 54 LRRM 2499 (CA 4, 1963).
[23] 58 LRRM at 2660–61.

erations and afford the employer a chance to discourage the exercising of bargaining or organizational rights among remaining employees.

The *Darlington* Court held that a decision to partially close is an unfair labor practice if (1) it is motivated by a purpose to chill unionism in any of the remaining plants of the single employer and, (2) the employer may reasonably have foreseen that such a closing would have that effect. The Court stated:

> If the persons exercising control over a plant being closed for anti-union reasons (1) have an interest in another business, whether or not affiliated with or engaged in the same line of commercial activity as the closed plant, of sufficient substantiality to give promise of their reaping a benefit from the discouragement of unionization in that business; (2) act to close their plant with the purpose of producing such a result; and (3) occupy a relationship to the other business which makes it realistically foreseeable that its employees will fear that such business will also be closed down if they persist in organizational activities, we think that an unfair labor practice has been made out.[24]

One reading of *Darlington* is that the NLRB may not find a Section 8(a)(5) violation in complete-plant-closing cases. On the other hand, one can read the decision to mean that while it is not an unfair labor practice to close an entire business, whatever management's motivation for so doing, the decision to close is still a mandatory subject of bargaining.[25]

First National Maintenance Corp. v. NLRB,[26] a 1981 case, is the Supreme Court's most recent pronouncement as of this writing on the overall subject of plant closings. In that case FNM, an employer in the business of providing housekeeping, cleaning, maintenance, and related services at its customer's premises, terminated a maintenance contract with the Greenpark Nursing Home and discharged the employees who had been working under that contract. An administrative law judge for the NLRB held that FNM failed to satisfy its duty to bar-

---

[24]Id. at 2661–62. One commentator has correctly noted that: "Darlington protects 'spectator' employees who are in a position to be intimidated by discrimination practiced against employees at *other* plants, but offers no protection to the direct victims of discrimination at the plant or department that is shut down." Miscimarra, supra note 11, at 173.

[25]See Miscimarra, supra note 11, at 137.

[26]452 U.S. 666, 107 LRRM 2705 (1981).

gain concerning both the decision to terminate the Greenpark contract and the effect of the decision upon the bargaining unit. The ALJ declared:

> That the discharge of a man is a change in his conditions of employment hardly needs comment. In these obvious facts, the law is clear. When an employer's work complement is represented by a union and he wishes to alter the hiring arrangements, be his reason lack of money or a mere desire to become richer, the law is no less clear that he must first talk to the union about it. . . . If [the union] had been given an opportunity to talk, something might have been worked out to transfer these people to other parts of [the] business.[27]

The ALJ also pointed out that FNM's business involved "taking on, finishing, or discontinuing this or that particular job," and that "there was no capital involved when it decided to terminate the Greenpark job. The closing of this one spot in no sense altered the nature of its business, nor did it substantially affect its total size."[28]

The NLRB adopted the administrative law judge's findings without further analysis.[29] The Second Circuit enforced the Board's order, but reasoned differently.[30] The appellate court stated that no *per se* rule could be formulated to govern an employer's decision to terminate part of its business. According to the court, the obligation to bargain creates a rebuttable presumption in favor of mandatory bargaining over the employer's decision:

> We believe that the determination whether to impose a duty to bargain should not depend on the relative injury to the employer and the employees, but rather on the relative merits of the arguments put forth as to those classic considerations of whether the purposes of the statute are furthered by the decision to impose a duty to bargain in a particular case.
>
> Accordingly, the presumption that the employer has an obligation to bargain over a decision partially to close the business may be rebutted by showing that the purposes of the statute would not be furthered by imposition of a duty to bargain.

The court of appeals went on to provide examples:

> The employer might overcome the presumption by demonstrating that bargaining over the decision would be futile, since the

---

[27]242 NLRB 462, 465, 101 LRRM 1177 (1979).
[28]Id. at 466.
[29]Id. at 462.
[30]NLRB v. First Nat'l Maintenance Corp., 627 F.2d 596, 104 LRRM 2924 (1980).

purposes of the statute would not be served by ordering the
parties to bargain when it is clear that the employer's decision
cannot be changed. Other relevant considerations would be that
the closing was due to emergency financial circumstances, or
that the custom of the industry, shown by the absence of such
an obligation from typical collective bargaining agreements, is
not to bargain over such decisions. The presumption might also
be rebutted if it could be demonstrated that forcing the employer to bargain would endanger the vitality of the entire
business, so that the purposes of the statute would not be fur-
thered by mandating bargaining to benefit some employees to
the potential detriment of the remainder. This might be a particularly significant point if the number to be laid off was small
and the number of the remainder was large.[31]

The Supreme Court reversed the Second Circuit and ruled
that an economically motivated *decision* to partially close was
beyond the requirements of bargaining. In other words, the
decision itself to partially close a business for economically-
motivated reasons is not part of Section 8(d)'s "terms and
conditions" over which Congress has mandated bargaining.

Writing for the majority, Justice Blackmun outlined various types of management decisions:

> Some management decisions, such as choice of advertising
> and promotion, product type and design, and financing arrange-
> ments, have only an indirect and attenuated impact on the
> employment relationship. . . . Other management decisions, such
> as the order of succession of layoffs and recalls, production quo-
> tas, and work rules, are almost exclusively "an aspect of the
> relationship" between employer and employee. . . . The present
> case concerns a third type of management decision, one that
> had a direct impact on employment, since jobs were inexorably
> eliminated by the termination, but had as its focus only the
> economic profitability of the contract with Greenpark, a concern
> under these facts wholly apart from the employment relation-
> ship. This decision, involving a change in the scope and direc-
> tion of the enterprise, is akin to the decision whether to be in
> business at all, "not in [itself] primarily about conditions of
> employment though the effect of the decision may be necessarily
> to terminate employment." . . . At the same time, this decision
> touches on a matter of central and pressing concern to the union
> and its member employees: the possibility of continued em-
> ployment and the retention of the employees' very jobs.[32]

---

[31]104 LRRM at 2928.
[32]107 LRRM at 2709 (citations omitted).

Justice Blackmun proposed a balancing test that, in his words, would not "serve either party's individual interest, but . . . [would] foster in a neutral manner a system in which the conflict between these interests may be resolved."[33] In stressing "an employer's need for unencumbered decision-making," Justice Blackmun said that "bargaining over management decisions that have a substantial impact on the continued availability of employment should be required only if the benefit, for labor-management relations and the collective bargaining process, outweighs the burden placed on the business." Although the union would "be impelled, in seeking these ends, to offer concessions, information, and alternatives that might be helpful to management or forestall or prevent the termination of jobs," Justice Blackmun thought it unlikely that requiring bargaining over the decision itself would "augment the flow of information and suggestions."[34]

Justice Blackmun noted that if labor costs are an important factor in the decision to close, management has an incentive to voluntarily discuss the decision with the union and to seek concessions that will permit continued operations. On the other hand, he said, particular circumstances may arise where "management may have great need for speed, flexibility, and secrecy in meeting business opportunities and exigencies." Further, he observed, "the employer also may have no feasible alternative to the closing, and even good faith bargaining over it may be both futile and cause the employer additional loss."[35]

Within the opinion the Court said the decision "intimate[d] no view as to other types of management decisions such as plant relocations, sales, subcontracting, automation, etc., which are to be considered on their facts."[36]

---

[33]Id. at 2710.
[34]Id. at 2710–11.
[35]Id. at 2711.
[36]Id. at 2713 n.22. The General Counsel of the NLRB has argued that the Court's decision in *First National Maintenance* covered economically motivated decisions to go wholly out of business, to terminate a distinct line of business, or to sell a business to another and no longer remain in it. NLRB, Office of the General Counsel Memorandum No. 81-57, Nov. 30, 1981, reprinted in 4 Lab. L. Rep. (CCH) ¶9271. In the latter two situations, the General Counsel asserted that the Board had come to the same conclusion prior to the *First National Maintenance* decision. See, e.g., Kingwood Mining Co., 210 NLRB 844, 86 LRRM 1203 (1974), affirmed, 515 F.2d 1018, 90 LRRM 2844 (CA DC, 1975)(employer ceased coal mining operations while continuing to operate its coal tipple); General Motors Corp., 191 NLRB 951 (1971), affirmed, Auto

Fibreboard, Darlington, and *First National Maintenance* consider, either directly or in dictum, the scope of the employer's duty to bargain over the decision to close all or a portion of its operations. Although it is difficult to determine whether an employer has a duty to bargain over a *decision* to close,[37] clearly an employer has the duty to bargain over the *effects* of a partial or total closing.

The First Circuit, in *Penntech Papers, Inc., v. NLRB,*[38] stated that "in order to meet its obligation to bargain over the effects on employees of a decision to close, an employer must conduct bargaining 'in a meaningful manner and at a meaningful time.' "[39] Thus, when an employer notified the union of its decision to close on the very same day it gave notice, the court of appeals, affirming the Board, held that the union was not given adequate opportunity to bargain over the effects of the decision.

In another decision, *Soule Glass and Glazing Co. v. NLRB*[40] the administrative law judge had previously found that a company announced its decision to close "without fully revealing and discussing all the effects of this closure on the employees and that although the company discussed with the Union some of the effects, . . . there was no meaningful bargaining since the company had already unilaterally decided upon the effects."[41] In its subsequent decision the First Circuit, while stating that the company had an obligation to bargain over the effects of the decision to close, nevertheless reversed the finding that there was bad faith bargaining since, in its opinion, the Union was given a "meaningful chance to offer counter-proposals and counter-arguments to the company's 'effects' proposals" and, according to the court, "[t]hat is all the Act requires."[42]

The Fourth Circuit, in *Universal Security Instruments v. NLRB,*[43] also addressed an employer's obligation to effects

---

Workers Local 864 v. NLRB, 470 F.2d 422, 81 LRRM 2439 (CA DC, 1972)(sale of retail outlet to franchise dealer).

[37]See text accompanying notes 71–77, infra.

[38]706 F.2d 18, 113 LRRM 2219 (CA 1, 1983).

[39]113 LRRM at 2225, citing First Nat'l Maintenance Corp. v. NLRB, 452 U.S. 666, 681-82, 107 LRRM 2705 (1981).

[40]652 F.2d 1055, 107 LRRM 2781 (CA 1, 1981).

[41]107 LRRM at 2797.

[42]Id. at 2797, citing NLRB v. W.R. Grace & Co., 571 F.2d 279, 282, 98 LRRM 2001 (CA 5, 1978).

[43]649 F.2d 247, 107 LRRM 2518 (CA 4, 1981).

bargain. The company recognized its duty to effects bargain its decision to close a warehouse, but questioned the NLRB's finding that the several labor-management meetings held prior to the closing did not constitute good-faith bargaining. These meetings failed to cover problems associated with such closing effects as transfer, severance pay, and seniority questions. Although the company claimed that it was willing to discuss these issues (the union did not bring them up at bargaining), the court upheld a finding that "these meetings were insufficient to satisfy the company's duty because they came too late for effective bargaining to take place."[44]

Transfer or Relocation of Unit Work

A typical transfer or relocation of bargaining-unit work involves two or more facilities, although the operational independence between the facilities may vary from complete control to complete independence. An employer may operate more than one unionized plant and, for whatever reasons, decide to transfer work from one unionized location to another. More commonly, an employer may wish to transfer work from a union facility to a facility that is not organized. A variant of either of the above situations involves a transfer or relocation that, on its face, appears to be between separate and distinct business entities but in reality involves an exchange between an employer and its "alter ego." In all three situations, if the employer's transfer of work is motivated by anti-union animus, or intended to undermine the union's status as collective bargaining representative, the statute is violated.[45] The more difficult cases are presented where anti-union animus is absent and the union alleges that by transferring work the employer is violating its statutory obligation to bargain.

Transfer From One Unit to Another

A company maintaining facilities represented by different locals of the same union may want to consider the respective bargaining agreements when deciding whether certain operations should be transferred. For example, in *Zipp v. Bohn*

---

[44]107 LRRM at 2526.
[45]See, e.g., NCR Corp., 271 NLRB 1212, 117 LRRM 1062, 1063 (1984).

Heat Transfer Group,[46] a producer of heat transfer coils in Danville, Illinois, was represented by Local 1271 of the United Auto Workers. The company also maintained a facility in Glasgow, Kentucky, that was represented by UAW Local 1847. After suffering a loss of business at its Illinois facility, the company concluded that it must either gain concessions from Local 1271 or transfer work to the Kentucky plant. Unable to gain concessions through bargaining with Local 1271, it negotiated an agreement with Local 1847 to relocate certain manufacturing operations to the Kentucky plant.

A federal district court in Illinois found that the company did not meet its duty to bargain about the effects of the relocation of work where the employer "withheld information from the Union and negotiated with Local 1847 about the bargaining unit work of Local 1271 while the 1271 collective bargaining agreement was still in effect."[47] Citing *Los Angeles Marine Hardware Co. v. NLRB,*[48] a decision by the Ninth Circuit, the court stated that a relocation motivated by an attempt to avoid the provisions of a collective bargaining agreement constitutes an unfair labor practice.

The duty to bargain over decisions involving the transfer or consolidation of bargaining unit work was addressed by the NLRB in 1984 in *Otis Elevator II.*[49] The Board held that an employer which transfers work from one plant to another has no statutory duty to bargain with the union about the *decision* itself, unless that decision is based solely on an attempt to reduce labor costs or a specific clause in the collective bargaining agreement creates a duty to bargain. However, the employer remains obligated to bargain about the *effects* of the transfer upon the bargaining unit.

Although the Board members agreed on the outcome in *Otis Elevator II,* they each stated a different rationale in reaching a decision. In the view of Chairman Dotson and Member Hunter, if an employer's decision turns upon a change in the nature and direction of a significant facet of its business, the decision is a nonmandatory subject, even if labor costs were one of the factors underlying the decision. Further, they stated

---

[46]110 LRRM 3013 (C.D. Ill., 1982).
[47]Id. at 3014.
[48]602 F.2d 1302, 102 LRRM 2498 (CA 9, 1979).
[49]269 NLRB 891, 115 LRRM 1281 (1984)(reversing Otis Elevator I, 255 NLRB 235, 106 LRRM 1343 (1981)).

that this rationale would apply to "decisions [by an employer] to sell a business or a part thereof, to dispose of its assets, to restructure or to reconsolidate operations, to subcontract, to invest in labor-saving machinery, to change the methods of finance or of sales, advertising, product design, and all other decisions akin to the foregoing."[50] The decision is a mandatory subject in their view if it does not turn upon a change in the nature and direction of a significant facet of the business, and it is motivated by labor costs.

In the view of Member Dennis, for a decision to be a mandatory subject of bargaining, the General Counsel must first prove that the decision is amenable to resolution through the bargaining process. Assuming that the General Counsel can prove this, it must then be established that the benefit for the collective bargaining process outweighs the burden on the business. Dennis further stated that this "balancing" test would apply to "decisions that have a direct impact on employment, but have as their focus only the economic profitability of the employer's operation."[51] Such decisions include plant relocations, consolidations, automation, and subcontracting.

Member Zimmerman reasoned that if a decision is amenable to resolution through the collective bargaining process, then the benefits of bargaining would outweigh the burdens, absent a showing by the employer that there is an urgent need for speed, flexibility, or secrecy, as referred to by the Supreme Court in *First National Maintenance*.[52]

The General Counsel has suggested an analytical framework for concluding whether a transfer decision is mandatory, arguably mandatory, or nonmandatory, posing three questions:

(1) Does the decision involve a change in the nature and direction of a significant facet of the business?
(2) Is the decision motivated by labor costs?
(3) Is the decision amenable to resolution through the process of collective bargaining, and if so, do the po-

---

[50]115 LRRM at 1283 n.5.
[51]Id. at 1287–88.
[52]Id. at 1285.

tential benefits of bargaining outweigh the burdens that such bargaining would place on the employer?[53]

Accordingly, only if the answer to the first question is "no" and the answers to the remaining questions are "yes" can it be definitely concluded that the decision is a mandatory subject. However, if reduction of labor costs is a major factor in the employer's decision to transfer/relocate or consolidate, then the decision is most likely a mandatory subject.

Double-Breasted Operations

A "double-breasted" or "open shop/closed shop" operation allows an employer to compete for both union and non-union work. For example, a subcontractor operates two corporations, one hiring union employees and bidding on jobs that require unionized subcontractors, and the other hiring non-union employees and bidding only on work from general contractors who use non-union workers.[54] In certain situations a double-breasted operation may violate a labor agreement. For example, a collective bargaining contract signed by one of the companies would not bind the other if each were a separate corporation, but would bind the other if both constituted a single employer and the employees of both companies constituted a single bargaining unit or the nonsignatory company were an alter ego of the signatory company.[55] Moreover, as part of its bargaining obligation, an employer may have to make available to the union information concerning its double-breasted operations.[56]

The District of Columbia Circuit in 1982 considered the statutory rights of a "single employer" operating union and non-union facilities. In *Plumbers Local 669 v. NLRB,*[57] the employer formed two corporations, a union company, Corcoran Automatic Sprinklers (CAS), and a non-union company, A-1 Fire Protection (A-1). With "grudging union consent," the em-

---

[53]"NLRB General Counsel on Otis Elevator Guidelines," Labor Relations Yearbook—1984, 363–66 (BNA Books, 1985), reprinting Memorandum GC 84-12, June 14, 1984.

[54]See the discussion by the Fifth Circuit in NLRB v. Leonard B. Hebert, Jr. & Co., 696 F.2d 1120, 112 LRRM 2672 (CA 5, 1983).

[55]Yoder & Sons, Inc., 270 NLRB 652, 117 LRRM 1066, 1067 n.2 (1984).

[56]NLRB v. Leonard B. Hebert, Jr. & Co., 696 F.2d 1120, 112 LRRM 2672 (CA 5, 1983); Yoder & Sons, Inc., 270 NLRB 652, 117 LRRM 1066 (1984).

[57]676 F.2d 826, 110 LRRM 2125 (CA DC, 1982).

ployer laid off a number of CAS employees and hired them at A-1 to work for union wages, but without union benefits. The effect was to increase work at A-1 and decrease the work at CAS. The union unsuccessfully demanded that the CAS collective bargaining agreement be applied to A-1. The union alleged that the employer had violated Section 8(a)(5) by withdrawing work from CAS and by refusing to apply the agreement to A-1 employees. The court of appeals upheld the Board's narrow finding that the union in one facility of a double-breasted operation does not have an independent statutory right to have its contract extended to the employees of the non-union facility. The fact that the two companies constitute a single employer does not define them as a single bargaining unit.[58]

The Fourth Circuit has held that the employer does have the duty to bargain with the union over the effects of a decision to transfer bargaining unit work to its non-union operations.[59] However, the area of double-breasted operations is filled with complexities which may influence an analysis of management's obligations, as the following analysis by the District of Columbia Circuit illustrates:

> The allocation of work to a bargaining unit is a "term and condition of employment," and an employer may not unilaterally attempt to divert work away from a bargaining unit without fulfilling his statutory duty to bargain. . . .
>   . . . The crucial determinant is whether the change in relative economic fortunes was due to external economic circumstances or to a change in the employer's established practices. It is easy to envision, for example, a double-breasted operation governed by the employer's established practice to assign to the union side of the operation only work that requires union labor, and to assign all other work, of whatever size or type, to the nonunion side. In that case, if certain customers (including even past customers of the union side) decided on their own no longer to require union labor, then it would not be a change in established practice for the employer to solicit that work on behalf of, and assign it to, the nonunion side of the operation.[60]

The court pointed out that the above-described hypothetical is not the only way a double-breasted operation can be organized. Union and non-union companies could have differ-

---

[58]110 LRRM at 2127.
[59]NLRB v. North Carolina Coastal Motor Lines, Inc., 542 F.2d 637, 93 LRRM 2411 (CA 4, 1976).
[60]110 LRRM at 2128, 2129 (citations omitted).

ent maximum dollar amounts that each will handle, or one
company could work on a large "bid-only" basis, while the
other company only handled non-industrial jobs. The court
also noted:

> Whether the solicitation of a given piece of work on behalf of,
> or the assignment of that work to, the nonunion side of a double-
> breasted operation constitutes a transfer of work from the union
> side must therefore depend on the pattern of allocation estab-
> lished by the past practice of the employer in that particular
> double-breasted operation.[61]

Transfer as a Midterm Contract Modification

In *Milwaukee Spring Division of Illinois Coil Spring Co.*
(*Milwaukee Spring II*),[62] a Board majority, reversing its earlier
Milwaukee Spring I decision,[63] held that an employer's decision to transfer assembly-operations work to another facility
for economically motivated reasons was not a contract modification under Taft-Hartley. The new Board ruled that, absent
a specific clause prohibiting midcontract transfers, the collective bargaining agreement had not been "modified" and therefore the union's consent was not required to effect the transfer.
It is of special note that the parties had stipulated that the
relocation decision was a mandatory subject of bargaining and
that the employer had satisfied its obligation to bargain over
the decision to relocate the assembly operations and had been
willing to engage in effects bargaining with the Union. Accordingly, the Board's holding did not specifically embrace the
"mandatory" bargaining issue. In dictum the Board further
declared that work reassignment and relocation decisions should
not be treated differently for purposes of determining whether
there has been a midcontract modification. The Board said:

> "[U]nless transfers are specifically prohibited by the bar-
> gaining agreement, an employer is free to transfer work out of
> the bargaining unit if: (1) the employer complies with *Fibre-
> board Paper Products v. NLRB* ... by bargaining in good faith
> to impasse; and (2) the employer is not motivated by anti-union
> animus ...."[64]

---

[61]Id. at 2129.
[62]268 NLRB 601, 115 LRRM 1065 (1984), affirmed, Auto Workers v. NLRB, 765
F.2d 175, 119 LRRM 2801 (CA DC, 1985).
[63]265 NLRB 206, 111 LRRM 1486 (1982).
[64]115 LRRM at 1068, quoting University of Chicago, 210 NLRB 190, 86 LRRM
1073 (1974), enforcement denied, 514 F.2d 942, 949, 89 LRRM 2113 (CA 7, 1975).

Transfers and the "Alter Ego" Doctrine

When two nominally separate business entities are treated as if they were a single employer, the companies constitute alter egos. The "alter ego" doctrine is designed to prevent an employer from gaining an unearned advantage in its labor activities simply by altering its corporate form.[65] If alter ego status is imposed upon two entities, the labor obligations of the original employer will be carried over to the subsequent entity, and both will be held liable for any violations of bargaining obligations. In determining whether alter ego status should be imposed, the initial question to be answered is whether the same entity substantially controls both the old and new employer after the transfer of business operations. If this control exists, then it must be determined whether the transfer resulted in an expected or reasonably foreseeable benefit to the old employer that is related to the elimination of its labor obligations. When no future benefit is gained, the transfer of ownership is bona fide.[66]

Circumstances surrounding the application of the alter ego doctrine vary. A partial transfer or relocation of operations to a parent or subsidiary, a "new" company resulting from a merger, or a transfer of work and assets through a sale-and-lease agreement are a few examples. While single-employer status ultimately depends on all the circumstances of the case, the courts apply a number of criteria in determining whether two or more business entities comprise a single employer: (1) interrelation of operations, (2) common management, (3) centralized control of labor relations, and (4) common ownership.

As stated by the First Circuit, "the fundamental inquiry is whether there exists overall control of critical matters at the policy level."[67] In most alter ego cases a court will set no minimum criteria for applying the doctrine but, rather, merely list the facts that form the basis for its decision.[68] For example,

---

[65]Southport Petroleum Co. v. NLRB, 315 U.S. 100, 9 LRRM 411 (1942); Howard Johnson Co. v. Detroit Local Joint Exec. Bd., 417 U.S. 249, 86 LRRM 2449 (1974); Alkire v. NLRB, 716 F.2d 1014, 114 LRRM 2180, 2183 (CA 4, 1983).
[66]114 LRRM at 2180.
[67]Penntech Papers v. NLRB, 706 F.2d 18, 113 LRRM 2219, 2224 (CA 1, 1983). See also J.M. Tanaka Constr. v. NLRB, 675 F.2d 1029, 110 LRRM 2296 (CA 9, 1982) ("most common single factor is centralized control of labor relations").
[68]Alkire v. NLRB, 716 F.2d 1014, 114 LRRM 2180 (CA 4, 1983).

in *NLRB v. Borg Warner Corp.*[69] the Sixth Circuit held that
Pony Express was the alter ego of another corporation, Wells
Fargo—both companies were wholly owned by a third corporation, Baker Industries, which in turn was 97 percent owned
by Borg Warner. The court of appeals, upholding the NLRB,
ruled that Borg Warner violated the statute when it failed to
give timely notice to the union and to bargain over the effects
of its decision to transfer courier work from Wells Fargo to
Pony Express. The court pointed out that Pony Express and
Wells Fargo shared top executives and had common offices,
post office boxes, and lock-boxes. Also, the vice-president of
personnel rendered labor advice for both companies.[70]

Summary

Under the Supreme Court's holding in *Darlington*, an employer is free to close its plant or business even if motivated
by anti-union animus. Although an employer has no obligation to bargain over the decision to close or sell its entire
operation,[71] an employer must nevertheless bargain over the
effects of that decision.

The reasoning of *Darlington*, however, is applicable only
when the closing is a bona fide closing and not merely a temporary suspension of operations. One appellate court stated
the law as follows:

> An employer who shuts down his plant in retaliation for union
> activity and subsequently reopens it does stand to gain from

---

[69]663 F.2d 666, 108 LRRM 2862 (CA 6, 1981), cert. denied, 457 U.S. 1105, 110
LRRM 2608 (1982).

[70]See also Air Express Int'l v. NLRB, 659 F.2d 610, 108 LRRM 2795 (CA 5, 1981)
(relocation and consolidation); NLRB v. Campbell-Harris Elec., Inc., 719 F.2d 292,
114 LRRM 2881 (CA 8, 1983)(dissolution of company and subsequent forming of new
business performing same services as former enterprise); J.M. Tanaka Constr. v.
NLRB, 675 F.2d 1029, 110 LRRM 2296 (CA 9, 1982)(alter ego established to eliminate
company's high cost of dealing with unions violative of statute); NLRB v. Al Bryant,
Inc., 711 F.2d 543, 113 LRRM 3690 (CA 3, 1983); Lapp Air Conditioning, 270 NLRB
641, 116 LRRM 1299 (1984)(failing to supply information where union suspected
employer and another company of having an alter ego relationship).

[71]The Court in *Darlington* specifically pointed out that it was not confronted
with a sale of a going concern, "which might present different considerations under
Sections 8(a)(3) and 8(a)(5)." Similarly, in *First National Maintenance*, the Court, in
a footnote, stated that plant sales were not controlled by its opinion and that they
were to be considered on their particular facts. 107 LRRM at 2713 n.22. Still, in view
of the dicta in *Darlington* and *First National Maintenance*, coupled with recent holdings by the NLRB, specifically Otis Elevator II, 115 LRRM 1281 (1984), it is reasonably clear that a bona fide sale is not a mandatory subject of bargaining.

the chilling effect on any future union activity by employees at that plant, and the "closing" becomes in reality a discriminatory action against employees for engaging in protected activity—a classic unfair labor practice under §8(a)(3). Thus, the *Darlington* Court was careful to note that it was not presented with the case of a "runaway shop," in which the employer transfers work from the closed plant to another plant . . . .[72]

With respect to a partial closing, the employer similarly is free to act with no obligation to bargain about that decision as long as it is economically motivated and the benefits to collective bargaining and labor-management relations do not outweigh the burden placed on the employer.[73] Again, the employer still has the obligation to bargain about the effects of that decision.

Milwaukee Spring II holds that an employer's relocation or transfer of bargaining unit work from a contract-covered facility to another facility is not a contract modification, unless it can be shown that the relocation modified a specific term of the collective bargaining agreement. The relocation may be unlawful if the decision to relocate is a mandatory subject of bargaining (the NLRB never reached this issue in *Milwaukee Spring II*), and if the employer refuses to bargain about the decision or makes the decision prior to reaching a good-faith impasse or agreement.

Under *Otis Elevator II*, the determination of whether the transfer decision is a mandatory subject rests upon (1) the extent to which the decision changes the nature of the business, (2) the motivation behind the transfer decision, and (3) the weighing of potential benefits to the bargaining unit against the burdens on the employer. Applying *Otis*, the Board in 1984 declared that "the critical factor in determining whether a management decision is subject to mandatory bargaining is 'the essence of the decision itself, i.e., whether it turns upon a change in the nature or direction of the business, or turns upon labor costs; *not* its effect on employees nor a union's ability to offer alternatives.' "[74] As in decisions involving total or partial plant closings, even if the decision is not subject to mandatory bargaining, the employer still has the duty to bar-

---

[72]Bruce Duncan Co. v. NLRB, 590 F.2d 1304, 101 LRRM 2033, 2034 (CA 4, 1979).
[73]First Nat'l Maintenance Corp. v. NLRB, 452 U.S. 666, 107 LRRM 2705 (1981).
[74]Bostrom Div., UOP, Inc., 272 NLRB 999, 117 LRRM 1429 (1984), quoting Otis Elevator II, 269 NLRB 891, 115 LRRM 1281 (1984) (emphasis in original).

gain over the effects of a transfer, relocation, or consolidation decision.[75]

The motive and intent of the employer in deciding to cease or transfer business operations are important considerations in determining whether the decision is subject to mandatory bargaining. If the decision turns on reducing labor costs and not on a change in the basic direction of the business, then the employer's decision to subcontract, reorganize, consolidate, or relocate will probably be held to be a mandatory subject.[76] All operation-type decisions (i.e., those decisions affecting the scope, direction, or nature of the enterprise) are excluded from the limited mandatory bargaining obligations of the statute, unless labor costs are a significant consideration in the decision.[77] The only situation in which motive does not influence an employer's duty to bargain is when the employer completely goes out of business and receives no further benefits from that business.

Arbitral Authority

Arbitrators have generally rejected the proposition that absent a specific restriction in the parties' contract, an em-

---

[75]See, e.g., Benchmark Indus., Inc., 269 NLRB 1096, 116 LRRM 1005 (1984), where a three-member Board held that an employer violated the statute by refusing to bargain the effects of a decision to close a plant and terminate the work force even though the plant was totally destroyed by fire. See also Creasey Co., 268 NLRB 1425, 115 LRRM 1131 (1984)(food distributor that elected to close produce division did not violate statute when it failed to bargain with union concerning effects of closure until final week of distribution).

[76]Pennsylvania Energy Corp., 274 NLRB No. 174, 119 LRRM 1042 (1985); Nurminco, Inc., 274 NLRB No. 112, 119 LRRM 1059 (1985).

[77]After Otis Elevator II, the Board has been consistent in holding that management decisions that affect the scope, direction, or nature of the enterprise are excluded from the limited mandatory bargaining obligations under §8(d) of the Act. See, e.g., Fraser Shipyards, Inc., 272 NLRB 496, 117 LRRM 1328 (1984)(decision by employer engaged in business of constructing and repairing vessels to close machine shop and to subcontract machine work to wholly-owned division non-mandatory where decision did not turn on labor costs but on significant change in nature and direction of business); Columbia City Freight Lines, 271 NLRB 12, 116 LRRM 1311 (1984) (trucking company did not violate statute by refusing to bargain about decision to close two terminals, lay off unit employees, and transfer work to main terminal, where decision not based on labor costs but on significant change in direction of business); Bostrom Div., UOP, Inc., 272 NLRB 999, 117 LRRM 1429 (1984); Hawthorn Mellody, Inc., 275 NLRB No. 55, 119 LRRM 1079 (1985)(decision to close delivery operation and transfer to another facility non-mandatory); Inland Steel Container Co., 275 NLRB No. 129, 119 LRRM 1293 (1985)(decision to relocate plant non-mandatory where labor costs not motivating factor in employer's decision); National Metalcrafters, Inc., 276 NLRB No. 14, 120 LRRM 1080 (1985)(no duty to bargain decision to relocate where union waived right to bargain).

ployer has the absolute right to determine all material changes in the operations of the business, including plant closings or relocations, subcontracting,[78] and termination or transfer of work. The policy supporting this view has been expressed by the Supreme Court as follows:

> "The objectives of national labor policy, reflected in established principles of federal law, require that the rightful prerogative of owners independently to rearrange their businesses and even eliminate themselves as employers be balanced by some protection to the employees from a sudden change in the employment relationship. The transition from one corporate organization to another will in most cases be eased and industrial strife avoided if employees' claims continue to be resolved by arbitration rather than by the 'relative strength . . . of the contending forces.' "[79]

This section examines the extent to which managerial prerogatives are limited by arbitrators. Although the general trend is to the contrary, some arbitrators have imposed a "rule of reason" on managerial discretion, even where an employer is not obligated to bargain over a specific decision affecting the nature of the enterprise.

Sale or Liquidation Where the Contract Is Silent

Employers have argued that when a collective bargaining agreement is silent, the right to sell or liquidate all or part of a business is absolute and not subject to any procedural or substantive limitation. Further, some advocates have asserted that even though the law may impose an obligation to bargain the decision or the effects of a sale or liquidation, the obligation of an arbitrator is to interpret the contract and not to import legal or moral obligations.

A case reported by Arbitrator Thomas Gallagher illustrates particularly well the approach taken by many arbitrators where the agreement is silent. In *Pioneer Holding Co.*,[80] the employer, which operated a taxi-cab business under the name "Blue & White Cabs," notified the union that it intended

---

[78]See Chapter 16, infra, for a comprehensive discussion on management rights and subcontracting.
[79]See Hill & Sinicropi, Remedies in Arbitration, 118 (BNA Books, 1981) quoting John Wiley & Sons v. Livingston, 376 U.S. 543, 549, 55 LRRM 2769, 2772 (1964) quoting in turn *Steelworkers v. Warrior & Gulf Navigation Co.*, 363 U.S. 574, 46 LRRM 2416, 2418 (1960).
[80]79 LA 292 (1982).

to sell all of its assets under a franchising plan, and that after the sale it would cease the business of owning and operating cabs. The announcement was made approximately five months before the contemplated sale.

The union argued that the proposed transaction was not a bona fide sale but, instead, a subcontracting of the bargaining unit's work in violation of several provisions of the agreement. The "new" corporation to be formed was named "Blue & White Service Corporation," with the former shareholders assuming the shares of the new company. The old building was to be leased by the new company. The net effect of the transaction was to eliminate the jobs of 85 percent of the bargaining unit. The employer, citing judicial authority holding that the sale was not a proper subject for bargaining, argued that it could not be barred from effecting this transaction by the labor agreement.

The arbitrator pointed out that the parties' agreement may cover subjects about which an employer has no statutory duty to bargain, and an employer may do what it is not required to do under a union contract. The arbitrator explained:

> [T]o decide that a certain subject is not one within the scope of the statutory phrase, "terms and conditions of employment," is not to decide that the terms of a particular labor agreement do not contain an agreement on that subject, made without any statutory requirement that it be made.
>
> . . .
>
> The reasoning of the courts in dealing with the statutory rights and obligations of union and employer when an employer proposes a sale of his business is not directly relevant to the issue that I must decide—whether *these* parties, in their labor contract, have expressed any relevant limitation on the right of the Employer to dispose of its cabs.[81]

The arbitrator's reasoning is of particular note, especially his discussion of the reserved rights doctrine and its relation to the management rights clause contained in this agreement:

> The doctrine of Reserved Rights is the starting point for most theorists on the law of labor relations. It holds that an employer is invested with all rights over the management of his affairs except those that are taken away by law and those that he has bargained away in his contract of employment with his employees, including any collective bargaining agreement with a representative of his employees. Thus, management's

---

[81]Id. at 294–95 (emphasis in original).

rights are inherent. The authority to manage exists independent of any grant, and it encompasses all that is not given up.

The usual management rights section of a labor agreement does no more than repeat this doctrine and does little to aid in the interpretation of other clauses that, in the view of the parties involved in grievance prosecution, either do or do not limit inherent management rights. In other words, where the general kind of management rights provision appears, the argument about meaning centers around the clauses that may or may not limit the right to manage. The right to manage exists whether or not the agreement contains a provision stating its existence. It is how that right is qualified by the rest of the contract that is the essence of the dispute.[82]

This is not to assert, however, that a management rights clause is of no effect when interpreting the parties' contract. Arbitrator Gallagher, reflecting the thinking of most arbitrators on the subject, stated that the management rights section of a few labor agreements "contains such an explicit and detailed list of powers retained that it becomes necessary to determine if the parties meant by their explicit statement of such powers to limit the meaning of the other clauses of the agreement."[83] Finding the parties' management rights clause nothing more than a restatement of the doctrine of reserved rights, the arbitrator indicated that the traditional "balancing of interests" test, similar to that applied by arbitrators in subcontracting disputes, could not be applied where the entire business was being sold:

> When what is proposed is the sale of all or almost all of the business, the parties rely upon the same clauses of the labor agreement and argue for the same inferences to be drawn from them—that the management rights clause preserves the employer's right to sell and that the recognition, seniority or other such clauses preserve the union's right to continue its status. Because, however, the change proposed is not a limited one, i.e., one of temporary or minor effect on the operation, it is not possible to apply the balancing-of-interests test developed in the subcontracting cases. It is not merely the erosion of the essential interests of the parties that is at stake, as it is in the case of the subcontracting of work. The entire fundamental interest of the employer and of the union may be at issue when a sale of the business is proposed.[84]

---

[82]Id. at 296.
[83]Id.
[84]Id. at 297–98.

Absent an express provision prohibiting the sale of a business, Arbitrator Gallagher, again reflecting the view of most arbitrators,[85] found that maintenance-of-standards, seniority, recognition, and other clauses that imply a continuation of the status of the union could not be used to abort a sale of the business.

Arbitrator Marvin Feldman, in *Bryan Custom Plastics*,[86] also relied on the reserved-rights theory in ruling that an employer did not violate the parties' labor agreement when it moved two pieces of production equipment from a union plant to a non-union site. The union's primary argument was that the removal violated the "recognition" clause. As a remedy it requested that the equipment that had been moved be returned, and that the employer bargain on the matter. In rejecting the union's claim, the arbitrator reasoned as follows:

> [T]o hold the Company responsible for negotiating the dismantling and shipping off of a piece or two of production equipment under the terms of a recognition clause would be to allow the Union the right to direct the manufacturing processes of the Company. It is noted in the management prerogative clause that the Company reserves and retains solely and exclusively all of its common law rights to manage a business except as may be expressly provided to the contrary in a specific provision of the contract. Thus, it appears that a dispute as is indicated under the recognition clause, must exist under some specific provision of the contract of collective bargaining under a past practice or under some previous arbitral decision. For example, if the Company and Union had agreed in the contract that the Company may not remove production equipment without negotiation prior to shipment, then in that event that would be a recognizable dispute within the terms and meanings of the recognition clause.
>
> However, when one considers a dispute under the terms and meanings of the instant contract, one cannot dispute those rights which are specially reserved to management under the management prerogative clause. In order for the activity of the Company to be violative of the contract, there must be some special provision in the contract that the Company is violative of and that is indicated by clear and unambiguous language of the contractor by past practice or by grievance settlement. One cannot be violative of the contract if there is no special clause under which an argument can be made. One cannot negotiate those items specifically retained for management. One can only

---

[85]See text accompanying notes 115–23, infra.
[86]84-1 ARB ¶8199 (1984).

negotiate those items which are negotiable under the terms and meanings of the contract.[87]

In *Lakeland Color Press, Inc.*,[88] the collective bargaining agreement provided:

> The Employer agrees that it will not physically transfer or install any equipment to or in any other plant for the purpose of avoiding the terms of this Agreement which results in the removal of jobs or work from under this Agreement.[89]

When Lakeland, a printer of religious books, sold all of its tangible assets to a non-union competitor, Bang Printing, and continued to do business as a "broker of printed materials" for Bang, the union filed a grievance contending that the sale was a transfer of equipment "for the purpose of avoiding the terms of this Agreement." The parties' bargaining history showed that the union had proposed provisions to protect the employees in the event of a sale of the business. Arbitrator Gallagher held that the language at issue was meant to prohibit a "runaway shop," and not to bar the sale of the assets by the employer.[90]

Likewise, in *Weis Manufacturing*,[91] Arbitrator Erwin Ellmann considered whether the following provision was violated when the company announced the sale of all its assets: "[I]f the company decides to move, the employees will have the right to remain with the Company, thus holding their seniority." In denying the grievance, Arbitrator Ellmann remarked:

> The fact that the parties saw fit to protect seniority and work opportunities if the Company itself were to move its operations suggests that they recognized a different result should

---

[87]Id. at 3909.

[88]82 LA 1151 (Gallagher, 1984).

[89]Id. at 1153.

[90]See also Address-O-Mat, 36 LA 1074 (Wolff, 1961)(employer may not subvert a labor agreement by a transfer of equipment to another business where transferee is alter ego of transferor); High Point Sprinkler Co. of Boston, 67 LA 239 (Connolly, 1976)(contract prohibiting "sale, transfer, lease, assignment, receivership or bankruptcy to evade terms of this agreement"); Hercules, Inc., 54 LA 517, 521 (Wolff, 1970)("[T]he proposed move [of a plastic laboratory] is occasioned by legitimate business motives and in no way by an improper desire by the Company to subvert the collective bargaining agreement and to discredit or weaken the Union."); Crown Cork & Seal Co., 43 LA 1264, 1268 (Woodruff, 1964)("The Company's decision and its subsequent actions in shifting this work were not for the purpose of harming, prejudicing or undermining the Union . . . ."); Safeway Stores, Inc., 42 LA 353 (Ross, 1964).

[91]64-3 ARB ¶8917 (1963).

follow if a plant is closed, machinery were sold, and the Company goes out of business. If they intended to limit the right of the employer to abandon business, it is fair to expect them to have said so explicitly. Under our economic system, such restrictions can hardly rest in implication or inference.[92]

Arbitrator Arthur Ross, in *Safeway Stores, Inc.*,[93] adopted a different approach to the issue whether an out-of-unit transfer of work violated a contract that was silent:

My own thinking begins with the proposition that the exercise of the managerial function is not absolute and unrestricted, even in the absence of explicit language limiting that specific function. This is another way of stating that it is possible for an employer to violate an agreement by subcontracting work, for example, without express language on the subject. Management prerogative clauses almost always provide that managerial rights must be exercised within the limitations of the agreement.

. . .

If there is no special evidence of intent one way or the other, the arbitrator must ask himself whether constructive intent should be assigned to the parties. Constructive intent is concededly a legal fiction but is sometimes an essential element of statutory as well as contractual interpretation. The arbitrator must consider whether an implied obligation should be extracted from the various articles of the agreement which have been negotiated for the benefit of the employees and the protection of the union. Such an implied obligation is often called the "covenant of good faith and fair dealing." It is implied in every contract that neither party will take any action which improperly impairs or destroys the right of the other party to receive the fruits of the bargain. In deciding whether the covenant of good faith and fair dealing has been violated, one must examine the employer's motive in taking action which adversely affects the employees. Objective effects as well as subjective purposes must be scrutinized, in order to ascertain whether the economic interests of the employees were so disproportionately impaired as to destroy the substance of the agreement for all practical purposes. Another test is whether the employer's action was in accordance with conventional and customary business practice.[94]

---

[92]Id. at 6167.
[93]42 LA 353 (1964).
[94]Id. at 357.

Sale or Liquidation: Contractual Restrictions

Some agreements specifically outline the parties' respective rights when all or part of a business is sold or liquidated. Not infrequently, "meet and discuss" or notice limitations are negotiated.[95] If the agreement does contain a meet-and-discuss limitation, the predominant view is that management is absolved of any further obligation once a bargaining impasse is reached with the union, although there is authority to the contrary.[96]

Sometimes the agreement will provide for recognition and even preferential-type hiring rights in the event of a sale or transfer of a part of the business.[97]

Even where the agreement does not limit management's right to close or transfer its business, equitable considerations may prompt an arbitrator to apply one of these remedies. Arbitrator John Sembower, in *Ex-Cell-O Corp.*,[98] held that an employer which closed two plants had to offer to the discharged employees the first available positions at the new locations with carryover of their old seniority rights, where the employer had exacted bargaining concessions from the union by promising to keep the plants in operation in return for such concessions. Arbitrator Joseph McGoldrick, in *John B. Stetson Co.*,[99] directed a company to set aside $100,000 to cover moving expenses for employees who lost their jobs as a result of a plant transfer.

The Third Circuit, in *Teamsters Local 115 v. DeSoto, Inc.*,[100] sustained an arbitrator's award that an employer's decision to close its plant and transfer all its production to its existing out-of-state plants violated the following provision of the parties' agreement:

---

[95]See, e.g., Lever Bros. Co., 65 LA 1299 (Edes, 1976)(two weeks advance written notice to arrange for applicable seniority moves).

[96]See Hill & Sinicropi, Remedies in Arbitration, 113 (BNA Books, 1981).

[97]See, e.g., the collective bargaining agreement in Federal-Mogul Corp., 61 LA 745, 747 (Cole, 1973). In a sampling by BNA, it reported that plant shutdown or relocation limitations were discussed in 18% of the agreements sampled. In 48% of these agreements, the displaced employee had transfer rights to a new location and in 20% the employee's moving expenses were paid by the company. Basic Patterns in Union Contracts, 65 (BNA Books, 1983).

[98]60 LA 1094 (1973).

[99]28 LA 514 (1957).

[100]725 F.2d 931, 115 LRRM 2449 (CA 3, 1984).

> The Company shall not move its plant from its present location beyond the radius of twenty-five (25) miles without the written consent of the Union, but the Union shall not withhold its consent for arbitrary and capricious reasons.[101]

The court of appeals rejected the employer's argument that the award should be overturned because an NLRB administrative law judge had found that the decision to close the plant was not a mandatory subject of bargaining. The court pointed out that the ALJ's ruling did not give the employer a statutory right to ignore a contract that dealt with non-mandatory subjects. It is of note that the Third Circuit overturned the district court, which, focusing on the waste of economic resources, had concluded that the arbitrator's reopening remedy was "irrational." The court of appeals reasoned that the lower court's analysis was incompatible with the policy of deference to arbitration.[102]

Work Preservation Clauses and Transfer of Operations

Many agreements contain "work preservation" clauses that, under certain fact situations, will prevent management from effecting structural changes in a business.[103] In *Pabst Brewing Co.*,[104] the contract provided:

> The Company shall not reassign any work presently being performed by employees covered by this Agreement, to other personnel to do such work who are not in the Bargaining Unit at this plant or other facilities as set forth and defined in the NLRB certification . . . .[105]

Arbitrator Sidney Wolff ruled that in transferring for economic reasons its brewery operation from its Peoria, Illinois to its Milwaukee, Wisconsin plant, the employer violated the above work preservation clause. The arbitrator rejected the employer's argument that the clause prohibited the company from using non-unit personnel at the Illinois plant only. As a

---

[101]115 LRRM at 2452.
[102]Id. at 2455.
[103]Besides the cases cited in this section, see Food Fair Stores, Inc., 71 LA 873, 874 (Hardy, 1978); Selb Mfg. Co., 37 LA 834 (Klamon, 1961); MacFadden-Bartell Corp., 58 LA 1061 (Friedman, 1972).
[104]78 LA 772 (Wolff, 1982).
[105]Id. at 774.

remedy the arbitrator ordered Pabst to re-open the Peoria facility and reinstate the displaced employees.

A similar result was reported by Arbitrator William Ellmann in *Douwe Egberts Superior Co.*,[106] under the following provision:

> For the purpose of preserving work and job opportunities for the employees covered by this agreement, the Employer agrees that no work or services presently performed by the collective bargaining unit for customers located in the State of Michigan will be subcontracted, transferred, assigned, leased or conveyed, in whole or part to any other plant, vendor, person or non-union employees except if equivalent work or services are substituted.[107]

The arbitrator found the employer, in closing its Detroit facility and moving to Chicago, violated the above-cited subcontracting provision.

The Eighth Circuit, in *Manhattan Coffee Co. v. Teamsters Local 688*,[108] sustained an arbitrator's award holding that the following language precluded an employer from transferring its payroll and accounting work to an out-of-state facility operated by its parent company while employees in the in-state facility were on layoff:

> The Employer agrees that no function or service presently performed, or hereafter assigned, to the bargaining unit shall be subcontracted, leased, assigned or conveyed in whole or in part to any other person or organization, if any member of the bargaining unit is, at the time of such action, on layoff due to lack of work. . . .
> The above language shall not be construed or interpreted to prohibit the Employer from adding or discontinuing manufacture, packaging, or processing of a product or performance of a service based on sound business considerations.

In *Continental Telephone System*,[109] an Indiana public utility consolidated its Petersburg service center with its Jasper center and in the process relocated two clerk positions to Jasper. The union argued that the employer, under the following language, had the power to abolish the jobs, but not to move them to another location.

---

[106]78 LA 1131 (1982).
[107]Id. at 1131.
[108]743 F.2d 621, 117 LRRM 2530, 2531 (1984), cert. denied, 471 U.S.___, 119 LRRM 2248 (1985).
[109]80 LA 1355 (Wren, 1983).

The management of the plant and the direction of the working forces, including the rights to establish new jobs, abolish or change existing jobs, increase or decrease the number of jobs, change materials, processes, products, equipment and operations shall be vested exclusively in the Company.[110]

Holding that the union's reading of the management rights clause was narrow and not consistent with the decisions of arbitrators who have dealt with similar charges, Arbitrator Harold Wren applied the reserved-rights doctrine as follows:

A management rights clause in a collective bargaining agreement represents the residuum of rights retained by management, other than those granted to the bargaining agent. To the extent that it seeks to show that a right has not been retained by management, the Union has the burden of proving its existence in other provisions of the collective bargaining agreement. Alternatively, it may argue that management's construction of the collective bargaining agreement is so unfair that equity demands the recognition of a particular right. Or, it might argue that there is some *inherent* right that exists apart from the collective bargaining agreement. It is not sufficient to state that the management rights clause does not provide for a particular power, such as the right to change the geographical location of certain jobs in the interest of economy or efficiency. No management rights clause can list *all* the rights of management. Rather, the rights of management are present because of the residual nature of the clause.[111]

Arbitrator Lynn Griffith, in *Liquid Carbonic Corp.*,[112] reported a decision in which an employer with operations in the Canton, Ohio, area established a new terminal some distance from Canton in order to better compete with other companies that had terminals in that area. Wages in the new area were substantially lower than in Canton. The union filed a grievance alleging that the employer violated the parties' agreement when it assigned drivers from the new terminal to make deliveries in the new territory thus having them perform work previously performed by the Canton bargaining unit. The union argued that the loss of work from the assignment of delivery duties violated the representation clause of the contract.

The arbitrator declared that if there are clauses according exclusive recognition of the union for employees performing

---

[110]Id. at 1357 (emphasis omitted).
[111]Id. at 1357 (emphasis in original).
[112]79 LA 180 (1982).

work within categories covered by the contract, then there is an implied prohibition against performance of such work by management personnel or other persons outside the bargaining unit. This was not the situation in the instant case, the arbitrator said, ruling against the union and balancing the rights of management against the rights of the bargaining unit, as follows:

> Obviously, if the Company had unlimited management rights and the representation clause had no force other than a mere identification of the representative agent, the Company could withdraw all the jobs from the bargaining unit personnel and render the contract a nullity. On the other hand, if the Union could freeze the work of the bargaining unit, the Company's right to determine the location of the plants and the continuance of any departments would be a nullity. . . . I believe this answer must be found as in most of the cases in which these two provisions of the contract (Management Rights Clause vs. Union Representation Clause) come into conflict in a determination of reasonable and prudent business practice. The bad faith that would tip the scale in favor of the Union is absent in this case.[113]

Effect of Recognition Clauses

Arbitrators have uniformly rejected claims that a recognition clause, standing alone, limits management's right to make changes in the operation of its business. For example, in *Leeds-Dixon Laboratories, Inc.*,[114] the management rights clause stated:

> The authority and right to manage the plant and direct the working forces, including but by no means whatever limited to the authority to . . . determine the extent to which the plant shall operate or be shutdown, is hereby vested exclusively in the Company, subject only to the limitations of this Agreement.[115]

When a parent company elected to discontinue production and laboratory operations at one subsidiary and allow another subsidiary to assume operations, Arbitrator Jay Kramer stated the general view of arbitrators when a labor organization is

---

[113]Id. at 182.
[114]74 LA 407 (1980).
[115]Id. at 408 (emphasis omitted).

alleging that a sale or discontinuance is violative of the "recognition clause":

> It has been virtually universally held that the recognition clause in collective bargaining agreements does not, per se, without more, inhibit or prohibit a management from moving a plant, discontinuing operations, adding operations, and otherwise operating as it may deem most efficient and profit promoting. What is required, as a minimum, to inhibit or prohibit such a move or discontinuance of operation is an absence of good faith.[116]

Perhaps Arbitrator Marion Beatty said it best when he declared:

> The purpose of this [the recognition] clause is to assure fulfillment of the Company's legal obligation to bargain with this Union and assure that this particular union may represent all hourly paid employees in this plant. It is stretching the point, I believe, to argue that it also means that the Union has jurisdiction over all work which this employer has or which is customarily done by these employees, or that all such work will remain with the employees. The contract does not provide jurisdiction over work or detract substantially from management's customary right to direct the working force, or to determine what work will be done and how.[117]

Arbitrators have similarly rejected attempts to construct a subcontracting clause out of a recognition clause. For example, in *National Cash Register Co.,*[118] the arbitrator stated:

> [C]ontracting out is not limited by the usual recognition clause, by the usual seniority provisions, or by the usual job descriptions, or by the listing of jobs on classifications or occupations or labor grades in the back of the contract, although we hear arguments to the contrary at times.[119]

Arbitrator Peter Kelliher also rejected claims based on the recognition or seniority clause in *Carbide and Carbon Chemicals Co.:*[120]

> Arguments with reference to the contracting out of work being a violation of the Recognition and Seniority clauses have been made in numerous cases under substantially similar factual situations. Arbitrators, including the Impartial Member of this Board, and the Courts of Law have held almost uniformly that

---

[116]Id. at 410. Accord: Kretschmar Brands, Inc., 83-2 ARB ¶8556 (Madden, 1983).
[117]American Sugar Ref. Co., 37 LA 334, 336 (1961).
[118]48 LA 1025 (Beatty, 1967).
[119]Id. at 1026.
[120]24 LA 158 (1955).

in the absence of a specific contractual restriction, Management has the right to contract out work.[121]

Contract Term-Duration Considerations

Arbitrator Jerome Klein, in *Babcock & Wilcox*,[122] reflected the thinking of most arbitrators where a business is liquidated before the expiration of a collective bargaining agreement, stating:

> Generally speaking, a Company has the right to close a plant during the term of a Collective Bargaining Agreement, or stating the foregoing another way, the fact that a Collective Bargaining Agreement for a particular plant encompasses a certain period of time is not a guarantee that the Company will keep that plant in operation for the entire term of the Agreement.[123]

It is of note that Arbitrator Klein found that the effect on the bargaining unit of decisions to subcontract and reallocate was not a factor sufficient to influence his decision, since any time a plant closes, the effect is substantial. Rather, the arbitrator said, a "rule of reason" analysis is applicable.

Arbitrator Donald Wollett, in *Louisiana-Pacific Corp.*,[124] found federal labor law controlling in concluding that, after a sawmill shut down permanently, the employer could deny all wages and other benefits for the duration of the contract period. Citing the decision of the Supreme Court in *J.I. Case v. NLRB*,[125] the arbitrator reasoned that, under federal labor law, a collective bargaining agreement which contains the type of provisions commonly found in labor agreements is not a true contract of employment, that no employee has a job or promise of a job by reason of its existence, and that it creates no obligation to provide work, benefits, or wages. The arbitrator pointed out that the parties' agreement contained no provision by which the employer guaranteed employment, or wages in lieu of employment, to any employees for any length of time, nor was there a provision by which the employer promised to maintain production at any level or to continue

---

[121]Id. at 159–60.
[122]80 LA 212 (1982).
[123]Id. at 218.
[124]83-1 ARB ¶8120 (1983).
[125]321 U.S. 332, 334–35 (1944).

in the business for the duration of the agreement. With respect to the "duration" provision, the arbitrator remarked:

> The duration provision upon which the Union relies simply specifies the period during which the agreement shall be in effect. Similar clauses are found in almost all collective bargaining agreements, and the decision of all courts (so far as I can ascertain) that have passed on the point clearly establish that such clauses neither create nor guarantee employment. They assure only that *if* employment exists, the terms of the agreement apply. The argument that such a clause obligates an employer, if not to stay in business, at least to continue to pay wages and benefits for the life of the agreement clashes directly with this overwhelming body of authority.[126]

One arbitrator ruled that a company did not violate the agreement when it closed its business prior to the expiration of the contract since the employees were, in effect, placed on permanent layoff and were entitled to any rights and benefits accruing under this status.[127]

Successor Clauses

One method unions have used in an attempt to preserve bargaining-unit jobs when a business is sold is to negotiate a "successor" provision in the contract whereby the employer agrees that, in the event of a sale or transfer to a successor employer, the terms of the contract will be applicable to the new employer. Unions have used the arbitral forum to enforce against the predecessor employer a labor agreement containing such a provision, as discussed below.

When the agreement is silent, the general rule applied by both arbitrators and the courts is that a successor employer is not bound either to the specific terms of the agreement or to bargain with the union unless there is substantial continuity of identity in the business enterprise, both before and after the transfer.[128]

Aside from the issue of whether the transfer or sale is to an independent employer, and not an "alter ego" of the seller,[129] even where the agreement addresses the successor issue, prob-

---

[126] 83-1 ARB ¶8120, at 3541 (emphasis in original).
[127] National Tea Co., 59 LA 1193, 1196 (Joseph, 1972).
[128] Howard Johnson Co. v. Detroit Local Joint Exec. Bd., 417 U.S. 249, 86 LRRM 2449 (1974).
[129] See, e.g., Leona Lee Corp., 60 LA 1310 (Gorsuch, 1972).

lems prevail. In *National Tea Co.,*[130] the contract contained the following successor clause:

> This Agreement shall be binding upon the parties hereto, their successors and assigns. It is the intent of the parties that the Agreement shall remain in effect for the full term of the Agreement, and shall bind the successors of the respective parties hereto.[131]

When an employer announced that its business would be sold and that its work force would be terminated, Arbitrator Myron Joseph ruled that this successor provision was not violated when the employer failed to incorporate in its sales agreement a provision requiring the buyer to assume the terms of the existing contract. The arbitrator reasoned that there was nothing in this successor clause that required that the employer undertake such a task. Since, moreover, not all buyers would be successors, Arbitrator Joseph said, the question of how effectively successor companies would be bound by the language of the contract would have to be determined after the sale took place and the parties were identified.

In *High Point Sprinkler Co. of Boston,*[132] the contract contained the following successor provision:

> This agreement shall be binding upon the parties hereto, their successors, administrators, executors and assigns. It is understood that the parties hereto shall not use any sale, transfer, lease, assignment, receivership, or bankruptcy to evade the terms of this Agreement.[133]

The arbitrator found that this provision created a duty in the seller to preserve the benefits of the agreement during its term. Because the seller had sold the business without requiring the purchaser to assume the contract, the arbitrator awarded the union damages to be paid by the seller.

Similarly, where the contract contained a clause requiring that "the Employer shall make it a condition of transfer that the successor or assigns be bound by the terms of this Agreement," Arbitrator Marshall Ross enjoined the employer from continuing with the sale of the business until compliance with the agreement was secured as a condition of the sale.[134]

---

[130]59 LA 1193 (Joseph, 1972).
[131]Id. at 1197–98.
[132]67 LA 239 (Connolly, 1976).
[133]Id. at 240.
[134]Sexton's Steak House, Inc., 76 LA 576, 577 (1981).

Consistent with the above-cited cases, the usual rule applied by arbitrators is that the mere inclusion of a general successor clause will not obligate an employer to secure agreement from the purchaser of the business and that the terms of the labor agreement will not be applicable to a "successor" employer. An employer will only be obligated to require assumption only if such an obligation is created by specific language.[135]

---

[135]See also Gallivan's, Inc., 79 LA 253 (Gallagher, 1982); Martin Podany Assocs., 80 LA 658 (Gallagher, 1983).

Chapter 16

Subcontracting

In arbitration terminology, as well as in general business parlance, subcontracting carries a connotation of third persons being hired to perform work. More specifically, it is work performed by individuals who are not part of the bargaining unit, whether or not such work is actually performed inside or outside the premises of the employer.[1] In *American Air Filter Co.*,[2] Arbitrator David Dolnick suggested that no fixed guidelines can be applied in subcontracting disputes.

> Subcontracting is one of the most troublesome and perplexing problems in labor-management relations. It affects the concern of the recognized collective bargaining agent and the preservation of the bargaining unit. It triggers the fear of job loss and unemployment. Although Arbitrators have extensively dealt with this subject, and although many excellent scholarly treatises have been written, there is no fixed guideline which may be applied in every subcontracting dispute. Each case must be examined in light of the applicable agreement, from the fixed, undisputed practices of the parties, from the implications that stem from either or both the contract and practice where

---

[1]Overhead Door Corp., 77 LA 619, 621 (Herrick, 1981); Rockwell Int'l, 71 LA 1024, 1025 (Cox, 1978); Food Mktg. Corp., 83 LA 671 (Chapman, 1984). See generally Fairweather, Practice and Procedure in Labor Arbitration, 2d Ed., 469–93 (BNA Books, 1983); Elkouri & Elkouri, How Arbitration Works, 4th Ed., 537–47 (BNA Books, 1985); Miscimarra, The NLRB and Managerial Discretion: Plant Closings, Relocations, Subcontracting, and Automation, Labor Relations and Public Policy Series, No. 24 (Philadelphia: Industrial Research Unit, The Wharton School, Univ. of Pa., 1983). See also the related discussions under "Transfer or Relocation of Unit Work" and "Work Preservation Clauses and Transfer of Operations," in Chapter 15, supra, and under "Supervisors Performing Bargaining-Unit Work" in Chapter 17, infra.
[2]54 LA 1251 (Dolnick, 1970).

they do not conflict, and from the circumstances and the evidence in each dispute.[3]

Grievances alleging improper subcontracting arise both in situations where the contract is silent on the issue of contracting out and where the parties have incorporated guidelines on subcontracting in their agreement. Although many of the standards that arbitrators use in resolving subcontracting disputes are applicable in either situation, still it is useful to examine both categories separately.

Where the Agreement Is Silent

While increasing percentages of collective bargaining agreements expressly mention subcontracting, management's ability to contract out work in the absence of specific provisions in the contract remains the subject of numerous arbitration cases. Nearly two decades ago, Arbitrator Saul Wallen characterized the dispute as follows:

> To the employer or his spokesman the contract's silence shouts an intent to preserve for him the untrammeled exercise of his "reserved rights" to determine, in the name of efficiency, what work should be done by his own employees and what should be done by other parties with whom the union has no direct relationship.
>
> To the union or its spokesman the silent contract is not silent at all. The recognition clause designates the union as bargaining agent for the employees engaged in production and maintenance work. The seniority clause confers on them the right to such work when it exists to be done. The union security clause guarantees the union as an entity. The wage clause puts a price on the work to be done. Singly or in concert, these provisions bespeak an intent to retain for the bargaining unit all production and maintenance work, the union argument runs.[4]

---

[3]Id. at 1254.

[4]Wallen, "How Issues of Subcontracting and Plant Removal and Handled by Arbitrators," 19 Indus. & Lab. Rel. Rev. 265, 265 (1966). For recent applications of the union argument, see Transit Auth. of River City, 74 LA 616 (Chapman, 1980); Rinker Materials Corp., 76 LA 1174 (Vause, 1981); Williams Pipe Line Co., 80 LA 338 (Ross, 1983); M.S. Ginn & Co., 82 LA 98 (Harkless, 1983); American Motor Sales Corp., 82 LA 662 (Thornell, 1984); Mid Am. Dairymen, Inc., 83 LA 804 (Yarowsky, 1984) (denying grievance). Even arbitrators sustaining grievances presented by unions in this fashion may downplay the argument's significance. See, e.g., Uniroyal Inc., 76 LA 1049 (Nolan, 1981). Cf. United Farm Tools, Inc., 80 LA 864 (Smith, 1983) (holding that recognition limits management's right to subcontract); City of Detroit, 79 LA 1273 (Mittenthal, 1982).

Arbitrator John Davies has reported that since the time
the passage above was written, arbitrators have changed their
thinking somewhat when ruling on management's right to
subcontract when the agreement is silent on the matter.

> [W]hen the matter was first considered by arbitrators, they
> found that since the employer had a common law right to sub-
> contract, he would retain that right unless it was specifically
> taken from him by direct provisions of the collective bargaining
> agreement. As time went on, however, arbitrators modified that
> reasoning. They came to the conclusion that to permit the
> wholesale subcontracting by an employer of jobs customarily
> performed by members of the bargaining unit, would be to com-
> pletely undermine the central reason for a collective bargaining
> agreement in the first place, namely, job security for the em-
> ployees involved. These arbitrators, when there was no specific
> language in the contract denying the employer's right to sub-
> contract, implied from general provisions of the contract itself
> that there must be some modification of the power to subcon-
> tract.[5]

Arbitral Criteria

In a paper presented to the National Academy of Arbitrators, Arbitrator Anthony Sinicropi stated that situations
where the agreement is silent on the issue of subcontracting
have been studied and researched with greater frequency than
any other area of subcontracting.[6] Citing studies by Crawford,
Dash, Greenbaum, Wallen, and others,[7] Sinicropi found the
following considerations to be those most frequently taken
into account by arbitrators when they examine the merits of
a subcontracting dispute where the labor agreement does not
contain a subcontracting clause:

1. *The discussion or treatment, if any, of the subject of
   subcontracting during contract negotiations.* (Is one

[5]Blue Diamond Coal Co., 78 LA 702, 704 (1982).
[6]Sinicropi, "Revisiting an Old Battle Ground: The Subcontracting Dispute,"
Proceedings of the 32d Annual Meeting of NAA, 125–66 (BNA Books, 1980).
[7]Crawford, "The Arbitration of Disputes Over Subcontracting," Proceedings of
the 13th Annual Meeting of NAA, 51–72 (BNA Books, 1960); Dash, "Arbitration of
Subcontracting Disputes," 16 Indus. & Lab. Rel. Rev. 221 (1963); Greenbaum, "Ar-
bitration of Subcontracting Disputes," 16 Indus. & Lab. Rel. Rev. 223 (1963); Wallen,
"How Issues of Subcontracting and Plant Removal Are Handled by Arbitrators," 19
Indus. & Lab. Rel. Rev. 265 (1966); McEachem, "The Arbitration of Subcontracting
Disputes," 19 Me. L. Rev. 62 (1967); Jacobs, "Subcontracting Arbitration: How Issues
Are Decided," 21 Clev. St. L. Rev. 162 (1962).

party attempting to obtain in arbitration something
that could not be obtained at the bargaining table?
In other words, does the history of negotiations between the parties indicate that the union has tried
unsuccessfully to insert a provision in the parties'
agreement prohibiting the company from subcontracting unit work?)[8]

2. *The "good faith" of the employer in subcontracting the
   work.* (Was the decision to subcontract motivated by
   anti-union bias or, alternatively, sound economic reasons? Was it designed to discriminate against the
   union? Is it aimed at the union's ability to enforce the
   union-security clause? Did management subcontract
   because of the union's unwillingness to surrender rights
   secured under the labor agreement?)[9]

3. *Whether there are any layoffs resulting from subcontracting.* (Were regular employees deprived of work?
   Alternatively, did the subcontracting result in employees who were already on layoff not being recalled
   by the employer?)[10]

4. *The effect or impact that subcontracting will have on
   the union and/or bargaining unit.* (Was the required
   work part of the main operation of the plant?)

5. *Possession by the company of the proper equipment,
   tools, or facilities to perform the subcontracted work.*
   (Did the employer own or lease the equipment that
   was used to perform the disputed work?)

6. *Whether the required work was an experiment into a
   specialty line.* (Was it sufficiently unique to require

---

[8]See, e.g., Pacific Tel. & Tel. Co., 78 LA 68, 69 (Koven, 1982); Burger Iron Co.,
78 LA 57, 59 (Van Pelt, 1982)("The evidence shows that there was an attempt to
include a provision against subcontracting by the Union in the contract negotiations
without success."); Chrysler Corp., 59 LA 629, 634 (Alexander, 1972)("[T]he fact that
no protest was voiced with respect to such divestitures . . . must be taken to mean
that the Union never previously believed that Chrysler was obligated by implication
not to contract out the operation of plant cafeterias."); Phillips Chem. Corp., 44 LA
102, 104 (Sartain, 1965)("An important consideration in this case, however, is what
the Union has tried without success to secure in previous years . . . .").

[9]See, e.g., City of Detroit, 79 LA 1273, 1277–78 (Mittenthal, 1982); Town of Van
Buren, 80 LA 105, 109 (Chandler, 1982)(finding bad faith where management negotiated a subcontract while contractual negotiations were in progress with the union).

[10]Super Valu Stores, Inc., 84 LA 738, 743 (Heinsz, 1985)("Here there is no new
venture in the form of increased business but rather a different method of performing
prior tasks which had been accomplished by refrigeration mechanics. Moreover, the
bargaining unit classification of refrigeration mechanics has been depleted and effectively eliminated as a result of this substitution . . . .").

outside expertise? Is the contracting out a one-time contract or does it involve a regular, continuing service?)[11]

7. *The existence of any compelling business reasons, economic considerations, or unusual circumstances justifying the subcontracting.* (Was the work subcontracted out performed at a substantially lower cost? Is the contracting out simply an attempt to find another person to do the same work at less pay? Or, alternatively, is the subcontractor charging lower prices simply because it is more efficient?)[12]

8. *Whether any special skill, experience, or techniques are required to perform the required work.* (Does the employer have qualified supervisors to oversee the project?)[13]

9. *The similarity of the required work to the work regularly performed by bargaining-unit employees.* (In this respect, one arbitrator commented that "Parties and arbitrators alike should have little trouble distinguishing between integral and ancillary functions, and prohibiting subcontracting of the former while permitting the latter."[14])

10. *Past practice in the plant with respect to subcontracting this type of work.* (Has the union accepted the contracting out of work by the employer in the past?)

11. *The existence of any emergency conditions such as a special job, a strike, or an unusual situation requiring special expertise.* (Were properly qualified bargaining-unit employees available to complete the work within the required time limits? Would management experience a "penalty" for not completing work on time?).[15]

12. *Whether the required work was included within the duties specified for a particular job classification.*

In another articulation of arbitral standards, Elkouri and Elkouri have argued that the thinking of arbitrators is that

---

[11]General Metals Corp., 25 LA 118 (Lennard, 1955).
[12]See, e.g., Continental Tenn. Lines, 72 LA 619 (Cocalis, 1979); White Bros., 32 LA 965 (Hogan, 1958).
[13]National Distillers Prods. Co., 79 LA 1216, 1220 (Katz, 1982).
[14]Uniroyal, Inc., 76 LA 1049, 1053 (Nolan, 1981).
[15]Commercial Constr. Co., 80 LA 565, 567 n.2 (Nicholas, 1983).

in the absence of language in the labor agreement relating to subcontracting, the general rule is that management has the right to subcontract as long as (1) the action is performed in good faith, (2) it represents a reasonable business decision, (3) it does not result in subversion of the labor agreement, and (4) it does not have the effect of seriously weakening the bargaining unit or important parts of it. Further, this general right to subcontract out may be explained or restricted by specific contractual language, according to Elkouri and Elkouri.[16]

Many arbitrators have at least paid lip service to this four-part test in balancing the employer's interest in an efficient business against the union's interest in job security and the stability of the bargaining unit. Illustrative is the following statement by Arbitrator Charles Chapman:

> The problems which have arisen as a result of subcontracting are so generally known in the labor-management field that it has become, in general, a recognized retained right of management to subcontract in the absence of language in the contract placing restrictions on subcontracting. Of course, the use of this right has to be considered in the context of its effect on the bargaining unit and whether the subcontracting was done in good faith for sound business reasons, which could include reasons of substantial economy among others.[17]

Another arbitrator concluded that arbitrators accept the practice of subcontracting if five criteria are met:

> a. There is an absence of language delimiting the right.
> b. The subcontracting is performed in good faith.
> c. It represents a reasonable decision in business.
> d. It does not result in subversion of the labor agreement, and
> e. It does not have the effect of seriously weakening the bargaining unit or important parts of it.[18]

Arbitrator Bruce Boals has correctly observed that "even with such criteria, arbitration decisions vary, because of varying weights afforded the several criteria in combination with the factual circumstances surrounding each case being different."[19]

[16]Elkouri & Elkouri, How Arbitration Works, 4th Ed., 540 (BNA Books, 1973), citing Shenango Valley Water Co., 53 LA 741, 744–45 (McDermott, 1969)(with supporting citations).
[17]Transit Auth. of River City, 74 LA 616, 619 (Chapman, 1980).
[18]Overhead Door Corp., 77 LA 619, 621 (Herrick, 1981).
[19]Delta Ref. Co., 78 LA 710, 714 (1982).

Contract Law Criteria

Some arbitrators, feeling that the suggested arbitral standards "offer a few general rules, a great many overlapping and sometimes contradictory guidelines, and far too many arbitration awards on both sides of the question to be of much help,"[20] choose, instead, to apply principles of contract law such as the "implied covenant of fair dealing" in resolving subcontracting disputes. This principle was best expressed by Arbitrator Dennis Nolan in the following excerpt from a decision holding that management did not have the right to subcontract janitorial work:

> [V]irtually all authorities agree that absent some explicit contractual prohibition management retains broad authority to subcontract work. Common sense tells us as much, else why would so many unions strive so vigorously to impose explicit contractual limitations on subcontracting? Similarly, virtually all authorities agree that even a silent contract imposes some limitations on management's freedom to subcontract. To take an extreme example, no one would seriously contend that immediately after signing a collective bargaining agreement an employer could lay off all employees and hire a subcontractor to perform all bargaining unit work simply to escape the burdens of the collective agreement.
>
> These polar positions are nicely described in the article by Archibald Cox cited by the Union, "The Legal Nature of Collective Bargaining Agreements," 57 Michigan Law Review 1 (1958). . . . Cox discusses the basic principle of contracts that every agreement contains an implied covenant of good faith and fair dealing. He states that this principle imposes an obligation "not to seek a substitute labor supply at lower wages or inferior standards." On the next page . . . Cox emphasizes that the implied covenant of fair dealing does not "reach subcontracting which is based on business considerations other than the cost of acquiring labor under the collective agreement. In such a case either management is free to act or some limitation must be found in the very nature of the collective bargaining agreement."[21]

Arbitrator Marshall Ross had this to say on the same subject:

---

[20]Uniroyal, Inc., 76 LA 1049, 1052 (Nolan, 1981). After examining studies on the issue of subcontracting, Arbitrator Kadish commented: "Like the town fair, there is something there for everyone." KVP Sutherland Paper Co., 40 LA 737, 740 (1963).
[21]Uniroyal Inc., 76 LA 1049, 1052 (Nolan, 1981).

Arbitrators recognize that there is [an] implied covenant of fair dealing between the contracting parties, and that one of the parties cannot subvert an agreement by conduct seeking to deprive the other party of the bargain that was struck. The published awards dealing with this problem indicate a subcontract that deprives the Union or its employed members of any contractual gains or benefits is suspect and will be denied unless an employer can demonstrate a special business need that outweighs the loss caused the members of the bargaining unit.[22]

Despite the lack of uniformity regarding standards articulated for evaluating subcontracting disputes, labor practitioners should make an effort to keep abreast of recent arbitral decisions in this area as a way of continuing to develop their own guidelines.

Good Faith From Results

In deciding whether management's decision to subcontract was made in good faith or, alternatively, motivated by anti-union bias, arbitrators tend to draw inferences in part from the effects of the subcontracting action on the bargaining unit and its employees. Rather than make an independent finding of motive, however, the decisions seem to indicate that many arbitrators examine the *results* of the subcontracting and find "good faith" when the effects are minimal. Common effects of contracting out include new or continuing layoffs, loss of overtime, or permanent elimination of bargaining-unit jobs. Where qualified employees already on layoff are recalled within a reasonable time after contracting out, the employer's decision to utilize subcontractors instead of regular unit employees may not be seen as an attempt to weaken or destroy the bargaining unit.[23] Even in the presence of "considerable layoffs," management may be permitted to subcontract where other considerations operate in the company's favor. Thus, Arbitrator Joseph Krislov articulated this view in *Roper Outdoor Products*,[24] as follows:

The union is understandably distressed that the regular bargaining employees who were laid off were not employed to

---

[22]Campbell Truck Co., 73 LA 1036, 1039 (1979). See also Town of Van Buren, 80 LA 105 (Chandler, 1982).
[23]Burger Iron Co., 78 LA 57 (Van Pelt, 1982)(employees recalled to work within six weeks).
[24]80 LA 363 (1983).

do the work. At a time when there were considerable lay-offs Union members regard the company's action as callous and indifferent. But the arbitrator cannot leap from this judgment to a conclusion that the company's action was unreasonable and thereby violated the contract.[25]

Where the decision to subcontract is followed by the elimination of bargaining-unit jobs, the job loss generally is attributed to an improper transfer of work outside the unit. However, if jobs are lost due to a lack of need for labor and not as a result of contracting out, the unit is not considered to be adversely affected by management's decision to subcontract.[26] One arbitrator analyzed harm to the bargaining unit in terms of whether the employees' work was "in any way impaired, or modified or reduced" by the subcontracting.[27] His words are particularly instructive.

> Was the bargaining unit seriously weakened by this subcontracting. Again, we cannot find that it was. The repairmen still work their full work week. Their work has been in no way impaired or modified or reduced because of this one act of subcontracting [replacement of a conveyor belt]. As a matter of fact, it was specifically stipulated that these men did not lose any work on the days when [the subcontractor] did its work. We therefore cannot come to the conclusion that either the collective bargaining agreement or the bargaining unit itself have been damaged by the actions of the Employer in this case.[28]

In this same respect, another arbitrator ruled that the bargaining unit suffered when it lost three unit jobs, "a small part of the total work force but a significant part of one department."[29] Arbitrator Richard Mittenthal in *City of Detroit* found a reduction by 69 tradesmen, approximately 10 percent of the bargaining unit, substantial. (It is of special note that the arbitrator also found that the city had dramatically reduced the size of the bargaining unit because of the union's unwillingness to surrender its rights under the agreement, i.e., it had rejected wage concessions sought by the City.) Still another arbitrator, declaring that "there is no absolute management right to contract out bargaining unit work," ruled

---

[25]Id. at 365.
[26]Joseph Horne Co., 78 LA 262, 266 (Ipavec, 1982).
[27]Blue Diamond Coal Co., 78 LA 702 (Davies, 1982).
[28]Id. at 705.
[29]Uniroyal, Inc., 76 LA 1049, 1054 (Nolan, 1981).

that the elimination of a job in the full-time janitor classification with a corresponding contracting out of the functions of that job was significant, even though no employee was laid off.[30]

The deprivation of overtime to unit employees may be seen as harmful to the bargaining unit,[31] although a decline in overtime hours does not necessarily represent an erosion of the unit.[32] However, when the decision to subcontract results, in part, from the company's difficulty in assigning overtime work, management's case is strengthened.[33]

Further, the harm from contracting out of unit work depends, to an extent, on the degree to which the work is "customarily" or "usually" performed by (or assigned to) the bargaining unit. If the work at issue is not of a marginal or incidental nature but, instead, is the type of work regularly performed by the bargaining unit, the union's position is stronger. When, however, the regular employees have never before performed the work contracted out, it is more difficult to establish detriment to the bargaining unit. Moreover, the better view is that such terms as "usually assigned" or "customarily assigned" do not mean that the disputed work must be exactly the same as that performed by unit employees before an arbitrator will find it should be done by the unit, but only that the work not be "wholly foreign" to the work done in the past by the unit.[34]

In some cases, even when management's decision to subcontract adversely affects the unit, the subcontracting nevertheless may be found to be justified. For example, in *H-N Advertising & Display Co., Inc.,*[35] the arbitrator held that management had the right to contract out silk screening work when the company could not otherwise meet a production deadline. Similarly, the need to act promptly, such as a need to remedy a citation from a regulatory agency, may override any adverse effect on the unit.[36] Arbitrators have also per-

---

[30]Mead Corp., 75 LA 665, 667 (Gross, 1980).
[31]See, e.g., United Farm Tools, Inc.,; 80 LA 864, 869 (Smith, 1983); Ilsco Corp., 74 LA 659 (Ipavec, 1980).
[32]Granite City Steel, 85-1 ARB ¶8172 (McDermott, 1985).
[33]Blue Diamond Coal Co., 78 LA 702, 705 (Davies, 1982).
[34]Climax Mfg. Co., 82 LA 992, 995 (Gross, 1984); Ed Friedrich, Inc., 39 LA 399, 401–02 (Williams, 1962).
[35]77 LA 1096 (Cyrol, 1981).
[36]Ilsco Corp., 74 LA 659 (Ipavec, 1980)(OSHA citation); Reserve Mining Co., 74 LA 1128 (R. Kahn, 1980)(state pollution control agency).

mitted management to subcontract in order to avoid penalties. Thus, Arbitrator Samuel Nicholas, Jr., offered the following justification in sustaining the company's decision to subcontract:

> [W]e have here an instance where Company has demonstrated good faith, perhaps best illustrated by it[s] having a full work force (Boilermakers) when the subject subcontract was executed and [by the fact that] no Boilermaker was laid off until some three weeks thereafter. At the same time, the proof denotes that Company would have stood to have lost significantly more if it had not engaged in the [subcontracting] .... To be sure, with Management facing a probable $4,000 per day penalty for not completing hull #65 on time, it must be said that a valid presumption runs with Management for its need to take the action necessary to see that the contractual completion date was met. As such, it would tax the sense of conscience to, therefore, say that Company was attempting to work a penalty on Union or show bad faith to its Boilermakers.[37]

Where there is no sudden or unexpected occasion requiring action, however, and where management could have planned ahead to have unit personnel perform the work, there may be no justification for contracting out.[38] There is also authority to the effect that when employees make themselves unavailable at needed times, they cannot subsequently complain when the employer elects to subcontract work.[39]

Economic Considerations

Employers frequently attempt to demonstrate that the contracting out was done in good faith and without discrimination by showing that the subcontracting resulted in improved business efficiency and economy. Thus, in *Transit Authority of River City*,[40] Arbitrator Charles Chapman held that management had the right to contract out the janitorial service at its terminal facility when the company demonstrated that savings of $70,000 (not including equipment and management costs) would be realized. And in *Roper Corp.*,[41] Arbitrator Julius Rezler found it significant that the company

---

[37]Todd Shipyard Corp., 80 LA 234, 237–38 (1983).
[38]Pennwalt Corp., 78 LA 1252 (Gibson, 1982).
[39]Rockwell Int'l, 71 LA 1024 (Cox, 1978); St. Regis Paper Co., 78 LA 1167 (Goodman, 1982).
[40]74 LA 616 (Chapman, 1980).
[41]80 LA 760, 764 (Rezler, 1983).

would realize cost savings of 50 percent by contracting out warranty repair work. It is of note in this respect that when a union contended that the figures used by the company to justify its subcontracting decision were in error (the union argued that it was incorrect for the company to use fixed costs in its comparisons between operating its own trucks and contracting out the deliveries), one arbitrator ruled that the accuracy or inaccuracy of the figures used by management was not relevant. The arbitrator reasoned that what was relevant was whether the employer used what it believed in good faith to be sound economic reasoning for subcontracting delivery service.[42]

Not all arbitrators, however, have found economic arguments to be dispositive of the issue. Illustrative of another viewpoint is *Mead Corp.*,[43] a decision reported by Arbitrator James Gross, in which the arbitrator made the following statement:

> An arbitrator would be most reluctant to render a decision denying a company the right to become more efficient through innovation or technological change. The Record in this case, however, does not reveal any such innovation or change—the sole change was that the Company contracted with an outsider to do the same job on the Company's premises for less money. If a company were permitted to contract out bargaining unit work on the basis of comparative wage rate advantages elsewhere, it would constitute a privilege to engage in a course of conduct that would nullify its collective bargaining contract. Followed to its extreme but logical conclusion, all bargaining unit work could be contracted out to cheaper labor. Simply beating the union prices set forth in the contract would be comparable to a unilateral reduction in a negotiated wage which a company has no right to make—and a company cannot accomplish by indirection what it would not be permitted to do directly under the terms of a contract.[44]

Similarly, Arbitrator Richard Mittenthal, in *City of Detroit*,[45] ruled that the refusal of city employees to accept a wage concession that was requested because of a deficit in funding did not justify the city in laying off the employees and subcontracting their work.

---

[42]Burger Iron Co., 78 LA 57, 59 (Van Pelt, 1982).
[43]75 LA 665 (Gross, 1980).
[44]Id. at 667.
[45]79 LA 1273 (1982).

The crucial issue is *not* whether the City had a right to lay off tradesmen in September 1981 *but rather* whether the City could engage contractors to perform the kind of repair and maintenance work the laid off tradesmen had customarily performed. These are entirely different questions. The layoff could well have been justified. However, that would not prove the contracting out was reasonable.[46]

In contrast, a private-sector employer facing a "severe financial crisis" was found to have the right to eliminate a janitor position and contract out these duties to a cleaning service, when the company produced evidence that the action resulted in savings of approximately $7,700 per year.[47] The arbitrator rejected the union's argument that the recognition clause, which specifically included the janitor position, and the wages clause, which specifically provided for a janitor classification, were violated by the company's unilateral action of farming out the janitor work.

Prior Negotiations

Management's claim to a right to subcontract is strengthened where the union has tried and failed in prior negotiations to obtain a provision restricting contracting out of work.[48] This is especially true where the union has unsuccessfully tried to obtain the deletion of the right to subcontract from an existing management rights provision.[49] Still, many arbitrators will not accord great weight to such evidence. Arbitrator Saul Wallen has observed that

> the unsuccessful demand for a limitation clause is not necessary or always an acknowledgment that in its absence there are no limitations on the right to contract out. The demand may well have been no more than an attempt to convert the implicit into

---

[46]Id. at 1277 (emphasis in original).

[47]American Motors Sales Corp., 82 LA 662 (Thornell, 1984).

[48]M.S. Ginn & Co., 82 LA 98 (Harkless, 1983). In Cleveland Builders Supply, 84-2 ARB ¶8337 (Hart, 1984), the arbitrator observed:

"[T]o say that a silent contract may imply some limitation on contracting out is not to say that it bars it. That is especially true considering why a contract is silent: that is, there is a difference between the case where a contract is 'absent a prohibition to contract out because the parties never considered the matter,' and the case, as at bar, where silence results from deliberate negotiation out of such a ban . . . ."
Id. at 4487.

[49]Hobart Mfg. Co., 73 LA 29 (Turkus, 1979).

the explicit, to crystalize and clarify that which may be uncertainly expressed though reasonably implied.[50]

Recognition, Job Classification, and Seniority Clauses

Unions have often argued that the right to subcontract, even in the absence of restrictions in the contract, is not absolute because of many other provisions in the labor agreement, including, but not limited to, the recognition, job classification, and seniority clauses. Most but not all arbitrators have consistently rejected such attempts by the union to construct a subcontracting clause where none exists. For example, in *National Cash Register Co.*,[51] Arbitrator Marion Beatty stated:

> [C]ontracting out is not limited by the usual recognition clause, by the usual seniority provisions, or by the usual job descriptions, or by the listing of jobs and classifications, or occupations or labor grades in the back of the contract, although we hear arguments to the contrary at times. Experienced counsel in our case at hand do not rely on such arguments.[52]

Similarly, Arbitrator Peter Kelliher has also rejected such claims.

> Arguments with reference to the contracting out of work being a violation of the Recognition and Seniority clauses have been made in numerous cases under substantially similar factual situations. Arbitrators, including the Impartial Member of this Board, the National Labor Relations Board, and the Courts of Law have held almost uniformly that in the absence of a specific contractual restriction, Management has the right to contract out work.[53]

In *KVP Sutherland Paper Co.*,[54] Arbitrator Sanford Kadish posed the issue and policy considerations as follows:

> What restrictions, if any, the very execution of a collective bargaining agreement and its typical recognition, wage, seniority and related clauses impose upon the authority of the Company to use outside contractors to perform work otherwise

---

[50]Wallen, "How Issues of Subcontracting and Plant Removal Are Handled by Arbitrators," 19 Indus. & Lab. Rel. Rev. 265, 271 (1966).
[51]48 LA 1025 (1967).
[52]Id. at 1026.
[53]Carbide & Carbon Chems. Co., 24 LA 158, 159–60 (1955).
[54]40 LA 737 (1963).

done by employers within the unit has generated vast differences of opinions among courts and arbitrators. . . .

Two extreme propositions concerning sub-contracting, neither of which we find acceptable, may serve as a point of departure. One is that the recognition clause, combined with the other clauses previously mentioned, entitle[s] the employees to all available work which falls within the collective bargaining unit. This work is, as it were, the fruits of the bargain, which may not be taken away by the Company contracting it out to other businesses. Such a wholesale interference with the authority of the Company to direct the business appears to us wholly unjustified, especially where, as here, the contract contains a management clause explicitly vesting the Company with the power to make and implement business decisions. Equally unpersuasive is the view at the other end of the spectrum that in the absence of express limitation the Company retains without limitation the full power to sub-contract, as it retains all authority not surrendered by the express terms of the agreement. Even those who assert the argument do not pursue its logic to the end, since it is virtually unanimously recognized that the execution of the contract, the recognition, seniority and wage, and related clauses do limit the Company's power to sub-contract in extreme cases where the decision was not made in good faith, but was part of a Company plan to undermine the Union and the scope of the bargain, rather than founded on ordinary business judgments.[55]

The resulting middle-ground approach taken by Arbitrator Kadish is illustrative of the thinking of many arbitrators.

Of course, the Company may use outside contractors, just as it may on other grounds find reason to increase, decrease or modify jobs within the bargaining unit. But this does not mean that it may abuse that right by so exercising it that the benefits of the bargain are taken from the union. And it is of course also true that the representation and related clauses do impose an obligation upon the Company not to sub-contract in circumstances in which the integrity of the bargain is undermined. But this does [not] mean that the Union may prevent all sub-contracting by the employer. Ultimately the question in this case, as in any case, entails weighing the Company's affirmative case for the particular decision to sub-contract against the impact that decision has upon the subject matter of the bargain. The integrity of the bargain, protected by the very execution of the contract, the recognition, wage and related clauses, may be said to have been violated where the balance favors the Union; otherwise not.[56]

---

[55]Id. at 739–40.
[56]Id. at 740. See also General Dynamics, 78-1 ARB ¶8136 (Gray, 1977)("[Contracting out] is not a case of absolutes one way or the other. Rather, it is a case of appropriate balancing of the legitimate interests of management, the bargaining unit employees, and their union representatives." Id. at 3645).

Summary

Management attorney and author Owen Fairweather has argued as follows:

> A balancing "good faith" test is used by some arbitrators to approve "subcontracting" if (1) job security is minimally affected, (2) strong economies are accomplished, and (3) no express contractual limitations are contained in the labor agreement. When the labor agreement does not describe specific restraints on subcontracting, most arbitrators that have used the "good faith-bad faith" test are attempting to protect the employment of employees in one unit from competition by employees in another.[57]

While the procedure that Fairweather describes may in some cases take place, the reported cases indicate that in the absence of a contractual provision on subcontracting, arbitral opinion continues to disallow management an unfettered right to contract out no matter what the effect is on the bargaining unit. In this regard the Ninth Circuit has spoken on the use of a "balancing" test under an agreement that is silent on subcontracting. During the economic recession of 1979–1982 when logging and other similar industries were heavily hit, the employer incurred losses which led to the closing of a sawmill and related logging operations. Motivated by economic considerations, the employer decided that the mill could not be opened unless the logging operations were subcontracted. Management re-opened the mill but eliminated the logging crews and replaced them with unrepresented subcontractors. A grievance was filed, and an arbitrator ruled in favor of the union, holding that the employer's right to subcontract was limited by the implied covenant not to seriously erode the bargaining unit found in every collective bargaining agreement. The award was vacated by the district court.

The Ninth Circuit, reversing the district court, ruled that a balancing-of-interests test was appropriate when an agreement is silent on the subcontracting issue. The court's reasoning is particularly instructive since it approved the use of the criteria noted by Sinicropi.

> To consider whether an award drew its essence from the collective bargaining agreement, the court must ensure that

---

[57]Fairweather, supra note 1, at 473–74.

the arbitrator looked to the words of the contract and to the conduct of the parties. . . .

In the case at bar the arbitrator did so. He examined the past practices of the parties. He noted that the employer had never before used subcontractors to the complete exclusion of bargaining unit loggers. He clearly based his decision in large part on the employer's undisputed historical practice of maintaining a 60–40 ratio [of company loggers to subcontractors] as indicated above. He discussed in his award past arbitral decisions favoring the employer and past negotiations, but found them to be distinguishable since none before had involved a permanent loss of so many bargaining unit positions. Additionally, the arbitrator found that other clauses, such as wages, recognition, union security, and seniority, taken together, constituted an implied covenant that the employer would not seriously erode the bargaining unit by subcontracting. The arbitrator considered the reserved rights theory of management, but rejected it after reviewing the applicable authorities.[58]

Still, when the agreement is silent arbitrators appear to accord great deference to the decision to subcontract, especially when management has discussed the matter with the union before contracting out. The issue is not so much a matter of good faith or bad faith. Rather, it is a realization that all acts of management must be reasonable rather than arbitrary or capricious. As such, if a decision to subcontract cannot be supported with some justification, economic or otherwise, it will likely be reversed by an arbitrator as violative of the agreement when that decision is shown to weaken the unit. Even when the agreement is completely silent on the matter of contracting out, arbitrators balance the interests of management against those of the bargaining unit in deciding whether the parties' labor agreement has been violated. The balance may (and usually is) invariably struck in favor of management, especially when the contract is silent, but an arbitrator faced with a subcontracting grievance when the agreement is silent is unlikely to reason simply that since the contract does not contain a subcontracting limitation the company must win. Most arbitrators require that management demonstrate some basis in fact for the decision.[59]

---

[58]Edward Hines Lumber Co. v. Lumber & Sawmill Workers Local 2588, 764 F.2d 631, 119 LRRM 3210, 3213 (CA 9, 1985)(citations omitted).

[59]See, e.g., General Dynamics, 78–1 ARB ¶8136 (Gray, 1977)(applying "balancing" test where contract silent on contracting out); Michigan State Univ., 82–2 ARB ¶8507 (Borland, 1982)("While Arbitrator Feldman stated strongly that 'any specific

Where Subcontracting Provisions Exist

Unions have made significant progress in bargaining over subcontracting since it was first declared a mandatory subject in 1964. Surveys by The Bureau of National Affairs, Inc. (BNA) indicate that the percentage of sample agreements containing some type of subcontracting clause doubled between 1965 and 1983. Classifications by type reveals the following breakdown as of 1983: clauses strictly prohibiting the contracting out of unit work (2 percent); clauses requiring advance discussion with, or notification to, the union (36 percent); clauses prohibiting subcontracting if layoffs exist or would result (23 percent); clauses permitting subcontracting only if the necessary skills and equipment are not available (25 percent); clauses permitting subcontracting only if contractual standards are met (22 percent); and clauses permitting subcontracting if it is in accordance with past practice (17 percent).[60]

Prior to the Supreme Court's decision in *Fibreboard Paper Products Corp. v. NLRB*,[61] the most common types of subcontracting clauses were those prohibiting contracting when the firm's own employees were on layoff or, alternatively, when the layoff or demotion of unit employees would result. Clauses imposing a limitation of "reasonableness" on company actions were also common.[62] Since *Fibreboard*, however, the "meet and confer" type of limitation has assumed predominant status, though other limitations are frequently found.

---

limitation upon management's ability to operate its facility must be in clear and unambiguous language,' he went on to state also that 'all acts of management must be reasonable and not arbitrary or capricious.'" Id. at 5271, discussing and quoting from University of Toledo, 730 Government Employee Relations Report (BNA) 22 (Feldman, 1977).); Binswanger Glass Co., 80 LA 1309 (Holman, 1983)(considering type of work subcontracted, reason for subcontracting, conditions of subcontract, and impact upon bargaining unit, even though contract silent on subcontracting); GTE Prod., 84–2 ARB ¶8514 (Florey, 1984)(applying "reasonableness" test to contracting out of maintenance).

[60]Basic Patterns in Union Contracts, 64 (BNA Books, 1983). The BNA survey also indicated that 45% of manufacturing agreements and 58% of nonmanufacturing agreements contained subcontracting provisions. Frequency of appearance by industry, in decreasing order, was: construction (93%); mining (83%); communication (80%); leather (75%); petroleum (71%); apparel and rubber (67%); utilities (60%); and transportation, services, foods, furniture, paper, chemicals, primary metals, fabricated metals, machinery, electrical machinery, and transportation equipment (at least 40%).

[61]379 U.S. 203, 57 LRRM 2609 (1964).

[62]See Crawford, supra note 7.

"Meet and Discuss" Limitations

In 1960 the late Donald Crawford, in a paper delivered to the National Academy of Arbitrators, categorized explicit subcontracting clauses. Crawford reported that the weakest limitation on contracting out is the "discussion before contracting out" type of clause.[63] His conclusion is verified by the outcome of recent arbitral decisions, most of which uphold the company's actions.

In *FMC Corp.*,[64] the agreement provided that the company "will notify and consult with the Grievance Committee before employing outside contractors to work in the plant, and any disagreement arising shall be subject to the grievance procedure."[65] FMC, an industrial chemicals manufacturer, informed the union of its plans to utilize an outside contractor for the reconstruction of a floor in a pump room. The company considered, but rejected, the union's suggestion as to how unit personnel might be utilized to do the work. The arbitrator found no contract violation, stating that

> [i]t must be realized that by this language the contract anticipates that there are situations which will result in proper subcontracting. . . . [W]hile the Company is required to "consult", it is not required to obtain agreement. The obligation is to listen to the Union's arguments, weigh them, and then the Company may make its decision.[66]

A similar result occurred when another company, after meeting with union representatives, subcontracted the construction and installation of a manufacturing storage shed. In *J.T. Baker Chemical Co.*,[67] the agreement provided as follows:

> Whenever the Company contemplates contracting out any type of work it shall inform the [union] . . . of its intentions and discuss the reasons for subcontracting prior to making a decision to award the contract.[68]

In holding that the employer met its contractual obligation, the arbitrator reasoned that the language does not mean that

[63]Id.
[64]75 LA 485 (LeWinter, 1980).
[65]Id. at 486.
[66]Id. at 492.
[67]76 LA 1146 (Mussmann, 1981).
[68]Id. at 1149.

no decision can be made by the company prior to discussion with the union.

> The word "contemplates" and "intentions" indicate mental processes which indicate some decision, even though preliminary, regarding the subcontracting of a work project. . . . [B]efore placing a subcontract with an outsider, the Company is obligated to inform the Union of its decision in order for the Union to have an opportunity to persuade the Company why it should keep the work "in house" if it so believes.[69]

Similarly, the U.S. Army Corps of Engineers was found in compliance with its contractual obligation to discuss subcontracting policies "when it is known that the contracting out will have an adverse effect on the employees of the unit" when it notified the union, met with its officials, and offered to provide relevant documents, figures, and backup data regarding a subcontracting proposal.[70]

In *National Distillers Products Co.*,[71] the agreement provided that no bargaining-unit work would be contracted out "except upon due consultation with the Union." The agreement further provided that "any disagreement not satisfactorily resolved shall be subject to arbitration." Even though management consulted with the union, the union argued that such consultation alone did not excuse the contracting out, unless the implied limitations of good faith and reasonableness had been met. Arbitrator Jonas Katz ruled that, where due consultation occurs, such bargaining-unit work may still be contracted out. In the words of the arbitrator, "'consultation' requires more than notification, but less than agreement."[72]

As can be seen from the cases discussed above, a major issue for consideration in this area is whether a "meet and discuss" or "notice" provision is merely a condition precedent to subcontracting. In other words, is management free to subcontract once it has given proper notice and engaged in good faith discussions with the union? Or, alternatively, is there still as in agreements which are silent concerning subcontracting an implied covenant not to contract out bargaining-unit work in the absence of compelling business justifications

---

[69]Id. at 1149.
[70]U.S. Army Corps of Eng's, 81 LA 510, 513 (Everitt, 1983).
[71]79 LA 1216 (Katz, 1982).
[72]Id. at 1218.

for doing so? If arbitrators take the latter view, management may validly argue in opposition that the "meet and discuss" provision is an additional limitation, and that for a company to agree to such a clause in addition to the implied-obligation concept is a "penalty" to which management would not have agreed if it had known beforehand that arbitrators would continue to impose implied-obligation constraints as well. On the other hand, unions could argue that if the "meet and discuss" clause cancels out the implied obligation to act reasonably, the clause is meaningless, since all management would be required to do is discuss the matter until impasse is reached.

There is support for both positions. For example, it might be argued that the primary purpose of the "meet and confer" clause is to allow the union an opportunity to persuade management to accede to the union's arguments. On the other hand, proponents of the view that "meet and confer" provisions do not cancel the implied-obligation standard might argue that, after the condition precedent of meeting and discussing is met, the arbitrator should limit management's action only if it is "reasonable" and does not cause a "serious detriment" to the bargaining unit.

As reported by Sinicropi in 1979[73] and by Hill and Sinicropi in 1981,[74] the predominant view is that "meet and discuss" limitations absolve management of any further obligation once an impasse is reached, but there is some authority to the contrary. Similarly, when the agreement contains a "meet and discuss" provision and the employer subcontracts without discussing the matter with the union, the better rule is that the union should be provided a remedy even though the contracting out was reasonable.[75]

Equipment/Employee Availability Limitations

The second most common type of subcontracting limitation, according to BNA survey results,[76] prohibits subcontracting except where the employer does not have available

[73]Sinicropi, supra note 6.
[74]Hill & Sinicropi, Remedies in Arbitration, 113 (BNA Books, 1981).
[75]See, e.g., Rockwell Int'l Corp., 85–1 ARB ¶8217 (Wren, 1985)(providing overtime remedy); North Star Steel Co., 83–2 ARB ¶8532 (Gallagher, 1983); Macomb Intermediate School Dist., 79–2 ARB ¶8620 (Roumell, 1979)(upholding grievance but denying monetary relief for failure to meet).
[76]Basic Patterns in Union Contracts, supra note 60.

equipment or personnel (including, in some cases, laid-off employees) with the skills necessary to perform the job. This type of restriction is common in the mining industry and is the subject of several recent decisions. In *Drummond Coal Co.*,[77] the company was found to have violated the following provision when it contracted out the fabrication of a broken metal bar, despite the availability of both equipment and employees:

> All construction of mine or mine related facilities . . . customarily performed by classified employees of the employer normally performing construction work in or about the mine in accordance with prior practice and custom, shall not be contracted out at any time unless all such Employees with necessary skills to perform the work are working no less than 5 days per week.[78]

Even though the work at issue had not been performed by classified employees for seven to eight years, the arbitrator ruled that the work was still within the union's jurisdiction.[79]

Likewise, in *Eaton Corp.*,[80] the agreement provided as follows:

> The Company agrees not to transfer any of its work to any of its other plants or to any other concern for the purpose of discrimination against the Union.[81]

Although the union in three separate negotiation periods proposed language limiting the company's right to subcontract work only to be successfully resisted each time by the company, the arbitrator nevertheless found that the above-cited language operated to prevent management from subcontracting yard maintenance work, even though that work was "incidental" to the company's main business—production of electromechanical products.

One issue in this area is whether management is obligated to renew leases on equipment rather than allowing them to expire and subcontracting the work previously done "in house" using the leased equipment. In a related case, one arbitrator held that management was precluded from subcon-

---

[77]82 LA 473 (Nicholas, 1984).
[78]Id. at 473.
[79]Id. at 475. See also Chemical Leaman Tank Lines, Inc., 81 LA 249 (Baroni, 1983); Quaker State Oil Ref. Corp., 81 LA 1054 (Katz, 1983). For decisions upholding the company's action, see Hobet Mining & Constr. Co., Inc., 80 LA 158 (Hayes, 1982); Shannopin Mining Co., 82 LA 725 (Hewitt, 1984); Peabody Coal Co., 82 LA 1251 (Roberts, 1984).
[80]80 LA 31 (Schedler, 1982).
[81]Id. at 33.

tracting even if it did not have all the necessary equipment and had to rent some items and then train the affected employees in the operation of such equipment.[82]

Layoff Limitations

Another common type of contractual limitation prohibits subcontracting if unit employees are currently on layoffs or if layoffs would result from contracting out. Two issues surface in these cases: (1) whether there are unit employees on layoff, and (2) whether the layoffs can be attributable to the subcontracting. Illustrative is *British West Indian Airways, Ltd.*,[83] where the subcontracting clause at issue provided as follows:

> The Company shall not subcontract any work which results directly or indirectly in the layoff of any employee currently on an active non-layoff status.[84]

The union learned of the airline's resumption of flights to San Juan and subcontracting of passenger-handling service there. It accordingly asked that recall notices be issued to all laid-off employees. However, all laid-off employees had accepted severance pay and, under the terms of the agreement, had been removed from the seniority lists and were no longer considered "employees." Moreover, no currently employed employee on active status was laid off as a result of the employer's action. Accordingly, the arbitrator ruled that the company had not violated the subcontracting provision.[85]

Likewise, in *United States Steel Corp.*,[86] the contract stated that the company "will not contract work which would require employees in the bargaining unit to be laid off, [or to be] reduced in rate of pay, [or which would] prevent laid-off employees from being recalled or prevent qualified employees from being upgraded." The union contended that the company's contracting out of mail-carrying duties to the Purolator Courier Corporation violated this provision because eight employees, including three "runners," had been laid off five months before the contracting out, as a result of a reorganization of

---

[82]Ashland Chems. Co., 64 LA 1244 (Carmichael, 1975).
[83]74 LA 1126 (Mackenzie, 1980).
[84]Id. at 1127.
[85]Id. at 1128.
[86]77 LA 77 (Helburn, 1981).

a company site. Arbitrator I.B. Helburn ruled that management had not violated this provision since, when the contract with Purolator was effected, the laid-off employees were either back at work or had been offered recall. Further, and more important, the arbitrator found no relationship between the reorganization decision and the subsequent contracting out.[87]

In considering a discussion of subcontracting and layoffs, an interesting point was made by Arbitrator Marlin Volz in *Champion Papers*.[88] Ruling that a company violated a comprehensive subcontracting provision, the arbitrator had this to say about timing a contracting-out decision to coincide with the retirement of employees:

> [T]he action [contracting out] cannot be justified merely because it was timed to coincide with the retirement of two employees so that no actual layoffs were required. If subcontracting could be substituted for the contractual procedures for filling job vacancies, the integrity of the bargaining unit could be eroded contrary to the intent of the parties . . . .[89]

The late and distinguished Arbitrator John Sembower also considered this issue and commented as follows:

> By far the most significant and novel issue presented by this arbitration is the question of whether so-called "attrition" can constitute an "erosion" of the bargaining unit. Here again, we have a head-on collision of basic concepts. On the one hand, it is axiomatic that an employer cannot be required to fill a job which because of economic reasons he thinks is no longer needed. To the contrary, from the very beginning of the Wagner Act days, deliberate erosion of a bargaining unit has been eschewed. Perhaps for the best economic motives imaginable, the Company here seems to have adopted a course of letting the bargaining unit "wither on the vine," by not replacing employees who leave for whatever reason. The Unit has consequently shrunken considerably in recent months during the pendency even of this arbitration. At the same time, sub-contractors have come into the plant itself and performed work which historically has been performed by the Company's own employees. It seems clear that the employer cannot disable himself to perform the customary work of his shop simply by letting his Unit members die off. . . . [T]he Arbitrator must award that "attrition" may not be used in this fashion to reduce the bargaining unit and have the work that customarily was performed by its members

---

[87]Id. at 83.
[88]51 LA 997 (1968).
[89]Id. at 1001.

taken over by sub-contractors, either outside or inside the plant, either union or non-union.[90]

Contractual Standards Limitations

Some agreements permit management to contract out only if the subcontractor is paid the same as if bargaining-unit employees had performed the work.[91] For example, in *Charles Righello Co.*, [92] Arbitrator Adolph Koven held that management violated the subcontracting clause when it timely terminated the collective bargaining agreement and contracted out bargaining unit work at rates less than that provided in the former agreement. Arbitrator Koven's lengthy analysis of whether a subcontracting provision survives the expiration of a labor agreement is especially noteworthy.

It has been held that those terms and conditions established by the contract, and governing the employer-employee relationship as opposed to the employer-Union relationship, survive the contract and establish the employer with a continuing obligation to apply those terms and conditions. . . .

The question, therefore, is whether a provision in a Contract prohibiting subcontracting is one which governs the "employer-employee" relationship or the "employer-Union" relationship. . . .

The Union argues that the prohibition against subcontracting survives the expiration of the Contract under the principles set forth above. It claims that subcontracting is a term and condition of employment which governs the employer-employee relationship because it is "a means by which a Union negotiates provisions to protect workers from the loss of jobs occasioned by subcontracting of bargaining unit work. It seeks to maintain the wages and conditions of employment in part in order to discourage subcontracting so as to preserve work opportunity for bargaining unit members . . . by requiring employers to contract only to those employers who do not have contracts with the Union."

This argument is persuasive. The prohibition against subcontracting lies at the very heart of the employer-employee relationship. If an employer may, after termination of the Contract freely subcontract work to non-Union subcontractors, the job security of the existing employees, their opportunity to over-

---

[90]Buhr Mach. Tool Corp., 61 LA 333, 339 (1973).

[91]Rohr Indus., Inc., 85-1 ARB ¶8115 (Gentile, 1984)("Such work performed by subcontractors within the plant, when skills are not available, shall not be paid for at a lessor rate than that established by the Company's rate and classification schedule . . . ." Id. at 3470.).

[92]78 LA 777 (Koven, 1982).

time benefits and to other protections of their employment status and conditions set forth in the Contract, could be eliminated
by the Company. . . . Such a wholesale and obvious avoidance
of the continuing obligations of an employer under the terminated contract would render meaningless the whole body of law
requiring the employer to continue to adhere to the terms and
conditions of the employer-employee obligation established by
the expired contract.[93]

Past Practice Limitations

Arbitrator Alfred Dybeck reports a decision where, in relevant part, the contract provided as follows:

> If plant production has in the past been performed within
> a plant under some circumstances by employees within a bar-
> gaining unit and under some circumstances by employees of
> contractors, or both, such contracting out shall be permissible
> under circumstances similar to those under which contracting
> out has been a practice unless mutually agreed . . . .[94]

The arbitrator found the provision inapplicable where U.S.
Steel closed two Youngstown plants, dismantled them, and
then contracted out the plant guard duties after the properties
were turned over to its own realty developer. The arbitrator
reasoned that the agreement secured to the union rights in
the company's steel-manufacturing plants, and that the total
change in the nature of the plants, in the process of being
dismantled and leased, extinguished management's obligation to the union.[95]

Strict Prohibition Provisions

Although infrequent, some contractual provisions strictly
prohibit the contracting out of work. However, *Cooey-Bentz
Co.*[96] demonstrates that even apparently ironclad language
preventing subcontracting may not operate to preserve work

---

[93]Id. at 778–79.
[94]United States Steel Corp., 77 LA 190, 191–92 (1981); See also Matson Navigation Co., 85-1 ARB ¶8112 (Sabo, 1984), where the agreement provided: "The association agrees that the work which has been historically performed by the members
of the bargaining unit will continue to be performed by the members of the bargaining
unit." Id. at 3462.
[95]77 LA at 194.
[96]76 LA 391 (Parkinson, 1981).

traditionally performed by the union. The subcontracting language at issue stated the following:

> The hiring of outside equipment shall not be done in such manner as to interfere with or discriminate against the seniority status of the Employer's employees. . . .[97]

In addition, at the time the agreement became effective, the company agreed that any work or services of the kind, nature or type covered by, presently performed by, or later assigned to members of the Union would not be "subcontracted," "transferred," "leased," "assigned," or "conveyed in whole or part," unless otherwise provided in the agreement.[98] At the execution of the labor agreement, the company provided not only floor covering but also installation service through its store. Four bargaining-unit employees were employed, at the time, in providing such service. When the service was discontinued, the union filed a grievance alleging violation of the subcontracting clause. In ruling for the company, the arbitrator pointed out the options that were available to management under this provision:

> The first item precluded as an option to the Company is subcontracting the work. This would mean that the Company had continued the service, but that the service is provided by another party for the Company. The Company, in other words would simply enter into a contract with another party for installation, as part of its carpet service provided *its* customers. In this situation, however, the Company does not offer installation services, but simply sells the floor covering. Currently, the customer can buy the floor covering at the Company, but the Company will not install [it] with its employees or provide for its installation by a third party whom it retains for such purposes. Consequently, the Company has not violated the subcontracting [provision] . . ., albeit the spirit in which the clause may have been negotiated [sic].[99]

The arbitrator did note, however, that by providing a list to its customers of potential floor covering installers the Company comes "perilously close to abridging its obligation not to transfer such work 'to any other plant, person or non-unit employees.'"[100]

---

[97]Id. at 392.
[98]Id. at 394.
[99]Id. at 395.
[100]Id.

Miscellaneous Subcontracting Provisions

It is not uncommon to see contractual provisions that outline mixed criteria to be applied in subcontracting decisions. For example, in *Champion Papers*,[101] the relevant subcontracting provision provided as follows:

It is agreed that no maintenance work or service functions normally performed by Maintenance Department employees or appropriate [service-type] department employees prior to this contract will be done within the plant by outside contracting services until all factors have been carefully considered, including but not limited to:
(1) Timely availability of required skills and personnel within the appropriate department;
(2) The timely availability of necessary tools and equipment;
(3) The time limits within which the work must be completed;
(4) Availability of related services;
(5) The continuity of mill operation while the work is being performed;
(6) Pertinent cost factors.
No qualified regular employees in the concerned departments will be laid off or caused to lose regular scheduled time as a direct result of using outside contracting services....
The Company will notify the Union of any decision to use outside contracting services prior to contracting the same.[102]

Two types of provisions not discussed in the BNA survey[103] but appearing frequently in recent decisions, invoke considerations employed in the "implied obligation" cases where the contract is silent as to subcontracting. One type of clause permits subcontracting only where "it can be demonstrated to have been the more reasonable course" of action. With regard to reasonableness-type clauses, arbitrators seem willing to defer to the company's judgment where it is able to demon-

---

[101]51 LA 997 (Volz, 1968).
[102]Id. See also Amax Coal Co., 83 LA 942 (Kilroy, 1984); Todd Shipyards Corp., 80 LA 234 (Nicholas, 1983)(contractual standards, notice, no subcontracting of work normally performed by unit where this would result in layoff or prevent recall of laid-off employees); Brown & Williamson Tobacco Corp., 81 LA 581 (Goldman, 1983)(no layoff, advise and discuss); Pickands Mather & Co., 78 LA 1183 (Garrett, 1982)(past practice for production, service, and day-to-day maintenance and repair work; reasonableness for day-to-day maintenance and repair work and installation, replacement and reconstruction; no restriction for new construction).
[103]Basic Patterns in Union Contracts, supra note 60.

strate that any of the factors similar to those listed in the *Champion Papers* contract operate in the employer's favor.

Another type of subcontracting clause is one in which contracting out is restricted if the work is normally performed by unit employees.[104] Several issues are of note in this area. The first is whether "work normally performed by unit employees" includes work of a similar nature but of a far greater magnitude than that which was previously performed by the unit. Arbitrators have ruled both ways on this issue.[105] A second issue is how to treat overtime. If the employees do not normally perform overtime, but overtime would be required to complete the task within the time limits necessary to meet the company's requirements, does this allow management to subcontract the entire job, or just the portion that can be accomplished by working the unit overtime? Again, the case decisions are split.[106] Two recent examples involving subcontracting of work "normally performed by unit employees" reflect the different twists these provisions can take.

In *Commercial Construction Co.*,[107] the agreement contained a "protection of work" clause which provided that management would "not bring an outside contractor into the shop to perform any work normally performed by the bargaining unit in the shop to the extent that any bargaining unit employee is sent home while such contractor is performing that work."[108] The arbitrator upheld the company's contracting out the installation of an overhead crane in a plant where it was shown that only one employee had any experience in installing such equipment and the company had never had an overhead crane in its plant. The fact that an employee was on layoff status while such work was being done was irrelevant, since the provision's major predicate ("work normally performed") had not been met.

In *Waller Brothers Stone Co.*,[109] the agreement stated that the company would not "contract for any work with any em-

---

[104]See, e.g., North Am. Coal Co., 84 LA 388 (Feldman, 1985); Laurel Run Mining Co., 85-1 ARB ¶8247 (Feldman, 1985).
[105]See, e.g., United States Steel Corp., 54 LA 1207 (Duff, 1970).
[106]See, e.g., Buhr Mach. Tool Corp., 61 LA 333 (Sembower, 1973); Goodyear Atomic Corp., 66 LA 598 (Volz, 1976); Ideal Elec. & Mfg. Co., 67 LA 227 (Chockley, 1976); Lehigh Portland Cement Co., 49 LA 967 (Crawford, 1967).
[107]80 LA 565 (Nicholas, 1983).
[108]Id. at 566.
[109]80 LA 1185 (Millious, 1983).

ployee or foreman or outside individual for any maintenance or construction work in and around the plant which its regular employees normally do."[110] The arbitrator held that management did not violate this clause when it subcontracted the remodeling of an office building. Even though the unit employees had, in the past, performed certain types of construction work, including remodeling of a house on company property, the arbitrator said the work was of an "intermittent nature" and thus "was not work regularly performed by unit employees."

Provisions Reserving Decision to Management

In *EG & G Sealol, Inc.*,[111] the contract contained the following management rights clause:

> The Company reserves to itself exclusively and solely all the rights pertaining to plans and decisions on all matters involving the products to be manufactured, the location of the operations, [and] subcontracting . . . .[112]

Arbitrator Lawrence Cohen recognized that, in the absence of controlling contractual language, many arbitrators have implied a limitation of reasonableness on the right to subcontract. Arbitrator Cohen nevertheless ruled that "where, however, the contract specifically sanctions subcontracting, either outright or subject to certain stated conditions, the arbitrator is precluded from engaging in weighing the equities of the situation."[113] The arbitrator accordingly allowed management to contract out maintenance work to an outside contractor who "could do a better job at less expense."

The Sixth Circuit has cautioned arbitrators against applying their own brand of industrial justice in subcontracting disputes. In *Sears v. Teamsters Local 243*,[114] the agreement contained a subcontracting clause which read, in its entirety, as follows:

> Section 10. A. The right to subcontract any type of work within the jurisdiction of the Union shall be vested exclusively with the Company, provided however, that such right to subcontract shall be restricted to work that can be performed more effi-

---

[110]Id.
[111]81 LA 1157 (Cohen, 1983).
[112]Id. at 1159.
[113]Id. at 1160, citing Electric Storage Battery Co., 44 LA 782 (Koven, 1965).
[114]683 F.2d 154, 110 LRRM 3175 (CA 6, 1982), cert. denied, 460 U.S. 1023 (1982).

ciently and economically outside of the bargaining unit, and no work shall be subcontracted solely to discriminate against the Union.

  B. The Company agrees, prior to the actual subcontracting, the Company will substantiate such action by submitting facts and figures that the work involved can be done more efficiently and economically.[115]

The arbitrator recognized that the agreement did not, on its face, limit Sears' authority to subcontract in the interest of efficiency and economy. Moreover, he specifically found that Sears acted in good faith in entering the subcontract at issue. (Sears had contracted out the work of its entire "MA" sales employees who sell Sears maintenance contracts by telephone, thereby eliminating 90 jobs.) Nevertheless, the arbitrator applied a "balancing" test and concluded that the costs to the union of the disputed subcontract outweighed its benefits to the employer. On this rationale, reinstatement of the MA sales unit with back pay was ordered.

In concluding that the arbitrator "exceeded his authority by amending the express terms of the agreement," the Sixth Circuit distinguished between those contracts that are silent on subcontracting and those which contain a subcontracting provision.

  The authorities cited by the arbitrator in support of his use of a "balancing test" in this case are inapposite. There is, as the District Court explained, a critical distinction in arbitration cases between collective bargaining agreements which are silent on the question of subcontracting and those which specifically address the issue.

  In the former instance, it is accepted practice for arbitrators to infer a "reasonableness" limitation on the employer's right to subcontract; "reasonableness" is determined by a "balancing test" or cost-benefit analysis. . . .

  On the other hand, when the parties to a collective bargaining agreement have negotiated a clear, unambiguous subcontracting provision, an arbitrator lacks discretion to alter the effect of that provision by performing, *sua sponte*, a "balancing test." The weight of authority supports this conclusion.[116]

---

[115]110 LRRM at 3176.
[116]Id. at 3177, citing Laclede Gas Co., 67 LA 461 (David, 1976); Electric Storage Battery Co., 44 LA 782 (Koven, 1965); Timken Co. v. Steelworkers Local 1123, 482 F.2d 1012, 1014, 83 LRRM 2814 (CA 6, 1973). Contra, Consolidated Aluminum Co., 66 LA 1170 (Boals, 1976).

Other courts have taken a similar approach where the agreement vests subcontracting decisions with management.[117] A decision of special note is *Jones Dairy Farm v. Food & Commercial Workers Local P-1236*,[118] a case reported by the Seventh Circuit. The contract provided that with respect to the subcontracting of work, each party retained its legal rights in effect prior to execution of the agreement. When the company contracted out janitorial work that was formerly performed by the union, Arbitrator John Flagler reasoned that any limitations on the employer's right to subcontract must be found in external law. Looking at the NLRB's decision in *Milwaukee Spring I*,[119] the arbitrator ruled that the parties' contractual language prohibited this subcontracting. On appeal, the Seventh Circuit majority found the law to be that, absent agreement to the contrary, management is free to subcontract, even if the motivation for the decision to subcontract is to pay lower labor costs. Since the arbitrator had followed *Milwaukee Spring I*,[120] which was then on appeal and later repudiated by the Board,[121] his award did not draw its essence from the collective bargaining agreement, according to the majority. The court went on to state that the arbitrator was simply "expressing his opinion on a legal question, and courts (the bearers of expertise in such matters) are free to correct a mere mistake of law. . . ."[122]

The authors believe the position of the majority in *Jones Dairy Farm* is incorrect under the federal standard of court

---

[117]See, e.g., Lever Bros. v. Oil Workers Local 7-336, 555 F.Supp. 295, 113 LRRM 2615 (N.D. Ind., 1983), rev'd without opinion, 745 F.2d 61, 118 LRRM 3232 (1984); Clinchfield Coal v. Mine Workers Dist. 28, 736 F.2d 998, 116 LRRM 2884 (CA 4, 1984). Cf. Lone Star Indus. v. Teamsters Local 291, ___ F.Supp. ___, 119 LRRM 2121 (N.D. Cal., 1985)(vacating award holding that company was precluded from transferring work outside jurisdiction of bargaining unit where contract was silent regarding transfers. But see Ethyl Corp. v. Steelworkers, 768 F.2d 180, 119 LRRM 3566 (CA 7, 1985)(enforcing award requiring vacation pay for workers terminated pursuant to plant closing).

[118]755 F.2d 583, 118 LRRM 2841 (CA 7, 1985).

[119]Milwaukee Spring Div. of Illinois Coil Spring Co., 265 NLRB 206, 111 LRRM 1486 (1982), discussed in Chapter 15, notes 62–64, and accompanying text.

[120]According to Judge Posner, dissenting in *Jones Dairy Farm*, *Milwaukee Spring I* was intended to state the rule for cases where the collective bargaining agreement does *not* waive the union's right to object to contracting out. It was unclear, in the eyes of the majority in *Jones Dairy Farm*, whether the union waived that right by agreeing to the contracting-out clause. 118 LRRM at 2843.

[121]Milwaukee Spring Div. of Illinois Coil Spring Co., 268 NLRB 601, 115 LRRM 1065 (1984), aff'd sub nom. Auto Workers v. NLRB, 765 F.2d 175, 119 LRRM 2801 (CA DC, 1985).

[122]118 LRRM at 2842.

review of arbitrators' awards. As pointed out by Judge Richard Posner in his dissent, the arbitrator looked at the parties' subcontracting clause, determined that it required him to look at *Milwaukee Spring I*, and then interpreted that case, although, according to the dissent, his interpretation was too broad.

> The arbitrator read Milwaukee Spring too broadly in thinking that it decides this case. He should have asked whether the clause in the collective bargaining agreement in this case was intended to give Jones Dairy Farm an absolute right to contract out, which would be permissible under Milwaukee Spring, or whether it merely incorporated current Board doctrine, whatever that might be, on collective bargaining agreements that are silent on the matter of contracting out. He did not ask the right question, and it is impossible to say therefore whether he came up with the right answer.[123]

Although the arbitrator may have "looked through rather than at the contracting-out clause,"[124] as the dissent stated, it is submitted that this did not justify a decision that the arbitrator's award did not draw its essence from the agreement. As noted by the dissent, courts have frequently deferred to the legal determinations of arbitrators and, on its face, the decision of the arbitrator did not require the parties to do something in violation of a statute.[125]

Arbitrability Considerations

Since the Supreme Court's decision in *Steelworkers v. Warrior & Gulf Navigation Co.*,[126] the courts have taken the position that subcontracting disputes are presumptively arbitrable even where the agreement does not contain a contracting-out restriction, provided that the arbitration clause is sufficiently broad that it gives the arbitrator jurisdiction over both the procedural and substantive questions that may arise, and provided that there is no express language in the

---

[123]Id. at 2843.
[124]Id.
[125]It is of note that, on rehearing, the Seventh Circuit ruled that its initial decision was wrong and that the district court should not have set aside the arbitrator's award. The case was thus remanded with directions to enforce the award. Jones Dairy Farm v. Food & Commercial Workers Local P-1236, 760 F.2d 173, 119 LRRM 2185 (CA 7, 1985), cert. denied, 474 U.S. ____, 120 LRRM 2632 (1985).
[126]363 U.S. 574, 46 LRRM 2416 (1960).

agreement barring arbitration of a subcontracting dispute.[127] Illustrative of the extent to which the judiciary has accommodated arbitration is a decision by the First Circuit. In *Mobil Oil v. Oil Workers Local 8-766*,[128] a union filed a grievance after Mobil had unilaterally decided to subcontract all delivery of fuel oil and gasoline at its Bangor, Maine, facility. Management argued that the dispute was not arbitrable because there was no express provision regarding subcontracting in the labor agreement and because the arbitration clause in the contract limited the scope of the arbitrator's power to the "express provisions of the agreement." Finding that the subcontracting could undercut the express terms of the agreement dealing with recognition, seniority, job classification, and wage scales, the arbitrator determined that the dispute was arbitrable. Mobil commenced an action in federal court to vacate the award. The district court denied the motion, and the court of appeals affirmed the decision, making the following statement:

> [A] dispute is arbitrable unless it can be said "with positive assurance that the arbitration clause is not susceptible of an interpretation that covers the asserted dispute" and unless there is an "express provision excluding a particular grievance from arbitration."[129]

Since the arbitration clause did not expressly exclude subcontracting from arbitration, the dispute was deemed arbitrable.[130]

---

[127]See, e.g., Ben Gutman Truck Serv. v. Teamsters Local 600, 636 F.2d 255, 106 LRRM 2240 (CA 8, 1980); George Day Constr. Co. v. Carpenters Local 354, 113 LRRM 2275 (N.D. Cal., 1982), aff'd, 722 F.2d 1471, 115 LRRM 2459 (CA 9, 1984) (holding arbitrable a grievance alleging breach of no-subcontracting clause in subcontracting unit work after expiration of agreement); Mine Workers 30 v. Sovereign Coal Corp., 704 F.2d 329, 113 LRRM 2140 (6th Cir. 1983). Cf. Auto Workers v. Lester Eng'g Co., 718 F.2d 818, 114 LRRM 2783 (CA 6, 1983)(denying union injunction to prevent employer from selling assets of manufacturing facility, holding decision to cease business operations was nonarbitrable where management rights clause gave company right "to decide the number and location of its plants").

[128]600 F.2d 322, 101 LRRM 2721 (1979).

[129]101 LRRM at 2725, quoting Steelworkers v. Warrior & Gulf Navigation Co., 363 U.S. 574, 582–83, 585, 46 LRRM 2416 (1960).

[130]See also George Day Constr. Co. v. Carpenters Local 354, 722 F.2d 1471, 115 LRRM 2459 (CA 9, 1984); Teamsters v. Washington Employers, Inc., 557 F.2d 1345, 96 LRRM 2096 (CA 9, 1977); Electrical Workers IBEW Local 323 v. Coral Elec. Corp., 576 F.Supp. 1128, 116 LRRM 2790 (S.D. Fla., 1983); cf. Elliot Int'l, Inc. v. Garment Workers Local 99, 120 LRRM 2498 (N.Y. Sup. Ct., 1984).

Duty to Bargain

At one time the bellwether case controlling the policy in this area was *Fibreboard Paper Products v. NLRB*,[131] a 1964 decision by the Supreme Court. In that case the Court ruled that an employer's decision to subcontract plant maintenance work formally performed by the bargaining unit was a mandatory subject of bargaining. The Court addressed the duty to bargain with regard to contracting out as follows:

> Experience illustrates that contracting out in one form or another has been brought, widely and successfully, within the collective bargaining framework. . . .
> We are thus not expanding the scope of mandatory bargaining to hold, as we do now, that the type of "contracting out" involved in this case—the replacement of employees in the existing bargaining unit with those of an independent contractor to do the same work under similar conditions of employment—is a statutory subject of collective bargaining. . . .[132]

Fibreboard was significant but, as subsequent cases indicated, it was restricted to its own facts, which included the following conditions:

1. the subcontracting did not alter the basic operation of the business;
2. the subcontracting occurred in the plant under situations that were similar to those that prevailed prior to the contracting out;
3. employee jobs were eliminated and taken over by the subcontractor's employees;
4. the reasons for the contracting out were related to the costs of labor, which might have been adjusted by negotiations with the union, thereby avoiding the need to subcontract; and
5. the employer was still in the same business-risk situation under the subcontract because the contracting out was done on a cost-plus basis.

One year later, in *Westinghouse Electric Corp.*,[133] the Board set forth five factors that it would consider in determining

---

[131]379 U.S. 203, 57 LRRM 2609 (1964).
[132]57 LRRM at 2612–13.
[133]150 NLRB 1574, 58 LRRM 1257 (1965).

whether an employer must bargain with the union over the decision to subcontract:

1. whether the contracting out was motivated solely by economic considerations;
2. whether it comported with the traditional methods by which the company conducted its business;
3. whether the subcontracting varied significantly from what had been customary under past practice;
4. whether it had a demonstrable adverse impact upon the employees in the unit; and
5. whether the union had the opportunity to bargain about changing existing subcontracting practices at negotiations.

Fibreboard and *Westinghouse Electric* made it clear that management is not obligated to consult and bargain with the union over every subcontracting decision. While no hard and fast rules exist, under these decisions subcontracting of unit work without notice to and consultation with the union is arguably permissible unless it results in a "significant detriment" to the bargaining unit.[134] At the same time, recent NLRB decisions indicate that "the critical factor in determining whether a management decision is subject to mandatory bargaining is 'the essence of the decision itself, i.e., whether it turns upon a change in the nature or direction of the business, or turns upon labor costs; *not* its effect on employees nor a union's ability to offer alternatives.' "[135] Thus, in *Griffith-Hope Co.*,[136] a three-member Board held that a company violated the NLRA by unilaterally subcontracting unit work without bargaining over the decision to do so and over its effects on the bargaining unit. The Board, citing its decision in *Otis Elevator Co. II*,[137] stated that "when a particular management decision turns upon labor costs, it falls within the scope of Section 8(d) and concerns a mandatory subject of bargaining."[138] A fair reading of management's bargaining ob-

---

[134]See, e.g., Olinkraft, Inc. v. NLRB, 666 F.2d 302, 109 LRRM 2573 (CA 5, 1982).

[135]Bostrom Div., UOP Inc., 272 NLRB 999, 117 LRRM 1429 (1984), quoting Otis Elevator Co. II, 269 NLRB 891, 115 LRRM 1281, 1283 (1984)(emphasis in original).

[136]275 NLRB No. 73, 119 LRRM 1197 (1985).

[137]269 NLRB 891, 115 LRRM 1281 (1984). *Otis Elevator* is discussed in Chapter 15, notes 49–53, and accompanying text.

[138]119 LRRM at 1198.

ligation under this line of cases is that a subcontracting decision that turns on labor costs, and does not alter the basic nature of the business, is subject to bargaining with the union if it results in a "significant detriment" to the unit.[139] Less clear is management's obligation when the decision alters the basic nature of the business and, at the same time, turns on labor costs.[140]

No-Subcontracting Provisions and Section 8(e)

Section 8(e) of the National Labor Relations Act, in relevant part, provides as follows:

> It shall be an unfair labor practice for any labor organization and any employer to enter into any contract or agreement, express or implied, whereby such employer ceases or refrains or agrees to cease or refrain from handling, using, selling, transporting or otherwise dealing in any of the products of any other employer, or to cease doing business with any other person, and any contract or agreement entered into heretofore or hereafter containing such an agreement shall be to such extent unenforceable and void. . . .[141]

In *Connell Construction Co., Inc., v. Plumbers (Plumbers and Steamfitters Local 100)*,[142] the Supreme Court made it clear that the proviso to Section 8(e)[143] provides only limited protection to the construction industry, and that clauses pro-

---

[139]See, e.g., Gottfried v. Echlin, Inc., 113 LRRM 2349 (E.D. Mich., 1983); P.W. Supermarkets, Inc., 269 NLRB 839, 115 LRRM 1315 (1984); Liberal Mkt., Inc., 264 NLRB 807, 111 LRRM 1326 (1982); Ausable Communications, 273 NLRB No. 166, 118 LRRM 1295 (1985)(subcontracting of increased installation work without affording union opportunity to bargain not violative of LMRA); Pennsylvania Energy Corp., 274 NLRB No. 174, 119 LRRM 1042 (1985)(finding violation when company laid off employees from strip-mining operation and thereafter subcontracted work; contracting out based on labor costs, did not involve change in nature of business, and was amenable to resolution through bargaining process without significant burden on employer). Cf. Nurminco, 274 NLRB No. 112, 119 LRRM 1059 (1985)(layoff of unit employees and transfer of work to non-unit employees violative of LMRA where decision based in substantial part on labor costs).

[140]In Griffith-Hope Co., 275 NLRB No. 73, 119 LRRM 1197 (1985), Chairman Dotson and Members Hunter and Dennis pointed out that the management "viewed the subcontracting program as a temporary one that did not effect a fundamental change in the nature of its operation." 119 LRRM at 1198.

[141]29 U.S.C. §158(e).

[142]421 U.S. 616, 89 LRRM 2401 (1975).

[143]"*Provided*, That nothing in this subsection shall apply to an agreement between a labor organization and an employer in the construction industry relating to the contracting or subcontracting of work to be done at the site of the construction, alteration, painting, or repair of a building, structure, or other work . . . ." 29 U.S.C. §158(e).

hibiting subcontracting are only legal where the employer and the union are in a collective bargaining relationship. This ruling was further clarified in 1982 when the Court, in *Woelke and Romero Framing, Inc. v. NLRB*,[144] held that no-subcontracting arrangements are legal as long as a collective bargaining relationship exists, including the situation where the parties' labor agreement has expired and they are in the process of bargaining. In light of these decisions, agreements not to subcontract parts, products, or services do not violate Section 8(e) of the Act. In this regard, the Supreme Court has recently pointed out that the purpose of Section 8(e) had been to close a loophole in the labor laws that allowed unions to employ "hot cargo" agreements to pressure neutral employers not to handle nonunion goods. As long as the union's efforts are directed at its own employer on a topic affecting employees' wages or hours or affecting working conditions that the primary employer can control, the union's conduct is considered "primary," and labor laws do not prohibit bona fide primary activity. Accordingly, when the objective of the unions is preserving work for its members through a no-subcontracting clause, it is presumptively legal even though the clause has secondary effects.[145]

---

[144]456 U.S. 645, 110 LRRM 2377 (1982).
[145]NLRB v. Longshoremen ILA, 473 U.S. ___, 119 LRRM 2915 (1985).

Chapter 17

Supervisors and Supervisory Directives

Selection of Supervisors[1]

Management's right to appoint supervisors is so universally recognized as part of its power to direct the work force that a union has a considerable burden to shoulder when challenging an appointment to a managerial position. As observed by one arbitrator,

> the general principle [is] that the Union has no more right to interfere concerning the appointment or retention of supervisors than the Company has to interfere with the retention of Union stewards, committeemen or officers.[2]

Even when the supervisor is a bargaining-unit employee, management has been accorded considerable discretion in appointing and removing supervisors.[3]

In this same respect there is authority for the proposition that, under certain situations, a union will be precluded from interfering with management's right to make temporary supervisory appointments. Thus, the First Circuit, in *NLRB v. Electrical Workers IBEW, System Council T-6 (New England Telephone Co.)*[4] held that a union violated its duty to bargain by unilaterally promulgating a rule prohibiting union members from accepting temporary management assignments to

---

[1]See also discussion under "Supervisory Classifications" in Chapter 14, supra.
[2]Electro Metallurgical Co., 19 LA 8, 10 (McCoy, 1952).
[3]Johnson Controls, Ltd., 57 LA 3 (Brown, 1971).
[4]599 F.2d 5, 101 LRRM 2413 (CA 1, 1979).

supervisory positions, where the past practice of the employer was to make temporary assignments and the practice had been recognized in a prior arbitration award.

While most cases in this area involve the method and criteria management uses for selecting supervisors, some decisions have addressed the company's motives. In *Chicago Electrotypers Division*,[5] for example, Arbitrator John Sembower ruled that management did not violate the seniority provisions of the agreement when it expanded its supervisory staff by promoting selected employees to the position of foreman, thus allowing the promoted employees to avoid an impending layoff.[6]

Where the agreement is silent, arbitrators are split on the issue of whether management may create a supervisory position and then transfer bargaining-unit work to that new position.[7] As discussed in another section, under an agreement that restricted management from performing bargaining-unit work, the better view has been stated by Arbitrator Tom Roberts when he held that absent a corresponding change in work duties, management may not transfer unit work to a non-unit employee through the device of promotion to supervisory status.[8]

Union Membership and Activities of Supervisors

The Taft-Hartley Act amended the National Labor Relations Act to exclude supervisors from the protections of the NLRA, and therefore freed management to discharge supervisors without violating it. In relevant part, Section 14(a) of the statute provides as follows:

> Nothing herein shall prohibit any individual employed as a supervisor from becoming or remaining a member of a labor organization, but no employer subject to this Act shall be compelled to deem individuals defined herein as supervisors as employees for the purpose of any law, either national or local, relating to collective bargaining.[9]

---

[5]51 LA 197, 199 (Sembower, 1968).
[6]See also SCM Corp., 58 LA 688 (Koven, 1972); Eastern Air Lines, Inc., 44 LA 145 (Seidenberg, 1964).
[7]See, e.g., Cotton Bros. Baking Co., 51 LA 220 (Hebert, 1968). See also the discussion under "Reassignment of Unit Work to Non-Unit Personnel" in Chapter 14.
[8]Crown Zellerbach Corp., 52 LA 1183, 1185 (1969).
[9]61 Stat. 137, 29 U.S.C. §164(a).

Under the NLRA, the term "supervisor" was broadly defined to include

[A]ny individual having authority, in the interest of the employer, to hire, transfer, suspend, lay off, recall, promote, discharge, assign, reward, or discipline other employees, or responsibly to direct them, or to adjust their grievances, or effectively to recommend such action, if in connection with the foregoing the exercise of such authority is not of a merely routine or clerical nature, but requires the use of independent judgment.[10]

The NLRB and the courts have held that an employee must manifest one or more of the above-cited criteria to be held a supervisor under the NLRA.[11]

In 1974 the Supreme Court issued three decisions that accorded significant discretion to management in discharging supervisors for union activity. In *NLRB v. Bell Aerospace Co.*,[12] the Court ruled that all employees properly classified as "managerial" are excluded from the protections of the NLRA. The Court further held, in *Beasley v. Food Fair of N.C., Inc.*,[13] that the Taft-Hartley amendments "excluded supervisors from the protections of the [NLRA] and thus freed employers to discharge supervisors without violating the Act's restraints against discharges on account of labor union membership." The Court reasoned that *"[m]anagement, like labor, must have faithful agents"* and that " 'there must be in management and loyal to it persons not subject to influence or control of unions.' "[14] In *Florida Power & Light Co. v. Electrical Workers IBEW Local 641*,[15] the Court confirmed that an employer "is at liberty to demand absolute loyalty from his supervisory personnel by insisting, on pain of discharge, that they neither participate in, nor retain membership in, a labor union. . . ."[16]

---

[10]29 U.S.C. §152(11).
[11]NLRB v. Rain-Ware, Inc., 732 F.2d 1349, 116 LRRM 2261 (CA 7, 1984), later proc., 275 NLRB No. 172, 119 LRRM 1288 (1985).
[12]416 U.S. 267, 85 LRRM 2945 (1974).
[13]416 U.S. 653, 86 LRRM 2196 (1974).
[14]Id. at 660, quoting H.R. Rep. No. 245, 80th Cong., 1st Sess., 16 (1947)(emphasis in original).
[15]417 U.S. 790, 86 LRRM 2689 (1974).
[16]Id. at 812, 86 LRRM at 2697. The NLRB has been faithful to this mandate. See Lucky Stores, Inc., 269 NLRB 942, 116 LRRM 1463 (1984)(holding discharge of confidential employee lawful); Harvey's Resort Hotel, 271 NLRB 306, 116 LRRM 1401 (1984)(discharge of casino floorman); Arroyo Grande Community Hosp., Inc., 260 NLRB 1183, 109 LRRM 1302 (1982)(discharge of supervisor-nurse who was active in union and organizing campaign lawful); Roma Baking Co., 263 NLRB 24, 110 LRRM 1523 (1982)(discharge of supervisor because of union activity upheld); Puro-

Former NLRB General Counsel John Irving, Jr., in an address before the American Bar Association, pointed out that the Board has nevertheless found supervisory discharges violative of the NLRA where (1) the discharges were part of a scheme to interfere directly with, or to clear the way for interfering directly with, the protected rights of employees, or (2) the discharge was designed to prevent the supervisor from engaging in conduct intended to protect employees from interference and from discrimination.[17] In this regard the Board has outlined the black-letter law as follows:

> [A]n employer may not discharge a supervisor for giving testimony adverse to an employer's interest either at an NLRB proceeding or during the processing of an employee's grievance under the collective bargaining agreement. Similarly an employer may not discharge a supervisor for refusing to commit unfair labor practices, or because the supervisor fails to prevent unionization. In all these situations, however, the protection afforded supervisors stems not from any statutory protection inuring to them, but rather from the need to vindicate employees' exercise of their Section 7 rights.[18]

At one time the Board would find that an employer violated the statute in dismissing a supervisor as part of a pattern of conduct aimed at coercing employees in the exercise of their bargaining rights.[19] The rationale for such a finding was that in an intentionally created atmosphere of coercion, employees could not be expected to perceive the distinction between the employer's right to prohibit union activity among supervisors and their right to engage freely in such activity themselves.

---

lator Prods., Inc., 270 NLRB 536, 117 LRRM 1036 (1984)(upholding discharge of four supervisors engaged in union activity).

[17]See J. Irving, Jr., Recent Significant NLRB Decisions, Developments and Changes, Remarks Before the American Bar Association, Section of Labor and Employment Law, New Orleans, La., May 1, 1980.

[18]Parker-Robb Chevrolet, 262 NLRB 402, 402–03, 110 LRRM 1289, 1290 (1982), enforced sub nom. Food & Commercial Workers (Automobile Salesmen's Union Local 1095) v. NLRB, 711 F.2d 383, 113 LRRM 3175 (CA DC, 1983). Recent applications of the law in this area include: Orkin Exterminating Co., 270 NLRB 428, 116 LRRM 1089 (1984)(ruling constructive discharge improper because supervisor announced intention to testify before NLRB); A&E Stores, Inc., 272 NLRB 737, 117 LRRM 1393 (1984)(holding discharge unlawful for giving testimony adverse to employer in NLRB proceeding); Datagraphic, Inc., 259 NLRB 1285, 109 LRRM 1099 (1982)(discharge unlawful for supervisor's refusal to commit unfair labor practices); Howard Johnson Motor Lodge, 261 NLRB 866, 110 LRRM 1135 (1982)(refusing to engage in surveillance in connection with organizing campaign), enforced, 702 F.2d 1, 112 LRRM 2904 (CA 1, 1983).

[19]See, e.g., DRW Corp. d/b/a Brothers Three Cabinets, 248 NLRB 828, 103 LRRM 1506 (1980); Empire Gas, Inc., 254 NLRB 626, 106 LRRM 1163 (1981).

In *Parker-Robb Chevrolet*,[20] however, the Board reversed its prior position. The Board reasoned that the "[s]upervisors in the 'integral part' or 'pattern of conduct' cases were, themselves, active for the union or participated in the concerted activity" and "it is difficult to distinguish these cases from those in which the Board has found that the discharge of a supervisor does not violate the Act."[21] The Board found that "[n]o matter what the employer's subjective hope or expectation, that circumstance cannot change the character of its otherwise lawful conduct."[22] The message is clear to supervisors: The "integral part" or "pattern of conduct" rationale for finding that a discharge violated the NLRA is no longer a safe harbor for supervisors.

Discharge and Discipline of Supervisors

Absent explicit contractual language to the contrary, an employee who is a management supervisor and not a member of the bargaining unit cannot be represented by the union and cannot utilize the contractual grievance procedure to challenge the propriety of discipline or discharge.[23] Further, when the recognition clause excludes supervisors from the bargaining unit, arbitrators are without jurisdiction to order discipline. Thus, Arbitrator Henry Sisk, in *U.S. Commission on Civil Rights*,[24] held that he had no jurisdiction to enter a ruling on whether an employer's issuance of a warning letter was a sufficient penalty for a supervisor who improperly issued an intent-to-terminate notice to a probationary employee. Similarly, Arbitrator Edward Archer reflected the thinking of most arbitrators in a case involving a supervisor who placed his

---

[20]262 NLRB 402, 110 LRRM 1289 (1982), enforced sub nom. Food & Commercial Workers (Automobile Salesmen's Union Local 1095) v. NLRB, 711 F.2d 383, 113 LRRM 3175 (CA DC, 1983).

[21]110 LRRM at 1290.

[22]Id. at 1291.

[23]New Jersey Zinc Co., 72 LA 914 (Malkin, 1979); Hotel Employer's Ass'n of San Francisco, 51 LA 701, 702 (Koven, 1968)(holding no presumption arises that grievant is a member of the bargaining unit since she voted in NLRB election). But see Chromalloy Am. Corp., 54 LA 965 (Elliott, 1970); Cedar Rapids Eng'g. Co., 58 LA 374 (Epstein, 1972)(union entitled to state discharged supervisor's claim to departmental seniority under agreement that provides for preserving departmental seniority rights of promoted employees). Of course, some agreements specifically reserve to management the exclusive right to discipline its officers and representatives. See, e.g., United States Steel Corp., 54 LA 640, 641 (Kreimer, 1970).

[24]67 LA 271 (1976).

hands on a union steward in order to prevent him from leaving the plant. Holding the grievance not arbitrable, Arbitrator Archer stated:

> The question in this case is, does the contract in question clearly provide for arbitrability of the Company's failure to impose greater discipline upon Supervisor M____. I find no provision in the contract which creates this authority under the facts of this case.
>
> . . .
>
> Article V sets forth the expressly reserved management rights. While management does not have the right to "man-handle" or in any way physically abuse employees under Article V, that is not the question in this case. The question is, does management have discretion in choosing what discipline, if any, to impose upon its supervisors. While this right may not be expressly spelled out in Article V, it is such an inherent function of management, arbitrators have uniformly held . . . that management retains this right absent a clear contractual restriction of the right. Article V in no way restricts or limits this inherent management right.[25]

Arbitrator Stephen Schoenfeld likewise declared that he was without authority to order the discharge of a supervisor who allegedly struck an employee during an argument. It was of no effect, the arbitrator stated, that the contract contained a provision stating that an employee may be dismissed for the offense charged by the union. The arbitrator's reasoning is particularly instructive.

> Even if A ___ came within the ambit of Article 4 [the article covering disciplinary action of employees], a careful examination of said article reveals that there is nothing therein that makes the remedy of discharge available to the Union. The initiative in disciplining employes resides exclusively with the Employer. The Union can scrutinize and challenge the actions of the Employer after discipline is imposed, but the initial determination concerning the disciplining of an employe—those covered by the agreement, and certainly those excluded from its coverage, as A ___—is the exclusive function of the Employer.
>
> Article 4 is a limitation on the exercise of management's rights. It affords employes protection so they cannot be arbitrarily and capriciously disciplined. It does not, however, make the remedy of discipline available to the Union or individual employe against a supervisor. Based on the aforesaid, the Ar-

---

[25]Merico, Inc., 67 LA 284, 286 (1976).

bitrator concludes that he is without authority to impose discipline of any nature on A ____.[26]

The arbitrator went on to comment:

> The Union has no more right to interfere concerning the discipline of supervisors than the Employer has to interfere with, for example, the appointment or retention of union stewards. The Employer cannot reach into the Union's internal affairs nor can the Union reach into the Employer's affairs. Misconduct on the part of a union steward toward a member of supervision would not justify the Arbitrator, at the request of the Employer, to order him removed from his union office.[27]

In summary, an employer has the unqualified right to discipline or discharge a non-unit supervisor in the absence of a specific limitation in the labor agreement. Further, both arbitrators and the courts have held that in the absence of such qualifying language, the discharge of a supervisor is not arbitrable.[28] When, however, the contract contains a clause preserving the seniority rights of an employee who is promoted out of the bargaining unit,[29] the better view is that bargaining-unit job rights are also retained. Under this view, while the decision to dismiss an employee from the supervisor position is not reviewable, a decision in addition not to allow the employee to revert back to the bargaining unit but instead to terminate the employee altogether, is reviewable under the seniority rights clause. As stated by Arbitrator George Fleischli,

> [i]n the case of a supervisor, who is not normally covered by a collective bargaining agreement, the employer retains the right to terminate the supervisor for any reason considered sufficient by the employer and such a decision is not reviewable under the collective bargaining agreement. However, if the employer's intent is to terminate the employee's retained seniority rights as well, the decision is reviewable for its compliance with the

---

[26]Marinette Gen. Hosp., 67 LA 785, 787–88 (1976).

[27]Id. at 787 n.4. See also Murdock Mach. Eng'g Co., 63 LA 65 (Dunn, 1974)(grievance requesting discipline of non-unit supervisor not arbitrable); Southern Iron & Equip. Co., 65 LA 694, 700 (Rutherford, 1975)("[T]his right to grieve does not give the Union the right to affect the employment status of management's representatives. Furthermore, Section 8(b)(1) of the National Labor Relations Act specifically prohibits Unions from restraining or coercing 'an employer in the selection of his representatives.'")

[28]Chromalloy Am. Corp., 54 LA 965, 968 (Elliott, 1970).

[29]See, e.g., American Metaseal Co., 70 LA 295, 295 (Kanner, 1978), where the contract, in relevant part, provided: "In the event they [supervisors] are subsequently demoted, they shall be permitted to use that seniority they had accumulated to return to the job they were promoted from, seniority permitting."

provisions of the collective bargaining agreement dealing with
the loss of seniority rights.

In a number of cases, employers have argued that such
clauses are intended to be "permissive" and do not create an
enforceable right to return to the bargaining unit. Although
such a result would be supportable if the language were drawn
with that intended meaning, it is clearly inconsistent with the
concept of seniority rights. Seniority, which is a creature of
collective bargaining agreements, constitutes a fundamental
form of job security. To say that an employee who is promoted
to a job which is outside the coverage of the collective bargaining agreement retains his accrued "seniority rights" but may
only exercise them if the employer concurs would be as anom-
alous as saying that a management rights clause gives the
employer the right to lay off employees for economic reasons
but only if the union concurs.[30]

Supervisors Performing Bargaining-Unit Work

The Bureau of National Affairs, Inc. reports that supervisory performance of bargaining-unit work is limited in 54
percent of the contracts surveyed, but that most of these clauses
provide that work may be performed by supervisory employees
on a limited basis under one or more of the following conditions: in case of emergency (72 percent); for instructional purposes (72 percent); to conduct experiments (28 percent); for
demonstration purposes (12 percent); and to develop new products (13 percent). Further, the BNA study found that 18 percent of the contracts limiting work by supervisors allow such
work if a regular employee is not displaced. Work by other
non-unit employees—for example, management trainees—was
allowed in 13 percent of the agreements sampled.[31]

When the Contract Is Silent

When the agreement is silent on the issue, arbitrators
have sometimes treated cases involving non-unit supervisors
performing unit work in the same manner as cases in which
management makes a permanent transfer of unit work to non-

---

[30]Rodman Indus., Inc., 59 LA 101, 105 (1972)(footnotes omitted).
[31]Basic Patterns in Union Contracts, 64–65 (BNA Books, 1983).

unit personnel, resulting in the same split of authority for both kinds of cases.[32]

On one side are the decisions that find no restriction on management's right to perform unit work in the absence of an express contractual provision to the contrary. This deference to management is often based on management's retention of express and implied powers within the collective bargaining agreement itself and on the basic assumption by arbitrators that the parties were free to have bargained otherwise had that been their intention.

On the other side, some arbitrators have held that the existence of the recognition, seniority, and job-classification provisions in a collective bargaining contract amount to an implied restriction on management's right to perform any bargaining unit work, except for situations involving emergencies, training and instructing of employees, or strikes.[33]

In the middle of the spectrum is the third approach requiring a balancing of the respective interests in any given case. In this approach the right to perform bargaining-unit work is not inferred from the absence of any limitation on management.[34]

Provisions Regarding Emergencies

Contractual provisions that permit non-unit supervisors to perform unit work during emergencies are common. Some agreements attempt a definition of "emergency,"[35] but, most contracts simply state that it is permissible for a non-unit employee to perform unit work when an emergency exists, because of the difficulty in defining the term, since emergencies by definition generally involve unanticipated situations and since a dispute over whether there was an actual emergency is likely to involve not so much a definition of the term as an application of the concept to facts which are not likely

---

[32]See the discussion under "Reassignment of Unit Work to Non-Unit Personnel," in Chapter 14, supra.
[33]Harman Packing Co., 12 LA 1000 (Bernstein, 1949)(owner's right to work and to use property as he wishes is subordinated by recognition clause); American Bemberg, 19 LA 372 (McCoy, 1952)(seniority provision implies restriction on performance of unit work by supervisors).
[34]Dayton Power & Light Co., 67-1 ARB ¶8259 (Bradley, 1967); Sundstrand Corp., 64-2 ARB ¶8861 (Updegraff, 1964); Pan Am. Airways, Inc., 13 LA 390 (Kerr, 1949); Bethlehem Steel Co., 14 LA 159 (Feinberg, 1949).
[35]See, e.g., Anheuser-Busch, Inc., 62 LA 1130, 1131 (Morris, 1974).

to be anticipated. A common procedure that arbitrators use to determine if an emergency required the performance of unit work by supervisors is to compare the factual situation to a dictionary definition.[36] Other arbitrators shun dictionary definitions of emergencies and focus solely on the facts and circumstances of each case.

In *Diamond National Corp.*,[37] Arbitrator Rankin Gibson ruled that a supervisor had the right under the parties' contract to replace a sprinkler head which had burst and was spilling water in a room where several electrical motors were present. The arbitrator noted that the past history of fires at the plant and the presence of flammables was enough to constitute an emergency even though a unit repairman could have been on the scene in thirty minutes.

On the other hand, under a provision that stated "company personnel excluded from the bargaining unit shall not perform bargaining work, except in an emergency endangering life or property," a company that had shut down for inventory was held to have violated the bargaining agreement by permitting supervisors to thaw frozen pipes before they burst. The arbitrator reasoned that freezing was a slow process which permitted time for a unit repairman to be brought in before property damage took place.[38]

While a large fire is usually conceded to constitute an emergency, questions as to the duration of the emergency situation may nonetheless arise. In *Alcolac, Inc.*,[39] the union contended that whatever emergency existed at the time of the fire ceased to exist once the fire had been extinguished. Arbitrator Robert Mullin first noted that damage in excess of $1 million had occurred at the chemical plant. He then noted the dangerous and flammable nature of the remaining chemicals and went on to decide the case as follows:

> [T]he accomplishment of the necessary clean-up required many on-the-scene decisions by the supervisors and foremen in the

---

[36]State of Mich., Department of Corrections, 83-2 ARB ¶8589 (Borland, 1983); Diamond Nat'l Corp., 61 LA 567, 571 (Gibson, 1973)("All of the dictionaries we have consulted seem to agree that an emergency arises when there is a sudden or unexpected occurrence or combination of occurrences which demand prompt action," citing Bruner v. McGlothin, 66 Ohio L. Abs. 477, 117 N.E.2d 476, 477 (Ohio Ct. App., 1951).
[37]61 LA 567 (Gibson, 1973).
[38]Louisville Cement Co., 79 LA 584, 586 (Archer, 1982).
[39]80 LA 171 (Mullin, 1983).

repair of damaged chemical lines, the removal of twisted and
dangling beams from the roof and the use of heavy equipment
such as front-end loaders and dump trucks to dispose of tons of
rubble and debris. . . . It is now found that on the morning after
the fire here involved the Company was confronted with an
"emergency" . . . and that the type of work which thereafter
had to be performed in order to restore production was not of
a type which was regularly assigned to members of the bargaining unit.[40]

At times, a company's precarious financial situation may
constitute an emergency. For example, in *Unit Parts Co.*,[41]
the company was undergoing an attempted revival following
bankruptcy. In the year prior to bankruptcy, the company had
lost some $300,000 and its overall debt was approximately
$14 million. During the time in dispute the company was in
the red by $331,000 and had no capacity to borrow. Its weekly
cash flow rarely exceeded $40,000, and it had an outstanding
weekly payroll of $30,000. Arbitrator Wallace Nelson per-
mitted the performance of the unit work by the supervisors
and stated succinctly, "The rationale was, and is, that the
Company is on the ragged edge of insolvency."[42]

However Arbitrator David Borland, in *State of Michigan,
Department of Corrections*,[43] reasoned that the length of time
involved in the development of a financial emergency subverts
the true meaning of "emergency." According to the arbitrator,
there should be a distinction between financial and operational emergencies, with only the latter qualifying as "emergencies" for purposes of application of a clause in the collective
bargaining agreement.

Although as can be seen from the above discussion the
determination that there is an "emergency" depends on the
facts and circumstances of each case, there are nonetheless
some common threads in arbitral thinking on what constitutes
an emergency. The reported decisions indicate that an emergency is generally defined as an unanticipated situation that
calls for sudden, immediate action.[44] Arbitrator Ralph Wil-

[40]Id. at 175–76.
[41]80 LA 1180 (Nelson, 1983).
[42]Id. at 1184.
[43]83-2 ARB ¶8589 (1983).
[44]See generally Elkouri & Elkouri, "Emergencies, Acts of God, and Conditions
Beyond the Control of Management," How Arbitration Works, 4th Ed., 529–31 (BNA
Books, 1985).

liams reflected the thinking of most neutrals when he stated that "it is an event or combination of circumstances which calls for immediate, prompt action or remedy without giving time for the deliberate exercise of judgment or discretion."[45] Another arbitrator said that an emergency was a condition "where life or property is endangered, or to prevent any phase from shutting down."[46] A mechanical breakdown where no other adequate machinery is available as a substitute is an emergency.[47] Some arbitrators, however, will find a violation of the contract if the breakdown is caused by management's neglecting routine maintenance. As stated by Arbitrator Sidney Cahn, "[o]nly circumstances which the Employer could not foresee and could not avoid would constitute an emergency."[48] Further, floods, fires, power failures, or explosions are situations that will usually permit management to perform tasks that are necessary to avoid danger to life or property. How much cleanup work can be performed by supervisors in any of the above situations is unclear.[49] So long as immediate or urgent action is required, the better rule would permit supervisors to perform what might otherwise be found to be unit work.[50] A rush order for a customer is generally not considered an emergency, unless there is a shortage of unit personnel and available employees refuse overtime assignments.[51]

The *De Minimis* Doctrine[52]

Arbitrators frequently apply the legal principle of *de minimis nom curat lex*, which means that the law does not care for, or take notice of, very small or trifling matters. This doctrine sometimes is applied to dismiss a grievance altogether

---

[45]Allied Mills, Inc., 49 LA 683, 685 (undated).

[46]John Deer Chem. Co., 61-3 ARB ¶8651 at 5970 (Quinlan, 1961).

[47]Ozark-Mahoning Co., 78-2 ARB ¶8345 (Hunter, 1978).

[48]Oxford Paper Co., 45 LA 609, 611 (Cahn, 1965); Coleman Co., 49 LA 431 (Lazar, 1967)(foreseeable parts shortage rejected as emergency).

[49]See, e.g., Alcolac, Inc., 80 LA 171 (Mullin, 1983)(cleanup after fire permitted).

[50]F.W. Means & Co., 54 LA 874 (Witney, 1970)(breakdown in hot water system); Union Camp Corp., 71 LA 454 (Volz, 1978).

[51]See, e.g., PHD, Inc., 74 LA 1175 (Witney, 1980); Avis Rent A Car System, Inc., 83 LA 294 (Schedler, 1984); Vulcan Material Co., 79 LA 1097, 1099 (Cabe, 1982)("A rush job does not in itself create an emergency.... If a qualified employee who was at work or on layoff had refused the operation, a nonunit employee would have been free to complete the job.").

[52]See generally Hill & Sinicropi, Remedies in Arbitration, 132–34 (BNA Books, 1981) for a discussion of the *de minimis* doctrine.

on the ground that the conduct complained of is so minor that it cannot reasonably be considered a violation of the parties' contract. However, one commentor has stated, in what appears to be the better reasoning, that the *de minimis* doctrine ought to be reserved for use only as a means of determining the amount of damages and should not be employed as a reason for dismissing the grievance altogether.[53]

By far the most common application of the *de minimis* rule is in situations where supervisors have performed bargaining-unit work. The reported decisions, however, do not lend themselves to the formulation of any set guidelines as to when the *de minimis* doctrine will defeat a grievance. According to Arbitrator Elmer Hilpert, an example of a "true" *de minimis* situation is an occurrence where a non-unit employee merely provided "a hand in passing" so that no unit employee lost a work opportunity.[54] Under an agreement that stated that "supervisory employees shall perform no production, classified or other work," Arbitrator Bernard Cantor found the *de minimis* rule inapplicable where a non-unit employee performed two or three minutes of work in cranking a welding machine onto a ball-headed connection on a truck. In finding the rule inapplicable, the arbitrator focused on the parties' intent as evidenced in their agreement, reasoning as follows:

> To an outsider, it would seem to be unspeakably minor.
> But the parties do not see it so. Of course, management now argues that it was trivial, and suggests the lawyers' concept of *de minimis*, something too small to invite the consideration of judge or arbitrator, but they are, directly, and through the agents who negotiate this agreement, parties to a document that evidences a much different attitude out of historical perspective. Somewhere back down the line, some management has so abused the situation as to outrage the people. The union has demanded, and the management people have acquiesced, that on a complaint of this nature, the management must prove the negative, an almost impossible task. Not that alone [sic], they have imposed a penalty provision [one shift's pay to the individual who should have performed the work] which requires far greater restitution than the offense might occasion. That contract provision is notable. . . . There is no concept of *de min-*

---

[53]Nolan, Labor Arbitration Law and Practice in a Nutshell, 191 (West, 1979).
[54]Acme Paper Co., 47 LA 238, 242 (1966).

imis here. The contract does not allow for it. The contract controls.[55]

Arbitrator James Altieri, in *Westinghouse Electric Corp.*,[56] ruled that the *de minimis* doctrine could not properly be applied where the work at issue, constituting no more than one minute of the supervisor's time, was a "principal" activity of the unit employees. In discussing the problems in evaluating *de minimis* claims on the basis of the time involved, Arbitrator Altieri offered the following hypothesis:

> Supposing the Company determines that it will increase production and make for a more efficient operation if, instead of ringing the bell at 10:30 A.M., that [sic] it do so at 10:31 A.M., and answers the Union's protest by saying that the extra minute is *de minimis*. . . .
> The foregoing analysis of course, stems necessarily from the conclusion that the tasks involved are integrally related with and constitute a part of, the principal activity. Once this conclusion is arrived at, there is no room, in the opinion of the undersigned, for application to unilateral Company action [non-unit personnel getting tools ready for use on assembly line] of the principle of "de minimis non curat lex" without doing gross violence to the contractual relationship between the parties.[57]

Where arbitrators have held that the *de minimis* rule operated to deny either a grievance or a remedy for a proven violation, they have stated that the work was of an insignificant nature and of short duration or that there were no measurable damages.[58]

Testing, Research, and Training Functions

It is not uncommon to find clauses that permit management to use supervisors to conduct tests and/or research and

---

[55]Roberts & Schafer Co., 72 LA 624, 626 (1979). See also Wheland Co., 34 LA 904 (Tatum, 1960)(10-second period of performing unit work was sufficient to make out violation under strict agreement).

[56]43 LA 84 (1964).

[57]Id. at 90.

[58]Superior Fiber Prods., Inc., 58 LA 582 (Johnson, 1972)(*de minimis* nature of work); National Lead Co., 62 LA 190 (High, 1974)(rule was applicable where work lasted 10 to 15 minutes); Acheson Dispersed Pigments Co., 36 LA 578 (Hale, 1960)(pay lost was inconsequential); General Chem., 61-3 ARB ¶8609 (McConnell, 1961)(work was minimal); Columbia Carbon Co., 65-1 ARB ¶8008 (Oppenheim, 1964)(work was *de minimis*); Pullman Inc., Trailmobile Div., 63-2 ARB ¶8661 (Stouffer, 1963)(minor nature of work); Oxford Paper Co., 45 LA 609 (Cahn, 1965)(damages were insignificant for 10 to 15 minutes of work); Marathon Oil Co., 70 LA 518 (Helburn, 1978)(refusing to apply *de minimis* rule to receipt of package by foreman).

carry out development tasks or, alternatively, to perform bargaining-unit work for training or instructional purposes.[59] The problem is ascertaining what activities constitute instruction, training, tests, research, or developmental tasks and what activities, in fact, constitute work that is reserved to the unit. One common approach is the following:

> It seems to me that the difference between bargaining unit work and nonbargaining unit work in this area lies in whether the work being done is for production purposes or for non-production purposes. Non-production purposes would be research and development. . . .[60]

Arbitrator Charles Morgan followed a different approach when he addressed the issue in *Dresser Industries, Inc.*[61] Disturbed by the casual use of the word "prototype" in reference to a number of compressors built by the non-unit research department, Arbitrator Morgan determined that there is no real prototype until the final product is released for production. All previous models would thus be experimental units rather than prototypes, and the number of such units to be produced by the research department, as determined by management, would accordingly depend on how many are needed for field testing. As stated by the arbitrator, "It is a well accepted fact that laboratory results are not the final criteria but that the final criteria [sic] is how the unit performs in the field."[62] Since the company completely turned the project over to the unit for production once the problems which the customers had identified in field testing were remedied, no violation was found.[63]

Many arbitrators have suggested that the proper question in determining if the work belongs to the unit is whether the supervisor's work directly relates to the testing or research to which he or she is assigned.[64] However, supervisors may not

---

[59]See, e.g., Oxford Paper Co., 45 LA 609 (Cahn, 1965); Western Kraft Paper Group, 74 LA 13 (Allen, 1980); Addison Prods. Co., 74 LA 1145, 1148–50 (Stephens, 1980).

[60]Philips Roxane, Inc., 73 LA 808, 810 (Cohen, 1979).

[61]80-2 ARB ¶8627 (Morgan, 1980).

[62]Id. at 5807.

[63]Id. at 5808. But see Klockner-Moeller Corp., 69–2 ARB ¶8751 (Larkin, 1969)(definition of prototype unimportant; question is whether work was normal production sold to customers or maintenance work commonly performed by unit).

[64]Union Carbide Corp., Nuclear Div., Oak Ridge Nat'l Laboratory, 70-1 ARB ¶8055 (Altieri, 1969)(removal of electric motor from radioactive cell during experiment proper for non-unit technician, as illustrated by past practice.).

perform unit work in tests or experiments that require no special research skills if the unit is fully qualified to perform this work.[65] Perhaps the best summary of arbitral thinking in this area is provided by Arbitrator John Boyer, Jr. In *Minnesota Mining & Manufacturing Co.*,[66] Arbitrator Boyer ruled that an employer did not violate a clause stating that "supervisory and other salaried employees will not perform the work of hourly production employees except in cases of emergency" when it assigned work on an experimental robotized automatic feeding machine to a non-unit engineer. Declaring that arbitrators have traditionally found that, in the absence of contractual restrictions, employers have the right to assign non-unit employees to projects broadly defined as experimental and/or in the process of research and development, Arbitrator Boyer went on to provide some guidelines as to the meaning of work termed "experimental."

> The basis for the consistent findings of neutrals relative to the unique qualities of work broadly defined as "experimental" in nature is generally predicated upon characterization of such as one (1) or more of the following: A) such work is reasonably and legitimately perceived as critical to the Employer's long-term stability . . . ; B) that Employer and/or research personnel have demonstrated the "hands on" method of development by individuals or employee teams is "beneficial" to the invention and product-development process . . . [;] and C) the Employer's utilization of bargaining unit employees would/could require and/or presence of research personnel to avoid the inherent characteristics of inefficiency and ineffectiveness that must of necessity be a subjective judgment.[67]

Training and Instructing Employees

There are a number of reported decisions dealing with supervisors doing unit work while training and instructing employees.[68] Arbitrator George Roberts, in *Atlanta Wire Works, Inc.*,[69] stated that training is "the act, process or methods of

---

[65]Pittsburgh Metallurgical Co., Div. of Air Reduction Co., 52 LA 40 (Shister, 1969)(installation of experimental furnace requires no special skills and is within qualifications of unit); Morris Bean & Co., 71-2 ARB ¶8591 (McDermott, 1971)(making mold and core for lab test is normal unit work and should have been performed by the unit).

[66]83 LA 74 (1984).

[67]Id. at 79–80. See also United States Steel Corp., 52 LA 880 (Garrett, 1969).

[68]See, e.g., the review of case authority by Arbitrator Elvis Stephens in Addison Prods. Co., 74 LA 1145 (1980).

[69]66 LA 365, 373 (1976).

one who trains." In the words of the arbitrator, "[T]he word training means that one person's action causes another person or persons to acquire certain knowledge or skill. It requires a teacher-pupil relationship."[70] Arbitrators have stated that the term "instruction" is synonymous with training.

Illustrative of the position taken by arbitrators in this area is *Roblin Steel Co.*,[71] a case reported by Arbitrator Howard Foster. Under a provision that stated that "foremen, or other supervisory personnel, shall not do production or maintenance work normally performed by employees except in connection with training or in emergency situations," Arbitrator Foster ruled that the contract was violated when two supervisors "set up" a bar straightener machine for the purpose of training themselves to operate the machine prior to instructing the employees. The arbitrator rejected the argument that the phrase "in connection with training" is broader than other language that could have been used to limit the performance of unit work by supervisors. Arbitrator Foster declared that

> there must be a clear, direct, and immediate nexus between the work of the supervisor and the instruction of bargaining unit members. It does not necessarily mean that a bargaining unit member must be present every time the supervisor is familiarizing himself with the work, but it does mean that the work must be done in such a way that, when it is finished, a bargaining unit member will emerge with more knowledge or ability than he had before.[72]

Generally, if a supervisor's conduct is primarily directed toward helping a unit employee acquire knowledge or skill in the work assigned, most arbitrators will conclude that the performance of unit work by supervisors is permissible even though in the instructional process some bargaining-unit employees may lose work they would otherwise perform. Common problems in this area include whether supervisors may set up machinery for training employees, the extent to which supervisors must be assisted by unit employees in the training process, and the amount of work necessary to instruct employees.

---

[70]Id. at 373.
[71]67 LA 1271 (Foster, 1976).
[72]Id. at 1273–74.

Working During a Strike

Arbitrators have recognized management's right to use supervisors to perform unit work during a strike. In a case where employees had refused to cross a "roving picket line," Arbitrator Bernard Cantor held that supervisors were permitted to install a safety device on a mine lift. Arbitrator Cantor reasoned that "[t]he employees may not both flout the contract and demand its benefits."[73] Furthermore, he explained,

> [t]here cannot be any doubt but what, in the event of a work stoppage, Management may do anything necessary in the mine. They may, in fact, dig coal, haul it, and sell it if they can. . . . If Management can achieve their purposes by other means, in the presence of a strike, they are entitled to do so.[74]

Likewise, in *Alfred M. Lewis, Inc.*,[75] when warehouse employees of a supermarket chain refused to cross the picket lines that had been set up by the union of one of the warehouse's customers, supervisors were used to make deliveries through the line. While the contract reserved unit work to unit members, the arbitrator found nothing in the facts or in the contract that restricted management's attempt to continue business by performing unit work with supervisors when the bargaining unit personnel declined to perform that work.

A different approach with the same answer to the question of whether supervisors may perform unit work during a strike relies on a determination of the effect that such work has on the unit employees. As Arbitrator Roy Ray explained,

> [b]y its very nature it would seem the primary purpose of the clause (restricting supervisors to unit work only in emergency and instructional situations) is to protect the job rights of members of the bargaining unit who are on duty and/or available for work, i.e., to prevent them from being displaced or deprived of promotions to which their seniority would entitle them. There would appear to be no need for such a clause in a situation where the bargaining unit employees have refused to work and are not being displaced by the supervisory personnel.[76]

---

[73]Centennial Constructors, Inc., 67 LA 771 (Cantor, 1976).
[74]Id. at 772.
[75]50 LA 553 (Meiners, 1968).
[76]Texas Gas Corp., 36 LA 1141, 1146 (Ray, 1961). See also Computer Sciences Corp., 79 LA 199 (Byars, 1982)(supervisors permitted to perform unit work of employees out on suspension).

In a similar case, Arbitrator Lloyd Byars, in *Computer Sciences Corp.*,[77] ruled that two non-unit supervisors were not barred from performing the unit work of the moving, hook-up, and on-line testing of a computer terminal while unit technicians were suspended because of a prior unauthorized absence. The arbitrator reasoned that to award any damages would effectively override the company's suspension. Likewise, Arbitrator Louis Yagoda, in *Interchemical Corp.*,[78] held that an employer did not violate a provision providing that "non bargaining unit employees shall not perform work usually performed by bargaining unit employees" when a supervisor operated a forklift truck to obtain materials needed for production after unit employees had refused his order to do so. The arbitrator pointed out that there was no clause in the contract stating that a foreman may not do bargaining-unit work when employees illegally and improperly refuse to perform the work they are ordered to do.[79]

However, management's right to use supervisors during strikes or other refusals to work is not unlimited. In a strike situation, for example, even though the use of supervisors may initially be justified, it is no longer permissible to perform unit work once the union indicates that its members desire to return to work.[80]

Work stoppages totally unrelated to the unit work have also been held to be situations where the use of supervisors is not appropriate. In *Central Appalachian Coal Co.*,[81] supervisors performed unit work on a conveyor belt after miners refused to cross a citizen group's picket line in protest over the school board's textbook policy. Arbitrator Ross Hunter analogized this situation to the unauthorized walkouts that had occurred on the anniversary of the assassination of Dr. Martin Luther King, Jr. in *Flint Steel Co.*[82] In *Flint Steel*, Arbitrator Wilber Bothwell had held that since there had been no intent to pressure the employer, the walkout did not constitute a work stoppage justifying discipline. Arbitrator Hunter reasoned that since the politically inspired walkout in *Flint*

---

[77]79 LA 199 (1982).
[78]48 LA 124 (1967).
[79]Id. at 132.
[80]National Lead Co., 69-1 ARB ¶8246 (Erbs, 1968).
[81]64 LA 787 (Hunter, 1975).
[82]60 LA 944 (Bothwell, 1973).

el Co. did not constitute a work stoppage, Central Appalachian employees also could not be considered as having conducted a work stoppage justifying forfeiture of their rights under the "exclusive work" jurisdiction principle, as the Central Appalachian work stoppage too was politically inspired and was not intended to pressure the employer.[83]

Supervisory Directives

Management has considered fundamental its right to direct the working force. As recognized by the distinguished arbitrator Carroll Daugherty, insubordination is considered a serious industrial offense because it violates this right.[84] While the term "insubordination" covers everything from an assault on a supervisor and refusal to obey work orders to the use of profanity when receiving managerial directives, most cases in the insubordination area involve an employee's outright refusal to follow the directives of a supervisor. The mere failure of an employee to carry out an order is generally not considered insubordination, although an arbitrator may conclude that such action is insubordination if coupled with other facts such as prior instances of abusive behavior toward supervision. One arbitrator outlined this principle as follows:

> [I]t is important to distinguish between failure to carry out an order and insubordination. Insubordination involves a refusal to carry out an order—a positive act of defiance[—]while failure to carry out an order involves no refusal but simply neglect in not performing an order or not carrying out the order in a satisfactory manner without any positive act of defiance. Based on the direct challenge to management's right to direct the work force, insubordination is considered a much more serious offense.[85]

The arbitrator correctly noted that three requirements must be satisfied before arbitrators uphold a discharge for insubordination: (1) the company must demonstrate that the instructions were clear and that the grievant understood the directives; (2) the instructions must be understood to be an order, not just a request; and (3) the individual must understand the

---

[83]See also Turner-Bear Corp., 75 LA 1302 (Heinsz, 1981).
[84]Combustion Eng'g, Inc., 49 LA 204, 206 (1967).
[85]Consolidation Coal Co., 77 LA 927, 932 (Nelson, 1981).
[86]Id.

penalty that may be imposed for being insubordinate.[86] Even when the three requirements are satisfied, the grievant's work record and length of service may still operate to reduce the penalty imposed by management.

"Obey Now, Grieve Later" Rule

Arbitrators have uniformly held that management is entitled to expect obedience by an employee to the directions and orders of those in a supervisory capacity, even though an employee believes that the orders, if carried out, would be unfair or would otherwise violate the labor agreement. The often-quoted rule, laid down by the late Dean Harry Shulman in 1944 while he was an umpire for Ford Motor Co. and the United Auto Workers, is as follows:

> No committeeman or other union officer is entitled to instruct employees to disobey Supervision's orders, no matter how strongly he may believe that the orders are in violation of agreement. If he believes that an improper order has been issued, his course is to take the matter up with Supervision and to seek to effect an adjustment. Failing to effect an adjustment, he may file a grievance. But he may not tell the employee to disregard the order.
>
> . . .
>
> Some men apparently think that when a violation of contract seems clear, the employee may refuse to obey and thus resort to self-help rather than the grievance procedure. That is an erroneous point of view. In the first place, what appears to one party to be a clear violation may not seem so at all to the other party. Neither party can be the final judge as to whether the Contract has been violated. The determination of that issue rests in collective negotiation through the grievance procedure. But in the second place, and more important, the grievance procedure is prescribed in the Contract precisely because the parties anticipated that there would be claims of violations which would require adjustment. The procedure is prescribed for all grievances, not merely for doubtful ones. Nothing in the Contract even suggests the idea that only doubtful violations need be processed through the grievance procedure and that clear violations can be resisted through individual self-help. The only difference between a "clear" violation and a "doubtful" one is that the former makes a clear grievance and the latter a doubtful one. But both must be handled in the regular prescribed manner.[87]

---

[87]Opinion A-116, Case No. 364 (June 30, 1944), reported in Opinions of the Umpire (New York State School of Industrial and Labor Relations).

Dean Shulman went on to declare that

> the grievance procedure is the orderly, effective and democratic
> way of adjusting such disputes within the framework of the
> collective labor agreement. It is the substitute of civilized col-
> lective bargaining for jungle warfare.
>
>   But an industrial plant is not a debating society. Its object
> is production. When a controversy arises, production cannot
> wait for exhaustion of the grievance procedure. While the pro-
> cedure is being pursued, production must go on. And some one
> must have the authority to direct the manner in which it is to
> go on until the controversy is settled. That authority is vested
> in Supervision. It must be vested there because the responsi-
> bility for production is also vested there; and responsibility
> must be accompanied by authority. It is fairly vested there
> because the grievance procedure is capable of adequately re-
> compensing employees for abuse of authority by Supervision.[88]

Shulman does recognize, however, that there are some
situations where an employee may engage in self-help. He
argues that an employee is not expected to obey an order that
is criminal or otherwise unlawful.[89] Further, an employee may
refuse to obey an order which involves a health hazard or
other serious sacrifice that is unusual to the normal job duties
of the grievant.[90] Other arbitrators have considered additional
exceptions. For example, exceptions have been urged where
the company violates a provision in the contract prohibiting
it from engaging in a specific act. Illustrative is *National Lead
Co. of Ohio*,[91] where Arbitrator Whitley McCoy held that the
"work now, grieve later" rule did not apply where the contract
provided "an employee may not be required to work overtime"
and an employee was disciplined for refusing to work overtime. Another arbitrator said that for the exception to apply
the order "must be in such flagrant disregard of the agreement
between the parties as to be oppressive of the employees'
rights."[92] An exception may also be appropriate where working and then grieving would make the very dispute covered

---

[88]Id.

[89]See, e.g., California Milk Producers, 65 LA 1139 (Gentile, 1975)(refusal to pick
up overload where punishable by statutory fine).

[90]See, e.g., Halstead Metal Prods., Inc., 49 LA 325 (Wagner, 1967)(unsafe machine); Hercules, Inc., 48 LA 788 (Hopson, 1967).

[91]48 LA 61, 62 (McCoy, 1966).

[92]Crescent Constr. Co., 55 LA 869, 873 (Shieber, 1970). See also Dwight Mfg.
Co., 12 LA 990, 996 (McCoy, 1949); West Penn Power Co., 27 LA 458 (Begley, chmn.,
1956) and A.D. Juilliard & Co., 17 LA 606 (Maggs, 1951), cited in National Lead
Co., 48 LA at 63.

by the grievance moot.[93] It is of note that when an exception is invoked, the burden shifts to the union to demonstrate its applicability.[94]

The exception most often claimed is that the work assigned involves a danger to the health or safety of the employee, an exception sometimes recognized in the parties' agreement.[95] The reasoning of arbitrators is that an employee is protecting his or her own health and safety and, thus, is not acting unreasonably and therefore is not in defiance of a reasonable work order. As so aptly put by one arbitrator, "such exception is recognition of the interest of self-preservation."[96] Various arbitrators differ, however, as to the exact scope of the safety exception. Some arbitrators take the position that despite the good-faith belief of the grievant concerning the safety hazard, if in fact no hazard exists the employee has acted insubordinately.[97] Other arbitrators have specifically held the employee need only have a reasonable belief that the work is hazardous in order to come within the exception. Reflecting the thinking of most arbitrators, Arbitrator Edwin Teple stated the following principle:

> This is not to say that an employee may claim that any task is dangerous and, on this basis alone, safely ignore his instructions. The circumstances must appear to furnish a reasonable basis for the claimed apprehension, and if they fail to do so, the employee will find that the general rule is considered applicable.[98]

Arbitrator Langston Hawley expressed this principle as follows:

> The fact that the task subsequently proved not to be dangerous is not determinative of the question before the arbitrator. The evidence shows that the Grievant honestly thought the assignment was dangerous. . . . It must be remembered that the Company has an added responsibility in safety matters not only to provide physically safe working conditions, but also to take

---

[93]See, e.g., Missouri Power & Light Co., 80 LA 297 (Westbrook, 1982); General Van & Storage Co., 51 LA 528 (Erbs, 1968)(attending funeral).
[94]T & J Indus., Inc., 79 LA 697, 699 (Clark, 1982).
[95]See, e.g., Mine Servs., Inc., 72 LA 215, 216–17 (Clarke, 1979); Halstead & Mitchell, 74 LA 946, 947 (Odom, 1980); National Can Corp., 68 LA 351 (Turkus, 1977); United States Steel Corp., 55 LA 61 (Dybeck, 1970).
[96]Goodyear Atomic Corp., 71 LA 619, 622 (Gibson, 1978).
[97]See, e.g., Hercules, Inc., 48 LA 788, 793 (Hopson, 1967); Griffin Pipe Prods. Co., 72 LA 1033, 1035 (Doyle, 1979); 3 M Co., 80 LA 926 (Gallagher, 1983).
[98]Ohio Edison Co., 70-2 ARB ¶8445, at 4461 (1970).

reasonable steps to allay the fears of employees who honestly believe that particular tasks are dangerous.[99]

A few neutrals have even been held that an employee has the right to be "extra cautious" in assessing the likelihood that a hazard exists.[100]

A major split in approach occurs in the situation where grievants, at the time they refused the work at issue, offered no reason as to why they refused. The better view in this situation is that if employees offer no reason when asked for one by management, their conduct will be considered insubordinate.[101]

Some employees resort to self-help simply because they believe that the grievance procedure will not provide an adequate remedy.[102] They believe, in other words, that unless they refuse the order, the subject matter of the grievance will be moot because it will be impossible for an arbitrator to restore the *status quo ante*. An example would be a situation in which an employee refuses an unscheduled Saturday work assignment because he has purchased tickets to the Iowa-Illinois football game to be held that day. The employee argues that the employer does not have the authority under the agreement to compel him to work an unscheduled assignment and, accordingly, refuses to work. Application of the "work now, grieve later" principle would require that he work the assignment and then file a grievance. This option, however, is of little utility to the employee since no remedy can restore the *status quo ante* if he elects to grieve rather than engage in self-help. An innovative arbitrator may award the employee the value of the tickets and may even include a monetary award to reflect the fact the employee had to work the contested hours. Still, the employee will have missed seeing Iowa

---

[99]Rome Kraft Co., 61-3 ARB ¶8792, at 6619–20 (1961). See also International Smelting & Ref. Co., 60 LA 341, 344 (Saracino, 1973); Hercules, Inc., 48 LA 788, 794–95 (1967); Fulton Seafood Indus., Inc., 74 LA 620 (Volz, 1980); LaClede Steel Co., 56 LA 407 (Volz, 1971); United States Steel Corp., 55 LA 61 (Dybeck, 1970)(refusal to remove dust respirator because of presence of smoke in meeting room).

[100]Union Carbide Plastics Co., 34 LA 504 (Luskin, 1960); Checker Motors Corp., 61 LA 33 (Daniel, 1973).

[101]See, e.g., C-E Glass, Inc., 71 LA 977 (Comey, 1978); Mine Servs., Inc., 72 LA 215 (Clarke, 1979). See also Firemen & Oilers Local 261 v. Great N. Paper Co., 118 LRRM 2317 (D. Me., 1984).

[102]See Hill & Sinicropi, "Remedies Where the Grievance Procedure Would Fail to Provide Adequate Relief," Remedies in Arbitration, 238–40 (BNA Books, 1981).

defeat Illinois[103] and not even an Iowa arbitrator is going to compensate him for this loss.

Further illustrative of the remedy problem in the "work now, grieve later" cases is the situation where a teacher requested a one-day personal leave to referee the Iowa Boys State Basketball Tournament, an assignment considered an honor among high school referees. His request for personal leave was refused by the school district. The "obey now, grieve later" principle is not a viable alternative for this teacher, since again there will be no adequate remedy by the time a grievance would come to arbitration.

There is no uniform solution to this problem other than to suggest that the parties take a common-sense approach and balance the competing interests. Prasow and Peters submit that in exceptional circumstances where there are problems with formulating a remedy, two criteria applied by the courts when considering petitions for injunctive relief may be resorted to by an arbitrator. The criteria are in the form of the following questions.

> 1. Will the damage suffered by the petitioner [grievant] be irreparable if he is subsequently proved to be the victim of an illegal wrongful action?
> 2. Will the damage to the petitioner be substantial enough to warrant restraining the other party, who might subsequently be proved to be in the right, and in turn suffer needless harassment, perhaps irreparable damage, by the restraining order?[104]

For arbitration purposes, the second question might be rephrased as follows: Is the damage the grievant would have suffered by obeying and then subsequently grieving substantial enough to warrant upholding the grievant's use of self-help against the employer, who may now be proved to have been in the right and, in turn, to have suffered needless harassment, perhaps irreparable damage, by the employee's use of self-help?

Prasow and Peters argue that if an aggrieved employee can meet these tests through a "yes" answer to both questions, it would seem inappropriate for an arbitrator to take an inflexible position against self-help. The authors submit that

---

[103]1985 score: Iowa 59, Illinois 0.
[104]Prasow & Peters, Arbitration and Collective Bargaining, 308 (McGraw-Hill, 1983).

iew represents the better position in those few cases
e the grievance procedure would fail to provide adequate
f.

As a final note, one arbitrator reported that in approximately 60 percent of the reported cases involving insubordination, management's response has been discharge. In those
cases where discharge was the decision of management, it was
upheld at arbitration slightly over 40 percent of the time, and
modified or reversed the rest of the time.[105] Still another study
reported that although the standard remedy is discharge, arbitrators either reversed or modified almost two-thirds of the
company rulings. A sizable majority of the decisions were in
favor of management when the penalty was less severe.[106]
This indicates a relatively strict interpretation by arbitrators
of management's right to discharge for insubordination. This
limiting of management's latitude in assessing the penalty of
discharge, as opposed to assessing a lesser penalty, may manifest itself in either of two ways: a strict interpretation of what
constitutes insubordination, or a finding that while there was
insubordination, it was not severe enough to warrant discharge. A common thread in this area is that insubordination
will not be found unless (1) the order or directive at issue was
clearly expressed, and (2) the grievant had notice of the possible consequences of the action. A variety of factors determine
whether the penalty assessed will be upheld if the facts indicate insubordination, including the nature of the insubordination (physical altercations with supervisors are considered
particularly serious by arbitrators), the existence of a specific
rule or contractual language prescribing the penalty for insubordination, the company's overall approach to discipline,
and mitigating circumstances favoring the employee such as
a good work record. In short, while insubordination is considered by managements to be a serious industrial offense for
which discharge is frequently assessed, a policy of discharging
all employees for any act of insubordination, regardless of how
minor the infraction may be, has not been supported by arbitrators. "Just cause" requires that each case be considered
on its own merits, and there are a number of exceptions to

---

[105]Prismo-William Armstrong Smith Co., 73 LA 581, 584 (Jedel, 1979)(cases were
reported from Labor Arbitration Reports (BNA), Volumes 61–70).
[106]Phillips, Discipline and Discharge in the Unionized Firm (1959), as cited in
Prismo-William Armstrong Smith Co., supra.

the "obey now, grieve later" rule that will work to mitigate or even excuse an insubordinate act by an employee.

Overtime Assignments

Management's right to require that an employee work overtime has been consistently recognized by arbitrators. Arbitrator Thomas Erbs' decision in *Pennwalt Corp.*[107] reflects the thinking of most arbitrators on the subject.

> A long line of arbitration decisions has fairly well established the right of management to require its employees to work overtime unless there is a contractual restriction which specifically takes away this right. This right of management, however, requires that the overtime so assigned be of a reasonable duration under reasonable circumstances. There is also a requirement that management accept certain reasonable excuses advanced by employees to be excused from such overtime.
>
> If there is no reference to management's right to require overtime, the provisions of the agreement establishing pay for overtime work certainly imply that occasional overtime work may be mandated.[108]

In this case the agreement contained a clause requiring an equal distribution of overtime. However, there was no written policy of mandatory overtime, and the practice of assigning mandatory overtime had been rare until this grievance. Arbitrator Erbs found the parties' practice of little relevance since the clause providing for overtime pay implied the right to require mandatory overtime. He supported this proposition by citing *Nebraska Consolidated Mills Co.*,[109] a 1949 case which, in relevant part, stated the following:

> This (pay rate for overtime) clearly recognizes an obligation on the Company to pay for overtime, and surely by implication, that workers are obligated to work reasonable necessary overtime unless specifically excused.[110]

The union's argument that the company had surrendered its power to require overtime by failing to exercise its prerogative was rejected by the arbitrator. In a holding similar to the position taken by most arbitrators, Arbitrator Erbs stated the

---

[107]77 LA 626 (1981).
[108]Id. at 631.
[109]13 LA 211 (Copelof, 1949).
[110]Id. at 214.

"black letter rule" to be that the mere failure to use a power does not constitute a waiver of a right.

Likewise, in *Van Dorn Co.*,[111] the arbitrator rejected the argument that the inclusion of a regular work week provision in the contract implies that overtime is voluntary. Stating the view of the majority of the arbitrators on the issue, the arbitrator ruled as follows:

> The section merely establishes the regular work day and the regular work week, and relates only to the hours to be considered in determining what constitutes the work day and the work week. The only relationship of the section to the subject of overtime is in the number of hours worked in determining premium pay for the premium hours. It must, therefore, be the finding that Section 24 contains no provisions that would be determinative of whether overtime is voluntary or mandatory.[112]

The arbitrator's analysis of the overtime issue and its relationship to the scheme of management rights also reflects the better weight of authority.

> It has been well recognized and accepted in arbitral matters that Management retains all of its inherent rights, except those which are specifically limited by express agreement or through the existence of an established past practice. . . .
>
> During the past twenty years this same question (of voluntary versus mandatory overtime) has arisen between many employers and Unions where their Labor Agreement is silent as it is here. The vast majority of arbitral awards have supported the position that overtime is compulsory in the absence of specific provision in the Collective Bargaining Agreement. The underlying theory behind the Awards is that Management has retained its inherent right to assign work and overtime. The Awards further hold that Management may enforce its right by the assessment of disciplinary action, if necessary, for the failure of an employee to comply.
>
> This Arbitrator is in full accord with these Awards and the theory underlying them. If such were not so, Management would be subject to the will of the individual employee where it was vital that important and necessary work be performed outside the regular work day.[113]

Similarly, in *City of Auburn Police Department*,[114] Arbitrator Joe Chandler found that management had the right to

---

[111]48 LA 925 (Kabaker, 1967).
[112]Id. at 927.
[113]Id. at 928.
[114]78 LA 537 (Chandler, 1982).

assign mandatory overtime, even when the overtime would conflict with the religious practices of a Seventh Day Adventist. In so holding, the arbitrator focused on the following considerations:

> We find no restriction on overtime in the contract. To the contrary, there is even an overtime provision (IX) and overtime pay is also provided for in [the agreement]. There can thus be no claim that overtime may not be given by management. The argument concerning the mandatory nature of overtime is similar. There are no contract restrictions or limitations. Further, the various "bulletins" indicate that mandatory overtime is and may be required. It has been shown that it has been used in the past, though infrequently, without the filing of any grievances since the bulletins were issued in 1974. The right has been utilized such that it would have become a past practice were it not a management right as above noted. The mere nonuse of such a right does not negate the right to make use of it.[115]

Of special note is the arbitrator's resolution of the union's claim that by exempting a Seventh Day Adventist from overtime during the twenty-four hour period beginning at sunset on Friday and ending at sunset on Saturday, the city was engaging in reverse discrimination against the other officers who were forced to work this Friday night shift in her place. In finding reverse discrimination, the arbitrator made reference to case law under Title VII and the holdings of other arbitrators.

> [E]ven without [a non-discrimination clause in the parties' contract], the parties are bound by the various statutes relating to the various forms of discrimination. . . . We find that the City has made an accommodation for religious beliefs to Ms. H ___ [an Adventist]. We do not consider this to be one that may be categorized as "reasonable", calling attention to the TWA citation [TWA v. Hardison, 423 U.S. 63, 14 FEP 1697 (1967)], supra. Arbitrators have made rulings indicating this view when they have ruled that employees were not discriminated against when denied leave to attend religious services during regular scheduled shifts (58 LA 143, 69 LA 325); when disciplined for refusing scheduled overtime to attend religious services (63 LA 157, 68 LA 171); for assigning [sic] Sunday work (67 LA 1031).[116]

---

[115]Id. at 540. Accord, Fruehauf Corp., 46 LA 15, 20 (Dworkin, 1966).

[116]78 LA at 541. See also Hurley Hosp., 70 LA 1061 (Roumell, 1978)(operating room technician objecting to scrub pants on religious basis entitled to present alternative uniform to employer committee); Pavey Envelope & Tag Corp., 78 LA 70 (Cull, 1982)(upholding dismissal of employee who failed to work overtime because of personal obligations, including religious work); Naval Amphibious Base, 74 LA 1131

Refusals to Work Overtime

Although the right to require overtime is a recognized management right, management is not absolved from its obligation to "observe fairness and reasonableness in demanding overtime, or [from its obligation not] to overlook the consideration of health and welfare when requiring that overtime be worked."[117] This principle was recognized by Arbitrator Harry Shulman in 1948 while serving as an umpire for Ford Motor Co. and the United Auto Workers.

> [W]hile an employee's refusal to work overtime may be a breach of duty for which he may properly be disciplined, his refusal may be justified and, if justified, is not a ground for disciplinary penalty. The refusal may be justified at least in the same way as absence from work during the normal scheduled eight hours. But it may also be justified by further considerations peculiarly applicable to overtime.[118]

Shulman went on to declare:

> Except when specifically so hired, employees are not on continuous call 24 hours a day. While they must recognize that they may be called upon to work overtime, they may properly plan their lives on the basis of their customary work schedules. Under the parties' present Agreement, when an employee is asked to work overtime, he may not refuse merely because he does not like to work more than eight hours, does not need the extra money, or for no reason at all. But if the overtime would unduly interfere with plans he made, then his refusal may be justified. If he is given advance notice sufficient to enable him to alter his plans, he must do so. But if the direction is given to him without such notice, then it would be arbitrary to require him to forgo plans which he made in justifiable reliance upon his normal work schedule—unless indeed, his commitments are

---

(Gregg, 1980)(demotion upheld for cashier who would not perform required Sunday work because of religious beliefs); Social Sec. Admin., 79 LA 449 (Mittelman, 1982)(ruling that federal agency properly directed supervisors to ask employees requesting time off to be made up by working overtime whenever request is based on personal religious beliefs in order to determine sincerity of employees' request); Alabama By-Prods. Corp., 79 LA 1320 (Clarke, 1982)(applying Title VII and holding that employer failed to make reasonable accommodation when it considered as unexcused employee's absence to preach at funeral); Building Owners & Managers Ass'n, 67 LA 1031 (Griffin, 1976)(employer justified in discharging Roman Catholic employee for refusing to work on Sunday, notwithstanding contention that employee's religion makes Sunday work unacceptable, under contract that contains no limitation on assigning work on Sunday).

[117]Van Dorn Co., 48 LA 925, 928 (Kabaker, 1967).
[118]Ford Motor Co., 11 LA 1158, 1160 (1948).

of such trivial importance as not to deserve consideration. A rule of thumb is not possible. What is required is sympathetic consideration of the individual's situation and make-up.[119]

A similar position was recognized by Arbitrator Robert Brecht. In *Vulcan Mold & Iron Co.*,[120] the arbitrator held that while management had the right to assign overtime, the right was subject to a reasonableness requirement. In the words of the arbitrators,

> [the right to require overtime] must be exercised in a reasonable way: reasonable with respect to requirements and reasonable with respect to employees' refusals to accept overtime assignments. Even though . . . the right to require overtime lies with the Company, disciplinary actions have been reversed *because of excessive overtime assignments, because of doubt as to their need, because the Company has not given reasonable notice in advance, and because the Company on the record has not given due and careful consideration to the reasons advanced by employees for refusing to accept the overtime assignments.*[121]

The arbitrator found that the employer violated the agreement when it required an employee, whose house was being moved to a new location, to work on her day off. In the opinion of the arbitrator, the company, when requiring overtime, must give full and good-faith consideration to the problems expressed by the employee.

Religious Objections and Title VII

Frequently an arbitrator will look to fair employment laws in resolving grievances that have religious implica-

[119]Id. at 1160.
[120]39 LA 292 (1962).
[121]Id. at 298 (emphasis in original). See also A.O. Smith Corp., 67-1 ARB ¶8115 (Howlett, 1961)(employer must accept reasonable excuses); Midcon Fabricators, Inc., 68 LA 1264 (Dugan, 1977)(requiring employees to work one hour of overtime on a regular basis unreasonable); Central Tel. Co., 69 LA 1133 (Daly, 1977)(mandatory six-day work schedule violated contract's normal work week provision); Hygrade Food Prods. Corp., 69 LA 414 (Harter, 1977)(failure to accord due process rights to employee who refused overtime because of health & safety concerns); Genesee County Personnel, 64 LA 458 (Roumell, 1975)(reversing suspension of clerk-typist who refused to work day off because she had "houseful of guests"); National Homes Corp., 65 LA 748 (Morgan, 1975)(dental appointment); Allied Paper, Inc., 80 LA 435 (Mathews, 1983)(ailing wife); American Mach. & Foundry Co., 50 LA 181, 184 (Geissinger, 1978)("Family and social obligations are entitled to greater consideration as reasons for not working extra hours"). But see Food Haven, Inc., 62 LA 1246 (May, 1974)(denying special treatment for employee who was minister having special duties to perform); Grocers Baking Co., 72 LA 591 (Daniel, 1979)(upholding discharge for grievant who refused overtime in order to attend painting class).

tions.[122] Because of its impact in the arbitral area, it is important to understand the law when employees cite religious grounds as a basis for refusing work assignments.

Title VII makes it an unlawful employment practice for an employer or labor union to discriminate against an employee or applicant on the basis of religion. The statute, as initially enacted, proscribed discrimination based upon religious belief, but did not specifically prohibit discriminatory treatment based on religious conduct. The statute, however, was amended in 1972 so that every aspect of religious observance and practice, as well as belief, is now protected.[123]

Under the amended statute, once employees or applicants for employment establish that a religious belief is sincerely held and that the belief or practice or observance had been used as the basis for discharging or otherwise discriminating against them, the burden shifts to the employer to "demonstrate that he is unable to reasonably accommodate to an employee's . . . religious observance without undue hardship on the conduct of the employer's business."[124] It is important to stress that the duty to accommodate only arises in those cases where an individual has first established that a belief or practice is religious and is sincerely held. Although the courts have been liberal in extending the protection of Title VII to religious beliefs and practices, this does not mean that an attempt to accommodate must be made merely because an individual characterizes some form of conduct as religious and asserts that it is sincerely held. As stated by one court, if one

---

[122]See, e.g., Hurley Hosp., 71 LA 1013 (Roumell, 1978)(allowing employer to transfer operating room technician who rejected modification of scrub-gown uniform as alternative to scrub pants which her religion prohibited, and stating that decision was consistent with Supreme Court's ruling in Hardison, discussed infra at note 127 and related text); Timken Co., 75 LA 801 (Morgan, 1980)(denying holiday pay for member of Worldwide Church of God when workday fell on his Sabbath; arbitrator declined to apply Title VII's reasonable accommodation mandate); Oolite Indus., Inc., 77 LA 838 (Greene, 1981)(reinstating truck driver for insubordination for failing to make delivery and leaving work five hours before end of shift to prepare for Sabbath, applying Title VII); Alabama By-Prods. Corp., 79 LA 1320 (Clarke, 1982)(employer failed to make reasonable accommodation required by Title VII when it considered as unexcused employee's absence to preach at funeral of church member); Kansas City Area Trans. Authority, 79 LA 299, 303 (Belkin, 1982)("both parties are aware that the ultimate determination of whether there was 'just cause' for discharge under the labor agreement depends on whether the Authority may be said to have violated Title VII of the Civil Rights Act of 1984."). See generally Hill & Sinicropi, "External Law as a Remedy in Labor Arbitration," Remedies in Arbitration, 207–25 (BNA Books, 1981).

[123]42 U.S.C. §2000e(17)(1970 Supp. V. 1975).

[124]§701(j), 42 U.S.C. §2000e(j).

were an avid sports fan, one could not use that enthusiasm, however intense, to require an accommodation to attend a sports event.[125] No court has indicated the point at which a philosophy or a conviction becomes a religious belief entitled to reasonable accommodation. However, all courts have indicated that employees do not have the final word with respect to what conduct will warrant protection under the statute.[126]

Employer's Duty to Accommodate. In *Trans World Airlines v. Hardison,*[127] the Supreme Court considered the extent of an employer's duty of reasonable accommodation and whether a collective bargaining agreement must be set aside to accommodate the religious beliefs of an employee. Hardison was hired by TWA and became subject to a collective bargaining agreement between TWA and the Machinists. The agreement contained provisions for a seniority system whereby the most senior employees had first choice for job and shift assignments and the most junior employees were required to work those job assignments and shifts that could not be filled voluntarily.

It was necessary to operate the Stores Department 24 hours a day and 365 days a year because of its essential role in the operation of the company. Whenever an employee's job in that department was not filled, an employee had to be shifted from another department or a supervisor had to cover that job, even if work in other areas suffered. Hardison, a member of the World Wide Church of God, normally worked the day shift in the Stores Department. He was subsequently called, however, to substitute for a vacationing co-worker. This required that he work on Friday evening and Saturday, which his religion prohibited. When he failed to appear for three consecutive Saturdays, Hardison was discharged on grounds of insubordination for refusing to work during his designated shift.

Alleging discrimination on the basis of religion, Hardison commenced an action in federal district court against TWA and the union. The district court ruled in favor of the defen-

---

[125]Gavin v. Peoples Natural Gas Co., 464 F.Supp. 622, 18 FEP 1431 (W.D. Pa., 1979), vacated, 613 F.2d 482, 21 FEP 1186 (CA 3, 1980).

[126]See, e.g., Wessling v. Kroger Co., 554 F.Supp. 548, 30 FEP 1222 (E.D. Mich., 1982)(upholding discharge of employee who left work early without permission on day before Christmas to set up for church play); McGinnis v. U.S. Postal Serv., 512 F.Supp. 517, 24 FEP 999 (N.D. Cal., 1980)(refusal to distribute draft registration material).

[127]432 U.S. 63, 14 FEP 1697 (1977).

dants.[128] The court of appeals reversed,[129] holding that TWA
had not made reasonable efforts to accommodate Hardison's
religious needs under the Equal Employment Opportunity
Commission (EEOC) guidelines in effect at the time the relevant events occurred. In its view, TWA had rejected three
reasonable alternatives, any one of which would have satisfied
its obligation without undue hardship. First, within the
framework of the seniority system TWA could have permitted
Hardison to work a four-day week, utilizing in his place the
fifth day a supervisor or another worker on duty elsewhere.
Second, TWA could have filled Hardison's Saturday shift from
other available personnel competent to do the job. Third, TWA
could have arranged a swap between Hardison and another
employee either for another shift or for Hardison's sabbath
days.

While affirmatively concluding that an employer does have
an obligation under Title VII to make reasonable accommodations to the religious needs of its employees, short of in-
curring an undue hardship, the Supreme Court nevertheless
reversed the court of appeals. The Court said that the employer
had no obligation under the statute to select one of the alternatives provided by the appeals court.

Answering Hardison's argument that the statutory obligation to accommodate religious needs takes precedence over
both the collective bargaining agreement and the seniority
rights of the other employees, the Court held that, absent a
congressional mandate, an agreed-upon seniority system cannot be abrogated in order to accommodate the religious needs
of others. Had TWA circumvented the seniority system by
relieving Hardison of Saturday work and ordering a senior
employee to replace him, the senior employee would have been
deprived of his contractual rights.

As mentioned above, the Eighth Circuit, in finding for
Hardison, had suggested that TWA could have permitted Har-
dison to work a four-day week to avoid working on his sabbath.
While acknowledging that this would have left the employer
shorthanded, the Eighth Circuit nevertheless concluded that
TWA would suffer no undue hardship if it were required to

---

[128]Hardison v. Trans World Airlines, 375 F.Supp. 877, 10 FEP 502 (W.D. Mo.,
1974).
[129]Hardison v. Trans World Airlines, 527 F.2d 33, 11 FEP 1121 (CA 8, 1975).

replace Hardison either with supervisory personnel or with qualified personnel from other departments. Alternatively, the appeals court had suggested that TWA could have replaced Hardison with other employees through the payment of premium wages.

The Supreme Court found that both of these alternatives would involve costs to TWA, either in the form of lost efficiency in other jobs or in the form of higher wages. The Court states that to require TWA to bear more than a *de minimis* cost in order to give Hardison Saturdays off was an undue hardship.

After *Hardison* it is clear that Title VII does not require an employer and a union who have agreed on a seniority system to deprive senior employees of their seniority rights in order to accommodate a junior employee's religious practices. Even more significant from the viewpoint of a practitioner, however, is the Court's analysis of the cost issue. Although the Court stated that TWA did not have to bear more than a *de minimis* cost to accommodate an employee's religious practices, it failed to note what constitutes more than *de minimis* costs.

The dissent (Justices Marshall and Brennan) in *Hardison* contended that the costs to TWA of either paying overtime or not replacing Hardison would not have been more than *de minimis*. The dissent argued that while the district court did state that both alternatives "would have created an undue burden on the conduct of TWA's business," the lower court did not explain its understanding of the phrase "undue burden," and may have believed that such a burden exists whenever any cost is incurred by the employer, no matter how slight. Since the district court never made a factual finding that the costs of these accommodations would be more than *de minimis*, the *Hardison* majority had no factual basis for ruling on the cost of the issue, the dissent argued.

The Supreme Court majority appears to have assumed that the employer would have incurred more than *de minimis* costs, based on a mere notion by the Court that TWA may have many employees whose religious observances prohibit them from working on Saturdays or Sundays. As stated by the dissent, this assumption was not only contrary to the record (which indicated that only one other case involving a conflict between work schedules and sabbath observances had arisen at TWA since 1945), but also irrelevant, since the real question was not whether such employees exist but whether they could be accommodated without significant expense. In this regard, after *Hardison* it is reasonably clear that an employer need not pay premium wages to accommodate an employee's religious beliefs, at least in the situation where premium payments would have to be made for any length of time.[130] This is not to say that any payment of premium wages would be considered an undue hardship. Again, the majority in Hardison was especially careful to use the phrase "*de minimis*" costs, and it remains to be seen what level of costs will not be exempt. As of this writing, the courts that have considered the issue of religious accommodation after Hardison have generally held that *any* premium payment would constitute undue hardship.[131]

Guidelines for the Practitioner. While the phrases "reasonable accommodation" and "undue hardship" are relative terms and therefore cannot be given any hard-and-fast meaning, a review of recent decisions indicated that the practitioner is not left totally in the dark. Four guidelines can be discerned.

First, after *Hardison*, Title VII does not require an employer to undertake activities that would violate a bona fide seniority system in the name of accommodation. The Court rejected the arguments of the EEOC and Hardison that the statutory obligation to accommodate religious needs takes precedence over both the collective bargaining contract and the seniority rights of TWA's other employees. While the Court agreed with the general proposition that neither a collective bargaining agreement nor a seniority system may be employed to violate the statute, it stated that the duty of accommodation did not require the employer to take steps inconsistent with a valid collective bargaining agreement.

Second, the Court made it clear that an employer is not obligated to take additional steps that would require it to bear extra costs, such as overtime pay for replacements, if such costs are more than *de minimis*. Although the Court did not

---

[130]The dissent noted that the cost to TWA would be approximately $150 for a three-month period, after which time Hardison would be allowed to return to his previous department. 14 FEP at 1709 n. 5.

[131]See, e.g., Beam v. General Motors Corp., 21 FEP 85 (N.D. Ohio, 1979)(upholding contractual provision that charges employees who refuse to work overtime on Saturdays); Guthrie v. Burger, 24 FEP 992 (D.D.C. 1980)(changing overtime schedule); Turpen v. M-K-T R.R. Co., 736 F.2d 1022, 35 FEP 492 (CA 5, 1984)(rejecting argument that §701(j) requires employer to hire overtime employees to accommodate Seventh Day Adventist).

SUPERVISORS AND DIRECTIVES 523

state what sum is more than a *de minimis* amount, the analysis taken in *Hardison* provides some guides. Arguably, the Court has indicated that whether a proposed accommodation would create costs that are more than *de minimis* is a matter to be determined on the basis of the projected number of instances of accommodation that a company may have to undertake, rather than the impact of a single case involving a particular employee. Justice Marshall, in his dissent in *Hardison*, estimated that the costs of overtime wages for replacements for Hardison for three months would have been $150; yet the majority, relying on the findings of the district court that such an alternative would have created an undue hardship on the conduct of TWA's business, held that the costs of such an accommodation were greater than *de minimis*.

Third, while the Supreme Court has not stated what kind of showing will suffice to establish undue hardship, an examination of court decisions subsequent to *Hardison* indicates that undue hardship will not be established by mere assumptions, opinions, or hypotheticals. Contrary to the approach taken by the majority in *Hardison*, the lower courts have generally demanded hard evidence that a specific accommodation does in fact create an undue hardship.

Finally, implicit within the accommodation context is the requirement that employees inform management of both their religious needs and their need for an accommodation. The Eighth Circuit has stated that a mutuality of obligation inheres in the employer-employee relationship, and that Section 701(j) of Title VII would have little meaning if it is considered only at the abstract level apart from complementary duties that employer and employee owe one another.[132] What is troublesome for the practitioner is that the statute does not explicitly address the corresponding duties of the employees, inherent in their relationship to their employers, in the entire process of arriving at a reasonable accommodation. Thus, in *Chrysler Corp. v. Mann*,[133] the Eighth Circuit held that an employee's "intransigent position" that resulted in "a disinterest in explaining his religious needs to his employer" and a "disinclination to utilize the provisions of the collective bar-

---

[132] 561 F.2d 1282, 15 FEP 788 (CA 8, 1977), cert. denied, 434 U.S. 1039, 16 FEP 501 (1978).
[133] Id.

gaining agreement pertaining to excused absences"[134] precluded the lower court from finding that the employer violated
the statute.

Refusal as a Protected Activity: LMRA

An additional consideration for management is whether
a concerted refusal to work overtime is protected activity under LMRA. In this regard the Eighth Circuit adopted as a
correct statement of the law the following conclusions of the
Trial Examiner:

> Employees may seek to change any term or condition of
> their employment and their ultimate sanction is the strike. If
> they choose to strike over hours of work, their strike is no
> different in quality or essence than is a strike over any other
> term of employment. What may make such a work stoppage
> unprotected is exactly what makes any work stoppage unpro-
> tected, that is, the refusal or failure of the employee to assume
> the status of strikers, with the consequent loss of pay and risk
> of being replaced. Employees who choose to withhold their ser-
> vices because of a dispute over scheduled hours may properly
> be required to do so by striking unequivocally. They may not
> simultaneously walk off their jobs but retain the benefits of
> working.[135]

The appellate court went on to state:

> We recognize the difficulty of drawing a line between pro-
> tected and unprotected activity in such situations. The task is
> even more difficult when the walkout occurs at or near the end
> of a regular day, and the employees return to work the next
> morning. The line is one which must nevertheless be drawn.
> Employees have the same right to engage in concerted activity
> to bring about a change in overtime policy as they do to bring
> about a change in wages or other working conditions. They have
> as much right to strike on this issue as any other, and they are
> not required to institute the strike at any particular time of
> the day or to maintain it for any particular period of time to
> be entitled to the protection of the Act. The test in each case
> is whether the employees have assumed the status of strikers.
> They cannot continue to work the regular hours of employment
> and refuse to work overtime.[136]

---

[134]15 FEP at 792, 791.
[135]First Nat'l Bank of Omaha v. NLRB, 413 F.2d 921, 71 LRRM 3019, 3020 (CA
8, 1969).
[136]71 LRRM at 3021.

The employer is not left defenseless in the event employees do strike over the issue of overtime. Employees acting as "economic strikers" may be replaced and, under the law, are entitled to reinstatement only if their jobs are open when they return to work. The bottom line is that employees cannot refuse to accept overtime assignments while continuing their regular hours. Nor can a union discipline employees for violating a union ban on working overtime.[137] When on the job the employee is subject to the authority and control of the employer. He cannot be "on strike" and at work simultaneously.[138]

[137]NLRB v. Graphic Arts GAIU Local 13-B, 682 F.2d 304, 110 LRRM 2984 (CA 2, 1982), cert. denied, 459 U.S. 1200, 112 LRRM 2752 (1983).
[138]See, e.g., C.G. Conn, Ltd. v. NLRB, 108 F.2d 390, 5 LRRM 806 (CA 7, 1939), discussed in First Nat'l Bank v. NLRB, 413 F.2d 921, 71 LRRM 3019, 3021 (CA 8, 1969); Excavation-Construction v. NLRB, 660 F.2d 1015 (CA 4, 1981); Avo Corp. v. Auto Workers Local 787, 459 F.2d 968, 974, 80 LRRM 2290 (CA 3, 1972).

Chapter 18

Conclusion

Throughout this text the authors have made numerous generalizations concerning arbitral and judicial thinking[1] on management rights. A concluding note is appropriate. Generalizations about management rights are, at best, often overbroad and, at worst, dangerous. As noted by Brown and Myers in their discussion of the changing industrial relations philosophy of American management,[2] not only is American management not a homogenous group ("it is possible to find particular managements lying at every point of each aspect of industrial relations"), but the same management may be non-homogenous in its different manifestations—"as 'plant management,' as spokesman for a large corporation, as an active participant in management associations such as the National Association of Manufacturers or the Chamber of Commerce, or as a best-foot-forward representative of American management abroad."[3] More important, the concept of "management prerogatives" frequently has a different meaning within different industries. Reflecting the view of management rights in the twenties and early thirties, in some

---

[1]Here one is reminded of Lippman's Law: "When all think alike, no one is thinking." Walter Lippmann, quoted by Ann Landers in the Poughkeepsie Journal, March 26, 1978, cited in Faber, The Book of Laws, 13 (Times Books, 1979).

[2]Brown & Myers, "The Changing Industrial Relations Philosophy of American Management," Proceedings of the 9th Annual Meeting, Industrial Relations Research Association (IRRA), 84, 84 (IRRA, 1956).

[3]Id. at 85. Wayne Horvitz, former president of the Industrial Relations Research Association (IRRA) stated this concept as follows:

"There is no monolith called American Management. There are, as we know, many managements, in and within large business and small, in public and in private enterprise. Therefore there isn't something, written or not, that we can easily identify as a 'management philosophy' in the United States, unlike our friends in

526

industries (agriculture, selected state governments) the term "management prerogative" is indeed a redundancy even today. In other industries (transportation, steel, auto, coal, and rubber) management has recognized and dealt with unions on a day-to-day basis and has accorded unions substantive rights which significantly limit managerial discretion.

The post-1960 period has been characterized by the growth of nonunion human resource management systems (corporate union-avoidance strategies) designed to increase the commitment, loyalty, and job satisfaction of employees. The human resource school is generally characterized by modern industrial designs and efficient work organization, conflict-resolution systems run by management, and extensive and open communication systems between supervision and the work force.[4] Moreover, according to Kochan, McKersie, and Katz, "The new nonunion model consists of personnel systems that either match union wage and fringe levels in labor markets where unions dominate or pay wages higher than competitive norms in rural or southern labor markets (but wages that are lower than the union rates found in the more highly unionized markets)."[5] To the extent that this union-avoidance effort is successful,[6] employees will have fewer incentives to unionize

---

Japan whom we admire, envy, and wish to emulate, at least if one examines the array of books in the Harvard Business School bookstore."
Horvitz, "Management's View of Industrial Relations in the U.S.," Proceedings of the 37th Annual Meeting, IRRA, 1, 1 (IRRA, 1985).

D. Quinn Mills has also observed: "It is hazardous to write about the philosophy of attitudes of American management for several reasons. First, not all managers share the same attitudes. Second, there are few, if any, careful studies of the topic, in part because attitudes can be quite difficult to measure accurately." Mills, "Management Performance," U.S. Industrial Relations 1950–1980: A Critical Assessment, 99, 108 (IRRA, 1981).

Of course, management is homogeneous in the following respect: "Much of American management is very explicit about its desire to avoid dealing with unions." Id. at 114.

[4]Lemuel Boulware, vice president of industrial relations for General Electric in the 1950s and main architect of the "take it or leave it" formula for bargaining was the forerunner of present advocates of comprehensive, corporate-wide communications systems characteristic of the human resources school.

[5]Kochan, McKersie & Katz, "U.S. Industrial Relations in Transition: A Summary Report," Proceedings of the 37th Annual Meeting, IRRA, 261, 266 (IRRA, 1985). See also Pestillo, "Learning to Live Without the Union," Proceedings of the 31st Annual Meeting, IRRA, 233, 238 (IRRA, 1979)("In a nonunion facility—regardless of location—wages are more often than not area competitive, or even a little higher. True, national rates are not paid, but national rates never made sense to me. Some people pay a premium in an effort at union avoidance; others do not.").

[6]While reports of organized labor's death are greatly exaggerated, the early returns indicate that the effort at union-avoidance is a success. As noted by Mills, "American management has been remarkably successful in its attempts to limit union organization." Mills, supra note 3, at 107. Private-sector union membership continues

and the term "management rights" will indeed be a redundancy and not a discussable issue. However, in those firms that have not implemented successful union-avoidance strategies, management rights disputes continue to reflect the adversarial struggle between labor with its quest for job security and management with its desire for flexibility in decision making.

Although the "power pendulum has swung sharply in management's direction," as noted by Horvitz,[7] the parties continue to argue over what rights management retains after the collective bargaining agreement is negotiated, and arbitrators, with some exceptions, still continue to hold that management is obligated to exercise its rights in a reasonable manner. Rather than taking the restrictive view that management retains all power not relinquished to the union and that this power can be exercised in any manner whatsoever, arbitrators have elected instead to impose what appears to be a "mere rationality" test on managerial conduct.[8] What results is not co-determination or even shared decision making between management and labor (although this form of employee participation through majority or minority stock ownership is not uncommon),[9] but a simple check against irrational man-

---

to erode—the unionized share of the work force is now about half of the 38% it was in 1954—and the legal environment, through its built-in opportunities for delay and inadequate system of remedies for statutory violations, is hostile to union organization. The only growth the labor movement has seen in recent years has been in the public sector. See generally Craver, "The Vitality of the American Labor Movement in the Twenty-First Century." U. Ill. L. Rev. 633 (1983); Weiler, "Promises to Keep: Securing Workers' Rights to Self-Organization Under the NLRA," 96 Harv. L. Rev. 1769 (1983); Weiler, "Striking a New Balance: Freedom of Contract and the Prospects for Union Representation," 98 Harv. L. Rev. 351 (1984); Piore, "Can the American Labor Movement Survive Re-Gomperization?" Proceedings of the 35th Annual Meeting, IRRA, 30–39 (IRRA, 1983); Prosten, "The Longest Season: Union Organizing in the Last Decade, a/k/a How Come One Team Has to Play With Its Shoelaces Tied Together?" Proceedings of the 31st Annual Meeting, IRRA, 240–249 (IRRA 1979). Kochan, McKersie & Katz, supra note 5, at 272–73 describe this phenomenon as follows: "[T]he dominant trend in strategic business and industrial relations decision-making at the highest levels within firms is to shift investments and jobs to nonunionized employment settings. Moreover, government policies are not creating an environment in which the labor movement can feel secure about its future as a viable force in American society. It is hard for us to see how unions can continue to act cooperatively in this environment while their basic security is being questioned and undermined."

[7]Horvitz, supra note 3, at 6–7.

[8]See, e.g., the discussion of Arbitrator Melvin Newmark in Pfizer, Inc., 79 LA 1225, 1232–36 (1982)(implying a "just cause" standard of discharge where none was explicitly mentioned in labor agreement).

[9]See Woodworth, "Promethean Industrial Relations: Labor, ESOPs, and the Boardroom," Proceedings of the 1985 Spring Meeting, IRRA, 618–24 (1985).

agerial behavior as that behavior affects employees. In the authors' view, this approach is neither radical nor a threat to managerial flexibility and indeed represents the better view today. The interest of management, labor, and the public are best served when all parties act reasonably and responsibly,[10] and in the end the debate over management rights may be nothing more than the rank and file simply wanting to avoid being victimized by the arbitrary and irrational exercise of managerial prerogatives. Unions may in fact complicate managers' lives, but it should not be concluded that industrial efficiency is impeded when unions, through the arbitration process, subject managerial decision making to a mere-rational-basis test.[11]

---

[10]Jack Barbash, citing John R. Commons, the founding father of industrial relations as a social science, observed: "There can be no question of reasonableness in maximum net income economies. It is only a question of economic power. But the institutional economics of willingness takes into account the ethical use of economic power . . . ." Barbash, "Values in Industrial Relations: The Case of the Adversary Principle," Proceedings of the 33rd Annual Meeting, IRRA 1, 7 (1981).

[11]According to Mills, "[The] studies suggest that an unqualified condemnation of unions as impeding industrial efficiency is not merited." Mills, supra note 3, at 113.

Appendix A

The United States Arbitration Act*

Chapter 1.—General Provisions

Section 1. "Maritime Transactions" and "Commerce" Defined; Exceptions to Operation of Title

"Maritime transactions," as herein defined, means charter parties, bills of lading of water carriers, agreements relating to wharfage, supplies furnished vessels or repairs of vessels, collisions, or any other matters in foreign commerce which, if the subject of controversy, would be embraced within admiralty jurisdiction; "commerce," as herein defined, means commerce among the several States or with foreign nations, or in any Territory of the United States or in the District of Columbia, or between any such Territory and another, or between any such Territory and any State or foreign nation, or between the District of Columbia and any State or Territory or foreign nation, but nothing herein contained shall apply to contracts of employment of seamen, railroad employees, or any other class of workers engaged in foreign or interstate commerce.

Section 2. Validity, Irrevocability, and Enforcement of Agreements to Arbitrate

A written provision in any maritime transaction or a contract evidencing a transaction involving commerce to settle by arbitration a controversy thereafter arising out of such contract or transaction, or the refusal to perform the whole or any part thereof, or an agreement in writing to submit to arbitration an existing controversy arising out of such a contract, transaction, or refusal, shall be valid, irrevocable, and enforceable, save upon such grounds as exist at law or in equity for the revocation of any contract.

---

*9 U.S.C.§§1–14.

Section 3. Stay of Proceedings Where Issue Therein Referable to Arbitration

If any suit or proceeding be brought in any of the courts of the United States upon any issue referable to arbitration under an agreement in writing for such arbitration, the court in which such suit is pending, upon being satisfied that the issue involved in such suit or proceeding is referable to arbitration under such an agreement, shall on application of one of the parties stay the trial of the action until such arbitration has been had in accordance with the terms of the agreement, providing the applicant for the stay is not in default in proceeding with such arbitration.

Section 4. Failure to Arbitrate Under Agreement; Petition to United States Court Having Jurisdiction for Order to Compel Arbitration; Notice and Service Thereof; Hearing and Determination

A party aggrieved by the alleged failure, neglect, or refusal of another to arbitrate under a written agreement for arbitration may petition any United States district court which, save for such agreement, would have jurisdiction under Title 28, in a civil action or in admiralty of the subject matter of a suit arising out of the controversy between the parties, for an order directing that such arbitration proceed in the manner provided for in such agreement. Five days' notice in writing of such application shall be served upon the party in default. Service thereof shall be made in the manner provided by the Federal Rules of Civil Procedure. The court shall hear the parties, and upon being satisfied that the making of the agreement for arbitration or the failure to comply therewith is not in issue, the court shall make an order directing the parties to proceed to arbitration in accordance with the terms of the agreement. The hearing and proceedings, under such agreement, shall be within the district in which the petition for an order directing such arbitration is filed. If the making of the arbitration agreement or the failure, neglect, or refusal to perform the same be in issue, the court shall proceed summarily to the trial thereof. If no jury trial be demanded by the party alleged to be in default, or if the matter in dispute is within admiralty jurisdiction, the court shall hear and determine such issue. Where such an issue is raised, the party alleged to be in default may, except in cases of admiralty, on or before the return day of the notice of application, demand a jury trial of such issue, and upon such demand the court shall make an order referring the issue or issues to a jury in the manner provided by the Federal Rules of Civil Procedure, or may specially call a jury for that purpose. If the jury find that no agreement in writing for arbitration was made or that there is no default in proceeding thereunder, the proceeding shall be dismissed. If the jury find that an agreement for arbitration was made in writing and that there is a default in proceeding thereunder, the court shall make an order summarily directing the parties to proceed with the arbitration in accordance with the terms thereof.

Section 5. Appointment of Arbitrators or Umpire

If in the agreement provision be made for a method of naming or appointing an arbitrator or arbitrators or any umpire, such method shall be followed; but if no method be provided therein, or if a method be provided and any party thereto shall fail to avail himself of such method, or if for any other reason there shall be a lapse in the naming of an arbitrator or arbitrators or umpire, or in filling a vacancy, then upon the application of either party to the controversy the court shall designate and appoint an arbitrator or arbitrators or umpire, as the case may require, who shall act under the said agreement with the same force and effect as if he or they had been specifically named therein; and unless otherwise provided in the agreement the arbitration shall be by a single arbitrator.

Section 6. Application Heard as Motion

Any application to the court hereunder shall be made and heard in the manner provided by law for the making and hearing of motions, except as otherwise herein expressly provided.

Section 7. Witnesses Before Arbitrators; Fees; Compelling Attendance

The arbitrators selected either as prescribed in this title or otherwise, or a majority of them, may summon in writing any person to attend before them or any of them as a witness and in a proper case to bring with him or them any book, record, document, or paper which may be deemed material as evidence in the case. The fees for such attendance shall be the same as the fees of witnesses before masters of the United States courts. Said summons shall issue in the name of the arbitrator or arbitrators, or a majority of them, and shall be signed by the arbitrators, or a majority of them, and shall be directed to the said person and shall be served in the same manner as subpoenas to appear and testify before the court; if any person or persons so summoned to testify shall refuse or neglect to obey said summons, upon petition the United States court in and for the district in which such arbitrators, or a majority of them, are sitting may compel the attendance of such person or persons before said arbitrator or arbitrators, or punish said person or persons for contempt in the same manner provided on February 12, 1925, for securing the attendance of witnesses or their punishment for neglect or refusal to attend in the courts of the United States.

Section 8. Proceedings Begun by Libel in Admiralty and Seizure of Vessel or Property

If the basis of jurisdiction be a cause of action otherwise justiciable in admiralty, then, notwithstanding anything herein to the contrary the party claiming to be aggrieved may begin his proceeding hereunder by libel and seizure of the vessel or other property of the other party according to the usual course of admiralty proceedings, and the court shall then have jurisdiction to direct the parties to proceed with the arbitration and shall retain jurisdiction to enter its decree upon the award.

Section 9. Award of Arbitrators; Confirmation; Jurisdiction; Procedure

If the parties in their agreement have agreed that a judgment of the court shall be entered upon the award made pursuant to the arbitration, and shall specify the court, then at any time within one year after the award is made any party to the arbitration may apply to the court so specified for an order confirming the award, and thereupon the court must grant such an order unless the award is vacated, modified, or corrected as prescribed in sections 10 and 11 of this title. If no court is specified in the agreement of the parties, then such application may be made to the United States court in and for the district within which such award was made. Notice of the application shall be served upon the adverse party, and thereupon the court shall have jurisdiction of such party as though he had appeared generally in the proceeding. If the adverse party is a resident of the district within which the award was made, such service shall be made upon the adverse party or his attorney as prescribed by law for service of notice of motion in an action in the same court. If the adverse party shall be a nonresident, then the notice of the application shall be served by the marshal of any district within which the adverse party may be found in like manner as other process of the court.

Section 10. Same; Vacation; Grounds; Rehearing

In either of the following cases the United States court in and for the district wherein the award was made may make an order vacating the award upon the application of any party to the arbitration—

(a) Where the award was procured by corruption, fraud, or undue means.

(b) Where there was evident partiality or corruption in the arbitrators, or either of them.

(c) Where the arbitrators were guilty of misconduct in refusing to postpone the hearing, upon sufficient cause shown, or in refusing to hear evidence pertinent and material to the controversy; or of any other misbehavior by which the rights of any party have been prejudiced.

(d) Where the arbitrators exceeded their powers, or so imperfectly executed them that a mutual, final, and definite award upon the subject matter submitted was not made.

(e) Where an award is vacated and the time within which the agreement required the award to be made has not expired the court may, in its discretion, direct a rehearing by the arbitrators.

Section 11. Same; Modification or Correction; Grounds; Order

In either of the following cases the United States court in and for the district wherein the award was made may make an order modifying or correcting the award upon the application of any party to the arbitration—

(a) Where there was an evident material miscalculation of figures or an evident material mistake in the description of any person, thing, or property referred to in the award.

(b) Where the arbitrators have awarded upon a matter not submitted to them, unless it is a matter not affecting the merits of the decision upon the matter submitted.

(c) Where the award is imperfect in matter of form not affecting the merits of the controversy.

The order may modify and correct the award, so as to effect the intent thereof and promote justice between the parties.

Section 12. Notice of Motions to Vacate or Modify; Service; Stay of Proceedings

Notice of a motion to vacate, modify, or correct an award must be served upon the adverse party or his attorney within three months after the award is filed or delivered. If the adverse party is a resident of the district within which the award was made, such service shall be made upon the adverse party or his attorney as prescribed by law for service of notice of motion in an action in the same court. If the adverse party shall be a nonresident then the notice of the application shall be served by the marshal of any district within which the adverse party may be found in like manner as other process of the court. For the purposes of the motion any judge who might make an order to stay the proceedings in an action brought in the same court may make an order, to be served with the notice of motion, staying the proceedings of the adverse party to enforce the award.

Section 13. Papers Filed with Order on Motions; Judgment; Docketing; Force and Effect; Enforcement

The party moving for an order confirming, modifying, or correcting an award shall, at the time such order is filed with the clerk for the entry of judgment thereon, also file the following papers with the clerk:

(a) The agreement; the selection or appointment, if any, of an additional arbitrator or umpire; and each written extension of the time, if any, within which to make the award.

(b) The award.

(c) Each notice, affidavit, or other paper used upon an application to confirm, modify, or correct the award, and a copy of each order of the court upon such an application.

The judgment shall be docketed as if it was rendered in an action.

The judgment so entered shall have the same force and effect, in all respects, as, and be subject to all the provisions of law relating to, a judgment in an action; and it may be enforced as if it had been rendered in an action in the court in which it is entered.

Section 14. Contracts Not Affected

This title shall not apply to contracts made prior to January 1, 1926.

Appendix B

Uniform Arbitration Act*

Act Relating to Arbitration and to Make Uniform
The Law With Reference Thereto

Section 1. (Validity of Arbitration Agreement.)

A written agreement to submit any existing controversy to arbitration or a provision in a written contract to submit to arbitration any controversy thereafter arising between the parties is valid, enforceable and irrevocable, save upon such grounds as exist at law or in equity for the revocation of any contract. This act also applies to arbitration agreements between employers and employees or between their respective representatives (unless otherwise provided in the agreement.)

Section 2. (Proceedings to Compel or Stay Arbitration.)

(a) On application of a party showing an agreement described in Section 1, and the opposing party's refusal to arbitrate, the Court shall order the parties to proceed with arbitration, but if the opposing party denies the existence of the agreement to arbitrate, the Court shall proceed summarily to the determination of the issue so raised and shall order arbitration if found for the moving party, otherwise, the application shall be denied.

(b) On application, the courts may stay an arbitration proceeding commenced or threatened on a showing that there is no agreement to arbitrate. Such an issue, when in substantial and bona fide dispute, shall be forthwith and summarily tried and the stay ordered

---

*Adopted by the National Conference of the Commissioners on Uniform State Laws, August 20, 1955, as amended August 24, 1956. Approved by the House of Delegates of the American Bar Association, August 26, 1955, and August 30, 1956.
Brackets and parenthesis enclose language which the Commissioners suggest may be used by those States desiring to do so.

if found for the moving party. If found for the opposing party, the court shall order the parties to proceed to arbitration.

(c) If an issue referable to arbitration under the alleged agreement is involved in action or proceeding pending in a court having jurisdiction to hear applications under subdivision (a) of this Section, the application shall be made therein. Otherwise and subject to Section 18, the application may be made in any court of competent jurisdiction.

(d) Any action or proceeding involving an issue subject to arbitration shall be stayed if an order for arbitration or an application therefore has been made under this section or, if the issue is severable, the stay may be with respect thereto only. When the application is made in such action or proceeding, the order for arbitration shall include such stay.

(e) An order for arbitration shall not be refused on the ground that the claim in issue lacks merit or bona fides or because any fault or grounds for the claim sought to be arbitrated have not been shown.

Section 3. (Appointment of Arbitrators by Courts.)

If the arbitration agreement provides a method of appointment of arbitrators, this method shall be followed. In the absence thereof, or if the agreed method fails or for any reason cannot be followed, or when an arbitrator appointed fails or is unable to act and his successor has not been duly appointed, the court on application of a party shall appoint one or more arbitrators. An arbitrator so appointed has all the powers of one specifically named in the agreement.

Section 4. (Majority Action by Arbitrators.)

The powers of the arbitrators may be exercised by a majority unless otherwise provided by the agreement or by this act.

Section 5. (Hearing.)

Unless otherwise provided by the agreement:

(a) The arbitrators shall appoint a time and place for the hearing and cause notification to the parties to be served personally or by registered mail not less than five days before the hearing. Appearance at the hearing waives such notice. The arbitrators may adjourn the hearing from time to time as necessary and, on request of a party and for good cause, or upon their own motion may postpone the hearing to a time not later than the date fixed by the agreement for making the award unless the parties consent to a later date. The arbitrators may hear and determine the controversy upon the evidence produced notwithstanding the failure of a party duly notified to appear. The court on application may direct the arbitrators to proceed promptly with the hearing and determination of the controversy.

(b) The parties are entitled to be heard, to present evidence material to the controversy and to cross-examine witnesses appearing at the hearing.

(c) The hearing shall be conducted by all the arbitrators but a majority may determine any question and render a final award. If, during the course of the hearing, an arbitrator for any reason ceases to act, the remaining arbitrator or arbitrators appointed to act as neutrals may continue with the hearing and determination of the controversy.

Section 6. *(Representation by Attorney.)*

A party has the right to be represented by an attorney at any proceeding or hearing under this act. A waiver thereof prior to the proceeding or hearing is ineffective.

Section 7. *(Witnesses, Subpoenas, Depositions.)*

(a) The arbitrators may issue (cause to be issued) subpoenas for the attendance of witnesses and for the production of books, records, documents and other evidence, and shall have the power to administer oaths. Subpoenas so issued shall be served, and upon application to the Court by a party or the arbitrators, enforced, in the manner provided by law for the service and enforcement of subpoenas in a civil action.

(b) On application of a party and for use as evidence, the arbitrators may permit a deposition to be taken, in the manner and upon the terms designated by the arbitrators, of a witness who cannot be subpoenaed or is unable to attend the hearing.

(c) All provisions of law compelling a person under subpoena to testify are applicable.

(d) Fees for attendance as a witness shall be the same as for a witness in the _____Court.

Section 8. *(Award.)*

(a) The award shall be in writing and signed by the arbitrators joining in the award. The arbitrators shall deliver a copy to each party personally or by registered mail, or as provided in the agreement.

(b) An award shall be made within the time fixed therefor by the agreement or, if not so fixed, within such time as the court orders on application of a party. The parties may extend the time in writing either before or after the expiration thereof. A party waives the objection that an award was not made within the time required unless he notifies the arbitrators of his objection prior to the delivery of the award to him.

Section 9. (Change of Award by Arbitrators.)

On application of a party or, if an application to the court is pending under Sections 11, 12, or 13, on submission to the arbitrators by the court under such conditions as the court may order, the arbitrators may modify or correct the award upon the grounds stated in paragraphs (1) and (3) of subdivision (a) of Section 13, or for the purpose of clarifying the award. The application shall be made within twenty days after delivery of the award to the applicant. Written notice thereof shall be given forthwith to the opposing party, stating he must serve his objection thereto if any, within ten days from the notice. The award so modified or corrected is subject to the provisions of Sections 11, 12 and 13.

Section 10. (Fees and Expenses of Arbitration.)

Unless otherwise provided in the agreement to arbitrate, the arbitrators' expenses and fees, together with other expenses, not including counsel fees, incurred in the conduct of the arbitration, shall be paid as provided in the award.

Section 11. (Confirmation of an Award.)

Upon application of a party, the court shall confirm an award, unless within the time limits hereinafter imposed grounds are urged for vacating or modifying or correcting the award, in which case the court shall proceed as provided in Sections 12 and 13.

Section 12. (Vacating an Award.)

(a) Upon application of a party, the court shall vacate an award where:

(1) The award was procured by corruption, fraud or other undue means;

(2) There was evident partiality by an arbitrator appointed as a neutral or corruption in any of the arbitrators or misconduct prejudicing the rights of any party;

(3) The arbitrators exceeded their powers;

(4) The arbitrators refused to postpone the hearing upon sufficient cause being shown therefor or refused to hear evidence material to the controversy or otherwise so conducted the hearing,

contrary to the provisions of Section 5, as to prejudice substantially the rights of a party; or

(5) There was no arbitration agreement and the issue was not adversely determined in proceedings under Section 2 and the party did not participate in the arbitration hearing without raising the objection;

But the fact that the relief was such that it could not or would not be granted by a court of law or equity is not ground for vacating or refusing to confirm the award.

(b) An application under this Section shall be made within ninety days after delivery of a copy of the award to the applicant, except that, if predicated upon corruption, fraud or other undue means, it shall be made within ninety days after such grounds are known or should have been known.

(c) In vacating the award on grounds other than stated in clause (5) of Subsection (a) the court may order a rehearing before new arbitrators chosen as provided in the agreement, or in the absence thereof, by the court in accordance with Section 3, or, if the award is vacated on grounds set forth in clauses (3), and (4) of Subsection (a) the court may order a rehearing before the arbitrators who made the award or their successors appointed in accordance with Section 3. The time within which the agreement requires the award to be made is applicable to the rehearing and commences from the date of the order.

(d) If the application to vacate is denied and no motion to modify or correct the award is pending, the court shall confirm the award.

Section 13. (Modification or Correction of Award.)

(a) Upon application made within ninety days after delivery of a copy of the award to the applicant, the court shall modify or correct the award where:

(1) There was an evident miscalculation of figures or an evident mistake in the description of any person, thing or property referred to in the award;

(2) The arbitrators have awarded upon a matter not submitted to them and the award may be corrected without affecting the merits of the decision upon the issues submitted; or

(3) The award is imperfect in a matter of form, not affecting the merits of the controversy.

(b) If the application is granted, the court shall modify and correct the award so as to effect its intent and shall confirm the award as so modified and corrected. Otherwise, the court shall confirm the award as made.

(c) An application to modify or correct an award may be joined in the alternative with an application to vacate the award.

Section 14. *(Judgment or Decree on Award.)*

Upon the granting of an order confirming, modifying or correcting an award, judgment or decree shall be entered in conformity therewith and be enforced as any other judgment or decree. Costs of the application and of the proceedings subsequent thereto, and disbursements may be awarded by the court.

[Section 15. *(Judgment Roll, Docketing.)*

(a) On entry of judgment or decree, the clerk shall prepare the judgment roll consisting, to the extent filled, of the following:
(1) The agreement and each written extension of the time within which to make the award;
(2) The award;
(3) A copy of the order confirming, modifying or correcting the award; and
(4) A copy of the judgment or decree.
(b) The judgment or decree may be docketed as if rendered in an action.]

Section 16. *(Applications to Court.)*

Except as otherwise provided, an application to the court under this act shall be by motion and shall be heard in the manner and upon the notice provided by law or rule of court for the making and hearing of motions. Unless the parties have agreed otherwise, notice of an initial application for an order shall be served in the manner provided by law for the service of a summons in an action.

Section 17. *(Court, Jurisdiction.)*

The term "court" means any court of competent jurisdiction of this State. The making of an agreement described in Section 1 providing for arbitration in this State confers jurisdiction on the court to enforce the agreement under this Act and to enter judgment on an award thereunder.

Section 18. *(Venue.)*

An initial application shall be made to the court of the (county) in which the agreement provides the arbitration hearing shall be held or, if the hearing has been held, in the county in which it was held. Otherwise the application shall be made in the (county) where the adverse party resides or has a place of business or, if he has no residence or place of business in this State, to the court of any (county). All subsequent applications shall be made to the court hearing the initial application unless the court otherwise directs.

Section 19. (Appeals.)

(a) An appeal may be taken from:
(1) An order denying an application to compel arbitration made under Section 2;
(2) An order granting an application to stay arbitration made under Section 2(b);
(3) An order confirming or denying confirmation of an award;
(4) An order modifying or correcting an award;
(5) An order vacating an award without directing a rehearing; or
(6) A judgment or decree entered pursuant to the provisions of this act.

(b) The appeal shall be taken in the manner and to the same extent as from orders or judgments in a civil action.

Section 20. (Act Not Retroactive.)

This act applies only to agreements made subsequent to the taking effect of this act.

Section 21. (Uniformity of Interpretation.)

This act shall be so construed as to effectuate its general purpose to make uniform the law of those states which enact it.

Section 22. (Constitutionality.)

If any provision of this act or the application thereof to any person or circumstance is held invalid, the invalidity shall not affect other provisions or applications of the act which can be given without the invalid provision or application, and to this end the provisions of the act are severable.

Section 23. (Short Title.)

This act may be cited as the Uniform Arbitration Act.

Section 24. (Repeal.)

All acts or parts of acts which are inconsistent with the provisions of this act are hereby repealed.

Section 25. (Time of Taking Effect.)

This act shall take effect _____

Appendix C

Titles of NAA Proceedings
1948–1985*

The Profession of Labor Arbitration, Selected Papers From the First Seven Annual Meetings of the National Academy of Arbitrators, 1948–1954 (BNA Books, 1957).

Arbitration Today, Proceedings of the 8th Annual Meeting, National Academy of Arbitrators (BNA Books, 1955).

Management Rights and the Arbitration Process, Proceedings of the 9th Annual Meeting, National Academy of Arbitrators (BNA Books, 1956).

Critical Issues in Labor Arbitration, Proceedings of the 10th Annual Meeting, National Academy of Arbitrators (BNA Books, 1957).

The Arbitrator and the Parties, Proceedings of the 11th Annual Meeting, National Academy of Arbitrators (BNA Books, 1958).

Arbitration and the Law, Proceedings of the 12th Annual Meeting, National Academy of Arbitrators (BNA Books, 1959).

Challenges to Arbitration, Proceedings of the 13th Annual Meeting, National Academy of Arbitrators (BNA Books, 1960).

Arbitration and Public Policy, Proceedings of the 14th Annual Meeting, National Academy of Arbitrators (BNA Books, 1961).

Collective Bargaining and the Arbitrator's Role, Proceedings of the 15th Annual Meeting, National Academy of Arbitrators (BNA Books, 1962).

Labor Arbitration and Industrial Change, Proceedings of the 16th Annual Meeting, National Academy of Arbitrators (BNA Books, 1963).

Labor Arbitration: Perspectives and Problems, Proceedings of the 17th Annual Meeting, National Academy of Arbitrators (BNA Books, 1964).

---

*A full listing of NAA titles is given here for the reader's reference to supplement the abbreviated titles used in footnotes of this Edition.

Proceedings of the 18th Annual Meeting of the National Academy of Arbitrators, 1965 (BNA Books, 1965).

Problems of Proof in Arbitration, Proceedings of the 19th Annual Meeting, National Academy of Arbitrators (BNA Books, 1967).

The Arbitrator, the NLRB, and the Courts, Proceedings of the 20th Annual Meeting, National Academy of Arbitrators (BNA Books, 1967).

Developments in American and Foreign Arbitration, Proceedings of the 21st Annual Meeting, National Academy of Arbitrators (BNA Books, 1968).

Arbitration and Social Change, Proceedings of the 22nd Annual Meeting, National Academy of Arbitrators (BNA Books, 1970).

Arbitration and the Expanding Role of Neutrals, Proceedings of the 23rd Annual Meeting, National Academy of Arbitrators (BNA Books, 1970).

Arbitration and the Public Interest, Proceedings of the 24th Annual Meeting, National Academy of Arbitrators (BNA Books, 1971).

Labor Arbitration at the Quarter-Century Mark, Proceedings of the 25th Annual Meeting, National Academy of Arbitrators (BNA Books, 1973).

Arbitration of Interest Disputes, Proceedings of the 26th Annual Meeting, National Academy of Arbitrators (BNA Books, 1974).

Arbitration—1974, Proceedings of the 27th Annual Meeting, National Academy of Arbitrators (BNA Books, 1975).

Arbitration—1975, Proceedings of the 28th Annual Meeting, National Academy of Arbitrators (BNA Books, 1976).

Arbitration—1976, Proceedings of the 29th Annual Meeting, National Academy of Arbitrators (BNA Books, 1976).

Arbitration—1977, Proceedings of the 30th Annual Meeting, National Academy of Arbitrators (BNA Books, 1978).

Truth, Lie Detectors, and Other Problems in Labor Arbitration, Proceedings of the 31st Annual Meeting, National Academy of Arbitrators (BNA Books, 1979).

Arbitration of Subcontracting and Wage Incentive Disputes, Proceedings of the 32nd Annual Meeting, National Academy of Arbitrators (BNA Books, 1980).

Decisional Thinking of Arbitrators and Judges, Proceedings of the 33rd Annual Meeting, National Academy of Arbitrators (BNA Books, 1981).

Arbitration Issues for the 1980s, Proceedings of the 34th Annual Meeting, National Academy of Arbitrators (BNA Books, 1982).

Arbitration 1982: Conduct of the Hearing, Proceedings of the 35th Annual Meeting, National Academy of Arbitrators (BNA Books, 1983).

Arbitration—Promise and Performance, Proceedings of the 36th

Annual Meeting, National Academy of Arbitrators (BNA Books, 1984).

Arbitration 1984: Absenteeism, Recent Law, Panels, and Published Decisions, Proceedings of the 37th Annual Meeting, National Academy of Arbitrators (BNA Books, 1985).

Arbitration 1985: Law and Practice, Proceedings of the 38th Annual Meeting, National Academy of Arbitrators (BNA Books, 1986).

Index

Dress and grooming codes—*Contd.*
 discriminatory standards 161–162
 dress codes 153–157
 grooming codes 159–161
 identification tags 157–159
Drug convictions 204, 205, 208, 213–214, 216, 217
Drug tests (*see* Alcohol and drug testing)
Due process (*see* Public sector employment)
Duff, Clair 30, 153, 154, 196, 203
Duff, James 157
Dybeck, Alfred 201, 474

E

Early quit 371
Edes, Samuel 210
Education requirements 306–307, 331–333
Edwards, Harry 217, 354–356
"Effects" bargaining 412–415, 422, 424, 430
Elkouri, Frank and Edna Asper 22–23, 366–367, 453–454
Ellmann, Erwin 370, 437–438
Ellmann, William 441
Elson, Alex 21
Employee benefits
 past practice, binding nature of 23, 45–48
Employee handbooks 132
Employee loyalty (*see* Loyalty)
Employee selection procedures (*see* Ability assessments; Testing)
Employment applications 298–301
Employment discrimination (*see* Discrimination in employment)
Equal Employment Opportunity Commission (EEOC) 88, 218–219, 303, 304, 307, 308, 314, 335, 384
Erbs, Thomas 513–514
Estoppel 21
Evidence
 polygraph tests 256–259, 273–274
 surveillance 285–289
Executive retirement 384

F

Fair employment (*see* Discrimination in employment)

Fair Labor Standards Act 92
Fairweather, Owen 16–17, 257, 464
Federal Contract Compliance Programs, Office of (OFCCP) 326
Federal contractors 326
Federal sector (*see* Public sector employment)
Federal Service Labor-Management Relations Act 295
Feldman, Marvin 35, 67, 321–322, 436–437
Feller, David 15
Ferguson, D. Emmett 194–195
Fifth Amendment rights 227, 265, 267
Fire departments
 affirmative action 315–317
 Stotts decision 381–383
Firearms possession 67–68, 214
First Amendment rights (*see* Speech rights)
Fitness and ability (*see* Ability assessments; Testing)
Flagler, John 356, 480
Fleischli, George 493–494
Fleming, R. W. 281
Forsythe, E. J. 160
Foster, Howard 67–68, 503
Foster, Robert 335–336
Fourteenth Amendment rights 184, 219–220, 227
Fourth Amendment rights 183–186, 227, 276, 280
Frankfurter, Felix 224
Freedom of Information Act 176
Freeman, Charles 208
Friedman, Milton 240

G

Gallagher, Thomas 433–437
Garnishment 92, 308–309
Garrett, Sylvester 323
Gersuny, Carl 351–352
Gibson, Rankin 320, 496
Gibson, Robert 197
Goldberg, Arthur 5, 12, 13
Good faith and fair dealing 128–132
Government employment (*see* Public sector employment)
Grether, Henry 47
Griffith, Lynn 442–443
Grooming codes (*see* Dress and grooming codes)
Gross, James 460
Gross, Jerome 105–106, 111

About the Authors

Marvin Hill, Jr., is currently Associate Professor of Industrial Relations at the College of Business Administration, Northern Illinois University, and an Iowa attorney. A member of the National Academy of Arbitrators, Hill is actively engaged in arbitration and mediation in the public and private sectors. Hill has contributed articles to many journals, including *The Arbitration Journal, Labor Law Journal, Indiana Law Review, DePaul Law Review*, and *Oklahoma Law Review*. He has also co-authored (with A.V. Sinicropi) two other books, *Evidence in Arbitration* and *Remedies in Arbitration*, both published by The Bureau of National Affairs, Inc. (BNA). To his credit, Hill is a Cubs fan.

Anthony V. Sinicropi is John F. Murray Professor of Industrial Relations at The University of Iowa and University Ombudsperson. In the past he has served the university in several administrative positions. He has also served as a consultant for several government organizations, is an arbitrator and umpire, and has acted as a mediator and fact finder in the public sector. He is a member of the National Academy of Arbitrators, having been a member of the Board of Governors and a vice president, and is a past president and founder of the Society of Professionals in Dispute Resolution. Among his publications are *Iowa Labor Laws,* "The Legal Status of Supervisors in Public Sector Labor Relations," "The Legal Framework of Public Sector Dispute Resolution," "Excluding Discriminational Grievances From Grievance and Arbitration Procedures: A Legal Analysis," and "Subcontracting in Labor Arbitration."